Library of Congress Cataloging-in-Publication Data

Newbold, Paul.
    Principles of management science.

    Includes index.
    1. Management science. I. Title.
HD30.23.N48 1986   658.4′001′51   85-28093
ISBN 0-13-701756-1

Editorial/production supervision by Margaret Rizzi
Cover and interior design by Suzanne Behnke
Manufacturing buyer: Ed O'Dougherty

© 1986 by Prentice-Hall
A Division of Simon & Schuster, Inc.
Englewood Cliffs, New Jersey 07632

Printed in the United States of America

10 9 8 7 6 5 4 3 2 1

ISBN 0-13-701756-1   01

Prentice-Hall International (UK) Limited, *London*
Prentice-Hall of Australia Pty. Limited, *Sydney*
Prentice-Hall Canada Inc., *Toronto*
Prentice-Hall Hispanoamericana, S.A., *Mexico*
Prentice-Hall of India Private Limited, *New Delhi*
Prentice-Hall of Japan, Inc., *Tokyo*
Prentice-Hall of Southeast Asia Pte. Ltd., *Singapore*
Editora Prentice-Hall do Brasil, Ltda., *Rio de Janeiro*
Whitehall Books Limited, *Wellington, New Zealand*

PRINCIPLES OF MANAGEMENT SCIENCE

Paul Newbold

University of Illinois, Urbana-Champaign

PRENTICE-HALL, Englewood Cliffs, New Jersey 07632

To Robbie and Gina

contents

9 DYNAMIC PROGRAMMING   305

10 PROBABILITY AND STATISTICAL DISTRIBUTIONS   331

11 DECISION THEORY   375

12 FORECASTING   423

13 NETWORK MODELS   448

14 INVENTORY MODELS   510

preface

This text is intended to introduce students to the principles of management science/operational research. The techniques discussed here are often described as "quantitative approaches to decision making in business," and constitute a powerful arsenal of weapons for attacking a wide range of management problems.

The book is aimed primarily at students of business: Its purpose is to provide a flavor of many management science techniques, and illustrate the potential for their application. Consequently, while effort is made to explain why procedures work, their theoretical development is not discussed in any depth. A college algebra course should provide an adequate mathematical preparation for the first nine chapters of the text. Much of the material in Chapters 11 through 17 requires also some introductory knowledge of probability and statistics. With this in mind, I have included in Chapter 10 a review of the pertinent material in these areas.

In introducing management science techniques throughout the text, I have chosen to proceed by immediately working through illustrative examples. These have been designed to permit the reader to develop a more concrete grasp of solution alogrithms, and of their potential for applications. Although, of necessity, these examples are simplified idealizations of real-world problems, it is hoped that they will convey insight into what can be achieved in practice with management science models. In addition, appended to many chapters are "Management Science in Action" sections, which provide discussions of more substantial applications.

There is more material in this text than can comfortably be covered in one semester, and, since the majority of the chapters are self-contained, a great deal of flexibility in designing a course is available. One possibility is

The book has benefited greatly from the advice of many people who have read some or all of the chapters in draft form. In particular, I would like to thank S. Christian Albright, James A. Bartos, Richard J. Coppins, Lori S. Franz, George Heitmann, Michael R. Middleton, Laurence D. Richards, Robert Schellenberger, Daniel G. Shimshak, and William A. Verdini.

Finally, I must thank Steve Hotopp for computational assistance, Dixie Trinkle for expert typing, and my Prentice-Hall editors, Dennis Hogan and Margaret Rizzi, for much-needed encouragement and support throughout the development of this project.

Next, we must account for the limited production capacities at the two plants. The total number of sets shipped from plant 1 is $(x_{1A} + x_{1B})$. However, given the capacity of this plant, this number cannot exceed 275. This constraint is written

$$x_{1A} + x_{1B} \leq 275 \qquad (1.4)$$

Similarly, as a result of the fact that plant 2 can produce at most 325 sets, we have

$$x_{2A} + x_{2B} \leq 325 \qquad (1.5)$$

There is one further constraint on the values that can be taken by the variables x_{1A}, x_{1B}, x_{2A}, and x_{2B}; they cannot be negative. Thus we write

$$x_{1A}, x_{1B}, x_{2A}, x_{2B} \geq 0 \qquad (1.6)$$

The objective of this corporation, then, is to find those values of x_{1A}, x_{1B}, x_{2A}, x_{2B} for which total shipment cost (1.1) is smallest, subject to the requirements that these values satisfy the constraints (1.2)–(1.6). Thus, the mathematical model of our problem is

$$\text{Minimize} \quad 10\, x_{1A} + 12\, x_{1B} + 14\, x_{2A} + 11\, x_{2B}$$

$$\text{subject to} \quad x_{1A} + x_{2A} = 300$$

$$x_{1B} + x_{2B} = 250$$

$$x_{1A} + x_{1B} \leq 275$$

$$x_{2A} + x_{2B} \leq 325$$

$$x_{1A}, x_{1B}, x_{2A}, x_{2B} \geq 0$$

The advantage of expressing our problem in symbolic form in this manner is that we can appeal to mathematical methods for its solution. This is a member of a broad class of problems, called **linear programming** problems, whose solution will be discussed in considerable detail in Chapters 2, 3, 4, and 5. (In fact, our problem belongs to a special subclass of linear programming problems called **transportation** problems. Solution algorithms for such problems will be considered in Chapter 6.)

1.3. DETERMINISTIC AND STOCHASTIC MODELS

In the previous section we illustrated, through a simple transportation problem, the technique of mathematical model building that will be central in our study of management science problems. As we have already noted, to be useful as an aid to solving real-world problems, a model must provide a faithful representation of the essential elements of those problems. The example of Section 1.2 excludes one important ingredient of a great many practical management problems—the element of **uncertainty**. The consequences of many management decisions will be felt months, or even years, into the future, and those future events that will determine the relative success of any decision cannot be known with certainty at the time the decision has to be taken. When the extent of any uncertainty is nonnegligible, it is crucial that it be factored into the decision-making process. Models that incorporate uncertainty are called **stochastic,** by contrast with **deterministic** models such as that of the previous section.

Let us illustrate this point through reference to an **inventory**[1] **management** problem. A distributor of tires orders from a manufacturer, and there is a delay of four days between the placing of an order and its receipt. Any unsold stock that the distributor has in hand will be held in inventory. In the context of inventory management, we can think of three types of costs that could be incurred:

1. *Ordering costs* will arise when a new order must be placed. These costs mainly comprise the time of employees in the purchasing and ordering departments.
2. *Holding costs* arise through the keeping of stocks that are surplus to immediate needs. This is so since money may have to be borrowed to finance inventory holding. However, if this expense is financed through internal resources, it remains the case that this sum could otherwise be profitably invested elsewhere. Other holding charges arise through the costs of storage, insurance, damage, and theft.
3. *Shortage costs* are losses in goodwill incurred through the failure to meet demand when stocks are exhausted.

In principle these different types of costs can be measured[2] for any ordering and inventory holding strategy, and the distributor will seek that strategy with the lowest possible total cost. Generally, when dealers must place orders for many products, a relatively straightforward strategy that can be routinely applied is needed. One possibility is the following:

(a) place orders of equal sizes, called the **order quantity.**
(b) Place a new order whenever inventory falls to a specific level, called the **reorder point.**

---

[1] Inventory models will be discussed in detail in Chapter 14.

[2] The measurement of ordering and holding costs is relatively straightforward. However, the determination of shortage costs, which involve customer goodwill losses, will necessarily be more subjective.

introducing management science

CHAPTER ONE

1.1. QUANTITATIVE MODELS FOR DECISION MAKING

Managers are paid to make decisions. In any organization, problems regularly arise for which a choice among alternative actions is possible, and different choices will impact differentially on the well-being of the organization. Consider, for example the following types of business problems:

1. In a multiproduct firm, what mix of products should be produced in the months ahead?
2. When, and in what quantities, should materials and parts required in the production process be ordered? What is the right balance between the costs associated with the exhaustion of stocks and those of holding large inventories?
3. Which research and development projects should be pursued, and what sums should be budgeted for those purposes?
4. How should a new product be marketed? What is the appropriate price, production level, and promotion strategy?
5. What is the most efficient system for the distribution of goods from factories to customer outlets?
6. How should members of a sales force be assigned to different regional territories?
7. At a customer service center, how many servers should be available at different times of the day?
8. How should an investment portfolio be constituted?

This partial listing is sufficient to display the range of problem types met by corporate management. Some, such as production scheduling and ordering are faced regularly, though that is not to imply that their appropriate solutions

1

will remain fixed. Rather, as the environment in which a corporation operates evolves over time, the essential problem specifications will change, and hence so will the appropriate solutions. Others of our problems, such as new product introduction are of a one-off nature, and must often be attacked from the ground up, rather than through the modification of existing practice.

In spite of this diversity of problems, it is useful to broadly categorize management approaches to decision making as either **informal** or **formal.** The informal approach is based on managers' intuition, insight, and experience. There is no doubt that these qualities, which to some extent will be both sharpened and deepened through his or her career development, are invaluable to a manager. However, in this text our attention will be concentrated on more formal approaches to management decision-making. The methodology that we will discuss is generally referred to as **management science,** as it involves the application of the **scientific method** to problem solving by managers. This methodology involves the careful formulation of a problem, the collection of relevant data, the analysis of that data, and the derivation of conclusions on the basis of this analysis. One important ingredient of the methodology of the laboratory scientist is, however, more difficult to translate to the sphere of corporate mangement. It is often prohibitively expensive to **experiment** with real business systems. However, a good understanding of the workings of a system can often be achieved by building a **model** of that system, and model building constitutes an essential element of management science. In Chapter 16, we will see how **simulation** can sometimes be employed to allow at modest cost experimentation with a model of a real-world system.

The rational approach to management decision-making that has come to be called management science is also referred to on occasion as **operations research** or **decision science.** The three terms are virtually synonymous, and are used interchangeably in the literature. In essence, a formal analysis is to be made of a business decision-making problem. Although we will concentrate in this book on the formal analysis of problems, it should not be inferred that informal subjective judgment of managers is not also of value. On the contrary, the methods of management science should be viewed as a valuable aid to decision-making, often most profitably employed in conjunction with less formal considerations.

The management scientist constructs **quantitative models** to formulate and analyze business problems. This approach is gaining increased acceptance as managers increasingly find themselves confronted by complex problems, involving many factors, which are not well understood, and for which informally developed solutions have little appeal. Quantitative model building is also attractive in the solution of repetitive problems, such as reordering decisions, where much time and money can be saved through the repeated use of a formal solution algorithm. The growing popularity of management science methods can be put down to two factors. First, as successful implementations of these methods are reported, managers have grown increasingly willing to consider their application to their own problems. Second, the rapid development of the capabilities of the electronic computer has allowed the efficient storage and retrieval of vast quantities of information, and the carrying out of complex computations that would otherwise have been prohibitively tedious. This development has allowed the possibility of the formal analysis of very large models in the study of problems that a few years ago, would of necessity have had to be attacked informally.

In the next section we will discuss and illustrate the nature of management model building.

1.2. MODEL BUILDING

A model is a representation of a real entity, and may be constructed in order to gain some understanding of, or insight into, that entity. Model building is at least as much an art as a science, requiring a balance between realism and simplicity. A model should be sufficiently realistic to incorporate the important characteristics of the real-world system it depicts, but not so complex as to obscure those characteristics.

Three types of models are generally distinguished:

(i) *Iconic models* are physical representations of real objects, designed to resemble in appearance those objects. For example, when a tall building is planned, engineers may construct a small scale model of that building, and of its surrounding area and environment, in order to conduct stress tests in a wind tunnel.

(ii) *Analog models* are also physical models, but represent the entities under study by analogy rather than by replica. An example is a graph showing the movements over time of stock market prices; this provides a pictorial representation of numerical data. A further example is a barometer which represents changes in atmospheric pressure through movements of a needle.

(iii) *Mathematical models,* or *symbolic models,* are more abstract representations than iconic or analog models. They attempt to provide, for example through an equation or system of equations, a description of a physical system.

Mathematical modeling is of central importance in management science, providing a means of describing and solving real-world problems. To illustrate, let us see how a problem can be expressed as a mathematical model.

A manufacturer of television sets has two plants and two distribution centers. For the coming week, distribution center A requires 300 sets, and center B, 250 sets. The maximum production capacities are 275 sets at plant 1, and 325 at plant 2. Television sets can be shipped from either plant to either distribution center, but shipping costs differ. Figure 1.1 shows the cost per set for shipments along each of the four possible routes. The manufacturer wants to supply the requirements at both distribution centers at the lowest possible total cost.

We now express this problem in mathematical form. The manufacturer must decide on four quantities—the numbers of sets to be shipped along each route. To develop a mathematical model of this problem, we must introduce symbols for each of these quantities. Let us set x_{1A} equal to the number of sets shipped from plant 1 to center A, x_{1B} the number from plant 1 to center B, x_{2A} the number from plant 2 to center A, and x_{2B} the number from plant 2 to center B.

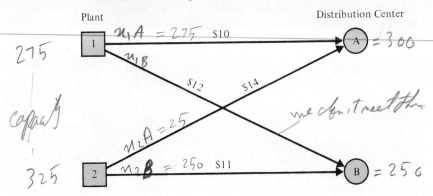

FIGURE 1.1 Costs per unit for shipments of television sets.

Handwritten annotations on figure:
Plant — 275 ; capacity ; 325
Distribution Center
$x_1A = 275$ $10 — A = 300
x_1B
$12 $14
we don't meet the
$x_2A = 25$
$x_2B = 250$ $11 — B = 256

Management is concerned about the total cost of the shipments. Since it costs $10 per set for shipments from plant 1 to distribution center A, if x_{1A} sets are sent along this route, the total cost will be $10 x_{1A}. Similarly, total shipment costs along the other three routes will be $12 x_{1B}, $14 x_{2A}, and $11 x_{2B}. Therefore, the total cost, in dollars, of all shipments will be

$C = 10 x_{1A} + 14 x_{2B} + 11 x_{2A}$ MINIMIZE

$$C = 10\,x_{1A} + 12\,x_{1B} + 14\,x_{2A} + 11\,x_{2B} \qquad (1.1)$$

The aim of this corporation is to choose x_{1A}, x_{1B}, x_{2A}, and x_{2B} so that the total cost given in equation (1.1) is as small as possible.

However, we do not as yet have a complete specification of the problem as limitations on the values that the variables x_{1A}, x_{1B}, x_{2A}, x_{2B} can take are imposed both by requirements at the two distribution centers and capacities of the two plants. Since 300 sets are needed at center A, this must be the total ($x_{1A} + x_{2A}$) of sets sent to that center from the two plants. We can therefore write

$$x_{1A} + x_{2A} = 300 \qquad (1.2)$$

Similarly, the requirement that 250 sets must be sent to distribution center B implies that

$$x_{1B} + x_{2B} = 250 \qquad (1.3)$$

The distributor then faces the problem of choosing the order quantity and the reorder point so as to minimize total order costs.

Now, the costs that will be incurred through any particular choice of these variables will depend on future product demand. If it were to be assumed that future demand were known with certainty, we could proceed to build and analyze a deterministic model of this system. However, for many products, demand levels fluctuate quite widely over time. Managers devote a great deal of effort to forecasting future product demand levels.[3] However, these forecasts are only estimates of future trends—they do not provide perfect foresight. In circumstances where there is much uncertainty about future demand, this should be incorporated in the system modeling, and a stochastic model will be appropriate.

In subsequent chapters of this book we will analyze management problems both through deterministic and stochastic models.

1.4. SOME MANAGEMENT SCIENCE PROBLEMS: A PREVIEW OF THINGS TO COME

In the previous two sections we have met two problems—the transportation problem, and the inventory management problem—that crop up rather frequently in business management. In this section we will outline several other problems. Our aim here is not to discuss the details of model building and problem solution—these must be postponed for later chapters. Rather we wish to provide a flavor of those activities in which the management scientist/operations researcher is engaged.

(i) THE PRODUCT MIX PROBLEM: LINEAR PROGRAMMING

Almost every modern manufacturing firm produces a range of products, and, for any production period, management has some discretion in the choice of product mix. Consider the following simple example, which we will begin to study in some detail in Chapter 2. An office furnishings company manufactures both desks and bookcases. For the coming week, management believes that within the feasible output ranges, each desk that is made can be sold at a profit of $30, and each bookcase at a profit of $20. These two products must pass through three departments—assembly, finishing, and inspection—and capacity constraints in these departments impose limitations on the quantities that can be produced. Each desk requires 8 man-hours of assembly time, 4 man-hours of finishing time, and one man-hour of inspection time. Also, each bookcase requires 4 man-hours of assembly time, 6 man-hours of inspection time, and one man-hour of finishing time. In total, for the coming week, this company expects to have available 640 man-hours of assembly time, 540 man-hours of finishing

---

[3] Some of the procedures employed will be discussed in Chapter 12.

time, and 100 man-hours of inspection time. Suppose, now, that management's objective is to find the product mix that will lead to the highest possible total profit. How many desks and bookcases should be made in this week?

As we have posed it, management needs to solve a **constrained optimization problem.** The aim is to find the product mix that maximizes total profits. However, capacity constraints in the three departments limit the choices of output levels. In fact, the special characteristics of our example place it in a subclass of constrained optimization problems called **linear programming** problems. In the next four chapters we will study linear programming in depth, showing how it can be applied to the solution of product mix problems, and to a wide range of other management problems.

(ii) MEETING MULTIPLE OBJECTIVES: GOAL PROGRAMMING

One element of the product mix problem just discussed was that management concentrated on a single objective—the maximization of short-run profit. Often the situation will not, in practice, be this straightforward. Rather, managers may have to concentrate on more than a single objective. Suppose, for example, that the office furnishings company has received from an important customer a large order for bookcases, and in the interests of customer goodwill wishes to go as far as possible towards meeting this demand. Management needs now to concentrate on two factors—the total profit, and the output of bookcases. One approach to this problem is to set targets, or **goals,** for the week's output. For instance, management may specify a total profit of at least $2500, and output of at least 60 bookcases.

Problems of this type, where multiple goals are set rather than optimization of a single objective, can often be formulated as **goal programming** problems. In Chapter 7 we will discuss and illustrate goal programming in some detail.

(iii) PROJECT PLANNING: NETWORK MODELS

It often happens that a project, involving many constituent interrelated activities, must be planned. The management of such projects raises important questions about the scheduling and costs of the individual activities, so that the whole project can be completed in a reasonable amount of time, within an overall budget. Consider, for example, the position of a manufacturer of detergent, planning a new promotional campaign for a product with sales that have recently been slipping. The campaign is to include new packaging for the product and intensive media advertising. This project will involve a number of activities. An overall budget must be determined and allocated, the new packages must be designed and produced, advertising copy must be written and advertisements prepared for radio, television, and newspapers. These activities are interrelated, in the sense that some cannot be started until others have been finished. For example, the new packages must be designed before they can be produced. Such interrelationships must be taken into account in assessing when the entire project can be completed.

In Chapter 13 we will see how **network models** can be employed to analyze such systems. The name derives from the fact that this, and many other problems, are most easily studied through a diagram called a network. It is often the case that a stochastic model is required for the analysis of a project planning problem. This will be so when there is uncertainty about the times that will be required to carry out the individual activities of the project.

(iv) CUSTOMER SERVICE: QUEUEING MODELS

A problem that is invariably most appropriately analyzed through a stochastic model arises in the study of the time spent by customers waiting for service. For example, trucks will arrive at a loading dock, and must be serviced; patients arrive at an emergency clinic to meet a physician. In either case, the precise times at which customers arrive, and the amounts of time they require for service will not be known with certainty. Nevertheless, it is important to have information on system service characteristics, such as the expected amount of time spent waiting in line.

In Chapter 15 we will consider **queueing models,** designed to provide a description of waiting line systems with uncertain arrival and service times. Such study helps in the design of systems with acceptable service characteristics.

The methods of management science provide the manager with powerful tools to aid in decision-making for a wide range of problems. In subsequent chapters of this book we will explore more fully the methods involved and illustrate their application.

linear programming: graphical solution

CHAPTER TWO

2.1. AREAS OF APPLICATION

In this chapter we will begin a detailed discussion of linear programming, a technique developed in 1947 by George Dantzig. It is one of the most commonly used of all quantitative management tools. Before introducing this procedure, we will discuss several of the multitude of areas of practical application in which the linear programming algorithm has proved to be valuable.

(i) *Product Mix*. Most manufacturing companies have the resources to produce more than one product and to adjust, to some extent at least, the proportions in which products are made. Such multi-product firms, then, have some flexibility in the choice of individual product output levels. The objective will be to choose that product mix which is most profitable. In making this choice, such a firm will be constrained by its resources of both equipment and labor. It will seek the most profitable output mix compatible with these constraints. In the following section, the linear programming problem will be illustrated through a specific product mix application.

(ii) *Blending*. Many products, for example those of the chemical, petroleum, pharmaceutical, and processed foods industries, contain mixtures of basic ingredients. The finished products will typically be required to meet certain specifications. Subject to these being met, the manufacturer is free to choose the blend of basic ingredients, perhaps being constrained also by their availability. The choice made will aim to produce a satisfactory product at as low a cost as possible. In Section 10 of this chapter, we will discuss a specific blending problem.

(iii) *Distribution Problems*. A company, for example a textbook publisher, may have warehouses at various places in the country. All orders received must be met by shipment from these warehouses. For example, copies of specific textbooks must be shipped to campus bookstores to meet the demand for fall classes. The company will want to minimize the distribution costs involved while meeting this demand. Thus, our textbook publisher will attempt to keep the cost of shipments as low as possible and seek the cheapest distribution system possible, given the availability of books in the various warehouses. We will discuss problems of this sort in some detail in Chapter 6.

(iv) *Purchasing*. The purchasing department of a corporation will have available many different sources of needed materials, in various quantities and qualities. Any number of different combinations of possibilities for purchase will be available. Subject to production requirements and budget restrictions, the combination sought is that for which the highest profit will result.

(v) *Portfolio Selection*. An investor faces the problem of deciding how to distribute his or her investments among such alternative assets as common stocks, bonds, and money market instruments. One strategy might be to seek the highest possible expected return on investment. However, such a strategy may also involve an unacceptably high level of risk to the investor. More prudently, the investor may seek to maximize expected return, subject to some tolerably high level of risk, in selecting an appropriate portfolio of investments.

(vi) *Advertising Media Mix*. Given a budget for product promotion, the marketing department of a corporation must decide how much to spend on advertising in newspapers and magazines, and on radio and television. The objective is to maximize the exposure of the product to potential customers, subject to budget constraints and media space and time availability.

(vii) *Production and Inventory Scheduling*. Corporations manufacturing several products will inevitably face variations through time in the market demands for these products. It is generally costly to make large changes in production schedules, so that inventory is carried to help meet fluctuations in demand. The problem is to minimize production and inventory holding costs, while meeting anticipated product demand.

Now, the range of applications just discussed is indeed diverse. Nevertheless, through all these problems we can trace two common threads.

First, each of the applications involves **optimization,** that is to say, in each case the objective is to **maximize,** or to **minimize,** something. For example, in the product mix and purchasing examples, the aim was to maximize profits. In the blending and distribution applications, the objective was to minimize costs.

There is also a further similarity. In none of the applications is it possible to go ahead and solve the optimization problem without paying attention to **constraints** on what is possible. In the product mix problem, availability of equipment and labor will restrict the range of possible combinations of output levels. For the blending problem, product specifications will impose constraints on what blends of materials it is feasible to employ.

A great many practical management problems can be characterized as problems of **constrained optimization.** Many of these can be set in a form for which the linear programming model is applicable. In the remainder of this and the next few chapters, we will consider this model and some of its applications.

2.2. A MAXIMIZATION PROBLEM

Let us now turn to detailed discussion of a specific product mix problem. A small company in the office furnishings field produces both desks and bookcases. There are three stages of production—assembly, finishing, and inspection. A

$\eta_1 =$

TABLE 2.1 Specifications for the product mix problem for the office furnishings company.

TOTAL MAN-HOURS AVAILABLE		MAN-HOURS PER UNIT	
		DESK	BOOKCASE
640	Assembly	8	4
540	Finishing	4	6
100	Inspection	1	1
	PROFIT PER UNIT ($)	30	20

desk requires 8 man-hours, and a bookcase 4 man-hours of assembly time. The finishing time needed is 4 man-hours for a desk and 6 man-hours for a bookcase. Finally, each product requires one man-hour per unit of inspection time. For the coming week, this company has available 640 man-hours in assembly, 540 man-hours in finishing, and 100 man-hours in inspection. The accountants of this company have determined that, within the range of its production possibilities, each desk can be sold for a profit of $30, and each bookcase for a profit of $20. For convenience, we summarize all of this information in Table 2.1.

The objective of the office furnishings company is to achieve as high a level of profit as possible, and to this end, the company is free to choose how many desks and how many bookcases are to be produced. However, this choice is not *completely* free. Rather, it is necessary to choose a combination of output levels that does not exceed the capacities available for assembly, finishing, or inspection. In fact, then, the company must solve a constrained optimization problem.

This company's task of selecting an optimal product mix fits into the general framework of linear programming. In the next three sections of this chapter we will introduce that framework by working out a solution to this specific problem.

2.3. SETTING UP THE PROBLEM

We must now express the optimization problem specifications of our office furnishings company in a convenient algebraic form. The company has some flexibility in the choice of two quantities—the amounts of desks and of bookcases to be produced in the week. We refer to such quantities as **decision variables.** We will denote by x_1 the number of desks to be produced, and by x_2 the number of bookcases.

Now, we have seen that for this company each desk made yields a profit of $30, and each bookcase a $20 profit. Hence, the total profit, in dollars, from an output of x_1 desks and x_2 bookcases will be

$$\text{Profit} = 30x_1 + 20x_2$$

The company's objective is to maximize profit, and this function of the decision variables is called the **objective function.**

Any choice of the decision variables is called a **solution** to the company's choice problem. For example, an output of $x_1 = 15$ desks and $x_2 = 18$ bookcases would yield a profit of

$$(30)(15) + (20)(18) = 810$$

dollars. However, the company, in seeking a practical solution is bound by **constraints** due to limited resources for assembly, finishing, and inspection. These constraints, too, can be expressed algebraically. Each desk requires 8 man-hours, and each bookcase 4 man-hours of assembly time. Hence, the total amount of assembly time required for the production of x_1 desks and x_2 bookcases is, in man-hours,

$$\text{Assembly Time Needed} = 8x_1 + 4x_2$$

The company has available at most 640 man-hours of assembly time. It is not able to use more than this, so that the assembly time actually employed must be no more than 640 hours. We can write this constraint, then, as

$$\text{Assembly Time Constraint: } 8x_1 + 4x_2 \leq 640$$

where the symbol $\leq$ denotes "less than or equal to." Similarly, finishing requires 4 man-hours for a desk and 6 man-hours for a bookcase with a total of 540 man-hours of finishing time available. The constraint thus imposed therefore can be written

$$\text{Finishing Time Constraint: } 4x_1 + 6x_2 \leq 540$$

Finally, the inspection time constraint is

$$\text{Inspection Time Constraint: } x_1 + x_2 \leq 100$$

We must also include in our problem specification two further constraints. It is obviously not possible to manufacture negative quantities of either bookcases or desks. The numbers produced must be at least zero. We can express these **nonnegativity constraints** as

$$\text{Nonnegativity Constraints: } x_1 \geq 0, x_2 \geq 0$$

The office furnishings company is free to select any combination of production levels for desks and bookcases which satisfies all of the constraints. It is not, however, able to choose a combination that violates any one of them. Thus, not all solutions for the decision variables are attainable. Any solution which satisfies all of the constraints is called a **feasible solution.** Consider the solution $x_1 = 50$, $x_2 = 50$; that is, the production of 50 desks and 50 bookcases. It can be directly verified that this requires 600 man-hours of assembly time, 500 man-hours of finishing time, and 100 man-hours of inspection time. Since it would violate none of the constraints, it is a feasible solution. By contrast, consider $x_1 = 25$, $x_2 = 75$, an output of 25 desks and 75 bookcases. This would require 500 man-hours of assembly time, 550 of finishing time, and 100 of inspection time. This solution would violate the finishing time constraint and so is not feasible.

Our company is free to choose any of the multitude of feasible solutions to the product mix problem. However, it will want to choose a feasible solution for which profits are as high as possible. Such a feasible solution is called an **optimal solution.** Gathering together the material in this section, we can succinctly formulate the aim of the office furnishings company, in algebraic form, as:

$$\text{Maximize } 30x_1 + 20x_2$$
$$\text{subject to} \quad 8x_1 + 4x_2 \leq 640$$
$$4x_1 + 6x_2 \leq 540$$
$$x_1 + x_2 \leq 100$$
$$x_1, x_2 \geq 0$$

Constrained optimization problems of this sort are referred to as **mathematical programming problems.** Our particular problem has a special feature. Notice that in the objective function and in all the constraints, the decision variables, x_1 and x_2, appear only in separate terms and raised to the first power. Functions of this sort are called linear functions,[1] and the corresponding problem formulation is then said to be a **linear program.**

Definitions

(i) Decision Variables: Quantities whose values can be chosen by a decision maker.

(ii) Objective Function: A function of the decision variables whose value is to be made as large (or, in some problems, as small) as possible.

(iii) Constraints: Restrictions on the values which can be taken by the decision variables.

(iv) Nonnegativity Constraints: Requirements that the decision variables not take negative values.

(v) Feasible Solution: Any set of values of the decision variables which satisfies all the constraints.

(vi) Optimal Solution: Any feasible solution such that the value of the objective function is as high (or, in minimization problems, as low) as possible.

(vii) Linear Program: A setup in which the objective function and the constraints involve only linear functions of the decision variables.

---

[1] Let $x_1, x_2, \ldots, x_K$ be a set of K variables. Then, any function of the form

$$a_1x_1 + a_2x_2 + \ldots + a_Kx_K$$

where $a_1, a_2, \ldots, a_K$ are fixed numbers, is called a linear function of the x_i.

In this section, we have algebraically formulated the position faced by our office furnishing company in attempting to determine the best possible product mix. Considerable further insight into such problems, and methods for their solution, can be obtained through a **graphical** analysis, to which we proceed in the following sections of this chapter.

2.4. GRAPHICAL DESCRIPTION OF THE PROBLEM

We will now set up our problem in graphical format. To do this, we will construct, as in Figure 2.1, a graph in which output of desks, x_1, is measured along the horizontal axis, and output of bookcases, x_2, along the vertical axis. Then, any output combination can be represented by a point on our graph. For example, in Figure 2.1, we show the point corresponding to production of 30 desks and 60 bookcases; that is, ($x_1 = 30$, $x_2 = 60$), which for simplicity we denote (30, 60).

Given this graphical framework, we will now depict the constraints faced by our office furnishings company. To begin, the non-negativity constraints, which imply that the numbers of both desks and bookcases must be at least zero, dictate that any feasible solution must be in the northeast quadrant of our graph. This is shown in Figure 2.2.

FIGURE 2.1 Graphical framework for output combinations of desks and bookcases: The point shown represents an output of 30 desks and 60 bookcases.

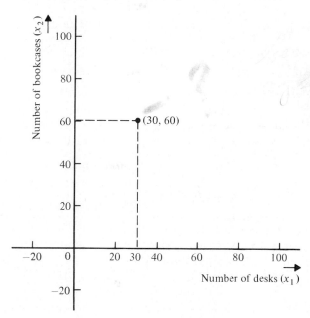

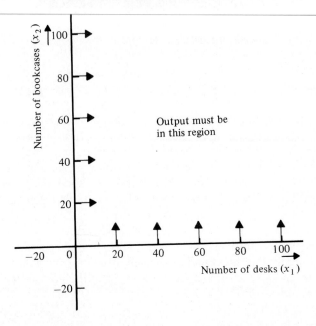

We now go on to draw in the other constraints, restricting attention to the case of nonnegative outputs. Recall that the assembly time constraint is

$$8x_1 + 4x_2 \leq 640$$

We can represent this by first drawing the line depicting the equation

$$8x_1 + 4x_2 = 640 \qquad (2.1)$$

Now, any line can be drawn by connecting a pair of points that lie on it. To obtain such a pair of points, we will find the value of x_2 when x_1 is zero, and the value of x_1 when x_2 is zero. Setting x_1 to zero in equation (2.1), we have

$$4x_2 = 640$$

so that

$$x_2 = 160$$

Hence, the point (0, 160) is on our line. The implication of this is that if no desks at all were to be made, there would be assembly time capacity for up to 160 bookcases. Similarly, setting x_1 to zero in equation (2.1) yields

$$8x_1 = 640$$

so that

$$x_1 = 80$$

It follows that the point (80, 0) is also on our line. Joining the points (0, 160) and (80, 0), we obtain, as in Figure 2.3, the line for equation (2.1).

Now, for any point lying along this line, we have an output combination for desks and bookcases that uses up precisely 640 man-hours of assembly time, and would therefore just be attainable, if the only constraint were imposed by limited assembly time. Next, consider any point to the northeast of our line, for example the point (50, 80), corresponding to 50 desks and 80 bookcases. Such output combinations violate the assembly time constraint. For the point (50, 80), the number of assembly man-hours needed would be

$$8x_1 + 4x_2 = (8)(50) + (4)(80) = 720$$

which exceeds the 640 man-hours available.

By contrast, consider now any point, such as (40, 60), to the southwest of the line (2.1). Such points depict output combinations which satisfy the assembly time constraint. This particular combination requires

$$8x_1 + 4x_2 = (8)(40) + (4)(60) = 560$$

FIGURE 2.3 Limitations on production possibilities imposed by the assembly time constraint: The shaded area shows all output combinations satisfying both the assembly time constraint and the nonnegativity constraints. The solution (50, 80) violates the assembly time constraint, the solution (40, 60) does not.

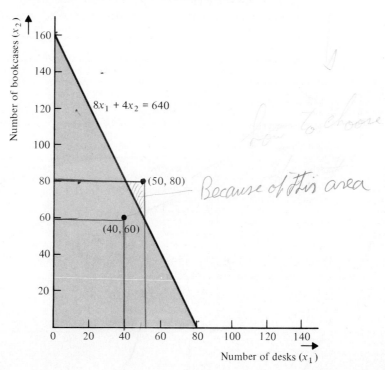

man-hours of assembly time. It follows, then, that any pair of output combinations in the region bounded by the line (2.1) and the vertical and horizontal axes, satisfies both the assembly time constraint and the nonnegativity constraints. This region is depicted by the shaded area in Figure 2.3.

Next, we turn to the finishing time constraint

$$4x_1 + 6x_2 \le 540$$

Proceeding as before, in Figure 2.4 the line

$$4x_1 + 6x_2 = 540 \qquad\qquad (2.2)$$

is drawn. Setting $x_1 = 0$ in equation (2.2) gives

$$6x_2 = 540$$

so that

$$x_2 = 90$$

FIGURE 2.4 Limitations on production possibilities imposed by the finishing time constraint: The shaded area shows all output combinations satisfying both the finishing time constraint and the nonnegativity constraints.

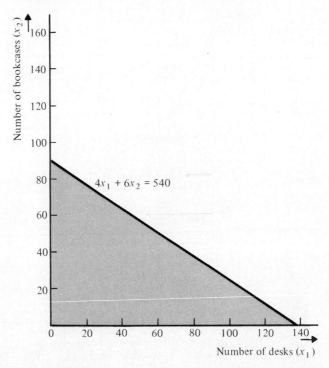

Setting $x_2 = 0$ in equation (2.2), we have

$$4x_1 = 540$$

so that

$$x_1 = 135$$

Therefore, we can draw the line (2.2) by connecting the points (0, 90) and (135, 0). In precisely analogous fashion to our discussion of the assembly time constraint, it follows that any pair of output combinations in the region bounded by the line (2.2) and the vertical and horizontal axes, satisfies both the finishing time constraint and the nonnegativity constraints. This region is depicted in Figure 2.4.

Arguing in precisely the same fashion as above, we can also show graphically the limitations on the production possibilities of the office furnishings company imposed by the final constraint—that for inspection time. This is done in Figure 2.5.

Now, any combination of outputs of desks and bookcases produced by our company must simultaneously satisfy *all* the constraints. That is to say, it must lie in *all* the shaded areas of Figures 2.3–2.5. We can show this requirement by

FIGURE 2.5 Limitations on production possibilities imposed by the inspection time constraint: The shaded area shows all output combinations satisfying both the inspection time constraint and the nonnegativity constraints.

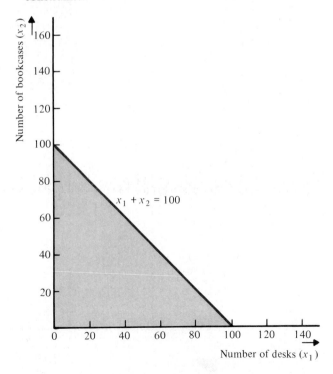

drawing a graph which superimposes these three figures on one another. This is precisely what is done in Figure 2.6. Any feasible solution to the product mix problem must lie in the area bounded by the two axes and the three lines

$$4x_1 + 6x_2 = 540$$

$$x_1 + x_2 = 100$$

$$8x_1 + 4x_2 = 640$$

This is the shaded area shown in Figure 2.6, and is known as the **feasible region.** Recall that in the previous section we showed that an output of 50 desks and 50 bookcases was a feasible solution, while an output of 25 desks and 75 bookcases was not. This is demonstrated graphically in Figure 2.6 where these two points are plotted. In summary, then, we have pictured in that figure the totality of possible output combinations which this company can produce, given its capacity limitations.

Definition

Feasible Region: The set of all possible feasible solutions.

FIGURE 2.6 Feasible region for the office furnishings company. The point (50, 50) is in the feasible region, the point (25, 75) is not.

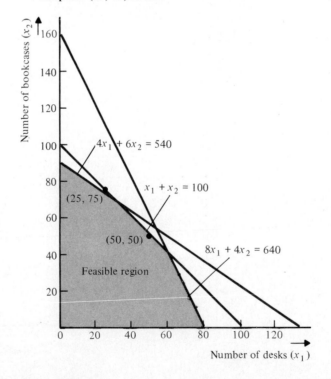

Having found a graphical representation of the constraints for our linear programming problem, we must now similarly represent the objective function. For the office furnishings company this is the function relating profit to output levels; that is

$$\text{Profit} = 30x_1 + 20x_2$$

where x_1 and x_2 are the respective quantities of desks and bookcases produced. It follows, for example, that any point on the line

$$30x_1 + 20x_2 = 1800$$

yields a profit of $1800. Similarly, output combinations on the lines

$$30x_1 + 20x_2 = 2600$$

and

$$30x_1 + 20x_2 = 3000$$

yield respective profits of $2600 and $3000. These three lines are drawn in Figure 2.7. Notice that these are parallel lines, and that the farther out the line from the origin the higher the profit. In this figure, then, we see that all output combinations lying on the same line yield the same profit, while an output combination on a line farther from the origin yields a higher profit than one on a line nearer the origin.

Combining the information in Figures 2.6 and 2.7, we are now in a position

FIGURE 2.7 Some values of the objective function for the office furnishings company.

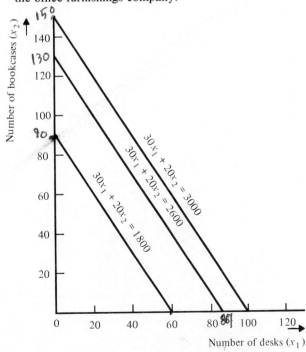

to provide a full graphical description of the product mix problem of the office furnishings company. First, the output combination that is to be produced must lie in the feasible region shown in Figure 2.6. Next, in order that profits be as high as possible, the output combination should be on a line, parallel to those of Figure 2.7, that is as far as possible from the origin.

2.5. THE GRAPHICAL SOLUTION

We have now covered the most difficult part of the route to the solution of our product mix problem. To travel the final mile, all that is necessary is to put together Figures 2.6 and 2.7. This is done in Figure 2.8 which shows the relation of the three profit lines of Figure 2.7 to the feasible region.

We see from the figure that the company can certainly have a profit of $1800. Any number of output combinations in the feasible region lie on the line which yields this profit. Now, in order to increase profits above this level, the company would have to move output to a parallel line farther from the origin. However, such a line must contain a point—that is, an output combination—in the feasible region. How far out is it possible to go, then, in increasing profits?

FIGURE 2.8 Solution of the product mix problem of the office furnishings company. Optimal solution is point (60, 40).

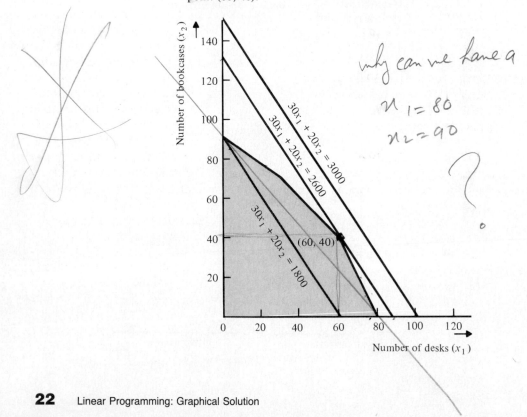

We see from the figure that a profit of $2600 is possible, as this profit line just touches the boundary of the feasible region. Any attempt to increase profits beyond this level is doomed to failure, for it would mean moving to a solution on a line, such as that yielding a profit of $3000, which lies entirely outside the feasible region.

This graphical analysis, then, has demonstrated that the highest profit that can be achieved is $2600. Furthermore, we see from the graph that this profit line touches the feasible region at the point (60, 40); that is, an output of 60 desks and 40 bookcases.

Let us pause to review what we have accomplished. The office furnishings company aimed to make as high a profit as possible, given the capacity restrictions imposed through limited availability of time for assembly, finishing, and inspection. We found that the best strategy for this company is to produce 60 desks and 40 bookcases, thereby generating a profit of $2600.

In fact, although we have studied and solved just a single specific problem, we have really learned a good deal and are in a position to infer a good deal more about more general linear programming problems and their solution. We will elaborate on this assertion in the next three sections of this chapter.

2.6. CHARACTERIZATIONS OF THE OPTIMAL SOLUTION

The office furnishings company faced three constraints, plus two nonnegativity constraints, on output. Taken together, we saw in Figure 2.6 that these five constraints imposed a feasible region bounded by a five-sided figure. Using Figure 2.8 we were able to solve the product mix problem. The optimal solution has a rather special feature. *This optimal solution to our problem is located at one of the corners of the feasible region.* Do you think that this is coincidental? A little reflection on the argument through which we obtained this solution should convince you that it is not. Recall that our approach was to consider parallel profit lines, and to move out from the origin from one such line to another until we reached the stage where any further movement would put us on a line lying entirely outside the feasible region. It necessarily follows that the outcome will be an optimal solution that is located at one of the corners of the feasible region.

The argument of the previous paragraph establishes an important conclusion about the nature of the optimal solution to linear programming problems of the kind we are considering. The office furnishings company could select a product mix from among a very large number of feasible solutions. However, *even without knowledge of the specific form of the objective function,* we know that an optimal solution can be found in one of five places, namely the output combinations corresponding to the five corners of the feasible region; that is, at the points at which the constraint lines cross. These five values are called **extreme points.**

Extreme Points are the corners of the feasible region.

In Figure 2.9 we show the extreme points for the problem of the office furnishings company. We can find the output combination values for these points in one of two ways. First, they can be read off directly from the graph. This, however, is a little imprecise. An alternative is to find these values algebraically. Beginning at the origin, we have the point (0, 0), corresponding to no output of either desks or bookcases.

We now proceed clockwise to identify the other four extreme points. The first of these is the point at which the line

$$4x_1 + 6x_2 = 540 \tag{2.3}$$

FIGURE 2.9 Extreme points for the office furnishings company.

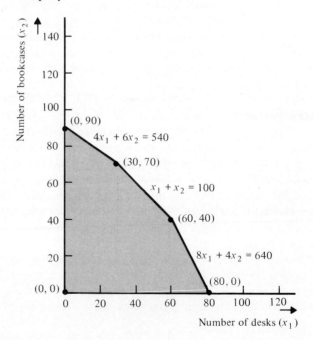

meets the vertical axis. We therefore require the value of x_2 on this line when x_1 is zero. Substituting $x_1 = 0$ in (2.3) yields

$$6x_2 = 540$$

or

$$x_2 = 90$$

so that $(0, 90)$ is the required point.

The next extreme point lies at the intersection of the lines (2.3) and

$$x_1 + x_2 = 100 \qquad (2.4)$$

To locate this point, we first multiply through (2.4) by 6, giving

$$6x_1 + 6x_2 = 600 \qquad (2.5)$$

Now, subtracting the left- and right-hand sides of (2.3) from those of (2.5) gives

$$(6x_1 - 4x_1) + (6x_2 - 6x_2) = 600 - 540$$

or

$$2x_1 = 60$$

so that

$$x_1 = 30$$

Hence the number of desks, x_1, produced at this extreme point is 30. To find the value of x_2 at this point, we multiply through (2.4) by 4, giving

$$4x_1 + 4x_2 = 400 \qquad (2.6)$$

Subtracting the left- and right-hand sides of (2.6) from those of (2.3) yields

$$(4x_1 - 4x_1) + (6x_2 - 4x_2) = 540 - 400$$

or

$$2x_2 = 140$$

so that

$$x_2 = 70$$

We therefore have identified this extreme point as the point (30, 70).
We now move on to the point where the line (2.4) meets the line

$$8x_1 + 4x_2 = 640 \tag{2.7}$$

You will recall that this point has already been shown to be the optimal solution to the constrained optimization problem of the office furnishings company. In Figure 2.8 we identified this as corresponding to an output of 60 desks and 40 bookcases. We now verify these figures algebraically. Multiplying through equation (2.4) by 4 yields once again (2.6). Subtracting the left- and right-hand sides of (2.6) from (2.7) then produces

$$(8x_1 - 4x_1) + (4x_2 - 4x_2) = 640 - 400$$

so that

$$4x_1 = 240$$

or

$$x_1 = 60$$

Next, multiplying through (2.4) by 8 gives

$$8x_1 + 8x_2 = 800 \tag{2.8}$$

Subtracting the left- and right-hand sides of (2.7) from those of (2.8) yields

$$(8x_1 - 8x_1) + (8x_2 - 4x_2) = 800 - 640$$

so that

$$4x_2 = 160$$

and hence

$$x_2 = 40$$

We have thus verified that this extreme point is indeed the point (60, 40).
The fifth and final extreme point for this problem is where the line (2.7) meets the horizontal axis, where x_2 is zero. Substituting $x_2 = 0$ in (2.7) gives

$$8x_1 = 640$$

so that

$$x_1 = 80$$

Hence, we have identified this point as (80, 0). The five values of our extreme points are shown in Figure 2.9.

EXTREME POINTS AND LOCATION OF OPTIMAL SOLUTION

Now that we understand that an optimal solution to our linear programming problem can be found at an extreme point, we have available a more straightforward means of locating an optimal solution than following a graphical argument such as that of Figure 2.8. All that is necessary is to evaluate the objective function at each of the extreme points. For problems where the objective is maximization, the extreme point yielding the highest value of the objective function is an optimal solution.

To illustrate, the objective of the office furnishings company is to maximize

$$\text{Profit} = 30x_1 + 20x_2 \qquad (2.9)$$

Let us determine the value of this function at the extreme point (30, 70); that is, we require to find the profit resulting from production of 30 desks and 70 bookcases. Substituting $x_1 = 30$ and $x_2 = 70$ into (2.9) gives

$$\text{Profit} = (30)(30) + (20)(70) = 2300$$

This particular output combination, then, leads to a profit of $2300. In the same way we can find the profit following from production at each of the other four extreme points. The results are summarized in Table 2.2.

We can read directly from Table 2.2 that the optimal solution to our linear programming problem is production of 60 desks and 40 bookcases, producing a profit of $2600.

We have already asserted that changing the objective function will not alter our conclusion that an extreme point will provide an optimal solution. Table 2.3 lists three different functions for which the respective extreme points (0, 90), (30, 70), and (80, 0) are optimal solutions. As an exercise the reader is invited to verify, both by a tabular analysis, like that of Table 2.2, and a graphical analysis, similar to that of Figure 2.8, that these solutions are indeed optimal

TABLE 2.2 Values of objective function at extreme points for the office furnishings company.

EXTREME POINTS		VALUE OF OBJECTIVE FUNCTION (PROFIT IN $)
x_1	x_2	
0	0	0
0	90	1800
30	70	2300
60	40	2600
80	0	2400

TABLE 2.3 Optimal solutions for different objective functions of the office furnishings company.

OBJECTIVE FUNCTION	OPTIMAL SOLUTION	VALUE OF OBJECTIVE FUNCTION AT OPTIMAL SOLUTION
$10x_1 + 40x_2$	(0, 90)	3600
$22x_1 + 28x_2$	(30, 70)	2620
$35x_1 + 15x_2$	(80, 0)	2800

Let us verify graphically the optimal solution to the first of the problems in Table 2.3. In this problem, we are considering the case where each desk produced yields a profit of $10, and each bookcase a profit of $40, so that the profit function is

$$\text{Profit} = 10x_1 + 40x_2$$

Now, the objective function has no effect on the constraints, so that our altering this function will not affect the feasible region. Figure 2.10 shows the feasible region, together with the line

$$10x_1 + 40x_2 = 3600$$

Now, all output combinations on this line yield a profit of $3600. We see from Figure 2.10 that this level of profit can be attained by the production of 90 book-

FIGURE 2.10 Optimal solution of the office furnishings company product mix problem for the objective function $10x_1 + 40x_2 = 3600$.

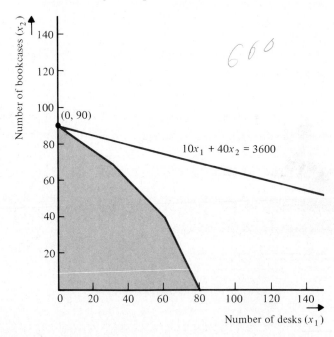

cases and no desks. However, it would not be possible to achieve a higher profit, for this would involve moving output to a parallel profit line farther from the origin. No such line contains a point in the feasible region.

The reader might be surprised that we have included among the extreme points to be checked in seeking the optimal solution to our linear programming problem, the origin (0,0). This implies no output at all of either desks or bookcases. Suppose, however, that each desk and each bookcase made yielded a loss (that is, a negative profit) to the company. In that case, the best strategy would be to produce nothing at all, so that the origin *is* the optimal solution here!

2.7. MULTIPLE OPTIMAL SOLUTIONS, INFEASIBILITY, AND UNBOUNDEDNESS

To this point we have discussed and illustrated a linear programming problem for which a unique optimal solution exists. Our office furnishings company is able to find a set of output combinations which satisfy all of its production constraints. Moreover, from among these feasible solutions, there exists a single optimal solution yielding a higher value of the objective function than any other. By producing 60 desks and 40 bookcases, this company can obtain a profit of $2600. Production at any other feasible solution would yield a lower profit. More often than not, in practice, linear programming problems lead to such solutions. However, this is not always the case. In this section we will discuss some types of problems for which unique optimal solutions do not exist.

MULTIPLE OPTIMAL SOLUTIONS

Suppose that the office furnishings company faces the same production constraints as before, but that now the market is such that a profit of $25 on each desk and $25 on each bookcase can be obtained. The objective function that we want to maximize is now

$$\text{Profit} = 25x_1 + 25x_2$$

Table 2.4 shows the values of this profit function at the five extreme points. In contrast with our earlier problem, we see now that the highest value for profits

TABLE 2.4 Values of the objective function $25x_1 + 25x_2$ at extreme points for the office furnishings company.

EXTREME POINTS		VALUE OF OBJECTIVE FUNCTION (PROFIT IN $)
x_1	x_2	
0	0	0
0	90	2250
30	70	2500
60	40	2500
80	0	2000

is attained not just at one, but at two, of these points. A profit of $2500 can be obtained by producing either 30 desks and 70 bookcases or 60 desks and 40 bookcases. Production at the other extreme points would lead to lower profits.

Already we have seen, then, that here is a linear programming problem with more than one optimal solution. The analysis of this problem can be taken further through a graph. Figure 2.11 shows the feasible region, together with the line

$$25x_1 + 25x_2 = 2500$$

It emerges from this picture that *any* output combination along this line between the points (30,70) and (60,40) is an optimal solution. A profit of $2500 can be obtained by producing 35 desks and 65 bookcases, 50 of each, and so on. Thus, there exists a multitude of optimal solutions.

The explanation of this phenomenon is clear from Figure 2.11. For this particular objective function, profit lines are parallel to one of the lines bounding the feasible region. In such circumstances linear programming problems can have multiple optimal solutions. This imposes no practical difficulties. Our company is simply free to choose from a range of product mix possibilities, and, if its only objective is profit maximization, the particular optimal solution chosen is a matter of indifference.

INFEASIBILITY

We have now met a linear programming problem with a unique optimal solution, and also a problem with multiple optimal solutions. It is pertinent to ask whether *any* optimal solution need necessarily exist. As we will see, the answer is "no." Indeed, it may be the case that no *feasible* solution exists. As a simple illustration of this point, consider once more our office furnishings company. This company faces production constraints imposed by limited amounts of time available for assembly, finishing, and inspection. Suppose, now, that the company has a customer whom it is desirable to satisfy in the hope of obtaining further orders. This customer requires delivery within the week of 120 bookcases. This requirement imposes the further constraint

$$x_2 \geq 120$$

The constrained optimization problem of the office furnishings company can now be written

$$
\begin{aligned}
\text{Maximize} \quad & 30x_1 + 20x_2 \\
\text{subject to} \quad & 8x_1 + 4x_2 \leq 640 \\
& 4x_1 + 6x_2 \leq 540 \\
& x_1 + x_2 \leq 100 \\
& x_2 \geq 120 \\
& x_1 \geq 0
\end{aligned}
$$

Unfortunately, this problem has no feasible solution. In Figure 2.6, and in subsequent figures, we have depicted the region of solutions satisfying all con-

FIGURE 2.11 Optimal solutions of the office furnishings company product mix problem for the objective function $25x_1 + 25x_2 = 2500$.

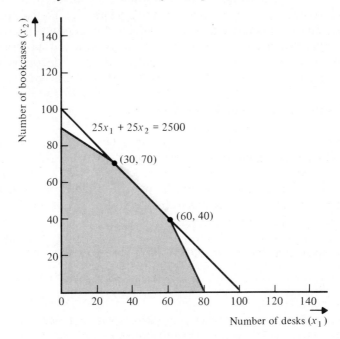

straints other than $x_2 \geq 120$. It can be seen from Figure 2.6 that, given these constraints, no output of bookcases in excess of 90 is possible. Hence, there is simply no way of satisfying simultaneously all five of the above constraints. We cannot proceed further with such problems. All we are able to do is demonstrate for the company the **infeasibility** of simultaneous satisfaction of all constraints. In itself this can be valuable, allowing the company a clearer understanding of the problem it faces.

UNBOUNDEDNESS

Consider the following problem:

$$\text{Maximize} \quad 30x_1 + 20x_2$$
$$\text{subject to} \quad x_1, x_2 \geq 0$$

This is simply the problem of the office furnishings company, but with the crucial distinction that the assembly time, finishing time, and inspection time constraints have all been removed. Indeed, the nonnegativity constraints now constitute the only restrictions on output, so that the feasible region is that area depicted in Figure 2.2.

How would you go about trying to solve this optimization problem? A little thought should convince you that this problem has an unusual, and implausible, feature. We can apparently raise the output of desks or bookcases, or both, to as high a level as we choose! It therefore follows that the objective function, that is, total profits, can be made larger and larger, with no upper bound.

This **unboundedness** of the values of the objective function that can be achieved is, as a practical matter, implausible. No corporation is truly in the position of being able to achieve infinitely high profits. Rather, if the appearance of unboundedness crops up in the formulation of a problem, it will almost certainly be the case that the problem has been incorrectly specified, perhaps through the inadvertent omission of one or more constraints. In such circumstances, it is necessary for the analyst to go back and think more carefully about the set up of the problem.

2.8. SLACK VARIABLES *to solve a series of linear eqs*

Let us consider, once again, the original problem of the office furnishings company. Recall that we set this up as

$$\text{Maximize} \quad 30x_1 + 20x_2$$
$$\text{subject to} \quad 8x_1 + 4x_2 \leq 640$$
$$4x_1 + 6x_2 \leq 540$$
$$x_1 + x_2 \leq 100$$
$$x_1, x_2 \geq 0$$

We found that the optimal solution to this problem is the production of 60 desks and 40 bookcases, that is

$$x_1 = 60, \, x_2 = 40$$

It is interesting to ask to what extent this product mix output will utilize the available resources of the company. Now, output of x_1 desks and x_2 bookcases uses an amount $8x_1 + 4x_2$ man-hours of assembly time. Hence the amount of assembly time required for the optimal solution is

$$8x_1 + 4x_2 = (8)(60) + (4)(40) = 640$$

man-hours. Notice that this is precisely the amount of time available. Similarly, the optimal product mix requires

$$4x_1 + 6x_2 = (4)(60) + (6)(40) = 480$$

man-hours of finishing time. However, 540 man-hours of finishing time are available to the company, so that 60 man-hours of this capacity will be unused when production is at the optimal product mix. Finally, the amount of inspection time used is

$$x_1 + x_2 = 60 + 40 = 100$$

man-hours, which completely exhausts the resources of the company in this department.

In terms of the optimal solution to its product mix problem, then, the three capacity constraints of this company do not all have the same status. An output of 60 desks and 40 bookcases will completely use up the capacity available for assembly and inspection. There will, however, remain 60 man-hours of unused capacity, or **slack,** in the finishing department.

For our problem, the optimal solution yields a profit of $2600. Given the existing constraints, any effort to obtain higher profits is doomed to failure. We can see now why this is so. Further resources for assembly and inspection are unavailable. (The company does have additional finishing time which could be used if extra capacity for assembly and inspection could be found.) In this problem, constraints, such as the assembly time and inspection time, are called **binding constraints.**

In fact, we could have identified the binding constraints from a review of our graphical derivation of the optimal solution in Figure 2.8. We see that this solution point is at the intersection of the lines

$$8x_1 + 4x_2 = 640$$

and

$$x_1 + x_2 = 100$$

These lines bound the feasible region as a consequence of the two binding constraints—limited time for assembly and inspection.

Definitions

(i) **Slack** is unused capacity in a "$\leq$" constraint.
(ii) **Binding Constraints** are those constraints which hold as equalities at a given point.

The concept of slack leads to an alternative statement of the linear programming problem, which we will find useful in later chapters. Essentially, the idea is that it will be convenient to replace the capacity constraint *inequalities* by *equalities*. Consider, for example, the total amount of time available for assembly. In any solution, some of this time could be used for producing desks, some for the production of bookcases, and some could be unused, or slack. Let us denote by s_1 the amount of slack time involved in the solution. We can then write the assembly time constraint as the equality

$$8x_1 + 4x_2 + s_1 = 640$$

In the same way, we can denote slack time in finishing and inspection by s_2 and s_3, respectively. Noting that in no case can slack time be negative, we now have an alternative algebraic formulation of our problem, namely

$$\text{Maximize} \quad 30x_1 + 20x_2$$

$$\text{subject to} \quad 8x_1 + 4x_2 + s_1 = 640$$

$$4x_1 + 6x_2 + s_2 = 540$$

$$x_1 + x_2 + s_3 = 100$$

$$x_1, x_2, s_1, s_2, s_3 \geq 0$$

The quantities s_1, s_2, s_3 are known as **slack variables,** and this formulation of the problem as the **standard form.**

Definitions

(i) **Slack Variables:** Variables introduced in a "$\leq$" constraint to represent the possibility of unused capacity.

(ii) **Standard Form:** A formulation of the problem involving slack variables, so that the capacity constraints are written as equalities.

This revision in the formulation of our problem does not, of course, alter its optimal solution. We have already seen that for the office furnishing company, the best strategy is to produce 60 desks and 40 bookcases, and that this leads to 60 man-hours of slack in finishing, but none in assembly or inspection. The optimal solution to the standard form of this problem is therefore

$$x_1 = 60, \, x_2 = 40, \, s_1 = 0, \, s_2 = 60, \, s_3 = 0$$

2.9. REDUNDANT CONSTRAINTS

We temporarily close our discussion of constrained maximization problems by considering one further elaboration of our product mix example. Suppose that in addition to its three capacity constraints, the office furnishings company faces one further constraint on production possibilities. This company markets its entire output through a distributor, who, in a particular week, informs the company that no more than 95 bookcases can be taken. Adding this constraint to the others, the complete specification of the problem can be written

$$\text{Maximize} \quad 30x_1 + 20x_2$$

$$\text{subject to} \quad 8x_1 + 4x_2 \leq 640$$

$$4x_1 + 6x_2 \leq 540$$

$$x_1 + x_2 \leq 100$$

$$x_2 \leq 95$$

$$x_1, x_2 \geq 0$$

Does this additional constraint impose any further limitation on product mix possibilities for the office furnishings company? We will see that it does not. Figure 2.12 shows the feasible region for the original problem, together with the line

$$x_2 = 95$$

Now, the new constraint simply implies that output combinations above this line are precluded. Notice, however, that given the other constraints, such output combinations were in any case not feasible. The addition of this constraint, then, has no effect at all on the feasible region which remains precisely as it was before. The new constraint is said, in these circumstances, to be **redundant.**

In the terminology of the previous section, redundant constraints can never be binding. In attempting to solve a linear programming problem, such constraints cannot possibly influence the optimal solution. We can therefore simplify matters by removing them from consideration before proceeding with further analysis. However, this is not always a good strategy. Often it is required to look at variants of linear programming problems obtained through modification of some of the original specifications. Constraints that are redundant in the original specification may not be so when this is modified.

FIGURE 2.12 The constraint $x_2 \leq 95$ is redundant in the office furnishings company problem.

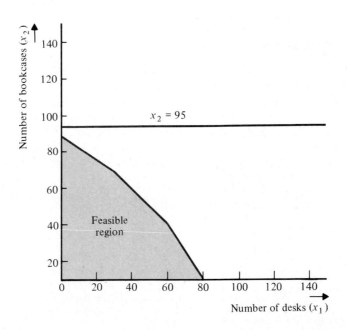

Redundant Constraints are constraints whose removal from a linear programming problem leaves the feasible region unchanged.

2.10. A MINIMIZATION PROBLEM AND ITS SOLUTION

We have now considered in some detail a linear programming problem of the constrained maximization type. In this section it is shown how some of the ideas just discussed can be applied when constrained *minimization* is required. We will illustrate this type of case through the study of a blending problem.

A processed food company has available two additives containing quantities of vitamins A, C, and D, and iron. Table 2.5 shows the percentage of U.S. Department of Agriculture (U.S.D.A.) daily requirements per gram of each nutrient in these additives, together with the minimum amounts of nutrient required by the food company in its product.

As we also show in Table 2.5, the first additive costs 2 cents and the second 3 cents per gram. This company is free to blend these additives in any proportions it chooses. What we now seek is the cheapest blend that will satisfy all of the standards that the company has set. We therefore have a problem requiring the minimization of costs, subject to these constraints.

Let us begin by algebraically formulating this problem. Denoting by x_1 the number of grams of additive I, and by x_2 the number of grams of additive II, to be used, the total cost in cents is

$$Cost = 2x_1 + 3x_2$$

This is the objective function to be minimized.

Now, vitamin A is available only through additive I, so that if at least 80% of U.S.D.A. requirements are needed, we must have

$$40x_1 \geq 80$$

TABLE 2.5 Specifications for the blending problem for the processed food company.

MINIMUM % U.S.D.A. REQUIREMENTS NEEDED IN PRODUCT		% U.S.D.A. REQUIREMENT PER GRAM	
		ADDITIVE I	ADDITIVE II
80	Vitamin A	40	0
80	Vitamin C	5	10
60	Vitamin D	10	5
80	Iron	0	20
PRICE PER GRAM (IN CENTS)		2	3

or simplifying,

$$\text{Vitamin A Constraint: } x_1 \geq 2$$

The requirement that at least 80% of the U.S.D.A. stipulated amount of vitamin C be added can be met through a combination of the additives. Since their respective contents are 5% and 10% of U.S.D.A. needs per gram, we must have

$$5x_1 + 10x_2 \geq 80$$

or, dividing through by 5,

$$\text{Vitamin C Constraint: } x_1 + 2x_2 \geq 16$$

Similarly, the vitamin D requirement dictates that we must have

$$10x_1 + 5x_2 \geq 60$$

or simplifying,

$$\text{Vitamin D Constraint: } 2x_1 + x_2 \geq 12$$

Finally, the second additive must be used to satisfy the standard for content of iron through

$$\text{Iron Constraint: } x_2 \geq 4$$

Putting together the objective function and the four constraints,[2] the linear programming problem for the processed food company can be set out algebraically as

$$
\begin{aligned}
\text{Minimize} \quad & 2x_1 + 3x_2 \\
\text{subject to} \quad & x_1 \geq 2 \\
& x_1 + 2x_2 \geq 16 \\
& 2x_1 + x_2 \geq 12 \\
& x_2 \geq 4
\end{aligned}
$$

We now have a complete formal description of this constrained minimization problem. The next step is to find a graphical representation of the feasible region. This is accomplished in Figure 2.13, where we graph the four lines

$$x_1 = 2; \; x_1 + 2x_2 = 16; \; 2x_1 + x_2 = 12; \; x_2 = 4$$

Now, any point on the same side as the origin of one of these lines cannot be a feasible solution. For example, no solution below the line $x_2 = 4$ is feasible. It then follows that the feasible region is the shaded area in Figure 2.13. The approach to the derivation of this feasible region is the same as that employed for the constrained maximization problem studied in earlier sections of this

---

[2] Of course, it is not possible to use negative amounts of either additive. However, the vitamin A and iron constraints render the nonnegativity constraints redundant.

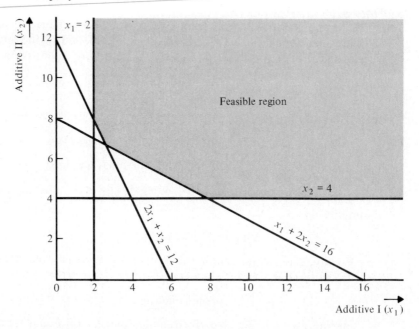

FIGURE 2.13 Derivation of the feasible region for the processed food company.

chapter. There is, however, one distinction between the two regions. The feasible region of Figure 2.13 is open; that is to say, it extends indefinitely. This is not surprising. It merely reflects the fact that there is nothing in the constraints imposing any *upper* limits on the quantities of the additives used. This need not disturb us. Although the use of vast amounts of both additives is feasible, the objective of keeping costs to a minimum will dictate against such a strategy.

The feasible region for the blending problem is shown again in Figure 2.14, where we have cut off the lines at the points at which they intersect. We also show in this figure the values of the extreme points of that feasible region. These values can be read off from the graph or determined algebraically, using precisely the same approach as in Section 2.6.

Now, just as for our earlier constrained maximization problem, one of the extreme points must constitute an optimal solution to the problem. Accordingly, in Table 2.6 we show the values of the objective function at the extreme points. These are obtained by direct substitution, so that, for example, the cost in cents of using 2 grams of additive I and 8 grams of additive II is

$$\text{Cost} = 2x_1 + 3x_2 = (2)(2) + (3)(8) = 28$$

Directly from Table 2.6, then, it can be seen that the optimal solution for the company is to use a blend of $2\frac{2}{3}$ grams of additive I and $6\frac{2}{3}$ grams of additive

FIGURE 2.14 Feasible region and extreme points for the blending problem of the processed food company.

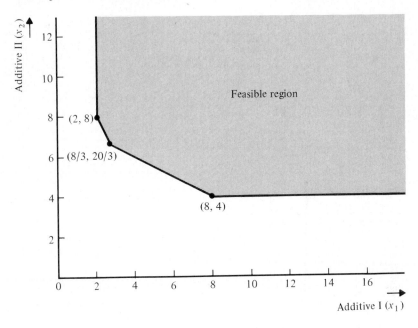

II, at a cost of $25\frac{1}{3}$ cents. In Figure 2.15 we verify that this solution is indeed optimal. The figure shows the feasible region, together with the line

$$2x_1 + 3x_2 = 25\frac{1}{3}$$

which represents all those blends of additives costing $25\frac{1}{3}$ cents. It can be seen that this line just touches the feasible region at the point $(\frac{8}{3}, \frac{20}{3})$. This must, therefore, be the optimal solution, for the only way to achieve a cheaper blend would be to move to a parallel cost line closer to the origin. Such a line, however, would contain no points in the feasible region.

TABLE 2.6 Values of the objective function at extreme points for the processed food company.

EXTREME POINTS		VALUE OF OBJECTIVE FUNCTION (COST IN CENTS)
x_1	x_2	
2	8	28
$\frac{8}{3}$	$\frac{20}{3}$	$25\frac{1}{3}$
8	4	28

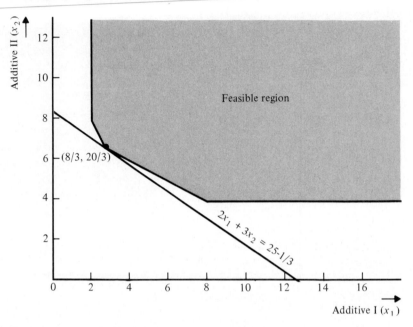

FIGURE 2.15 Solution of the blending problem of the processed food company. Optimal solution is point (8/3, 20/3).

2.11. SURPLUS VARIABLES

Let us continue to explore the optimal solution of our constrained minimization problem. We see from Figure 2.15 that the optimal solution $(\frac{8}{3}, \frac{20}{3})$ is at the intersection of the two lines.

$$x_1 + 2x_2 = 16; \quad 2x_1 + x_2 = 12$$

Now, as we saw in the previous section, these particular lines bound the feasibility region as a consequence of the vitamin C and vitamin D constraints. Recalling the discussion of Section 2.8, this suggests that these two constraints are binding, while the others are not. In the context of the present problem then, we should expect to find that the optimal blend will contain the minimum requirements of the company for vitamins C and D, while the minimum requirements for vitamin A and iron will be exceeded. We will now verify directly that this is indeed the case.

At the optimal solution, the content of vitamin C will be

$$5x_1 + 10x_2 = (5)(\tfrac{8}{3}) + (10)(\tfrac{20}{3}) = 80$$

the minimum desired percent of U.S.D.A. requirements. Similarly, vitamin D content is

$$10x_1 + 5x_2 = (10)(\tfrac{8}{3}) + (5)(\tfrac{20}{3}) = 60$$

again just hitting the minimum standard set by the company. The vitamin A content at the optimum solution is

$$40x_1 = (40)(\tfrac{8}{3}) = 106\tfrac{2}{3}$$

This exceeds by $26\tfrac{2}{3}$ the company standard that a minimum of 80% of U.S.D.A. requirements of vitamin A be added. This excess is referred to as **surplus.** Finally, the iron content in the optimal blend is

$$20x_2 = (20)(\tfrac{20}{3}) = 133\tfrac{1}{3}$$

providing a surplus of $53\tfrac{1}{3}$ over the minimum standard of 80.

The concept of surplus can be used to express a constrained minimization problem in standard form. To illustrate, for the blending problem let s_1 denote the amount of surplus over the vitamin A company standard, and s_2, s_3, s_4 the corresponding surpluses for vitamin C, vitamin D, and iron. The vitamin A constraint can then be written

$$40x_1 - s_1 = 80$$

Similarly, the other constraints can be expressed in such a fashion. Noting that adherence to the constraints prohibits negative surpluses, it follows that the standard form of the blending linear programming problem is

$$
\begin{aligned}
\text{Minimize} \quad & 2x_1 + 3x_2 \\
\text{subject to} \quad & 40x_1 - s_1 && = 80 \\
& 5x_1 + 10x_2 - s_2 && = 80 \\
& 10x_1 + 5x_2 - s_3 && = 60 \\
& 20x_2 - s_4 && = 80 \\
& x_1, x_2, s_1, s_2, s_3, s_4 \geq 0
\end{aligned}
$$

We have already seen that the optimal solution to this problem is

$$x_1 = 2\tfrac{2}{3},\ x_2 = 6\tfrac{2}{3},\ s_1 = 26\tfrac{2}{3},\ s_2 = 0,\ s_3 = 0,\ s_4 = 53\tfrac{1}{3}$$

The variables s_1, s_2, s_3, s_4 used in this way are called **surplus variables.**

Definitions

(i) Surplus is excess over minimum requirements in a "≥" constraint.
(ii) Surplus Variables are variables introduced in a "≥" constraint to represent the possibility of excess over the mininum requirements.

The product mix problem introduced in this chapter is a constrained maximization problem involving "≤", but not "≥", constraints. Thus, its standard form contained slack variables, but not surplus variables. Also, the blending problem studied here is a constrained minimization problem involving "≥", but not "≤" constraints. Its standard form therefore contained surplus variables, but not slack variables. However, constrained maximization problems with "≥" as well as "≤" constraints are often encountered in practice. Similarly, constrained minimization problems may have "≤" constraints.

To illustrate, suppose that for the coming week, to fill an order from an important customer, management of the office furnishings company decides that at least 50 bookcases must be produced. Adding this constraint to the other specifications, the problem to be solved is now

$$\text{Maximize} \quad 30x_1 + 20x_2$$
$$\text{subject to} \quad 8x_1 + 4x_2 \leq 640$$
$$4x_1 + 6x_2 \leq 540$$
$$x_1 + x_2 \leq 100$$
$$x_2 \geq 50$$
$$x_1, x_2 \geq 0$$

The standard form of this problem is

$$\text{Maximize} \quad 30x_1 + 20x_2$$
$$\text{subject to} \quad 8x_1 + 4x_2 + s_1 = 640$$
$$4x_1 + 6x_2 + s_2 = 540$$
$$x_1 + x_2 + s_3 = 100$$
$$x_2 - s_4 = 50$$
$$x_1, x_2, s_1, s_2, s_3, s_4 \geq 0$$

Here s_4 is a surplus variable, representing production of bookcases in excess of 50 units.

This problem can be solved graphically by finding the new feasible region and evaluating the objective function at the corners of that region. We leave the details as an exercise to the reader.

EXERCISES

2.1. For the linear programming problem

$$\text{Maximize} \quad x_1 + x_2$$
$$\text{subject to} \quad 2x_1 + 3x_2 \leq 960$$
$$x_1, x_2 \geq 0$$

كيف يصل

(a) Construct a graph showing the feasible region.
(b) Find the values of x_1 and x_2 at the extreme points.

(c) Using the results in (b), find an optimal solution to this constrained maximization problem.

(d) Verify graphically that the solution found in (c) is optimal.

2.2. For the linear programming problem

$$\text{Maximize} \quad x_1 + x_2 \quad \rightarrow D.\checkmark$$
$$\text{subject to} \quad 2x_1 + 3x_2 \leq 960$$
$$4x_1 + x_2 \leq 600$$
$$x_1, x_2 \geq 0$$

(a) Construct a graph showing the feasible region.
(b) Find the values of the decision variables at the extreme points.
(c) Using the results in (b), find an optimal solution to this problem.
(d) Find the value of the objective function at this optimal solution.
(e) Verify graphically that the solution found in (c) is optimal.

2.3. For the constrained maximization problem

$$\text{Maximize} \quad 4x_1 + 5x_2$$
$$\text{subject to} \quad 3x_1 + 5x_2 \leq 1200$$
$$x_1 + x_2 \leq 300$$
$$x_1, x_2 \geq 0$$

(a) Construct a graph showing the feasible region.
(b) Find the values of the decision variables at the extreme points.
(c) Using the results in (b), find an optimal solution to the problem.
(d) Find the value of the objective function at the optimal solution.
(e) Verify graphically that the solution found in (c) is optimal.

2.4. For the constrained maximization problem

$$\text{Maximize} \quad 2x_1 + 3x_2$$
$$\text{subject to} \quad 3x_1 + 2x_2 \leq 1800$$
$$x_1 + x_2 \leq 750$$
$$x_1, x_2 \geq 0$$

(a) Construct a graph showing the feasible region.
(b) Find the values of the decision variables at the extreme points.
(c) Using the results in (b), find an optimal solution to this problem.
(d) Find the value of the objective function at the optimal solution.
(e) Verify graphically that the solution found in (c) is optimal.
(f) Express this problem in standard form and provide a complete optimal solution.

2.5. For the linear programming problem

$$\text{Maximize} \quad 3x_1 + 4x_2$$
$$\text{subject to} \quad 3x_1 + 2x_2 \leq 1800$$
$$2x_1 + 3x_2 \leq 1500$$
$$x_1, x_2 \geq 0$$

(a) Construct a graph showing the feasible region.

(b) Find the values of the decision variables at the extreme points.

(c) Using the results in (b) find an optimal solution to this constrained maximization problem.

(d) Find the value of the objective function at the optimal solution.

(e) Verify graphically that the solution found in (c) is optimal.

(f) Express the problem in standard form and provide a complete optimal solution.

2.6. For the linear programming problem

$$\text{Maximize} \quad 4x_1 + 3x_2$$

$$\text{subject to} \quad 3x_1 + 2x_2 \leq 1800$$

$$x_1 + x_2 \leq 750$$

$$3x_1 + 4x_2 \leq 2400$$

$$x_1, x_2 \geq 0$$

(a) Construct a graph showing the feasible region.

(b) Find the values of the decision variables at the extreme points.

(c) Using the results in (b) find an optimal solution to this problem.

(d) Find the value of the objective function at the optimal solution.

(e) Verify graphically that the solution found in (c) is optimal.

2.7. For the constrained maximization problem

$$\text{Maximize} \quad 5x_1 + 3x_2$$

$$\text{subject to} \quad 2x_1 + 3x_2 \leq 1500$$

$$2x_1 + x_2 \leq 1000$$

$$4x_1 + 3x_2 \leq 2400$$

$$x_1, x_2 \geq 0$$

(a) Construct a graph showing the feasible region.

(b) Find the values of the decision variables at the extreme points.

(c) Using the results in (b) find an optimal solution to this problem.

(d) Find the value of the objective function at the optimal solution.

(e) Verify graphically that the solution found in (c) is optimal.

(f) Express the problem in standard form and provide a complete optimal solution.

2.8. For the constrained maximization problem

$$\text{Maximize} \quad 4x_1 + 5x_2$$

$$\text{subject to} \quad 5x_1 + 3x_2 \leq 3000$$

$$x_1 + 2x_2 \leq 900$$

$$6x_1 + 5x_2 \leq 4200$$

$$x_1, x_2 \geq 0$$

(a) Construct a graph showing the feasible region.

(b) Find the values of the decision variables at the extreme points.

(c) Using the results in (b) find an optimal solution to the problem.

(d) Find the value of the objective function at the optimal solution.

(e) Verify graphically that the solution found in (c) is optimal.

(f) Express the problem in standard form and provide a complete optimal solution.

2.9. For the linear programming problem

$$\text{Maximize} \quad 2x_1 + x_2$$

$$\text{subject to} \quad x_1 + 2x_2 \leq 1000$$

$$5x_1 + 2x_2 \leq 2000$$

$$x_1 + 3x_2 \leq 1200$$

$$3x_1 + 2x_2 \leq 1800$$

$$x_1, x_2 \geq 0$$

(a) Construct a graph showing the feasible region.

(b) Find the values of the decision variables at the extreme points.

(c) Using the results in (b) find an optimal solution to the problem.

(d) Find the value of the objective function at the optimal solution.

(e) Verify graphically that the solution found in (c) is optimal.

(f) Express the problem in standard form and provide a complete optimal solution.

2.10. Consider, again, the constrained optimization problem of Exercise 2.2. Leaving the constraints unchanged, provide an example of an objective function such that the modified problem has multiple optimal solutions. Verify your answer graphically.

2.11. Returning to the problem of Exercise 2.3, and leaving the other specifications unchanged, provide an example of an additional constraint such that the modified problem would have no feasible solution.

2.12. Returning to the problem of Exercise 2.4, and leaving the other specifications unchanged, provide an example of an additional constraint that would be redundant. Draw a graph to illustrate your answer.

2.13. A company faces a constrained maximization problem for which the constraints are

$$2x_1 + 3x_2 \leq 1200$$

$$3x_1 + 4x_2 \leq 2400$$

$$x_1 + x_2 \leq 1000$$

$$x_1, x_2 \geq 0$$

Draw a graph showing the feasible region and determine which, if any, of these constraints are redundant.

2.14. A constrained maximization problem involves the constraints

$$3x_1 + 5x_2 \leq 3600$$

$$2x_1 + 3x_2 \leq 2400$$

$$5x_1 + 4x_2 \leq 5600$$

$$2x_1 + x_2 \leq 1200$$

Draw a graph showing the feasible region and determine which, if any, of these constraints are redundant.

2.15. Consider the office furnishings company whose problem specifications are set out in Table 2.1. Leaving all other specifications unchanged, to what level would inspection time capacity have to be increased before the inspection time constraint became redundant?

2.16. Consider, once again, the product mix problem of the office furnishings company. For the coming week, this company has increased its capacity for assembly to 720 man-hours. The remaining problem specifications are those given in Table 2.1. Provide a full analysis of the new constrained optimization problem for this company. Your answer should include derivation of the optimal solution, calculation of the resulting profit, and computation of the amounts of any slack times at the optimal solution.

2.17. A manufacturer of canned foods produces cans of peas in two sizes. The smaller size contains 10 ounces of peas per can, and the larger size 16 ounces of peas per can. For the next week, this manufacturer has available a total of 64,000 ounces of peas. The marketing department for this company estimates that it will be unable to sell more than 5000 of the smaller size cans, or more than 3000 of the larger size cans. Each can sold of the smaller size yields a profit of 12 cents, and each can of the larger size a profit of 17 cents. The objective of the manufacturer is to maximize profits.

(a) How many cans of each size should be produced?

(b) Discuss the concept of slack in relation to this problem and calculate and interpret any amounts of slack involved in the optimal solution.

2.18. A distributor handles two types of television sets—large color and portable black and white—purchased directly from an importer. The distributor has available for his purchases next month a total of 5000 cubic feet of storage space. Each large color set requires 8 cubic feet, and each black and white portable 4 cubic feet, of storage space. Each large color set costs the distributor $360, and each black and white portable costs $80. The distributor calculates that he can make $50 profit on each large color, and $20 on each black and white portable, set. It is also felt, due to restrictions on marketing possibilities, that no more than 450 color sets can be taken for the coming month. If the distributor has $180,000 available for the purchase of television sets, and the objective is to maximize profits:

(a) How many television sets of each type should be purchased?

(b) Discuss the concept of slack, as it applies to this particular constrained optimization problem, and calculate and interpret any amounts of slack involved in the optimal solution.

2.19. A record club intends to advertise an introductory offer. It faces the problem, however, that many people take up such offers and then immediately discontinue membership, leading to promotional losses. Advertisements can be placed both in newspapers and magazines. The club has calculated that each thousand dollars spent on newspaper advertisements generates 280 customers who will take up the offer and continue club membership, and 200 who will take up the offer but immediately discontinue membership. Each thousand dollars spent on magazine advertisements produces 300 customers taking up the offer and subsequently retaining membership, and 250 taking up the offer and immediately discontinuing membership. The club has a maximum of $50,000 to spend on advertising, and feels that it wants no more than 12,000 responses from people who will accept the introductory offer but immediately discontinue membership. Given these constraints:

(a) How should the advertising budget be distributed to maximize the total number of responses from people who will continue club membership after taking up the introductory offer?

(b) Find and interpret the value of the objective function at the optimal solution.

(c) Discuss the concept of slack in relation to the problem of the record club, and calculate and interpret any amounts of slack involved in the optimal solution.

2.20. A supermarket manager has available a maximum of 20 square feet of shelf display space to allocate to detergents. This space must be allocated between national and generic brands. The owners of the chain, to which this supermarket belongs, stipulate that at least a quarter of the total display space used must be allocated to the generic brand. Further, the manager believes that a minimum of 10 square feet is necessary for the adequate display of national brands. It has been calculated that each square foot of display space allocated to national brands yields a profit of $50 per week, with the generic brand yielding $40. The manager's intention is to allocate shelf space so as to maximize total profit.

(a) Set out this linear programming problem in algebraic form.

(b) Draw a graph showing the feasible region.

(c) Find the optimal solution and the amount of weekly profits at this solution.

2.21. An investor has to allocate $100,000 among three investment opportunities. Two common stock funds—one high risk, and one low risk—are available. The respective expected annual returns from these funds are 20% and 15% of the amounts invested. Any money not invested in these funds will be deposited in fixed interest securities, yielding a 10% annual rate of return. This investor requires that no more than one-fifth of the total invested in the common stock funds be in the high risk fund, and, in any case, does not want to invest more than $15,000 in the high risk fund. Given these constraints, the investor's objective is to maximize total expected annual return. [Assume that the entire $100,000 must be invested.]

(a) Set out in algebraic form the linear programming problem for this investor.

(b) Draw a graph showing the feasible region.

(c) Find the optimal solution and the total expected annual return at this solution.

2.22. Suppose, now, that you have solved the problem of the previous exercise for the investor. However, having been presented with your solution, he now announces that it is essential that at least $30,000 of his money be deposited in fixed interest securities. Reanalyze the problem in light of this additional constraint.

2.23. A company produces two products, each of which requires time on four different machines. This company wishes to determine the product output mix which maximizes profits, given the specifications shown in the table below.

TOTAL MACHINE-HOURS AVAILABLE	MACHINE	MACHINE-HOURS PER UNIT	
		PRODUCT I	PRODUCT II
500	A	2	1
400	B	1	1
600	C	1	2
1100	D	2	3
PROFIT PER UNIT ($)		60	40

(a) Draw a graph showing the feasible region for this problem indicating which, if any, of the constraints are redundant.

(b) Find the optimal solution and verify your result graphically.

(c) Express the problem in standard form and set out the full optimal solution.

2.24. Consider again the product mix problem of the previous exercise. Given these constraints, and a profit per unit of $60 for product I, for what values of profit per unit of product II would the constrained maximization problem have multiple optimal solutions?

2.25. A manufacturing company produces two products, each of which must be processed through four departments. The company must determine the product mix yielding the highest possible profit, given the specifications shown in the following table.

TOTAL MAN-HOURS AVAILABLE	DEPARTMENT	MAN-HOURS PER UNIT	
		PRODUCT I	PRODUCT II
5000	A	4	1
4200	B	3	1
1400	C	1	1
1700	D	1	2
PROFIT PER UNIT ($)		3	2

(a) Draw a graph showing the feasible region for this product mix problem and state which, if any, of the constraints are redundant.

(b) Find the optimal solution and verify your answer graphically.

(c) Express the problem in standard form and set out the full optimal solution.

2.26. Continuing Exercise 2.25, take the constraints as given. If the profit per unit is $3 for product I, for what values of profit per unit of product II would the constrained maximization problem have multiple optimal solutions?

2.27. A drug company has a maximum of $250,000 to invest in research and development on two drugs—one aimed at relief of flu symptoms, the other an aspirin substitute. Management has stipulated that at most $150,000 can be made available for each project. Company forecasts suggest that the respective returns on investment for these two drugs will be 8% and 10%. Assume that the aim is to maximize total return on investment.

(a) Formulate the problem of this drug company in standard form, and derive and discuss the optimal solution.

(b) Can you modify this problem so as to produce a linear programming problem with unbounded feasible region? Comment on the practical implications of your modified problem.

2.28. A company produces two brands of perfumed bath oils. Each brand contains a combination of three of four perfume essences, the quantities required per bottle being those set out in the table below.

BATH OIL	QUANTITY OF PERFUME ESSENCE (IN OUNCES)			
	1	2	3	4
A	0.2	0.4	0	0.2
B	0.5	0	0.2	0.1

While the remaining ingredients are readily available, quantities of these essences are in limited supply for the coming week. Supplies are shown as follows:

AVAILABILITY OF ESSENCE (IN OUNCES)			
1	2	3	4
200	200	150	100

Each bottle of bath oil A produced yields a profit of $1.20 and each bottle of bath oil B a profit of $1.50. The objective of this company is to maximize profits.

(a) Set out in algebraic form the linear programming problem.

(b) Draw a graph showing the feasible region and indicate which, if any, of the constraints are redundant.

(c) Find the optimal solution, together with the resulting profits, and the amounts of any slack.

2.29. Consider again the problem of the previous exercise, with the constraints as before. If each bottle of bath oil A yields a profit of $1.20, for what values of profit of bath oil B would the constrained optimization problem have multiple optimal solutions?

2.30. Let us return to the office furnishings company whose problem specification is set out in Table 2.1. For the next week, a union representative offers to allow the movement of 24 man-hours from finishing to inspection, provided that a bonus is paid. What, if any, is the largest amount of bonus payment the company should agree to make for such a move?

2.31. For the linear programming problem

$$\text{Minimize} \quad x_1 + x_2$$
$$\text{subject to} \quad x_1 + 2x_2 \geq 400$$
$$x_1 \geq 100$$
$$x_2 \geq 120$$

(a) Construct a graph showing the feasible region.

(b) Find the values of the decision variables at the extreme points.

(c) Using the results in (b), find an optimal solution to this problem.

(d) Find the value of the objective function at the optimal solution.

(e) Verify graphically that the solution found in (c) is optimal.

2.32. For the constrained minimization problem

$$\text{Minimize} \quad 2x_1 + 3x_2$$
$$\text{subject to} \quad x_1 + x_2 \geq 80$$
$$x_1 + 2x_2 \geq 130$$
$$x_1 \geq 20$$
$$x_2 \geq 40$$

(a) Construct a graph showing the feasible region.

(b) Find the values of the decision variables at the extreme points.

(c) Using the results in (b), find an optimal solution to this linear programming problem.

(d) Find the value of the objective function at the optimal solution.

(e) Verify graphically that the solution found in (c) is optimal.

2.33. For the linear programming problem

$$\text{Minimize} \quad 2x_1 + 5x_2$$

$$\text{subject to} \quad 2x_1 + 3x_2 \geq 340$$

$$x_1 + 2x_2 \geq 200$$

$$x_1 \geq 50$$

$$x_2 \geq 50$$

(a) Construct a graph showing the feasible region.
(b) Find the values of the decision variables at the extreme points.
(c) Using the results in (b), find an optimal solution to this constrained minimization problem.
(d) Find the value of the objective function at the optimal solution.
(e) Verify graphically that the solution found in (c) is optimal.

2.34. For the constrained optimization problem

$$\text{Minimize} \quad x_1 + 2x_2$$

$$\text{subject to} \quad x_1 + x_2 \geq 70$$

$$x_1 + 3x_2 \geq 150$$

$$x_1 \geq 10$$

$$x_2 \geq 30$$

(a) Construct a graph showing the feasible region.
(b) Find the values of the decision variable at the extreme points.
(c) Using the results in (b), find an optimal solution to this problem.
(d) Find the value of the objective function at the optimal solution.
(e) Verify graphically that the solution found in (c) is optimal.
(f) Express the problem in standard form, and provide a complete optimal solution.

2.35. For the linear programming problem

$$\text{Minimize} \quad 2x_1 + 5x_2$$

$$\text{subject to} \quad x_1 + 2x_2 \geq 40$$

$$x_1 + x_2 \geq 25$$

$$x_1 + 3x_2 \geq 45$$

$$x_1 \geq 10$$

$$x_2 \geq 10$$

(a) Construct a graph showing the feasible region and indicate which, if any, of the constraints are redundant.
(b) Find the values of the decision variables at the extreme points.
(c) Using the results in (b), find an optimal solution to this problem.
(d) Find the value of the objective function at the optimal solution.
(e) Verify graphically that the solution found in (c) is optimal.
(f) Express this problem in standard form and provide a complete optimal solution.

2.36. Consider again the constrained minimization problem of Exercise 2.31. Leaving the constraints unchanged, provide an example of an objective function such that the modified problem has multiple optimal solutions. Verify your answer graphically.

2.37. Returning to the problem of Exercise 2.32, and leaving the other specifications unchanged, provide an example of an additional constraint, of the form

$$a_1x_1 + a_2x_2 \geq K$$

with a_1, a_2 and K positive numbers, such that this further constraint would be redundant. Draw a graph to illustrate your answer.

2.38. Consider, once again, the blending problem of the processed food company. This company faces an increase in price from 3 cents to 4 cents per gram for additive II, with the remaining problem specifications the same as in Table 2.5. Provide a full analysis of the new constrained minimization problem. Your answer should include derivation of an optimal solution, calculation of the resulting total cost, and discussion of any surplus involved in the optimal solution.

2.39. A dog owner wants to provide each day for his pet a diet containing at least 6 ounces of protein and 4 ounces of carbohydrate. At the beginning of each week he plans to make up enough food for the next seven days by mixing together quantities of two kinds of dog food—Tailwagger and Petsup. Each package of Tailwagger contains 7 ounces each of protein and carbohydrate, and costs 55 cents. Each package of Petsup contains 6 ounces of protein and 2 ounces of carbohydrate and costs 35 cents. The dog owner wants to make up a mixture that contains the minimum weekly requirements of both protein and carbohydrate for his pet at the lowest possible cost. Provide a full analysis of this problem.

2.40. A large travel agency employs telephone operators who work 8-hour shifts, either from 8:00 a.m. to 4:00 p.m., or from 2:00 p.m. to 10:00 p.m. Those working the earlier shift are paid $40 per day, while those on the later shift are paid $45 per day. The manager of this agency has determined that the minimum numbers of operators that must be available at various times of the day are:

TIME	MINIMUM NUMBER OF OPERATORS
8 a.m.–10 a.m.	3
10 a.m.– 2 p.m.	4
2 p.m.– 4 p.m.	12
4 p.m.– 8 p.m.	5
8 p.m.–10 p.m.	2

The objective is to meet these requirements at the lowest possible cost. Provide a full analysis of this problem, giving the optimal solution and the amounts of any surpluses.

2.41. The union representing the telephone operators of the previous exercise is offering a different work schedule in which each operator employed works the early shift and late shift in alternate weeks. The same daily wage will then be paid to each employee whichever shift is worked. What is the maximum daily wage per operator the travel agency should offer under this arrangement?

2.42. The processed food company of Section 2.10 is considering raising the amount of vitamin C in its product to 100% of U.S.D.A. requirements. Assuming the other specifications in Table 2.5 remain unchanged, and the additives are blended in the most cost-effective manner, what is the additional cost involved in meeting this more stringent requirement?

2.43. Consider again the product mix problem of the office furnishings company, with the specifications of Table 2.1. In the coming week, management requires that at least 50 bookcases must be made.

(a) Draw a graph showing the feasible region for this augmented problem.

(b) Find the optimal solution.

(c) Find the values of the slack and surplus variables at the optimal solution.

2.44. An editor has 10,000 pages of copyediting work, all of which must be completed in at most 30 days. This editor has available three freelance copyeditors to whom the work can be assigned. For each copyeditor, the table shows the numbers of pages per day that can be handled, and the daily fee charged for this work.

	COPYEDITOR		
	1	2	3
Pages per Day	100	180	150
Fee per Day	$40	$81	$54

The editor must decide how many pages to assign to each copyeditor so that the work can be completed within 30 days at the lowest possible total cost.

(a) Formulate the editor's problem as a linear programming problem with two decision variables.

(b) How many pages should be assigned to each copyeditor?

linear programming: the simplex method

CHAPTER THREE

3.1. INTRODUCTION TO THE SIMPLEX METHOD

In the text of Chapter 2 we discussed in considerable detail two constrained optimization problems. You met several other such problems in the exercises from that chapter. These certainly revealed a wide array of potential applications of linear programming. They also had a common special feature which allowed the use of graphical methods in the derivation of their optimal solutions. *In each case there were only two decision variables.* It is for this reason that we could represent these problems graphically in two dimensions. Although such a graphical formulation allows valuable insights into the general nature of linear programming problems, we will want to be able to accomplish rather more, by tackling problems involving several decision variables. For such purposes, the graphical approach of the previous chapter is inadequate. Given three decision variables, we could, in principle, represent a linear programming problem through a three-dimensional picture. With more decision variables, a pictorial representation is not possible. Therefore, we require an alternative approach to the solution of general linear programming problems. To that end, we introduce in this chapter **the simplex method.**

In linear programming problems the aim is to maximize (or minimize) an objective function, subject to limitations imposed by the problem constraints. Essentially, the simplex method involves a process of **iteration,** in which we start by picking out any solution, then try to find a second solution, and so on, until we reach a point at which no further improvement is possible. As you can imagine, however, such an unstructured procedure would be unreasonably tedious. There are too many possible solutions, and it is necessary to find some way of limiting the number that need to be examined. Fortunately, help is at hand. As we saw in Chapter 2, one of the extreme points of the feasible region must constitute an optimal solution, provided such a solution exists, This fact limits considerably the domain of our search. We begin by picking an extreme point, and then attempting to move to a second extreme point to obtain an improved solution. The process of iteration continues until we reach an extreme point from which further movement fails to yield any improvement in the solution.

The details of the iterative solution algorithm, which makes up the simplex method, are a little involved. We will begin our introduction to this algorithm through the analysis of the product mix problem of our office furnishings company. Of course, since this problem has just two decision variables, it can readily be attacked graphically. However, its relatively simple structure allows us to conveniently introduce the simplex method as a prelude to looking at more complicated problems.

3.2. A CONSTRAINED MAXIMIZATION PROBLEM: INITIAL BASIC FEASIBLE SOLUTION

In Chapter 2 we discussed the product mix problem of an office furnishings company, which makes both desks and bookcases with respective profits per unit of \$30 and \$20. For any week the output potential of this company is restricted by limited availability of time for assembly, finishing, and inspection. In algebraic form, the linear programming problem is

$$\text{Maximize} \quad 30x_1 + 20x_2$$
$$\text{subject to}$$

Assembly Time Constraint: $\quad 8x_1 + 4x_2 \leq 640$

Finishing Time Constraint: $\quad 4x_1 + 6x_2 \leq 540$

Inspection Time Constraint: $\quad x_1 + x_2 \leq 100$

$$x_1, x_2 \geq 0$$

where the decision variables, x_1 and x_2, denote respective outputs of desks and bookcases.

We also saw in Chapter 2 that an alternative, but equivalent, formulation of this problem, known as the standard form, can be obtained through the introduction of slack variables. Specifically, let s_1, s_2, s_3 denote any amounts of unused assembly, finishing, and inspection time capacities. Then, the standard form of the product mix problem is

$$\text{Maximize} \quad 30x_1 + 20x_2$$
$$\text{subject to} \quad 8x_1 + 4x_2 + s_1 = 640 \tag{3.1}$$
$$4x_1 + 6x_2 + s_2 = 540 \tag{3.2}$$
$$x_1 + x_2 + s_3 = 100 \tag{3.3}$$
$$x_1, x_2, s_1, s_2, s_3 \geq 0$$

Let us pause to examine the general nature of the linear programming problem as thus posed. We are required to find the values of five variables (the two decision variables, and the three slack variables) so that the objective function is made as large as possible. The values of these variables must, however, satisfy the nonnegativity constraints and the three production constraints represented by equations (3.1)–(3.3). More generally, we can conceive of constrained maximization problems in which there are a total of n variables (some decision, and some slack) and m constraints, in addition to the nonnegativity constraints. A general linear programming maximization problem is then of the form

Maximize
subject to

$$c_1 x_1 + c_2 x_2 + \ldots + c_n x_n$$
$$a_{11} x_1 + a_{12} x_2 + \ldots + a_{1n} x_n = b_1$$
$$a_{21} x_1 + a_{22} x_2 + \ldots + a_{2n} x_n = b_2 \qquad (3.4)$$
$$\cdots\cdots\cdots\cdots$$
$$a_{m1} x_1 + a_{m2} x_2 + \ldots + a_{mn} x_n = b_m$$
$$x_1, x_2, \ldots, x_n \geq 0$$

where the c_j, b_i and a_{ij} are fixed numbers. The standard form of the product mix problem of the office furnishings company fits into this framework. Denoting the slack variables s_1, s_2, s_3 by x_3, x_4, x_5, respectively, we have, with $m = 3$ and $n = 5$,

Maximize
subject to

$$30x_1 + 20x_2 + 0x_3 + 0x_4 + 0x_5$$
$$8x_1 + 4x_2 + 1x_3 + 0x_4 + 0x_5 = 640$$
$$4x_1 + 6x_2 + 0x_3 + 1x_4 + 0x_5 = 540 \qquad (3.5)$$
$$1x_1 + 1x_2 + 0x_3 + 0x_4 + 1x_5 = 100$$
$$x_1, x_2, x_3, x_4, x_5 \geq 0$$

where

$$x_1 = \text{Number of desks}$$
$$x_2 = \text{Number of bookcases}$$
$$x_3 = \text{Slack time in assembly } (s_1)$$
$$x_4 = \text{Slack time in finishing } (s_2)$$
$$x_5 = \text{Slack time in inspection } (s_3)$$

Notice in (3.5) that the objective function coefficients associated with the slack variables are all zero. This follows from the fact that in our problem formulation, unused capacity makes no contribution to total profit.

One particular feature of these problems should be noted. The number of constraint equations (ignoring the nonnegativity constraints) is less than the number of variables. For instance, for our product mix example, the three equations (3.1)–(3.3) involve the five variables x_1, x_2, s_1, s_2, s_3. In general, such systems of equations will have infinitely many solutions. Here we will concentrate on a specific set of solutions. Suppose that in equations (3.1)–(3.3), we set the values of any two of the variables to zero. This will result in a system of three equations in the remaining three variables, and this system will generally have a unique solution in these three variables. Such a solution is called a **basic solution.** The variables set to zero are called **nonbasic variables,** and the others **basic variables.**

To illustrate, let us choose x_1 and s_3 as nonbasic variables. Setting the values of these quantities to zero in (3.1)–(3.3) produces the set of equations

$$4x_2 + s_1 = 640$$
$$6x_2 + s_2 = 540$$
$$x_2 = 100$$

The third equation of this set provides directly the solution for x_2, and substituting $x_2 = 100$ in the other two equations yields $s_1 = 240$, $s_2 = -60$. We have therefore found that a basic solution is

$$x_1 = 0, \, x_2 = 100, \, s_1 = 240, \, s_2 = -60, \, s_3 = 0$$

The basic solution just found necessarily satisfies the three production constraints. Notice, however, that it is *not* a feasible solution to our product mix problem, for it violates one of the nonnegativity constraints. This solution would require a *negative* amount of slack time of -60 man hours in finishing, which is, of course, not possible.

We have not, to this point, made much of a start in our effort to solve the product mix problem of the office furnishings company. To get things rolling, we must find a basic solution that *is* feasible. Such a solution is termed a **basic feasible solution.** Can you find one? In fact, there are five, corresponding to the five corners of the feasible region. Looking again at equations (3.1)–(3.3), the most obvious and easy to find of these is where x_1 and x_2 are the nonbasic variables. Setting their values to zero in these equations, we have immediately the basic solution

$$x_1 = 0, \, x_2 = 0, \, s_1 = 640, \, s_2 = 540, \, s_3 = 100 \tag{3.6}$$

which satisfies the nonnegativity constraints. This is the initial solution to the product mix problem from which we will attempt to iterate to the optimal solution.

Why are we so interested in finding a basic feasible solution? The answer lies in a crucially important result. *The basic feasible solutions correspond to the extreme points of the feasible region.* We have already seen in Chapter 2

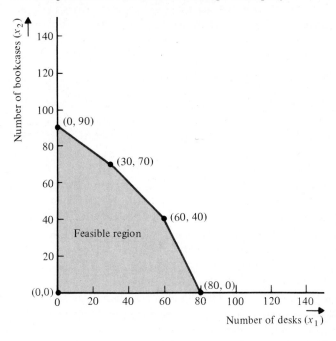

FIGURE 3.1 The five extreme points for the product mix problem of the office furnishings commpany.

that in seeking the optimal solution, we need concern ourselves only with these extreme points. It follows, then, that we can concentrate our attention on the basic feasible solutions. Figure 3.1 shows the extreme points of the feasible region for the problem of the office furnishings company. Our initial basic feasible solution (3.6) is simply the point $(0, 0)$, corresponding to no output of either desks or bookcases.

Definitions
1. *Basic Solution:* Suppose that in standard form, a linear programming problem has m equality constraints involving n variables. Any solution to these equations in which $n - m$ of the variables take the value zero is called a basic solution.
2. *Nonbasic Variables* are variables forced to take the value zero in a basic solution.
3. *Basic Variables* are variables whose values are determined from the constraints, given that the nonbasic variables are zero.
4. *Basic Feasible Solution* is a basic solution that satisfies the nonnegativity constraints. Such solutions correspond to the extreme points of the feasible region.

Having found an initial basic feasible solution our intention is to make progress by moving to a better one. Before doing so, however, we pause to set our problem in a tabular form which will prove extremely useful in deriving the path to the optimal solution.

3.3. THE SIMPLEX TABLEAU

Why was it so easy to identify the solution (3.6) as a basic feasible solution? Recall that when there are n variables and m equality constraints, a basic feasible solution has $n - m$ of the variable values set to zero, with the values of the remaining m variables satisfying the nonnegativity constraints. Now, for our problem, we have $n = 5$ and $m = 3$, and the standard form (3.5) is of a very convenient type. Notice that there are three variables, s_1, s_2, s_3 (that is, x_3, x_4, x_5 in (3.5)) such that each equality constraint involves one of these variables with coefficient 1 and the others with coefficient zero. Further, the right-hand sides of these three constraint equations are all nonnegative. Hence, by making s_1, s_2, s_3 the basic variables, and setting x_1 and x_2 to zero, the basic feasible solution (3.6) immediately follows.

A linear programming problem whose constraints are in this form is said to be in **tableau form.** Thus, if s_1, s_2, s_3 are to be used as basic variables, or as the **basis,** for a solution, we see that the standard form of the product mix problem of the office furnishings company is already in tableau form.[1] When the constraints have been put in such a form, a tabular representation, known as the **simplex tableau,** provides a very convenient and efficient description of the problem, and an invaluable tool for moving toward its optimal solution.

Let us see how to build a simplex tableau. Part of such a tableau includes describing the problem in tableau form with the initial basic feasible solution. This is shown in Table 3.1. This tableau is very much a short-hand description of the information we have acquired to this point, and we must pause to elaborate on its construction.

First, the five columns in the central portion of the table, one column for each variable, describe the objective function and the left-hand sides of the equality constraints when these are set in tableau form. In the context of our problem, the first row, labelled c_j, relates to the objective function, implying a contribution to profits of $30 for each desk produced and $20 for each bookcase produced. The c_j values for the three slack variables are all zero, since each man-hour of slack time in assembly, finishing, or inspection adds nothing to company profits.

Turning now to rows three through five of this central portion of the table, these entries show the amount of available resources used up by each unit of

---

[1] It is frequently the case that the standard form of a linear programming problem will be in tableau form. However, in general, a set-up such as (3.4) need not be. In Section 3.4 we will see how to translate a set of constraints to tableau form.

TABLE 3.1 Part of the simplex tableau for the initial basic feasible solution for the office furnishings company.

		c_j	30	20	0	0	0	
c_B		BASIS	x_1	x_2	s_1	s_2	s_3	SOLUTION
0		s_1	8	4	1	0	0	640
0		s_2	4	6	0	1	0	540
0		s_3	1	1	0	0	1	100
								0 Profit

the variables. For example, each desk and each bookcase produced uses up, respectively, 8 and 4 man-hours of assembly time. Further, each man-hour of slack in assembly also exhausts one man-hour of the total available.

Next, the two columns in the left-hand portion of the table relate to the basic variables. These are identified, and the contribution to profits of each noted, so that the entries in the c_B (where B denotes "basis") column are the same as those for the basic variables in the c_j row.

The final column of the table, headed "Solution," gives the values of the basic variables at the basic feasible solution, and consists simply of those solutions shown in equations (3.6). The final three rows of Table 3.1, then, simply set out the constraints in equations (3.5). Finally, the bottom right-hand corner of Table 3.1 gives the profit resulting from the basic feasible solution. Since this solution involves 640 units of s_1, each contributing 0 to profits, and so on, we have

$$\text{Profit} = (640)(0) + (540)(0) + (100)(0) = 0$$

This result simply confirms that if no desks and no bookcases are produced, there will be no profit.

So far we have succeeded in describing the position at the initial basic feasible solution. The next job is to figure out what would happen if we altered that solution. We need to ask if it would be more profitable to move away from this solution to some other. How could such a move be accomplished? We could consider adding to the quantity of a particular variable an amount in addition to that set by the basic feasible solution. For example, we could contemplate the production of more desks. Here it is necessary to consider a balance between two factors. Each additional desk made will add $30 to profits. However, there may be a price to pay. Given the production constraints, an addition in the quantity of one variable must be compensated for by a reduction in the quantities of others, a decision which could subtract from profits. What we need to ask is whether a *net gain* in profits would result from the output of an additional desk.

To answer questions of this sort, it is necessary to extend Table 3.1. This is done in Table 3.2, through the addition of two further rows at the bottom of

TABLE 3.2 Simplex tableau for the initial basic feasible solution for the office furnishings company.

c_B	BASIS	c_j 30 x_1	20 x_2	0 s_1	0 s_2	0 s_3	SOLUTION
0	s_1	8	4	1	0	0	640
0	s_2	4	6	0	1	0	540
0	s_3	1	1	0	0	1	100
	z_j	0	0	0	0	0	0 Profit
	$c_j - z_j$	30	20	0	0	0	

the table. We have already noted that the top row, c_j, of the table shows the contribution to profit per unit for each of the variables. We now have to worry about any reductions in profit which might also arise from the addition to our solution of one unit of each variable. Any such reduction must come from a compensating decrease in the basic variables. The nonbasic variables cannot be decreased further, for they are already at zero, their lowest feasible value.

What would we have to give up in order to produce one additional desk? The answer can be read directly from the x_1 column of the simplex tableau. Each additional unit of x_1 added to our solution would involve the sacrifice of 8 units of s_1, 4 units of s_2, and 1 unit of s_3. The costs of these sacrifices are shown in the c_B column. In fact, since the slack variables contribute nothing to profits, the total loss to profit involved in the production of an extra desk is simply

$$(0)(8) + (0)(4) + (0)(1) = 0$$

These costs, which in this particular case are all zero, are entered in the row labelled z_j in Table 3.2. It is no surprise to learn that we need to give up nothing in order to produce an extra desk or bookcase. The only effect will be a reduction in slack values.

Finally, the deductions from profits, z_j, are subtracted from the contributions to profits, c_j, to yield the row $c_j - z_j$. This row shows the net change in profit resulting from a unit increase in each of the variables. We see, therefore, that taking our initial basic feasible solution as a starting point, profit will increase by \$30 for each additional desk produced, by \$20 for each extra bookcase, and will be unchanged by adding to the slack values.

We have set out in Table 3.2 the simplex tableau for the initial basic feasible solution to our product mix problem. To make clear how, in general, the various elements of a constrained maximization problem are incorporated into a simplex tableau, we show the form of such a tableau in Table 3.3.

At this stage, we have a pretty full description of the nature of our initial basic feasible solution. The next step is to try to move to a better solution. We will see how this can be accomplished in the following section.

TABLE 3.3 General form of the simplex tableau for a profit maximization problem.

		c_j	GROSS CONTRIBUTION PER UNIT TO PROFIT	SOLUTION
c_B	BASIS		LABELS FOR ALL VARIABLES	
Contributions per unit to profit for basic variables	Labels for basic variables		Resource uses per unit for each variable for all constraints	Values of basic variables at basic feasible solution
		z_j $c_j - z_j$	Profit lost per unit increase in variables Net change in profit per unit increase in variables	Profit at basic feasible solution

3.4. IMPROVING THE INITIAL SOLUTION

Having obtained a basic feasible solution, we must ask whether any improvement is possible, and if so, in what direction we should now move. The simplex algorithm proceeds by first testing a basic feasible solution for optimality. If the solution is indeed optimal, then the job is finished. If it is not, the next step is to move to an *adjacent* basic feasible solution. It is necessary only to look at basic feasible solutions, since if there exists an optimum solution, it must be at one of the extreme points of the feasible region. In the context of our product mix problem, the initial basic feasible solution is at the point (0, 0) of Figure 3.1. The next step would be to move to one or the other adjacent extreme points— either (0, 90) or (80, 0). We will next test the new basic feasible solution for optimality, and so on.

In this section, then, we have to answer three questions:

1. How do we test for optimality the initial basic feasible solution?
2. If this solution is not optimal, to which extreme point do we next move?
3. How do we set up the simplex tableau for the new basic feasible solution?

The first two questions are a good deal more easily answered than the third. Let us return to the product mix problem of the office furnishings company, and in particular, to the simplex tableau of Table 3.2. The last row of that table provides a ready answer to our first question. An increase in either x_1 or x_2 will have a positive net effect on profits. Hence, our initial basic feasible solution cannot be optimal. It could be improved either by increasing x_1 (production of desks) or x_2 (production of bookcases). This suggests a general rule for checking optimality.

Checking the Optimality of a Basic Feasible Solution for Maximization Problems

A basic feasible solution is optimal if, and only if, none of the elements in the $c_j - z_j$ row of the simplex tableau is greater than zero.

علم (handwritten)

Having ascertained that our initial solution is not optimal, the next step is to move on to another basic feasible solution. As already noted, the simplex algorithm moves to an adjacent extreme point. In practice, this means replacing *one* member of the basis by a variable that was nonbasic in the previous solution. Which variable would be most sensible to bring into the basis? Each additional unit of x_1 increases profits by \$30, while each additional unit of x_2 produces only a \$20 increase. Given just this information it seems sensible to increase x_1; that is, to produce more desks. Again, a general rule follows.

Bringing a New Variable into the Basis

If a basic feasible solution is not optimal, we proceed by bringing one of the previously nonbasic variables into the basis. The variable chosen is that for which $c_j - z_j$ is largest.

We now have to ask which member of the current basis is to be replaced. This is determined by increasing the value of the new basic variable to the point where further increase would violate a constraint. Now, each unit of x_1 uses up 8 man-hours of assembly time, and since there are just 640 available, the maximum permitted output of desks if this were the only constraint would be 640/8 = 80. On the other hand, the finishing time constraint would allow the production of 540/4 = 135 desks, and, by itself, the inspection time constraint would permit output of 100 desks. It follows that the best that can be done before hitting a constraint is to produce 80 desks. Production of more desks would be infeasible, as this would require more than the available amount of assembly time. Thus, choosing s_1 as the variable to leave the basis ensures that we move to a feasible solution.

We set out these calculations in an addition to our simplex tableau in Table 3.4. The final column of this table provides the additional information.

TABLE 3.4 Simplex tableau deriving the entering and leaving variables for the product mix problem.

	c_j	30	20	0	0	0		
c_B	BASIS	x_1	x_2	s_1	s_2	s_3	SOLUTION	
0	s_1	⑧	4	1	0	0	640	$\frac{640}{8} = 80$
0	s_2	4	6	0	1	0	540	$\frac{540}{4} = 135$
0	s_3	1	1	0	0	1	100	$\frac{100}{1} = 100$
	z_j	0	0	0	0	0	0 Profit	
	$c_j - z_j$	30	20	0	0	0		

What is the consequence of producing 80 desks? Recall that the assembly time constraint is

$$8x_1 + 4x_2 + s_1 = 640$$

The value of x_2 is to remain at 0, but, if x_1 is to be set at 80, this equation can only be satisfied if s_1 is zero. In our terminology, this implies that s_1 leaves the basis and becomes nonbasic. We could have deduced this by noticing in Table 3.4 that s_1 appears with coefficient 1 in that row for which the entry in the final column is smallest. In Table 3.4, we have indicated that x_1 is to enter the basis and s_1 to leave, by circling the element in the x_1 column and s_1 row. We call this the **pivotal element.**

Moving to an Improved Solution

If a basic feasible solution is nonoptimal, we move to an improved solution by bringing one variable into, and removing one variable from, the basis. The former is called the **entering variable** and the latter the **leaving variable.** The element in the simplex tableau in the column of the entering, and row of the leaving, variable is called the **pivotal element.**

We have seen that the leaving variable is to be that one for which the value in the final column of tables, such as Table 3.4, is smallest. However, later we will encounter examples in which the values in this final column can be negative. Now, because of the nonnegativity constraint, the value of the entering variable cannot be negative. Hence, stated in full, our rule should be that the leaving variable is the one corresponding to the smallest *positive* value in the final column of tables such as Table 3.4.

We have now moved to a second basic feasible solution which has x_1, s_2, s_3 as basis, that is, the values of x_2 and s_1 are zero at this solution. To make further progress, it is necessary to compute the simplex tableau for this solution. Part of that task is straightforward, part less so. The difficulty arises because in terms of our new basis, the standard form for the constraints is not in tableau form.

To see how to get around this problem, we write out again the constraints in standard form as

$$8x_1 + 4x_2 + 1s_1 + 0s_2 + 0s_3 = 640 \qquad (3.7)$$

$$4x_1 + 6x_2 + 0s_1 + 1s_2 + 0s_3 = 540 \qquad (3.8)$$

$$1x_1 + 1x_2 + 0s_1 + 0s_2 + 1s_3 = 100 \qquad (3.9)$$

Now, as far as two of the members of our basis go, we are in good shape. The variable s_2 appears with coefficient 1 in (3.8) and coefficient zero in the other two equations. Similarly s_3 appears with coefficient 1 in (3.9) and zero in the other two equations. Our objective now is to leave that happy state of affairs undisturbed, while arranging things so that we have a system of equations in which x_1 appears with coefficient 1 in the first equation and zero in the others. The initial part of this task is easily accomplished. Dividing through (3.7) by 8 gives

$$1x_1 + \tfrac{1}{2}x_2 + \tfrac{1}{8}s_1 + 0s_2 + 0s_3 = 80 \qquad (3.7)^*$$

Next, we multiply through (3.7)* by 4, yielding

$$4x_1 + 2x_2 + \tfrac{1}{2}s_1 + 0s_2 + 0s_3 = 320$$

Subtracting the left- and right-hand sides of this equation from those of equation (3.8) yields

$$0x_1 + 4x_2 - \tfrac{1}{2}s_1 + 1s_2 + 0s_3 = 220 \qquad (3.8)^*$$

in which x_1 appears with coefficient zero. Finally, subtracting the left- and right-hand sides of (3.7)* from those of (3.9) produces

$$0x_1 + \tfrac{1}{2}x_2 - \tfrac{1}{8}s_1 + 0s_2 + 1s_3 = 20 \qquad (3.9)^*$$

Equations (3.7)*–(3.9)* set out the constraints in tableau form, with x_1, s_2, s_3 as basis.

We are now in a position to set up the new simplex tableau. However, before doing so we note how the changes just derived could have been developed from the old tableau. Three rows from Table 3.4 are, in part,

x_1	x_2	s_1	s_2	s_3	SOLUTION	
8	4	1	0	0	640	Row 1
4	6	0	1	0	540	Row 2
1	1	0	0	1	100	Row 3

The corresponding part of the new tableau, in which x_1 enters and s_1 leaves the basis, is, where we have described how the new entries were formed,

x_1	x_2	s_1	s_2	s_3	SOLUTION	
1	$\frac{1}{2}$	$\frac{1}{8}$	0	0	80	Row 1* = (Row 1)/8
0	4	$-\frac{1}{2}$	1	0	220	Row 2* = Row 2 $-$ 4(Row 1*)
0	$\frac{1}{2}$	$-\frac{1}{8}$	0	1	20	Row 3* = Row 3 $-$ Row 1*

Row 3

These entries, of course, correspond to the coefficients in equations (3.7)*–(3.9)*. However, we can now see how to move directly from one tableau to the next. This involves two steps:

STEP 1: ☐ Divide each element in the row in which the pivot element lies by the value of the pivot element.

STEP 2: ☐ For every other row, subtract from each initial value the product of the initial value appearing in the same column as the pivot element and the value found in the column of interest in step 1. For example, the entry $-\frac{1}{2}$ in the second row and the s_1 column is found from $0 - (4)(\frac{1}{8}) = -\frac{1}{2}$. This procedure follows from our discussion leading to equations (3.7)*–(3.9)*.

We are now in a position to complete the new simplex tableau. This is done in Table 3.5. The following points should be noted:

1. The top row of the tableau lists the contributions to profits of a unit of each variable and remains unchanged from one tableau to the next.

2. In the left-hand portion of the tableau, we now show that x_1 is in the basis, together with its associated contribution per unit to profit.

3. We can read directly from the table the solution values for the basic variables. Hence the complete basic feasible solution is

$$x_1 = 80, x_2 = 0, s_1 = 0, s_2 = 220, s_3 = 20$$

Notice that this is the extreme point (80, 0) in Figure 3.1.

4. The profit at this basic feasible solution is then obtained by multiplying each solution value by the corresponding contribution per unit to profit and summing, giving

$$\text{Profit} = (30)(80) + (0)(220) + (0)(20) = 2400$$

Hence we have improved from an initial basic feasible solution yielding zero profit to one giving profit $2400.

5. The elements in the z_j row again show any subtractions from profits incurred from increasing each variable by one unit. For example, an increase of one in output of bookcases (x_2) would lead to foregone profits of

$$(30)(\tfrac{1}{2}) + (0)(4) + (0)(\tfrac{1}{2}) = 15$$

dollars. Finally, these z_j values are subtracted from the corresponding contributions per unit to profits, c_j, yielding the net contributions $c_j - z_j$.

What, then, can we conclude from the simplex tableau of Table 3.5? Perhaps the most important message is that our journey to the optimal solution has not yet ended. It can be seen that a unit increase in x_2 (production of bookcases) will yield a net increase (of $5) in profits. It therefore follows, as we discussed earlier, that our basic feasible solution is not optimal.

TABLE 3.5 Simplex tableau with x_1, s_2, s_3 in basis for the office furnishings company.

c_B	BASIS	c_j 30 x_1	20 x_2	0 s_1	0 s_2	0 s_3	SOLUTION
30	x_1	1	$\frac{1}{2}$	$\frac{1}{8}$	0	0	80
0	s_2	0	4	$-\frac{1}{2}$	1	0	220
0	s_3	0	$\frac{1}{2}$	$-\frac{1}{8}$	0	1	20
	z_j	30	15	$3\frac{3}{4}$	0	0	2400 Profit
	$c_j - z_j$	0	5	$-3\frac{3}{4}$	0	0	

3.5. ITERATING TO THE OPTIMAL SOLUTION

If the current basic feasible solution is not optimal, it is necessary to move to an adjacent extreme point and test the corresponding solution for optimality. This **iterative** process then continues until a basic feasible solution passing the optimality test is found. The iterative cycle is described schematically in Figure 3.2.

Up to this point, for our product mix problem, we have found an initial basic feasible solution and completed one circuit of the loop in Figure 3.2. Moreover, we have just discovered that at least one further circuit will be necessary, since the second basic feasible solution tested also turned out to be suboptimal. We continue, therefore, in the same fashion as in the previous section. First, it is clear from the tableau of Table 3.5 that the entering variable should be x_2, since this is the only variable for which an addition would lead to a positive net contribution to profits. To determine which variable should leave the basis, we augment the tableau with an additional column in Table 3.6.

The final column of Table 3.6 is found by dividing the entries in the solution column by the corresponding values in the x_2 column. Since the smallest

TABLE 3.6 Determination of new entering and leaving variables for the product mix problem, and the indication of the pivotal element.

c_B	BASIS	c_j 30 x_1	20 x_2	0 s_1	0 s_2	0 s_3	SOLUTION	
30	x_1	1	$\frac{1}{2}$	$\frac{1}{8}$	0	0	80	$80 \div \frac{1}{2} = 160$
0	s_2	0	4	$-\frac{1}{2}$	1	0	220	$\frac{220}{4} = 55$
0	s_3	0	$\frac{1}{2}$	$-\frac{1}{8}$	0	1	20	$20 \div \frac{1}{2} = 40$
	z_j	30	15	$3\frac{3}{4}$	0	0	2400	
	$c_j - z_j$	0	5	$-3\frac{3}{4}$	0	0	Profit	

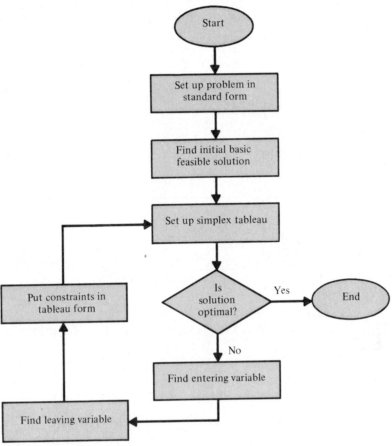

FIGURE 3.2 Schematic representation of the simplex algorithm.

result is in the s_3 row, this variable leaves the basis. Hence, the basic variables for the next solution to be tested will be x_1, s_2, x_2.

We now have to set up the simplex tableau for this new basis. The trickiest part of this exercise, as before, is to find the portion of the new tableau corresponding to the production constraints. The procedure used is the same as in the previous section. From Table 3.5 we have

x_1	x_2	s_1	s_2	s_3	SOLUTION	
1	$\frac{1}{2}$	$\frac{1}{8}$	0	0	80	Row 1
0	4	$-\frac{1}{2}$	1	0	220	Row 2
0	$\frac{1}{2}$	$-\frac{1}{8}$	0	1	20	Row 3

TABLE 3.7 Simplex Tableau with x_1, s_2, x_2 in basis for the office furnishings company.

	c_j	30	20	0	0	0	
c_B	BASIS	x_1	x_2	s_1	s_2	s_3	SOLUTION
30	x_1	1	0	$\frac{1}{4}$	0	-1	60
0	s_2	0	0	$\frac{1}{2}$	1	-8	60
20	x_2	0	1	$-\frac{1}{4}$	0	2	40
	z_j	30	20	$2\frac{1}{2}$	0	10	2600 Profit
	$c_j - z_j$	0	0	$-2\frac{1}{2}$	0	-10	

rich at optimum level

This portion of the new tableau is then determined as indicated below:

x_1	x_2	s_1	s_2	s_3	SOLUTION	
1	0	$\frac{1}{4}$	0	-1	60	Row 1* = Row 1 $-\frac{1}{2}$(Row 3*)
0	0	$\frac{1}{2}$	1	-8	60	Row 2* = Row 2 $-$ 4(Row 3*)
0	1	$-\frac{1}{4}$	0	2	40	Row 3* = (Row 3) $\div \frac{1}{2}$

Since s_3 is replaced by x_2 in the basis, the initial row 3 is divided by $\frac{1}{2}$, so that the coefficient on x_2 is now 1. Operations on the other two rows then produce 0 coefficients on x_2.

The simplex tableau for this basic feasible solution can now be completed, precisely as we did in the previous section. The full tableau is shown in Table 3.7.

From Table 3.7, we read that this basic feasible solution is

$$x_1 = 60, \ x_2 = 40, \ s_1 = 0, \ s_2 = 60, \ s_3 = 0$$

This implies production of 60 desks and 40 bookcases, with 60 man-hours of slack in finishing. There is no slack time in either assembly or inspection. It can also be seen from the table that this solution yields a profit of $2600.

Finally, we find from the $c_j - z_j$ row of Table 3.7 that in no case will the addition of a unit to any nonbasic variable produce a positive increase in net profit. It follows, therefore, that our solution is optimal. This solution is the point (60,40) in Figure 3.1, confirming the conclusion of our graphical analysis of this problem in Chapter 2.

In Figure 3.3 we recap the route taken by the simplex method to this optimal solution.

3.6. A FURTHER EXAMPLE

The product mix problem of the office furnishings company can be solved graphically because it involves only two decision variables. With more than two decision variables, this route to the optimal solution is not really practicable.

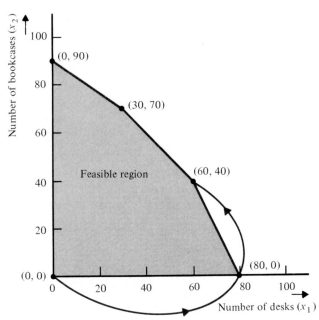

In this section, we show the simplex algorithm solution to a media mix advertising problem with three decision variables. An automobile dealer intends to launch a promotion campaign which is to cost no more than $50,000. The problem is to decide the allocation of this budget among three local media outlets—television, radio, and newspapers. Given time and availability restrictions, it is not possible to spend more than $40,000 on television, $20,000 on radio, or $5,000 on newspaper advertisements. Within the limits of these amounts, the dealer estimates that each thousand dollars spent on television advertising brings an extra 12 customers into the showroom. The corresponding numbers for radio and newspapers are 10 and 15. Given the problem constraints, the dealer wants to determine the media mix that will generate as many extra customers as possible.[2]

First we set the problem in algebraic form. Let x_1, x_2, x_3 denote the

---

[2] This is a simplified version of an advertising media mix problem. In particular we have ignored such complications as the possibility of potential customers being reached by more than one media outlet. We will put this problem in algebraic form and proceed with the simplex algorithm analysis. However, if you think a little first about the problem, you should be able to deduce the optimal solution. It should be instructive to compare your intuition with our formal development of an optimal solution.

amounts, in thousands of dollars, spent respectively on television, radio, and newspapers. The media mix problem can then be formulated as

$$\text{Maximize} \quad 12x_1 + 10x_2 + 15x_3$$

$$\text{subject to} \quad x_1 \leq 40$$

$$x_2 \leq 20$$

$$x_3 \leq 5$$

$$x_1 + x_2 + x_3 \leq 50$$

$$x_1, x_2, x_3 \geq 0$$

The next step is to put the problem in standard form, by introducing four slack variables. Let s_1, s_2, s_3 denote the respective amounts, in thousands of dollars, of unused potential for advertising for television, radio, and newspapers. Finally, denote by s_4 the unspent amount, in thousands of dollars, of the total advertising budget. The standard form of the media mix problem is then

$$\text{Maximize} \quad 12x_1 + 10x_2 + 15x_3$$

$$\text{subject to} \quad x_1 + s_1 = 40$$

$$x_2 + s_2 = 20$$

$$x_3 + s_3 = 5$$

$$x_1 + x_2 + x_3 + s_4 = 50$$

$$x_1, x_2, x_3, s_1, s_2, s_3, s_4 \geq 0$$

For our initial basic feasible solution, the four slack variables will constitute the basis. Since the standard form is then in tableau form, we can proceed immediately to build up the simplex tableau. Table 3.8 shows the derivation of the optimal solution through the simplex algorithm. In part (i) of the table we see that the initial solution produces no customers and is not optimal. The entering variable at the next stage should be x_3, and the leaving variable s_3.

Part (ii) of Table 3.8 shows the simplex tableau when s_1, s_2, x_3, s_4 are in the basis. This basic feasible solution generates 75 customers and again is not optimal. We see that the entering variable should be x_1 and the leaving variable s_1.

Moving to part (iii) of the table, in which x_1, s_2, x_3, s_4 are in the basis, we see that we now have a basic feasible solution yielding 555 customers, but that this solution is still not optimal. For the next stage, the entering variable should be x_2 and the leaving variable s_4.

Finally, part (iv) of Table 3.8 presents an optimal solution yielding 605 customers. This solution is

$$x_1 = 40, \; x_2 = 5, \; x_3 = 5, \; s_1 = 0, \; s_2 = 15, \; s_3 = 0, \; s_4 = 0$$

Hence, we conclude that the dealer should spend \$40,000 on television, \$5000 on radio, and \$5000 on newspaper advertising. The only nonzero slack remaining at this optimal solution is \$15,000 of available radio time.

TABLE 3.8 Simplex algorithm derivation of the optimal solution to advertising media mix problem of the automobile dealer.

(i)

c_j		12	10	15	0	0	0	0		
c_B	BASIS	x_1	x_2	x_3	s_1	s_2	s_3	s_4	SOLUTION	
0	s_1	1	0	0	1	0	0	0	40	$\frac{40}{0}$
0	s_2	0	1	0	0	1	0	0	20	$\frac{20}{0}$
0	s_3	0	0	①	0	0	1	0	5	$\frac{5}{1} = 5$
0	s_4	1	1	1	0	0	0	1	50	$\frac{50}{1} = 50$
	z_j	0	0	0	0	0	0	0	0	
	$c_j - z_j$	12	10	15	0	0	0	0	Customers	

(ii)

c_j		12	10	15	0	0	0	0		
c_B	BASIS	x_1	x_2	x_3	s_1	s_2	s_3	s_4	SOLUTION	
0	s_1	①	0	0	1	0	0	0	40	$\frac{40}{1} = 40$
0	s_2	0	1	0	0	1	0	0	20	$\frac{20}{0}$
15	x_3	0	0	1	0	0	1	0	5	$\frac{5}{0}$
0	s_4	1	1	0	0	0	-1	1	45	$\frac{45}{1} = 45$
	z_j	0	0	15	0	0	15	0	75	
	$c_j - z_j$	12	10	0	0	0	-15	0	Customers	

(iii)

c_j		12	10	15	0	0	0	0		
c_B	BASIS	x_1	x_2	x_3	s_1	s_2	s_3	s_4	SOLUTION	
0	s_1	1	0	0	1	0	0	0	40	$\frac{40}{1} = 40$
0	s_2	0	1	0	0	1	0	0	20	$\frac{20}{0}$
15	x_3	0	0	1	0	0	1	0	5	$\frac{5}{0}$
0	s_4	1	①	0	0	0	-1	1	45	$\frac{45}{1} = 45$
	z_j	0	0	15	0	0	15	0	75	
	$c_j - z_j$	12	10	0	0	0	-15	0	Customers	

(iv)

c_j		12	10	15	0	0	0	0	
c_B	BASIS	x_1	x_2	x_3	s_1	s_2	s_3	s_4	SOLUTION
12	x_1	1	0	0	1	0	0	0	40
0	s_2	0	0	0	1	1	1	-1	15
15	x_3	0	0	1	0	0	1	0	5
10	x_2	0	1	0	-1	0	-1	1	5
	z_j	12	10	15	2	0	5	10	605
	$c_j - z_j$	0	0	0	-2	0	-5	-10	Customers

GREATER THAN OR EQUAL TO AND EQUALITY CONSTRAINTS IN MAXIMIZATION PROBLEMS: ARTIFICIAL VARIABLES

We have learned how to solve a wide range of constrained maximization linear programming problems. Now that the simplex algorithm is available to us, it is no longer necessary to restrict attention to problems with only two decision variables. However, the examples considered to this point still contain a restrictive common feature. All of the constraints (apart from the nonnegativity constraints) are of the "less than or equal to" form. This precludes attacking problems with other types of constraints, though in the real world these frequently crop up.

To illustrate, suppose that in addition to its other production constraints, our office furnishings company must produce at least 50 bookcases in a particular week in order to meet a rush order from an important customer. It is easy enough to set up the modified problem in algebraic form. We have

$$\text{Maximize} \quad 30x_1 + 20x_2$$
$$\text{subject to} \quad 8x_1 + 4x_2 \leq 640$$
$$4x_1 + 6x_2 \leq 540$$
$$x_1 + x_2 \leq 100$$
$$x_2 \geq 50$$
$$x_1, x_2 \geq 0$$

In Figure 3.4 we show the feasible region and extreme points for the modified problem. Notice that a different product mix will be required here, as the previous optimal solution is now infeasible, given the additional constraint.

With the introduction of a surplus variable, it is straightforward to put this problem in standard form. Let s_4 denote the number of desks produced over the minimum requirement. Then we can write the problem in standard form as

$$\text{Maximize} \quad 30x_1 + 20x_2$$
$$\text{subject to} \quad 8x_1 + 4x_2 + s_1 = 640$$
$$4x_1 + 6x_2 + s_2 = 540$$
$$x_1 + x_2 + s_3 = 100$$
$$x_2 - s_4 = 50 \tag{3.10}$$
$$x_1, x_2, s_1, s_2, s_3, s_4 \geq 0$$

You will recall that we began our journey to the optimal solution of constrained maximization problems by choosing the slack variables as basis. By

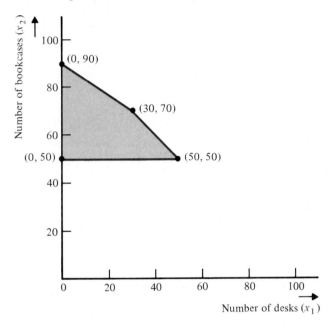

FIGURE 3.4 Feasible region for the product mix of the office furnishings company when at least 50 bookcases must be produced.

analogy, it would be tempting here to let s_1, s_2, s_3, s_4 be the basic variables at the initial stage. This will not do, however, as the constraints in the standard form are not in tableau form. This is so, since the variable s_4 does not appear with coefficient one in (3.10). Moreover, it is not possible to transpose these constraints to tableau form. For example, writing (3.10) as

$$s_4 - x_2 = -50$$

will not do the trick, as the right-hand side of this equation is negative.

We get around this difficulty through the use of an artifice.[3] Specifically, we introduce an additional variable into the problem. Suppose that the variable a_1 is added to the left-hand side of (3.10). Then, with s_1, s_2, s_3, a_1 as basis, the constraints will be in tableau form. Now, in terms of our problem, this new variable has no physical interpretation, and is known as an **artificial variable.** Its sole purpose is to provide us with a basis such that the constraints are in tableau form. However, we certainly do not want this variable to remain in the basis. It would be ridiculous to commit resources to a quantity with no concrete interpretation. To ensure that the artificial variable does indeed leave the basis, we associate a heavy penalty with any nonzero value of this variable. Specifically, we modify the objective function so that each unit of the artificial variable in the

---

[3] We will see in the next section that the same trick can be exploited to solve minimization problems.

solution leads to a decrease of M in profits, where M represents a very large positive number. Taking these considerations together, the tableau form of the problem is

$$\text{Maximize} \quad 30x_1 + 20x_2 + Ma_1$$
$$\text{subject to} \quad 8x_1 + 4x_2 + s_1 = 640$$
$$4x_1 + 6x_2 + s_2 = 540$$
$$x_1 + x_2 + s_3 = 100$$
$$x_2 - s_4 + a_1 = 50 \qquad (3.11)$$
$$x_1, x_2, s_1, s_2, s_3, s_4, a_1 \geq 0$$

Beginning with a solution using s_1, s_2, s_3, a_1 as basis, we can now employ the simplex algorithm in the usual way to find the optimal solution to this constrained maximization problem. Before doing so, however, a feature of the initial solution must be noted. If x_2 is to be nonbasic in our solution, then, by definition, it takes the value zero. However, in terms of our original problem, this solution is not feasible, since at least 50 bookcases must be produced!

The reader can be excused if he or she is perplexed at this point! We have complicated our problem by adding a further variable which admittedly has no physical interpretation. This was done to allow the formulation of the problem in tableau form. Yet, the resulting initial solution is infeasible. In mitigation, it should be said that

(a) the simplex algorithm will not know that the initial solution is infeasible in terms of the original problem, and therefore will not take offense;

(b) any artificial variables introduced will be associated with a large penalty in the objective function, so that they will quickly leave the basis, and the algorithm will move to basic solutions that *are* feasible. Once the artificial variables leave the basis, they will not enter again.

We illustrate these points in Table 3.9, where the simplex algorithm is employed in the derivation of the optimal solution to our modified product mix problem. In part (i) of the table, the initial solution is given as

$$x_1 = 0, x_2 = 0, s_1 = 640, s_2 = 540, s_3 = 100, s_4 = 0, a_1 = 50$$

Now, this is a basic feasible solution to the tableau version of the problem, where the artificial variable a_1 is introduced. It is not, however, a feasible solution to our real problem, since (3.10) is not satisfied. Such solutions are sometimes called **pseudofeasible.** Now, we see from the table that this solution is not optimal. Indeed, by associating the high cost M with membership of the artificial variable in the basis, we have ensured that it cannot be. The simplex algorithm proceeds, as before, by moving to an adjacent basic feasible solution. This will involve driving artificial variables out of the basis, and hence, moving eventually to basic feasible solutions at the extreme points of the feasible region of the real problem. The use of artificial variables, then, can be viewed as a device for starting up the simplex algorithm, which will then evolve to the systematic checking for optimality of extreme points of the actual feasible region. In the context of our present problem, from part (i) of Table 3.9, the new entering variable should be x_2. This is so since the net addition to profit, $20 + M$, can be

TABLE 3.9 Simplex algorithm derivation of the optimal solution to the product mix problem of the office furnishings company when at least 50 bookcases must be produced.

(i)

c_B	BASIS	c_j 30 x_1	20 x_2	0 s_1	0 s_2	0 s_3	0 s_4	$-M$ a_1	SOLUTION	
0	s_1	8	4	1	0	0	0	0	640	$\frac{640}{4} = 160$
0	s_2	4	6	0	1	0	0	0	540	$\frac{540}{6} = 90$
0	s_3	1	1	0	0	1	0	0	100	$\frac{100}{1} = 100$
$-M$	a_1	0	①	0	0	0	-1	1	50	$\frac{50}{1} = 50$
	z_j	0	$-M$	0	0	0	M	$-M$	$-50M$	
	$c_j - z_j$	30	$20 + M$	0	0	0	$-M$	0	Profit	

(ii)

c_B	BASIS	c_j 30 x_1	20 x_2	0 s_1	0 s_2	0 s_3	0 s_4	$-M$ a_1	SOLUTION	
0	s_1	8	0	1	0	0	4	-4	440	$\frac{440}{8} = 55$
0	s_2	4	0	0	1	0	6	-6	240	$\frac{240}{4} = 60$
0	s_3	①	0	0	0	1	1	-1	50	$\frac{50}{1} = 50$
20	x_2	0	1	0	0	0	-1	1	50	$\frac{50}{0}$
	z_j	0	20	0	0	0	-20	20	1000	
	$c_j - z_j$	30	0	0	0	0	20	$-M-20$	Profit	

(iii)

c_B	BASIS	c_j 30 x_1	20 x_2	0 s_1	0 s_2	0 s_3	0 s_4	$-M$ a_1	SOLUTION
0	s_1	0	0	1	0	-8	-4	4	40
0	s_2	0	0	0	1	-4	2	-2	40
30	x_1	1	0	0	0	1	1	-1	50
20	x_2	0	1	0	0	0	-1	1	50
	z_j	30	20	0	0	30	10	-10	2500
	$c_j - z_j$	0	0	0	0	-30	-10	$10 - M$	Profit

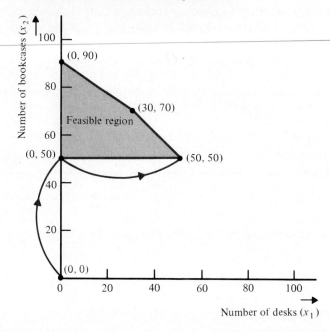

FIGURE 3.5 Route taken by the simplex method to the optimal solution of the office furnishings company when at least 50 bookcases must be produced.

made bigger than any other $c_j - z_j$ value by choosing a large enough M. It also emerges, as predicted, that the leaving variable is the artificial variable a_1.

Part (ii) of Table 3.9 shows the simplex tableau for the modified product mix problem when s_1, s_2, s_3, x_2 are in the basis. This solution, involving just the production of 50 bookcases, yields a profit of $1000, and is not optimal. It can be seen that at the next step, x_1 should enter and s_3 leave the basis.

Finally, in part (iii) of this table, it can be seen that an optimal solution has been reached. This solution yields a profit of $2500, and is

$$x_1 = 50, \ x_2 = 50, \ s_1 = 40, \ s_2 = 40, \ s_3 = 0, \ s_4 = 0$$

This implies production of 50 desks and 50 bookcases, with 40 man-hours of slack in assembly, 40 man-hours of slack in finishing, and no slack in inspection. The zero value for the surplus variable, s_4, implies no production of bookcases above the minimum requirement of 50.

The path taken by the simplex algorithm to the optimal solution is shown in Figure 3.5. Initially, we began with the solution (0, 0), which is not in the feasible region. The artificial variable was then driven out of the basis, moving us to the point (0, 50)—that is, output of no desks and 50 bookcases—which is an extreme point of the feasible region. Finally, the algorithm moves to the optimal solution, production of 50 desks and 50 bookcases.[4]

---

[4] The reader may want to verify graphically that this solution is indeed optimal.

The example we have just studied involves just a single greater than or equal to constraint. There is, however, no difficulty in handling several such constraints. In addition to surplus variables, we need to bring in one artificial variable for each such constraint. Hence, if there are K greater than or equal to constraints, K artificial variables, $a_1, a_2, \ldots, a_K$, will be needed. Each of these should be associated with a large cost, M, in the objective function. This will ensure that they are all driven out of the basis.

EQUALITY CONSTRAINTS

Equality constraints in linear programming problems can also be handled through the introduction of artificial variables. Suppose that the office furnishings company wants to produce *exactly* 50 bookcases, hence imposing the constraint

$$x_2 = 50$$

The standard form of the problem will then be precisely as before, except that (3.10) is replaced by

$$x_2 = 50$$

The surplus variable s_4 no longer appears in the problem specification, as production in excess of 50 bookcases is prohibited by the equality constraint. To put the problem in tableau form, the artificial variable, a_1, again with a high associated unit cost M, is introduced. The tableau form, then, is as before, except that the surplus variable, s_4, does not appear, and (3.11) is replaced by

$$x_2 + a_1 = 50$$

The initial simplex tableau can then be set up, and the simplex algorithm used to derive the optimal solution. In fact, the optimal solution is the same in this particular case as when production in excess of 50 bookcases was permitted. This is not surprising, since that solution dictated production of exactly 50 bookcases. The simplex tableau approach to the problem with the equality constraint is exactly the same as that of Table 3.9, with the s_4 column deleted.

Definition

   Artificial Variables are variables introduced into linear programming problems with greater than or equal to, or equality, constraints. They have no physical interpretation, but constitute a valuable device for initializing the simplex algorithm solution routine. Such variables are associated with a high cost in the objective function to ensure that they will be driven out of the basis.

3.8. APPLICATION OF THE SIMPLEX METHOD TO A CONSTRAINED MINIMIZATION PROBLEM

We have come a long way in this chapter, and many readers will have found the going a little rough in places. But, good news is at hand! Although you may not yet realize it, you now know how to use the simplex method to solve constrained **minimization,** as well as maximization, problems. All we need, in addition to the procedures already developed, is one little trick. Stated in words, we need to note only that minimization of a quantity is precisely equivalent to maximization of the negative of that quantity. For example, if our objective is to make "cost" as small as possible, we can just as well make "−cost" as large as possible. Armed with this device, and the further procedure of introducing artificial variables when there are greater than or equal to constraints, we can attack minimization problems along by now familiar lines.

Simplex Solution of Minimization Problems

Suppose we require to minimize y, a linear function of decision variables. The problem can be solved through the simplex algorithm by maximizing $-y$. ·

To illustrate, let us return to the blending problem of the processed food company, discussed in Sections 2.10 and 2.11. This company set minimum standards for the amounts of vitamins A, C, and D, and iron in its product. These were to be met through blending two additives, in quantities x_1 and x_2. In standard form, we wrote the blending problem for this company as

$$
\begin{aligned}
\text{Minimize} \quad & 2x_1 + 3x_2 \\
\text{subject to} \quad & 40x_1 - s_1 = 80 \\
& 5x_1 + 10x_2 - s_2 = 80 \\
& 10x_1 + 5x_2 - s_3 = 60 \\
& 20x_2 - s_4 = 80 \\
& x_1, x_2, s_1, s_2, s_3, s_4 \geq 0
\end{aligned}
\tag{3.12}
$$

The surplus variables s_1, s_2, s_3, s_4 represent excesses of company minimum standards for vitamins A, C, D, and iron in the blend. The objective function in (3.12) follows from the fact that the costs per unit for the two additives are 2 and 3 cents, and the aim is to produce the blend of lowest possible cost, satisfying the constraints.

Now, to convert this requirement to a maximization problem, we must maximize

$$-(2x_1 + 3x_2) = -2x_1 - 3x_2$$

Further, since the constaints in (3.12) are not in tableau form, as they are of the "greater than or equal to" type, we must add four artificial variables—a_1, a_2, a_3, a_4. The blending problem can then be expressed as[5]

Maximize $-2\,x_1 - 3x_2 - Ma_1 - Ma_2 - Ma_3 - Ma_4$

subject to

$$40x_1 - s_1 + a_1 = 80$$
$$5x_1 + 10x_2 - s_2 + a_2 = 80 \qquad (3.13)$$
$$10x_1 + 5x_2 - s_3 + a_3 = 60$$
$$20x_2 - s_4 + a_4 = 80$$
$$x_1, x_2, s_1, s_2, s_3, s_4, a_1, a_2, a_3, a_4 \geq 0$$

Since the formulation (3.13) is that of a linear programming constrained maximization problem in tableau form, we can proceed directly to the application of the simplex algorithm. This is done in Table 3.10. Since the problem involves 10 variables—two decision, four surplus, and four artificial—and since the four artificial variables that are initially basic must be driven one at a time out of the basis, the reader might suspect that the path to the optimal solution is quite lengthy. This is indeed the case.

Let us examine, one at a time, the six stages set out in Table 3.10.

(i) We begin with a basis consisting of the four artificial variables. The cost of this, and subsequent solutions is denoted as negative "profit." Clearly this solution is not optimal; indeed, since a high cost is associated with each artificial variable, there is no possibility that an optimal solution will be reached until all these variables have been driven from the basis. It emerges that x_1 should enter, and a_1 leave, the basis.

(ii) The new solution is, of course, not optimal. We see that at the next step, the entering variable is x_2, while the artificial variable, a_4 leaves the basis.

(iii) Naturally, our third pseudofeasible solution remains suboptimal. The new variable to enter the basis should be the surplus variable s_4. Notice that there is a negative value in the final column of this portion of the table. The implication is that s_4 cannot displace x_2 in the basis, for in doing so it would take a negative value which is not permitted by the problem constraints. Recall, rather, that the leaving variable should be the one associated with the smallest *positive* value in this final column. This is the artificial variable a_2.

---

[5] As before, we associate with each unit of each artificial variable a very high cost, M, to ensure that these variables will be driven out of the basis.

(iv) At this stage we find that the last artificial variable, a_3, is to leave the basis, with the surplus variable, s_2, entering.

(v) At last, then, we have a solution whose basis contains no artificial variables. This solution is for a blend of 2 grams of additive I and 8 grams of additive II, at a cost of 28 cents. It is, however, not optimal. Instead, we must move to a solution with s_1 replacing s_2 in the basis.

(vi) Finally, we have arrived at an optimal solution, requiring $2\frac{2}{3}$ grams of additive I and $6\frac{2}{3}$ grams of additive II, at a cost of $25\frac{1}{3}$ cents. This solution also involves $26\frac{2}{3}$ of slack over the minimum vitamin A standard and $53\frac{1}{3}$ over the minimum standard for iron. Notice that if our arithmetic is correct, this conclusion agrees with our findings through the graphical analysis of the problem in Chapter 2.

In terms of the decision variables (x_1, x_2), it can be seen from Table 3.10 that the six successive solutions examined by the simplex algorithm are $(0, 0)$, $(2, 0)$, $(2, 4)$, $(2, 7)$, $(2, 8)$, and finally the optimal solution $(\frac{8}{3}, \frac{20}{3})$. In Figure 3.6, we show the route taken to the optimal solution. The feasible region for this problem is, of course, that shown earlier in Figure 2.14.

We see from Figure 3.6 that the first four solutions examined are not in the

FIGURE 3.6 Route taken by the simplex algorithm to the optimal solution of the blending program of the processed food company.

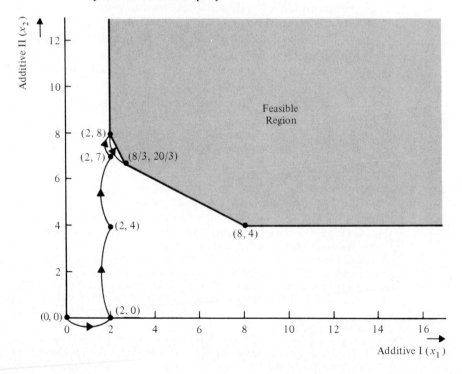

feasible region. It is only when all four artificial variables have left the basis that a feasible solution is reached. Notice that this solution, 2 grams of additive I and 8 grams of additive II, is an extreme point of the feasible region. Since this solution is not optimal, the algorithm moves on to an adjacent extreme point which turns out to be the optimal solution.

3.9. SOME SPECIAL SITUATIONS

The problems studied in this chapter all lead to straightforward application of the simplex algorithm. There are, however, four special situations which can arise, and of which the reader must be aware in interpreting the simplex analysis. Three of these have already been met in Section 2.7.

TABLE 3.10 Simplex algorithm derivation of the optimal solution to the blending problem of the processed food company.

(i)

c_B	BASIS	c_j -2 x_1	-3 x_2	0 s_1	0 s_2	0 s_3	0 s_4	$-M$ a_1	$-M$ a_2	$-M$ a_3	$-M$ a_4	SOLUTION	
$-M$	a_1	40	0	-1	0	0	0	1	0	0	0	80	$\frac{80}{40}=2$
$-M$	a_2	⑤	10	0	-1	0	0	0	1	0	0	80	$\frac{80}{5}=16$
$-M$	a_3	10	5	0	0	-1	0	0	0	1	0	60	$\frac{60}{10}=6$
$-M$	a_4	0	20	0	0	0	-1	0	0	0	1	80	$\frac{80}{0}$
	z_j	$-55M$	$-35M$	M	M	M	M	$-M$	$-M$	$-M$	$-M$	$-300M$	
	$c_j - z_j$	$55M-2$	$35M-3$	$-M$	$-M$	$-M$	$-M$	0	0	0	0	"Profit"	

(ii)

c_B	BASIS	c_j -2 x_1	-3 x_2	0 s_1	0 s_2	0 s_3	0 s_4	$-M$ a_1	$-M$ a_2	$-M$ a_3	$-M$ a_4	SOLUTION	
-2	x_1	1	0	$-\frac{1}{40}$	0	0	0	$\frac{1}{40}$	0	0	0	2	$\frac{2}{0}$
$-M$	a_2	0	10	$\frac{1}{8}$	-1	0	0	$\frac{1}{8}$	1	0	0	70	$\frac{70}{10}=7$
$-M$	a_3	0	5	$\frac{1}{4}$	0	-1	0	$-\frac{1}{4}$	0	1	0	40	$\frac{40}{5}=8$
$-M$	a_4	0	⑳	0	0	0	-1	0	0	0	1	80	$\frac{80}{20}=4$
	z_j	2	$-35M$	$-\frac{3}{8}M + \frac{1}{20}$	M	M	M	$\frac{3}{8}M - \frac{1}{20}$	$-M$	$-M$	$-M$	$-190M-2$	
	$c_j - z_j$	0	$35M-3$	$\frac{3}{8}M - \frac{1}{20}$	$-M$	$-M$	$-M$	$-1\frac{3}{8}M + \frac{1}{20}$	0	0	0	"Profit"	

TABLE 3.10 (Continued)

(iii)

c_B	c_j → BASIS	-2 x_1	-3 x_2	0 s_1	0 s_2	0 s_3	0 s_4	-M a_1	-M a_2	-M a_3	-M a_4	SOLUTION
-2	x_1	1	0	$-\frac{1}{40}$	0	0	0	$\frac{1}{40}$	0	0	0	2 $\frac{2}{8}$
-M	a_2	0	0	$\frac{1}{8}$	-1	0	$\left(\frac{1}{2}\right)$	$-\frac{1}{8}$	1	0	$-\frac{1}{2}$	30 $30/\frac{1}{2}=60$
-M	a_3	0	0	$\frac{1}{4}$	0	-1	$\frac{1}{4}$	$-\frac{1}{4}$	0	1	$-\frac{1}{4}$	20 $20/\frac{1}{4}=80$
-3	x_2	0	1	0	0	0	$-\frac{1}{20}$	0	0	0	$\frac{1}{20}$	4 $4/-\frac{1}{20}=-80$
	z_j	-2	-3	$-\frac{3}{8}M+\frac{1}{20}$	M	M	$-\frac{3}{4}M+\frac{3}{20}$	$\frac{3}{8}M-\frac{1}{20}$	-M	-M	$\frac{3}{4}M-\frac{3}{20}$	$-50M-16$
	c_j-z_j	0	0	$\frac{3}{8}M-\frac{1}{20}$	-M	-M	$\frac{3}{4}M-\frac{3}{20}$	$-1\frac{3}{8}M+\frac{1}{20}$	0	0	$-1\frac{3}{4}M+\frac{3}{20}$	"Profit"

(iv)

c_B	c_j → BASIS	-2 x_1	-3 x_2	0 s_1	0 s_2	0 s_3	0 s_4	-M a_1	-M a_2	-M a_3	-M a_4	SOLUTION
-2	x_1	1	0	$-\frac{1}{40}$	0	0	0	$\frac{1}{40}$	0	0	0	2 $\frac{2}{8}$
0	s_4	0	0	$\frac{1}{4}$	-2	0	1	$-\frac{1}{4}$	2	0	-1	60 $60/-2=-30$
-M	a_3	0	0	$\frac{3}{16}$	$\left(\frac{1}{2}\right)$	-1	0	$-\frac{3}{16}$	$-\frac{1}{2}$	1	0	5 $5/\frac{1}{2}=10$
-3	x_2	0	1	$\frac{1}{80}$	$-\frac{1}{10}$	0	0	$-\frac{1}{80}$	$\frac{1}{10}$	0	0	7 $7/-\frac{1}{10}=-70$
	z_j	-2	-3	$-\frac{3}{16}M+\frac{1}{80}$	$-\frac{1}{2}M-\frac{3}{10}$	M	0	$\frac{3}{16}M-\frac{1}{80}$	$\frac{1}{2}M+\frac{3}{10}$	-M	0	$-5M-25$
	c_j-z_j	0	0	$\frac{3}{16}M-\frac{1}{80}$	$\frac{1}{2}M+\frac{3}{10}$	-M	0	$-1\frac{3}{16}M+\frac{1}{80}$	$-1\frac{1}{2}M-\frac{3}{10}$	0	M	"Profit"

(v)

c_B	BASIS	-2 x_1	-3 x_2	0 s_1	0 s_2	0 s_3	0 s_4	$-M$ a_1	$-M$ a_2	$-M$ a_3	$-M$ a_4	SOLUTION	
-2	x_1	1	0	$-\frac{1}{40}$	0	0	0	$\frac{1}{40}$	0	0	0	2	$2/-\frac{1}{40} = -80$
0	s_4	0	0	1	0	-4	1	-1	0	4	-1	80	$\frac{80}{1} = 80$
0	s_2	0	0	$\left(\frac{1}{8}\right)$	1	-2	0	$-\frac{3}{8}$	-1	2	0	10	$10/\frac{1}{8} = \frac{80}{3}$
-3	x_2	0	1	$\frac{1}{20}$	0	$-\frac{1}{5}$	0	$-\frac{1}{20}$	0	$\frac{1}{5}$	0	8	$8/\frac{1}{20} = 160$
	z_j	-2	-3	$-\frac{1}{10}$	0	$\frac{3}{5}$	0	$\frac{1}{10}$	0	$-\frac{3}{5}$	0	-28	
	$c_j - z_j$	0	0	$\frac{1}{10}$	0	$-\frac{3}{5}$	0	$-M - \frac{1}{10}$	$-M$	$-M + \frac{3}{5}$	$-M$	"Profit"	

(vi)

c_B	BASIS	-2 x_1	-3 x_2	0 s_1	0 s_2	0 s_3	0 s_4	$-M$ a_1	$-M$ a_2	$-M$ a_3	$-M$ a_4	SOLUTION
-2	x_1	1	0	0	$\frac{1}{15}$	$-\frac{2}{15}$	0	0	$-\frac{1}{15}$	$\frac{2}{15}$	0	$2\frac{2}{3}$
0	s_4	0	0	0	$-\frac{8}{3}$	$\frac{4}{3}$	1	0	$\frac{8}{3}$	$-\frac{4}{3}$	-1	$53\frac{1}{3}$
0	s_1	0	0	1	$-\frac{8}{3}$	$-\frac{16}{3}$	0	-1	$\frac{8}{3}$	$\frac{16}{3}$	0	$26\frac{2}{3}$
-3	x_2	0	1	0	$-\frac{2}{15}$	$\frac{1}{15}$	0	0	$\frac{2}{15}$	$-\frac{1}{15}$	0	$6\frac{2}{3}$
	z_j	-2	-3	0	$\frac{4}{15}$	$\frac{1}{15}$	0	0	$-\frac{4}{15}$	$-\frac{1}{15}$	0	$-25\frac{1}{3}$
	$c_j - z_j$	0	0	0	$-\frac{4}{15}$	$-\frac{1}{15}$	0	$-M$	$-M + \frac{4}{15}$	$-M + \frac{1}{15}$	$-M$	"Profit"

It is not necessarily the case that a constrained optimization problem has a *unique* optimal solution. In Section 2.7, we saw that if the office furnishings company product mix problem is modified so that profit per unit is $25 for both desks and bookcases, there will be multiple optimal solutions. We noted how such a circumstance appears in a graphical analysis, and now ask what will be the effect on the simplex algorithm. Before reading further, you might sharpen your understanding of the simplex method by trying to figure out the way in which multiple optimal solutions influence the tableaux.

In standard form, the problem to be solved is

$$\text{Maximize} \quad 25x_1 + 25x_2$$

$$\text{subject to} \quad 8x_1 + 4x_2 + s_1 = 640$$

$$4x_1 + 6x_2 + s_2 = 540$$

$$x_1 + x_2 + s_3 = 100$$

$$x_1, x_2, s_1, s_2, s_3 \geq 0$$

The simplex algorithm derivation of the optimal solution is given in Table 3.11. In part (i) we see that the net gain $(c_j - z_j)$ from increasing either x_1 or x_2 by one unit is $25. Since the constraints allow a higher output for x_2, we choose to bring this variable into the basis, with the slack variable s_2 leaving. At step (iii) in the table we find that the solution

$$x_1 = 30, \ x_2 = 70, \ s_1 = 120, \ s_2 = 0, \ s_3 = 0$$

is optimal, yielding a profit of $2500. Do you notice anything special about the simplex tableau at this step? Certainly the solution is optimal. None of the values $c_j - z_j$, which measure net additions to profits from an increase of one unit in the variables, is positive. However, for one nonbasic variable, s_2, this value is zero. The implication is that an increase in s_2, while adding nothing to profits, will not decrease profits. This is precisely what we would expect when there are multiple optimal solutions—a nonbasic variable can be substituted for one of the basic variables, with no net effect on the value of the objective function, at an optimal solution.

The reader can verify that entering s_2 into the basis, with s_1 leaving, yields the basic feasible solution

$$x_1 = 60, \ x_2 = 40, \ s_1 = 0, \ s_2 = 60, \ s_3 = 0$$

which also produces a profit of $2500. As we saw in Section 2.7, it will be the case that when two basic feasible solutions are optimal, intermediate solutions are also optimal.

TABLE 3.11 Simplex algorithm derivation of an optimal solution for office furnishings company problem when profit per unit is $25 for both desks and bookcases.

(i)

c_B	c_j BASIS	25 x_1	25 x_2	0 s_1	0 s_2	0 s_3	SOLUTION	
0	s_1	8	4	1	0	0	640	$\frac{640}{4} = 160$
0	s_2	4	⑥	0	1	0	540	$\frac{540}{6} = 90$
0	s_3	1	1	0	0	1	100	$\frac{100}{1} = 100$
	z_j	0	0	0	0	0	0	
	$c_j - z_j$	25	25	0	0	0	Profit	

(ii)

c_B	c_j BASIS	25 x_1	25 x_2	0 s_1	0 s_2	0 s_3	SOLUTION	
0	s_1	$\frac{16}{3}$	0	1	$-\frac{2}{3}$	0	280	$280/\frac{16}{3} = 52\frac{1}{2}$
25	x_2	$\frac{2}{3}$	1	0	$\frac{1}{6}$	0	90	$90/\frac{2}{3} = 135$
0	s_3	$\textcircled{\tfrac{1}{3}}$	0	0	$-\frac{1}{6}$	1	10	$10/\frac{1}{3} = 30$
	z_j	$16\frac{2}{3}$	25	0	$4\frac{1}{6}$	0	2250	
	$c_j - z_j$	$8\frac{1}{3}$	0	0	$-4\frac{1}{6}$	0	Profit	

(iii)

c_B	c_j BASIS	25 x_1	25 x_2	0 s_1	0 s_2	0 s_3	SOLUTION
0	s_1	0	0	1	2	-16	120
25	x_2	0	1	0	$\frac{1}{2}$	-2	70
25	x_1	1	0	0	$-\frac{1}{2}$	3	30
	z_j	25	25	0	0	25	2500
	$c_j - z_j$	0	0	0	0	-25	Profit

Infeasibility arises when a constrained optimization problem has no feasible solution. In Section 2.7 we saw an example of such a problem, where the office furnishings company, in addition to its other constraints, requires the production of at least 120 bookcases. How does the simplex algorithm react to such a problem? To see, let us express it in tableau form as

$$
\begin{aligned}
\text{Maximize} \quad & 30x_1 + 20x_2 - Ma_1 \\
\text{subject to} \quad & 8x_1 + 4x_2 + s_1 = 640 \\
& 4x_1 + 6x_2 + s_2 = 540 \\
& x_1 + x_2 + s_3 = 100 \\
& x_2 - s_4 + a_1 = 120 \\
& x_1, x_2, s_1, s_2, s_3, s_4, a_1 \geq 0
\end{aligned}
\tag{3.14}
$$

In this formulation, s_4 is a surplus variable, denoting any production of bookcases over the required minimum, and a_1 is an artificial variable, with associated high cost per unit M.

In Table 3.12, we apply the simplex algorithm to this problem. A superficial look at the second tableau suggests that an optimal solution has been reached. Since M is an arbitrarily large positive number, the net gains $c_j - z_j$ in this second tableau are at most zero. However, two peculiarities of this solution need to be noted. First, since only 90 bookcases are to be made, the requirement that x_2 be at least 120 is not met, so that the solution is not feasible. Moreover, contrary to our earlier claims, the artificial variable has *not* been driven from the basis. This finding is typical of problems for which no feasible solution exists. The simplex algorithm will iterate to an apparent optimal solution involving artificial variables in the basis. Such solutions have no value, other than to convey the information that the problem has no feasible solution.

UNBOUNDEDNESS

Suppose that the office furnishings company can sell every desk produced at a profit of $30, and every bookcase at a profit of $20, and that the *only* constraints faced by this company are that it must produce at least 40 desks and 60 bookcases. In algebraic form, the profit maximization problem can then be written as

$$
\begin{aligned}
\text{Maximize} \quad & 30x_1 + 20x_2 \\
\text{subject to} \quad & x_1 \geq 40 \\
& x_2 \geq 60
\end{aligned}
$$

TABLE 3.12 The simplex algorithm applied to Problem (3.14).

(i)

c_j		30	20	0	0	0	0	$-M$	
c_B	BASIS	x_1	x_2	s_1	s_2	s_3	s_4	a_1	SOLUTION
0	s_1	8	4	1	0	0	0	0	640	$\frac{640}{4} = 160$
0	s_2	4	⑥	0	1	0	0	0	540	$\frac{540}{6} = 90$
0	s_3	1	1	0	0	1	0	0	100	$\frac{100}{1} = 100$
$-M$	a_1	0	1	0	0	0	-1	1	120	$\frac{120}{1} = 120$
	z_j	0	$-M$	0	0	0	M	$-M$	$-120M$	
	$c_j - z_j$	30	$M + 20$	0	0	0	$-M$	0	Profit	

(ii)

c_j		30	20	0	0	0	0	$-M$	
c_B	BASIS	x_1	x_2	s_1	s_2	s_3	s_4	a_1	SOLUTION
0	s_1	$\frac{16}{3}$	0	1	$-\frac{2}{3}$	0	0	0	280
20	x_2	$\frac{2}{3}$	1	0	$\frac{1}{6}$	0	0	0	90
0	s_3	$\frac{1}{3}$	0	0	$-\frac{1}{6}$	1	0	0	10
$-M$	a_1	$-\frac{2}{3}$	0	0	$-\frac{1}{6}$	0	-1	1	30
	z_j	$\frac{2}{3}M + \frac{40}{3}$	20	0	$\frac{1}{6}M + \frac{10}{3}$	0	M	$-M$	$-30M + 1800$
	$c_j - z_j$	$-\frac{2}{3}M + \frac{50}{3}$	0	0	$-\frac{1}{6}M - \frac{10}{3}$	0	$-M$	0	Profit

Now, from our discussion of Section 2.7, you will recognize the feature of unboundedness in this problem. Given no further constraints, the company is apparently able to increase output, and hence profit, without bound.

To see how the simplex algorithm is influenced by such a situation, we introduce two surplus variables and two artificial variables, each, as usual, associated with a high cost M. The tableau form of the problem can then be written

$$
\begin{aligned}
&\text{Maximize} \quad 30x_1 + 20x_2 - Ma_1 - Ma_2 \\
&\text{subject to} \qquad\qquad\qquad x_1 - s_1 + a_1 = 40 \qquad\qquad (3.15) \\
&\qquad\qquad\qquad\qquad\qquad\quad x_2 - s_2 + a_2 = 60 \\
&\qquad\qquad\qquad\quad x_1, x_2, s_1, s_2, a_1, a_2 \geq 0
\end{aligned}
$$

The simplex algorithm analysis of our problem is shown in Table 3.13. The algorithm proceeds uneventfully until the third stage is reached. Here, with x_1 and x_2 in the basis, the net gains, $c_j - z_j$, indicate that profit can be increased by raising the value of either of the surplus variables. It appears, then, that s_1 should be brought into the basis. Look, however, at the values in the final column of the table. The infinite value implies, as usual, that it is not possible to increase s_1 at the expense of any reduction in x_2. Further, the negative value implies that we cannot bring s_1 into the basis by having x_1 leave. Indeed, if s_1 is to increase, then x_1 must also *increase* in order for the first constraint to remain satisfied. This will lead to higher profit, and the process of increasing output and profit can continue indefinitely.

The simplex algorithm, then, is telling us that the value of the objective function can be made arbitrarily high. If such a phenomenon arises in the analysis of a problem, one should reexamine the specifications to see if any constraints have been inadvertently omitted.

DEGENERACY

We conclude this chapter by mentioning one more special situation that can arise in the simplex solution of constrained optimization linear programming problems. Let us return again to the product mix problem of the office furnishings company. Leaving the remainder of the original specifications in their original form, let us assume that finishing time capacity is only 480 man-hours. In standard form, then, the problem is

$$
\begin{aligned}
&\text{Maximize} \qquad 30x_1 + 20x_2 \\
&\text{subject to} \quad 8x_1 + 4x_2 + s_1 = 640 \\
&\qquad\qquad\quad 4x_1 + 6x_2 + s_2 = 480 \\
&\qquad\qquad\qquad\quad x_1 + x_2 + s_3 = 100 \\
&\qquad\qquad\quad x_1, x_2, s_1, s_2, s_3 \geq 0
\end{aligned}
$$

TABLE 3.13 Simplex algorithm analysis of problem (3.15).

(i)

c_j		30	20	0	0	$-M$	$-M$		
c_B	BASIS	x_1	x_2	s_1	s_2	a_1	a_2	SOLUTION	
$-M$	a_1	①	0	-1	0	1	0	40	$\frac{40}{1}=40$
$-M$	a_2	0	1	0	-1	0	1	60	$\frac{60}{0}$
	z_j	$-M$	$-M$	M	M	$-M$	$-M$	$-100M$	
	$c_j - z_j$	$M+30$	$M+20$	$-M$	$-M$	0	0	Profit	

(ii)

c_j		30	20	0	0	$-M$	$-M$		
c_B	BASIS	x_1	x_2	s_1	s_2	a_1	a_2	SOLUTION	
30	x_1	1	0	-1	0	1	0	40	$\frac{40}{0}$
$-M$	a_2	0	①	0	-1	0	1	60	$\frac{60}{1}=60$
	z_j	30	$-M$	-30	M	30	$-M$	$-60M + 1200$	
	$c_j - z_j$	0	$M+20$	30	$-M$	$-M-30$	0	Profit	

(iii)

c_j		30	20	0	0	$-M$	$-M$		
c_B	BASIS	x_1	x_2	s_1	s_2	a_1	a_2	SOLUTION	
30	x_1	1	0	-1	1	1	0	40	$\frac{-40}{1}=-40$
20	x_2	0	1	0	-1	0	1	60	$\frac{60}{0}$
	z_j	30	20	-30	-20	30	20	2400	
	$c_j - z_j$	0	0	30	20	$-M-30$	$-M-20$	Profit	

The simplex algorithm solution to this modified problem is set out in Table 3.14. Let us first look at the second tableau, where x_1, s_2, s_3 are in the basis. We see that this solution is not optimal, and that x_2 should enter the basis. When we come to ask which variable should leave the basis, we find, from the final column of this tableau, no clear-cut answer. Rather, we learn that the value of x_2 can be raised to 40 by setting either s_2 or s_3 to zero. Given this tie, the choice as to which of these two variables to remove from the basis is arbitrary. We select the first. The consequence of the tie is revealed in the third, and final, tableau of Table 3.14. In this solution, the basic variable s_3 takes the value zero.

When one or more variables in the basis has solution value zero, the solution is said to be **degenerate.** In our particular example, degeneracy causes no problems. The third tableau of Table 3.14 shows that the solution of producing 60 desks and 40 bookcases, with all three slack variables zero, is optimal. However, it is *theoretically* possible, if a degenerate solution is obtained before

TABLE 3.14 Simplex algorithm solution of the office furnishings company problem when 480 man-hours are available for finishing.

(i)

c_B	BASIS	c_j 30 x_1	20 x_2	0 s_1	0 s_2	0 s_3	SOLUTION	
0	s_1	⑧	4	1	0	0	640	$\frac{640}{8} = 80$
0	s_2	4	6	0	1	0	480	$\frac{480}{4} = 120$
0	s_3	1	1	0	0	1	100	$\frac{100}{1} = 100$
	z_j	0	0	0	0	0	0	
	$c_j - z_j$	30	20	0	0	0	Profit	

(ii)

c_B	BASIS	c_j 30 x_1	20 x_2	0 s_1	0 s_2	0 s_3	SOLUTION	
30	x_1	1	$\frac{1}{2}$	$\frac{1}{8}$	0	0	80	$80/\frac{1}{2} = 160$
0	s_2	0	④	$-\frac{1}{2}$	1	0	160	$\frac{160}{4} = 40$
0	s_3	0	$\frac{1}{2}$	$-\frac{1}{8}$	0	1	20	$20/\frac{1}{2} = 40$
	z_j	30	15	$3\frac{3}{4}$	0	0	2400	
	$c_j - z_j$	0	5	$-3\frac{3}{4}$	0	0	Profit	

TABLE 3.14 *(Continued)*

(iii)

c_B	BASIS	c_j 30 x_1	20 x_2	0 s_1	0 s_2	0 s_3	SOLUTION
30	x_1	1	0	$\frac{3}{16}$	$-\frac{1}{8}$	0	60
20	x_2	0	1	$-\frac{1}{8}$	$\frac{1}{4}$	0	40
0	s_3	0	0	$-\frac{1}{16}$	$-\frac{1}{8}$	1	0
	z_j	30	20	$3\frac{1}{8}$	$1\frac{1}{4}$	0	2600
	$c_j - z_j$	0	0	$-3\frac{1}{8}$	$-1\frac{1}{4}$	0	Profit

reaching the optimum, that the simplex algorithm will not iterate to the optimal solution, but rather **cycle** repeatedly through a set of suboptimal solutions. Special techniques have been devised to get around this difficulty. However, since it arises very infrequently in practice, we will not devote space to their discussion.

EXERCISES

3.1. Use the simplex algorithm to find an optimal solution to the linear programming problem

$$\text{Maximize} \quad x_1 + 2x_2$$
$$\text{subject to} \quad 2x_1 + 3x_2 \leq 900$$
$$x_1, x_2 \geq 0$$

3.2. Using the simplex algorithm, find an optimal solution to the constrained maximization problem

$$\text{Maximize} \quad x_1 + x_2$$
$$\text{subject to} \quad 2x_1 + 3x_2 \leq 900$$
$$x_1 + x_2 \leq 500$$
$$x_1, x_2 \geq 0$$

3.3. Using the simplex algorithm, determine the largest attainable value of the objective function in the linear programming problem

$$\text{Maximize} \quad 4x_1 + 5x_2$$
$$\text{subject to} \quad 2x_1 + 3x_2 \leq 1800$$
$$x_1 + x_2 \leq 750$$
$$x_1, x_2 \geq 0$$

3.4. Find an optimal solution to the problem

$$\text{Maximize} \quad x_1 + 2x_2 + 3x_3$$
$$\text{subject to} \quad x_1 + x_2 \le 400$$
$$x_2 + x_3 \le 300$$
$$x_1, x_2, x_3 \ge 0$$

3.5. For the constrained maximization problem

$$\text{Maximize} \quad x_1 + x_2 + x_3$$
$$\text{subject to} \quad x_1 + 2x_2 \le 600$$
$$x_2 + 2x_3 \le 900$$
$$2x_1 + x_2 + x_3 \le 1200$$
$$x_1, x_2, x_3 \ge 0$$

(a) Find an optimal solution.
(b) Find the value of the objective function at the optimal solution.

3.6. For the linear programming problem

$$\text{Maximize} \quad x_1 + 2x_2 + x_3$$
$$\text{subject to} \quad x_1 + x_2 \le 500$$
$$x_1 + x_2 + x_3 \le 800$$
$$2x_1 + x_2 + 2x_3 \le 1400$$
$$x_1, x_2, x_3 \ge 0$$

(a) Find an optimal solution.
(b) Find the value of the objective function at the optimal solution.

3.7. For the constrained maximization problem

$$\text{Maximize} \quad 2x_1 + 3x_2 + 2x_3$$
$$\text{subject to} \quad x_1 + 2x_2 \le 700$$
$$x_1 + x_3 \le 600$$
$$2x_1 + x_2 + x_3 \le 1000$$
$$x_1, x_2, x_3 \ge 0$$

(a) Find an optimal solution.
(b) Find the value of the objective function at the optimal solution.

3.8. For the linear programming problem

$$\text{Maximize} \quad 3x_1 + x_2 + 3x_3$$
$$\text{subject to} \quad x_1 + x_2 + x_3 \le 800$$
$$x_1 + 2x_2 + x_3 \le 1100$$
$$x_1 + x_2 + 2x_3 \le 1200$$
$$x_1, x_2, x_3 \ge 0$$

(a) Find an optimal solution.
(b) Find the value of the objective function at the optimal solution.

3.9. For the constrained optimization problem

$$\text{Maximize} \quad x_1 + x_2 + x_3 + x_4$$
$$\text{subject to} \quad x_1 + x_2 \le 500$$
$$x_2 + x_3 \le 600$$
$$x_3 + x_4 \le 400$$
$$x_1, x_2, x_3, x_4 \ge 0$$

(a) Find an optimal solution.

(b) Find the value of the objective function at the optimal solution.

3.10. Our office furnishings company decides to expand its capacity to a total of 800 man-hours for assembly, 670 man-hours for finishing, and 160 man-hours for inspection. At the same time a new product, chairs, yielding a profit of $16 per unit, is introduced. Each chair requires 2 man-hours of assembly time, 4 man-hours of finishing time, and one man-hour of inspection time. The previous problem specifications are unchanged. That is, desks require 8, 4, and 1 man-hours, and bookcases 4, 6, and 1 man-hours of assembly, finishing, and inspection time respectively. Profits per unit are $30 for desks and $20 for bookcases. Given these specifications:

(a) Find the optimal output levels for desks, bookcases, and chairs.

(b) Find and interpret any amounts of slack capacity at the optimal solution.

(c) Find the maximum attainable profit.

3.11. Referring to the previous exercise, suppose that the company has available a total of 1630 man-hours of production time and is able to allocate this time in any way it chooses among assembly, finishing, and inspection. Without producing a detailed solution, show how you would set up the new constrained optimization problem.

3.12. A canned foods company produces cans of beans in three sizes—small, medium, and large—containing respectively 10, 16, and 20 ounces of beans per can. For the coming week, the company has available a total of 80,000 ounces of beans. The marketing department estimates that it will be unable to sell more than 5000 of the small size cans, or more than 2000 of the large size cans. It is further estimated that combined sales of medium and large cans cannot exceed 5000. Each can sold of the small size yields a profit of 10 cents, each of the medium size a profit of 12 cents, and each of the large size a profit of 15 cents. The objective of the company is to maximize profits.

(a) How many cans of each size should be produced?

(b) What is the maximum attainable level of profits?

(c) Find and interpret the values of the slack variables at the optimal solution.

3.13. A distributor handles three types of television sets—large color, small color, and portable black and white—which take up respectively 8, 5, and 4 cubic feet of storage space. For the coming month the distributor has available a total of 8000 cubic feet of storage space. He also has available a total of $320,000 for the purchase of these sets. Large color sets cost him $360 each, while costs per unit are $300 for small color and $80 for black and white portable sets. Profits per unit for sales of these sets are $50 for large color, $40 for small color, and $20 for black and white portable. The distributor feels that he will not be able to sell more than 500 large color sets. If the objective is profit maximization:

(a) How many sets of each type should be purchased?

(b) What is the maximum attainable level of profits?

(c) Find and interpret the values of the slack variables at the optimal solution.

3.14. Consider the problem of the record club of Exercise 2.19. Set out the simplex algorithm analysis of this problem and verify that the optimal solution you derive agrees with the findings of your earlier graphical analysis.

3.15. A supermarket manager has available a total of at most 30 square feet of shelf space to be allocated among two national brand products—A and B—and a competing generic brand. He does not want to allocate more than 15 square feet of space to any single brand. Company policy also dictates that the total space allocated to the national brands may not exceed that devoted to the generic brand by more than 10 square feet. It is calculated that profits per square foot of shelf space are $50 for brand A, $40 for brand B, and $30 for the generic brand. The object is to maximize profits.

(a) How much space should be allotted to each brand?

(b) Find and interpret the amounts of slack at the optimal solution.

3.16. Consider the constrained maximization problem

$$\text{Maximize} \quad x_1 + 2x_2$$

$$\text{subject to} \quad x_1 + x_2 \leq 10$$

$$x_2 - x_1 \leq 0$$

$$x_1, x_2 \geq 0$$

(a) Develop a graphical solution to this problem.

(b) How can the simplex algorithm be employed in deriving the optimal solution?

3.17. An investor has to allocate $100,000 among four investment opportunities. Two common stock funds—one high risk, and one low risk—and a corporate bond fund are available. The respective expected annual rates of return from these three funds are 20%, 15%, and 12%. Any money not invested in these funds will be deposited in fixed interest securities, yielding a 10% annual rate of return. The investor wants to invest no more than $30,000 in the high risk common stock fund, and also requires that the total amount invested in the two common stock funds not exceed that invested in the corporate bond fund by more than $20,000. Subject to these constraints, the objective is to maximize total expected annual return. Find the optimal solution to this problem.

3.18. The investor of the previous exercise is dissatisfied with the solution obtained, claiming that he wishes to invest at most $35,000 in the corporate bond fund. If this constraint is added, by how much is the maximum possible expected rate of return decreased?

3.19. A company produces three products, each of which requires time on four different machines. The company wants to find the product mix yielding the highest attainable profits, subject to the problem specifications set out in the following table

TOTAL MACHINE-HOURS AVAILABLE	MACHINE	MACHINE-HOURS PER UNIT		
		PRODUCT 1	PRODUCT 2	PRODUCT 3
800	A	1	2	1
600	B	1	1	1
900	C	2	1	1
1,200	D	1	2	2
PROFIT PER UNIT ($)		30	25	20

Find the optimal product mix.

3.20. A manufacturing company produces three products, each of which has to be processed through four departments. Find the optimal product mix, given the specifications in the following table.

TOTAL MAN-HOURS AVAILABLE	DEPARTMENT	MAN-HOURS PER WEEK		
		PRODUCT 1	PRODUCT 2	PRODUCT 3
6000	A	4	1	1
4500	B	3	1	1
2000	C	1	2	1
2500	D	1	2	2
PROFIT PER UNIT ($)		3	2	2

3.21. A company produces three brands of perfume, each containing a combination of three or four essences. The quantities of essences required per bottle are set out in the table below.

PERFUME	QUANTITY OF ESSENCE (IN OUNCES)			
	1	2	3	4
A	0.2	0.4	0	0.2
B	0.5	0	0.2	0.1
C	0.2	0.2	0.2	0.1

Quantities of these essences are in limited supply for the coming week. Available supplies are shown below.

AVAILABILITY OF ESSENCE (IN OUNCES)			
1	2	3	4
270	180	160	160

Each bottle of perfume A yields a profit of $1.20, each bottle of B a profit of $1.50, and each bottle of C a profit of $1.00. If the object is to maximize total profits, how many bottles of each brand of perfume should be produced?

3.22. Use the simplex algorithm to find an optimal solution to the linear programming problem

$$\text{Maximize} \quad x_1 + 2x_2$$
$$\text{subject to} \quad 2x_1 + 3x_2 \leq 900$$
$$x_1 + x_2 \leq 400$$
$$x_1 + x_2 \geq 350$$
$$x_1, x_2 \geq 0$$

3.23. Using the simplex algorithm, find an optimal solution to the constrained maximization problem

$$\text{Maximize} \quad x_1 + x_2$$
$$\text{subject to} \quad 2x_1 + 3x_2 \leq 900$$
$$4x_1 + x_2 \leq 500$$
$$x_1 \geq 45$$
$$x_1, x_2 \geq 0$$

3.24. Using the simplex algorithm, find an optimal solution to the constrained optimization problem

$$\text{Maximize} \quad 4x_1 + 5x_2$$
$$\text{subject to} \quad 2x_1 + 3x_2 \leq 1800$$
$$x_1 + x_2 \leq 750$$
$$7x_1 + 9x_2 = 5550$$
$$x_1, x_2 \geq 0$$

3.25. Find an optimal solution to the problem

$$\text{Maximize} \quad x_1 + 2x_2 + 3x_3$$
$$\text{subject to} \quad x_1 + x_2 \leq 400$$
$$x_2 + x_3 \leq 300$$
$$x_1 + x_3 \geq 500$$
$$x_1, x_2, x_3 \geq 0$$

3.26. For the constrained maximization problem

$$\text{Maximize} \quad x_1 + x_2 + x_3$$
$$\text{subject to} \quad x_1 + 2x_2 \leq 600$$
$$x_2 + 2x_3 \leq 900$$
$$2x_1 + x_2 + x_3 \leq 1200$$
$$x_1 \geq 400$$
$$x_1, x_2, x_3 \geq 0$$

(a) Find an optimal solution.
(b) Find the value of the objective function at the optimal solution.

3.27. Refer again to Exercise 3.12. In a particular week the canned foods company receives from an important distributor an order for 1000 large cans of beans. The constraints on production are revised so that at least 1000 large cans must be produced. The maximum number of large cans allowed is increased to 3000, and the maximum combined total for medium and large cans is increased to 6000. If the remaining specifications are unchanged, find the profit maximizing product mix subject to the modified constraints.

3.28. In order to satisfy an important customer, the television set distributor of Exercise 3.13 feels that he must purchase at least 1000 portable black and white sets. If the remaining problem specifications are unchanged, and the objective remains profit maximization subject to the modified constraints, how many sets of each type should be purchased?

3.29. A company produces three products, each of which requires time on three different machines. It is required to find the product mix yielding the highest obtainable profits, subject to the requirement that at least 400 units of product 3 be produced. The problem specifications are set out in the following table.

TOTAL MACHINE-HOURS AVAILABLE	MACHINE	MACHINE-HOURS PER UNIT		
		PRODUCT 1	PRODUCT 2	PRODUCT 3
800	A	1	2	1
600	B	1	1	1
900	C	2	1	1
PROFIT PER UNIT ($)		30	25	20

Find the optimal product mix.

3.30. A manufacturing company produces three products, each of which has to be processed through three departments. If at least 800 units of product 3 must be produced, find the optimal product mix, given the following specifications.

TOTAL MAN-HOURS AVAILABLE	DEPARTMENT	MAN-HOURS PER WEEK		
		PRODUCT 1	PRODUCT 2	PRODUCT 3
4500	A	3	1	1
2000	B	1	2	1
2500	C	1	2	2
PROFIT PER UNIT ($)		3	2	2

3.31. Suppose that in addition to the other problem specifications, the perfume company of Exercise 3.21 must produce a combined total of at least 600 bottles of perfumes A and B. How, if at all, does this requirement influence the optimal solution to the problem?

3.32. Use the simplex algorithm to find an optimal solution to the linear programming problem.

$$\text{Minimize} \quad x_1 + x_2$$
$$\text{subject to} \quad 2x_1 + x_2 \geq 400$$
$$x_1 \geq 120$$
$$x_2 \geq 100$$

3.33. Using the simplex algorithm, find an optimal solution to the constrained minimization problem.

$$\text{Minimize} \quad 2x_1 + 3x_2$$
$$\text{subject to} \quad x_1 + x_2 \geq 80$$
$$2x_1 + x_2 \geq 130$$
$$x_1 \geq 40$$
$$x_2 \geq 20$$

3.34. Using the simplex algorithm, determine the smallest attainable value of the objective function in the linear programming problem

$$\text{Minimize} \quad 5x_1 + 2x_2$$
$$\text{subject to} \quad 3x_1 + 2x_2 \geq 340$$
$$2x_1 + x_2 \geq 200$$
$$x_1 \geq 50$$
$$x_2 \geq 50$$

3.35. Use the simplex algorithm to find an optimal solution to the constrained minimization problem

$$\text{Minimize} \quad x_1 + 2x_2 + 3x_3$$
$$\text{subject to} \quad x_1 \geq 50$$
$$x_1 + x_2 \geq 100$$
$$x_1 + x_2 + x_3 \geq 150$$
$$x_1, x_2, x_3 \geq 0$$

3.36. Using the simplex algorithm, find an optimal solution to the linear programming problem

$$\text{Minimize} \quad x_1 + 2x_2 + x_3$$
$$\text{subject to} \quad x_1 + x_2 \geq 400$$
$$x_1 \geq 100$$
$$x_2 \geq 200$$
$$x_3 \geq 300$$

3.37. A company wishes to produce a diet blend containing amounts of three nutrients, through the mixture of three basic products. If the objective is to find the blend with the lowest possible cost, subject to nutritional requirements, find the optimal solution given the specifications in the following table.

MINIMUM QUANTITIES REQUIRED (OUNCES)	NUTRIENT	NUTRIENTS PER UNIT (OUNCES)		
		PRODUCT 1	PRODUCT 2	PRODUCT 3
10	A	0.2	0.1	0.2
15	B	0.3	0.2	0.2
20	C	0.4	0.2	0.4
COST PER UNIT (IN CENTS)		10	5	8

3.38. Refer again to the previous exercise. Suppose that no more than 10 units of product 1 are available. Without doing the detailed calculations, show how you would go about using the simplex algorithm to find the optimal solution to the modified constrained optimization problem.

3.39. A company employs telephone operators who work 8-hour shifts, from 6:00 a.m. to 2:00 p.m., from 10:00 a.m. to 6:00 p.m., or from 2:00 p.m. to 10:00 p.m. Those working the first shift are paid $40 per day, those working the second $35 per day, and those working the third $45 per day. The company has determined that the minimum number of operators that must be available at various times of day are:

TIME	MINIMUM NUMBER OF OPERATORS
6 a.m.–10 a.m.	8
10 a.m.– 2 p.m.	12
2 p.m.– 6 p.m.	15
6 p.m.–10 p.m.	6

The objective of the company is to meet these requirements at the lowest possible cost. Produce a complete optimal solution to this problem.

3.40. The company of the previous exercise is considering offering an alternative work schedule in which telephone operators alternate shifts in three week cycles. The same daily wage will then be paid to each operator, whichever shift is worked. What is the maximum daily wage per operator that should be offered under this alternative work schedule?

3.41. A constrained maximization problem has a redundant constraint. Explain how this will influence, if at all, the simplex algorithm solution.

3.42. A manufacturer of television sets has two plants and two distribution centers. For the coming week, distribution center A requires 300 sets, and center B 250 sets. At most, 275 sets will be available at plant 1, and at most, 325 sets will be available at plant 2. Television sets can be shipped from either plant to either distribution center. However, unit shipping costs differ along the four routes. It costs $10 per set for shipments from plant 1 to center A, $12 per set for shipments from plant 1 to center B, $14 per set for shipments from plant 2 to center A, and $11 per set for shipments from plant 2 to center B. If demand at the two centers is to be fully met at the lowest possible total shipment cost, how many sets should be shipped along each route?

Assigning Telephone Operators to Shifts: Betting by Phone in Australia[1]

A commonly occurring problem, for which linear programming methods have been successfully employed, arises when telephone operators are assigned to shifts in order to meet fluctuating demand.

In the state of Victoria, Australia, all legal off-track betting is provided by the Victorian Totalizator Agency Board (TAB). A growing percentage of TAB turnover has come from telephone betting. Customers can directly dial a telephone betting center and place bets through an operator. The betting centers have a total capacity of 440 operators. The demand for operator services fluctuates widely from day to day, depending, for example, on what races are being run on a particular day. There is also considerable fluctuation of demand over the 15 hours of a day during which the TAB center is open. Past experience provides a reasonable guide as to what demand levels might be expected for each 15-minute period of a given day.

The TAB can assign operators to any one of 60 possible shifts, varying in length from 3 to 6 hours. For late evening work, overtime rates that exceed by 50% normal time rates, must be paid to operators. The aim is to assign operators to shifts so that total cost for the day is minimized. Thus if

x_i = number of operators assigned to shift i ($i = 1, 2, \ldots, 60$)
c_i = cost per operator of shift i ($i = 1, 2, \ldots, 60$)

the objective is

$$\text{Minimize } c_1 x_1 + c_2 x_2 + \ldots + c_{60} x_{60}$$

The decision variables x_i ($i = 1, 2, \ldots, 60$) are required to satisfy three types of constraints. These are:

1. For each 15-minute period there must be enough operators available to meet anticipated demand.
2. At any particular time of the day, there is a limit to the number of operators that can be assigned. Thus, for each 15-minute period, an upper bound is also placed on the number of operators.
3. Disruption is caused by a large volume of staff movement, through shifts either beginning or ending, at any time. It is desirable, therefore, to set limits on the total number of movements at the beginning of each 15-minute period.

---

[1] This discussion is based on E. J. G. Wilson and R. J. Willis, "Scheduling of Telephone Betting Operators—A Case Study," *Journal of the Operational Research Society, 34*, (1983), 991–998.

For any day, given information on demand patterns, numbers of operators that can be assigned, and desired limits on staff movement, a linear programming model can be specified and solved to yield the minimum cost assignments. When this procedure was adopted by the TAB, it was found that on average for each working day, operator cost was reduced by 10% compared with previous practice. This amounted to savings of approximately $350,000 per year.

sensitivity analysis and duality

CHAPTER FOUR

4.1. INTRODUCTION TO SENSITIVITY ANALYSIS

When faced with a linear programming problem, we have seen how an optimal solution can be derived. However, this is not all that can be accomplished; it is possible to produce further valuable information. A desire for such additional information arises when we consider uncertainty in problem specification and when a problem is viewed in a dynamic context. For example, management may be somewhat unsure of the precise values of some elements, such as profits per unit resulting from sales, in the problem set-up. Moreover, in practice, these specifications are likely to change through time. It is therefore of considerable interest to learn how much deviation from the original specifications would be required before the optimal solution altered. In other words, we would like to assess the **sensitivity** of this solution to departures from the original problem formulation. In this chapter we will see, through **sensitivity analysis,** the impact of altering a single specification in a linear programming problem when the other specifications remain unchanged.

In the previous two chapters, we analyzed for an office furnishings company a product mix problem which, in standard form, was expressed as

$$\text{Maximize} \quad 30x_1 + 20x_2$$

$$\text{subject to} \quad 8x_1 + 4x_2 + s_1 = 640$$

$$4x_1 + 6x_2 + s_2 = 540$$

$$x_1 + x_2 + s_3 = 100$$

$$x_1, x_2, s_1, s_2, s_3 \geq 0$$

where, for production in a given week,

x_1 = number of desks;
x_2 = number of bookcases;
s_1 = slack time in assembly;
s_2 = slack time in finishing;
s_3 = slack time in inspection

We saw that the optimal solution to this problem is

$$x_1 = 60,\ x_2 = 40,\ s_1 = 0,\ s_2 = 60,\ s_3 = 0$$

Now, in fact, management may not *know* that desks can be sold at a profit of $30 each. Rather, they may feel that a likely outcome is somewhere in the range from $28 to $32. It would be of interest to know if the optimum solution would be exactly the same for all profit levels in this range. In addition, the profit per unit that can be obtained for these products may well not remain constant through time. It is also quite likely that the right-hand sides of the constraints will change from week to week. For instance, the number of man-hours available for assembly might vary between 600 and 680 a week. Again, it would be helpful to learn how this affects the optimal solution.

In subsequent sections of this chapter, we will consider separately changes in objective function specifications and in the right-hand sides of the constraints. Of course, in principle, for any respecification of the problem, it is possible to reapply the simplex algorithm. This, however, would be very tedious, and we will see how the simplex solution *of the original problem* can be used to provide valuable insights into sensitivity. Moreover, for simple problems involving just a pair of decision variables the question of sensitivity can also be analyzed graphically, as a further aid to understanding.

4.2. SENSITIVITY TO CHANGES IN OBJECTIVE FUNCTION COEFFICIENTS

Since we intend to illustrate our discussion of sensitivity analysis by reference to the product mix problem of the office furnishings company, it is convenient here to reproduce our description of the optimal solution to the original. problem. Figure 4.1 shows the graphical analysis, while the final tableau of the simplex algorithm solution is given in Table 4.1. This is precisely the same as Table 3.7.

In this section, the question to be explored concerns the effect on the optimum solution of a change in one or another of the coefficients of the objective function, that is, of the c_j, in the notation of Table 4.1. Specifically, we will allow one of these coefficients to change, *while holding the other coefficients and the remaining problem specifications fixed.*

In fact, it turns out to be convenient to consider separately coefficients on those variables that are basic and nonbasic at the optimal solution.

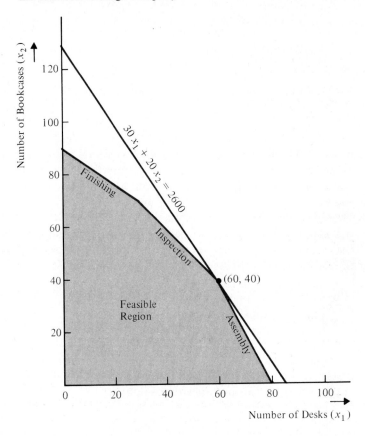

FIGURE 4.1 Graphical solution of the product mix problem of the office furnishings company.

COEFFICIENTS ON THE NONBASIC VARIABLES

Consider now the possibility of modifying the specification of a linear programming problem by changing the value of the objective function coefficient on one of the nonbasic variables. For the original problem the value of this variable is, by definition, zero at the optimal solution. This solution can only be altered by our specification change through the nonbasic variable entering the basis.

Recall the simplex algorithm procedure for testing whether a variable should enter the basis. It is required that for that variable to enter,

$$c_j - z_j > 0$$

Now, changing the c_j value for a nonbasic variable does not influence the corresponding z_j, which depends only on the objective function coefficients of the basic variables. It follows that the optimal solution will be unchanged for any

TABLE 4.1 Final tableau of the simplex algorithm solution to the product mix problem of the office furnishings company.

c_B	BASIS	c_j					SOLUTION
		30	20	0	0	0	
		x_1	x_2	s_1	s_2	s_3	
30	x_1	1	0	$\frac{1}{4}$	0	-1	60
0	s_2	0	0	$\frac{1}{2}$	1	-8	60
20	x_2	0	1	$-\frac{1}{4}$	0	2	40
	z_j	30	20	$2\frac{1}{2}$	0	10	2600 Profit
	$c_j - z_j$	0	0	$-2\frac{1}{2}$	0	-10	

value of c_j for a nonbasic variable up to z_j. The following general conclusion therefore holds.

> Let c_j denote the objective function coefficient[1] on a variable that is nonbasic in the optimal solution of a constrained optimization problem. That optimal solution will be the same, if the original specifications are otherwise unaltered, for all
>
> $$-\infty < c_j \le z_j$$
>
> where the z_j value is that for the nonbasic variable in the final tableau of the simplex algorithm solution to the problem.

This aspect of sensitivity analysis turns out not to be relevant for our office furnishings product mix problem. We see from Table 4.1 that at the optimal solution, the only nonbasic variables are the slack variables s_1 and s_3, which necessarily are associated with coefficient zero in the objective function.

COEFFICIENTS ON THE BASIC VARIABLES

Next, we ask by how much the objective function coefficient on a basic variable can change without altering the optimal solution to a linear programming problem. To see how such a question can be answered, let us look again at the office furnishings company problem. In the original specification, each desk could be sold for a profit of $30. We will consider varying this amount and representing the new profit per unit by $\$c_1^*$. The only effects of this change on the tableau of Table 4.1 are on the z_j (and hence the $c_j - z_j$), and on the profit at the solution. Substituting c_1^* for 30, the new values are calculated in Table 4.2.

---

[1] For constrained minimization problems, it is assumed that the problem has first been written as a constrained maximization problem, so that c_j will be negative. For example, in previous chapters we considered a blending problem in which the aim was to minimize $2x_1 + 3x_2$. This is equivalent to maximizing $-2x_1 - 3x_2$, so that $c_1 = -2$ and $c_2 = -3$.

TABLE 4.2 Revision of tableau of Table 4.1 for profit per desk of $\$c_1^*$.

c_j		c_1^*	20	0	0	0	
c_B	BASIS	x_1	x_2	s_1	s_2	s_3	SOLUTION
c_1^*	x_1	1	0	$\frac{1}{4}$	0	-1	60
0	s_2	0	0	$\frac{1}{2}$	1	-8	60
20	x_2	0	1	$-\frac{1}{4}$	0	2	40
	z_j	c_1^*	20	$\frac{1}{4}c_1^* - 5$	0	$40 - c_1^*$	$60c_1^* + 800$ Profit
	$c_j - z_j$	0	0	$5 - \frac{1}{4}c_1^*$	0	$c_1^* - 40$	

Now, the original optimal solution to the problem will remain optimal provided none of the $c_j - z_j$ is positive. Hence, we see from the last line of Table 4.2 that production of 60 desks and 40 bookcases will still be optimal provided that *both* conditions

$$5 - \tfrac{1}{4} c_1^* \le 0; \; c_1^* - 40 \le 0$$

hold. We can rewrite these requirements as

$$5 \le \tfrac{1}{4} c_1^*$$

so that

$$20 \le c_1^*$$

and

$$c_1^* \le 40$$

It therefore follows from this pair of requirements that our solution is optimal provided that

$$20 \le c_1^* \le 40$$

Given that other problem specifications remain unaltered, we have shown that if the profit per desk is anywhere in the range from $20 to $40, production of 60 desks and 40 bookcases will be optimal.[2]

This result can also be shown graphically. Changing the objective function leads to new profit lines, but does not, of course, alter the feasible region. Figure 4.2 shows that when profit per desk is reduced to $20 the problem has multiple optimal solutions. Comparison with Figure 4.1 makes it clear that if there is a

---

[2] Of course, as can be read from Table 4.2, the level of profits at the optimal solution will depend on the value of c_1^*.

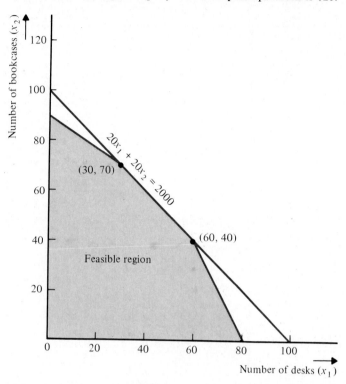

FIGURE 4.2 Graphical solution of the product mix problem for the office furnishings company when the profit per desk is $20.

further reduction in profit per desk, production of 30 desks and 70 bookcases will be preferable to the original optimal solution. At the other extreme of our range, Figure 4.3 shows the position when profit per desk is $40. Again there are multiple optimal solutions. By comparison with Figure 4.1 we see that if profit per desk increases further, the optimal strategy will be to produce 80 desks and no bookcases.

In exactly the same way, we can consider variations in the profit per bookcase, given that the other problem specifications are set at their original values. A parallel argument to that just employed leads to the conclusion that our original solution remains optimal provided profit per bookcase is in the range from $15 to $30. Verification of this contention is left as an exercise to the reader.

We have succeeded in showing, then, that profit per unit of one or the other of these products can deviate quite a bit from the initial values without changing the optimal solution. We might say, therefore, that this solution is not terribly sensitive to such changes.

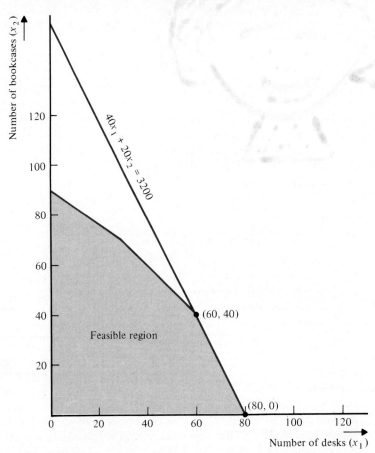

4.3. SENSITIVITY TO CHANGES IN RIGHT-HAND SIDE VALUES OF CONSTRAINTS

The next step in our sensitivity analysis concerns the study of certain changes in the feasible region. How, for example, would the optimal solution to the office furnishings company problem be affected by changes in the number of man-hours available for assembly?

The answer to questions of this sort depends on whether the constraint in which we are interested is binding at the optimal solution. If it is not, things are very straightforward. Referring to Figure 4.1, it can be seen that while the assembly time and inspection time constraints for the office furnishings company are binding at the optimal solution, the finishing time constraint is not. This conclusion is reflected in Table 4.1, where we find that at the optimal solution, the amount of slack time in finishing, s_2, is 60 man-hours. What would be the consequence if, holding everything else constant, the company increased available finishing time beyond the current 540 man-hours? Clearly, none at all, except to increase the amount of finishing time slack at the optimal solution. It is similarly obvious that any reduction, up to 60 man-hours, in finishing time capacity will reduce this slack but leave the optimal solution otherwise undisturbed.

We turn now to deal with the more difficult problem of analyzing capacity changes in those constraints that are binding at the optimal solution. It is clear from Figure 4.1 that the optimal solution *will* be altered if capacity in either inspection or assembly is changed. To begin, let us ask what the value is to the company of an additional man-hour of time in assembly, inspection, or finishing. We saw in the previous paragraph that an extra man-hour of finishing time is worth nothing at all. However, increasing the time available for inspection or assembly will broaden the range of production possibilities and produce higher profits.

To find the value of an additional unit of capacity in a particular constraint, all we need to do is look at the $c_j - z_j$ row of the simplex tableau at the optimal solution. Suppose, for example, that the office furnishings company were to increase inspection time available by one man-hour. What does a man-hour of inspection time contribute to profits? Now, the $c_j - z_j$ row of the simplex tableau shows the net changes in profits when the column variables increase from their optimal values by one unit. From Table 4.1 we can see that raising slack time, s_3, in inspection from zero to one man-hour leads to a reduction of $10 in profit. But this would simply be the equivalent of dispensing with one of the available man-hours for inspection. We can therefore argue that the value to this company of an extra man-hour of inspection time is $10. This is known as the **shadow price** of this resource, and is the maximum price the company should be prepared to pay for an additional unit of the resource. Our analysis has demonstrated that with all other problem specifications held at their initial levels, an extra man-hour of inspection time allows an additional $10 of profit to be made. The company should, then, be prepared to pay up to $10 for a further unit of this resource.

Definition

The **shadow price** of a resource is the value of the contribution made by an additional unit of that resource to the objective function. It can be found as the negative of the $c_j - z_j$ value for the corresponding slack variable at the optimal solution.

It can also be seen directly from Table 4.1 that the shadow price of a man-hour of assembly time is $2.50, and, as we would expect, that for inspection time is zero.

We are now apparently in a position to tell management of the office furnishings company that all else equal, each additional man-hour of inspection will increase profits by $10, and conversely, each man-hour reduction will decrease profits by $10. A little thought, however, should convince you that this conclusion is *not true for changes of any amount in inspection time.* Suppose, for instance, that inspection time were reduced from the current 100 man-hours to zero. Then nothing at all could be produced, so that profit would fall, not by $1000, but from $2600 to zero. Conversely, increasing inspection time capacity indefinitely would not continue to increase profits, as after a point, the constraint would simply become redundant, while production possibilities would still be limited by assembly and finishing time constraints. What we would like to do is find a **range** of values for inspection time capacity in which the shadow price of $10 per unit is valid.

To find the ranges of validity for the shadow prices, it is necessary to turn again to the simplex tableau at the optimal solution. Directly from that tableau it is possible to see the effect on the optimal solution of the addition of a unit of capacity anywhere. Suppose that the office furnishings company adds one man-hour of inspection time. To see the impact of this additional capacity, let us look in equation form, at the constraints implied by the tableau of Table 4.1. These are

$$
\begin{aligned}
x_1 + \tfrac{1}{4} s_1 - s_3 &= 60 \\
\tfrac{1}{2} s_1 + s_2 - 8 s_3 &= 60 \\
x_2 - \tfrac{1}{4} s_1 + 2 s_3 &= 40
\end{aligned}
\tag{4.1}
$$

At the optimal solution, s_1 and s_3 are zero; so that $x_1 = 60$, $s_2 = 60$, and $x_2 = 40$. Suppose now that an additional man-hour of inspection time is available. The inspection time constraint is now

$$x_1 + x_2 \le 101$$

so that, in the form

$$x_1 + x_2 + s_3 = 100$$

the variable s_3 could be as low as -1. We see, then, that provision of an extra unit of a resource is equivalent to allowing a value of -1 for the slack variable associated with that resource in the original specification.

Let us examine the effects of setting $s_3 = -1$ in (4.1), while keeping s_1 at zero. We then have from the first equation

$$x_1 - (-1) = 60$$

so that

$$x_1 = 59$$

Similarly, from the other two equations,

$$s_2 - 8(-1) = 60$$

giving

$$s_2 = 52$$

and

$$x_2 + 2(-1) = 40$$

yielding

$$x_2 = 42$$

Notice that this new solution, production of 59 desks and 42 bookcases with 52 man-hours of slack in finishing, could have been obtained by adding the entries in the s_3 column of Table 4.1 to those of the "Solution" column of that table. This new solution, then, involves the production of two additional bookcases and one fewer desk, compared with the solution to the original problem. The extra bookcases add \$40 to profit, while \$30 is lost through producing one fewer desk. The net change in profit, then, is the shadow price, \$10, as expected. Table 4.3 shows the complete simplex tableau when inspection time is increased from 100 to 101 man-hours.

Let us pause to compare the solutions in Tables 4.1 and 4.3. The additional man-hour of inspection time has allowed the company to increase profits by producing two extra bookcases, while sacrificing production of only one desk. Notice that this solution also involves taking up 8 man-hours of the slack in finishing. If we continue to add inspection time capacity, the same consequences will follow *up to the point at which finishing time capacity is exhausted.* Beyond that point, however, the finishing time constraint will become binding, and further increases inspection time capacity of no value.

Let us continue our analysis by considering the "addition" of K man-hours of inspection time to the original 100, where K may be either positive or negative. Setting $s_1 = 0$ and $s_3 = -K$ in equations (4.1) yields

$$x_1 - (-K) = 60$$

TABLE 4.3 Final tableau of the simplex algorithm solution to product mix problem of the office furnishings company when inspection time capacity is increased by one man-hour.

c_B	c_j BASIS	30 x_1	20 x_2	0 s_1	0 s_2	0 s_3	SOLUTION
30	x_1	1	0	$\frac{1}{4}$	0	-1	59
0	s_2	0	0	$\frac{1}{2}$	1	-8	52
20	x_2	0	1	$-\frac{1}{4}$	0	2	42
	z_j	30	20	$2\frac{1}{2}$	0	10	2610 Profit
	$c_j - z_j$	0	0	$-2\frac{1}{2}$	0	-10	

so that

$$x_1 = 60 - K$$

Also,

$$s_2 - 8(-K) = 60$$

giving

$$s_2 = 60 - 8K$$

and

$$x_2 + 2(-K) = 40$$

yielding

$$x_2 = 40 + 2K$$

This solution

$$x_1 = 60 - K, \ s_2 = 60 - 8K, \ x_2 = 40 + 2K \qquad (4.2)$$

could have been obtained by adding K times the entries in the s_3 column of Table 4.1 to the entries of the solution column of that table. We have shown, then, as set out in the simplex tableau of Table 4.4, that addition of K man-hours of inspection time yields the solution (4.2), *provided that solution is feasible*. Now, for this solution to be feasible, the values of x_1, x_2, and s_2 must be nonnegative. We therefore require that the conditions

$$60 - K \geq 0; \ 40 + 2K \geq 0; \ 60 - 8K \geq 0 \qquad (4.3)$$

all hold.

TABLE 4.4 Final tableau of the simplex algorithm solution to the product mix problem of the office furnishings company when inspection time capacity is increased by K man-hours.

c_B	c_j BASIS	30 x_1	20 x_2	0 s_1	0 s_2	0 s_3	SOLUTION
30	x_1	1	0	$\frac{1}{4}$	0	-1	$60 - K$
0	s_2	0	0	$\frac{1}{2}$	1	-8	$60 - 8K$
20	x_2	0	1	$-\frac{1}{4}$	0	2	$40 + 2K$
	z_j	30	20	$2\frac{1}{2}$	0	10	$2600 + 10K$
	$c_j - z_j$	0	0	$-2\frac{1}{2}$	0	-10	Profit

The first condition in (4.3) implies

$$K \leq 60$$

The second condition is

$$2K \geq -40$$

so that

$$K \geq -20$$

The third condition is

$$8K \leq 60$$

or

$$K \leq 7\tfrac{1}{2}$$

We therefore require for the solution of Table 4.4 to be feasible

$$K \leq 60, \; K \geq -20, \; K \leq 7\tfrac{1}{2}$$

Now, the first of these is redundant, since it must be satisfied if the third is satisfied. Our requirements can therefore be summarized as

$$-20 \leq K \leq 7\tfrac{1}{2}$$

where K is the "addition" to the originally available capacity. Since we started with 100 man-hours, the range of values in which the shadow price is valid is

$$100 - 20 \leq \text{Inspection Time} \leq 100 + 7\tfrac{1}{2}$$

or

$$80 \leq \text{Inspection Time} \leq 107\tfrac{1}{2}$$

We have shown that provided it does not take us outside the range from 80 to $107\tfrac{1}{2}$ man-hours, each extra man-hour of inspection time capacity adds $10 to profit, and each man-hour reduction in inspection time cuts profit by $10, when all other problem specifications are kept at their original levels.

To see the need for the lower limit of this range, consider Figure 4.4, where we illustrate the impact of reductions in inspection time capacity on the feasible region and optimal solution. For the original problem, the optimal solution is production of 60 desks and 40 bookcases. However, if inspection time capacity is reduced to 90 man-hours, this solution is no longer feasible. Optimally, the company should now make 70 desks and 20 bookcases. Reducing inspection time further, to 80 man-hours, leads optimally to production of 80 desks and no bookcases. Up to this point, then, each man-hour reduction in inspection time has resulted in the production of two fewer bookcases, and one additional desk. Since the respective profits per unit are $20 and $30, the net effect is a reduction of $10 in profit. However, beyond this point the picture changes. If inspection time is reduced further, to 70 man-hours, the best that can be done is to manufacture just 70 desks. Hence, each man-hour decrease in inspection time capac-

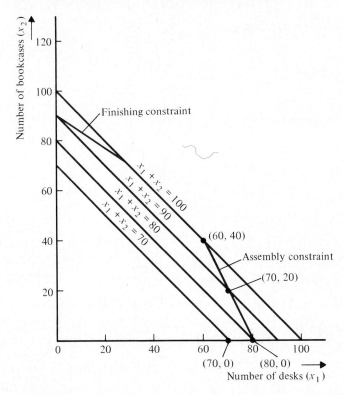

FIGURE 4.4 Reduction of inspection time capacity from 100 to 70 manhours for the office furnishings company.

ity below 80 leads to the output of one less desk, and hence a reduction of $30 in profit. We see, then, that our result showing a $10 value to the company of a man-hour of inspection time is not valid when this time falls below 80 man-hours.

As an exercise, the reader is invited to verify graphically that the upper bound of the applicability of the $10 shadow price for a man-hour of inspection time is $107\frac{1}{2}$ man-hours.

We have seen that the shadow price of a man-hour of assembly time is $2.50. Using an algebraic argument of precisely the same form as that employed above, it can be shown that the range in which this result is valid is

$$520 \leq \text{Assembly Time} \leq 800$$

We leave the verification of this contention as an exercise to the reader. In words, what the result says is that each man-hour of added assembly time, up to a total capacity of 800 man-hours, yields an additional $2.50 profit. Similarly, each man-hour reduction, down to a total of 520, leads to a reduction of $2.50 in total profits, with all other problem specifications held at their original levels.

4.4. ADDING A NEW DECISION VARIABLE

It is not uncommon to want to consider the possibility of adding a new decision variable to a linear programming problem. We can easily determine whether such a variable would enter the basis; that is, take a nonzero value at the optimal solution. To illustrate the kind of problem we have in mind, suppose the office furnishings company is considering adding a new product—chairs. It has been calculated that each chair requires 3 man-hours of assembly time, 2 man-hours finishing time, and 1 man-hour of inspection time. If the company does not intend to increase its available resources in these departments, what profit per unit would have to be obtained from the sale of chairs for their production to be economically desirable?

Now, we could certainly solve this problem by setting out the augmented problem in algebraic form, and employing the simplex algorithm to derive an optimal solution for any specific value of profit per unit of chairs. However, a simpler line of attack is available through a modest extension of our discussion of the previous section. The heart of the solution lies in the notion of **opportunity cost.** In order to produce a chair, the office furnishings company will have to give up some production of other lines. Resources will have to be re-allocated from production of desks and bookcases to production of chairs. The value of this foregone production is termed "opportunity cost." Using the resource shadow prices calculated in Section 4.3, we can easily work out the opportunity cost of producing a chair. The calculations are set out in Table 4.5.

Production of a chair requires 3 man-hours of assembly time, and since the value per man-hour to the company is the shadow price, $2.50, it follows that the total value of foregone production will be $7.50. Similarly, since 1 man-hour of inspection time, at a shadow price of $10.00, is required, this amount must be added to the opportunity cost of producing a chair. On the other hand, since there is spare capacity in finishing, it costs nothing further to use 2 man-hours of this time in the manufacture of a chair. Hence, the total opportunity cost is $17.50 per chair. It follows that it will pay this company to add this product line if, and only if, profit per unit in excess of $17.50 can be derived from the sale of chairs. In that case, the profit derived will exceed the value of foregone production in other lines.

TABLE 4.5 Opportunity cost for the production of a chair by the office furnishings company.

RESOURCE	QUANTITY REQUIRED (MAN-HOURS)	SHADOW PRICE ($)	OPPORTUNITY COST ($)
Assembly time	3	2.50	7.50
Finishing time	2	0.00	0.00
Inspection time	1	10.00	10.00
			17.50

4.5. SENSITIVITY ANALYSIS FOR A CONSTRAINED MINIMIZATION PROBLEM

In Chapters 2 and 3, we discussed the blending problem of a processed food company intending to mix quantities, x_1 and x_2, of two additives to produce a blend satisfying specified standards for content of vitamins A, C, and D, and iron. In standard form, the problem was specified as

$$\text{Minimize} \qquad 2x_1 + 3x_2$$

subject to

Vitamin A:	$40x_1 - s_1 = 80$	
Vitamin C:	$5x_1 + 10x_2 - s_2 = 80$	
Vitamin D:	$10x_1 + 5x_2 - s_3 = 60$	
Iron:	$20x_2 - s_4 = 80$	

$$x_1, x_2, s_1, s_2, s_3, s_4 \geq 0$$

We found that the optimal solution is

$$x_1 = 2\tfrac{2}{3},\ x_2 = 6\tfrac{2}{3},\ s_1 = 26\tfrac{2}{3},\ s_2 = 0,\ s_3 = 0,\ s_4 = 53\tfrac{1}{3}$$

Optimally, the blend should contain $2\tfrac{2}{3}$ grams of additive I and $6\tfrac{2}{3}$ grams of additive II, resulting in surpluses over the minimum requirements for vitamin A and iron. For convenience, the final tableau of the simplex algorithm solution is reproduced in Table 4.6. The optimal solution is also illustrated in Figure 4.5.

SENSITIVITY TO CHANGES IN OBJECTIVE FUNCTION COEFFICIENTS

We begin by considering the possibility of changes in one or another of the objective function coefficients. As before, it is useful to consider separately coefficients on variables that are and are not basic at the optimal solution.

TABLE 4.6 Final tableau of simplex algorithm solution to blending problem of the processed food company.

c_B	BASIS	$c_j \to$ x_1 (-2)	x_2 (-3)	s_1 (0)	s_2 (0)	s_3 (0)	s_4 (0)	a_1 ($-M$)	a_2 ($-M$)	a_3 ($-M$)	a_4 ($-M$)	SOLUTION
-2	x_1	1	0	0	$\frac{1}{15}$	$-\frac{2}{15}$	0	0	$-\frac{1}{15}$	$\frac{2}{15}$	0	$2\frac{2}{3}$
0	s_4	0	0	0	$-\frac{8}{3}$	$\frac{4}{3}$	1	0	$\frac{8}{3}$	$-\frac{4}{3}$	-1	$53\frac{1}{3}$
0	s_1	0	0	1	$\frac{8}{3}$	$-\frac{16}{3}$	-1	0	$-\frac{8}{3}$	$\frac{16}{3}$	0	$26\frac{2}{3}$
-3	x_2	0	1	0	$-\frac{2}{15}$	$\frac{1}{15}$	0	0	$\frac{2}{15}$	$-\frac{1}{15}$	0	$6\frac{2}{3}$
	z_j	-2	-3	0	$\frac{4}{15}$	$\frac{1}{15}$	0	0	$-\frac{1}{15}$	$-\frac{1}{15}$	0	$-25\frac{1}{3}$
	$c_j - z_j$	0	0	0	$-\frac{4}{15}$	$-\frac{1}{15}$	0	$-M$	$-M+\frac{1}{15}$	$-M+\frac{1}{15}$	$-M$	"Profit"

FIGURE 4.5 Graphical solution of the blending problem of the processed food company.

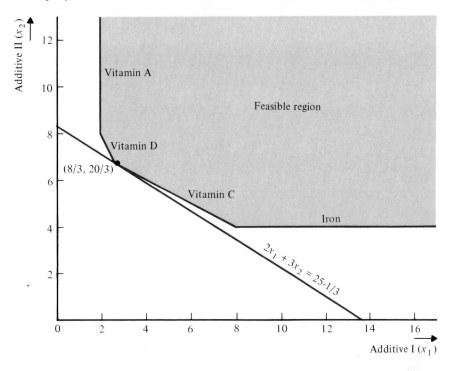

For the nonbasic variables, the position is exactly the same as for constrained maximization problems. It pays to enter a nonbasic variable into the basis only if the corresponding

$$c_j - z_j > 0$$

where here c_j *refers to the negative of the cost per unit of the variable.* Hence, for any nonbasic variable, the optimal solution will remain unaltered, provided the other problem specifications remain the same, for all c_j satisfying

$$-\infty < c_j \leq z_j$$

In this particular example, we see from Table 4.6 that aside from the artificial variables, the only nonbasic variables at the optimal solution are s_2 and s_3. These surplus variables are necessarily associated with coefficients zero in the objective function for our problem.

Let us turn now to the possibility of changes in the objective function coefficients of the basic variables. Specifically, we will consider departures from the respective unit prices of 2 and 3 cents for additives I and II. Preserving the notation that the c_j refer to the negatives of the costs, suppose that, rather than

2 cents per gram, the cost per gram of additive I is $-c_1^*$ cents. The resulting modifications to the tableau of Table 4.6 are shown in Table 4.7. Again, we need to concentrate on the $c_j - z_j$ evaluation row of Table 4.7. In order that the solution of a blend of $2\frac{2}{3}$ grams of additive I and $6\frac{2}{3}$ grams of additive II remain optimal, the entries in this row must not exceed zero. We therefore require the two conditions

$$-\tfrac{2}{5} - \tfrac{1}{15} c_1^* \leq 0; \tfrac{1}{5} + \tfrac{2}{15} c_1^* \leq 0$$

to both hold. From the first of these restrictions, we have

$$\tfrac{1}{15} c_1^* \geq -\tfrac{2}{5}$$

or

$$c_1^* \geq -6$$

The second restriction gives

$$\tfrac{2}{15} c_1^* \leq -\tfrac{1}{5}$$

so that

$$c_1^* \leq -1\tfrac{1}{2}$$

Thus, the solution remains optimal provided

$$-6 \leq c_1^* \leq -1\tfrac{1}{2}$$

Hence, holding the other specifications fixed, the solution of a mix of $2\frac{2}{3}$ grams of additive I and $6\frac{2}{3}$ grams of additive II is optimal for any price per gram of additive I in the range from $1\frac{1}{2}$ to 6 cents.

Figure 4.6 reveals the position when the price is increased to 6 cents per gram, the upper limit of that range. We see that there will then be multiple optimal solutions, at a total cost of 36 cents. However, increase beyond this level in the price of additive I will lead the company to move to a blend of 2 grams of additive I and 8 grams of additive II.

Using precisely the same line of reasoning, we can also find that holding the remaining problem specifications fixed at their original values, the solution

TABLE 4.7 Revision of the tableau of Table 4.6 for a cost per gram of additive I of $-c_1^*$ cents.

	c_j	c_1^*	-3	0	0	0	0	$-M$	$-M$	$-M$	$-M$	
c_B	BASIS	x_1	x_2	s_1	s_2	s_3	s_4	a_1	a_2	a_3	a_4	SOLUTION
c_1^*	x_1	1	0	0	$\frac{1}{15}$	$-\frac{2}{15}$	0	0	$-\frac{1}{15}$	$\frac{2}{15}$	0	$2\frac{2}{3}$
0	s_4	0	0	0	$-\frac{8}{3}$	$\frac{4}{3}$	1	0	$\frac{8}{3}$	$-\frac{4}{3}$	-1	$53\frac{1}{3}$
0	s_1	0	0	1	$\frac{8}{3}$	$-\frac{16}{3}$	0	-1	$-\frac{8}{3}$	$\frac{16}{3}$	0	$26\frac{2}{3}$
-3	x_2	0	1	0	$-\frac{2}{15}$	$\frac{1}{15}$	0	0	$\frac{2}{15}$	$-\frac{1}{15}$	0	$6\frac{2}{3}$
	z_j	c_1^*	-3	0	$\frac{1}{15}c_1^* + \frac{2}{5}$	$-\frac{2}{15}c_1^* - \frac{1}{5}$	0	0	$-\frac{1}{15}c_1^* - \frac{2}{5}$	$\frac{2}{15}c_1^* + \frac{1}{5}$	0	$2\frac{2}{3}c_1^* - 20$
	$c_j - z_j$	0	0	0	$-\frac{2}{5} - \frac{1}{15}c_1^*$	$\frac{1}{5} + \frac{2}{15}c_1^*$	0	$-M$	$-M + \frac{1}{15}c_1^* + \frac{2}{5}$	$-M - \frac{2}{15}c_1^* - \frac{1}{5}$	$-M$	"Profit"

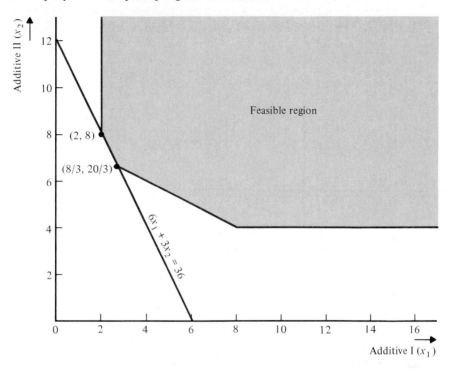

FIGURE 4.6 Graphical solution of the blending problem of the processed food company when the price per gram of Additive I is 6 cents.

of a blend of $2\frac{2}{3}$ grams of additive I and $6\frac{2}{3}$ grams of additive II is optimal for all prices per gram of additive II between one and 4 cents.

SENSITIVITY TO CHANGES IN RIGHT-HAND SIDE VALUES OF CONSTRAINTS

It can be seen from Table 4.6 that whereas the vitamin C and D constraints are binding at the optimal solution, the vitamin A and iron constraints are not. Indeed, given the surpluses involved, the standard for vitamin A can be raised from 80% to $106\frac{2}{3}$%, and that for iron from 80% to $133\frac{1}{3}$%, of U.S.D.A. requirements at no additional cost. However, raising the standard for either vitamin C or D will involve the company in further cost. We proceed now to assess these costs.

From Table 4.6 it emerges that adding one unit of s_2, surplus in the vitamin C constraint, leads to a reduction of $\frac{4}{15}$ cent in "profit"; that is, an addition of $\frac{4}{15}$ cent to total cost. It follows that each unit increase in the vitamin C requirement costs the company $\frac{4}{15}$ cent. The shadow price per unit of this requirement is, then, $-\frac{4}{15}$ cent. Similarly, the shadow price per unit of the vitamin D constraint is $-\frac{1}{15}$ cent. Notice that here the shadow prices are negative, since raising the standards will lead to higher costs, or reduced profits.

We must now determine the ranges in which these shadow prices are valid. Suppose that the vitamin C standard is raised from 80% to $(80 + K)\%$ of U.S.D.A. requirements. To see the impact of this increase in the standard, consider, in equation form, the constraints implied by the tablueau of Table 4.6. These are

$$x_1 + \tfrac{1}{15}s_2 - \tfrac{2}{15}s_3 - \tfrac{1}{15}a_2 + \tfrac{2}{15}a_3 = 2\tfrac{2}{3}$$

$$-\tfrac{8}{3}s_2 + \tfrac{4}{3}s_3 + s_4 + \tfrac{8}{3}a_2 - \tfrac{4}{3}a_3 - a_4 = 53\tfrac{1}{3} \qquad (4.4)$$

$$s_1 + \tfrac{8}{3}s_2 - \tfrac{16}{3}s_3 - a_1 - \tfrac{8}{3}a_2 + \tfrac{16}{3}a_3 = 26\tfrac{2}{3}$$

$$x_2 - \tfrac{2}{15}s_2 + \tfrac{1}{15}s_3 + \tfrac{2}{15}a_2 - \tfrac{1}{15}a_3 = 6\tfrac{2}{3}$$

At the optimal solution, s_2, s_3, a_1, a_2, a_3, a_4 are zero, so that $x_1 = 2\tfrac{2}{3}$, $s_4 = 53\tfrac{1}{3}$, $s_1 = 26\tfrac{2}{3}$, and $x_2 = 6\tfrac{2}{3}$. Suppose now that the vitamin C requirement is increased from 80 to $(80 + K)$. The vitamin C constraint is now

$$5\,x_1 + 10x_2 \geq 80 + K$$

so that in the form

$$5\,x_1 + 10\,x_2 - s_2 = 80$$

the variable s_2 must be at least equal to K. Thus, raising by K the vitamin C standard is equivalent to requiring a value of at least K for the surplus variable associated with the vitamin C constraint in the original formulation.

Consider, now, the effects of setting $s_2 = K$ in (4.4), while keeping s_3 and the four artificial variables at zero. From the first equation of (4.4)

$$x_1 + \tfrac{1}{15}K = 2\tfrac{2}{3}$$

so that

$$x_1 = 2\tfrac{2}{3} - \tfrac{1}{15}K$$

Similarly, for the other three equations

$$-\tfrac{8}{3}K + s_4 = 53\tfrac{1}{3}$$

and so

$$s_4 = 53\tfrac{1}{3} + \tfrac{8}{3}K$$

Also

$$s_1 + \tfrac{8}{3}K = 26\tfrac{2}{3}$$

giving

$$s_1 = 26\tfrac{2}{3} - \tfrac{8}{3}K$$

and

$$x_2 - \tfrac{2}{15}K = 6\tfrac{2}{3}$$

yielding

$$x_2 = 6\tfrac{2}{3} + \tfrac{2}{15}K$$

Notice that this new solution, a blend of $(2\frac{2}{3} - \frac{1}{15}K)$ grams of additive I and $(6\frac{2}{3} + \frac{2}{15}K)$ grams of additive II, with a surplus of $(26\frac{2}{3} - \frac{8}{3}K)$ in the vitamin A requirement and $(53\frac{1}{3} + \frac{8}{3}K)$ in the iron requirement, could have been obtained by *subtracting* K times the entries in the s_2 column of Table 4.6 from those of the "Solution" column of that table.

The new solution involves the use of $\frac{2}{15}K$ extra grams of additive II, at a cost of 3 cents per gram, and $\frac{1}{15}K$ fewer grams of additive I, saving 2 cents per gram. The net effect is an increase in total cost of $(\frac{6}{15}K - \frac{2}{15}K) = \frac{4}{15}K$ cents. The new solution is set out in the simplex tableau of Table 4.8.

From Table 4.8 we see that each unit increase in the vitamin C standard leads to the use of $\frac{1}{15}$ gram less of additive I and $\frac{2}{15}$ gram more of additive II, the net effect being a reduction of $\frac{4}{15}$ cent in profit, as predicted by the shadow price. We must now find whether this solution is feasible. Feasibility requires

$$2\frac{2}{3} - \frac{1}{15}K \geq 0; \quad 53\frac{1}{3} + \frac{8}{3}K \geq 0;$$

$$26\frac{2}{3} - \frac{8}{3}K \geq 0; \quad 6\frac{2}{3} + \frac{2}{15}K \geq 0$$

Equivalently, these requirements can be written as

$$K \leq 40; \quad K \geq -20;$$

$$K \leq 10; \quad K \geq -50$$

Therefore, for all these constraints to hold, the increase K in the vitamin C standard must satisfy

$$-20 \leq K \leq 10$$

Since the initial standard was 80% of U.S.D.A. requirements, the range of values for the standard in which the shadow price is valid is

$$60 \leq \% \text{ U.S.D.A. Vitamin C Requirement} \leq 90$$

Our calculations, then, have shown that each additional percentage point increase in the vitamin C standard, within a range running from 60% to 90% of U.S.D.A. requirements, involves a cost of $\frac{4}{15}$ cent.

The need for the upper bound of this range is illustrated in Figure 4.7. If the vitamin C standard is set at 80% of U.S.D.A. requirements, the optimal

TABLE 4.8 Final tableau of the simplex algorithm solution to the blending problem of the processed food company when the vitamin C standard is raised by K percentage points.

c_j		-2	-3	0	0	0	0	$-M$	$-M$	$-M$	$-M$	
c_B	BASIS	x_1	x_2	s_1	s_2	s_3	s_4	a_1	a_2	a_3	a_4	SOLUTION
-2	x_1	1	0	0	$\frac{1}{15}$	$-\frac{2}{15}$	0	0	$-\frac{1}{15}$	$\frac{2}{15}$	0	$2\frac{2}{3} - \frac{1}{15}K$
0	s_4	0	0	0	$-\frac{8}{3}$	$\frac{4}{3}$	1	0	$\frac{8}{3}$	$-\frac{4}{3}$	-1	$53\frac{1}{3} + \frac{8}{3}K$
0	s_1	0	0	1	$\frac{8}{3}$	$-\frac{16}{3}$	0	-1	$-\frac{8}{3}$	$\frac{16}{3}$	0	$26\frac{2}{3} - \frac{8}{3}K$
-3	x_2	0	1	0	$-\frac{2}{15}$	$\frac{1}{15}$	0	0	$\frac{2}{15}$	$-\frac{1}{15}$	0	$6\frac{2}{3} + \frac{2}{15}K$
	z_j	-2	-3	0	$\frac{4}{15}$	$\frac{1}{15}$	0	0	$-\frac{4}{15}$	$-\frac{1}{15}$	0	$-25\frac{1}{3} - \frac{4}{15}K$
	$c_j - z_j$	0	0	0	$-\frac{4}{15}$	$-\frac{1}{15}$	0	$-M$	$-M + \frac{4}{15}$	$-M + \frac{1}{15}$	$-M$	"Profit"

blend contains $2\frac{2}{3}$ grams of additive I and $6\frac{2}{3}$ grams of additive II. However, if the vitamin C standard is raised, this solution will no longer be feasible. If the standard is increased to 90% of U.S.D.A. requirements, the optimal solution is a blend of 2 grams of additive I and 8 grams of additive II. Thus, while the company has had to use an extra $1\frac{1}{3}$ grams of additive II, adding 4 cents to costs, as partial compensation $\frac{2}{3}$ gram less of additive I is used, saving $1\frac{1}{3}$ cents. The net effect, then, is an increase of $2\frac{2}{3}$ cents in total cost. This amounts, as predicted, to $\frac{4}{15}$ cent for each percentage point increase in the vitamin C standard.

However, the picture changes if the vitamin C standard is raised beyond this point. This will require additional amounts of additive II. However, as can be seen from Figure 4.7, the vitamin A constraint prohibits reduction below 2 grams in the amount of additive I in the blend. For example, moving from 90% to 100% of U.S.D.A. vitamin C requirements leads, optimally, to a blend of 2 grams of additive I and 9 grams of additive II. The extra gram of additive II adds 3 cents to total costs; that is, $\frac{3}{10}$ cent for each percentage point increase, beyond 90%, in the vitamin C standard.

Using the same approach employed previously, it can also be shown that each additional percentage point increase in the vitamin D standard, within a

FIGURE 4.7 Raising of the Vitamin C standard for the processed food company from 80% to 100% of U.S.D.A. requirements.

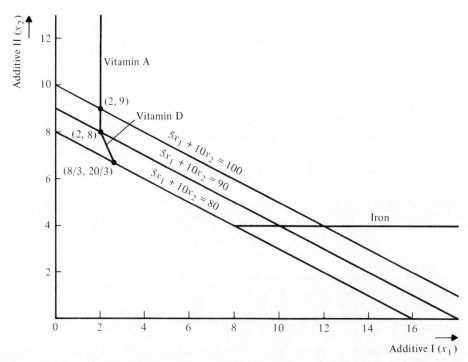

TABLE 4.9 Opportunity cost for the use of a gram of the third additive by the processed food company.

REQUIREMENT	QUANTITY AVAILABLE (% U.S.D.A. REQUIREMENTS)	SHADOW PRICE (CENTS)	OPPORTUNITY COST (CENTS)
Vitamin A	10	0	0
Vitamin C	10	$-\frac{4}{15}$	$-2\frac{2}{3}$
Vitamin D	10	$-\frac{1}{15}$	$-\frac{2}{3}$
Iron	10	0	0
			$-3\frac{1}{3}$

range running from 55% to 100% of U.S.D.A. requirements and with the other problem specifications set at their initial values, involves a cost of $\frac{1}{15}$ cent.

ADDING A NEW DECISION VARIABLE

We close our discussion of sensitivity analysis for this problem by examining the possibility that the processed food company has a third additive available for potential use in its blend. Each gram of this additive contains 10% of U.S.D.A. requirements for all three vitamins and for iron. What is the maximum price per gram the company should be prepared to pay for this additive?

The calculations are set out in Table 4.9 which utilizes the shadow prices we have already obtained. Each gram used of the third additive will allow the company to use less of the other additives in its blend. The opportunity cost to the company is the "cost" of this reduced usage of additives I and II, and is, of course, negative. This opportunity cost is calculated in Table 4.9. Since the current blend contains surpluses of vitamin A and iron, their presence in the new additive is of no value. However, each one percent of vitamin C is worth $\frac{4}{15}$ cent, and each one percent of vitamin D $\frac{1}{15}$ cent. We find, then, that use of a gram of the new additive reduces by $3\frac{1}{3}$ cents the total costs of needed amounts of additives I and II. It will, therefore, pay the company to use this new additive provided its price per gram is less than $3\frac{1}{3}$ cents.

4.6. A FURTHER EXAMPLE

We conclude our discussion of sensitivity analysis with an elaboration of the product mix problem of the office furnishings company. Specifically, we will add two elements to the original problem specifications:

(a) The company is able to produce a third product—chairs. Each chair requires 3 man-hours of assembly time, 2 man-hours of finishing time, and 1 man-hour of inspection time, and can be sold at a profit of $12.

(b) In order to fill an important order, at least 50 bookcases must be produced.

The complete specification is set out in Table 4.10.

TABLE 4.10 Specifications for the office furnishings company modified product mix problem.

TOTAL MAN-HOURS AVAILABLE	DEPARTMENT	MAN-HOURS PER UNIT		
		DESKS	BOOKCASES	CHAIRS
640	Assembly	8	4	3
540	Finishing	4	6	2
100	Inspection	1	1	1
PROFIT PER UNIT ($)		30	20	12
MINIMUM PRODUCTION		0	50	0

Denoting output of desks, bookcases, and chairs by x_1, x_2, and x_3, respectively, the constrained maximization problem to be solved is

$$\text{Maximize} \quad 30x_1 + 20x_2 + 12x_3$$

$$\text{subject to} \quad 8x_1 + 4x_2 + 3x_3 \leq 640$$

$$4x_1 + 6x_2 + 2x_3 \leq 540$$

$$x_1 + x_2 + x_3 \leq 100$$

$$x_2 \geq 50$$

$$x_1, x_2, x_3 \geq 0$$

In tableau form, our problem is expressed as

$$\text{Maximize} \quad 30x_1 + 20x_2 + 12x_3 - Ma_1$$

$$\text{subject to} \quad 8x_1 + 4x_2 + 3x_3 + s_1 = 640$$

$$4x_1 + 6x_2 + 2x_3 + s_2 = 540$$

$$x_1 + x_2 + x_3 + s_3 = 100$$

$$x_2 - s_4 + a_1 = 50$$

$$x_1, x_2, x_3, s_1, s_2, s_3, s_4, a_1 \geq 0$$

In this formulation, s_1, s_2 and s_3 are slack variables, s_4 is a surplus variable, and a_1 is an artificial variable.

The final tableau for the simplex algorithm solution of this problem is displayed in Table 4.11. Directly from the table, we read that the optimal solution is

$$x_1 = 50, \, x_2 = 50, \, x_3 = 0, \, s_1 = 40, \, s_2 = 40, \, s_3 = 0, \, s_4 = 0$$

The profit maximizing strategy, then, is to manufacture 50 desks and 50 bookcases, giving a total profit of $2500. No chairs will be produced. At the optimal solution, 40 man-hours of assembly time and 40 man-hours of finishing time will

TABLE 4.11 Final tableau of the simplex algorithm solution for the modified product mix problem of the office furnishings company.

		30	20	12	0	0	0	0	$-M$	
c_B	BASIS	x_1	x_2	x_3	s_1	s_2	s_3	s_4	a_1	SOLUTION
0	s_1	0	0	-5	1	0	-8	-4	4	40
0	s_2	0	0	-2	0	1	-4	2	-2	40
30	x_1	1	0	1	0	0	1	1	-1	50
20	x_2	0	1	0	0	0	0	-1	1	50
	z_j	30	20	30	0	0	30	10	-10	2500
	$c_j - z_j$	0	0	-18	0	0	-30	-10	$10 - M$	Profit

be unused. There will be no unused inspection capacity, and no bookcases in addition to the required minimum will be produced.

SENSITIVITY TO CHANGES IN OBJECTIVE FUNCTION COEFFICIENTS

We now examine the impact on the optimal solution of changing the coefficient on one of the decision variables in the objective function; that is, of altering the profit per unit of a product while leaving all other problem specifications at their original levels.

(i) COEFFICIENTS ON THE NONBASIC VARIABLES

The only nonbasic variable at the optimal solution is x_3—output of chairs. In order to make production of a positive number of chairs profitable, the $c_j - z_j$ value associated with the variable x_3 would have to be positive. From Table 4.11, it emerges that $z_3 = 30$. Therefore, provided the profit per unit, c_3, for chairs remains no more than $30, chairs will not be manufactured, and the optimal solution will be unchanged; that is, the optimal solution is the same for all

$$-\infty < c_3 \leq z_3$$

i.e.,

$$-\infty < c_3 \leq 30$$

We conclude, then, that if all other problem specifications are kept at their original levels, our solution will remain optimal provided that profit per chair does not exceed $30.

(ii) COEFFICIENTS ON THE BASIC VARIABLES

Next we consider the effect of changing the coefficient in the objective function on one of the basic variables. To illustrate, suppose, while keeping all other specifications at their original levels, we contemplate deviations from the $20

TABLE 4.12 Revision of the tableau of Table 4.11 for profit per bookcase of c_2^*.

c_j		30	c_2^*	12	0	0	0	0	$-M$	
c_B	BASIS	x_1	x_2	x_3	s_1	s_2	s_3	s_4	a_1	SOLUTION
0	s_1	0	0	-5	1	0	-8	-4	4	40
0	s_2	0	0	-2	0	1	-4	2	-2	40
30	x_1	1	0	1	0	0	1	1	-1	50
c_2^*	x_2	0	1	0	0	0	0	-1	1	50
	z_j	30	c_2^*	30	0	0	30	$30 - c_2^*$	$c_2^* - 30$	$1500 + 50c_2^*$
	$c_j - z_j$	0	0	-18	0	0	-30	$c_2^* - 30$	$30 - c_2^* - M$	Profit

per unit profit for bookcases. We will denote by c_2^* the profit per bookcase. Replacing this entry in Table 4.11, we need only recompute the z_j and $c_j - z_j$ entries, and modify the total profit appropriately. This is done in Table 4.12.

The original optimal solution will remain optimal provided none of the $c_j - z_j$ entries in Table 4.12 is positive. This requires only that

$$c_2^* - 30 \le 0$$

or

$$c_2^* \le 30$$

It follows, then, that if all other problem constraints are held at their original levels, our solution will remain optimal provided that profit per bookcase does not exceed $30. The reason that there is no lower bound on profit per bookcase is that 50 units *must* be made, however low is unit profit.

By a similar argument, it can be shown that our solution remains optimal provided that profit per desk is not less than $20, when all other problem specifications are fixed at their original levels. We leave the demonstration of this result as an exercise for the reader.

SENSITIVITY TO CHANGES IN RIGHT-HAND SIDE VALUES OF CONSTRAINTS

The effect on profits of adjusting the right-hand sides of any of the constraints can be read from the entries for the corresponding slack or surplus variables in the $c_j - z_j$ row of Table 4.11. At the optimal solution, the assembly and finishing constraints are not binding, so that the shadow prices of these resources are zero. The inspection time constraint is, however, binding at the optimal solution. Table 4.11 shows that increasing the slack variable, s_3, by one unit, which is equivalent to decreasing inspection time by one man-hour, leads to a reduction of $30 in profit. Hence, each extra man-hour in inspection is worth $30, and is, therefore, the shadow price of this resource.

Also from Table 4.11 we see that increasing the surplus variable, s_4, by one unit, which is equivalent to requiring production of an additional bookcase, leads to a fall of $10 in total profit. Thus, each extra bookcase that must be made costs $10 in foregone profits, so that the associated shadow price is -10.

Next, we need to find the ranges in which these shadow prices hold. To illustrate, consider the addition of K man-hours of assembly time. Recall that we can solve the modified optimization problem by adding K times the entries in the s_1 column of Table 4.11 to those of the "Solution" column. The modified tableau is shown in Table 4.13.

The solution in Table 4.13 is feasible provided that all the entries in the "Solution" column are nonnegative. We therefore require

$$40 + K \geq 0$$

or

$$K \geq -40$$

Since 640 man-hours of assembly time were originally available, it follows that the shadow price of zero is valid in the range

$$\text{Assembly Time} \geq 640 - 40 = 600$$

We conclude, then, that with all other specifications at their original levels, and for any level of assembly time at least 600 man-hours, each additional man-hour of assembly time adds nothing to total profit.

By a similar argument it can be shown that the shadow price of zero for finishing time is valid in the range

$$\text{Finishing Time} \geq 500$$

and that the shadow price of $30 for inspection time is valid in the range

$$50 \leq \text{Inspection Time} \leq 105$$

We leave it as an exercise to the reader to verify these conclusions.

Finally, consider the addition of K units to the number of bookcases that must be produced. Since s_4 is a surplus variable, the modified problem is solved

TABLE 4.13 Final tableau of the simplex algorithm solution to the modified product mix problem of the office furnishings company when the assembly time capacity is increased by K man-hours.

c_j		30	20	12	0	0	0	0	$-M$	
c_B	BASIS	x_1	x_2	x_3	s_1	s_2	s_3	s_4	a_1	SOLUTION
0	s_1	0	0	-5	1	0	-8	-4	4	$40 + K$
0	s_2	0	0	-2	0	1	-4	2	-2	40
30	x_1	1	0	1	0	0	1	1	-1	50
20	x_2	0	1	0	0	0	0	-1	1	50
	z_j	30	20	30	0	0	30	10	-10	2500
	$c_j - z_j$	0	0	-18	0	0	-30	-10	$10 - M$	Profit

TABLE 4.14 Final tableau of the simplex algorithm solution to the modified product mix problem of the office furnishings company when the minimum number of bookcases that must be produced is increased by K.

c_B	BASIS	c_j → x_1 (30)	x_2 (20)	x_3 (12)	s_1 (0)	s_2 (0)	s_3 (0)	s_4 (0)	a_1 (-M)	SOLUTION
0	s_1	0	0	-5	1	0	-8	-4	4	$40 + 4K$
0	s_2	0	0	-2	0	1	-4	2	-2	$40 - 2K$
30	s_3	1	0	1	0	0	1	1	-1	$50 - K$
20	s_4	0	1	0	0	0	0	-1	1	$50 + K$
	z_j	30	20	30	0	0	30	10	-10	$2500 - 10K$
	$c_j - z_j$	0	0	-18	0	0	-30	-10	$10 - M$	Profit

by subtracting K times the entries in the s_4 column of Table 4.11 from those of the "Solution" column. The new tableau is shown in Table 4.14.

Again, the solution in Table 4.14 is feasible if all the entries in the "Solution" column are nonnegative. We therefore need

$$40 + 4K \geq 0; \, 40 - 2K \geq 0$$

$$50 - K \geq 0; \, 50 + K \geq 0$$

Equivalently,

$$K \geq -10; \, K \leq 20$$

$$K \leq 50; \, K \geq -50$$

For all four of these conditions to hold, we must have

$$-10 \leq K \leq 20$$

Then, since the original requirement is production of 50 bookcases, it follows that the shadow price of $\$-10$ is valid in the range

$$50 - 10 \leq \text{Minimum Number of Bookcases} \leq 50 + 20$$

or

$$40 \leq \text{Minimum Number of Bookcases} \leq 70$$

We conclude, then, that with all other problem specifications at their initial levels, each additional bookcase that must be produced, within a range from 40 to 70 bookcases, leads to a fall of $10 in maximum attainable total profit.

4.7. DUALITY

We have learned, using the simplex algorithm, how to solve a linear programming problem. As a matter of fact, rather remarkably, it will emerge that in solving the problem of interest, we have also solved a second associated linear programming problem! This associated problem is termed the **dual,** while in this context, the original problem is called the **primal.**

To illustrate how the dual arises, consider once again the office furnishings company, for which the primal problem is

$$\text{Maximize} \quad 30x_1 + 20x_2$$

$$\text{subject to} \quad 8x_1 + 4x_2 \leq 640$$

$$4x_1 + 6x_2 \leq 540$$

$$x_1 + x_2 \leq 100$$

$$x_1, x_2 \geq 0$$

Suppose, now, that this company must purchase its total weekly capacity of 640 man-hours of assembly time, 540 man-hours of finishing time, and 100 man-hours of inspection time at prices per man-hour of y_1, y_2 and y_3, respectively. The total dollar amount to be paid will then be

$$640y_1 + 540y_2 + 100y_3$$

The company will want to set its bids y_1, y_2, y_3 for the resources so as to make this total cost as small as possible. On the other hand, sellers of these resources know that by using 8 man-hours of assembly time, 4 man-hours of finishing time, and 1 man-hour of inspection time, it is possible to produce a desk at a profit of $30. Sellers will therefore demand at least $30 for this combination of resources. Similarly, they will require at least $20 for a package of 4 man-hours of assembly time, 6 man-hours of finishing time and 1 man-hour of inspection time. Hence, in determining the bids per unit for each resource, the company faces the problem

$$\text{Minimize} \quad 640y_1 + 540y_2 + 100y_3$$

$$\text{subject to} \quad 8y_1 + 4y_2 + y_3 \geq 30$$

$$4y_1 + 6y_2 + y_3 \geq 20$$

$$y_1, y_2, y_3 \geq 0$$

This is the dual of the original problem.

Can you see how the dual was formed from the primal? A general formulation emerges if we consider the constrained maximization problem

$$\text{Maximize} \quad c_1x_1 + c_2x_2 + \ldots + c_nx_n$$

$$\text{subject to} \quad a_{11}x_1 + a_{12}x_2 + \ldots + a_{1n}x_n \leq b_1$$

$$a_{21}x_1 + a_{22}x_2 + \ldots + a_{2n}x_n \leq b_2$$

$$\cdot \quad \cdot \quad \cdot \quad \cdot \quad \cdot$$

$$a_{m1}x_1 + a_{m2}x_2 + \ldots + a_{mn}x_n \leq b_n$$

$$x_1, x_2, \ldots, x_n \geq 0$$

(4.5)

The dual problem involves the m decision variables, $y_1, y_2, \ldots, y_m$, and can be written as

$$
\begin{aligned}
\text{Minimize} \quad & b_1 y_1 + b_2 y_2 + \ldots + b_m y_m \\
\text{subject to} \quad & a_{11} y_1 + a_{21} y_2 + \ldots + a_{m1} y_m \geq c_1 \\
& a_{12} y_1 + a_{22} y_2 + \ldots + a_{m2} y_m \geq c_2 \\
& \qquad \cdot \qquad \cdot \qquad \cdot \qquad \cdot \qquad \cdot \\
& a_{1n} y_1 + a_{2n} y_2 + \ldots + a_{mn} y_m \geq c_n \\
& y_1, y_2, \ldots, y_m \geq 0
\end{aligned}
\tag{4.6}
$$

The concept of duality is important because, as we will see in the next section, once we have the solution to one of the two problems, we also have the solution to the other. We can, then, choose to which problem the simplex algorithm is applied. In fact, in terms of computation time, it will generally pay to attack directly the problem with fewer constraints.

GENERAL RULE FOR FINDING THE DUAL OF A LINEAR PROGRAMMING PROBLEM

We have seen how to find the dual of a constrained maximization problem in which all constraints are of the $\leq$ type. To see how this procedure may be applied more generally, we will show how any linear programming problem can be converted to this form.

(i) *Minimization Problems:* If the aim is minimization of some objective, this must first be converted to an objective maximization problem. For example, if the problem is

$$\text{Minimize } 2x_1 + 3x_2$$

we have, on multiplying through this function by -1,

$$\text{Maximize } -2x_1 - 3x_2$$

(ii) *Greater than or Equal to Constraints:* A $\geq$ constraint can be formulated as a $\leq$ constraint by multiplying through by -1. For example,

$$5x_1 + 10x_2 \geq 80$$

is equivalent to

$$-5x_1 - 10x_2 \leq -80$$

(iii) *Equal to Constraints:* An equal to constraint must first be replaced by a $\geq$ and a $\leq$ constraint. For example, in place of

$$x_1 + 2x_2 = 20$$

we write

$$x_1 + 2x_2 \geq 20$$

$$x_1 + 2x_2 \leq 20$$

The first of these is modified as in (ii), so that finally the equal to constraint is replaced by

$$x_1 + 2x_2 \geq 20$$

$$-x_1 - 2x_2 \geq -20$$

Once a linear programming problem has been expressed as a constrained maximization problem with only $\leq$ constraints, we can convert from the form (4.5) to the dual (4.6).

4.8. OPTIMAL SOLUTIONS OF PRIMAL AND DUAL PROBLEMS

Let us begin by deriving, through the simplex algorithm, the optimal solution to the dual problem of the office furnishings company. To do so we introduce a pair of surplus variables, denoted s_1^* and s_2^* to avoid confusion with the slack variables of the primal problem, and a pair of artificial variables, a_1 and a_2. The dual problem can then be expressed as

Maximize $\quad -640y_1 - 540y_2 - 100y_3 - Ma_1 - Ma_2$

subject to $\qquad 8y_1 + 4y_2 + y_3 - s_1^* + a_1 = 30$

$\qquad 4y_1 + 6y_2 + y_3 - s_2^* + a_2 = 20$

$\qquad y_1, y_2, y_3, s_1^*, s_2^*, a_1, a_2 \geq 0$

In Table 4.15 the simplex algorithm is applied in solving this dual problem. The optimal solution is reached at the fourth step, and is

$$y_1 = 2\tfrac{1}{2}, \; y_2 = 0, \; y_3 = 10, \; s_1^* = 0, \; s_2^* = 0$$

As the dual problem was described in the previous section, the solution for minimizing total cost, given the constraints, is to bid for additional resources at $2.50 per man-hour for assembly time, $0 per man-hour for finishing time, and $10 per man-hour for inspection time.

We now explore the connection between the primal and dual problems by looking at the final tableaux of the simplex algorithm solutions to the two problems. For convenience, the tableau for the primal problem is reproduced in Table 4.16. Can you find any relationship between the final tableau of Table 4.15 and that of Table 4.16? Perhaps the most obvious similarity is in the bottom right-hand corners of the two tableaux. The maximum profit the company can make from the allocation of resources to an optimal product mix is $2600. We see also from Table 4.15 that the lowest price at which the resources can be acquired is $2600. On reflection, this finding is not too surprising. If the resources could be used to produce $2600 worth of profit in desks and bookcases, why sell them for less? The conclusion reached for this specific example is quite general.

The values of the objective functions at the optimal solutions of the primal and dual problems are identical.

TABLE 4.15 Simplex algorithm solution to the dual problem of the office furnishings company.

(i)

c_j		-640	-540	-100	0	0	$-M$	$-M$		
c_B	BASIS	y_1	y_2	y_3	s_1^*	s_2^*	a_1	a_2	SOLUTION	
$-M$	a_1	⑧	4	1	-1	0	1	0	30	$\frac{30}{8} = 3\frac{3}{4}$
$-M$	a_2	4	6	1	0	-1	0	1	20	$\frac{20}{4} = 5$
	z_j	$-12M$	$-10M$	$-2M$	M	M	$-M$	$-M$	$-50M$	
	$c_j - z_j$	$12M - 640$	$10M - 540$	$2M - 100$	$-M$	$-M$	0	0	"Profit"	

(ii)

c_j		-640	-540	-100	0	0	$-M$	$-M$		
c_B	BASIS	y_1	y_2	y_3	s_1^*	s_2^*	a_1	a_2	SOLUTION	
-640	y_1	1	$\frac{1}{2}$	$\frac{1}{8}$	$-\frac{1}{8}$	0	$\frac{1}{8}$	0	$3\frac{3}{4}$	$3\frac{3}{4}/\frac{1}{2} = 7\frac{1}{2}$
$-M$	a_2	0	④	$\frac{1}{2}$	$\frac{1}{2}$	-1	$-\frac{1}{2}$	1	5	$\frac{5}{4} = 1\frac{1}{4}$
	z_j	-640	$-4M - 320$	$-\frac{1}{2}M - 80$	$-\frac{1}{2}M + 80$	M	$\frac{1}{2}M - 80$	$-M$	$-5M - 2400$	
	$c_j - z_j$	0	$4M - 220$	$\frac{1}{2}M - 20$	$\frac{1}{2}M - 80$	$-M$	$-\frac{1}{2}M + 80$	0	"Profit"	

(iii)

c_j		-640	-540	-100	0	0	$-M$	$-M$		
c_B	BASIS	y_1	y_2	y_3	s_1^*	s_2^*	a_1	a_2	SOLUTION	
-640	y_1	1	0	$\frac{1}{16}$	$-\frac{3}{16}$	$\frac{1}{8}$	$\frac{3}{16}$	$-\frac{1}{8}$	$3\frac{3}{8}$	$3\frac{3}{8}/\frac{1}{16} = 50$
-540	y_2	0	1	⑧	$\frac{1}{8}$	$-\frac{1}{4}$	$-\frac{1}{8}$	$\frac{1}{4}$	$1\frac{1}{4}$	$1\frac{1}{4}/\frac{1}{8} = 10$
	z_j	-640	-540	$-107\frac{1}{2}$	$52\frac{1}{2}$	55	$-52\frac{1}{2}$	-55	-2675	
	$c_j - z_j$	0	0	$7\frac{1}{2}$	$-52\frac{1}{2}$	-55	$-M + 52\frac{1}{2}$	$-M + 55$	"Profit"	

(iv)

c_j		-640	-540	-100	0	0	$-M$	$-M$	
c_B	BASIS	y_1	y_2	y_3	s_1^*	s_2^*	a_1	a_2	SOLUTION
-640	y_1	1	$-\frac{1}{2}$	0	$-\frac{1}{4}$	$\frac{1}{4}$	$\frac{1}{4}$	$-\frac{1}{4}$	$2\frac{1}{2}$
-100	y_3	0	8	1	1	-2	-1	2	10
	z_j	-640	-480	-100	60	40	-60	-40	-2600
	$c_j - z_j$	0	-60	0	-60	-40	$-M + 60$	$-M + 40$	"Profit"

TABLE 4.16 Final tableau of the simplex algorithm solution to the primal problem of the office furnishings company.

c_j		30	20	0	0	0	
c_B	BASIS	x_1	x_2	s_1	s_2	s_3	SOLUTION
30	x_1	1	0	$\frac{1}{4}$	0	-1	60
0	s_2	0	0	$\frac{1}{2}$	1	-8	60
20	x_2	0	1	$-\frac{1}{4}$	0	2	40
	z_j	30	20	$2\frac{1}{2}$	0	10	2600
	$c_j - z_j$	0	0	$-2\frac{1}{2}$	0	-10	Profit

This important result far from exhausts the relationship between the two problems. Perhaps, from looking at Tables 4.15 and 4.16, you have already found further connections. To make the position transparent, we set out in Table 4.17 the relevant details. It emerges that the negatives of the $c_j - z_j$ values for one problem provide the optimal solution to the other.

Now, each slack variable in the primal problem is associated with a decision variable in the dual problem. For instance, the variable s_1 denotes slack in assembly, while y_1 is price per man-hour bid for assembly time in the dual problem. Recall that in Section 4.3, we identified the negatives of the $c_j - z_j$ values for the slack variables as the **shadow prices** of the corresponding resources. These shadow prices represent the values of an additional unit of the resources. Looked at in this way, it should occasion no surprise at all to learn that these are precisely the prices that would be bid for these resources.

In addition, each decision variable in the primal problem is associated with a surplus variable in the dual problem. For example, x_1 denotes the number of desks made, while s_1^* is the difference between what the company would bid for the combination of resources needed to make a desk and the profit that can be derived from its manufacture. In our particular problem, the optimal solutions for all of these variables are zero.

Suppose, however, that the company could, if it chose, make a third product—chairs. Assume, further, that in the final tableau of the simplex algorithm

TABLE 4.17 Some aspects of the optimal solutions of primal and dual problems of the office furnishings company.

PRIMAL PROBLEM			DUAL PROBLEM		
VARIABLE	SOLUTION	$c_j - z_j$	VARIABLE	SOLUTION	$c_j - z_j$
x_1	60	0	s_1^*	0	-60
x_2	40	0	s_2^*	0	-40
s_1	0	$-2\frac{1}{2}$	y_1	$2\frac{1}{2}$	0
s_2	60	0	y_2	0	-60
s_3	0	-10	y_3	10	0

solution to the primal problem the $c_j - z_j$ value for chairs was negative, say -15. This would imply that the net effect of producing a chair would, as a result of foregone profits elsewhere, be a reduction of $15 in total profits. Another way to put this is that the combination of resources needed to make a chair is worth $15 more than the profit from a chair when these resources are optimally employed in the production of desks and bookcases. Since the company would be prepared to bid for these resources at *their value when optimally used*, it follows that the optimal value of the surplus variable, corresponding to chairs in the dual problem, will be 15.

Let us emphasize the generality of the conclusions which have just been illustrated. Quite generally, if the primal problem has an optimal solution, then so will the dual. As we have already seen, the objective functions have the same values at the optimal solutions to the two problems. Furthermore, the following result also holds.

Suppose we are given a primal problem and corresponding dual. The optimal solutions for the decision variables for one problem are the negatives of the $c_j - z_j$ values of the corresponding surplus/slack variables at the optimal solution of the other. In addition, the optimal solutions for the slack/surplus variables for one problem are the negatives of the $c_j - z_j$ values of the corresponding decision variables at the optimal solution of the other.

Example 4.1

The blending problem of the processed food company, which we have already discussed extensively, is

$$\text{Minimize} \quad 2x_1 + 3x_2$$
$$\text{subject to} \quad 40x_1 \geq 80$$
$$5x_1 + 10x_2 \geq 80$$
$$10x_1 + 5x_2 \geq 60$$
$$20x_2 \geq 80$$
$$x_1, x_2 \geq 0$$

The optimal solution to this problem is

$$x_1 = 2\tfrac{2}{3}, \ x_2 = 6\tfrac{2}{3}, \ s_1 = 26\tfrac{2}{3}, \ s_2 = 0, \ s_3 = 0, \ s_4 = 53\tfrac{1}{3}$$

where the s_i are the surplus variables for the four constraints. From Table 4.6, it can be seen that at the optimal solution, the $c_j - z_j$ values are $-\tfrac{4}{15}$ for s_2 and $-\tfrac{1}{15}$ for s_3, and are zero for the other variables. Also, the value of the objective function at this solution is $25\tfrac{1}{3}$.

The dual of this problem can be found by applying the general procedure of Section 4.7. First, the primal must be expressed as a constrained maximization problem with only $\leq$ constraints. The objective is

$$\text{Maximize } -2x_1 - 3x_2$$

Multiplying through each of the four constraints by -1 allows us to express them in $\leq$ form. Hence, the primal is

$$
\begin{aligned}
\text{Maximize} \quad & -2x_1 - 3x_2 \\
\text{subject to} \quad & -40x_1 \leq -80 \\
& -5x_1 - 10x_2 \leq -80 \\
& -10x_1 - 5x_2 \leq -60 \\
& -20x_2 \leq -80 \\
& x_1, x_2 \geq 0
\end{aligned}
$$

Thus, by reference to the formulations (4.5) and (4.6), it follows that the dual is

$$
\begin{aligned}
\text{Minimize} \quad & -80y_1 - 80y_2 - 60y_3 - 80y_4 \\
\text{subject to} \quad & -40y_1 - 5y_2 - 10y_3 \geq -2 \\
& -10y_2 - 5y_3 - 20y_4 \geq -3 \\
& y_1, y_2, y_3, y_4 \geq 0
\end{aligned}
$$

This is equivalent to

$$
\begin{aligned}
\text{Maximize} \quad & 80y_1 + 80y_2 + 60y_3 + 80y_4 \\
\text{subject to} \quad & 40y_1 + 5y_2 + 10y_3 \leq 2 \\
& 10y_2 + 5y_3 + 20y_4 \leq 3 \\
& y_1, y_2, y_3, y_4 \geq 0
\end{aligned}
$$

As a result of our analysis of the primal problem, we, know immediately that the highest attainable value of the objective function for the dual is $25\frac{1}{3}$, and that this is achieved by the optimal solution

$$y_1 = 0, \, y_2 = \tfrac{4}{15}, \, y_3 = \tfrac{1}{15}, \, y_4 = 0, \, s_1^* = 0, \, s_2^* = 0$$

where s_1^* and s_2^* are the slack variables associated with the two dual problem constraints.

The reader is invited to verify these results through the application of the simplex algorithm to the dual problem.

4.1. Consider the product mix problem of the office furnishings company. Holding the remaining problem specifications at their initial values, examine the sensitivity of the optimal solution to variations in the profit per unit for bookcases:

(a) Show that the optimal solution is to produce 60 desks and 40 bookcases, provided profit per unit for bookcases is in the range from $15 to $30.

(b) Confirm graphically your conclusions of (a).

4.2. Keeping the feasible region for the office furnishings company problem fixed at its initial state, consider now the possibility of variations in profits per unit for *both* desks and bookcases. Show that the optimal solution is to produce 60 desks and 40 bookcases whenever the profit per unit for desks is both no less than that for bookcases and no more than twice that for bookcases.

4.3. In Section 4.3 it was shown that the shadow price of $10 per man-hour of inspection time for the office furnishings company is valid in a range running from 80 to $107\frac{1}{2}$ man-hours. Produce a graphical analysis justifying the need for the upper limit of this range. Explain how the situation changes when inspection time capacity is increased beyond $107\frac{1}{2}$ man-hours.

4.4. (a) Using the simplex tableau, show that the shadow price of $2.50 per man-hour of assembly time for the office furnishings company is valid in a range running from 520 to 800 man-hours.

(b) Produce graphical analyses justifying the need for both limits of this range. Explain how the position changes when assembly time capacity is reduced below 520 man-hours, and when this capacity is increased above 800 man-hours.

(c) Holding the other problem specifications fixed at their original values, what is the value to the office furnishings company of an additional man-hour of assembly time beyond 800 man-hours?

4.5. The office furnishings company has the opportunity to add a further item, cabinets, to its product mix. The company does not, however, intend to add to its production resources. Each cabinet requires 2 man-hours of assembly time, 4 man-hours of finishing time, and 1 man-hour of inspection time. It is believed that each cabinet made can be sold at a profit of $20. Should the company manufacture cabinets if its only objective is to maximize total profit?

4.6. Consider the blending problem of the processed food company. In Section 4.5 we saw that holding the other problem specifications fixed at their original values, a blend of $2\frac{2}{3}$ grams of additive I and $6\frac{2}{3}$ grams of additive II is optimal for any price per gram of additive I in the range from $1\frac{1}{2}$ to 6 cents. Show graphically the situation as the price falls below $1\frac{1}{2}$ cents.

4.7. In the blending problem of the processed food company, examine the sensitivity of the optimal solution to variations in the price of additive II, when all other specifications are set at their original levels.

(a) Show that the optimal solution is to blend $2\frac{2}{3}$ grams of additive I and $6\frac{2}{3}$ grams of additive II, provided price per gram of additive II is in the range from 1 to 4 cents.

(b) Confirm graphically your conclusions of (a).

4.8. Keeping the feasible region for the processed food company problem fixed at its initial state, consider the possibility of variation in the prices of *both* additives. Show that the optimal solution is to blend $2\frac{2}{3}$ grams of additive I and $6\frac{2}{3}$ grams of additive II whenever the price per gram of additive I is both no less than half and no more than twice that of additive II.

4.9. In section 4.5 it was shown that for the processed food company, each additional percentage point increase in the vitamin C standard, within a range from 60% to

90% of U.S.D.A. requirements, raises cost by $\frac{4}{15}$ cent. Through a graphical analysis, justify the need for the lower bound of this range. Explain how the position changes when the vitamin C standard is reduced below 60% of U.S.D.A. requirements.

4.10. (a) Using the simplex tableau, show for the processed food company, that each additional percentage point increase in the vitamin D standard, within a range from 55% to 100% of U.S.D.A. requirements, raises cost by $\frac{1}{15}$ cent, holding the other problem specifications at their initial settings.

(b) Produce graphical analyses justifying the need for both limits of this range. Explain how the position changes when the vitamin D standard is raised above 100% of U.S.D.A. requirements, and when it is lowered to less than 55% of U.S.D.A. requirements.

(c) Holding the other problem specifications fixed at their original values, how much is saved by the company for an extra percentage point reduction in the vitamin D standard below 55% of U.S.D.A. requirements?

4.11. The processed food company has the opportunity to employ in its blend a third additive. Each gram of this additive contains 5% of U.S.D.A. requirements for vitamin A, 10% for vitamin C, 15% for vitamin D, and 5% for iron. This additive would cost the company 3 cents per gram. Should the company use the new additive if its only objective is to produce, at the lowest possible cost, a blend meeting all its standards?

4.12. Suppose that the processed food company has available the two original additives, and also the third additive described in the previous exercise.

(a) Set up, and solve through the simplex algorithm, the new constrained minimization problem for this company.

(b) Analyze the effects on the optimal solution to the new problem of individual variations in the prices of the three additives.

(c) Find the cost to the company of a percentage point increase in the standards for each of vitamin A, vitamin C, and iron, and determine the ranges in which these results are valid.

4.13. A company manufactures two products, each of which needs time on four different machines. The company wants to determine the product output mix which yields maximum possible profits, given the specifications in the following table.

TOTAL MACHINE-HOURS AVAILABLE	MACHINE	MACHINE-HOURS PER UNIT	
		PRODUCT I	PRODUCT II
600	A	2	1
400	B	1	1
500	C	1	2
1000	D	3	2
PROFIT PER UNIT ($)		50	40

(a) Use the simplex algorithm to derive the optimal solution to this problem and verify your findings graphically.

(b) Analyze the effects on the optimal solution of individual variations in the profits per unit of the two products. Produce a graphical analysis to verify your results.

(c) Find the shadow price for a machine-hour for each of the four machines.

(d) Use the final tableau of the simplex algorithm solution to determine the ranges in which these shadow prices are valid. Illustrate your results graphically.

4.14. A manufacturing company produces three products, each of which must be processed through four departments. The aim is to find the product mix yielding the maximum possible profit, given the specifications shown in the table below.

TOTAL MAN-HOURS AVAILABLE	DEPARTMENT	MAN-HOURS PER WEEK		
		PRODUCT I	PRODUCT II	PRODUCT III
6000	A	1	3	2
4000	B	2	1	2
3000	C	2	1	1
2000	D	1	1	1
PROFIT PER UNIT ($)		2	3	2

(a) Use the simplex algorithm to derive the optimal solution to this problem.
(b) Analyze the effects on the optimal solution of individual variations in the profits per unit of the three products.
(c) Find the shadow price of a man-hour in each of the four departments.
(d) Determine the ranges in which the shadow prices are valid.

4.15. A company produces three brands of perfumed bath oils. Each brand contains a combination of three of four perfume essences. The quantities required per bottle are set out in the following table.

BATH OIL	QUANTITY OF PERFUME ESSENCE (IN OUNCES)			
	1	2	3	4
A	0.2	0.4	0	0.2
B	0.5	0	0.2	0.1
C	0	0.2	0.3	0.3

Quantities of these essences are in limited supply for the coming week. Supplies are shown in the following table

AVAILABILITY OF ESSENCE (IN OUNCES)			
1	2	3	4
200	200	150	150

The profits per bottle (in dollars) for the three bath oils are:

PROFIT PER BOTTLE ($)		
A	B	C
1.80	1.50	1.20

(a) If the objective is to maximize total profits, find the optimal solution.

(b) Analyze the effects on the optimal solution of individual variations in the profits per bottle of the three bath oils.

(c) Find the shadow price per ounce for each of the four essences.

(d) Determine the ranges in which the shadow prices are valid.

4.16. Find the dual of the linear programming problem

$$\text{Maximize} \quad x_1 + 2x_2 + 3x_3$$
$$\text{subject to} \quad 2x_1 + x_2 \le 400$$
$$3x_1 + x_3 \le 600$$
$$x_1, x_2, x_3 \ge 0$$

4.17. Find the dual of the constrained minimization problem

$$\text{Minimize} \quad x_1 + 3x_2 + 2x_3$$
$$\text{subject to} \quad x_1 + x_2 + x_3 \ge 100$$
$$2x_1 + x_3 \ge 120$$
$$x_1, x_2, x_3 \ge 0$$

4.18. Consider the constrained maximization problem

$$\text{Maximize} \quad x_1 + x_2$$
$$\text{subject to} \quad 2x_1 + 3x_2 \le 960$$
$$4x_1 + x_2 \le 600$$
$$x_1, x_2 \ge 0$$

(a) Use the simplex algorithm to find the optimal solution to this problem.

(b) Write down the dual problem.

(c) Using the results of (a), find the optimal solution to the dual problem.

(d) Verify your answer to (c) by solving the dual problem through the simplex algorithm.

4.19. Consider again the problem of Exercise 4.12, where the processed food company has available for its blend three additives.

(a) Write down the dual problem.

(b) Using your solution to the primal problem, find the optimal solution to the dual problem.

(c) Verify your answer to (b) by solving the dual problem directly through the simplex algorithm.

4.20. Given the constrained minimization problem

$$\text{Minimize} \quad 2x_1 + 3x_2$$
$$\text{subject to} \quad x_1 + x_2 \ge 80$$
$$x_1 + 2x_2 \ge 130$$
$$x_1 \ge 20$$
$$x_2 \ge 40$$

(a) Use the simplex algorithm to find the optimal solution to this problem.

(b) Write down the dual problem.

(c) Based on the results in (a), find the optimal solution to the dual problem.

(d) Verify your answer to (d) by solving the dual problem directly through the simplex algorithm.

4.21. Consider again the linear programming problem of Exercise 4.13.

(a) Write down the dual problem.

(b) Based on your solution to the primal problem, find the optimal solution to the dual problem.

(c) Verify your answer to (b) by directly solving, through the simplex algorithm, the dual problem.

4.22. Return to the constrained maximization problem of Exercise 4.14.

(a) Write down the dual problem.

(b) Using your solution to the primal problem, find the optimal solution to the dual.

(c) Confirm your answer in (b) by solving directly, through the simplex algorithm, the dual problem.

4.23. For the constrained optimization problem of Exercise 4.15

(a) Write down the dual problem.

(b) Given your solution to the primal problem, obtain the optimal solution to the dual.

(c) Confirm the answer to (b) by directly solving the dual problem through use of the simplex algorithm.

4.24. Consider again the problem of the distributor of television sets of Exercise 3.13.

(a) Provide a full sensitivity analysis of the optimal solution to this problem.

(b) Write out the dual problem, and find and interpret its optimal solution.

4.25. Consider again the problem of Exercise 3.39, where a company must schedule its telephone operators.

(a) Provide a full sensitivity analysis of the optimal solution to this problem.

(b) Write out the dual problem, and find and interpret its optimal solution.

4.26. Refer to the modified product mix problem of the office furnishings company of Section 4.6.

(a) Show that with all other specifications at their initial levels, the same solution remains optimal provided that profit per desk is at least $20.

(b) Show that the shadow price of zero for finishing time is valid provided that finishing time available is at least 500 man-hours.

(c) Show that for any level of inspection time in the range from 50 man-hours to 105 man-hours, with all other specifications at their original levels, each extra man-hour of inspection time adds $30 to total profit. Discuss the position when

(i) Inspection time available is less than 50 man-hours.

(ii) Inspection time available is more than 105 man-hours.

(d) Write down the dual of this problem, and find and interpret its optimal solution.

computer solution of linear programming problems, formulation, and applications

CHAPTER FIVE

5.1. USING THE COMPUTER TO SOLVE LINEAR PROGRAMMING PROBLEMS

In Chapter 2 we saw how graphical procedures could be used to solve linear programming problems with only two decision variables. For more than two decision variables, this approach is impracticable, but, as was illustrated in Chapter 3, it is possible to attack such problems through the use of the simplex algorithm. For relatively small problems, the simplex algorithm computations are fairly easily manageable, but, for larger problems, the arithmetic burden can become very heavy, and of course the chance of arithmetic errors very high. In many real-world business applications, linear programming problems involving large numbers of decision variables and constraints are formulated. Because of the widespread demand for solutions to linear programming problems, many computer programs have been written to allow the analysis of such problems. Access to such a program greatly extends the range of problems that can be handled, and has been responsible for the growth in the use of linear programming to solve practical business problems. In this chapter we will illustrate the use of linear programming computer algorithms, and discuss their application to a range of business problems.

The computer programs available differ in terms of the format for entering problem specifications, program mode (batch or interactive), output format, and the options available to the user. To implement such a program, it is necessary to specify in a designated form, the objective function, with instructions as to whether this is to be maximized or minimized, and the constraints (though the nonnegativity constraints are typically assumed, and therefore need not be formally stated).

In this chapter, we will discuss the implementation of one widely used program, LINDO (Linear Interactive Discrete Optimizer).[1] The output of the program available to the reader may differ somewhat from that of LINDO, but the differences are not likely to be very substantial.

We will illustrate the program output through the product mix problem of the office furnishings company discussed in the previous three chapters. Of course, this small problem can be comfortably handled without recourse to a computer program. It does, however, provide us with a convenient basis for interpreting the computer output in the context of our earlier manually derived results.

The office furnishings company manufactures desks and bookcases, with respective unit profits $30 and $20. Weekly output potential is restricted, as man-hours available for assembly, finishing, and inspection are, respectively, 640, 540, and 100. Each desk requires 8 hours of assembly time, 4 hours of finishing time, and one hour of inspection time, while hourly time requirements in these three departments for a bookcase are, respectively, 4, 6, and one.

Table 5.1 shows the LINDO program output for this problem. The LINDO program is interactive. Information supplied by the user is printed in lower case, while the program output is in capitals. The user specifies the constrained optimization problem in algebraic form. Here we have labeled the numbers of desks and bookcases by $X1$ and $X2$, respectively. Notice that since many printers do not have the symbol $\leq$, the program uses $<=$. The instruction "look" requests the printout of the problem specification, while "all" demands the whole of that specification. Note that the program has labeled the assembly, finishing, and inspection constraints $R2$, $R3$, and $R4$.

Following the instruction "go," details of the problem solution are printed out. The algorithm iterates to an optimal solution, which in this case was found at the second step. The OBJECTIVE FUNCTION VALUE tells us that at the optimal solution, profit per week is $2600.

The next part of the output shows the values of the decision variables at the optimal solution. Hence, it can be seen that the best strategy is a product mix of 60 desks and 40 bookcases. Also shown under the heading REDUCED COST, is the amount by which the profit per unit for a decision variable must be improved before that variable enters the optimal solution with a nonzero value. In this case, since the optimal solution dictates the production of positive numbers of both desks and bookcases, these reduced costs are necessarily zero.

The following portion of output gives the values of the slack or surplus variables at the optimum solution. Here, the only slack is in finishing ($R3$), where 60 of the available man-hours will not be used. Also printed out are the DUAL PRICES (or, shadow prices) associated with the three constraints. In the

---

[1] The LINDO program is described in detail in L. Schrage, *Linear Programming Models with LINDO* (Palo Alto, Calif.: The Scientific Press, 1981), and L. Schrage, *User's Manual for LINDO* (Palo Alto, Calif.: The Scientific Press, 1981).

context of our maximization problem, these are the values of the contributions made to profit by additional units of each resource, when the amounts of all other resources are held fixed at their original levels. Thus, adding one man-hour of assembly time, with everything else remaining fixed, increases weekly profit by $2.50, while a $10 increase in profit follows from adding a man-hour of inspection time. Since at the optimal solution, there is positive slack in assembly, the addition of further resources there alone will add nothing to total profits.

At this stage the user is asked whether further sensitivity analysis is required. An answer in the affirmative produces the remainder of the output shown in Table 5.1. This section is headed RANGES IN WHICH THE BASIS IS UN-CHANGED, and is in two portions.

The first portion examines the sensitivity of the optimal solution to changes in the objective function coefficients. The column CURRENT COEF shows, for each decision variable, the associated coefficient in the objective function. For our product mix problem, these are the unit profits. The columns ALLOW-ABLE INCREASE and ALLOWABLE DECREASE show by how much a coefficient can be increased or reduced, when the other problem specifications are fixed at their initial values, without changing the values of the decision var-

TABLE 5.1 LINDO program output for the product mix problem of the office furnishings company.

```
max 30 x1 + 20 x2
st
8 x1 + 4 x2 < = 640
4 x1 + 6 x2 < = 540
x1 + x2 < = 100
end
look
ROW
all


MAXIMIZE

OBJ  )    30 X1 + 20 X2

SUBJECT TO

    R2  )    8 X1 + 4 X2 < = 640
    R3  )    4 X1 + 6 X2 < = 540
    R4  )      X1 +   X2 < = 100

       go


    LP OPTIMUM FOUND AT STEP 2
```

TABLE 5.1 (*Continued*)

OBJECTIVE FUNCTION VALUE

1)   2600.00000

VARIABLE	VALUE	REDUCED COST
X1	60.000000	0.000000
X2	40.000000	0'000000

ROW	SLACK OR SURPLUS	DUAL PRICES
R2)	0.000000	2.500000
R3)	60.000000	0.000000
R4)	0.000000	10.000000

NO. ITERATIONS = 2

DO RANGE (SENSITIVITY) ANALYSIS?

        yes

RANGES IN WHICH THE BASIS IS UNCHANGED

OBJ COEFFICIENT RANGES

VARIABLE	CURRENT COEF	ALLOWABLE INCREASE	ALLOWABLE DECREASE
X1	30.000000	10.000000	10.000000
X2	20.000000	10.000000	5.000000

RIGHTHAND SIDE RANGES

ROW	CURRENT RHS	ALLOWABLE INCREASE	ALLOWABLE DECREASE
R2	640.00000	160.00000	120.00000
R3	540.00000	INFINITY	60.00000
R4	100.00000	7.50000	20.00000

iables at the optimal solution. It can be seen, therefore, that any value for profit per desk in the range from $20 to $40, with all other problem parameters set at their initial values, yields the same optimal product mix. Also, this solution remains optimal for all values of profit per bookcase between $15 and $30 if the other problem specifications are unchanged. This confirms our findings in Section 4.2.

The final segment of output provides the ranges in which the dual prices are valid. For this particular problem, we calculated these quantities in Section 4.3. The column headed CURRENT RHS shows, for each constraint, the original right-hand side in the algebraic specification. For the office furnishings company, these are the available man-hours in the three departments. We see, then, that each extra man-hour of assembly time capacity adds $2.50 to total profit, provided capacity in assembly is between $640 - 120 = 520$ and $640 + 160 = 800$ man-hours, with all other problem specifications kept at their original levels. Similarly, if inspection time capacity is between 80 and 107.5 man-hours, an additional man-hour adds $10 to profit. Finally, provided available finishing time is at least 480 man-hours, adding further capacity does not change maximum achievable profit if the other problem specifications remain at their original levels.

APPLICATION TO A CONSTRAINED MINIMIZATION PROBLEM

Linear programming computer programs can also be employed to analyze constrained minimization problems, as we will now illustrate through an example met in the previous three chapters. A processed food company has two additives containing quantities of vitamins A, C, and D, and iron. Given the problem specifications reproduced in Table 5.2, the aim is to find the lowest cost blend.

The LINDO program output is shown in Table 5.3, from which it can be seen that the cheapest possible blend meeting all the requirements costs 25.333333 cents, and uses 2.666667 grams of additive I and 6.666667 grams of additive II. Since the values of the decision variables at the optimum solution are greater than zero, the associated "reduced costs" are zero.

TABLE 5.2 Blending problem specifications for the processed food company.

	MINIMUM % U.S.D.A. REQUIREMENTS IN PRODUCT	% U.S.D.A. REQUIREMENTS PER GRAM	
		ADDITIVE I	ADDITIVE II
Vitamin A	80	40	0
Vitamin C	80	5	10
Vitamin D	60	10	5
Iron	80	0	20
PRICE (IN CENTS) PER GRAM		2	3

The values of the surplus variables at the optimum solution indicate that the minimum vitamin A standard is exceeded by 26.666667 percentage points, while that for iron is exceeded by 53.333333 percentage points. The other two standards are met precisely. Also it can be seen that there are two nonzero dual prices. Notice that their values are negative. The implication is that with all other specifications fixed at their original levels, a one percentage point increase in the vitamin C requirement will lead to a *reduction* in profit—that is, an increase in cost—of 0.2666667 cent. Similarly, raising the vitamin D standard by one percentage point will cost an additional 0.066667 cent.

The next portion of output analyzes the effects of changes in the objective function. The current optimal solution will remain unchanged at any cost per gram of additive I ranging from 1.5 to 6 cents, when the cost per gram of additive II is 3 cents, or for any cost per gram of additive II in the range from 1 to 4 cents, when the cost per gram of additive I is held at 2 cents.

TABLE 5.3 LINDO program output for the blending problem of the processed food company.

```
MINIMIZE
OBJ   )   2 X1  3 X2
SUBJECT TO
R2   )    40 X1 > = 80
R3   )     5 X1 + 10 X2 > = 80
R4   )    10 X1 +  5 X2 > = 60
R5   )    20 X2 > = 80
END
```

LP OPTIMUM FOUND AT STEP 4

OBJECTIVE FUNCTION VALUE

1)   25.333333

VARIABLE	VALUE	REDUCED COST
X1	2.666667	0.00000
X2	6.666667	0.00000

ROW		SLACK OR SURPLUS	DUAL PRICES
R2	)	26.666667	0.000000
R3	)	0.000000	-.266667
R4	)	0.000000	-.066667
R5	)	53.333333	0.000000

TABLE 5.3 *(Continued)*

```
NO, ITERATIONS = 4

            RANGES IN WHICH THE BASIS IS UNCHANGED

                OBJ COEFFICIENT RANGES

                    CURRENT      ALLOWABLE      ALLOWABLE
        VARIABLE      COEF        INCREASE       DECREASE

          X1         2,000000     4,000000        ,500000
          X2         3,000000     1,000000       2,000000

                RIGHTHAND SIDE RANGES

                    CURRENT      ALLOWABLE      ALLOWABLE
        ROW          RHS         INCREASE       DECREASE

          R2        80,000000    26,666667       INFINITY
          R3        80,000000    10,000000      20,000000
          R4        60,000000    40,000000       5,000000
          R5        80,000000    53,333333       INFINITY
```

Finally, we see the ranges in which the shadow prices are valid. Thus, it follows that:

1. For any standard up to 106.666667% of U.S.D.A. requirements for vitamin A, a one percentage point increase in the standard can be achieved at no additional cost, when the other three standards are fixed at their initial levels.
2. For any standard from 60% to 90% of U.S.D.A. requirements for vitamin C, a one percentage point increase in the standard costs an additional 0.266667 cent, when the other three standards are fixed at their initial levels.
3. For any standard from 55% to 100% of U.S.D.A. requirements for vitamin D, a one percentage point increase in the standard costs an extra 0.066667 cent, when the other three standards are fixed at their initial levels.
4. For any standard up to 133.333333% of U.S.D.A. requirements for iron, a one percentage point increase in the standard is achieveable at no extra cost, provided the other three standards are fixed at their initial levels.

5.2. APPLICATION TO PRODUCTION PLANNING

One of the most common industrial applications of linear programming is to the planning of production schedules. Corporations face, over time, varying demand levels for their products; to some extent, it is possible, using methods to be

TABLE 5.4 Monthly demand for stereo speakers.

	SMALL	LARGE
January	400	200
February	500	320
March	550	400

discussed in Chapter 12, for example, to forecast future demand. It should there-fore be possible to plan production schedules such that anticipated demand can be met. A number of considerations are relevant to the choice of a specific pro-duction plan. First, it may be impossible to sharply increase production from one month to the next. It may be feasible, at additional cost, to achieve addi-tional production through overtime working, but capacity constraints will limit what is possible. Next, any output that cannot be sold at once will have to be held in inventory, and the firm will thus incur storage and other carrying costs on this inventory.[2] Although there may also be various economic reasons argu-ing in favor of a production schedule that is as smooth as possible, we will illustrate the problem in this section through an example which takes into ac-count only production costs and constraints, and inventory holding costs.

A company produces stereo speakers of two sizes and anticipates demand for the first three months of the year at the levels shown in Table 5.4. Over this short time horizon, it is not possible to increase plant capacity, and monthly production is constrained by that capacity. A production manager has computed that each month, during normal working time, capacity dictates that:

2(Number of Small Speakers) + Number of Large Speakers $\leq$ 1200   (5.1)

However, some overtime can be worked, production during these additional hours each month being constrained by

2(Number of Small Speakers) + Number of Large Speakers $\leq$ 240   (5.2)

Next, we must specify the costs involved with alternative possible produc-tion plans. For normal working time, it costs $60 to produce each small speaker and $80 for each large speaker. However, for overtime working, these figures increase to $70 and $95, respectively. Further, it is computed that for each month a small speaker is held in inventory an additional cost of $3 is incurred,

---

[2] We will discuss inventory costs in much more detail in Chapter 14.

TABLE 5.5 Unit production and inventory costs (in dollars) for stereo speakers.

	SMALL	LARGE
Normal Production Cost	60	80
Overtime Production Cost	70	95
Monthly Inventory Cost	3	5

while the corresponding figure for large speakers is $5. This information is summarized in Table 5.5.

The objective of this corporation is to find the lowest-cost, feasible production schedule that will allow demand to be fully satisfied in each of the three months. There are a number of ways of specifying this problem. One approach is illustrated in Table 5.6, where we introduce twenty-four decision variables, $x_1, x_2, \ldots, x_{24}$. Each one of these refers to the quantity of one or the other speaker to be produced in a given month, either in normal time or overtime, and to be sold in a specific month. Thus, for example, x_{17} is the number of small speakers that are to be made in normal time in February, for sale the following month. Notice, of course, that it is not possible to manufacture speakers one month for sale in an earlier month.

In Table 5.7 we set out the unit costs associated with each of these decision variables. These costs will depend on whether production is in normal working hours or in overtime, and on the length of time a speaker is held in inventory before it is sold. For example, for each small speaker made in normal time in February, for sale in March, total cost is $63, made up of $60 production cost, plus an additional $3 for one month of inventory holding.

TABLE 5.6 Decision variables (numbers of speakers) for the production scheduling problem of the manufacturer of stereo speakers.

PRODUCTION		SALE					
		JANUARY		FEBRUARY		MARCH	
		SMALL	LARGE	SMALL	LARGE	SMALL	LARGE
January:	Normal Small	x_1		x_5		x_9	
	Overtime Small	x_2		x_6		x_{10}	
	Normal Large		x_3		x_7		x_{11}
	Overtime Large		x_4		x_8		x_{12}
February:	Normal Small			x_{13}		x_{17}	
	Overtime Small			x_{14}		x_{18}	
	Normal Large				x_{15}		x_{19}
	Overtime Large				x_{16}		x_{20}
March:	Normal Small					x_{21}	
	Overtime Small					x_{22}	
	Normal Large						x_{23}
	Overtime Large						x_{24}

TABLE 5.7 Unit costs (in dollars) associated with decision variables for the production scheduling problem of the manufacturer of stereo speakers.

PRODUCTION		SALE				
		JANUARY		FEBRUARY		MARCH
		SMALL	LARGE	SMALL	LARGE	SMALL	LARGE
January:	Normal Small	60		63		66	
	Overtime Small	70		73		76	
	Normal Large		80		85		90
	Overtime Large		95		100		105
February:	Normal Small			60		63	
	Overtime Small			70		73	
	Normal Large				80		85
	Overtime Large				95		100
March:	Normal Small					60	
	Overtime Small					70	
	Normal Large						80
	Overtime Large						95

It follows that the total cost of a solution in which the decision variables take the values $x_1, x_2, \ldots, x_{24}$, is, using Tables 5.6 and 5.7:

$$
\begin{aligned}
C = {} & 60\,x_1 + 70\,x_2 + 80\,x_3 + 95\,x_4 + 63\,x_5 + 73\,x_6 + 85\,x_7 \\
& + 100\,x_8 + 66\,x_9 + 76\,x_{10} + 90\,x_{11} + 105\,x_{12} + 60\,x_{13} \\
& + 70\,x_{14} + 80\,x_{15} + 95\,x_{16} + 63\,x_{17} + 73\,x_{18} + 85\,x_{19} \\
& + 100\,x_{20} + 60\,x_{21} + 70\,x_{22} + 80\,x_{23} + 95\,x_{24}
\end{aligned}
\tag{5.3}
$$

This is the objective function that must be minimized to find the production schedule with the lowest possible total cost.

Next, we must specify the constraints on the decision variables. These are:

(i) $x_1 + x_2 = 400$

(ii) $x_3 + x_4 = 200$

(iii) $x_5 + x_6 + x_{13} + x_{14} = 500$

(iv) $x_7 + x_8 + x_{15} + x_{16} = 320$

(v) $x_9 + x_{10} + x_{17} + x_{18} + x_{21} + x_{22} = 550$

(vi) $x_{11} + x_{12} + x_{19} + x_{20} + x_{23} + x_{24} = 400$

(vii) $2(x_1 + x_5 + x_9) + (x_3 + x_7 + x_{11}) \leq 1{,}200$

(viii) $2(x_2 + x_6 + x_{10}) + (x_4 + x_8 + x_{12}) \leq 240$

(ix) $2(x_{13} + x_{17}) + (x_{15} + x_{19}) \leq 1{,}200$

(x) $2(x_{14} + x_{18}) + (x_{16} + x_{20}) \leq 240$

(xi) $2x_{21} + x_{23} \leq 1{,}200$

(xii) $2x_{22} + x_{24} \leq 240$

(xiii) $x_i \geq 0 \ (i = 1, 2, \ldots, 24)$

The first six of these restrictions require that the quantities of speakers of each type sold in any month must be equal to the quantity demanded. For example, the number of small speakers sold in February is $x_5 + x_6 + x_{13} + x_{14}$, which must be equal to the quantity demanded. Thus, from Table 5.4, the constraint (iii) follows. The next six constraints, two for each month in turn, express the limitations on production possibilities for normal time and overtime working. Thus, constraint (vii) follows from the fact that in January, during normal working hours, a total of $(x_1 + x_5 + x_9)$ small speakers and $(x_3 + x_7 + x_{11})$ large speakers are to be made. Then (vii) results from (5.1). Similarly, the constraint (viii) refers to January overtime production, and follows from (5.2). Finally, (xiii) is the usual nonnegativity constraint, since the decision variables must all be at least zero in any feasible solution.

The linear programming problem that must be solved in order to find the lowest cost production schedule is the minimization of the objective function (5.3), subject to the constraints (i)–(xiii). Solution of a problem of this size through manual application of the simplex algorithm is extremely time consuming. However, problems of this size are very easily managed by computer programs. Using the CYBER system at the University of Illinois, the problem analysis was completed in seven-tenths of a second of execution time. Part of the computer program output is displayed in Table 5.8.

The lowest cost feasible solution to our problem entails a total cost of $162,120. The optimal solutions for the twenty-four decision variables are set out in a more readily digested form in Table 5.9. We see that this solution calls for overtime working only in March, when 110 small speakers are to be made through overtime working. All large speakers are to be manufactured in the months in which they will be sold, while 100 small speakers made in January, and 40 in February, will be carried in inventory for a month. The final column of Table 5.9 shows production totals for each type of speaker in normal hours and overtime for the three months.

Since the first six constraints are equalities, there can be no associated slack or surplus in any feasible solution. The three nonzero slack variables in the optimal solution provide a measure of unused overtime capacity in January, February, and March. Notice that in each month, normal time working capacity is fully exhausted in the optimal solution.

The REDUCED COSTS, given in Table 5.8, show for each decision variable, the amount by which its associated unit cost in the objective function must be reduced before the variable enters the optimal solution with a nonzero value. These will generally be greater than zero. For example, the reduced cost of $6 is associated with the variable x_2. The implication is that it will not pay to produce in overtime in January small speakers, for sale in that month, unless the unit cost can be reduced from $70 to $64 or less.

Notice that the variable x_9 takes the value zero in our optimal solution, but that its associated reduced cost is zero. This implies that nothing would be lost by producing, in January for sale in March, small speakers in normal working hours. This suggests that the problem has multiple optimal solutions. Looking at the solution displayed in Table 5.9, a moment's thought should convince you

TABLE 5.8 LINDO program output for the production scheduling problem of the manufacturer of stereo speakers.

MINIMIZE

```
OBJ  )  60 X1 + 70 X2 + 80 X3 + 95 X4 + 63 X5 + 73 X6 + 85 X7
        + 100 X8 + 66 X9 + 76 X10 + 90 X11 + 105 X12 + 60 X13
        + 70 X14 + 80 X15 + 95 X16 + 63 X17 + 73 X18 + 85 X19
        + 100 X20 + 60 X21 + 70 X22 + 80 X23 + 95 X24
```

SUBJECT TO

```
R2   )  X1 + X2 = 400
R3   )  X3 + X4 = 200
R4   )  X5 + X6 + X13 + X14 = 500
R5   )  X7 + X8 + X15 + X16 = 320
R6   )  X9 + X10 + X17 + X18 + X21 + X22 = 550
R7   )  X11 + X12 + X19 + X20 + X23 + X24 = 400
R8   )  2 X1 + X3 + 2 X5 + X7 + 2 X9 + X11 < = 1200
R9   )  2 X2 + X4 + 2 X6 + X8 + 2 X10 + X12 < = 240
R10  )  2 X13 + X15 + 2 X17 + X19 < = 1200
R11  )  2 X14 + X16 + 2 X18 + X20 ≤ = 240
R12  )  2 X21 + X23 < = 1200
R13  )  2 X22 + X24 < = 240
END
```

LP OPTIMUM FOUND AT STEP 12

OBJECTIVE FUNCTION VALUE

1)   162120.000

VARIABLE	VALUE	REDUCED COST
X1	400.000000	0.000000
X2	0.000000	6.000000
X3	200.000000	0.000000
X4	0.000000	13.000000
X5	100.000000	0.000000
X6	0.000000	6.000000
X7	0.000000	3.500000
X8	0.000000	16.500000
X9	0.000000	0.000000
X10	0.000000	6.000000
X11	0.000000	7.000000

TABLE 5.8 (*Continued*)

VARIABLE	VALUE	REDUCED COST
X12	0.000000	20.000000
X13	400.000000	0.000000
X14	0.000000	3.000000
X15	320.000000	0.000000
X16	0.000000	11.500000
X17	40.000000	0.000000
X18	0.000000	3.000000
X19	0.000000	3.500000
X20	0.000000	15.000000
X21	400.000000	0.000000
X22	110.000000	0.000000
X23	400.000000	0.000000
X24	0.000000	10.000000

ROW	SLACK OR SURPLUS	DUAL PRICES
R2)	0.000000	-64.000000
R3)	0.000000	-82.000000
R4)	0.000000	-67.000000
R5)	0.000000	-83.000000
R6)	0.000000	-70.000000
R7)	0.000000	-85.000000
R8)	0.000000	2.000000
R9)	240.000000	0.000000
R10)	0.000000	3.500000
R11)	240.000000	0.000000
R12)	0.000000	5.000000
R13)	20.000000	0.000000

NO. ITERATIONS = 12

RANGES IN WHICH THE BASIS IS UNCHANGED

VARIABLE	OBJ COEFFICIENT RANGES		
	CURRENT COEF	ALLOWABLE INCREASE	ALLOWABLE DECREASE
X1	60.000000	6.000000	INFINITY
X2	70.000000	INFINITY	6.000000
X3	80.000000	13.000000	INFINITY
X4	95.000000	INFINITY	13.000000

TABLE 5.8 (*Continued*)

VARIABLE	CURRENT COEF	ALLOWABLE INCREASE	ALLOWABLE DECREASE
X5	63.000000	0.000000	6.000000
X6	73.000000	INFINITY	6.000000
X7	85.000000	INFINITY	3.500000
X8	100.000000	INFINITY	16.500000
X9	66.000000	INFINITY	0.000000
X10	76.000000	INFINITY	6.000000
X11	90.000000	INFINITY	7.000000
X12	105.000000	INFINITY	20.000000
X13	60.000000	3.000000	0.000000
X14	70.000000	INFINITY	3.000000
X15	80.000000	3.500000	INFINITY
X16	95.000000	INFINITY	11.500000
X17	63.000000	0.000000	3.000000
X18	73.000000	INFINITY	3.000000
X19	85.000000	INFINITY	3.500000
X20	100.000000	INFINITY	15.000000
X21	60.000000	10.000000	7.000000
X22	70.000000	3.000000	4.000000
X23	80.000000	3.500000	INFINITY
X24	95.000000	INFINITY	10.000000

RIGHTHAND SIDE RANGES

ROW	CURRENT RHS	ALLOWABLE INCREASE	ALLOWABLE DECREASE
R2	400.000000	10.000000	110.000000
R3	200.000000	20.000000	200.000000
R4	500.000000	10.000000	110.000000
R5	320.000000	20.000000	220.000000
R6	550.000000	10.000000	110.000000
R7	400.000000	20.000000	220.000000
R8	1200.000000	220.000000	20.000000
R9	240.000000	INFINITY	240.000000
R10	1200.000000	220.000000	20.000000
R11	240.000000	INFINITY	240.000000
R12	1200.000000	220.000000	20.000000
R13	240.000000	INFINITY	20.000000

TABLE 5.9 Values of decision variables at the optimal solution to the production scheduling problem of the manufacturer of stereo speakers.

PRODUCTION	SALE						
	JANUARY		FEBRUARY		MARCH		
	SMALL	LARGE	SMALL	LARGE	SMALL	LARGE	TOTALS
January: Normal Small	400		100		0		500
Overtime Small	0		0		0		0
Normal Large		200		0		0	200
Overtime Large		0		0		0	0
February: Normal Small			400		40		440
Overtime Small			0		0		0
Normal Large				320		0	320
Overtime Large				0		0	0
March: Normal Small					400		400
Overtime Small					110		110
Normal Large						400	400
Overtime Large						0	0
Totals	400	200	500	320	550	400	

that this is so. Since 40 previously made small speakers are to be carried forward for sale in March, it is a matter of indifference, given the structure of our solution, whether these were made in January or February. Thus, without altering the total cost of the solution, we can increase x_9 by as much as 40, while reducing x_5, increasing x_{13}, and reducing x_{17} by the same amount.

The dual prices for the six equality constraints ($R2$–$R7$) show the effect on "profit"—that is, the negative of cost—of adding one to the right-hand side of these constraints. Thus, for example, the first of these ($R2$) implies that production of an extra small speaker for sale in January will add $64 to total costs. The dual prices for the six inequality constraints indicate the value of increasing normal and overtime capacity in each month. We see ($R12$) that most valuable would be an increase of normal time capacity in March. Each unit by which

$$2(\text{Number of Small Speakers}) + \text{Number of Large Speakers}$$

can be raised is worth $5.

The penultimate segment of Table 5.8 shows the amount by which an individual objective function coefficient can be changed, with all other specifications unchanged, without altering the optimal solution. For example, referring to the result for x_1, it is seen that the same solution will result for any unit cost that is at most $66 for producing small speakers in normal working time in January for sale in that month. Similarly, referring to the result for x_{21}, the same optimal solution follows for any unit cost from $53 to $70 for producing small speakers in normal working time in March for sale in that month.

The final segment of Table 5.8 shows the ranges in which the dual prices are valid. For example, for constraint $R2$, we find that the production of an additional small speaker for sale in January will add $64 to total costs for any production level between 290 and 410. Similarly, from $R12$, it follows that the shadow price of \$5 for normal time capacity in March applies in the range

$$1180 \leq 2(\text{Number of Small Speakers}) + \text{Number of Large Speakers} \leq 1420$$

5.3. LABOR SCHEDULING

An increasingly widespread application of linear programming methods is to the assignment of workers to tasks. This possibility arises when employees can work one of several shifts, or have the skills to work in more than one department of a company. In previous chapters of this book, and again in the first section of this chapter, we considered the product mix problem of an office furnishings company. Our analyses were based on the assumption that manpower resources in each of three departments were fixed. A rather more elaborate problem would have arisen had the company possessed the flexibility to shift some employees from one department to another. We saw that in the optimal solution to that problem, 60 of the available man-hours in finishing were not used. If some of these resources could have been switched to the other two departments, it would have been possible to make more desks and bookcases, and hence generate higher profits. In this section we will consider a problem in which some flexibility in labor assignment is possible.

A company manufactures four types of drugs, and, at the beginning of each month, must decide how much of each drug to produce and how to allocate its labor resources among the three departments involved in the production process. Table 5.10 shows some of the relevant specifications for the coming month. An order from an important customer dictates that at least 1000 pounds of drug B must be produced, while, since a high level of inventory is already on hand, no more than 500 pounds of drug D are needed. As we have set it out so far, our problem is of the standard product mix type. Denoting by x_1, x_2, x_3, and x_4 production quantities (in pounds) of drugs A, B, C, and D, the objective function to be maximized is

$$\text{Total Profit} = 10x_1 + 12x_2 + 13x_3 + 14x_4 \qquad (5.4)$$

Indeed, if labor resources in the three departments were fixed, we could simply maximize the objective function (5.4) subject to three capacity constraints, plus the two production limits specified in Table 5.10. However, the drugs company has some freedom in the allocation of its labor resources among the three departments. This capability is set out in Table 5.11. A total of 40,000 man-hours is available, of which the departmental allocation of 28,000 man-hours are fixed. However 4000 man-hours are available for allocation to either of departments I or II. We will denote by x_5 and x_6 the respective allocations made from this total. Similarly 3000 man-hours can be allocated between departments I and III, and a further 3000 between departments II and III. Finally, for 2000 man-hours there is the possibility of allocation to any one of the three

TABLE 5.10 Some specifications for the product mix/labor scheduling problem of the drugs company.

DEPARTMENT	DRUG A	DRUG B	DRUG C	DRUG D
	MAN-HOURS PER POUND			
I	2	2	3	3
II	2	3	1	2
III	1	2	2	3
PROFIT PER POUND ($)	10	12	13	14
LIMITS ON PRODUCTION (POUNDS)	None	At Least 1,000	None	At Most 500

departments. Notice that since there is flexibility in determining some labor resource assignments, nine further decision variables, $x_5, x_6, \ldots, x_{13}$ have been created to represent the allocations made. The capacity constraints in the three departments can now be written as:

$$2x_1 + 2x_2 + 3x_3 + 3x_4 \leq 12,000 + x_5 + x_7 + x_{11}$$
$$2x_1 + 3x_2 + x_3 + 2x_4 \leq 7,000 + x_6 + x_9 + x_{12} \quad (5.5)$$
$$x_1 + 2x_2 + 2x_3 + 3x_4 \leq 9,000 + x_8 + x_{10} + x_{13}$$

The left-hand sides of these constraints, which follow from Table 5.10, show man-hour requirements in each department, while the right-hand sides, which are the column totals of Table 5.11, show the available resources.

We are now in a position to set out, in algebraic form, the profit maximization problem of the drugs manufacturer. This is:

Maximize $\quad 10x_1 + 12x_2 + 13x_3 + 14x_4 + 0x_5 + 0x_6 + 0x_7$

$$+ 0x_8 + 0x_9 + 0x_{10} + 0x_{11} + 0x_{12} + 0x_{13}$$

subject to $\quad 2x_1 + 2x_2 + 3x_3 + 3x_4 - x_5 - x_7 - x_{11} \leq 12,000$

$$2x_1 + 3x_2 + x_3 + 2x_4 - x_6 - x_9 - x_{12} \leq 7,000$$

$$x_1 + 2x_2 + 2x_3 + 3x_4 - x_8 - x_{10} - x_{13} \leq 9,000$$

$$x_2 \geq 1,000$$

$$x_4 \leq 500$$

$$x_5 + x_6 \leq 4,000$$

$$x_7 + x_8 \leq 3,000$$

$$x_9 + x_{10} \leq 3,000$$

$$x_{11} + x_{12} + x_{13} \leq 2,000$$

$$x_i \geq 0 \ (i = 1, 2, \ldots, 13)$$

TABLE 5.11 Labor resources of drugs company.

AVAILABLE MAN-HOURS		ALLOCATION		
		I	II	III
I	12,000	12,000	0	0
II	7,000	0	7,000	0
III	9,000	0	0	9,000
I or II	4,000	x_5	x_6	0
I or III	3,000	x_7	0	x_8
II or III	3,000	0	x_9	x_{10}
I, II or III	2,000	x_{11}	x_{12}	x_{13}
Totals	40,000	$12,000 + x_5 + x_7 + x_{11}$	$7,000 + x_6 + x_9 + x_{12}$	$9,000 + x_8 + x_{10} + x_{13}$

The objective function is simply (5.4), but with the nine labor allocation decision variables added. These variables appear in the objective function with zero coefficients, as they make no *direct* contribution to profit. Their presence, however, emphasizes the fact that we can *simultaneously* determine product mix and labor allocations so as to make total profit as high as possible. The first three constraints are merely algebraic rearrangements of the department capacity constraints (5.5), while the next two set out the production limits in the bottom portion of Table 5.10. The final four constraints (apart from the usual nonnegativity constraints) recognize the limited quantities of flexible labor resources, and follow from Table 5.11.

The computer output for this problem solution is shown in Table 5.12. The maximum attainable profit is $83,500, achieved through the production of 1000 pounds of drug B and 5500 pounds of drug C. The other two drugs are not produced at this optimal solution. The decision variables x_5, x_6, . . . , x_{13} refer to the allocations of flexible labor resources, and their values at the optimal solution can be interpreted by reference to Table 5.11. Thus, of the 4000 man-hours that can be assigned to departments I or II, 2500 should be allocated to the former. Of the 3000 man-hours that can be assigned to departments I or III, 2000 should be allocated to the former. All 3000 man-hours that can be assigned to departments II or III should be allocated to the latter. Finally, all 2000 of the most flexible man-hours are employed in department I. The optimal solution, therefore, calls for a total of 18,500 man-hours in department I, 8500 in department II, and 13,000 in department III.

The only nonzero slack or surplus variable at the optimal solution relates to the requirement that no more than 500 pounds of drug D should be produced. Since the optimal solution requires no production of this drug, the slack of 500 naturally results. As things turn out, this constraint is irrelevant.

Moving on to the sensitivity analysis, the two nonzero REDUCED COSTS for the decision variables show, for drugs A and D, the amounts by which their profit per pound must be increased before it pays to produce them. Thus, all else the same, drug A will not be produced unless its profit per pound is above $10.83333. Similarly, in order for production of drug D to lead to a solution with higher profits, its profit per pound would have to exceed $17.33333. Now, the

TABLE 5.12 LINDO program output for the product mix/labor scheduling problem of the drugs company.

```
MAXIMIZE

OBJ   )    10 X1 + 12 X2 + 13 X3 + 14 X4

SUBJECT TO

R2    )    2 X1 + 2 X2 + 3 X3 + 3 X4 - X5 - X7 - X11 < = 12000
R3    )    2 X1 + 3 X2 + X3 + 2 X4 - X6 - X9 - X12 < = 7000
R4    )    X1 + 2 X2 + 2 X3 + 3 X4 - X8 - X10 - X13 < = 9000
R5    )    X2 > = 1000
R6    )    X4 < = 500
R7    )    X5 + X6 < = 4000
R8    )    X7 + X8 < = 3000
R9    )    X9 + X10 < = 3000
R10   )    X11 + X12 + X13 < = 2000
END
```

```
            LP OPTIMUM FOUND AT STEP 14

              OBJECTIVE VALUE FUNCTION

1)                    83500.000

        VARIABLE          VALUE          REDUCED COST

        X1              0.000000             .833333
        X2           1000.000000            0.000000
        X3           5500.000000            0.000000
        X4              0.000000            3.333333
        X5           2500.000000            0.000000
        X7           2000.000000            0.000000
        X11          2000.000000            0.000000
        X6           1500.000000            0.000000
        X9              0.000000            0.000000
        X12             0.000000            0.000000
        X8           1000.000000            0.000000
        X10          3000.000000            0.000000
        X13             0.000000            0.000000

        ROW        SLACK OR SURPLUS         DUAL PRICES

        R2    )        0.000000              2.166667
        R3    )        0.000000              2.166667
        R4    )        0.000000              2.166667
        R5    )        0.000000             -3.166667
```

TABLE 5.12 (*Continued*)

ROW		SLACK OR SURPLUS	DUAL PRICES
R6	)	500.000000	0.000000
R7	)	0.000000	2.166667
R8	)	0.000000	2.166667
R9	)	0.000000	2.166667
R10	)	0.000000	2.166667

NO ITERATIONS = 14

RANGES IN WHICH THE BASIS IS UNCHANGED

OBJ COEFFICIENT RANGES

VARIABLE	CURRENT COEF	ALLOWABLE INCREASE	ALLOWABLE DECREASE
X1	10.000000	.833333	INFINITY
X2	12.000000	3.166667	INFINITY
X3	13.000000	INFINITY	1.000000
X4	14.000000	3.333333	INFINITY
X5	0.000000	0.000000	.714286
X7	0.000000	0.000000	0.000000
X11	0.000000	INFINITY	0.000000
X6	0.000000	.714286	0.000000
X9	0.000000	0.000000	INFINITY
X12	0.000000	0.000000	INFINITY
X8	0.000000	0.000000	0.000000
X10	0.000000	INFINITY	0.000000
X13	0.000000	0.000000	INFINITY

RIGHTHAND SIDE RANGES

ROW	CURRENT RHS	ALLOWABLE INCREASE	ALLOWABLE DECREASE
R2	12000.000000	6000.000000	3000.000000
R3	7000.000000	1800.000000	3000.000000
R4	9000.000000	1500.000000	3000.000000
R5	1000.000000	1363.636364	818.181818
R6	500.000000	INFINITY	500.000000
R7	4000.000000	6000.000000	3000.000000
R8	3000.000000	15000.000000	3000.000000
R9	3000.000000	1500.000000	3000.000000
R10	2000.000000	6000.000000	2000.000000

decision variables x_9, x_{12}, and x_{13} must necessarily enter the objective function with zero coefficients, so that the associated reduced costs have no meaning in the context of our problem. Notice, however, that the zero values do suggest the possibility of multiple optimal solutions. This is not surprising, as can be seen by referring to Table 5.11. For example, an increase from zero of x_{13}, accompanied by a reduction in x_{11}, an increase in x_7, and a reduction in x_8 of any amount up to 1000 man-hours will leave the total allocations to the three departments, and hence the quantities of drugs that can be produced, unchanged.

The dual prices for constraints $R2$–$R4$ and $R7$–$R10$ show the value of an additional man-hour of each of the seven types of labor. In every case, addition of an extra man-hour will increase profit by $2.16667. Since the constraint $R6$ is not binding at the optimal solution, its associated dual price is zero. The constraint $R5$ requires that at least 1000 pounds of drug B must be produced. We see that for each pound by which this requirement could be reduced, an increase in profit of $3.16667 can be achieved.

Turning, now, to the objective coefficient ranges segment of Table 5.12, the first four rows show profit per pound ranges for the individual drugs such that the optimal solution will be unchanged when the other problem parameters are fixed at their initial values. For example, with the other problem specifications unchanged, we see that the same optimal solution results for any value of profit per pound of drug A up to $10.83333. Since the objective function coefficients associated with the decision variables x_5, x_6, . . . , x_{13} must necessarily be zero, the final nine rows of this portion of the table are meaningless in the context of our problem.

The final segment of Table 5.12 shows the ranges in which the shadow prices are valid. For example, referring to constraint $R7$, it follows that with the other problem parameters set at their initial values, each additional man-hour of labor that can be assigned to either of departments I or II, within the range 1000–10,000 man-hours, adds $2.16667 to maximum achieveable total profit. From the figures for constraint $R5$, it emerges that if the remaining problem parameters are fixed at their original levels, each additional pound of drug B that must be produced, in a range from 181.81818 to 2,363.63636 pounds leads to a reduction of $3.16667 in maximum possible total profit.

The framework we have just discussed is extremely useful in determining month to month production schedules and labor allocations. The specifications can readily be modified in the events of changing labor availability or new minimum and maximum requirements for production levels of individual drugs.

5.4. FINANCIAL PLANNING APPLICATION

In this section we introduce the reader to the application of linear programming to financial planning.[3] Consider a corporation which has the opportunity to

---

[3] Here we are only able to provide a simplified introduction to an important financial planning model developed by S. C. Myers and G. A. Pogue, "A Programmatic Approach to Corporate Financial Management," *Journal of Finance, 29* (1974), 579–599.

invest in two projects. This investment can be financed through new borrowing, the issue of new equity, and the use of cash in hand. This corporation also intends to pay a dividend to equity holders.

Before deciding on an appropriate strategy, management has made the following decisions:

(a) The most that can be invested in the first project is $2 million, and the most that can be invested in the second is $3 million.

(b) Because of the risk involved, the corporation is willing to borrow no more than 30% of the amount to be invested in the first project and 20% of the amount to be invested in the second.

(c) Each dollar invested in the first project is expected to add 6 cents to the net present value of the firm, and each dollar invested in the second is expected to add 8 cents.

(d) Because of the shield provided by corporate taxes, it can be argued[4] that each dollar borrowed adds an amount equal to the corporate tax rate to the net present value of a corporation. Assuming a tax rate of 50%, each dollar borrowed adds 50 cents to net present value.

(e) The corporation has $0.5 million cash in hand, and wants to pay out $1 million in dividends.

(f) The objective is to maximize the net present value of the corporation.

As we have described it, our problem involves four decision variables. These are:

x_1 = amount invested in first project
x_2 = amount invested in second project
x_3 = amount of new borrowing
x_4 = amount of new equity to be issued

where all will be measured in millions of dollars.

THE OBJECTIVE FUNCTION

The objective of this corporation is to maximize net present value. From (c) above, it follows that if x_1 is to be invested in the first project and x_2 in the second, net present value is raised by $0.06x_1 + 0.08x_2$. Further, from (d), if x_3 is borrowed, this will increase net present value by a further $0.5x_3$. The function to be maximized is, then,

$$\text{Addition to Net Present Value} = 0.06x_1 + 0.08x_2 + 0.5x_3 \quad (5.6)$$

---

[4] This argument is due to F. Modigliani and M. H. Miller, "Corporate Income Taxes and the Cost of Capital: A Correction," *American Economic Review, 53* (1963), 433–443. This finding is based on somewhat idealized assumptions, which in practice will not always be appropriate. We will assume that within the borrowing range of interest, our corporation believes that the Modigliani-Miller finding is relevant to its own position. Our subsequent analysis can be modified in an obvious way to incorporate the possibility of any or no impact of borrowing on the net present value of the firm.

THE CONSTRAINTS

Given the limits on the amounts that can be invested in the two projects, we have immediately

$$x_1 \leq 2 \qquad\qquad (5.7)$$

and

$$x_2 \leq 3 \qquad\qquad (5.8)$$

The requirement in (b) above that borrowing be limited implies that

$$x_3 \leq 0.3x_1 + 0.2x_2$$

or

$$x_3 - 0.3x_1 - 0.2x_2 \leq 0 \qquad\qquad (5.9)$$

Finally, the corporation is subject to the constraint that its total uses of funds cannot exceed the total value of sources. Funds are to be used on investment in the two projects and a dividend payment of $1 million. Hence

Total Uses = Investment in First Project + Investment in Second Project
+ Dividend Payment
$$= x_1 + x_2 + 1$$

Available funds are made up of the amount borrowed, the amount raised from new equity issued, and $0.5 million cash in hand. Thus

Total Sources = Amount Borrowed + Amount of New Equity + Cash in Hand
$$= x_3 + x_4 + 0.5$$

The corporation is therefore subject to the constraint

$$x_1 + x_2 + 1 \leq x_3 + x_4 + 0.5$$

or

$$x_1 + x_2 - x_3 - x_4 \leq -0.5 \qquad\qquad (5.10)$$

THE OPTIMAL SOLUTION

Putting together (5.6)–(5.10), this corporation's constrained optimization problem can be expressed as

$$\text{Maximize} \quad 0.06x_1 + 0.08x_2 + 0.5x_3$$

$$\text{subject to} \quad x_1 \leq 2$$

$$x_2 \leq 3$$

$$x_3 - 0.3x_1 - 0.2x_2 \leq 0$$

$$x_1 + x_2 - x_3 - x_4 \leq -0.5$$

$$x_i \geq 0 \ (i = 1, 2, 3, 4)$$

Table 5.13 shows the LINDO program output for this constrained maximization problem. Given the constraints involved, the most that can be added to net present value of the corporation is $0.96 million. This outcome would result from investment of $2 million in the first project and $3 million in the second. A total of $1.2 million is to be borrowed and $4.3 million of new equity is to be issued. Notice that since all four decision variables enter the optimal solution with positive values, their associated REDUCED COSTS are necessarily zero. All four slack variables are zero, implying that at the optimal solution, the four constraints are all binding.

The dual price associated with the first constraint indicates that with all other problem specifications fixed at their initial values, each additional million dollars that could be invested in the first project would add $0.21 million to net present value. Similarly, $0.18 million would be added to net present value for each additional million dollars that could be invested in the second project.

The constraint R4, derived as equation (5.9), follows from the requirement that at most 30% of the amount invested in the first project and 20% of the amount invested in the second project may be borrowed. The dual price 0.5 implies that each additional million dollars that is borrowed adds $0.5 million to

TABLE 5.13 LINDO program output for the corporate financial planning problem.

```
        MAXIMIZE
        OBJ     )  .06 X1 + .08 X2 + .5 X3
        SUBJECT TO
        R2      )  X1 < = 2
        R3      )  X2 < = 3
        R4      )  - .3 X1 - .2 X2 + X3 < = 0
        R5      )  X1 + X2 - X3 - X4 < = - .5
        END
```

TABLE 5.13 (*Continued*)

LP OPTIMUM FOUND AT STEP 4

OBJECTIVE FUNCTION VALUE

1)   .9600000

VARIABLE	VALUE	REDUCED COST
X1	2.000000	0.000000
X2	3.000000	0.000000
X3	1.200000	0.000000
X4	4.300000	0.000000

ROW	SLACK OR SURPLUS	DUAL PRICES
R2)	0.000000	.210000
R3)	0.000000	.180000
R4)	0.000000	.500000
R5)	0.000000	0.000000

NO. ITERATIONS = 4

RANGES IN WHICH THE BASIS IS UNCHANGED

OBJ COEFFICIENT RANGES

VARIABLE	CURRENT COEF	ALLOWABLE INCREASE	ALLOWABLE DECREASE
X1	.060000	INFINITY	.210000
X2	.080000	INFINITY	.180000
X3	.500000	INFINITY	.500000
X4	0.000000	0.000000	.225000

RIGHTHAND SIDE RANGES

ROW	CURRENT RHS	ALLOWABLE INCREASE	ALLOWABLE DECREASE
R2	2.000000	INFINITY	2.000000
R3	3.000000	INFINITY	3.000000
R4	0.000000	4.300000	1.200000
R5	−.500000	4.300000	INFINITY

net present value, a result that follows from our treatment of the corporate tax shield.

The constraint $R5$, which was obtained in equation (5.10), follows from the requirement that the total uses of funds cannot exceed the current sources. The right-hand side of this equation, $-\$0.5$ million, is the difference between cash in hand and dividend payment. The dual price of zero tells us that any change in cash in hand less dividend payment will have no impact on net present value.

Turning to the objective coefficient ranges, we see first that if all other problem specifications are held fixed at their initial values, the optimal solution will be unchanged for any value above -15 cents for the addition to net present value of the firm resulting from each dollar invested in the first project.[5] Similarly, the optimal solution will be unchanged for any value above -10 cents for the addition to net present value resulting from each dollar invested in the second project. Next, we see that the optimum solution remains the same, provided all other specifications are at their original values, for any nonnegative corporate tax rate.

As we have specified it, the decision variable, x_4, does not appear in the objective function. Thus, it has been assumed that the amount of new equity issued has no direct impact on the net present value of the corporation. It can be seen from Table 5.13 that, in fact, the optimal solution would be the same if the effect on net present value of each million dollars of equity issued was anything from a drop of $225,000 to no impact.

The final portion of Table 5.13 shows the ranges in which the shadow prices are valid. We therefore conclude that:

1. With all other specifications fixed at their initial levels, each additional dollar that can be invested in the first project adds 21 cents to net present value, for any positive level of investment.

2. With all other specifications fixed at their initial levels, each additional dollar that can be invested in the second project adds 18 cents to net present value, for any positive level of investment.

3. With all other specifications fixed at their initial levels, each additional dollar that can be borrowed in the range from 30% of the amount invested in the first project plus 20% of the amount invested in the second project, less $1.2 million, to 30% of the investment in the first project plus 20% of the investment in the second project, plus $4.3 million, adds 50 cents to net present value.

4. With all other specifications fixed at their initial levels, provided cash in hand less dividend payment remains below $3.8 million, any change in this quantity will have no effect on net present value.

5.5. PORTFOLIO SELECTION APPLICATION

A further application of linear programming methods in the field of finance arises when an individual investor, or the manager of an investment fund, makes decisions on the composition of a portfolio. In planning their strategies, managers

---

[5] The implication here that it may pay to borrow money to invest in unprofitable projects is a consequence of the corporate tax shield.

TABLE 5.14 Expected rates of return for the portfolio selection problem.

SECURITY	QUANTITY PURCHASED ($ THOUSANDS)	EXPECTED RATE OF RETURN (%)
General Motors Stock	x_1	10.3
Ford Stock	x_2	10.1
Texas Instruments Stock	x_3	11.8
Xerox Stock	x_4	11.4
National Medical Care Stock	x_5	12.7
Shared Medical Systems Stock	x_6	12.2
General Motors Bonds	x_7	9.5
Xerox Bonds	x_8	9.9
Short-term Government Bonds	x_9	8.6
Long-term Government Bonds	x_{10}	9.2

of different funds have different objectives. However, we can broadly characterize the aim as achieving as high an expected return as possible, subject to the provision of some safeguards provided by diversification and the inclusion in a portfolio of some low-risk assets.

We will illustrate some of the considerations involved through the case of an investment fund manager, who currently has available $500,000 for the purchase of securities to add to an existing portfolio. The manager is considering investment in the stock of two automobile companies (General Motors and Ford), of two electronic office equipment manufacturers (Texas Instruments and Xerox), and of two medical care providers (National Medical Care and Shared Medical Systems). Also under consideration are two corporate bonds (General Motors and Xerox), as well as short- and long-term government bonds. Table 5.14 shows the manager's expectations of annual rates of return for these ten securities.

The expected annual return for the whole portfolio is

$$
\begin{aligned}
\text{Expected Portfolio Return} &= 0.103x_1 + 0.101x_2 + 0.118x_3 \\
&+ 0.114x_4 + 0.127x_5 + 0.122x_6 + 0.095x_7 + 0.099x_8 \\
&+ 0.086x_9 + 0.092x_{10}
\end{aligned} \tag{5.11}
$$

This is the quantity that must be maximized. Since $500,000 is available for investment, we have immediately the constraint:

$$
x_1 + x_2 + x_3 + x_4 + x_5 + x_6 + x_7 + x_8 + x_9 + x_{10} = 500 \tag{5.12}
$$

The fund manager also wishes to impose the following constraints:

(i) Not more than $150,000 should be invested in automobile company stock. Thus

$$x_1 + x_2 \leq 150 \qquad (5.13)$$

(ii) Not more than $150,000 should be invested in electronic office equipment stock. Hence

$$x_3 + x_4 \leq 150 \qquad (5.14)$$

(iii) Not more than $100,000 should be invested in the stock of medical care providers. Then

$$x_5 + x_6 \leq 100 \qquad (5.15)$$

(iv) At least $100,000 should be invested in corporate bonds. This implies

$$x_7 + x_8 \geq 100 \qquad (5.16)$$

(v) At least $125,000 should be invested in government bonds. Thus

$$x_9 + x_{10} \geq 125 \qquad (5.17)$$

(vi) At least 40% of the amount invested in long-term government bonds should be invested in short-term government bonds. This implies that

$$x_9 \geq 0.4x_{10}$$

or

$$x_9 - 0.4x_{10} \geq 0 \qquad (5.18)$$

(vii) Not more than $250,000 should be invested in General Motors securities, so that

$$x_1 + x_7 \leq 250 \qquad (5.19)$$

(viii) Not more than \$200,000 should be invested in electronic office equipment securities. Hence

$$x_3 + x_4 + x_8 \leq 200 \qquad\qquad (5.20)$$

Putting together equations (5.11)–(5.20), the constrained optimization problem can be set out as:

Maximize $\quad 0.103x_1 + 0.101x_2 + 0.118x_3 + 0.114x_4 + 0.127x_5 + 0.122x_6$
$$+ 0.095x_7 + 0.099x_8 + 0.086x_9 + 0.092x_{10}$$

subject to $\quad x_1 + x_2 + x_3 + x_4 + x_5 + x_6 + x_7 + x_8 + x_9 + x_{10} = 500$

$$x_1 + x_2 \leq 150$$
$$x_3 + x_4 \leq 150$$
$$x_5 + x_6 \leq 100$$
$$x_7 + x_8 \geq 100$$
$$x_9 + x_{10} \geq 125$$
$$x_9 - 0.4x_{10} \geq 0$$
$$x_1 + x_7 \leq 250$$
$$x_3 + x_4 + x_8 \leq 200$$
$$x_i \geq 0 \ (i = 1, 2, \ldots, 10)$$

The LINDO program output is shown in Table 5.15. Given the constraints, the highest possible expected return on the \$500,000 investment is \$53,961, or 10.79%. To achieve this return, \$25,000 must be invested in General Motors stock, \$150,000 in Texas Instruments stock, \$100,000 in National Medical Care stock, \$50,000 each in the bonds of General Motors and Xerox, \$35,714 in short-term and \$89,286 in long-term government bonds.

The REDUCED COSTS for the nonbasic decision variables show the amounts by which the associated returns per dollar must be improved before the variables enter the optimal solution with positive values. For example, with all other specifications unchanged, it will only pay to include Ford stock in the portfolio if the expected return per dollar increases from \$0.101 to \$0.103.

The only nonzero slack or surplus variables at the optimal solution are associated with the constraints $R3$ and $R9$; that is, (5.13) and (5.19). The implication of the former is that the amount invested in automobile company stock is \$125,000 below the maximum allowable. The latter implies that the amount invested in General Motors securities is \$175,000 below the permitted limit.

TABLE 5.15 LINDO program output for the portfolio selection problem.

```
MAXIMIZE

OBJ        )       .103 X1 + .101 X2 + .118 X3 + .114 X4 + .127 X5
                   + .122 X6 + .095 X7 + .099 X8 + .086 X9 + .092 X10


SUBJECT TO

R2         )       X1 + X2 + X3 + X4 + X5 + X6 + X7 + X8 + X9 + X10 = 500
R3         )       X1 + X2 < = 150
R4         )       X3 + X4 < = 150
R5         )       X5 + X6 < = 100
R6         )       X7 + X8 > = 100
R7         )       X9 + X10 > = 125
R8         )       X9 _ .4 X10 > = 0
R9         )       X1 + X7 < = 250
R10        )       X3 + X4 + X8 < = 200
END
```

LP OPTIMUM FOUND AT STEP 7

OBJECTIVE FUNCTION VALUE

1)   53.9607143

VARIABLE	VALUE	REDUCED COST
X1	25.000000	0.000000
X2	0.000000	.002000
X3	150.000000	0.000000
X4	0.000000	.004000
X5	100.000000	0.000000
X6	0.000000	.005000
X7	50.000000	0.000000
X8	50.000000	0.000000
X9	35.714286	0.000000
X10	89.285714	0.000000

ROW	SLACK OR SURPLUS	DUAL PRICES
R2)	0.000000	.103000
R3)	125.000000	0.000000
R4)	0.000000	.011000

TABLE 5.15 (*Continued*)

ROW	SLACK OR SURPLUS	DUAL PRICES
R5)	0.000000	.024000
R6)	0.000000	−.008000
R7)	0.000000	−.012714
R8)	0.000000	−.004286
R9)	175.000000	0.000000
R10)	0.000000	.004000

NO. ITERATIONS = 7

RANGES IN WHICH THE BASIS IS UNCHANGED

OBJ COEFFICIENT RANGES

VARIABLE	CURRENT COEF	ALLOWABLE INCREASE	ALLOWABLE DECREASE
X1	.103000	.011000	.002000
X2	.101000	.002000	INFINITY
X3	.118000	INFINITY	.004000
X4	.114000	.004000	INFINITY
X5	.127000	INFINITY	.005000
X6	.122000	.005000	INFINITY
X7	.095000	.004000	.011000
X8	.099000	.011000	.004000
X9	.086000	.006000	INFINITY
X10	.092000	.017800	.006000

RIGHTHAND SIDE RANGES

ROW	CURRENT RHS	ALLOWABLE INCREASE	ALLOWABLE DECREASE
R2	500.000000	125.000000	25.000000
R3	150.000000	INFINITY	125.000000
R4	150.000000	25.000000	50.000000
R5	100.000000	25.000000	100.000000
R6	100.000000	25.000000	50.000000
R7	125.000000	25.000000	125.000000
R8	0.000000	125.000000	50.000000
R9	250.000000	INFINITY	175.000000
R10	200.000000	50.000000	50.000000

The DUAL PRICES show the effect on maximum attainable return of a unit increase in the values of the right-hand side of each constraint, when all other problem specifications are set at their original levels. We illustrate with three examples:

1. For constraint $R2$, that is (5.12), it can be seen that if the other constraints are kept in their present form, each additional thousand dollars available for investment will produce an additional expected return of $103.
2. For constraint $R5$, that is (5.15), we see that all else the same, each additional thousand dollars that can be invested in the stock of medical care providers yields an extra $24 in maximum achieveable total expected return.
3. For constraint $R6$, that is (5.16), it emerges that with all other specifications set at their initial levels, each additional thousand dollars that must be invested in corporate bonds will lead to a decrease of $8 in maximum attainable total return. From the final portion of Table 5.15 it can be seen that this conclusion holds for any lower limit on corporate bond purchases between 50 thousand and 125 thousand dollars.

The penultimate section of Table 5.15 shows the objective coefficient ranges for which the optimal solution remains unchanged. For example

(a) All else the same, the solution is unchanged for any expected rate of return on General Motors stock between 10.1% and 11.4%.
(b) With other specifications held at their initial levels, the optimal solution is unaltered for any expected return on Texas Instruments stock above 11.4%.

The linear programming model has been successfully employed to a wide range of business problems. In this chapter we have attempted to provide a flavor of these applications.

EXERCISES

5.1. A company produces six products, each of which requires time on five different machines. The aim is to find the product mix yielding the highest possible total profit, subject to the specifications set out in the following table, for the coming week.

TOTAL MACHINE-HOURS AVAILABLE	TYPE OF MACHINE	MACHINE-HOURS PER UNIT PRODUCT					
		1	2	3	4	5	6
1,500	A	1	1	2	2	1	2
2,400	B	3	2	1	1	1	1
1,800	C	1	1	2	2	2	1
2,100	D	2	2	1	1	2	2
2,700	E	2	3	1	3	1	2
PROFIT PER UNIT ($)		30	25	20	40	25	30

The LINDO program has been used to analyze this problem, yielding the output shown below.

```
MAXIMIZE

OBJ      )    30 X1 + 25 X2 + 20 X3 + 40 X4 + 25 X5 + 30 X6

SUBJECT TO

R2       )    X1 + X2 + 2 X3 + 2 X4 + X5 + 2 X6 < = 1500
R3       )    3 X1 + 2 X2 + X3 + X4 + X5 + X6 < = 2400
R4       )    X1 + X2 + 2 X3 + 2 X4 + 2 X5 + X6 < = 1800
R5       )    2 X1 + 2 X2 + X3 + X4 + 2 X5 + 2 X6 < = 2100
R6       )    2 X1 + 3 X2 + X3 + 3 X4 + X5 + 2 X6 < = 2700
END


               LP OPTIMUM FOUND AT STEP 3

               OBJECTIVE FUNCTION VALUE

    1)                    37500.0000


       VARIABLE          VALUE          REDUCED COST

         X1           600.000000          0.000000
         X2             0.000000          2.500000
         X3             0.000000         20.000000
         X4           300.000000          0.000000
         X5           300.000000          0.000000
         X6             0.000000         12.500000


       ROW          SLACK OR SURPLUS     DUAL PRICES

       R2   )          0.000000         17.500000
       R3   )          0.000000          2.500000
       R4   )          0.000000          0.000000
       R5   )          0.000000          2.500000
       R6   )        300.000000          0.000000


       NO. ITERATIONS = 3
```

```
          RANGES IN WHICH THE BASIS IS UNCHANGED

                   OBJ COEFFICIENT RANGES
```

VARIABLE	CURRENT COEF	ALLOWABLE INCREASE	ALLOWABLE DECREASE
X1	30.000000	15.000000	5.000000
X2	25.000000	2.500000	INFINITY
X3	20.000000	20.000000	INFINITY
X4	40.000000	7.500000	18.750000
X5	25.000000	5.000000	3.000000
X6	30.000000	12.500000	INFINITY

```
                   RIGHTHAND SIDE RANGES
```

ROW	CURRENT RHS	ALLOWABLE INCREASE	ALLOWABLE DECREASE
R2	1500.000000	0.000000	450.000000
R3	2400.000000	600.000000	0.000000
R4	1800.000000	INFINITY	0.000000
R5	2100.000000	0.000000	360.000000
R6	2700.000000	INFINITY	300.000000

(a) What is the largest profit that can be made?

(b) What product mix yields this maximum profit?

(c) Interpret the nonzero slack variable at the optimal solution.

(d) Interpret the REDUCED COST associated with $X2$.

(e) Interpret the dual price associated with $R2$. In what range does this price apply?

(f) At the optimal solution the slack for constraint $R4$ is zero, and yet the associated dual price is zero. Explain this finding.

(g) Interpret the objective coefficient range for variable $X1$.

(h) Management is considering increasing the weekly capacity of machine type B from 2400 to 3400 machine-hours. Can the LINDO program output be used to find the effect of this strategy on total profit for the week? Explain your answer.

5.2. The company of Exercise 5.1 receives from a valued customer an order for 200 units of product 2, to be delivered at the end of the week.

(a) If management wants to fill this order, write down the algebraic form of the new constrained optimization problem.

(b) Use a computer program to solve the new problem.

(i) What is the new optimal product mix?

(ii) How much will be lost in profits for the week if the order is filled?

5.3. A company produces five products, each of which must be processed through four departments. Management wants to find the product mix for the coming week that will yield the highest possible total profit, given the specifications in the following table.

TOTAL MAN-HOURS AVAILABLE	DEPARTMENT	MAN-HOURS PER UNIT				
		PRODUCT				
		1	2	3	4	5
6,000	A	3	2	2	2	1
5,000	B	2	1	3	2	1
4,000	C	2	1	2	2	1
4,000	D	1	3	1	1	2
	PROFIT PER UNIT ($)	4	3	3	4	2

The LINDO program has been used to analyze this problem. The output is shown below

```
MAXIMIZE

OBJ      )   4 X1 + 3 X2 + 3 X3 + 4 X4 + 2 X5

SUBJECT TO

R2       )   3 X1 + 2 X2 + 2 X3 + 2 X4 + X5 < = 6000
R3       )   2 X1 + X2 + 3 X3 + 2 X4 + X5 < = 5000
R4       )   2 X1 + X2 + 2 X3 + 2 X4 + X5 < = 4000
R5       )   X1 + 3 X2 + X3 + X4 + 2 X5 < = 4000
END
```

```
          LP OPTIMUM FOUND AT STEP 3

             OBJECTIVE FUNCTION VALUE

    1)                  8800.00000

VARIABLE              VALUE            REDUCED COST

    X1             1200.000000           0.000000
    X2              800.000000           0.000000
    X3                0.000000           2.800000
    X4              400.000000           0.000000
    X5                0.000000            .600000
```

ROW		SLACK OR SURPLUS	DUAL PRICES
R2	)	0.000000	.000000
R3	)	1000.000000	0.000000
R4	)	0.000000	1.800000
R5	)	0.000000	.400000

NO ITERATIONS = 3

RANGES IN WHICH THE BASIS IS UNCHANGED

OBJ COEFFICIENT RANGES

VARIABLE	CURRENT COEF	ALLOWABLE INCREASE	ALLOWABLE DECREASE
X1	4.000000	1.000000	.000000
X2	3.000000	9.000000	1.000000
X3	3.000000	2.800000	INFINITY
X4	4.000000	.000000	.750000
X5	2.000000	.600000	INFINITY

RIGHTHAND SIDE RANGES

ROW	CURRENT RHS	ALLOWABLE INCREASE	ALLOWABLE DECREASE
R2	6000.000000	400.000000	1200.000000
R3	5000.000000	INFINITY	1000.000000
R4	4000.000000	1000.000000	285.714286
R5	4000.000000	3000.000000	2000.000000

(a) What is the largest profit that can be made?

(b) What product mix yields the maximum profit?

(c) Interpret the nonzero slack variable at the optimal solution.

(d) To what level must the profit per unit of product 3 rise before it will pay to produce any of that product?

(e) Interpret the dual price associated with $R5$. In what range does this price apply?

(f) Suppose that it is possible to double the profit per unit of product 2. What will be the effect on the maximum achieveable weekly profit? Explain your answer.

(g) What is the effect on total profits of adding 200 man-hours in department C?

5.4. The company of Exercise 5.3 has been experiencing sluggish demand, and inventories have built up. Management has instituted a policy requiring that for any week, output of a product should not exceed projected demand. For the coming week the following demand levels are expected:

PRODUCT	1	2	3	4	5
DEMAND	1,000	600	500	600	200

(a) If this policy is instituted, write down the algebraic form of the new constrained optimization problem.

(b) Use a computer program to solve this new problem.

   (i) What is the new optimal product mix?

   (ii) Interpret the values of the slack variables at the optimal solution.

5.5. A company produces six brands of bath oil, each containing a combination of three of the five essences that the company employs. The quantities of essences required per pint of bath oil are shown in the table below.

BATH OIL	QUANTITY OF ESSENCE (IN OUNCES)				
	A	B	C	D	E
1	0.2	0.4	0.2	0	0
2	0.3	0	0.5	0.4	0
3	0	0.3	0.3	0	0.5
4	0.1	0	0	0.5	0.4
5	0	0.4	0	0.5	0.3
6	0.5	0	0.2	0.4	0

For the coming week quantities of these essences are in limited supply. The amounts available are shown below.

AVAILABILITY OF ESSENCE (IN OUNCES)				
A	B	C	D	E
250	225	275	300	250

Profits per pint for the six bath oils are, respectively, $1, $1.20, $0.75, $1.10, $1.20, and $1. The objective is to find the product mix that maximizes total profit for the week. The LINDO program output for this problem is shown below.

```
MAXIMIZE


OBJ       )    X1 + 1.2 X2 + .75 X3 + 1.1 X4 + 1.2 X5 + X6

SUBJECT TO

R2        )    .2 X1 + .3 X2 + .1 X4 + .5 X6 < = 250
R3        )    .4 X1 + .3 X3 + .4 X5 < = 225
R4        )    .2 X1 + .5 X2 + .3 X3 + .2 X6 < = 275
R5        )    .4 X2 + .5 X4 + .5 X5 + .4 X6 < = 300
R6        )    .5 X3 + .4 X4 + .3 X5 < = 250
```

```
                 LP OPTIMUM FOUND AT STEP 4

                   OBJECTIVE FUNCTION VALUE

   1)                    1326.50000

   VARIABLE               VALUE            REDUCED COST

   X1                   562.500000          0.000000
   X2                   325.000000          0.000000
   X3                     0.000000           .096000
   X4                   340.000000          0.000000
   X5                     0.000000           .772000
   X6                     0.000000           .008000

   ROW             SLACK OR SURPLUS         DUAL PRICES

   R2    )              6.000000            0.000000
   R3    )              0.000000            2.180000
   R4    )              0.000000             .640000
   R5    )              0.000000            2.200000
   R6    )            114.000000            0.000000

   NO. ITERATIONS = 4

            RANGES IN WHICH THE BASIS IS UNCHANGED

                   OBJ COEFFICIENT RANGES
   VARIABLE      CURRENT       ALLOWABLE        ALLOWABLE
                  COEF         INCREASE         DECREASE

   X1           1.000000       INFINITY          .128000
   X2           1.200000       1.930000          .020000
   X3            .750000        .096000         INFINITY
   X4           1.100000        .400000          .016667
   X5           1.200000        .772000         INFINITY
   X6           1.000000        .008000         INFINITY

                   RIGHTHAND SIDE RANGES
   ROW           CURRENT       ALLOWABLE        ALLOWABLE
                  COEF         INCREASE         DECREASE

   R2          250.000000      INFINITY         6.000000
   R3          225.000000      21.428571      225.000000
   R4          275.000000      13.636364      162.500000
   R5          300.000000      30.000000      170.000000
   R6          250.000000      INFINITY       114.000000
```

Write, for a manager who is not familiar with the details of linear programming, a report summarizing the findings of this analysis.

5.6. Refer to Exercise 5.5. The purchasing department of this company has the opportunity to buy, for immediate delivery, up to 50 additional ounces of essence B. However, each additional ounce purchased will cost $2 more than the usual price. Accordingly, for each additional ounce of essence B purchased and used, profits will be $2 lower than had the same product mix been produced from normal supplies of essences. The company must decide how much, if any, additional essence B should be purchased.

(a) Write down the algebraic form of the constrained optimization problem.

(b) Use a computer program to solve the modified problem.

(i) How many additional ounces of essence B should be purchased?

(ii) What now should be the product mix for the week?

5.7. A company intends to produce a tonic blend containing amounts of six nutrients through the mixture of five basic ingredients. The objective is to find the blend with the lowest possible cost, subject to nutritional requirements, given the specifications in the following table.

MINIMUM QUANTITIES REQUIRED (OUNCES)	NUTRIENT	NUTRIENTS PER UNIT (OUNCES)				
		INGREDIENT				
		1	2	3	4	5
20	A	0.2	0.3	0.1	0.1	0.2
10	B	0.1	0.2	0.3	0.1	0.1
15	C	0.1	0.1	0.1	0.2	0.2
15	D	0.1	0.1	0.2	0.2	0.1
20	E	0.3	0.1	0.1	0.1	0.3
15	F	0.1	0.2	0.2	0.2	0.1
COST PER UNIT (IN CENTS)		6	8	10	6	8

The LINDO program output for this problem is shown below.

```
MINIMIZE

OBJ     )   6 X1 + 8 X2 + + 10 X3 + 6 X4 + 8 X5

SUBJECT TO

R2      )   .2 X1 + .3 X2 + .1 X3 + .1 X4 + .2 X5 > = 20
R3      )   .1 X1 + .2 X2 + .3 X3 + .1 X4 + .1 X5 > = 10
R4      )   .1 X1 + .1 X2 + .1 X3 + .2 X4 + .2 X5 > = 15
R5      )   .1 X1 + .1 X2 + .2 X3 + .2 X4 + .1 X5 > = 15
R6      )   .3 X1 + .1 X2 + .1 X3 + .1 X4 + .3 X5 > = 20
R7      )   .1 X1 + .2 X2 + .2 X3 + .2 X4 + .1 X5 > = 15
END
```

```
                        OBJECTIVE FUNCTION VALUE

   1)                            700.000000

   VARIABLE                VALUE              REDUCED COST

   X1                   83.333333              0.000000
   X2                    0.000000              0.000000
   X3                    0.000000              6.000000
   X4                   33.333333              0.000000
   X5                    0.000000              0.000000

   ROW               SLACK OR SURPLUS          DUAL PRICES

   R2    )               0.000000             -20.000000
   R3    )               1.666667               0.000000
   R4    )               0.000000             -20.000000
   R5    )               0.000000               0.000000
   R6    )               8.333333               0.000000
   R7    )               0.000000               0.000000

   NO. ITERATIONS = 6

            RANGES IN WHICH THE BASIS IS UNCHANGED

                    OBJ COEFFICIENT RANGES
   VARIABLE       CURRENT          ALLOWABLE          ALLOWABLE
                   COEF            INCREASE           DECREASE

   X1           6.000000           0.000000           0.000000
   X2           8.000000           INFINITY           0.000000
   X3          10.000000           INFINITY           6.000000
   X4           6.000000           6.000000           0.000000
   X5           8.000000           0.000000           2.000000

                    RIGHTHAND SIDE RANGES
   ROW           CURRENT           ALLOWABLE          ALLOWABLE
                   RHS             INCREASE           DECREASE

   R2    )      20.000000          10.000000          5.000000
   R3    )      10.000000           1.666667          INFINITY
   R4    )      15.000000           8.333333          0.000000
   R5    )      15.000000           0.000000          5.000000
   R6    )      20.000000           8.333333          INFINITY
   R7    )      15.000000           INFINITY          0.000000
```

(a) What is the lowest possible cost at which a blend satisfying all of the requirements can be made?

(b) Find a blend yielding the minimum possible total cost.

(c) Interpret the reduced cost associated with variable $X3$.

(d) Interpret the nonzero surplus variables at the optimum solution.

(e) Interpret the dual price associated with constraint $R2$. In what range is this price valid?

(f) It appears that this problem has multiple optimal solutions. How can this be deduced from the output? Trace the effect of this phenomenon on the output.

5.8. Refer to Exercise 5.7. Analysts at this corporation claim to be able to develop, at very low cost, an ingredient containing 0.5 ounce per unit of nutrient A, but none of the other nutrients. Management wishes to know how low must be the cost per unit of this new ingredient in order to make its use in the blend worthwhile.

(a) Explain how the LINDO program could be used to provide an answer to this question.

(b) Use a computer to discover the highest possible cost of the new ingredient for its use in the blend to be cost-effective.

5.9. Refer to the production planning example of Section 5.2, and to the LINDO program output of Table 5.8.

(a) Interpret the REDUCED COST associated with decision variable $X4$.

(b) Interpret the DUAL PRICE associated with constraint $R10$.

(c) Interpret the objective coefficient range associated with decision variable $X6$.

(d) Interpret the right-hand side ranging associated with constraint $R9$.

5.10. A company produces both small and large photocopiers. Projected demand for the last three months of the year is shown in the table below:

	SMALL	LARGE
October	250	100
November	300	180
December	320	175

Production costs during normal time working are $400 for small copiers and $750 for large copiers. Inventory holding costs are $10 per month for large copiers and $6 per month for small copiers. It is possible to produce both types of copiers through overtime working, the unit costs being $450 for small copiers and $820 for large copiers. Each month, during normal working time, it has been computed that a maximum of 300 copiers (small plus large) can be made. Total overtime capacity is 200 copiers per month. Management wishes to find the production schedule that will meet demand at the lowest possible total cost.

(a) Set out the algebraic form of the constrained optimization problem.

(b) Use a computer program to solve this problem, and write a report summarizing your findings.

5.11. Refer to Exercise 5.10. Union representatives at this firm have complained about the effect on employee morale of widely fluctuating monthly overtime requirements. Management has decided to take account of this concern by considering month to month changes in the total number of copiers made in overtime. Specifically, for each copier made in overtime in one month over or above the number of copiers made in overtime in the previous month, an additional "cost" of $12 is added to total costs. In September, 80 copiers were made in overtime. The objective is to minimize total costs incorporating this new factor.

(a) Write down the algebraic form of the constrained optimization problem.

(b) Use a computer program to solve this problem, and discuss your findings.

5.12. A company produces carpets, using both normal and overtime working, and a production schedule for the first four months of the year must be set. The table shows, in terms of hundreds of man-hours of working time, projected demand, regular time and overtime production capacity, and storage capacity for unsold output. Each man-hour of normal working time costs $10, and each man-hour of overtime costs $12.50. Storage of each unsold man-hour's worth of output costs $2 per month. The aim is to meet projected demand at the lowest possible total cost. The company begins the year with two hundred man-hours of output in storage, and wishes to have the same quantity in storage at the end of April.

MONTH	PROJECTED DEMAND	PRODUCTION CAPACITY		END OF MONTH STORAGE CAPACITY
		NORMAL TIME	OVERTIME	
January	25	18	8	5
February	18	20	10	5
March	28	20	10	5
April	28	24	10	5

(a) Set out the algebraic form of the constrained optimization problem.

(b) Use a computer program to solve this problem, and discuss in detail the program output.

5.13. Refer again to Exercise 5.12. Management is concerned about the possibility of not being able to meet a potential rush order, over and above the projected demand levels. Accordingly, it is decided that at least 200 man-hours worth of output should be held in storage at the end of each month. Subject to this and the other constraints, the objective remains to meet projected demand at the lowest possible total cost.

(a) Set out the algebraic form of the modified constrained optimization problem.

(b) Use a computer program to solve this problem. Discuss the output of this program.

5.14. Refer to the labor scheduling example of Section 5.3, and, in particular, to the computer output in Table 5.12. A manager has noticed that the dual prices associated with constraints $R2$–$R4$, $R7$–$R10$ are the same. These constraints refer to the seven different categories of workers. The manager then asserts that since versatile workers seem to be no more valuable than workers who can work in only one department, there is no point in going to the expense of training workers in more than one skill.

(a) Discuss verbally this point of view.

(b) Consider two extreme cases:

(i) Each of the 40,000 man-hours of available labor can be assigned to any department.

(ii) There is no flexibility whatever: 14,000 man-hours are available in department I, and 13,000 in each of the other two departments.

In each case, write out the new constrained optimization problem (assuming all other constraints are unchanged.) Use a computer program to solve these problems, and compare your solutions with those of Table 5.12.

5.15. Refer again to Exercise 5.3. In departments A and B, a total of 11,000 man-hours are available. Suppose now that each of these can be allocated to either one of these two departments, but that there is no flexibility in the allocation of the other 8000 man-hours.

(a) Set out the algebraic form of the new constrained optimization problem.

(b) Use a computer program to solve this problem and discuss your findings.

5.16. A city fire department employs officers who work 8-hour shifts. The table below shows the wage per hour that must be paid each employee on the six possible shifts.

SHIFT	HOURLY WAGE ($)
Midnight–8:00 a.m.	15.00
4:00 a.m.–Noon	12.50
8:00 a.m.–4:00 p.m.	10.00
Noon–8:00 p.m.	11.25
4:00 p.m.–Midnight	12.50
8:00 p.m.–4:00 a.m.	15.00

The fire chief has estimated, for each 4-hour period of the day, the minimum number of officers required to provide adequate coverage. These estimates are shown in the table below.

PERIOD	MINIMUM NUMBER NEEDED
Midnight–4:00 a.m.	40
4:00 a.m.–8:00 a.m.	30
8:00 a.m.–Noon	25
Noon–4:00 p.m.	25
4:00 p.m.–8:00 p.m.	30
8:00 p.m.–Midnight	50

The chief requires to find the numbers of officers to allocate to each shift so that total daily wage cost is minimized, subject to the coverage requirements.

(a) Write out the algebraic form of the constrained optimization problem.

(b) Use a computer program to solve this problem, and discuss the results.

5.17. A drug company makes three products, each of which requires work in four departments. The table below shows man-hour requirements and unit profits.

DEPARTMENT	MAN-HOURS PER POUND		
	DRUG		
	A	B	C
I	2	4	2
II	3	2	5
III	4	2	3
IV	2	3	4
PROFIT PER POUND ($)	10	12	12

Currently 10,000 man-hours per month of labor are available in each department. However, the company is planning to expand by hiring an additional 5000 man-hours of labor. After suitable training, it will be possible to assign each new man-hour of labor to any one of the four departments. For the foreseeable future, management expects, even with the additional capacity, to be able to sell its entire output at the profit levels shown in the above table. The problem is to find how to allocate the new resources so as to maximize total monthly profits.

(a) Write down the algebraic form of the constrained optimization problem.

(b) Use a computer program to solve this problem and comment on the results.

5.18. Refer to Exercise 5.17. Management of the drug company is afraid that it may be difficult to recruit additional labor at the current wage rate (The same rate is paid in every department). Accordingly, the company may, if it is profitable to do so, ask some of its current employees to work overtime. Suppose this option is adopted in place of the recruitment of new labor. Up to 2000 man-hours per month of overtime working in each department is possible. However, each overtime man-hour costs $1 more than a man-hour of normal time working, and this amount must be subtracted from total profits. The problem is to find how much, if any, overtime should be worked in each department so as to maximize monthly profits.

(a) Write down the algebraic form of the constrained optimization problem.

(b) Use a computer program to solve this problem and discuss the results.

5.19. A corporation has the opportunity to invest in three projects, the investments to be financed through new borrowing, issue of new equity, and use of cash in hand. The most that can be invested in any one of these projects is $2 million. The corporation is willing to borrow no more than 30% of the amount to be invested in the first project, no more than 25% of the amount to be invested in the second project, and no more than 20% of the amount to be invested in the third project. Also management does not want to borrow more than 25% of the total amount to be invested in the three projects. Each dollar invested in the first project is expected to add 6 cents to the net present value of the firm, each dollar invested in the second project is expected to add 8 cents, and each dollar invested in the third project is expected to add 10 cents. Management of this corporation believes that within the ranges contemplated for these variables, the amount of borrowing and the size of the dividend payment will have no effect on net present value. This corporation has $1.5 million cash in hand, and wants to pay $1 million in dividends to stockholders. Management has been advised by financial consultants that it will not be possible to sell more than $3 million in new equity. This company wants to decide how to proceed, given the objective of maximizing net present value.

(a) Write down the algebraic form of the constrained optimization problem.

(b) Use a computer program to solve this problem and discuss the results.

5.20. Refer to the portfolio selection application of Section 5.5, and to the LINDO program output of Table 5.15.

(a) Interpret the DUAL PRICES for the constraints $R4$, $R7$, $R8$, and $R10$, and find the ranges in which these prices are valid.

(b) Interpret the OBJECTIVE COEFFICIENT RANGES associated with $X5$, $X6$, and $X7$.

5.21. A corporation manufactures fertilizer, and currently has quantities available at three depots. There are 600 bags available at depot 1, 500 bags available at depot 2, and 400 bags at depot 3. Orders have been placed by three distribution centers. There are 300 bags required at center A, 700 bags at center B, and 450 bags at center C. The table below shows the cost per bag, in dollars, of shipping fertilizer from each depot to each distribution center.

DEPOT	DISTRIBUTION CENTER		
	A	B	C
1	10	7	5
2	8	6	9
3	6	7	4

The fertilizer manufacturer wants to meet total demand at the lowest possible total shipping cost.

(a) Write out the algebraic form of the linear programming problem that must be solved.

(b) Use a computer program to solve this problem and comment on your findings.

5.22. A manufacturer of stereos has three plants with differing production capacities. For the coming week it is anticipated that maximum capacities are 400 units at plant 1, 300 units at plant 2, and 200 units at plant 3. These stereos are sold through three distribution centers. Total demand is 250 units at center A, 350 units at center B, and 450 units at center C. (Notice that total production capacity is insufficient to meet total demand.) Unit production costs differ from plant to plant, and selling prices differ from distribution center to distribution center. Taking into account these factors, and differences in shipment costs from the production plants to the distribution centers, management has calculated the profits (in dollars) per unit for each plant-distribution center combination.

PLANT	DISTRIBUTION CENTER		
	A	B	C
1	40	35	30
2	35	30	45
3	25	25	30

The problem is to find how many stereos should be shipped from each plant to each distribution center to achieve the highest total profit, subject to plant capacity constraints and the requirement that the total number of stereos shipped to any distribution center should not exceed demand at that center.

(a) Write out the algebraic form of the linear programming problem that must be solved.

(b) Use a computer program to find the optimal solution and discuss the output.

5.23. The manufacturer of Exercise 5.22 is able to increase, for the coming week, production capacity at either plant 1 or plant 2 (or both) by up to 40 units. However, each additional unit produced in this way costs an additional $20 at plant 1 and $25 at plant 2. These amounts must therefore be subtracted from the profits that otherwise would have resulted. The aim is still to maximize total profits, subject to the constraints.

(a) Write out the algebraic form of the new constrained optimization problem.

(b) Use a computer program to solve this problem and discuss the program output.

5.24. A distributor stocks three types of television sets—large color, portable color, and portable black and white. The same distributor also stocks microwave ovens, wash machines, and tumble dryers. The table below shows, for each type of appliance, the cost per unit to the distributor, the profit per unit that can be made, and the storage capacity per unit required.

APPLIANCE	COST ($)	PROFIT ($)	STORAGE SPACE (CUBIC FEET)
Large color T.V.	360	50	8
Portable color T.V.	280	30	4
Portable black and white T.V.	80	20	4
Microwave oven	250	40	6
Wash machine	270	60	12
Tumble dryer	220	45	12

This distributor currently has available 12,000 cubic feet of storage capacity, and $600,000 for the purchase of new stock. However, difficulties in marketing lead the distributor to feel that at most 300 wash machines should be purchased. Further, to maintain some inventory balance, it is felt that of the total cost of all purchases made, between 25% and 75% should be devoted to television sets, of one type or another. Subject to storage capacity and the other constraints, the aim is to order that mix of appliances that will lead to the highest possible profit.

(a) Set out the algebraic form of the constrained optimization problem.

(b) Use a computer program to solve this problem and discuss the output.

5.25. A supermarket manager has available a total of at most 60 square feet of shelf space to be allocated among four national brand products—A, B, C, and D—and a competing generic brand. Company policy dictates that at least 10% of the space used should be devoted to each national brand, that no national brand should receive more than half the total space devoted to all national brands, and that no national brand should receive more than twice the space devoted to the generic brand. It has been calculated that profits per square foot of shelf space are $60 for brand A, $55 for brand B, $50 for brand C, $45 for brand D, and $45 for the generic brand. The manager wants to find, subject to the above constraints, the shelf allocation yielding the largest possible total profit.

(a) Write down the algebraic form of the constrained optimization problem.

(b) Use a computer program to solve this problem and discuss the program output.

5.26. A fast food company is planning to mount an advertising campaign featuring a new product—passion fruit flavored shakes. A total of $500,000 is available for the campaign and is to be spread among newspapers, television, radio, and magazines. Company policy requires that at least 10% of the total expenditure be devoted to each medium, and that no more than 60% of the total should be devoted to either the broadcast media or the print media. Also, since the campaign must be mounted quickly, it will be impossible to spend more than $100,000 on magazine advertisements. This company has developed, for similar products, an index which measures audience exposure per dollar spent on advertising. This index has the value 80 for newspapers, 120 for magazines, 90 for radio, and 100 for television. The aim, subject to the above constraints, is to allocate the advertising budget so as to maximize total audience exposure.

(a) Formulate algebraically the constrained optimization problem.

(b) Use a computer program to solve this problem and comment on the computer output.

5.27. A drugs company has three products—A, B, and C—that must be made into pills. Three machines—1, 2, and 3—are available for this purpose, and each machine can be used to process each product. However, the processing costs per pound differ for each machine-product combination, as indicated in the table below.

MACHINE	TIME PER POUND (HOURS)		
	PRODUCT		
	A	B	C
1	1	1.25	1
2	0.75	1	1.25
3	0.75	1.5	1

Further, the times per pound for processing also differ according to machine-product combination, as shown in the following table.

MACHINE	COST PER POUND ($)		
	PRODUCT		
	A	B	C
1	5	4	3
2	4	4.5	3.5
3	3.5	3.5	3

For the coming day, a total of 8 hours are available on the first machine, and 6 hours on each of the other two. Management requires that during the day, 6 pounds of each product must be processed. The objective is to achieve this target as cheaply as possible, and the supervisor must decide how much of each product should be processed on each machine.

(a) Formulate algebraically the constrained optimization problem.

(b) Use a computer program to solve this problem, and discuss the program output.

5.28. A publisher is planning to print copies of a very specialized academic book. Capacity is limited, and it is not possible to print more than 5000 copies in the initial print run, of which it is felt that at least 1000 should go to libraries. Maximum possible library sales are estimated at 2000 copies. The book is also to be sold to professors in North America, and in the overseas market. Management has estimated that advertising costs per book sold to libraries will be $1, advertising costs per book sold to professors in North America will be $1.50, and advertising costs per book sold in the overseas market will be $1.25. A maximum of $6000 is available for expenditure on advertising. Other marketing costs (for which a total of $2000 is available) are $0.25 per book for libraries, $0.50 per book for professors in North America, and $0.40 per book overseas. Taking into account these factors, together with differences in distribution costs and pricing in different markets, it is estimated that each book sold to libraries yields a profit of $6, each book to professors in North America $5, and each book overseas $4.50. Given the constraints, the aim is to find how many books should be produced, and how they should be distributed among the three markets in order to maximize total profit.

(a) Formulate algebraically the constrained optimization problem.

(b) Use a computer program to solve this problem and analyze the program output.

5.29. When portfolio managers make decisions about investment opportunities, not only expected returns, but uncertainty about future returns, are relevant. A manager has $250,000 to invest and is considering six investment projects. The table below shows the expected rate of return (as a proportion) for each project, and also the standard deviation of rate of return (as a measure of uncertainty).

PROJECT	1	2	3	4	5	6
EXPECTED RATE OF RETURN	.095	.108	.112	.120	.131	.119
STANDARD DEVIATION OF RATE OF RETURN	.016	.021	.030	.036	.040	.034

Let x_i denote the amount (in dollars) invested in the i-th project, and μ_i and σ_i the expected rate of return and standard deviation of rate of return for that project. Then, the expected return for the total investment is $(\mu_1 x_1 + \mu_2 x_2 + \ldots + \mu_6 x_6)$, and the maximum possible standard deviation of return for the total investment is $(\sigma_1 x_1 + \sigma_2 x_2 + \ldots + \sigma_6 x_6)$, where both are measured in dollars. The portfolio manager wishes to invest the $250,000 among the six projects in such a way that the standard deviation of return on the total investment will certainly not exceed $8000. Other considerations dictate that at least $25,000 must be invested in project 1, at most $50,000 can be invested in project 5, and that the total investment in projects 2 and 3 should be at least half that in projects 4 and 6. Subject to these constraints, it is required to find the investment mix with the highest expected total return.

(a) Formulate algebraically the constrained optimization problem that the manager must solve.

(b) Use a computer program to solve this problem, and discuss your findings.

5.30. An office furnishings company manufactures desks and bookcases, each of which requires time for assembly, finishing, and inspection. Monthly output potential is restricted by resource limitations in these three departments: 2560 man-hours are available each month for assembly, 2160 for finishing, and 400 for inspection. Each desk requires 8 man-hours of assembly, 4 man-hours of finishing, and one man-hour of inspection. Each bookcase requires 4 man-hours of assembly, 6 man-hours of finishing, and one man-hour of inspection. A production manager is planning output schedules for the final three months of the year. There is no inventory at the beginning of this period, and none is required at the end. Anticipated demand for desks is 250 in October, 290 in November, and 300 in December. Anticipated demand for bookcases is 120 in October, 150 in November, and 200 in December. Each desk made and sold yields a profit of $30 if it is sold in the month it is produced. However, each month the desk is held in inventory before it is sold, reduces this profit by $4. Each bookcase made and sold yields a profit of $20 if it is sold in the month it is produced. Each month the bookcase is held in inventory before it is sold, reduces this profit by $2.50. If an order for a desk or bookcase is received in one month, and cannot be met in that month, the order is lost, and the company counts this as a goodwill loss of $2.50 per desk or bookcase. This amount must be subtracted from total profit. The aim is to find the production schedule that maximizes total profits over these three months.

(a) Formulate algebraically the constrained optimization problem.

(b) Use a computer program to solve this problem and discuss the program output.

5.31. A corporation produces rolls of clear plastic of a standard length. The production process is such that the only width that can be produced is 7 feet. However, orders have been received from distributors for rolls of $1\frac{1}{2}$ feet, $2\frac{1}{2}$ feet and $3\frac{1}{2}$ feet in width. In order to fill these orders, the 7 foot rolls must be cut into sections. A number of cutting strategies, some of which will involve wastage, are possible. For example, it is possible to cut 2 rolls of width $1\frac{1}{2}$ feet and 1 roll of width $3\frac{1}{2}$ feet, leading to $\frac{1}{2}$ foot of wastage. In total, the corporation has orders for 1000 rolls of width $1\frac{1}{2}$ feet, 3000 rolls of width $2\frac{1}{2}$ feet, and 2000 rolls of width $3\frac{1}{2}$ feet. Any excess production over these amounts is also considered as wastage, and will be thrown away.

(a) Write down the possible cutting strategies and the associated amounts of wastage.

(b) Formulate the linear programming problem that must be solved if these orders are to be met with the minimum possible amount of total wastage.

5.32. A machine shop has just taken delivery of two machines which are to be operated together as a system. Each machine must be installed and checked, and the integrated system checked. The checking of a machine cannot begin until it has been installed, and the system cannot be checked until each individual machine has been checked. Management has estimated the following times for each of these five activities under normal working conditions:

Installation of Machine A:	9 working days
Installation of Machine B:	8 working days
Checking of Machine A:	4 working days
Checking of Machine B:	6 working days
Checking of System:	7 working days

A manager notices that under normal working conditions, the whole project will take 21 working days to complete. This is regarded as unacceptable. Management sees it as essential that the project be completed in at most 14 working days, and is prepared to devote additional resources to this end. It is possible to cut time for installation of machine A by up to 4 working days. However this will involve a cost of $400 for each day saved below the normal time of 9 working days. Other possible reductions are up to 3 working days for installation of machine B at a cost of $350 per day saved, up to 2 working days for checking of machine A at a cost of $250 per day saved, up to 3 working days for checking machine B at a cost of $200 per day saved, and up to 3 working days for checking of the system at a cost of $300 per day saved. If management wishes to complete this project in at most 14 working days at the lowest possible cost, formulate the linear programming problem that must be solved.

Planning Life Insurance Purchases:
An Application of Linear Programming[1]

How much life insurance should an individual purchase in a year? The answer to this question will depend on a number of factors, including desired size of the estate on death, funds available (possibly through borrowing) for insurance purchase, and value of other assets and investments. Consider, for example, a relatively young individual whose accumulated assets are of modest value. Should such a person wish to provide a sizeable estate in the event of death, purchase of a large insurance policy may be the only viable option. However, in future years, as this person accumulates savings from income, these can be invested to generate some "self-insurance" coverage. If the expected return on such investments is sufficiently high, it may be preferable to purchase less term life insurance, or to take out loans on the cash value of existing whole life insurance, or perhaps to cancel some fraction of this insurance.

The author of this study views the life insurance purchase decision as one that is to be made now for current and future purchases. The objective is to make that decision which yields the highest possible present value of future cash flows over the planning horizon. The decision variables for each period are:

1. the amount of new whole life insurance purchased in the period
2. the amount of whole life insurance bought back from insurance purchased in earlier periods
3. the amount of money invested in an alternative investment, for "self-insurance"
4. the amount of money withdrawn from the alternative investment
5. the amount borrowed from the cash value of policies taken out in earlier periods
6. the amount repaid of loans taken out on cash values for policies from earlier periods
7. the amount of new term insurance purchased in the period
8. the amount of term insurance cancelled from policies taken out in earlier periods.

Given information on, or assumptions about, premium rates on loans, and expected rate of return on the alternative investment, the present value of future cash flows can be computed as a function of these decision variables. This function can then be maximized, subject to a number of constraints being satisfied. These constraints are of two types. First a death benefit requirement for each year must be met. Second, a number of accounting constraints must be satisfied. For example, the available budget in any period cannot be exceeded, the loan

---

[1] This discussion is based on H. J. Schleef, "Using Linear Programming for Planning Life Insurance Purchases," *Decision Sciences, 11* (1980), 522–534.

balance for any policy should not exceed its value, the amount of term insurance canceled cannot exceed the amount taken out, and so on.

The author shows how this model can be employed to develop optimal insurance strategies for individuals with different death benefit requirements and availability of funds.

Planning Hospital Admissions: A Constrained Maximization Problem[2]

The authors of this study are concerned with the problem of long patient waiting lists for hospital treatment—a common situation in the National Health Service in Great Britain. They develop a linear programming model designed to plan patient admissions. Patients on the hospital waiting list are classified into one of 37 diagnostic categories. Within these categories patients are also classified according to the level of urgency of the case and whether treatment will be as an inpatient or day patient. The decision to be made is how many patients of each category, type, and urgency level to admit to the hospital. The objective is to maximize a weighted sum of patient throughput, where weights are determined subjectively according to diagnostic category and seriousness of case.

This objective function is maximized subject to a number of types of constraints. The number of patients admitted of any type cannot exceed the number of that type on the waiting list. The available bed space cannot be exceeded, and constraints are also imposed by the limited availability of surgeons' time and operating theater availability.

The authors discuss the application of this model to two hospitals. In particular, they demonstrate its use in estimating changes in the patient throughput that would arise from changes in such parameters as availability of beds, theater time, and surgeons' time.

---

[2] This discussion is based on J. A. George, D. R. Fox and R. W. Canvin, "A Hospital Throughput Model in the Context of Long Waiting Lists," *Journal of Operational Research Society, 34* (1983), 27–35.

special linear programming algorithms: transportation and assignment problems

6.1. INTRODUCTION

abstain

In earlier chapters, we have seen how to set up and solve quite general linear programming problems. For problems of modest size, solutions can be achieved by hand through the simplex algorithm, while computer programs can be employed in the solution of larger problems. In spite of the widespread availability of such computer programs, it is worthwhile seeking, wherever possible, computational shortcuts. These will lead to reductions in computational costs and to an increase in the size of the problems that can be handled.

When linear programming problems take certain specific structures, it is possible to find solution methods, or **algorithms,** that are computationally very much more efficient than the general simplex algorithm. In this chapter we will discuss the solution of two special problems of this sort—the **transportation problem** and the **assignment problem.** The special-purpose algorithms we will introduce for their solutions have substantial computational advantages over the simplex algorithm. In addition, these special-purpose algorithms can have a further important advantage over the simplex algorithm. For many problems met in practice, the solutions must be **integers;** we cannot, for example, ship a fraction of a refrigerator to a customer. The necessity for integer solutions is not directly catered for by the simplex algorithm. However, in the algorithms discussed in the present chapter, no difficulty of this sort arises.

6.2. THE TRANSPORTATION PROBLEM

The transportation algorithm was originally developed to handle a class of problems in which quantities of material or goods are available at various **origins,** and are required at several **destinations.** It is assumed that the costs per unit of transporting goods from each origin to each destination are known. The objective, then, is to minimize total transportation costs.

We will illustrate the general setup and solution to the transportation problem through the case of a washing machine manufacturer who has three plants—in New York, Denver, and Baltimore. Monthly production capacities at these plants are shown in Table 6.1.

The washing machines are marketed through four distribution centers—in Boston, Atlanta, Chicago, and Los Angeles. Demand forecasts for the coming month indicate the requirements of these centers shown in Table 6.2.

Notice that as we have set up the problem, the total demand for washing machines is precisely equal to the total supply. Later it will be shown how this restriction can be relaxed. For the present, the method of solution described will assume a balance between total demand and supply.

In principle, the manufacturer can ship washing machines from any origin to any destination. Therefore, as illustrated in Figure 6.1, there are twelve possible routes. In general, the number of possible routes will be the product of the number of origins and the number of destinations. To complete the problem specifications, Table 6.3 shows the costs per unit for each of the twelve possible transportation routes for the washing machine manufacturer.

Given the problem specifications set out in Tables 6.1–6.3, the question to be answered in the following sections of this chapter is easily stated. Which

TABLE 6.1 Production capacities for the washing machine manufacturer.

ORIGIN	PRODUCTION CAPACITY
New York	700
Denver	400
Baltimore	600
Total Supply	1700

TABLE 6.2 Distribution center requirements for the washing machine manufacturer.

DESTINATION	REQUIREMENTS
Boston	300
Atlanta	300
Chicago	600
Los Angeles	500
Total Demand	1700

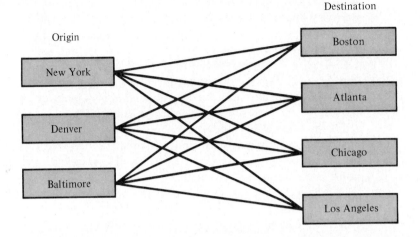

TABLE 6.3 Unit transportation costs (in dollars) for the washing machine manufacturer.

ORIGIN	DESTINATION			
	BOSTON	ATLANTA	CHICAGO	LOS ANGELES
New York	6	9	8	13
Denver	12	17	10	9
Baltimore	7	8	11	15

choice of routes will yield the lowest possible total transportation cost? The general problem is now stated in the box.

The Transportation Problem

Suppose that quantities of goods are available in m different origins, and are required at n different destinations. Let a_i ($i = 1, 2, \ldots, m$) denote the quantity that can be supplied at the i-th point of origin, and b_j ($j = 1, 2, \ldots, n$) be the quantity demanded at the j-th destination. Then, assuming total demand is equal to total supply,

$$a_1 + a_2 + \ldots + a_m = b_1 + b_2 + \ldots + b_n$$

Denote by c_{ij} the cost per unit of transportation from the i-th origin to the j-th destination. Then, the problem is to minimize total transportation costs, subject to the requirement that totals of a_i ($i = 1, 2, \ldots, m$) be shipped from the origins, and totals of b_j ($j = 1, 2, \ldots, n$) be shipped to the destinations.

That the transportation problem is a linear programming problem can easily be seen through denoting by x_{ij} the quantity to be shipped from origin i to destination j. For example, in the problem of the manufacturer of washing machines, x_{23} denotes the number of machines sent from Denver to Chicago. Since, from Table 6.3, the cost per machine on this route is \$10, the total cost of transporting x_{23} washing machines from Denver to Chicago will be $10x_{23}$. The transportation problem can therefore be expressed algebraically as

$$\text{Minimize} \quad 6x_{11} + 9x_{12} + 8x_{13} + 13x_{14}$$
$$+ 12x_{21} + 17x_{22} + 10x_{23} + 9x_{24}$$
$$+ 7x_{31} + 8x_{32} + 11x_{33} + 15x_{34}$$

$$\text{subject to} \quad x_{11} + x_{12} + x_{13} + x_{14} = 700$$
$$x_{21} + x_{22} + x_{23} + x_{24} = 400$$
$$x_{31} + x_{32} + x_{33} + x_{34} = 600$$
$$x_{11} + x_{21} + x_{31} = 300$$
$$x_{12} + x_{22} + x_{32} = 300$$
$$x_{13} + x_{23} + x_{33} = 600$$
$$x_{14} + x_{24} + x_{34} = 500$$
$$x_{ij} \geq 0$$
$$(i = 1, 2, 3; j = 1, 2, 3, 4)$$

The function to be minimized is the total cost of transportation. The first three constraints ensure that the supply at each point of origin is exhausted, while the next four require that the demand at each destination point is met. We have, therefore, a linear programming problem with twelve decision variables, x_{ij}, and seven constraints, in addition to the nonnegativity constraints.

For the more general problem, with m points of origin and n destination points, the algebraic formulation is

$$\text{Minimize} \quad c_{11}x_{11} + c_{12}x_{12} + \ldots + c_{1n}x_{1n}$$
$$+ c_{21}x_{21} + c_{22}x_{22} + \ldots + c_{2n}x_{2n}$$
$$+ \cdots \cdots$$
$$+ c_{m1}x_{m1} + c_{m2}x_{m2} + \ldots + c_{mn}x_{mn}$$

$$\text{subject to} \quad x_{11} + x_{12} + \ldots + x_{1n} = a_1$$
$$x_{21} + x_{22} + \ldots + x_{2n} = a_2$$
$$\cdots$$
$$x_{m1} + x_{m2} + \ldots + x_{mn} = a_m \quad\quad (6.1)$$
$$x_{11} + x_{21} + \ldots + x_{m1} = b_1$$
$$x_{12} + x_{22} + \ldots + x_{m2} = b_2$$
$$\cdots$$
$$x_{1n} + x_{2n} + \ldots + x_{mn} = b_n$$
$$x_{ij} \geq 0$$
$$(i = 1, 2, \ldots, m; j = 1, 2, \ldots, n)$$

The general problem, then, has mn decision variables, and, as we have written it, $m + n$ equality constraints. In fact, however, given the requirement that total demand is equal to total supply, one of these constraints is redundant; that is, if any $m + n - 1$ of them are satisfied, then so must be the other. Therefore, without any loss of generality, one of the equality constraints can be dropped, so that there are $m + n - 1$ *effective* constraints.

We see, then, that the transportation problem is simply a linear programming problem with a special structure, which can be written as

Minimize
$$\sum_{i=1}^{m} \sum_{j=1}^{n} c_{ij} x_{ij}$$

subject to
$$\sum_{j=1}^{n} x_{ij} = a_i \ (i = 1, 2, \ldots, m)$$
$$\sum_{i=1}^{m} x_{ij} = b_j \ (j = 1, 2, \ldots, n)$$
$$x_{ij} \geq 0 \ (i = 1, 2, \ldots, m; j = 1, 2, \ldots, n)$$

Any problem with this special structure is referred to as a "transportation problem," irrespective of the context in which it arises. The algorithm employed in the solution of the transportation problem is an adaptation of the simplex algorithm to this structure. It involves considerable computational simplification and, moreover, guarantees that the solutions will be integer-valued. The outline structure of the algorithm is depicted in Figure 6.2 (see page 198). Like the simplex algorithm, it begins with an initial solution which is then tested for optimality. Should this solution be suboptimal, an improved solution is found, and the algorithm **iterates** until the optimal solution is achieved.

Since the transportation problem is a linear programming problem, we know that it is only necessary to examine basic feasible solutions. It follows, then, since there are $m + n - 1$ effective constraints, that the solutions we seek will have at most $m + n - 1$ decision variables taking nonzero values; that is, at most $m + n - 1$ of the available mn routes will actually be used. For example, in the case of the washing machine manufacturer, at most six of the twelve routes will be employed in such solutions. It is certainly not difficult to find an initial feasible solution of this sort. However, given our objective of computational efficiency, it is worthwhile to spend a little effort looking for an initial solution that is likely to be quite close to the optimal solution. In that case, relatively few iterations would be required before the algorithm converges on the optimal solution. The procedure we will describe for finding an initial solution is known as **Vogel's Approximation Method.** Next, we can iterate to the optimal solution using the **Modified Distribution Method.**

It is convenient to set out the transportation problem in a rectangular tableau form, as in Table 6.4. We will build on this tableau in deriving the optimal solution to the transportation problem. The first column of Table 6.4 shows the origins, while the final column lists the supply of washing machines at each. Similarly, the first row of the table gives the destinations, and the bottom row the demand at each. In the main body of the table, there are twelve squares—

TABLE 6.4 Specification of the transportation problem for the washing machine manufacturer.

From \ To	Boston	Atlanta	Chicago	Los Angeles	Supply
New York	6	9	8	13	700
Denver	12	17	10	9	400
Baltimore	7	8	11	15	600
Demand	300	300	600	500	Total 1700

one for each origin-destination route. The main bodies of these squares will be used later to show the numbers of washing machines to be transported on each route. In their upper right-hand corners, smaller squares have been drawn containing the costs of transportation on the various routes. As we will see, this tabular scheme will provide us with a convenient worksheet for the solution of the transportation problem.

6.3. INITIAL FEASIBLE SOLUTION FOR TRANSPORTATION PROBLEMS: VOGEL'S APPROXIMATION METHOD (VAM)

Referring to Figure 6.2, our first task is to find an initial feasible solution to the transportation problem. The procedure we will employ, **Vogel's Approximation Method (VAM)**, is a little cumbersome to work through. However, the time taken is very likely to be rewarded by the achievement of a solution that is quite close to optimal.

To see how this procedure works, notice that the lowest cost destination for shipments out of New York is Boston, at $6 per unit. The second lowest cost route out of New York is to Chicago, at $8 per unit. The difference, $2 per unit, is known as the **opportunity cost** of shipping to Chicago rather than to Boston. In the same way, the lowest cost source of shipments to Atlanta is Baltimore, at $8 per unit. The next cheapest source is New York, at $9 per unit. Here, then, the opportunity cost of not using the lowest cost route is $1. Continuing in this fashion we can find opportunity costs for each origin and for each destination. In Table 6.5, we extend Table 6.4 to show these opportunity costs.

FIGURE 6.2 General approach to the solution of the transportation problem.

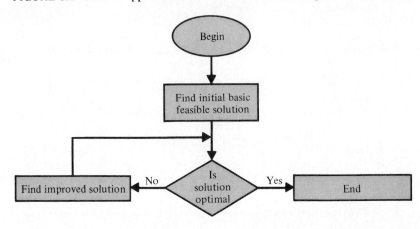

Looking at Table 6.5, it can be seen that the highest of these seven opportunity costs is in the Los Angeles column. The implication is that if washing machines are not sent from Denver to Los Angeles, the additional cost per unit for the next cheapest source is $4. Accordingly, the VAM solution dictates that as many machines as possible be sent from Denver to Los Angeles. The most that can be done is to ship 400 machines, the entire Denver capacity, along this route. This figure is therefore entered in the body of the table. Since the entire Denver supply is now exhausted, a line is drawn through both the supply and the transportation costs from Denver, as they are no longer relevant for the remainder of our calculations. Further, the total Los Angeles demand is reduced by 400, to 100 washing machines.

TABLE 6.5 First step of VAM for the problem of the washing machine manufacturer.

To / From	Boston	Atlanta	Chicago	Los Angeles	Supply	Opportunity Cost
New York	6	9	8	13	700	2
Denver	~~12~~	~~17~~	~~10~~	~~9~~ 400	~~400~~	1
Baltimore	7	8	11	15	600	1
Demand	300	300	600	~~500~~ 100		
Opportunity Cost	1	1	2	4		

TABLE 6.6 Second step of VAM for the problem of the washing machine manufacturer.

To / From	Boston	Atlanta	Chicago	Los Angeles	Supply	Opportunity Cost
New York	6	9	8 / 600	13	~~700~~ 100	2
Denver	~~12~~	~~17~~	~~10~~	~~9~~ / 400	~~400~~	~~1~~
Baltimore	7	8	1|1	15	600	1
Demand	300	300	~~600~~	~~500~~ 100		
Opportunity Cost	1	1	~~2~~ 3	~~4~~ 2		

Where necessary, we must now recompute the opportunity costs with Denver eliminated as a possible source of supply. This is done in Table 6.6. As we see, two of the opportunity costs have changed with the elimination of the Denver origin. Moreover, we now ignore opportunity costs for shipment from Denver, so that there is no entry for this row. The highest of the six remaining opportunity costs is in the Chicago column. This value, of $3, arises as the difference between unit costs for shipments from New York and Baltimore to Chicago. In consequence, VAM requires as large a shipment as possible from New York to Chicago. This amounts to 600 washing machines, the entire amount demanded in Chicago. The facts that these are to be shipped, and that the full demand for Chicago has, in consequence, been met are indicated in the table. Also noted is that now only 100 washing machines remain from the original New York supply.

Continuing in exactly the same manner, the opportunity costs are recomputed in Table 6.7, with Denver eliminated as a possible origin and Chicago as a potential destination. The biggest opportunity cost is now in the New York row, indicating a difference of $3 per unit between transporting washing machines from New York to Boston and from New York to Atlanta. Therefore, as many machines as possible should be sent from New York to Boston. In fact, only 100 of the original New York supply remains, so that this quantity is entered in the appropriate cell of the table. The total New York capacity is now exhausted, and the unmet demand in Boston is now 200 washing machines.

In fact, a further look at Table 6.7 reveals that our task has been completed. The only remaining supply of washing machines is in Baltimore, and these must therefore be used to meet the remaining demands in Boston, Atlanta,

TABLE 6.7 Third step of VAM for the problem of the washing machine manufacturer.

To / From	Boston	Atlanta	Chicago	Los Angeles	Supply	Opportunity Cost
New York	~~6~~ 100	~~9~~	~~8~~ 600	~~13~~	~~700~~ ~~100~~	~~2~~ 3
Denver	~~12~~	~~17~~	~~10~~	~~9~~ 400	~~400~~	~~1~~
Baltimore	7	8	11	15	600	1
Demand	~~300~~ 200	300	600	~~500~~ 100		
Opportunity Cost	1	1	~~2~~ 3	~~4~~ 2		

and Los Angeles. At this stage, then, the only feasible solution involves ship-
ments from Baltimore of 200 machines to Boston, 300 to Atlanta, and 100 to Los
Angeles. The complete solution is entered in the transportation tableau of
Table 6.8.

The procedure through which the VAM solution to the transportation problem was constructed ensures that the solution is feasible. Notice also that the
solution of Table 6.8 involves, as required for a basic feasible solution, just

TABLE 6.8 VAM solution for the problem of the washing machine manufacturer.

To / From	Boston	Atlanta	Chicago	Los Angeles	Supply
New York	6 100	9	8 600	13	700
Denver	12	17	10	9 400	400
Baltimore	7 200	8 300	11	15 100	600
Demand	300	300	600	500	Total 1700

TABLE 6.9 Summary of the VAM solution for the problem of the washing machine manufacturer.

ROUTE	QUANTITY SHIPPED	COST PER UNIT	TOTAL COST ($)
New York–Boston	100	6	600
New York–Chicago	600	8	4800
Denver–Los Angeles	400	9	3600
Baltimore–Boston	200	7	1400
Baltimore–Atlanta	300	8	2400
Baltimore–Los Angeles	100	15	1500
	1700		14,300

$m + n - 1 = 6$ of the available routes being used. In Table 6.9, these routes are listed, and the total transportation cost of the VAM solution is calculated. We see that total transportation costs at this solution amount to $14,300.

Summary of VAM Approach

(i) Set out the transportation problem in a rectangular array.

(ii) For each row (column) find the opportunity cost as the difference in unit transportation costs between the least expensive and next least expensive routes in that row (column).

(iii) Identify the largest of all these opportunity costs and ship the maximum amount possible along the least expensive route in the corresponding row or column.

(iv) For this route, reduce by the amount shipped the supply at the origin and the demand at the destination.

(v) The supply at the point of origin or the demand at the destination point will now be fully exhausted. Delete all of the unit transportation costs in the exhausted row or column. If both supply and demand are exhausted, delete the row and column costs.

(vi) Repeat steps (ii)–(v) until a complete feasible solution is achieved.

6.4. FINDING THE OPTIMAL SOLUTION FOR TRANSPORTATION PROBLEMS: THE MODIFIED DISTRIBUTION (MODI) METHOD

In Section 6.3, we derived the VAM solution to the transportation problem of the washing machine manufacturer. This procedure generally gives a good start to finding an optimal solution, though the VAM solution itself is not necessarily the best that can be achieved. The solution described in Tables 6.8 and 6.9 shows how the washing machines can be transported from the three origins to the four destinations at a total cost of $14,300. The next step is to test this solution for optimality.

The procedure we will employ is known as the **Modified Distribution (MODI) Method.** The MODI method requires the introduction of a total of $m + n$ variables—one for each origin and one for each destination. For the problem of the washing machine manufacturer, then, we must define three row variables, r_1, r_2, and r_3, and four column variables, k_1, k_2, k_3, and k_4. The values of these variables are found by solving the equations

$$r_i + k_j = c_{ij}$$

where the c_{ij} are the unit transportation costs *of those routes that are actually used in the solution that is being tested for optimality.* Therefore, for the six routes of Table 6.9, we have:

New York–Boston	$r_1 + k_1 = 6$
New York–Chicago	$r_1 + k_3 = 8$
Denver–Los Angeles	$r_2 + k_4 = 9$
Baltimore–Boston	$r_3 + k_1 = 7$
Baltimore–Atlanta	$r_3 + k_2 = 8$
Baltimore–Los Angeles	$r_3 + k_4 = 15$

Since there are 6 equations in 7 variables (r_i, k_j), one of these variables can be set arbitrarily, and the resulting system of 6 equations in 6 variables solved. The approach employed is to set one of the variables to zero. Here we will let $r_1 = 0$. Then, immediately from the New York–Boston equation, $k_1 = 6$ and, using the New York–Chicago equation, $k_3 = 8$. Next, from the Baltimore–Boston equation

$$r_3 + 6 = 7$$

so that

$$r_3 = 1$$

From the Baltimore–Atlanta equation we then find

$$1 + k_2 = 8$$

and so

$$k_2 = 7$$

Similarly, from the Baltimore–Los Angeles equation

$$1 + k_4 = 15$$

giving

$$k_4 = 14$$

Finally, using the Denver–Los Angeles equation,

$$r_2 + 14 = 9$$

yielding

$$r_2 = -5$$

A complete solution then is given by

$$r_1 = 0, r_2 = -5, r_3 = 1, k_1 = 6, k_2 = 7, k_3 = 8, k_4 = 14$$

We can interpret these results as implying that using the routes in the solution being tested is equivalent to a system in which $0 is "paid" for each washing machine leaving New York, $-$5$ is "paid" for each unit leaving Denver, and $1 is paid for each unit leaving Baltimore. In addition, $6 is paid for each machine entering Boston, $7 for each unit entering Atlanta, $8 for each unit entering Chicago, and $14 for each unit entering Los Angeles. This information is easily incorporated into our worksheet by the addition of an extra row and column to the tableau, as in Table 6.10. In fact, the MODI method is simply a streamlined version of the simplex algorithm and, for any route, $(r_i + k_j)$ is, in effect, a z entry in the simplex tableau. For example, since $r_1 = 0$ and $k_2 = 7$, $(r_1 + k_2) = 7$, implying that for each unit shipped from New York to Atlanta, a savings of $7 can be achieved through the net reduction of one unit in the numbers to be shipped on the routes currently in use.

Now, to test our solution for optimality, it is necessary to check whether employment of one of the unused routes would be less expensive than this scheme of payments. Accordingly, for each such route we calculate the differences

$$d_{ij} = c_{ij} - (r_i + k_j)$$

If any of these differences is negative, then a solution with lower total cost can be found. Since the aim is to minimize total cost, any negative d_{ij} value will

TABLE 6.10 MODI optimality test of VAM solution for the problem of the washing machine manufacturer.

r_i	From \ To	Boston (k_j 6)	Atlanta (7)	Chicago (8)	Los Angeles (14)	Supply
0	New York	6 / 100	9 / 2	8 / 600	13 / -1	700
-5	Denver	12 / 11	17 / 15	10 / 7	9 / 400	400
1	Baltimore	7 / 200	8 / 300	11 / 2	15 / 100	600
	Demand	300	300	600	500	Total 1700

imply that the current solution is not optimal. For example, for the New York–Atlanta route, we find

$$d_{12} = 9 - (0 + 7) = 2$$

The d_{ij} are displayed in the bottom left-hand corners of the route squares in the main body of Table 6.10.

Looking at Table 6.10, we see that there is one negative d_{ij} value—for the New York–Lost Angeles route. The implication is that the current solution is not optimal, and that we should proceed by bringing this route into the solution.

The MODI Test for Optimality

Suppose we have a transportation problem with m points of origin and n destination points. Denote by c_{ij} the unit cost of shipments from the i-th origin to the j-th destination. A feasible solution involving the use of $m + n - 1$ of the available routes is to be tested for optimality.

(i) Define the variables r_i $(i = 1, \ldots, m)$ and k_j $(j = 1, \ldots, n)$ through the $m + n - 1$ equations

$$r_i + k_j = c_{ij}$$

for the basic routes in the solution. This set of equations is solved when one of the variables (say, r_1) is set to zero.

(ii) For each nonbasic route in the solution, calculate the differences

$$d_{ij} = c_{ij} - (r_i + k_j)$$

If none of these differences is negative, the solution is optimal.

(iii) If any of the d_{ij} is negative, move to a solution in which the route corresponding to the largest negative d_{ij} is brought into use.

MOVING TO AN IMPROVED SOLUTION: THE STEPPING-STONE METHOD

The next step toward the optimal solution of the transportation problem of the washing machine manufacturer is to bring the New York–Los Angeles route into use. How can this be achieved? Referring to Table 6.10, we can ship washing machines from New York to Los Angeles by sending less machines from New York to Boston. To compensate for this, more machines can be sent from Baltimore to Boston, and correspondingly less from Baltimore to Los Angeles. In fact, since at present just 100 machines are shipped on each of the New York–Boston and Baltimore–Los Angeles routes, the adjustments just described to the original solution can be made with at most 100 washing machines.

In Table 6.11 we see graphically how this conclusion was reached. In that table we have connected four routes at the corners of a rectangle, using a dotted

TABLE 6.11 Stepping-stone method applied to the problem of the washing machine manufacturer.

To From	Boston		Atlanta	Chicago	Los Angeles		Supply
New York	− 100 100	6	9	8 600	+ 100	13	700
Denver		12	17	10	400	9	400
Baltimore	+ 100 200	7	8 300	11	− 100 100	15	600
Demand	300		300	600	500		Total 1700

line. One of these routes is that which we want to bring into the solution, while the other three are routes that are already in the solution. We move in steps from one of these four routes to the next, adding and subtracting quantities to be shipped. It is for this reason that the procedure is called the **stepping-stone method.** In order to ship machines from New York to Los Angeles, we reduce by the same amount shipments from Baltimore to Los Angeles. Instead, more machines are sent from Baltimore to Boston, and correspondingly less from New York to Boston. These adjustments can be made to the point where the quantity to be shipped on one of the routes of the stepping-stone path falls to zero. It is clear from Table 6.11 that the maximum possible size of the adjustments to be made is 100 units. Accordingly, in the next solution, 100 machines will be sent from New York to Los Angeles, none from New York to Boston, 300 from Baltimore to Boston, and none from Baltimore to Los Angeles. This solution is set out in the tableau of Table 6.12.

Table 6.13 summarizes the new solution in terms of the routes actually in use and derives the total transportation cost of $14,200. As expected this is lower[1] than the total cost of the VAM solution of Table 6.9.

At this point then, we have produced a solution that improves over the initial VAM solution. The next step in the analysis of the transportation problem is to test the new solution for optimality.

---

[1] In fact, we could have deduced earlier that the new solution would yield $100 savings over the other. The implication of the d_{ij} value of -1 for the New York-Los Angeles route, as shown in Table 6.10, is that each unit sent along this route will yield a saving of $1. Since 100 units are to be transported in the new solution, the total gain must be $100.

TABLE 6.12 Second solution to the problem of the washing machine manufacturer.

To From	Boston	Atlanta	Chicago	Los Angeles	Supply
New York	6	9	8 600	13 100	700
Denver	12	17	10	9 400	400
Baltimore	7 300	8 300	11	15	600
Demand	300	300	600	500	Total 1700

TABLE 6.13 Summary of the second solution for the problem of the washing machine manufacturer.

ROUTE	QUANTITY SHIPPED	COST PER UNIT	TOTAL COST ($)
New York–Chicago	600	8	4800
New York–Los Angeles	100	13	1300
Denver–Los Angeles	400	9	3600
Baltimore–Boston	300	7	2100
Baltimore–Atlanta	300	8	2400
	1700		14,200

The Stepping-Stone Method

Suppose that we have a suboptimal solution to a transportation problem and want to being a new route into the solution.

(i) In the transportation tableau, construct a closed figure, with the route to be brought into solution at one corner, and routes already in the solution at the other corners.

(ii) Moving from corner to corner of this figure, add and subtract equal amounts from the original shipment quantities. Make these adjustments as large as possible subject to the requirement that the new solution must be feasible.

DEGENERATE SOLUTIONS

Typically, the new solution can be checked for optimality using the MODI method precisely as before. However, the solution of Table 6.12 has a special feature—namely that less than $m + n - 1 = 6$ routes are in use. In fact, we see that five routes are used in this solution. Such solutions are said to be **degenerate.**

Definition:

A **degenerate solution** is one in which less than $m + n - 1$ routes are used.

Before applying the MODI method, we artificially bring up to $m + n - 1$ the number of routes in the solution by adding a route along which the quantity of items to be transported is zero. The choice, however, is not arbitrary. To check the solution for optimality, we must be able to compute all of the r_i and k_j. The route with zero shipment is chosen to ensure that this is possible. From the routes that are in use in the solution of Table 6.12, we obtain the equations

New York–Chicago	$r_1 + k_3 = 8$
New York–Los Angeles	$r_1 + k_4 = 13$
Denver–Los Angeles	$r_2 + k_4 = 9$
Baltimore–Boston	$r_3 + k_1 = 7$
Baltimore–Atlanta	$r_3 + k_2 = 8$

Since now there are only 5 equations in 7 variables, setting any one of these variables to zero will not allow us to solve for the other six. We see that the first three equations involve only r_1, r_2, k_3, and k_4, and the second two involve only r_3, k_1, and k_2. What we require is a sixth equation linking these two sets. For example,

$$r_2 + k_3 = 10$$

will not do, as it involves only variables in the first set. Suppose, instead we use the New York–Boston route as the route with zero shipment. Then, adding

$$r_1 + k_1 = 6$$

to the original five equations yields a system that can be solved. We do this by setting $r_1 = 0$ and solving for the other six variables. Next, for the non-basic routes, we compute the differences

$$d_{ij} = c_{ij} - (r_i + k_j)$$

The results are shown in Table 6.14, from which it emerges that none of these differences is negative. It therefore follows that the solution of Table 6.13 is optimal. The lowest possible transportation cost that can be achieved is $14,200. This optimal solution is shown graphically in Figure 6.3.

FIGURE 6.3 Optimal solution for the problem of the washing machine manufacturer.

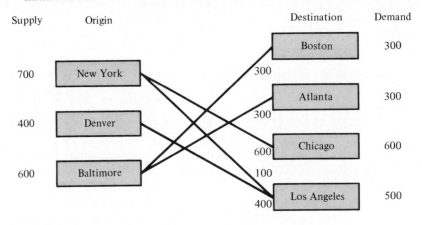

TABLE 6.14 MODI optimality test for the second solution of the problem of the washing machine manufacturer.

r_i	k_j / From \ To	6 / Boston	7 / Atlanta	8 / Chicago	13 / Los Angeles	Supply
0	New York	6 / 0	9 / / 2	8 / 600	13 / 100	700
−4	Denver	12 / / 10	17 / / 14	·10 / / 6	9 / 400	400
1	Baltimore	7 / 300	8 / 300	11 / / 2	15 / / 1	600
	Demand	300	300	600	500	Total 1700

6.5. UNBALANCED DEMAND AND SUPPLY IN TRANSPORTATION PROBLEMS

The transportation problem that we solved in the earlier sections of this chapter had the special feature that total demand was equal to total supply. It very often happens in practice that we want to deal with transportation problems in which

Special Linear Programming Algorithms: Transportation and Assignment Problems demand and supply are not in balance. The object is still to ship material as inexpensively as possible, but now, inevitably, any feasible solution will involve either excess supply or unmet demand.

It is not difficult to modify our algorithms to handle problems of unbalanced supply and demand. This is done by creating **dummy routes,** that is, routes which will actually not be used, and with which, therefore, transportation costs of zero are associated. Specifically, there are two cases:

- **(a)** *Total demand exceeds total supply.* In this case a **dummy origin** is created, together with the fiction that the amount of the excess demand is to be shipped from this origin. Since no such shipments can occur, of course, the unit shipment costs from the dummy origin to each destination are set at zero.
- **(b)** *Total supply exceeds total demand.* Here we create a **dummy destination,** along with the fiction that the amount of the excess supply will be sent to this destination. Again, since no such transfers will really be made, we set at zero the unit transportation costs to this dummy destination.

We now proceed to illustrate the techniques involved through minor modifications of the original specifications to the transportation problem of the washing machine manufacturer.

TOTAL DEMAND EXCEEDS TOTAL SUPPLY

Suppose that for a particular month, sales forecasts of the washing machine manufacturer indicate that an additional 100 units are required in Boston. Demand at the other three destination centers remains unchanged, while the production capacities at the three plants cannot be altered. The problem specifications, then, are precisely those of Tables 6.1–6.3, with the single exception that 400 machines are now required in Boston.

We are now in the position where total demand exceeds total supply, and there will necessarily be 100 units of unmet demand. Our problem is to ship the total output of 1700 washing machines as cheaply as possible, subject to the limitations imposed by demand and supply at the destinations and origins. In order to solve this problem, the transportation tableau is extended through the addition of a dummy origin, as shown in Table 6.15. Unit transportation costs from the dummy origin are set at zero.

Once the tableau has been extended in this fashion, the VAM procedure and MODI method can be employed, along precisely the same lines as in Sections 6.3–6.4, to derive the optimum solution. We leave as an exercise to the reader the details of these derivations. Table 6.15 displays the optimum solution. The implication, in that solution, of the "shipment" of 100 units from the dummy origin to Los Angeles is that 100 units of the total Los Angeles demand will be unmet in this solution.

Table 6.15 also shows the MODI check for optimality of the solution. Notice that since the solution is degenerate, we have entered the shipment of zero units from New York to Los Angeles. That the solution is indeed optimal follows

TABLE 6.15 Problem of the washing machine manufacturer when 100 additional machines are required in Boston. Shown are the optimal solution and the MODI test for optimality.

r_i	To / From	k_j = 6 Boston	7 Atlanta	8 Chicago	13 Los Angeles	Supply
0	New York	6 / 100	9 / (2)	8 / 600	13 / 0	700
−4	Denver	12 / (10)	17 / (14)	10 / (6)	9 / 400	400
1	Baltimore	7 / 300	8 / 300	11 / (2)	15 / (1)	600
−13	Dummy	0 / (7)	0 / (6)	0 / (5)	0 / 100	100
	Demand	400	300	600	500	Total 1800

from the fact that none of the d_{ij} values, displayed in the bottom left-hand corners of the cells corresponding to the unused routes, are negative.

TOTAL SUPPLY EXCEEDS TOTAL DEMAND

Now let us assume that the washing machine manufacturer can increase production capacity in New York from 700 to 800 machines, with the original problem specifications remaining unchanged, as in Tables 6.1–6.3. The position now is that total supply exceeds total demand, so that 100 of the available units will not be required. In order to find the lowest possible total transportation costs, the tableau is extended by adding a dummy destination, as shown in Table 6.16. All unit transportation costs to this destination are set at zero.

Given this extended tableau, the VAM procedure and MODI method can be used in the usual way to derive the optimum solution displayed in Table 6.16. We leave, as an exercise to the reader, the details of the derivations and the verification that the solution is indeed optimal. In Table 6.16, the implication of the "shipment" of 100 units from Baltimore to the dummy destination is that only 500 units of the 600 available in Baltimore will be required.

TABLE 6.16 Optimal solution to the problem of the washing machine manufacturer when 100 additional machines are available in New York.

From \ To	Boston	Atlanta	Chicago	Los Angeles	Dummy	Supply
New York	6 — 100	9	8 — 600	13 — 100	0	800
Denver	12	17	10	9 — 400	0	400
Baltimore	7 — 200	8 — 300	11	15	0 — 100	600
Demand	300	300	600	500	100	Total 1800

6.6. MAXIMIZATION PROBLEMS AND THE TRANSPORTATION ALGORITHM

The transportation algorithm, with minor modifications, can also be used to solve a class of constrained maximization problems. To illustrate, consider the problem of a manufacturer of portable televisions, with three plants and four distribution centers. Table 6.17 shows, for the coming week, the production capacities of the plants and demand forecasts at the distribution centers. Notice that total demand exceeds total supply.

The manufacturer again must ship units from plants to distribution centers, and transportation costs will differ from route to route. However, unit production costs also differ from plant to plant, and the selling prices at the distribution centers are not all the same. For each origin–destination route, the manufacturer is able to take into account all these factors and compute the profit per unit that

TABLE 6.17 Production capacities and distribution center requirements for the manufacturer of television sets.

PLANT	PRODUCTION CAPACITY	DISTRIBUTION CENTER	DEMAND FORECAST
Kansas City	600	New Orleans	600
Newark	600	Philadelphia	700
Dallas	800	San Francisco	400
	2000	Minneapolis	500
			2200

TABLE 6.18 Unit profits (in dollars) for the television set manufacturer.

ORIGIN	DESTINATION			
	NEW ORLEANS	PHILADELPHIA	SAN FRANCISCO	MINNEAPOLIS
Kansas City	10	12	14	18
Newark	13	11	12	14
Dallas	15	15	14	16

can be achieved from sales of the television sets. These profit figures are set out in Table 6.18.

Given these problem specifications, the objective of the company is to transport television sets from origins to destinations so that total profits are as high as possible. Thus, although the framework of the problem is that of a transportation tableau, the aim here is objective function **maximization.**

In fact, maximization problems can be solved through relatively minor modifications of the procedures we presented for the solution of constrained minimization problems. Again, we begin by finding a feasible solution. This solution is tested for optimality, and, should it prove suboptimal, we then iterate to an optimal solution.

Vogel's Approximation Method can be used to develop an initial feasible solution which should often be quite close to the optimal solution. The only difference from the approach used in Section 6.3 follows from the fact that our interest is now in the highest possible profits, rather than the lowest possible costs. Accordingly, the opportunity costs for any origin or destination are now computed as *the difference between the highest and next highest profits*. For example, from Table 6.18 we see that for shipments from Kansas City, the most profitable route, at $18 per unit, is to Minneapolis, while the next most profitable, at $14, is to San Francisco. Hence, at the outset, the opportunity cost associated with the Kansas City origin is $4. The VAM approach is then to ship as much as possible along the most profitable route corresponding to the highest opportunity cost.

Table 6.19 shows the completed VAM worksheet. Notice that because demand exceeds supply, we have introduced a dummy origin associated with zero profits. The VAM solution involves the use of $m + n - 1 = 7$ routes, and is therefore not degenerate. The "shipment" of 200 units from the dummy origin to San Francisco implies that in this solution, there will be 200 units of unmet demand in San Francisco.

The VAM solution is not necessarily the best that can be achieved and must be checked for optimality. We will now show how the Modified Distribution Method can be employed for this purpose. We begin, as before, by defining row and column variables r_i and k_j. These are computed by solving, for the routes actually used in the tested solution, equations

$$r_i + k_j = c_{ij}$$

TABLE 6.19 VAM solution to the problem of the television set manufacturer.

From \ To	New Orleans	Philadelphia	San Francisco	Minneapolis	Supply	Opportunity Cost
Kansas City	~~10~~	~~12~~	14 100	18 500	~~600~~ ~~100~~	~~4~~ ~~2~~ ~~4~~
Newark	13 500	~~11~~	12 100	14	~~600~~ 100	1
Dallas	~~15~~ 100	~~15~~ 700	~~14~~	~~16~~	~~800~~ ~~100~~	~~1~~ ~~0~~ ~~1~~
Dummy	0	0	0 200	0	200	0
Demand	~~600~~ ~~500~~	~~700~~	~~400~~ 300	~~500~~	Total 2200	
Opportunity Cost	~~2~~ 13	~~3~~	~~0~~ ~~2~~ 12	~~2~~		

where c_{ij} denotes unit *profit* for shipments from the i-th origin to the j-th destination. As before, to achieve a solution to these equations, we set r_1 equal to zero. The complete solution is displayed in Table 6.20. These values can be interpreted as implying that the VAM solution is equivalent to a system in which $0 "profit" is received for each unit shipped from Kansas City, $-$2 "profit" for each unit out of Newark, and so on. In addition, $15 profit is derived from each unit entering New Orleans, and so forth.

Just as for the minimization problem, the differences

$$d_{ij} = c_{ij} - (r_i + k_j)$$

are computed for each unused route. However, in seeking a better solution, we now look for *positive* values of these differences since this would imply that increased profits could be achieved by bringing the corresponding routes into the solution. Looking at the entries in the bottom left-hand corners of the route cells in Table 6.20, we see that none of the d_{ij} values is positive. It follows that on this occasion, the VAM solution is optimal. This solution is displayed graphically in Figure 6.4. The total profit that can be obtained is

$$(100)(14) + (500)(18) + (500)(13) + (100)(12) + (100)(15) + (700)(15) = \$30,100$$

TABLE 6.20 MODI optimality test for the VAM solution to the problem of the television set manufacturer.

r_i / From	k_j →	New Orleans (15)	Philadelphia (15)	San Francisco (14)	Minneapolis (18)	Supply
0	Kansas City	10 −5	12 −3	14 100	18 500	600
−2	Newark	13 +100 500	11 −2	12 −100 100	14 −2	600
0	Dallas	15 −100 100	15 700	14 +100 0	16 −2	800
−14	Dummy	0 −1	0 −1	0 200	0 −4	200
	Demand	600	700	400	500	Total 2200

In Table 6.20, notice that the d_{ij} value for the Dallas–San Francisco route is zero. The implication is that bringing this route into the solution will leave total profits unchanged. It follows, therefore, that our problem has multiple optimal solutions. To see this, Table 6.20 shows the stepping-stone path for the Dallas–San Francisco route to enter the solution. The most that can be transported along this route, making the stepping-stone adjustments, is 100 units. The new solution obtained in this fashion is displayed in Table 6.21. The total profit for this solution is

$$(100)(14) + (500)(18) + (600)(13) + (700)(15) + (100)(14) = \$30,100$$

As predicted, this is precisely the total profit resulting from the solution of Table 6.20. In this particular case, then, the manufacturer has some flexibility in the choice of routes employed without reducing total profit.[2]

---

[2] The reader is invited to verify directly, using the MODI test, that the solution of Table 6.21 is indeed optimal. In doing so, keep in mind that this solution is degenerate.

FIGURE 6.4 An optimal solution for the problem of the television set manufacturer.

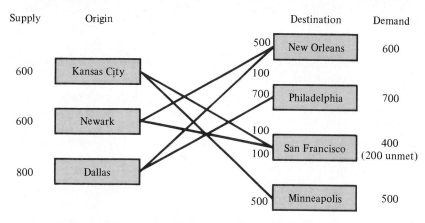

TABLE 6.21 A second optimal solution to the problem of the television set manufacturer.

From \ To	New Orleans	Philadelphia	San Francisco	Minneapolis	Supply
Kansas City	10	12	14 100	18 500	600
Newark	13 600	11	12	14	600
Dallas	15	15 700	14 100	16	800
Dummy	0	0	0 200	0	200
Demand	600	700	400	500	Total 2200

Modification of the Transportation Algorithm for Maximization Problems

Suppose we have a transportation problem in which the objective is maximization of a function which we will refer to as "profit." Then VAM and MODI can be applied as for the function minimization problem, with the following modifications:

(i) In VAM, the opportunity costs are computed as the differences between the most profitable and the next profitable routes. The most profitable route corresponding to the highest opportunity cost is then selected for the largest feasible shipment.

(ii) In MODI, with c_{ij} denoting the unit profits, a solution is optimal if none of the differences

$$d_{ij} = c_{ij} - (r_i + k_j)$$

is positive. If the solution is suboptimal, proceed by bringing in the route with the highest d_{ij}.

6.7. PRODUCTION PLANNING AND THE TRANSPORTATION ALGORITHM

As its name suggests, the transportation algorithm was originally designed to tackle problems in which shipments were to be physically made from specific origins to particular destinations. However, the algorithm does have broader applicability. In this section we will see how it can be applied in **production planning.**

A manufacturer of electronic components is planning its production schedule for the first four months of the year. One hundred units can be made in January, while increasing capacity to 120 units is planned for each of the next three months. This manufacturer also has available forecasts of demand for each of these four months. Table 6.22 shows production capacities and demand forecasts.

It can be seen from Table 6.22 that the total production capacity over this period exceeds total demand. The company does not wish, however, to end the period carrying additional inventory so it will not produce to full capacity over the entire four months.

The manufacturer has calculated that each component costs $20 to produce. In addition, for each month that a component is held in storage before it is sold, an additional $3 cost is incurred. Table 6.23 summarizes the total costs for various months of production–month of sale combinations.

The objective of the electronics component manufacturer is to schedule production so as to minimize total costs. Set up in this way, the problem is, with

TABLE 6.22 Production capacities and demand forecasts for the electronic components manufacturer.

MONTH	PRODUCTION CAPACITY	DEMAND FORECAST
January	100	90
February	120	100
March	120	120
April	120	130
Totals	460	440

TABLE 6.23 Total costs of the month of production–month of sale combinations for the electronic components manufacturer.

SUPPLY	DEMAND			
	JANUARY	FEBRUARY	MARCH	APRIL
January	20	23	26	29
February	M	20	23	26
March	M	M	20	23
April	M	M	M	20

one exception, in the form of a transportation minimization problem, with supply exceeding demand, as discussed in Section 6.5. The single difference is that some "routes" cannot be used. For example, it is not possible to sell any of the March output in January. For each supply-demand combination that cannot be used, we attach a cost M, which can be made sufficiently large to ensure that these cells are not brought into the solution. We have employed this notation in Table 6.23.

In Table 6.24, the transportation tableau is set up, with a dummy demand point to take care of the excess supply. To find an initial solution, we will use, on this occasion, a simpler approach than VAM. The **Northwest Corner Method** begins by entering the largest feasible amount in the top left-hand (Northwest) corner of the table. We then move in single steps, right and down, entering the

TABLE 6.24 Northwest corner solution to the problem of the electronic components manufacturer.

Production \ Sale	January	February	March	April	Dummy	Supply
January	20 / 90	23 / 10	26	29	0	100
February	M	20 / 90	23 / 30	26	0	120
March	M	M	20 / 90	23 / 30	0	120
April	M	M	M	20 / 100	0 / 20	120
Demand	90	100	120	130	20	Total 460

largest feasible amount in each cell of the table until a complete solution has been attained. Those supply-demand combinations, which cannot be utilized, are associated with high cost M. The implication of 20 units in the April production—dummy sale category is that in April, only 100 units will actually be produced in this solution.

The Northwest corner solution of Table 6.24 is further investigated in Table 6.25, where the MODI optimality test is applied in exactly the manner described in Section 6.4. In fact, since there are three cells with negative d_{ij} values, the solution clearly is not optimal. The largest of these negative differences (-9) is in the January production-dummy sale cell, which must therefore be brought into the solution. The stepping-stone path for doing so is also illustrated in Table 6.25. It can be seen from the table that the largest feasible adjustments, to be added and subtracted from the values in the cells at the corners of the stepping-stone path, are ten units.

The new solution, obtained in this manner, is displayed in Table 6.26 together with the optimality check. The solution is suboptimal, so we must bring the February production-dummy sale cell into the solution. The stepping-stone path for doing so is given in Table 6.26, which shows that adjustments of ten units can be made.

TABLE 6.25 MODI optimality test applied to the northwest corner solution of the problem of the electronic components manufacturer.

r_i	Production / Sale	k_j = 20 January	23 February	26 March	29 April	9 Dummy	Supply
0	**January**	20 / 90	−10 | 23 / 10	26 / 0	29 / 0	+10 | 0 / −9	100
−3	**February**	M / M − 17	+10 | 20 / 90	−10 | 23 / 30	26 / 0	0 / −6	120
−6	**March**	M / M − 14	M / M − 17	+10 | 20 / 90	−10 | 23 / 30	0 / −3	120
−9	**April**	M / M − 11	M / M − 14	M / M − 17	+10 | 20 / 100	−10 | 0 / 20	120
	Demand	90	100	120	130	20	Total 460

TABLE 6.26 Second solution to the problem of the electronic components manufacturer.

k_j		20	14	17	20	0	
r_i	Sale / Production	January	February	March	April	Dummy	Supply
0	January	20 90	23 9	26 9	29 9	0 10	100
6	February	M $M-26$	20 100	-10 | 23 20	26 0	$+10$ | 0 -6	120
3	March	M $M-23$	M $M-17$	$+10$ | 20 100	-10 | 23 20	0 -3	120
0	April	M $M-20$	M $M-14$	M $M-17$	$+10$ | 20 110	-10 | 0 -10	120
	Demand	90	100	120	130	20	Total 460

Finally, in Table 6.27, we see that an optimal solution to our production planning problem has been achieved. From the entries in the dummy sales column, it can immediately be inferred that the lowest cost production schedule involves the manufacture of 90 components in January, 110 components in February, and 120 components in each of the next two months.[3]

6.8. THE ASSIGNMENT PROBLEM

We turn now to another class of problems for which a special purpose solution algorithm is available. The **assignment problem** can arise when:

(a) Machines or workers must be assigned to jobs
(b) Salespersons are to be assigned to territories
(c) Contracts must be assigned to bidders

---

[3] In fact, as can be seen from the zero d_{ij} value in the February production-April sale cell, the solution in Table 6.27 is not uniquely optimal. We leave it to the reader to verify that all of the optimal solutions lead to the same production quantities for each month as that shown in the table.

TABLE 6.27 Optimal solution to the problem of the electronic components manufacturer.

r_i \ k_j	Production \ Sale	20 January	20 February	23 March	26 April	0 Dummy	Supply
0	January	20 / 90	23 / (3)	26 / (3)	29 / (3)	0 / 10	100
0	February	M / (M − 20)	20 / 100	23 / 10	26 / (0)	0 / 10	120
−3	March	M / (M − 17)	M / (M − 17)	20 / 110	23 / 10	0 / (3)	120
−6	April	M / (M − 14)	M / (M − 14)	M / (M − 17)	20 / 120	0 / (6)	120
	Demand	90	100	120	130	20	Total 460

Taking the first of these for illustration, the distinctive feature of the assignment problem is that only one job can be assigned to any machine, and only one machine to any job. It will further be assumed, for the time being, that the number of jobs to be done is equal to the number of machines available.

To illustrate, on a particular morning a machine shop has four jobs, each of which must be assigned to one of four machines. Management has been able, for each job-machine combination, to calculate the costs of carrying out the jobs. These costs are displayed in Table 6.28.

TABLE 6.28 Costs (in dollars) of the assignments of jobs to machines.

JOB	MACHINE A	B	C	D
1	81	75	69	77
2	74	74	63	73
3	85	77	66	74
4	66	63	58	62

The objective of the machine shop management is to assign jobs to machines in such a way that the total cost of carrying out the four jobs is as small as possible. How many different assignments are in fact possible? There are four machines to which the first job could be assigned. Given that this job has been assigned to a particular machine, a choice from three machines is available for the second job. It follows that the total number of possibilities for the first two jobs is $4 \times 3 = 12$. Continuing in this way, given that the first two jobs have been assigned, there remain two machines on which the third job can be carried out. Finally, just one machine is left for the last job. It follows, then, that the total number of possible assignments if $4 \times 3 \times 2 \times 1 = 24$. More generally, if n jobs are to be assigned to n machines, the total number of possible assignments is $n(n - 1)(n - 2) \ldots 2.1$, which we denote $n!$

The Assignment Problem

Suppose that there are n "jobs" to be assigned to n "machines" in such a way that one job is to be assigned to one machine. The total number of possible assignments is $n!$, and the problem is to find the assignment combination with the lowest total cost.

Now, one possible approach to our machine shop assignment problem would be to compute the total costs of each of the 24 possible combinations. However, this is quite tedious, and of course would be even more so in problems involving more jobs. For example, if there were eight jobs to be assigned to eight machines, it would be necessary to look at $8! = 40,320$ possibilities. Fortunately, an algorithm, to be discussed in the following section, affords a computationally efficient method of solution.

Before proceeding, however, we will see how the assignment problem can be expressed in the constrained minimization linear programming framework. Let c_{ij} denote the cost of assigning the i-th job to the j-th machine, and define the variables x_{ij} so that

$$x_{ij} = \begin{cases} 1 & \text{if job } i \text{ is assigned to machine } j \\ 0 & \text{otherwise} \end{cases}$$

Then, the total assignment cost is the sum of $c_{ij}x_{ij}$ over all possible job-machine combinations. The problem to be solved can then be written:

$$
\begin{aligned}
\text{Minimize} \quad & c_{11}x_{11} + c_{12}x_{12} + \ldots + c_{1n}x_{1n} \\
& + c_{21}x_{21} + c_{22}x_{22} + \ldots + c_{2n}x_{2n} \\
& + \cdot \quad\quad\quad \cdot \quad \cdot \quad\quad \cdot \quad\quad \cdot \quad \cdot \\
& + c_{n1}x_{n1} + c_{n2}x_{n2} + \ldots + c_{nn}x_{nn}
\end{aligned}
$$

$$\text{subject to} \quad x_{11} + x_{12} + \ldots + x_{1n} = 1$$

$$x_{21} + x_{22} + \ldots + x_{2n} = 1$$

$$\cdot \quad\quad \cdot \quad\quad \cdot \quad\quad \cdot \quad\quad \cdot$$

$$x_{n1} + x_{n2} + \ldots + x_{nn} = 1$$

$$x_{11} + x_{21} + \ldots + x_{n1} = 1$$

$$x_{12} + x_{22} + \ldots + x_{n2} = 1$$

$$\cdot \quad\quad \cdot \quad\quad \cdot \quad\quad \cdot \quad\quad \cdot$$

$$x_{1n} + x_{2n} + \ldots + x_{nn} = 1$$

$$x_{ij} \geq 0$$

$$(i = 1, 2, \ldots, n; j = 1, 2, \ldots, n)$$

where the first set of n constraints follows because each job is assigned to just one machine, and the second set because each machine is used for just one job.

Viewed in this fashion, then, it can be seen by comparison with equations (6.1) of Section 6.2 that the assignment problem is in fact a special case of the transportation problem. We could, therefore, employ the MODI method in its solution since this algorithm yields integer solutions. However, a far more efficient algorithm, to be discussed in the following section, is available for this special class of problems.

6.9. FINDING THE OPTIMAL SOLUTION FOR ASSIGNMENT PROBLEMS: THE HUNGARIAN METHOD

The Hungarian method for solving assignment problems proceeds using the notion of **opportunity costs,** by operating on the complete set of costs. The eventual objective is to reduce the position to one in which it is possible to find a complete assignment with zero opportunity costs. We proceed in steps.

STEP 1 □ For each row, replace the costs by the difference between the original costs and the lowest cost assignment in that row. This is done in the first part of Table 6.29. For example, we see that job 1 costs \$6 more on machine B than on the lowest cost machine C. Next, working on this new table, replace the values by their differences from the smallest number in the corresponding column. The results are shown in the second part of Table 6.29. For example, for the machine A column, the smallest value in part (i) of Table 6.29 is 8. Hence, for the job 1-machine A combination, we enter in part (ii) of the table 12 − 8 = 4.

STEP 2 □ Find the smallest possible number of straight lines, extending over whole rows or columns, needed to cover all the zeros in the table achieved in step 1. If the number of lines needed is the same as the number of rows (or, equivalently, the number of columns) in the table, then an optimal solution has been reached. This check for optimality has been applied in Table 6.30. Since only two lines are needed

TABLE 6.29 Step 1 of the Hungarian method solution to the machine-shop problem.

(i)

JOB	MACHINE			
	A	B	C	D
1	12	6	0	8
2	11	11	0	10
3	19	11	0	8
4	8	5	0	4

(ii)

JOB	MACHINE			
	A	B	C	D
1	4	1	0	4
2	3	6	0	6
3	11	6	0	4
4	0	0	0	0

to cover the zeros in the table, we have not yet reached the position where it is possible to determine the optimal solution to our problem.

STEP 3 □ If, according to the test of step 2, an optimal solution has not been reached, find the smallest of the table entries not covered by a line. This is the value circled in Table 6.30. Subtract this value from all those entries not covered by a line and add it to all those values covered by two lines. Those entries covered by a single line are left unchanged. Continue steps 2 and 3 iteratively until an optimal solution has been achieved. The necessary computations for the machine shop problem are set out in Table 6.31. In the first part of that table, we have added one to the entry in Table 6.30 that is covered by two lines, and subtracted one from those entries not covered by lines. From part (i) of Table 6.31, we see that at least three lines are now needed to cover every zero. An optimal solution has, therefore, still not been attained. We proceed, then, to the second part of Table 6.31. The entries there have been derived by subtracting two from those entries in part (i) that are not covered by lines, and adding two to those entries that are covered by two lines. In this table it is possible to cover all the zeros only by using four lines, so that an optimal solution has been reached.

TABLE 6.30 Step 2 of the Hungarian method solution to the machine shop problem.

JOB	MACHINE			
	A	B	C	D
1	4	①	0	4
2	3	6	0	6
3	11	6	0	4
4	0	0	0	0

TABLE 6.31 Step 3 and the derivation of the optimal solution to the machine shop problem.

(i)

JOB	MACHINE			
	A	B	C	D
1	3	0	0	3
2	2	5	0	5
3	10	5	0	3
4	0	0	1	0

(ii)

JOB	MACHINE			
	A	B	C	D
1	3	0	0	3
2	0	3	0	3
3	3	3	0	1
4	0	0	3	0

Having reached the position in part (ii) of Table 6.31, it must now be possible to find a complete set of assignments with zero opportunity costs. It is generally pretty clear how such a solution can be achieved. A systematic procedure begins by looking for any row or column with just a single zero. The corresponding assignment must necessarily be made, and the row and column of that assignment need no longer be considered. Continuing in this way a complete solution can be deduced. In part (ii) of Table 6.31, the only 0 in the job 3 row is for machine C. Therefore job 3 must be assigned to machine C. Deleting the job 3 row and machine C column leaves us with:

JOB	MACHINE		
	A	B	D
1	3	0	3
2	0	3	3
4	0	0	0

Now, the only 0 in the job 1 row is for machine B, so that job 1 has to be assigned to machine B. Also, job 2 must be assigned to machine A, as the only 0 in the job 2 row is for machine A. This leaves job 4 to be assigned to machine D.

The solution, together with its associated cost, is set out in Table 6.32. The total cost is obtained by referring back to the original values of Table 6.28. It emerges that the best possible solution costs $277 to carry out the four jobs.

TABLE 6.32 Optimal solution to the machine-shop assignment problem.

JOB	MACHINE	COST
1	B	75
2	A	74
3	C	66
4	D	62
		277

6.10. UNBALANCED ASSIGNMENT PROBLEMS

We now relax our assumption that the number of rows in the assignment table must be equal to the number of columns. In the context of the example of the previous section there may be more jobs than machines or more machines than jobs. It is possible to attack such problems by creating either dummy rows or dummy columns, so that the table can again be set up as a square array. Thus, if the machine shop has a fifth machine potentially available for work on one of the four jobs, we create a dummy job. Since this job will not actually be carried out, we associate with it zero costs.

To illustrate, suppose that the machine shop has available a fifth machine, for which the dollar costs of the four jobs are 62, 58, 65, and 60. The problem is then set up, as in Table 6.33, with a dummy job. Since this job will not be carried out, but rather one of the machines will be unused, we set at zero the cost of this job on each machine.

Once the setup of the problem has been modified in this way, the Hungarian method can be employed in its solution exactly as in Section 6.9. The details are set out in Table 6.34. Part (i) of that table shows the results of the application of the first two steps. Notice that three lines are required to cover the zeros. Three lines are also required in part (ii), while parts (iii)–(v) each require just four lines. It is not until part (vi) of the table that we finally find ourselves in a position to determine the optimum assignment. This requires that the corresponding opportunity costs are zero, and hence, that job 1 is done on machine B, job 2 on machine E, job 3 on machine C, job 4 on machine D, and the dummy

TABLE 6.33 Assignment costs for the machine-shop with a fifth machine.

JOB	MACHINE				
	A	B	C	D	E
1	81	75	69	77	62
2	74	74	63	73	58
3	85	77	66	74	65
4	66	63	58	62	60
Dummy	0	0	0	0	0

(i)

JOB	MACHINE				
	A	B	C	D	E
1	19	13	7	15	0
2	16	16	5	15	0
3	20	12	(1)	9	0
4	8	5	0	4	2
Dummy	0	0	0	0	0

(ii)

JOB	MACHINE				
	A	B	C	D	E
1	18	12	6	14	0
2	15	15	4	14	0
3	19	11	0	8	0
4	8	5	0	(4)	3
Dummy	0	0	0	0	1

(iii)

JOB	MACHINE				
	A	B	C	D	E
1	14	8	6	10	0
2	11	11	4	10	0
3	15	7	0	(4)	0
4	4	1	0	0	3
Dummy	0	0	4	0	5

job on machine A. Therefore, the optimal solution involves machine A being unused. The total cost of this solution is

$$75 + 58 + 66 + 62 = \$261$$

Notice that this solution is less expensive by $16 than that of Table 6.32, where the fifth machine was unavailable.

6.11. SOLVING MAXIMIZATION ASSIGNMENT PROBLEMS

In the previous two sections we have discussed assignment problems in which an objective function was to be minimized. The same type of problem, but with a maximization objective, also occurs very frequently in management applications. Such problems can, by a very simple modification, be converted to minimization problems, and hence solved by familiar methods.

TABLE 6.34 (*Continued*)

(iv)

JOB	MACHINE				
	A	B	C	D	E
1	10	4	6	6	0
2	7	7	4	6	0
3	11	3	0	0	0
4	4	(1)	4	0	7
Dummy	0	0	8	0	9

(v)

JOB	MACHINE				
	A	B	C	D	E
1	9	3	5	6	0
2	6	6	(3)	6	0
3	11	3	0	1	1
4	3	0	3	0	7
Dummy	0	0	8	1	10

(vi)

JOB	MACHINE				
	A	B	C	D	E
1	6	0	2	3	0
2	3	3	0	3	0
3	11	3	0	1	4
4	3	0	3	0	10
Dummy	0	0	8	1	13

To illustrate, consider a company with four sales representatives to be assigned to four territories. Given the characteristics of both the representatives and the territories, a manager estimates, for the various possible assignments, the monthly profit figures shown in Table 6.35. The problem here is to assign representatives to territories so as to maximize total monthly profits.

TABLE 6.35 Estimated monthly profits (in thousands of dollars) from the assignments of representatives to territories.

REPRESENTATIVE	TERRITORY			
	A	B	C	D
1	25	23	20	18
2	24	22	19	15
3	28	24	22	19
4	30	26	25	20

REPRESENTATIVE	TERRITORY			
	A	B	C	D
1	5	3	5	2
2	6	4	6	5
3	2	2	3	1
4	0	0	0	0

To convert the problem to one of minimization, we find the **opportunity costs** of not making the most profitable allocation for each territory. For example, the most profitable assignment, at 25 thousand dollars, to territory C would be representative 4. If representative 1 were assigned to this territory, then, the opportunity cost would be 25 − 20 = 5 thousand dollars. The complete set of opportunity costs is shown in Table 6.36.

The original problem has now been converted from one of the maximization of total profits to an equivalent problem of minimization of total opportunity costs. Once it is in this form, the Hungarian method of solution can be applied directly. The details are set out in Table 6.37. The first part of this table shows the results of steps 1 and 2. Since only three lines are required to cover all of the zeros in this array, it is necessary to proceed to the next step. In the second part of Table 6.37, it emerges that no further manipulations of the opportunity costs are necessary, as four lines are now required to cover all of the zeros in the array. It is therefore now possible to find a solution for which all of the

TABLE 6.37 Hungarian method solution to the sales representative assignment problem.

(i)

REPRESENTATIVE	TERRITORY			
	A	B	C	D
1	3	⓪	3	0
2	2	0	2	1
3	1	1	2	0
4	0	0	0	0

(ii)

REPRESENTATIVE	TERRITORY			
	A	B	C	D
1	2	0	2	0
2	2	0	2	2
3	0	0	1	0
4	0	0	0	1

opportunity costs are zero. Referring to the second part of Table 6.37, then, we see that the optimal solution is to assign representative 1 to territory D, representative 2 to territory B, representative 3 to territory A, and representative 4 to territory C. From Table 6.35, we find the total profit from this solution to be

$$20 + 22 + 28 + 25 = \$95,000$$

EXERCISES

6.1. For the coming month, the washing machine manufacturer of Section 6.2 is able to produce an additional 200 machines in New York, and requires a further 200 machines in Atlanta. Therefore, production capacity in New York is now 900 units, and demand in Atlanta is 500 units. The remaining problem specifications are those of Tables 6.1–6.3.

(a) Use the VAM approach to find an initial feasible solution.

(b) Use the MODI method to check the initial solution, and, if necessary, iterate to an optimal solution.

(c) What is the minimum possible total transportation cost?

6.2. A manufacturer of stereos has plants in Atlanta, New Haven, and Dallas, and distribution centers in San Francisco, Boston, Washington, D.C., and Cleveland. The tables show weekly production capacities, demand requirements, and unit transportation costs (in dollars).

ORIGIN	PRODUCTION CAPACITY	DESTINATION	REQUIREMENTS
Atlanta	65	San Francisco	50
New Haven	75	Boston	35
Dallas	45	Washington, D. C.	35
		Cleveland	65

UNIT TRANSPORTATION COSTS				
	SAN FRANCISCO	BOSTON	WASHINGTON, D.C.	CLEVELAND
Atlanta	13	9	6	5
New Haven	11	6	7	4
Dallas	7	8	15	10

The objective is to minimize total transportation costs.

(a) Employ the VAM approach to find an initial feasible solution.

(b) Using the MODI method, check the initial solution, and, if necessary, iterate to an optimal solution.

(c) What is the smallest possible total transportation cost?

6.3. A manufacturer of cookers has plants in Boston, Denver, Cleveland, and Baltimore, and distribution centers in New York, San Francisco, Houston, and Chicago. The tables show weekly production capacities, demand requirements, and unit transportation costs (in dollars).

ORIGIN	PRODUCTION CAPACITY	DESTINATION	REQUIREMENTS
Boston	310	New York	230
Denver	250	San Francisco	320
Cleveland	160	Houston	190
Baltimore	300	Chicago	280

	UNIT TRANSPORTATION COSTS			
	NEW YORK	SAN FRANCISCO	HOUSTON	CHICAGO
Boston	9	18	15	12
Denver	13	10	11	12
Cleveland	10	14	15	7
Baltimore	12	13	12	11

The objective is to minimize total transportation costs.

(a) Find the optimal solution to this problem.

(b) What is the lowest possible total transportation cost?

6.4. A company has four plants and four distribution centers. The accompanying table shows weekly production capacities, demand requirements, and unit transportation costs (in dollars).

From \ To	A	B	C	D	Supply
I	10	18	15	12	260
II	13	10	10	12	240
III	11	14	15	7	250
IV	12	12	12	10	300
Demand	320	330	200	200	Total 1050

The objective is the minimization of total transportation costs.

(a) Find an optimal solution to this problem.

(b) Is the optimal solution of part (a) unique?

(c) Find the smallest possible total transportation cost.

6.5. A corporation has three plants and four distribution centers. The accompanying table shows weekly production capacities, demand requirements, and unit transportation costs (in dollars).

From \ To	A	B	C	D	Supply
I	9	7	4	5	300
II	5	4	9	8	280
III	4	7	6	7	160
Demand	340	220	100	80	Total 740

The objective is to make total transportation costs as low as possible.

(a) Find the optimal solution to this problem.

(b) Find the smallest possible total transportation costs.

6.6. The accompanying table shows a feasible solution to a transportation minimization problem in which the unit costs are expressed in dollars.

From \ To	A	B	C	D	Supply
I	13 250	13	13	11	250
II	12 60	15 200	16	8	260
III	11	19 140	16 100	13	240
IV	14	11	11 120	15 180	300
Demand	310	340	220	180	Total 1050

(a) Use the MODI method to check this solution for optimality.

(b) If the solution given is suboptimal, iterate to an optimal solution.

(c) What is the minimum achievable total transportation cost?

6.7. A company has three plants and three warehouses. The following table shows weekly demand and supply at each

PLANT	SUPPLY	WAREHOUSE	DEMAND
I	70	A	130
II	210	B	100
III	140	C	190

Unit transportation costs (in dollars) are given in the table below.

PLANT	WAREHOUSE		
	A	B	C
I	7	9	15
II	21	17	13
III	5	7	7

(a) Use the VAM approach to find an initial feasible solution.

(b) Use the MODI method to check the initial solution, and, if necessary, iterate to an optimal solution.

(c) What is the lowest possible total transportation cost?

6.8. Because of labor troubles, the manufacturer of stereos of Exercise 6.2 is unable to use the Dallas–San Francisco route. Given this additional constraint, find the optimal solution to the transportation problem.

[Hint: This problem can be solved either by inserting a prohibitively high cost for the impermissible route, or by ignoring the route altogether, in the manner of Section 6.7.]

6.9. Refer to the problem discussed in Section 6.5 of the washing machine manufacturer when 100 additional units are required in Boston. Derive the optimal solution displayed in Table 6.15.

6.10. Refer to the problem discussed in Section 6.5 of the washing machine manufacturer when 100 additional machines are available in New York. Derive the optimal solution displayed in Table 6.16, and verify its optimality.

6.11. The manufacturer of cookers, of Exercise 6.3, faces for the coming week, a demand for 30 additional cookers in Houston. The total Houston demand is then 220, the other problem specifications remaining unchanged.

(a) Find the optimal solution to the transportation problem.

(b) At which distribution center(s) will there be unmet demand at the optimal solution?

6.12. For the coming week, the company of Exercise 6.4 is able to increase by 40 units, to a total of 280, production at plant II. The remaining problem specifications are unchanged.

(a) Find the optimal solution to the transportation problem.

(b) At which plant(s) will there be surplus capacity at the optimal solution?

6.13. The corporation of Exercise 6.5 faces, for the coming week, demand for an additional 20 units at distribution center D. The other problem specifications are unchanged.

(a) Find the optimal solution to the transportation problem.

(b) At which distribution center(s) will there be unmet demand at the optimal solution?

6.14. The company of Exercise 6.7 is able, in the coming week, to produce 30 additional units in plant I. The remaining problem specifications are unchanged.

(a) Find the optimal solution to the transportation problem.

(b) At which plant(s) will there be excess capacity at the optimal solution?

6.15. A company has three plants and four warehouses. The following table shows weekly production capacities and demand forecasts.

PLANT	CAPACITY	WAREHOUSE	DEMAND
I	620	A	730
II	550	B	490
III	340	C	250
		D	460

Unit transportation costs (in dollars) are given below.

PLANT	WAREHOUSE			
	A	B	C	D
I	8	6	4	7
II	5	3	10	8
III	3	8	7	5

The company calculates that for each unit sold, gross profit (exclusive of transportation costs) is $15. A new plant is to be built, from which unit transportation costs are $7 to warehouse A, $9 to warehouse B, $8 to warehouse C, and $6 to warehouse D. The new plant is to have the capacity to produce 450 units. By how much will net weekly profits (total gross profits from sales less total transportation costs) increase after this plant has been constructed?

6.16. An importer of video cassette recorders has a contract allowing the purchase of up to 400 recorders at $350 each in each of the first two months of the coming year. For March and April, the importer expects to be permitted to import up to 450 recorders with an increase in price to $375 per recorder. Demand forecasts suggest that sales of 380 recorders can be expected in January, 390 in February, 440 in March, and 460 in April. For each month that a recorder is held in storage, the importer calculates that an additional $20 cost is incurred. The importer wants to end the first four months of the year with no additional inventory.

Find the lowest cost allocation of purchases that will allow the importer to meet total demand in each of the first four months of the year.

6.17. The importer of the previous exercise is offered the opportunity to purchase up to 20 additional recorders at a cost of $360 each, in either or both of the first two months of the year. To what extent should the importer take up this offer?

6.18. Continuing exercises 6.16 and 6.17, the importer is advised that in April, it will be possible to increase by $15 the price that he charges customers for the video cassette recorders, without reducing demand. What now is the best strategy?

6.19. Refer to the example of the manufacturer of electronic components in Section 6.7. This manufacturer is afraid of the possibility of labor disputes in April, when a union contract is due for renegotiation. In that case it is estimated that production capacity for April will fall to 100 units. If the manufacturer plans to produce a maximum of 100 units in April, what will be the total additional cost, compared with the optimal solution when April capacity was 120 units? Can you see how the answer to this question can be inferred from Table 6.27?

6.20. A manufacturer of mattresses has plants in New Orleans, Boston, and Seattle, and distribution centers in Los Angeles, Philadelphia, Baltimore, and Milwaukee. The following table shows monthly production capacities, demand requirements, and unit profits (in dollars) for the various origin-destination combinations.

From \ To	Los Angeles	Philadelphia	Baltimore	Milwaukee	Supply
New Orleans	17	23	22	28	95
Boston	19	26	21	29	110
Seattle	23	24	10	20	80
Demand	75	70	65	75	Total 285

The objective is to maximize total profits

(a) Employ the VAM approach to find an initial feasible solution.

(b) Using the MODI method, check the initial solution, and, if necessary, iterate to an optimal solution.

(c) What is the largest possible total monthly profit?

6.21. Due to an industrial dispute on the west coast, the manufacturer of mattresses of the previous exercise is unable, in the coming month, to use the Seattle–Los Angeles route. How much does this dispute cost the manufacturer in lost profits? [Hint: One way to proceed is to ensure that the Seattle–Los Angeles route does not enter the optimal solution by associating with it zero unit profits.]

6.22. A company produces dining tables of a standard size and design. The company has four production centers and four distribution outlets, for which monthly production capacities and demand requirements are shown below.

PRODUCTION CENTER	CAPACITY	DISTRIBUTION OUTLET	DEMAND
Newark	320	Boston	250
Seattle	260	San Francisco	340
Detroit	180	Dallas	200
Charlotte	300	Minneapolis	310

The unit profits for sales from each production center-distribution outlet route are given in the following table

	BOSTON	SAN FRANCISCO	DALLAS	MINNEAPOLIS
Newark	41	34	33	35
Seattle	37	42	37	35
Detroit	40	38	33	40
Charlotte	38	39	36	36

(a) Use the VAM approach to find an initial feasible solution.

(b) Use the MODI method to check the initial solution, and, if necessary, iterate to an optimal solution.

(c) Find the largest possible total monthly profit.

6.23. For the coming month, the company of the previous exercise is unable to use the Newark–Boston route. What is the resulting decrease in total profit for that month?

6.24. A company has four plants and four distribution centers. The accompanying table shows weekly production capacities, demand requirements, and unit profits (in dollars).

From \ To	A	B	C	D	Supply
I	50	40	41	50	270
II	47	48	46	50	250
III	49	44	41	53	260
IV	48	46	44	52	300
Demand	320	330	190	200	

The objective is maximization of total profits

(a) Find an optimal solution to this problem

(b) Is the optimal solution of part (a) unique?

(c) Find the largest possible total weekly profit.

6.25. The accompanying table shows a feasible solution to a transportation maximization problem in which the unit profits are expressed in dollars.

To From	A	B	C	D	Dummy	Supply
I	17 260	15	19	15	0	260
II	18 40	13 210	16	20	0	250
III	19	9 120	16 130	15	0	250
IV	16	17	20 80	13 180	0 30	290
Demand	300	330	210	180	30	Total 1050

(a) Use the MODI method to check this solution for optimality.

(b) If the solution given is suboptimal, iterate to an optimal solution.

(c) What is the maximum attainable total profit?

6.26. An investor has $100,000 which she intends to invest in three corporations—General Motors, I.B.M., and Mobil. She is able to invest in common stocks, preferred stocks, and bonds of all three corporations. This investor wants to invest a total of $40,000 in General Motors and $30,000 in each of the other two corporations. She also intends to invest $50,000 in common stocks, $25,000 in preferred stocks, and $25,000 in bonds. The table below shows the returns (in cents) that are expected over a year for each dollar invested.

	GENERAL MOTORS	IBM	MOBIL
Common stocks	11.4	10.8	12.0
Preferred stocks	10.3	10.6	11.0
Bonds	9.3	9.5	9.8

If the aim is to maximize total expected return on investments over the year, given the above constraints, how should this investor proceed?

6.27. A company has four jobs, each of which must be assigned to a single employee.

Taking into account job specifications and employee skills, a manager calculates the following dollar costs for carrying out the work.

JOB	EMPLOYEE			
	JOHN	PAUL	GEORGE	MARY
1	86	78	70	71
2	77	72	64	70
3	87	73	67	75
4	69	65	59	64

Find the set of assignments for which total costs are as small as possible and compute the minimum achievable total costs.

6.28. A local government agency asks four contractors to bid on each of four projects, with the intention of awarding one project to each contractor. The table shows the bids in thousands of dollars

PROJECT	CONTRACTOR			
	A	B	C	D
1	12	14	15	13
2	15	16	19	18
3	17	17	19	20
4	21	26	24	25

If the objective is to achieve the smallest possible total cost for carrying out the four projects, how should contractors be assigned to projects?

6.29. A company has five jobs, each of which must be assigned to a single machine. The table shows dollar costs for each possible job-machine assignment.

JOB	MACHINE				
	A	B	C	D	E
1	138	127	118	121	143
2	157	138	129	132	160
3	143	129	131	130	172
4	111	119	123	107	120
5	102	120	100	100	119

(a) Use the Hungarian method to find the set of assignments with the lowest possible total cost.

(b) What is the minimum attainable total cost?

6.30. The manager of a work shop must plan to carry out five jobs, and has available five machines, one of which must be assigned to each job. The table shows dollar costs for each possible assignment. It is not possible to carry out job 2 on machine D or job 4 on machine B.

MACHINE					
	A	B	C	D	E
1	235	210	206	238	227
2	263	239	230		234
3	249	238	227	240	243
4	261		248	251	257
5	250	240	245	249	260

Find the set of assignments with the lowest possible total cost.
[Hint: The Hungarian method can be used if the costs associated with the impermissible assignments are set at very high values, thus ensuring that these assignments do not enter the optimal solution.]

6.31. A manager has available five employees for possible assignment to four jobs. She calculates the dollar assignment costs shown in the following table.

JOB	EMPLOYEE				
	TAVARE	FOWLER	GOWER	LAMB	BOTHAM
1	120	125	132	118	110
2	132	138	143	124	119
3	137	140	144	132	128
4	108	112	115	112	101

(a) Use the Hungarian method to find the set of assignments with the smallest possible total cost.

(b) What is the lowest possible total cost?

6.32. The director of a research laboratory has six potential project leaders, one to be assigned to each of four research contracts. The director, taking into account the nature of the research and the skill and experience of the candidates to lead the projects, estimates the costs of successful completion shown, in thousands of dollars, in the accompanying table.

RESEARCH CONTRACT	PROJECT LEADER					
	RANDALL	EDMONDS	DILLEY	TAYLOR	WILLIS	COWANS
1	28	37	29	41	32	46
2	19	27	26	34	27	41
3	26	29	30	36	25	40
4	31	36	34	39	33	45

(a) Use the Hungarian method to find the set of assignments with the lowest possible total cost.

(b) Find the minimum attainable total cost.

6.33. A company solicits bids on each of four projects from five contractors. Only one project may be assigned to any contractor. The bids received (in thousands of dollars) are given in the accompanying table. Contractor D feels unable to carry out project 3, and therefore submits no bid.

PROJECT	CONTRACTOR				
	A	B	C	D	E
1	18	25	22	26	25
2	26	29	26	27	24
3	28	31	30		31
4	26	28	27	26	29

(a) Use the Hungarian method to find the set of assignments with the smallest possible total cost.

(b) What is the minimum achievable total cost?

6.34. A corporation has five salespersons to be assigned to five territories. The following table shows projected monthly profits (in thousands of dollars) resulting from the possible assignments.

SALESPERSON	TERRITORY				
	A	B	C	D	E
1	34	37	41	32	46
2	33	35	40	32	41
3	37	39	44	37	48
4	39	39	47	38	49
5	36	37	46	34	47

(a) Use the Hungarian method to find the set of assignments with the largest possible total profit.

(b) What is the maximum attainable total profit?

6.35. A conference attracts 100 delegates. Four sessions are planned on the first day, and the organizers must decide how to schedule the four speakers. Estimated attendances for the various speaker-session combinations are shown in the accompanying table. Brown is not able to speak at the late session, as he must leave early for an engagement the next day.

SESSION TIMES	SPEAKER			
	SMITH	BROWN	JONES	BLACK
8:30–10:00 a.m.	64	72	70	68
10:30–12:00 a.m.	87	93	90	87
2:00–3:30 p.m.	79	84	85	86
4:00–5:30 p.m.	74		81	80

Find the set of assignments that maximizes total attendance at the four sessions.
[Hint: Setting at zero attendance for Brown in the late session allows the Hungarian
method to be used, while ensuring that this combination does not occur in
the optimal solution.]

6.36. A corporate personnel officer has available six candidates to fill four positions.
Each candidate is given four aptitude tests, thought to be relevant in assessing
suitability for carrying out the duties of the four positions. The accompanying table
gives the scores achieved by the candidates.

POSITION	CANDIDATE					
	BANKS	COHEN	WILSON	STILES	CHARLTON	MOORE
1	86	82	84	86	84	87
2	79	80	82	80	83	81
3	84	83	80	79	80	82
4	77	76	79	78	77	75

Use the Hungarian method to find the set of assignments yielding the highest possible sum of aptitude test scores.

Assigning Students to Company Interviews: Student Placement at the University of Minnesota[1]

The assignment problem discussed in the text, where, for example, a single operator is to be assigned to a single machine, is just the most straightforward variant of this type of problem. More elaborate versions of the assignment problem are frequently encountered.

To illustrate, consider the problem of a student placement office. Companies visit campus to recruit students for potential future employment and will request certain numbers of half-hour interview slots. Many of these companies will also impose restrictions such as limitation to particular major fields, on the types of students they are willing to interview. For any company, then, student interview assignment possibilities will be restricted by the number of available slots and, perhaps, by student types. The individual student will probably want to interview with only a small fraction of the companies visiting the campus, and will often have quite strong preferences for a few specific companies. Historically, the University of Minnesota had solved the problem of assigning students to interview slots by having students line up at the placement office (often through the night), and sign up for slots on a first-come, first-served basis. Whatever might be said in favor of such a solution, it was unpopular with many students, and its scientific merit was rather dubious.

An alternative procedure was developed in which students were required to quantify their preferences for interviews with different companies. Specifically, students were asked to allocate 1000 "utility points" among at most 20 companies for interviews. This allocation was to reflect preference order and intensity of preference. The optimization algorithm employed then sought to assign students to interview slots so that total "utility points" over all students was as high as possible. There were three types of constraints:

1. Individual students can have at most 20 interview assignments, and must have at least one assignment.
2. Each individual company fixes the number of interview slots it has available.
3. Each company may specify that it wishes to interview particular numbers of students with specific characteristics.

The constrained optimization problem may then be solved by maximizing utility over all students. Alternatively, as in the present case, some account can

---

[1] This discussion is based on A. V. Hill, J. D. Naumann, and N. L. Chervany, "SCAT and SPAT: Large-scale Computer-based Optimization Systems for the Personnel Assignment Problem," *Decision Sciences, 14,* (1983), 207–220.

also be taken of the rankings of companies by students. This procedure was applied at the University of Minnesota in a quarter in which 181 companies visited campus, with a total of 3142 interview slots. At the same time, 744 students requested a total of 8046 interviews with these companies. The solution algorithm generated a total of 3015 assignments. Almost 20% of these were with companies ranked 1 by the student, over 50% were with companies ranked 3 or better, and over 75% with companies ranked 6 or better. Of the 744 students, 594 were assigned interviews with their highest rank company.

goal programming

CHAPTER SEVEN

7.1. CONCEPTS OF GOAL PROGRAMMING

The linear programming problems that we have discussed so far all involve *the optimization of a single objective function*. For example, the aim may be to maximize profit, or to minimize cost. Such problems inevitably constitute important elements of management activity. Nevertheless, it is generally overly simplistic to view a corporation as having just a single objective. While considerations of short-run profit are naturally important, corporate management will almost certainly want to take account also of other factors which influence the longer term well-being of the business. For instance, production of the most immediately profitable product mix today may detract from the possibility of taking up fruitful opportunities in the future. In many management applications, therefore, it is more realistic to consider a company as having **multiple objectives.**

Goal programming is designed to deal with problems where several targets, or **goals,** are set by management for corporate performance. The goal programming approach for analyzing problems with multiple objectives has been applied to both linear and nonlinear programming problems. However, here we will restrict attention to the analysis of linear programming problems. To illustrate the distinction between goal programming and the one-dimensional optimization problems discussed in earlier chapters, consider again the office furnishings company which manufactures desks and bookcases. The profit maximization problem of this company was written as

$$\text{Maximize} \quad 30x_1 + 20x_2$$

$$\text{subject to} \quad 8x_1 + 4x_2 \leq 640$$

$$4x_1 + 6x_2 \leq 540$$

$$x_1 + x_2 \leq 100$$

$$x_1, x_2 \geq 0$$

where x_1 denotes the number of desks, and x_2 the number of bookcases produced, and the capacity constraints reflected limited resources in assembly, finishing, and inspection. In Chapters 2 and 3, we saw that the optimal solution to this profit maximization problem was to produce 60 desks and 40 bookcases, at a total profit for the week of $2600.

Now, suppose that in the near future this company anticipates large orders for bookcases, and, to maintain customer goodwill, would like to go as far as possible toward meeting this potential demand. The office furnishings company might, therefore, be interested in two factors—the level of profit, and the output level of bookcases. Rather than aiming simply to maximize total profit, management of the office furnishings company decides for next week to set two targets, or goals. These are:

(a) Profit of at least $2500
(b) Production of at least 60 bookcases

Algebraically, these goals can be expressed as

$$\text{Profit} = 30x_1 + 20x_2 \geq 2{,}500$$

$$\text{Output of Bookcases} = x_2 \geq 60$$

Definition

   A **goal** is a performance target.

When several corporate goals are set, it is often the case that the targets cannot be simultaneously met. For the current example, this is illustrated in Figure 7.1. This figure shows the feasible region, determined by the capacity constraints, as well as lines depicting the two targets of the office furnishings company. In order to achieve a profit of at least $2500, production must be at a point to the northeast of the line $30x_1 + 20x_2 = 2500$. Similarly, output of at least 60 bookcases dictates a point on or above the line $x_2 = 60$. It is clear from Figure 7.1 that no point simultaneously satisfying these requirements lies in the feasible region.

It can be seen from this simple example that it may not be possible to simultaneously meet all targets. Our objective in these circumstances is to get,

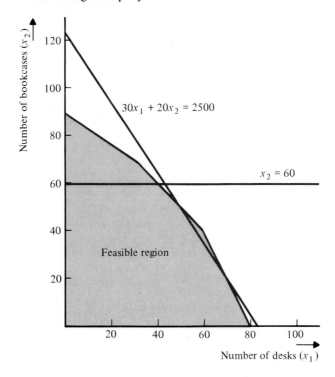

FIGURE 7.1 Feasible region and goals for the office furnishings company.

in a sense to be formalized later, as close as possible to the targets. This concept is known as **satisficing.**

To account for the possibility of targets not being met, it is necessary to introduce additional variables which represent the difference between actual outcomes and targets. For the profit target, define

$$d_1^+ = \begin{cases} 0 \text{ if profit is at or below \$2500} \\ (\text{Profit} - 2500) \text{ if profit is above \$2500} \end{cases}$$

and

$$d_1^- = \begin{cases} 0 \text{ if profit is at or above \$2500} \\ (2500 - \text{Profit}) \text{ if profit is below \$2500} \end{cases}$$

Hence d_1^+ measures the extent to which the target value is exceeded, and d_1^- the amount of any profit below the target level. Using this notation we can therefore write

$$\text{Profit} = 30x_1 + 20x_2 = 2500 + d_1^+ - d_1^-$$

or, equivalently,

$$30x_1 + 20x_2 - d_1^+ + d_1^- = 2500 \qquad (7.1)$$

In exactly the same way, let us define

$$d_2^+ = \begin{cases} 0 \text{ if output of bookcases is at or below 60} \\ (\text{Output of bookcases} - 60) \text{ if output of bookcases is above 60} \end{cases}$$

and

$$d_2^- = \begin{cases} 0 \text{ if output of bookcases is at or above 60} \\ (60 - \text{Output of bookcases}) \text{ if output of bookcases is below 60} \end{cases}$$

It therefore follows that we can write

$$\text{Output of Bookcases} = x_2 = 60 + d_2^+ - d_2^-$$

and hence

$$x_2 - d_2^+ + d_2^- = 60 \qquad (7.2)$$

We have now added to the original decision variables, x_1 and x_2, four additional decision variables, d_1^+, d_1^-, d_2^+, and d_2^-, representing discrepancies from targets. Moreover, equations (7.1) and (7.2) are a pair of **goal constraints** which must be satisfied along with the original production constraints. The complete set of constraints can therefore be written

$$
\begin{aligned}
8x_1 + 4x_2 &\leq 640 \\
4x_1 + 6x_2 &\leq 540 \\
x_1 + x_2 &\leq 100 \\
30x_1 + 20x_2 - d_1^+ + d_1^- &= 2{,}500 \\
x_2 - d_2^+ + d_2^- &= 60 \\
x_i, d_i^+, d_i^- &\geq 0 \ (i = 1, 2)
\end{aligned}
\qquad (7.3)
$$

In order that the problem be set in the linear programming framework, it remains only to specify an objective function. By contrast with the simple profit maximization problem, there are now two goals. The target profit is \$2500. Therefore, the smaller d_1^- is, the closer the company will be to this target.[1] Similarly, the smaller d_2^- is, the closer the company will be to the goal of producing at least 60 bookcases. The aim, then, is to find that solution which makes these two discrepancies as small as possible. Of course, there may be some tradeoff involved, in the sense that movement toward one particular goal might only be possible at the expense of movement away from another. We will consider in this chapter two distinct ways of specifying objective functions in goal programming.

(a) *Goal Programming Without Priorities.* Here it is assumed that management can specify tradeoffs to which it is indifferent. For example, it may be that the office furnishings company regards each bookcase produced below target as comparable with each \$5 below target in profits.

(b) *Goal Programming With Priorities.* It often happens that the levels of importance of the various goals are of different orders of magnitude. For instance, the company may feel that meeting the profit target, if at all possible, is of the highest priority. In that case it will only be concerned with lower priority goals once it has moved as close as possible to the highest priority goal.

Additional Variables and Constraints in Goal Programming Problems

For each goal, two additional variables, d_i^+ and d_i^-, are introduced, representing respectively the amounts above and below target of actual outcomes. For each goal, these variables are incorporated in an additional constraint.

7.2. GOAL PROGRAMMING WITHOUT PRIORITIES

We begin by examining a class of goal programming problems whose optimal solutions can be derived by familiar application of the simplex algorithm. The assumption needed is that it is possible to set dollar amounts to the costs of failure to meet goals, and that these "penalty costs" are proportional to the amounts by which the targets are missed.

Consider again our office furnishings company, with targets of \$2500 profit and production of 60 bookcases. Management of this company asserts that each bookcase produced below the target figure of sixty can be regarded as the equivalent of \$5 profit below the goal of \$2500. Suppose, then, that profits are below the target figure by an amount d_1^-, and that production of bookcases falls d_2^- below target. The "penalty costs" will therefore be d_1^- and $5d_2^-$, the latter value constituting \$5 for each bookcase below target. Summing these components, the total penalty cost is $d_1^- + 5d_2^-$. Our objective is to find the product mix for which this total is as small as possible.

---

[1] Notice that we do not consider d_1^+ here, because any profit in excess of \$2500 will not, all other things equal, cause concern.

The constrained minimization problem can now be set out in algebraic form as

$$d_1^- + 5d_2^-$$

$$8x_1 + 4x_2 + s_1 = 640$$

$$4x_1 + 6x_2 + s_2 = 540$$

$$x_1 + x_2 + s_3 = 100 \tag{7.4}$$

$$30x_1 + 20x_2 - d_1^+ + d_1^- = 2{,}500$$

$$x_2 - d_2^+ + d_2^- = 60$$

$$x_i, d_i^+, d_i^-, s_i \geq 0 \text{ (for all } i)$$

The constraints in (7.4) are the same as those in (7.3) except that we have now put the capacity constraints into standard form, in the usual way, using slack variables. Notice that the objective function in (7.4) does not directly involve x_1 and x_2, the outputs of desks and bookcases, but rather is expressed exclusively in terms of the relevant deviations from targets.

Once the problem has been expressed as a linear programming minimization formulation, it can be solved routinely, either through use of a computer program or manual application of the simplex algorithm. We have set out the simplex algorithm computations in Table 7.1. As in Section 3.8, we begin by converting to a constrained maximization problem, so that the objective is

$$\text{Maximize } -d_1^- - 5d_2^-$$

This is reflected in the top row of each part of Table 7.1, where the c_j values associated with d_1^- and d_2^- are, respectively, -1 and -5. Since the other variables do not enter the objective function, their associated c_j values are all zero.

TABLE 7.1 Simplex algorithm solution to a goal programming problem without priorities of the office furnishings company.

(i)

c_B	BASIS	c_j									SOLUTION	
		0	**0**	**0**	**0**	**0**	**0**	**−1**	**0**	**−5**		
		x_1	x_2	s_1	s_2	s_3	d_1^+	d_1^-	d_2^+	d_2^-		
0	s_1	⑧	4	1	0	0	0	0	0	0	640	$\frac{640}{8} = 80$
0	s_2	4	6	0	1	0	0	0	0	0	540	$\frac{540}{4} = 135$
0	s_3	1	1	0	0	1	0	0	0	0	100	$\frac{100}{1} = 100$
−1	d_1^-	30	20	0	0	0	−1	1	0	0	2500	$\frac{2500}{30} = 83\frac{1}{3}$
−5	d_2^-	0	1	0	0	0	0	0	−1	1	60	$\frac{60}{0} = \infty$
	z_j	−30	−25	0	0	0	1	−1	5	−5	−2800	
	$c_j - z_j$	30	25	0	0	0	−1	0	−5	0	"Profit"	

TABLE 7.1 *(Continued)*

(ii)

c_B	BASIS	c_j 0 x_1	0 x_2	0 s_1	0 s_2	0 s_3	0 d_1^+	-1 d_1^-	0 d_2^+	-5 d_2^-	SOLUTION	
0	x_1	1	$\frac{1}{2}$	$\frac{1}{8}$	0	0	0	0	0	0	80	$80/\frac{1}{2} = 160$
0	s_2	0	4	$-\frac{1}{2}$	1	0	0	0	0	0	220	$\frac{220}{4} = 55$
0	s_3	0	$\frac{1}{2}$	$-\frac{1}{8}$	0	1	0	0	0	0	20	$20/\frac{1}{2} = 40$
-1	d_1^-	0	⑤	$-\frac{15}{4}$	0	0	-1	1	0	0	100	$\frac{100}{5} = 20$
-5	d_2^-	0	1	0	0	0	0	0	-1	1	60	$\frac{60}{1} = 60$
	z_j	0	-10	$\frac{15}{4}$	0	0	1	-1	5	-5	-400	
	$c_j - z_j$	0	10	$-\frac{15}{4}$	0	0	-1	0	-5	0	"Profit"	

(iii)

c_B	BASIS	c_j 0 x_1	0 x_2	0 s_1	0 s_2	0 s_3	0 d_1^+	-1 d_1^-	0 d_2^+	-5 d_2^-	SOLUTION	
0	x_1	1	0	$\frac{1}{2}$	0	0	$\frac{1}{10}$	$-\frac{1}{10}$	0	0	70	$70/\frac{1}{2} = 140$
0	s_2	0	0	$\frac{3}{2}$	1	0	$\frac{4}{5}$	$-\frac{4}{5}$	0	0	140	$140/\frac{3}{2} = 56$
0	s_3	0	0	④	0	1	$\frac{1}{10}$	$-\frac{1}{10}$	0	0	10	$10/\frac{1}{4} = 40$
0	x_2	0	1	$-\frac{3}{4}$	0	0	$-\frac{1}{5}$	$\frac{1}{5}$	0	0	20	$20/-\frac{3}{4} = -26\frac{2}{3}$
-5	d_2^-	0	0	$\frac{3}{4}$	0	0	$\frac{1}{5}$	$-\frac{1}{5}$	-1	1	40	$40/\frac{3}{4} = 53\frac{1}{3}$
	z_j	0	0	$-\frac{15}{4}$	0	0	-1	1	5	-5	-200	
	$c_j - z_j$	0	0	$\frac{15}{4}$	0	0	1	-2	-5	0	"Profit"	

(iv)

c_B	BASIS	c_j 0 x_1	0 x_2	0 s_1	0 s_2	0 s_3	0 d_1^+	-1 d_1^-	0 d_2^+	-5 d_2^-	SOLUTION
0	x_1	1	0	0	0	-2	$-\frac{1}{10}$	$\frac{1}{10}$	0	0	50
0	s_2	0	0	0	1	-10	$-\frac{1}{5}$	$\frac{1}{5}$	0	0	40
0	s_1	0	0	1	0	4	$\frac{2}{5}$	$-\frac{2}{5}$	0	0	40
0	x_2	0	1	0	0	3	$\frac{1}{10}$	$-\frac{1}{10}$	0	0	50
-5	d_2^-	0	0	0	0	-3	$-\frac{1}{10}$	$\frac{1}{10}$	-1	1	10
	z_j	0	0	0	0	15	$\frac{1}{2}$	$-\frac{1}{2}$	5	-5	-50
	$c_j - z_j$	0	0	0	0	-15	$-\frac{1}{2}$	$-\frac{1}{2}$	-5	0	"Profit"

Since equations (7.4) involve five constraints (apart from the nonnegativity constraints) there must be five elements in the basis. Notice that the constraints are already in tableau form, with s_1, s_2, s_3, d_1^- and d_2^- as basic variables. Accordingly, we begin with this basis in part (i) of Table 7.1, and proceed to the point where an optimal solution, with no positive $c_j - z_j$ values, has been reached.

The optimal solution is displayed in part (iv) of Table 7.1, from which we find

$$x_1 = 50, \; x_2 = 50, \; s_1 = 40, \; s_2 = 40,$$

$$s_3 = 0, \; d_1^+ = 0, \; d_1^- = 0, \; d_2^+ = 0, \; d_2^- = 10$$

The best available solution, then, is to produce 50 desks and 50 bookcases. At this solution there are 40 hours of slack time in both assembly and finishing, but none in inspection. The fact that d_1^- is zero implies that the profit target of \$2500 has been reached, while the zero value for d_1^+ tells us that at this solution, profit does not exceed the target figure. It follows, of course, that profit for this product mix is precisely \$2500. Since d_2^- is equal to 10, this is the amount by which the target of 60 bookcases has not been met. It necessarily follows in these circumstances, of course, that d_2^+ must be zero. We see, then, that in this solution the profit goal has been reached, but the production goal for bookcases has not.[2]

Notice that the solution to this goal programming problem differs from our solution to the profit maximization problem of the office furnishings company. In the latter case, a profit of \$2600 was achieved through the manufacture of 60 desks and 40 bookcases. Now, with a lower profit goal, the company is able to increase production of bookcases.

7.3. GOAL PROGRAMMING WITH PRIORITIES

We now turn to the case where there are multiple goals which are of different orders of magnitude of importance to the organization in question. For example, suppose that the office furnishings company regards coming as close as possible to the target profit of \$2500 as extremely important. Achieving an output close to 60 bookcases is seen as a desirable goal, *but one which should not interfere with the objective of getting as close as possible to the profit target*. In these circumstances, the profit goal is said to be **first priority,** and the bookcase output goal **second priority.** The distinction between this framework and that of the previous section is that the company will now accept no sacrifice whatever in profit below the target level in order to get closer to the bookcase output goal. Problems in which goals are ranked absolutely in this fashion require some modifications of the usual simplex algorithm for their solution.

The schematic outline of the solution method is shown in Figure 7.2. We first turn to, and solve, the high priority problem by moving as close as possible to the specified goal. Only when this has been accomplished is attention focused on the lower priority target. An attempt is now made to get closer to that target, *but we move in this direction only if doing so carries us no further from the higher priority goal*.

---

[2] This is a consequence of the fact that the penalty cost per bookcase produced below the target of 60 is set at the relatively low value of \$5. The reader is invited to verify, as an exercise, that a different result would arise if this cost were set at \$15.

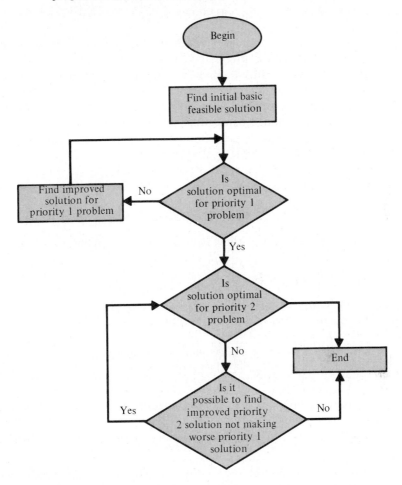

FIGURE 7.2 General approach to the solution of the goal programming problem with priorities.

Formally, we set up our problem for the office furnishings company as

Minimize $\qquad\qquad P_1d_1^- + P_2d_2^-$

subject to $\qquad\qquad 8x_1 + 4x_2 + s_1 = 640$

$$4x_1 + 6x_2 + s_2 = 540$$

$$x_1 + x_2 + s_3 = 100$$

$$30x_1 + 20x_2 - d_1^+ + d_1^- = 2{,}500$$

$$x_2 - d_2^+ + d_2^- = 60$$

$$x_i, d_i^+, d_i^-, s_i \geq 0 \text{ (for all } i\text{)}$$

The constraints are precisely the same as those in (7.4). In this formulation, $P_1 d_1^- + P_2 d_2^-$ is often called an **achievement function.** The P_1, P_2 notation here implies that the profit target has a higher priority than the bookcase output goal.

The setup of the simplex tableau for goal programming with priorities differs slightly from the usual structure. Incorporated in the tableau are evaluation rows for each priority level. The solution method proceeds by first working on the highest priority problem, before moving to those with lower priorities. Table 7.2 develops the optimal solution for the priority goal programming problem of the office furnishings company. Notice that the tables contain two sets of calculations for the $c_j - z_j$ evaluations. That labelled P_1 is for the higher priority goal of achieving a profit of at least \$2500, while the other is for the lower priority target of producing at least 60 bookcases. The problem is transposed to that of maximizing

$$-P_1 d_1^- - P_2 d_2^-$$

but the treatment of P_1 and P_2 is unorthodox. When carrying out computations for the priority one problem, the objective is to make d_1^- as small as possible. Accordingly, in these calculations we set P_1 equal to one and P_2 to zero. Similarly, in the priority two problem, the aim is to minimize d_2^-, so that the calculations here are carried out with P_1 set at zero and P_2 at one. We now consider in some detail the solution algorithm set out in Table 7.2.

(i) In the first part of the table the priority one evaluations are carried out with P_1 set at one and P_2 at zero. Since there are positive $c_j - z_j$ values, the initial basic feasible solution is not optimal, and we must move to an improved solution by bringing x_1 into the basis in place of s_1. The $c_j - z_j$ values for the second priority problem are obtained by setting P_1 to zero and P_2 to one. However, since an optimal solution to the priority one problem has not yet been achieved, these results are ignored.

(ii) In the second part of Table 7.2, the evaluations of the new solution are carried out as before. It turns out that this solution, producing 80 desks and no bookcases, is not optimal for the higher priority problem. The calculations show that x_2 should replace d_1^- in the basis. Again, the $c_j - z_j$ values for the lower priority problem are not used, since an optimal solution of the higher priority problem has not yet been attained.

(iii) From the third part of Table 7.2, we see that the new solution, a product mix of 70 desks and 20 bookcases, is optimal for the higher priority problem. Indeed, the value 0 "profit" for the objective function at this solution implies that the target profit of \$2500 has been reached. Having obtained an optimal solution for the higher priority problem, we can now turn our attention to the lower. We see from part (iii) of Table 7.2 that the solution is not optimal with regard to the target of 60 bookcases, as two of the $c_j - z_j$ values are positive. However, before bringing either of the corresponding variables, s_1 or d_1^+, into the basis, we must assure that doing so will not move us away from the higher priority target. Referring to the priority one $c_j - z_j$ evaluations, we find values of zero corresponding to these two variables. The implication is that bringing either one of them into the basis will yield a solution which remains optimal for the higher priority problem. Accordingly, at the next step, s_1 enters the basis in place of s_3.

(iv) The new solution, displayed in part (iv) of Table 7.2, remains as predicted, optimal for the P_1 problem. It is not, on the other hand, optimal for the P_2 problem, as a positive

TABLE 7.2 Simplex algorithm solution to a goal programming problem with priorities of the office furnishings company.

(i)

c_B	c_j BASIS	0 x_1	0 x_2	0 s_1	0 s_2	0 s_3	0 d_1^+	$-P_1$ d_1^-	0 d_2^+	$-P_2$ d_2^-	SOLUTION	
0	s_1	⑧	4	1	0	0	0	0	0	0	640	$\frac{640}{8}=80$
0	s_2	4	6	0	1	0	0	0	0	0	540	$\frac{540}{4}=135$
0	s_3	1	1	0	0	1	0	0	0	0	100	$\frac{100}{1}=100$
$-P_1$	d_1^-	30	20	0	0	0	-1	1	0	0	2500	$\frac{2500}{30}=83\frac{1}{3}$
$-P_2$	d_2^-	0	1	0	0	0	0	0	-1	1	60	$\frac{60}{0}=\infty$
P_2	z_j	0	-1	0	0	0	0	0	1	-1	-60	
	$c_j - z_j$	0	1	0	0	0	0	0	-1	0	"Profit"	
P_1	z_j	-30	-20	0	0	0	1	-1	0	0	-2500	
	$c_j - z_j$	30	20	0	0	0	-1	0	0	0	"Profit"	

(ii)

c_B	c_j BASIS	0 x_1	0 x_2	0 s_1	0 s_2	0 s_3	0 d_1^+	$-P_1$ d_1^-	0 d_2^+	$-P_2$ d_2^-	SOLUTION	
0	x_1	1	$\frac{1}{2}$	$\frac{1}{8}$	0	0	0	0	0	0	80	$80/\frac{1}{2}=160$
0	s_2	0	4	$-\frac{1}{2}$	1	0	0	0	0	0	220	$\frac{220}{4}=55$
0	s_3	0	$\frac{1}{2}$	$-\frac{1}{8}$	0	1	0	0	0	0	20	$20/\frac{1}{2}=40$
$-P_1$	d_1^-	0	⑤	$-\frac{15}{4}$	0	0	-1	1	0	0	100	$\frac{100}{5}=20$
$-P_2$	d_2^-	0	1	0	0	0	0	0	-1	1	60	$\frac{60}{1}=60$
P_2	z_j	0	-1	0	0	0	0	0	1	-1	-60	
	$c_j - z_j$	0	1	0	0	0	0	0	-1	0	"Profit"	
P_1	z_j	0	-5	$\frac{15}{4}$	0	0	1	-1	0	0	-100	
	$c_j - z_j$	0	5	$-\frac{15}{4}$	0	0	-1	0	0	0	"Profit"	

(iii)

c_B	c_j BASIS	0 x_1	0 x_2	0 s_1	0 s_2	0 s_3	0 d_1^+	$-P_1$ d_1^-	0 d_2^+	$-P_2$ d_2^-	SOLUTION	
0	x_1	1	0	$\frac{1}{2}$	0	0	$\frac{1}{10}$	$-\frac{1}{10}$	0	0	70	$70/\frac{1}{2}=140$
0	s_2	0	0	$\frac{5}{2}$	1	0	$\frac{4}{5}$	$-\frac{4}{5}$	0	0	140	$140/\frac{5}{2}=56$
0	s_3	0	0	④	0	1	$\frac{1}{10}$	$-\frac{1}{10}$	0	0	10	$10/\frac{1}{4}=40$
0	x_2	0	1	$-\frac{3}{4}$	0	0	$-\frac{1}{5}$	$\frac{1}{5}$	0	0	20	$20/-\frac{3}{4}=-26\frac{2}{3}$
$-P_2$	d_2^-	0	0	$\frac{3}{4}$	0	0	$\frac{1}{5}$	$-\frac{1}{5}$	-1	1	40	$40/\frac{3}{4}=53\frac{1}{3}$
P_2	z_j	0	0	$-\frac{3}{4}$	0	0	$-\frac{1}{5}$	$\frac{1}{5}$	1	-1	-40	
	$c_j - z_j$	0	0	$\frac{3}{4}$	0	0	$\frac{1}{5}$	$-\frac{1}{5}$	-1	0	"Profit"	
P_1	z_j	0	0	0	0	0	0	0	0	0	0	
	$c_j - z_j$	0	0	0	0	0	0	-1	0	0	"Profit"	

TABLE 7.2 (*Continued*)

(iv)

c_j		0	0	0	0	0	0	$-P_1$	0	$-P_2$	
c_B	BASIS	x_1	x_2	s_1	s_2	s_3	d_1^+	d_1^-	d_2^+	d_2^-	SOLUTION
0	x_1	1	0	0	0	-2	$-\frac{1}{10}$	$\frac{1}{10}$	0	0	50
0	s_2	0	0	0	1	-10	$-\frac{1}{5}$	$\frac{1}{5}$	0	0	40
0	s_1	0	0	1	0	4	$\frac{2}{5}$	$-\frac{2}{5}$	0	0	40
0	x_2	0	1	0	0	3	$\frac{1}{10}$	$-\frac{1}{10}$	0	0	50
$-P_2$	d_2^-	0	0	0	0	-3	$-\frac{1}{10}$	$\frac{1}{10}$	-1	1	10
P_2	z_j	0	0	0	0	3	$\frac{1}{10}$	$-\frac{1}{10}$	1	-1	-10
	$c_j - z_j$	0	0	0	0	-3	$-\frac{1}{10}$	$\frac{1}{10}$	-1	0	"Profit"
P_1	z_j	0	0	0	0	0	0	0	0	0	0
	$c_j - z_j$	0	0	0	0	0	0	-1	0	0	"Profit"

$c_j - z_j$ is associated with d_1^-. This variable cannot, however, be brought into the basis, since the negative priority one $c_j - z_j$ value implies that doing so would yield a suboptimal solution to the higher priority problem. Therefore, given the two goals and their respective priorities, we have come as far as possible toward their satisfaction.

The optimal solution to the priority goal programming problem of the office furnishings company is set out in the final part of Table 7.2. It involves the production of 50 desks and 50 bookcases, and happens, on this occasion, to be identical to the solution reached for the problem without priorities in the previous section. This is to be expected, since in the earlier problem we obtained a solution for which the profit target was met. This solution is displayed in Figure 7.3, where it can be seen that the profit target of $2500 has been reached. Any feasible solution that would move nearer to the target output of 60 bookcases would move us below the profit target. Since the profit goal has the higher priority, no further movement toward an output of 60 bookcases is made.

The procedures described in this section can be extended to deal with problems in which there are several goals and ordered priorities. In the simplex tableau, an evaluation row is set up for each goal, and we proceed by attacking the optimization problems of getting as close as possible to the targets, in order of priority.

Solution of Goal Programming Problems with Priorities

Suppose that we have K goals, with priorities ordered $P_1, P_2, \ldots, P_K$ from most to least important. Proceed as follows:

(i) Set up a simplex tableau with $c_j - z_j$ evaluation rows for each priority level. In computing these values for the i-th priority, set P_i to one and all other P_j to zero.

(ii) Solve the problems in order of priority, by improving the current solution. However, do not move to an improved solution at one priority level if this results in moving further away from a higher priority goal.

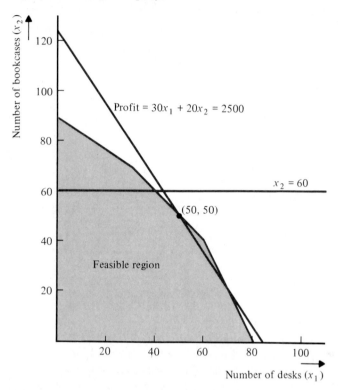

FIGURE 7.3 Production of 50 desks and 50 bookcases as the solution to a priority goal programming problem of the office furnishings company.

Number of bookcases (x_2)

Profit = $30x_1 + 20x_2 = 2500$

$x_2 = 60$

(50, 50)

Feasible region

Number of desks (x_1)

EXERCISES

7.1. Consider again the problem of the office furnishings company discussed in Section 7.2. As before, the company has targets of $2500 profit and production of 60 bookcases. Suppose that management now believes that each bookcase produced below the target figure is equivalent to $15 in lost profit below the goal of $2500. Find the optimal solution to this new goal programming problem.

7.2. In Chapters 2 and 3 we discussed a constrained minimization problem in which a processed food company sought the blend of two additives with the lowest possible total cost, subject to four nutrition requirements being met. The problem specifications are set out in Table 2.5. This company remains concerned about the cost of the blend used, but because of a potential shortage in the future, is anxious not to use too much of additive II in its blend. Two targets are set for the coming week's production:

(i) A blend costing no more than 26.5 cents

(ii) A blend containing no more than 5 grams of additive II

The company regards each gram of additive II used above the target amount as equivalent to 1.5 cents of additional cost above the target figure. In these circumstances, what blend should the processed food company employ?

7.3. A company produces two products, each of which requires time on three different machines. The company wants to determine the product output mix, given two goals:

(i) Profit of at least $14,500

(ii) Output of at least 220 units of product II

and the specifications shown in the accompanying table.

TOTAL MACHINE HOURS AVAILABLE	MACHINE	MACHINE-HOURS PER UNIT	
		PRODUCT I	PRODUCT II
500	A	2	1
300	B	1	1
550	C	1	2
PROFIT PER UNIT ($)		60	40

The company views each unit of product II produced below the target level as equivalent to $20 of profit below the profit goal. What product mix should be chosen?

7.4. A manufacturing company produces two products, each of which must be processed through three departments. This company wants to find the best product mix, given two goals:

(i) Profit of at least $2900

(ii) Output of at least 600 units of product II

and the specifications shown in the following table.

TOTAL MAN-HOURS AVAILABLE	DEPARTMENT	MAN-HOURS PER WEEK	
		PRODUCT I	PRODUCT II
5000	A	4	1
1400	B	1	1
1700	C	1	2
PROFIT PER UNIT ($)		2	3

The company regards each unit of product II produced below the goal as equivalent to $1 of profit below target. Which is the optimal product mix in these circumstances?

7.5. A company produces two brands of perfumed bath oils. Each brand contains a combination of three of four perfume essences. The quantities required are set out in the following table.

BATH OIL	QUANTITY OF PERFUME ESSENCE (IN OUNCES)			
	1	2	3	4
A	0.2	0.4	0	0.2
B	0.5	0	0.2	0.1

Quantities of these essences are in limited supply for the coming week, as shown below

AVAILABILITY OF ESSENCE (IN OUNCES)			
1	2	3	4
200	200	150	100

Each bottle of bath oil A yields a profit of $1.20, and each bottle of bath oil B a profit of $1.50. The company has the following three goals:

(i) Profit of at least $775

(ii) Production of at least 400 bottles of bath oil A

(iii) Production of at least 350 bottles of bath oil B

Each bottle of either bath oil produced below the target levels is viewed as equivalent to 50 cents in foregone profit below the goal figure. Find the optimal product mix.

7.6. A large travel agency employs telephone operators who work 8-hour shifts, either from 8:00 a.m. to 4:00 p.m., or from 2:00 p.m. to 10:00 p.m. Operators on the earlier shift are paid $40 per day, and those on the later shift $45 per day. The manager of the travel agency estimates minimum numbers of operators needed in various time periods as shown in the accompanying table.

TIME	MINIMUM NUMBER OF OPERATORS
8 a.m.–10 a.m.	3
10 a.m.– 2 p.m.	4
2 p.m.– 4 p.m.	12
4 p.m.– 8 p.m.	5
8 p.m.–10 p.m.	2

The travel agency manager has two goals:

(i) Daily cost of no more than $510

(ii) At least 7 operators on the second shift

Each operator below target on the second shift is viewed as equivalent to an addition of $3 to total cost above the goal. How many operators should be allocated to each shift?

7.7. An agent selling fire protection insurance contacts both households and businesses. Each household contact requires one hour, and each business contact 3 hours. The agent has available during the month a total of 150 hours for such contacts. He sets, as monthly goals, contact of 90 households and 40 businesses. The agent counts the cost of each business contact below target at twice that of each household contact below target. How should he proceed?

7.8. Return to the goal programming problem of the office furnishings company of Section 7.3, but now assume that the target of producing 60 bookcases has first priority, while the profit goal is of lower priority. What now should be the product mix?

7.9. The office furnishings company still has available only 640 hours of assembly time and 540 hours of finishing time, but is able, though management is reluctant to do so, to increase capacity for inspection through overtime working beyond 100 man-hours. Management sets two goals, which are, in order of priority

  (i) A profit of at least $2700

  (ii) As little overtime working in inspection as possible

  Solve this goal programming problem.

7.10. Extending the previous exercise, suppose that management has, in order of priority, the following three goals

  (i) A profit of at least $2700

  (ii) As little overtime working in inspection as possible

  (iii) Production of at least 60 bookcases

  What product mix should now be produced?

7.11. Repeat Exercise 7.10, but with the priorities for goals (ii) and (iii) reversed. Draw a graph to demonstrate the rationale behind your solutions to this and the previous exercise.

7.12. Refer to Exercise 7.2. Suppose that the processed food company views achieving a blend costing no more than 26.5 cents as first priority, while the target of a blend containing no more than 5 grams of additive II is a lower priority. What blend should be used?

7.13. Repeat Exercise 7.12, but with the orders of priority reversed. Draw a graph to justify your solutions to this and the previous exercise.

7.14. Refer to Exercise 7.3. Assume that the company regards the profit goal of $14,500 as first priority, and output of at least 220 units of product II as a lower priority. In these circumstances what should be the product mix?

7.15. Repeat Exercise 7.14, but with the orders of priority of the two goals reversed. Draw a graph illustrating the logic behind your solutions to this and the previous exercise.

7.16. Refer to Exercise 7.4. Assume now that the manufacturing company views the profit target of $2900 as a high priority, and the output goal of production of at least 600 units of product II as a lower priority. What then should be the product mix?

7.17. Repeat Exercise 7.16, but with the orders of priority of the two goals reversed. Sketch a graph to illustrate your answers to this and the previous exercise.

7.18. Refer to Exercise 7.5. Suppose that the company views the profit goal of $775 as the highest priority. The second priority is production of at least 400 bottles of bath oil A, while output of at least 350 bottles of bath oil B has the lowest priority of the three targets. What product mix should the company produce?

7.19. Repeat Exercise 7.18, but with the orders of priority for production targets for the two bath oils reversed. The profit goal retains the highest priority.

7.20. Refer to Exercise 7.6. Suppose the travel agency sees a daily cost of no more than $510 as first priority, while the target of at least seven operators on the second shift is a lower priority. How many operators should be allocated to each shift?

7.21. Repeat Exercise 7.20, but with the orders of priority for the two goals reversed. How many operators now should be allocated to each shift?

Public Health Resource Allocation: The Special Supplemental Food Program for Women, Infants, and Children[1]

The Special Supplemental Food Program for Women, Infants, and Children (WIC) is administered by the United States Department of Agriculture. Its aim is to provide food supplements and education on nutrition for low income pregnant and breastfeeding women, and infants and children up to five years of age. Funds from WIC are distributed to the states, and state agencies must then decide how to allocate these funds among local WIC programs.

Typically, local WIC agencies will identify more potential program participants than can be served with available funds. These potential participants can be classified into six priority groups, according to degree of nutritional risk. Target values can be set for the number of participants served in each priority group. (These target values may simply be the total numbers of cases identified in each group.) Penalties for failures to meet targets can then be established, depending on state officials' views on the differences in degrees of need among the six groups. Allocation of resources to local WIC agencies can then be determined in such a way that the total penalty over all groups is as small as possible, subject to the budget constraint. This model allows the allocation of additional dollars to expand the caseloads of existing local agencies, or to establish new agencies.

The model was applied to the WIC program in the state of Indiana, where a possible additional $960,000 of funding were anticipated. Allocations were computed first by setting as target values total numbers of potential participants identified in each priority group, and penalties for failure to meet targets suggested by state officials. Sensitivity analysis was also carried out to show the effects of lowering the target values and of modifying the priority weights. The authors of this study also show how their approach can be employed in the allocation of *reductions* in budget.

---

[1] This discussion is based on K. M. Tingley and J. S. Liebman, "A Goal Programming Example in Public Health Resource Allocation," *Management Science, 30,* (1984), 279–289.

Balanced Nutrients: Diet Planning in the Third World[2]

Diet mixes are frequently chosen so that specific nutritional requirements are met at the lowest possible cost. Diet planning of this sort is particularly important in third world countries where food is not plentiful. This approach was applied to formulate a food product for Thais. A total of 150 raw material ingredients were available, and standards were set for 26 nutrients. These nutrients included protein, fat, calories, fiber, minerals, vitamins, and amino acids. Using linear programming, the mininum cost diet satisfying all standards was found. One feature of this solution, often found for such problem formulations, was that the diet contained quantities of some nutrients considerably *in excess* of the standards set. Nutritionists would not support such a solution, preferring a more balanced diet of nutrients, as the dangers of overdoses of certain nutrients are now well established.

Goal programming provides an alternative approach to this problem. The standards for each nutrient are still retained as lower levels that a diet must satisfy. However, these standards are now viewed as targets to be met. For the Thai diet problem, in place of the cost minimization objective was substituted the aim of minimizing the total of the percentage deviations of all nutrients from their target levels. For the linear programming solution to the cost minimization problem, this total of percentage deviations had been 2038%. The goal programming problem solution reduced this figure to 372%.

The simple linear programming and goal programming approaches just described for the diet problem may both be unsatisfactory. The simple linear programming formulation pays no attention to the desirability of balance in the diet. It could, however, be made to do so by specifying upper as well as lower limits for each nutrient in the diet. However, there exists the danger that the addition of many further constraints will lead to infeasibility. On the other hand, the simple goal programming approach we have discussed pays no attention to cost, which is certainly not desirable in applications to third world countries. In fact, the goal programming solution to the Thai diet problem yielded a diet with a cost three times that of the linear programming solution. One way around this difficulty is to add to the goal programming formulation a further constraint—setting an upper limit on the cost of the diet.

---

[2] This discussion is based on A. M. Anderson and M. D. Earle, "Diet Planning in the Third World by Linear and Goal Programming," *Journal of Operational Research Society, 34,* (1983), 9–16.

integer linear programming

CHAPTER EIGHT

8.1. SOME INTEGER LINEAR PROGRAMMING PROBLEM FORMULATIONS

Many linear programming problems met in practice involve additional constraints of a type we have not yet discussed in any detail. It is often necessary to restrict attention to solution values that are whole numbers, or **integers.** For example, in some earlier chapters we discussed the product mix problem of an office furnishings company that manufactures desks and bookcases. Now, this company cannot produce fractions of a desk or bookcase, so that of necessity, any feasible solution to its product mix problem must involve integer numbers. In our analysis, we glossed over this point, and in fact it turned out that the optimum solution derived did indeed yield integer numbers of desks and bookcases. This, however, was entirely fortuitous. There was nothing in our problem specification or solution method to guarantee such an outcome. In this chapter we will examine constrained optimization linear programming problems of the type discussed in Chapters 2 and 3, *but where the solutions are required to be integers.*

Here, we will introduce three important classes of problems and in subsequent sections of this chapter, discuss methods for their solution.

(i) ALL-INTEGER LINEAR PROGRAMMING PROBLEMS

An all-integer linear programming problem is one in which *every* decision variable is required to take an integer value. As an illustration of such a problem, consider a small scientific research laboratory whose director must plan to take

TABLE 8.1 Problem specifications for the research laboratory.

TOTAL MAN-HOURS AVAILABLE IN YEAR (THOUSANDS)	MANPOWER	MAN-HOURS PER UNIT (THOUSANDS)	
		DRUGS	AGRICULTURAL CHEMICALS
30	Scientists	4	5
40	Technicians	6	4
10	Managers	1	2
PROFIT PER UNIT ($'000)		20	30

on projects for the coming year. Research of two types—on drugs, and on agricultural chemicals (fertilizers, insecticides, and the like)—can be carried out. Table 8.1 shows the expected profitability per project of each type, together with annual resources, and requirements of scientific, technical, and managerial manpower. The decision to be made is how many drugs projects and agricultural chemicals projects should be taken on to maximize expected total profits, subject to the resource constraints being satisfied.

Denoting by x_1 the number of drugs projects and by x_2 the number of agricultural chemicals projects, we can write out the constrained maximization problem in the usual way, but with the additional proviso that the numbers of projects of each type must be integers. The algebraic formulation is, therefore

$$
\begin{aligned}
\text{Maximize} \quad & 20x_1 + 30x_2 \\
\text{subject to} \quad & 4x_1 + 5x_2 \leq 30 \\
& 6x_1 + 4x_2 \leq 40 \\
& x_1 + 2x_2 \leq 10 \\
& x_1, x_2 \geq 0 \\
& x_1, x_2 \text{ integer}
\end{aligned}
\qquad (8.1)
$$

Suppose, for the moment, we ignore the requirement that the solutions must be integers. The resulting problem is called the **linear programming relaxation** of the integer programming problem. It can be solved using the simplex algorithm, or, since there are only two decision variables, by graphical methods.

Definitions

(i) An **all-integer linear programming problem** is one in which every decision variable is required to take an integer value.

(ii) The **linear programming relaxation** of an integer programming problem is the original problem with the integer requirements ignored.

It is straightforward to show that the optimal solution to the linear programming relaxation of our research laboratory problem is:

$$x_1 = 3\tfrac{1}{3},\ x_2 = 3\tfrac{1}{3},\ \text{Objective Function} = 166\tfrac{2}{3}$$

This solution requires $3\tfrac{1}{3}$ drugs projects and $3\tfrac{1}{3}$ agricultural chemicals projects, and yields an expected annual profit of $166\tfrac{2}{3}$ thousand dollars. This is not, however, a feasible solution to the actual problem faced by the research laboratory, as it is not possible to take on fractions of projects.

The position is illustrated in Figure 8.1, which shows the feasible region for the linear programming relaxation, together with the profit line

$$20x_1 + 30x_2 = 166\tfrac{2}{3}$$

This line just touches the feasible region at the point $(3\tfrac{1}{3}, 3\tfrac{1}{3})$ which is therefore the optimal solution to the linear programming relaxation. However, the original problem (8.1) requires the solution values to be integers. Figure 8.1 shows all possible feasible integer solutions, marked by points. This is just the set of integer solutions lying in the feasible region of the linear programming relaxation.

Since there are just two decision variables, it is possible to solve graphically this particular integer linear programming problem. Using precisely the same approach as was employed in Chapter 2, we can draw parallel profit lines

FIGURE 8.1 Graphical analysis of the all-integer linear programming problem of the research laboratory.

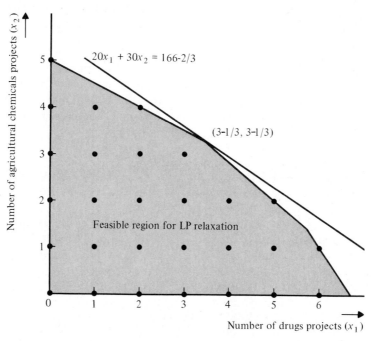

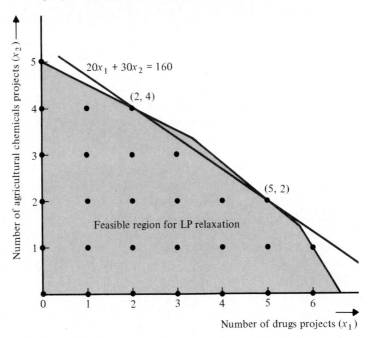

FIGURE 8.2 Optimal solutions to the all-integer linear programming problem of the research laboratory.

closer and closer to the origin until one is found to pass through a feasible solution point. In fact, this problem has a pair of jointly optimal solutions:

$$x_1 = 2,\ x_2 = 4 \text{ and } x_1 = 5,\ x_2 = 2$$

Each of these solutions yields a value 160 for the objective function. Hence the laboratory can achieve an expected profit of 160 thousand dollars by taking either two drugs and four agricultural chemicals projects, or five drugs and two agricultural chemicals projects. This conclusion can be verified by reference to Figure 8.2, where we have drawn in the line

$$20x_1 + 30x_2 = 160$$

This line passes through the points (2, 4) and (5, 2), while all other feasible solution points lie between the line and the origin, implying associated expected profits of less than 160 thousand dollars.

For more complex problems involving several decision variables, it will not be possible to use graphical methods of solution. A solution algorithm which can be applied to such problems is described in the following section.

(ii) MIXED-INTEGER LINEAR PROGRAMMING

A mixed-integer linear programming problem is one in which *some, but not all,* of the decision variables are required to take integer values. Consider, for example, the problem of a scientific consulting group planning to take on contracts

TABLE 8.2 Problem specifications for the scientific consulting group.

TOTAL MAN-HOURS AVAILABLE IN YEAR (THOUSANDS)	MANPOWER	MAN-HOURS PER UNIT (THOUSANDS)	
		CONTRACTS	BIDS
40	Technicians	3	4
36	Scientists	4	3
16	Managers	2	1
PROFIT PER UNIT ($'000)		18	20

for the coming year. It is required that work on any contract be completed during the year. Since it is not feasible to carry work over to the next year, the number of contracts undertaken in the year must be an integer. The consulting group is planning to expand into more profitable areas, so that management wants to spend some effort in preparing bids for work which is eventually expected to yield higher returns. Moreover, work begun on any bid during the year can be carried forward, if not completed, to the next year. Hence the number of complete bids prepared during the year need not be an integer. Table 8.2 shows expected profitability for contracts and new bids, together with resource requirements and availability. The objective is to find the allocation of effort between current contract work and bid preparation that yields the highest possible expected profit, given the resource constraints.

If we denote by x_1 the number of contracts taken, and by x_2 the number of bids prepared during the year, the constrained optimization problem can be expressed algebraically as

$$\text{Maximize} \quad 18x_1 + 20x_2$$
$$\text{subject to} \quad 3x_1 + 4x_2 \le 40$$
$$4x_1 + 3x_2 \le 36$$
$$2x_1 + x_2 \le 16 \tag{8.2}$$
$$x_1, x_2 \ge 0$$
$$x_1 \text{ integer}$$

Notice that by contrast with the problem set out in (8.1), one of the decision variables in (8.2) is required to take an integer value, but the other is not.

Definition

A **mixed-integer linear programming problem** is one in which some decision variables are required to take integer values, while others may take any values satisfying the problem constraints.

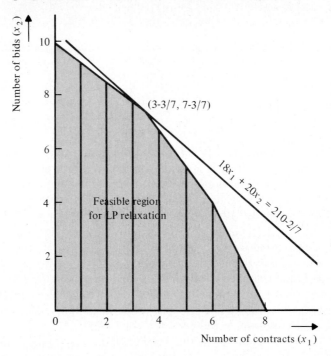

FIGURE 8.3 Graphical analysis of the mixed-integer linear programming problem of the scientific consulting group.

Again, it is useful to examine the linear programming relaxation of our integer programming problem. This is done by dropping the requirement in (8.2) that x_1 must be an integer. It is then straightforward to show that the optimal solution to the resulting constrained maximization problem is:

$$x_1 = 3\tfrac{3}{7}, x_2 = 7\tfrac{3}{7}, \text{Objective Function} = 210\tfrac{2}{7}$$

This solution involves work on $3\tfrac{3}{7}$ contracts, and the preparation of $7\tfrac{3}{7}$ bids, yielding an expected profit of $210\tfrac{2}{7}$ thousand dollars. However, this does not constitute a feasible solution to the problem (8.2), where x_1 is required to be an integer.

In Figure 8.3 the position is illustrated. We show the feasible region for the linear programming relaxation, together with the profit line

$$18x_1 + 20x_2 = 210\tfrac{2}{7}$$

Since this line just touches the feasible region at the point $(3\tfrac{3}{7}, 7\tfrac{3}{7})$, that point constitutes the optimal solution to the linear programming relaxation. The original problem (8.2), however, requires the solution for x_1 to be integer. This requirement is shown by drawing the lines $x_1 = 0$, $x_1 = 1$, . . . , $x_1 = 7$, $x_1 = 8$ within the feasible region. Any solution must lie on one of these line segments in order to satisfy the problem constraints and the requirement that x_1 be integer.

Since there are just two decision variables, an optimal solution to our prob-

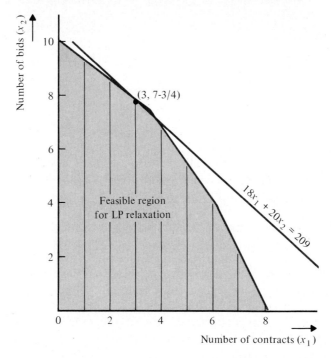

FIGURE 8.4 Optimal solution to the mixed-integer linear programming problem of the scientific consulting group.

lem can be derived graphically. If parallel profit lines are drawn closer and closer to the origin, the first point at which a feasible solution to the mixed-integer linear programming problem is touched yields the optimal solution

$$x_1 = 3, x_2 = 7\tfrac{3}{4}, \text{Objective Function} = 209$$

Therefore, at this solution, three contracts are carried out, $7\tfrac{3}{4}$ bids prepared, and an expected profit of 209 thousand dollars results. This is illustrated in Figure 8.4, which shows the line

$$18x_1 + 20x_2 = 209$$

touching the point $(3, 7\tfrac{3}{4})$. All other feasible solutions lie between this line and the origin, establishing the optimality of our solution. In Section 8.3 we will discuss a procedure for solving more general mixed-integer linear programming problems.

(iii) ZERO-ONE INTEGER LINEAR PROGRAMMING PROBLEMS

Some constrained optimization problems are formulated so that each decision variable must take one of two values—generally zero or one. Such problems arise naturally if decisions of the "yes or no" type must be made. To illustrate

TABLE 8.3 Costs and expected profits from research and development projects.

PROJECT	RESEARCH AND DEVELOPMENT COSTS ($ MILLION)	EXPECTED PROFITS ($ MILLION)
1	1.2	5.0
2	3.2	4.5
3	1.8	4.8
4	4.0	8.0
5	2.5	4.2

how questions of this sort might be formulated, consider a large corporation with a total budget of $6.5 million for research and development expenditures on new products. There are five possible projects. Table 8.3 shows research and development costs and the expected present values of future profits (allowing for development costs) from the five projects.

The objective of this corporation is to carry out research and development on those projects with the highest total expected present value of future profits, subject to the budget constraint that total costs must not exceed $6.5 million. The position therefore is that research and development on any particular project either will or will not be carried out. Although it is clear that this problem involves constrained optimization, it is less obvious how we would go about formulating it in the familiar linear programming framework. To achieve this end, we define the decision variables in a special way, introducing variables restricted to take values of either zero or one. Specifically, we define

$$x_i = \begin{cases} 0 & \text{if project } i \text{ is not adopted} \\ 1 & \text{if project } i \text{ is adopted} \end{cases} \quad (i = 1, 2, \ldots, 5)$$

With these definitions, the total research and development cost, in millions of dollars, can be written

$$\text{Total Cost} = 1.2x_1 + 3.2x_2 + 1.8x_3 + 4.0x_4 + 2.5x_5$$

Similarly, the total expected present value of profits (in millions of dollars) is

$$\text{Total Expected Profit} = 5.0x_1 + 4.5x_2 + 4.8x_3 + 8.0x_4 + 4.2x_5$$

Our problem can therefore be expressed algebraically as

Maximize $\quad 5.0x_1 + 4.5x_2 + 4.8x_3 + 8.0x_4 + 4.2x_5$

subject to $\quad 1.2x_1 + 3.2x_2 + 1.8x_3 + 4.0x_4 + 2.5x_5 \leq 6.5 \qquad (8.3)$

$$x_i = 0 \text{ or } 1 \ (i = 1, 2, \ldots, 5)$$

In (8.3) we have a constrained maximization problem involving five decision variables. It is required, however, that these decision variables each take the values zero or one. Such problems are called zero-one integer linear programming problems, and are special cases of the general integer linear programming problems discussed earlier in this section. The problem discussed here is an example of a **capital budgeting problem.**

Definition

A **zero-one integer linear programming problem** is one in which decision variables are required to take values zero or one.

The linear programming relaxation of the zero-one integer programming problem (8.3) requires only that the decision variables be nonnegative and not exceed one. It is written therefore as

Maximize $\quad 5.0x_1 + 4.5x_2 + 4.8x_3 + 8.0x_4 + 4.2x_5$

subject to $\quad 1.2x_1 + 3.2x_2 + 1.8x_3 + 4.0x_4 + 2.5x_5 \leq 6.5$

$$x_i \leq 1 \quad (i = 1, 2, \ldots, 5)$$
$$x_i \geq 0 \quad (i = 1, 2, \ldots, 5)$$

The optimal solution to this linear programming relaxation is[1]

$$x_1 = 1, x_2 = 0, x_3 = 1, x_4 = \tfrac{7}{8}, x_5 = 0$$

yielding a total profit of \$16.80 million. This solution is not, however, feasible for the zero-one problem (8.3), as it involves a fractional value for one of the decision variables. In Section 8.4 we will see how optimal feasible solutions to zero-one integer linear programming problems can be derived.

DIFFICULTY IN SOLVING INTEGER LINEAR PROGRAMMING PROBLEMS

At first sight it might appear that finding the optimal solution of an integer linear programming problem should be easier than finding the optimal solution of the corresponding linear programming relaxation. After all, in all-integer or zero-one problems there is only a finite number of possible solutions. However, such intuition is misleading. In fact, integer linear programming problems are considerably more difficult to solve than their linear programming relaxations.

One obvious possibility is to simply ignore, at first, the integer requirements, apply the simplex algorithm, and then round the solutions to the nearest

---

[1] For problems of this form a short-cut method of solution is available, circumventing the need for application of the simplex algorithm. For the five projects, the profits per unit cost are, respectively, $5.0/1.2 = 4.167$, 1.406, 2.667, 2, and 1.68. Ordering the projects by profit per unit cost, we set the corresponding x_i at their highest possible values, until the total available resources are used up. Hence, we set x_1 and x_3 to 1, which yields a total cost of 3 million dollars. The remaining 3.5 million dollars is allocated to project 4, so that $x_4 = 3.5/4 = 7/8$.

integers. Unfortunately, however, the resulting solution may not be feasible. Even when rounding yields a feasible solution, that solution may not be optimal. For example, consider the research laboratory problem of Table 8.1 and equations (8.1). As we have seen, the optimal solution of the linear programming relaxation is $x_1 = 3\frac{1}{3}$, $x_2 = 3\frac{1}{3}$. Rounding, then, suggests the solution $x_1 = 3$, $x_2 = 3$. However, as we have already noted, the solutions $x_1 = 2$, $x_2 = 4$ and $x_1 = 5$, $x_2 = 2$ both yield higher profits. For larger problems, rounding may produce a solution that is far from optimal.

A further difficulty in attacking integer linear programming problems arises from the fact that it is hard to check any feasible solution for optimality. In Chapter 3 we saw how the simplex tableau could be used to test a solution of a linear programming problem for optimality. This approach, however, is not directly applicable to the case where some decision variables are required to take integer values.

One approach that has been applied in solving integer linear programming problems employs the **cutting plane** technique. Essentially, the strategy is to first solve the linear programming relaxation. If this solution is an integer, then nothing more need be done. However, if it is not, the problem specification is modified by adding a new constraint, or **cut,** such that the feasible region for the modified problem includes all possible integer solutions of the original problem, *but does not include the optimal solution of the linear programming relaxation of that problem.*

To illustrate, consider the simple problem

$$\text{Maximize} \quad 20x_1 + 30x_2$$
$$\text{subject to} \quad 3x_1 + 4x_2 \leq 23$$
$$x_1, x_2 \geq 0$$
$$x_1, x_2 \text{ integer}$$

Figure 8.5 shows the feasible region for the linear programming relaxation and the feasible solutions to the all-integer problem. It is straightforward to show graphically that the optimal solution to the linear programming relaxation is

$$x_1 = 0, x_2 = 5\frac{3}{4}$$

Since this does not yield an integer value for x_2, we must proceed further. Specifically, the aim is to add a further constraint in such a way that the point $(0, 5\frac{3}{4})$ is excluded from the feasible region, but all integer solutions to the original problem are still included. One way to achieve this is to require that x_2 be at most 5.

Consider, then, the problem

$$\text{Maximize} \quad 20x_1 + 30x_2$$
$$\text{subject to} \quad 3x_1 + 4x_2 \leq 23$$
$$x_2 \leq 5$$
$$x_1, x_2 \geq 0$$

FIGURE 8.5 Shaded area is feasible region $3x_1 + 4x_2 \leq 23$; $x_1, x_2 \geq 0$. The ● are the all-integer solutions in that region.

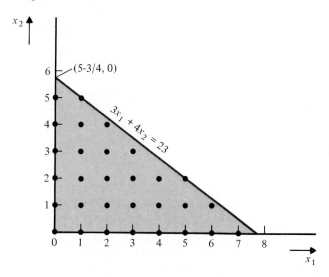

In Figure 8.6, the line $x_2 = 5$ cuts the original feasible region. As can be seen, the point $(0, 5\frac{3}{4})$ is not in the feasible region of the new problem. Now, if the optimal solution to the modified problem is all-integer, this solution must also be optimal for the original all-integer problem. This is so since our new constraint has not eliminated any feasible all-integer solutions of the original problem.

FIGURE 8.6 Shaded area is feasible region $3x_1 + 4x_2 \leq 23$, $x_2 \leq 5$; $x_1, x_2 \geq 0$. The ● are the all-integer solutions in the region $3x_1 + 4x_2 \leq 23$; $x_1, x_2 \geq 0$.

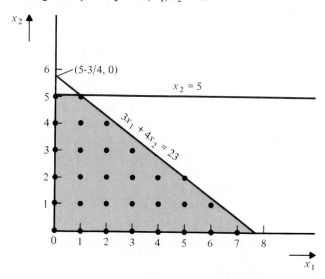

In fact, it is easily seen that the optimal solution to the modified problem is

$$x_1 = 1, x_2 = 5$$

Therefore, this is the optimal solution to the original all-integer programming problem.

Had this solution not been all-integer, it would have been necessary to proceed by making a second cut, again making sure that the new feasible region included all feasible solutions to the original integer programming problem. For larger problems, the cutting plane approach can be extremely time consuming, requiring many applications of the simplex algorithm before an optimal solution is found. In the next section we will introduce an alternative solution algorithm which is generally more efficient.

8.2. SOLVING ALL-INTEGER LINEAR PROGRAMMING PROBLEMS: THE BRANCH-AND-BOUND METHOD

In this and the following two sections we will illustrate a procedure for deriving the optimal solution to integer linear programming problems. We begin by considering problems for which every decision variable is required to take an integer value. To provide a specific example, in Section 8.1 we considered a research laboratory wanting to optimally allocate effort between drugs and agricultural chemicals projects. The all-integer linear programming problem for this laboratory is set out in equations (8.1). A direct line of attack would be to simply evaluate the objective function for all feasible values of the decision variables[2]; that is, for all those points shown in Figure 8.1. However, unless the number of decision variables in the problem is very small, such an approach would, in general, involve computations unnecessarily burdensome.

In fact, the algorithms commonly employed for solving integer linear programming problems use a procedure known as the **branch-and-bound method** which searches systematically for an optimal solution. The starting point is the optimal solution to the linear programming relaxation. For the problem of the research laboratory, we found this to be:

$$x_1 = 3\tfrac{1}{3}, x_2 = 3\tfrac{1}{3}, \text{Objective Function} = 166\tfrac{2}{3}$$

where x_1 and x_2 denote respectively the numbers of drugs and agricultural chemicals projects. Now, although this is not a feasible solution to our integer linear programming problem, it does give us useful information. Since this solution provides the highest possible value of the objective function for *any* nonnegative values of the decision variables satisfying the problem constraints, it follows that no integer solution satisfying those constraints can yield a higher objective function value. We therefore say that the profit of $166\tfrac{2}{3}$ thousand constitutes an

---

[2] In fact, it is not necessary to go this far. For example, since $x_1 = 3$, $x_2 = 3$ is a feasible solution, it is pointless to consider those solutions in which one of these variables is less that 3 and the other does not exceed 3.

upper bound for the value of the objective function at the optimal solution to the integer linear programming problem. Next, for our constrained maximization problem, we can find a feasible solution to the all-integer problem by rounding down to the next integers, the solution values to the linear programming relaxation. This yields the solution $x_1 = 3$, $x_2 = 3$, at which the objective function is $(20)(3) + (30)(3) = \$150$ thousand. We therefore have, as a feasible solution to our problem,

$$x_1 = 3, \; x_2 = 3, \; \text{Objective Function} = 150$$

Since this solution is feasible, it follows that the optimal solution to the integer linear programming problem must yield a profit of at least $150 thousand. This figure, then, constitutes a **lower bound** to the value of the objective function at the optimal solution.

We have now shown that the optimal solution to the problem of the research laboratory must yield a profit in the interval from $150 to $166⅔ thousand. This information is summarized in Figure 8.7. The box shows the values of the decision variables and objective function at the optimal solution to the linear programming relaxation. It is labelled "1" to indicate that it is the first step in our solution algorithm. We now proceed by moving, in steps, further from the optimal solution to the linear programming relaxation.

Starting with the information that the optimal solution to our problem must produce a profit in the range from $150 to $166⅔ thousand, the branch-and-bound method provides a systematic procedure for finding that solution. The principles behind this approach are as follows:

(i) The feasible region of the linear programming relaxation is partitioned into segments. This partitioning is accomplished by adding further constraints.

(ii) The optimum value of the objective function can be found over each segment. However, it is not necessary to consider those segments in which no solution satisfies the integer requirements.

(iii) At any stage in the process we will be in a position to compute the following two numbers:

(a) The optimum value that the objective function could possibly take for any solution satisfying the integer requirements.

(b) The optimum value taken by the objective function for all solutions satisfying the integer requirements that have been examined to date.

FIGURE 8.7 Preliminary format for the branch-and-bound solution to the problem of the research laboratory.

Upper bound: 166-2/3
Lower bound: 150

```
              1
    ─────────────────────
      x₁ = 3-1/3
      x₂ = 3-1/3
    Ob. Fn. = 166–2/3
```

$x_1 = 3\text{-}1/3$
$x_2 = 3\text{-}1/3$
Ob. Fn. $= 166\text{–}2/3$

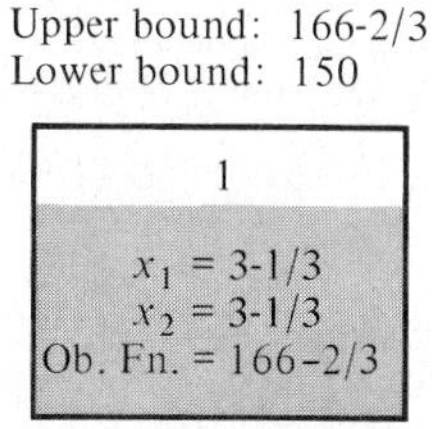

When the two numbers are equal, the optimal solution to the problem has been found.

(iv) If, over any segment of the feasible region, the optimum value of the objective function is inferior to that of a solution satisfying the integer requirements, solutions in this segment can be eliminated from further consideration.

The branch-and-bound method proceeds by *branching* from the current solution. We choose to branch on that decision variable whose solution value is furthest from being an integer. At one branch we require that variable to be, at most, the integer below its solution value, while at the other, the variable is required to be at least the integer above its solution value. In this particular case, both decision variables happen to take the same value at the current solution. We will choose, arbitrarily, to branch on x_1.

At the first branch, we add to the constraints of the linear programming relaxation the requirement that x_1 not exceed 3, so that the problem to be solved is

$$\text{Maximize} \quad 20x_1 + 30x_2$$
$$\text{subject to} \quad 4x_1 + 5x_2 \leq 30$$
$$6x_1 + 4x_2 \leq 40$$
$$x_1 + 2x_2 \leq 10$$
$$x_1 \leq 3$$
$$x_1, x_2 \geq 0$$

It is straightforward, either graphically or through the simplex algorithm, to show that the optimal solution to this problem is

$$x_1 = 3, x_2 = 3\tfrac{1}{2}, \text{Objective Function} = 165$$

Next, we add to the constraints of the linear programming relaxation the requirement that x_1 be at least 4, yielding the problem

$$\text{Maximize} \quad 20x_1 + 30x_2$$
$$\text{subject to} \quad 4x_1 + 5x_2 \leq 30$$
$$6x_1 + 4x_2 \leq 40$$
$$x_1 + 2x_2 \leq 10$$
$$x_1 \geq 4$$
$$x_1, x_2 \geq 0$$

The optimal solution to this problem is

$$x_1 = 4, x_2 = 2\tfrac{4}{5}, \text{Objective Function} = 164$$

What we have done here is to partition the feasible region of the linear programming relaxation into three segments:

1. The segment containing all solutions satisfying $x_1 \leq 3$.
2. The segment containing all solutions satisfying $x_1 \geq 4$.
3. The segment containing all solutions satisfying $3 < x_1 < 4$.

Notice, however, that we need not consider the third of these segments, since no solution in it will be integer-valued for x_1. Any integer-valued solution must be in one or the other of the first two segments.

In Figure 8.8, the position to date is illustrated. Boxes 2 and 3 set out the solutions to the two problems just discussed. In the context of the branch-and-bound method, these boxes are referred to as **nodes.** In branching down from node 1 to node 2 or 3, an additional constraint has been added. It necessarily follows, when we branch in this way, that *the optimal objective function value on a descendant node cannot be higher than that of the node from which it branches.* Now, we have not yet achieved an integer solution to our problem, and must branch down further to do so, by adding additional constraints. As we have just argued, such branching cannot raise the value of the objective function. Hence $165 thousand must constitute an upper bound on the optimal value of the objective function for the integer programming problem. In general, this upper bound is *the largest objective function value at any node from which there are no descending branches.* The only all-integer solution we have seen so far yields a profit of $150 thousand, so that this remains the lower bound for the optimal solution to our problem. What we have been able to demonstrate thus far, then, is that the optimal solution to our problem cannot yield a profit of more than 165 thousand dollars.

We must now continue the branching process, branching from node 2, since it has a higher objective function value than node 3, and hence appears to offer the better prospect of achieving a solution with high profits. At node 2, the

FIGURE 8.8 First step for the branch-and-bound solution to the problem of the research laboratory.

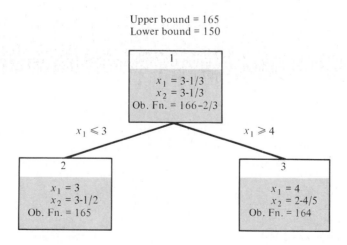

Upper bound = 165
Lower bound = 150

solution for x_1 is an integer, so that we branch on x_2. The constraint $x_1 \leq 3$, leading to node 2, is retained, and we consider, in turn, adding the constraints $x_2 \leq 3$ and $x_2 \geq 4$. The first problem to be solved, then, is

$$\text{Maximize} \quad 20x_1 + 30x_2$$
$$\text{subject to} \quad 4x_1 + 5x_2 \leq 30$$
$$6x_1 + 4x_2 \leq 40$$
$$x_1 + 2x_2 \leq 10$$
$$x_1 \leq 3$$
$$x_2 \leq 3$$
$$x_1, x_2 \geq 0$$

The optimal solution is

$$x_1 = 3, x_2 = 3, \text{Objective Function} = 150$$

The second problem is

$$\text{Maximize} \quad 20x_1 + 30x_2$$
$$\text{subject to} \quad 4x_1 + 5x_2 \leq 30$$
$$6x_1 + 4x_2 \leq 40$$
$$x_1 + 2x_2 \leq 10$$
$$x_1 \leq 3$$
$$x_2 \geq 4$$
$$x_1, x_2 \geq 0$$

and yields the optimal solution

$$x_1 = 2, x_2 = 4, \text{Objective Function} = 160$$

We have now achieved a solution—2 drugs projects and 4 agricultural chemicals projects—which is an integer and yields a higher profit than the previous lower bound. Hence, the new lower bound on the value of the objective function is, as shown in Figure 8.9, $160 thousand. In Figure 8.9, integer solutions have been obtained at nodes 4 and 5. There is no need for any further branching from such nodes, as this cannot generate superior solutions. However, we cannot yet infer that the solution $x_1 = 2$, $x_2 = 4$ is optimal, since the objective function at node 3 is $164 thousand. It is therefore possible that there exists an all-integer solution with profit between $160 and $164 thousand lying in the segment of the feasible region where $x_1 \geq 4$.

FIGURE 8.9 Second step for the branch-and-bound solution to the problem of the research laboratory.

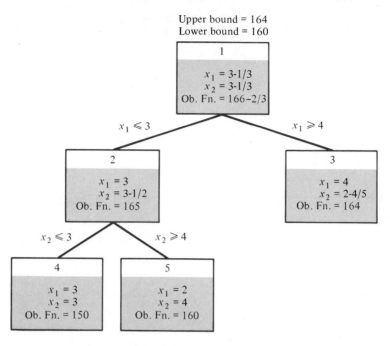

In order to check this possibility, we must branch from node 3, requiring in turn $x_2 \leq 2$ and $x_2 \geq 3$, while retaining the constraint $x_1 \geq 4$. For the problem

$$
\begin{array}{ll}
\text{Maximize} & 20x_1 + 30x_2 \\
\text{subject to} & 4x_1 + 5x_2 \leq 30 \\
& 6x_1 + 4x_2 \leq 40 \\
& x_1 + 2x_2 \leq 10 \qquad\qquad (8.4) \\
& x_1 \geq 4 \\
& x_2 \leq 2 \\
& x_1, x_2 \geq 0
\end{array}
$$

the optimal solution is

$$x_1 = 5, \ x_2 = 2, \text{ Objective Function} = 160$$

FIGURE 8.10 Branch-and-bound derivation of the optimal solutions to the problem of the research laboratory.

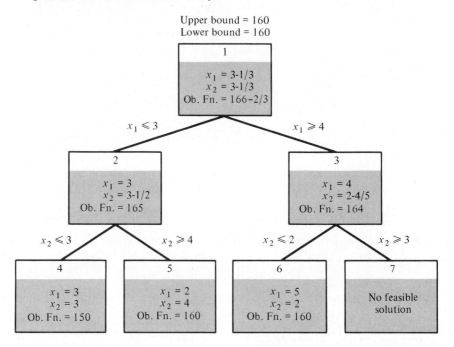

The second branch from node 3 provides a problem that differs from (8.4) only in that the constraint $x_2 \geq 3$ replaces $x_2 \leq 2$. This problem, however, has no feasible solution.

Figure 8.10 shows the situation at this stage. The upper bound for the objective function is the highest value at any node not having descending branches. The lower bound is the highest objective function value found for all-integer solutions. Since these are equal, it follows that the optimal solution to the all-integer linear programming problem yields a profit of $160 thousand. Notice that in fact, there is a pair of jointly optimal solutions. The research laboratory can achieve a profit of $160 thousand from 2 drugs and 4 agricultural chemicals projects, or from 5 drugs and 2 agricultural chemicals projects.

Branch-and-Bound Method for All-Integer Linear Programming Maximization Problems

1. *Initial Stage.* Find the optimal solution to the linear programming relaxation. The optimal objective function value constitutes an initial **upper bound** to the objective function at the optimal solution to the integer programming problem. An initial **lower bound** is obtained by reducing each decision variable solution to the next integer and substituting in the objective function.

2. *Development of Branch-and-Bound Algorithm*
   (a) Branch from the available node with the highest objective function value.
   (b) Branch on the decision variable whose solution is furthest from an integer.
   (c) For the branching variable, augment the previous optimization problem by, in turn, requiring: (i) that this variable not exceed the integer immediately below its present solution value; (ii) that this variable be at least equal to the integer immediately above its present solution value.
   (d) The upper bound is the highest value of the objective function at any node from which there are not descending branches.
   (e) The lower bound is the highest value of the objective function found for all-integer solutions.
3. *Termination of Algorithm.* The algorithm terminates when the upper bound and lower bound are equal.

8.3. USING THE BRANCH-AND-BOUND METHOD TO SOLVE MIXED-INTEGER LINEAR PROGRAMMING PROBLEMS

There is no difficulty in applying the branch-and-bound algorithm to mixed-integer linear programming problems. The procedure of Section 8.2 can be applied, with the proviso that we do not branch on those decision variables that are not required to take integer solutions. We will illustrate by returning to the problem of the scientific consulting group set out in equations (8.2). This group had to decide the number (x_1) of contracts on which to work, and the number (x_2) of bids to prepare. The decision variable, x_1, was required to be an integer, but x_2 was not, since work begun in one year on bid preparation could be carried forward to the following year.

We saw in Section 8.1 that the linear programming relaxation to the problem of the scientific consulting group has the optimal solution

$$x_1 = 3\tfrac{3}{7}, \ x_2 = 7\tfrac{3}{7}, \ \text{Objective Function} = 210\tfrac{6}{7}$$

Since x_1 is required to be an integer, an initial feasible solution to the mixed-integer linear programming problem can be obtained by setting $x_1 = 3$, and $x_2 = 7\tfrac{3}{7}$, yielding a total profit of $(18)(3) + (20)(7\tfrac{3}{7}) = \$202\tfrac{4}{7}$ thousand. Hence, at this solution, we have

$$x_1 = 3, \ x_2 = 7\tfrac{3}{7}, \ \text{Objective Function} = 202\tfrac{4}{7}$$

This information is summarized in Figure 8.11, which provides the starting point for the application of the branch-and-bound algorithm. The above feasible solution and the optimal solution to the linear programming relaxation provide, respectively, initial lower and upper bounds for profits at the optimal solution to the mixed-integer linear programming problem.

Since there is just a single decision variable required to take an integer value, that is the variable we must branch on. We do so by adding, in turn, to

Upper Bound: 210 2/7
Lower Bound: 202 4/7

1
$x_1 = 3\text{-}3/7$
$x_2 = 7\text{-}3/7$
Ob. Fn. = 210-2/7

the linear programming problem the constraints $x_1 \leq 3$ and $x_1 \geq 4$. The first of these problems is, then,

$$\text{Maximize} \quad 18x_1 + 20x_2$$
$$\text{subject to} \quad 3x_1 + 4x_2 \leq 40$$
$$4x_1 + 3x_2 \leq 36$$
$$2x_1 + x_2 \leq 16$$
$$x_1 \leq 3$$
$$x_1, x_2 \geq 0$$

with the optimal solution

$$x_1 = 3, x_2 = 7\tfrac{3}{4}, \text{Objective Function} = 209$$

The second branch yields the problem

$$\text{Maximize} \quad 18x_1 + 20x_2$$
$$\text{subject to} \quad 3x_1 + 4x_2 \leq 40$$
$$4x_1 + 3x_2 \leq 36$$
$$2x_1 + x_2 \leq 16$$
$$x_1 \geq 4$$
$$x_1, x_2 \geq 0$$

which has the optimal solution

$$x_1 = 4, x_2 = 6\tfrac{2}{3}, \text{Objective Function} = 205\tfrac{1}{3}$$

These results are set out in Figure 8.12, from which we conclude that an optimal solution to our mixed-integer linear programming problem has been reached. No descendant node can yield a profit higher than $209 thousand which has been obtained with an integer value for x_1. The scientific consulting group should, therefore, work on 3 contracts and prepare $7\tfrac{3}{4}$ bids during the year, a conclusion which confirms our graphical analysis of Section 7.1.

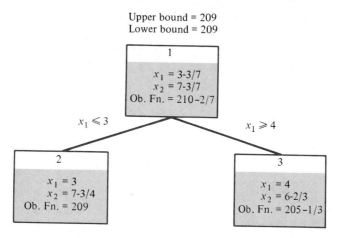

FIGURE 8.12 Branch-and-bound derivation of the optimal solution to the problem of the scientific consulting group.

8.4. USING THE BRANCH-AND-BOUND METHOD TO SOLVE ZERO-ONE INTEGER LINEAR PROGRAMMING PROBLEMS

In essence, the procedure for solving zero-one integer linear programming problems is the same as the methodology outlined in the previous two sections. The only difference is that we branch on a decision variable by forcing it, in turn, to take the values zero and one. To illustrate, we will consider the research and development problem set out in equations (8.3). The linear programming relaxation is

$$
\begin{aligned}
\text{Maximize} \quad & 5.0x_1 + 4.5x_2 + 4.8x_3 + 8.0x_4 + 4.2x_5 \\
\text{subject to} \quad & 1.2x_1 + 3.2x_2 + 1.8x_3 + 4.0x_4 + 2.5x_5 \le 6.5 \\
& x_i \le 1 \quad (i = 1, 2, \ldots, 5) \\
& x_i \ge 0 \quad (i = 1, 2, \ldots, 5)
\end{aligned}
\tag{8.5}
$$

As we saw in Section 8.1, this problem has the optimal solution

$x_1 = 1$, $x_2 = 0$, $x_3 = 1$, $x_4 = \frac{7}{8}$, $x_5 = 0$, Objective Function $= 16.8$

Thus \$16.8 million is the upper bound for the optimal solution to our zero-one programming problem. To obtain a lower bound, we have

$x_1 = 1$, $x_2 = 0$, $x_3 = 1$, $x_4 = 0$, $x_5 = 0$, Objective Function $= 9.8$

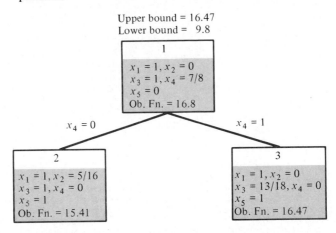

FIGURE 8.13 First three nodes in the branch-and-bound algorithm solution to the research and development problem.

We begin the branch-and-bound algorithm, then, by branching on x_4. Adding the constraint $x_4 = 0$ to (8.5) yields a problem with optimal solution

$$x_1 = 1, \ x_2 = \tfrac{5}{16}, \ x_3 = 1, \ x_4 = 0, \ x_5 = 1, \ \text{Objective Function} = 15.41$$

Adding the constraint $x_4 = 1$ to (8.5) produces a problem with optimal solution

$$x_1 = 1, \ x_2 = 0, \ x_3 = \tfrac{13}{18}, \ x_4 = 1, \ x_5 = 0, \ \text{Objective Function} = 16.47$$

We are therefore at the position illustrated in Figure 8.13, the upper bound to the optimal solution now being $16.47 million.

The next step is to branch from node 3, by adding in turn the constraints $x_3 = 0$ and $x_3 = 1$. Table 8.4 sets out the derivation of nodes 4 through 9, and these results are summarized in Figure 8.14, which, for the sake of brevity, shows only the values of the objective function at each node. Notice that the

TABLE 8.4 Derivation of nodes 4 – 9 in the branch-and-bound algorithm for the research and development problem.

NEW NODE	NODE BRANCHED FROM	BRANCHING VARIABLE	OPTIMAL SOLUTION					OBJECTIVE FUNCTION	UPPER BOUND	LOWER BOUND
			x_1	x_2	x_3	x_4	x_5			
4	3	$x_3 = 0$	1	0	0	1	$\tfrac{13}{25}$	15.18		
5		$x_3 = 1$	$\tfrac{7}{12}$	0	1	1	0	15.72	15.72	9.8
6	5	$x_1 = 0$	0	0	1	1	$\tfrac{7}{25}$	13.98		
7		$x_1 = 1$	No Feasible Solution					—	15.41	9.8
8	2	$x_2 = 0$	1	0	1	0	1	14		
9		$x_2 = 1$	1	1	0	0	$\tfrac{21}{25}$	13.03	15.18	14

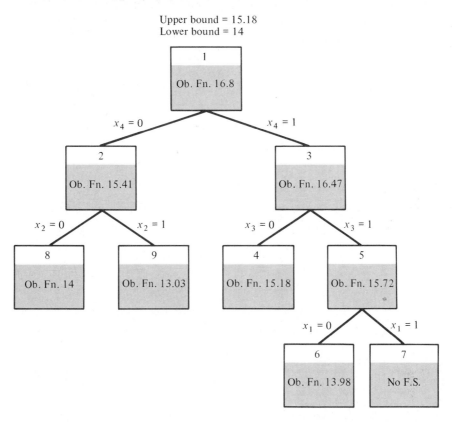

solution at node 8 has all decision variable values at either zero or one. The lower bound for the optimal solution to our problem is therefore now $14 million. We can further see from Figure 8.14 that node 4 is the only node with an objective function bigger than $14 million from which there are no descending branches. It follows that this is the only node from which we need to consider further branching.

In Figure 8.15, the algorithm is completed. We have reached a point where there are no nodes, without descendant branches, for which the objective function exceeds $14 million. The optimal solution to our problem, then, can be read from node 8. Expected total profits are maximized by carrying out research and development on projects 1, 3, and 5.

The calculations needed to reach this conclusion were somewhat tedious. However, their repetitive nature makes them ideally suited to programming on an electronic computer. The branch-and-bound algorithm generally forms the basis for computer programs designed to solve integer programming problems. Such programs have been successfully applied in the solution of far more complex problems than those discussed in this chapter.

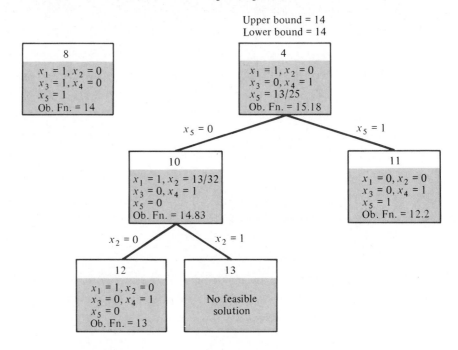

FIGURE 8.15 Branch-and bound derivation of nodes 10–13, and the optimal solution of the research and development problem.

Upper bound = 14
Lower bound = 14

8
$x_1 = 1, x_2 = 0$
$x_3 = 1, x_4 = 0$
$x_5 = 1$
Ob. Fn. = 14

4
$x_1 = 1, x_2 = 0$
$x_3 = 0, x_4 = 1$
$x_5 = 13/25$
Ob. Fn. = 15.18

$x_5 = 0$

$x_5 = 1$

10
$x_1 = 1, x_2 = 13/32$
$x_3 = 0, x_4 = 1$
$x_5 = 0$
Ob. Fn. = 14.83

11
$x_1 = 0, x_2 = 0$
$x_3 = 0, x_4 = 1$
$x_5 = 1$
Ob. Fn. = 12.2

$x_2 = 0$

$x_2 = 1$

12
$x_1 = 1, x_2 = 0$
$x_3 = 0, x_4 = 1$
$x_5 = 0$
Ob. Fn. = 13

13
No feasible
solution

8.5. INTEGER LINEAR PROGRAMMING PROBLEMS: FORMULATION AND APPLICATIONS

In this section we will see how some commonly met classes of problems can be formulated in the integer linear programming framework.

CAPITAL BUDGETING

In sections 1 and 4 of this chapter we discussed a relatively simple example of a capital budgeting problem. Here we will see how to formulate a more elaborate problem of this type. When managers contemplate the purchase of new capital equipment, the available options are likely to be limited to a very small number of possibilities. It is for this reason that the integer programming framework is often appropriate for such decisions.

To illustrate, Table 8.5 shows data for a company that produces three products, each of which requires time on four different machines for which weekly capacity is limited.

As it stands, the data of Table 8.5 can be used to formulate a product mix problem whose solution will yield the weekly profit maximizing output mix. This company is considering increasing capacity through the purchase of additional machinery. For machine types A and B two different capacity sizes may be purchased, while only one size is available for each of the other two machine

TABLE 8.5 Current weekly data for a company considering capital expansion.

TOTAL MACHINE-HOURS AVAILABLE	MACHINE	MACHINE-HOURS PER UNIT		
		PRODUCT 1	PRODUCT 2	PRODUCT 3
700	A	2	1	1
500	B	1	1	1
1,000	C	1	2	1
1,300	D	1	2	2
PROFIT PER UNIT ($)		25	35	30

types. The possibilities, together with the associated costs, are shown in Table 8.6.

This company has available at most $350 thousand for capital expansion, and, subject to this budget constraint, wishes to make a capital investment that will lead to the highest possible weekly profit.

We begin to formulate this problem by setting

x_1 = Weekly output of product 1
x_2 = Weekly output of product 2
x_3 = Weekly output of product 3

The objective, then, is

$$\text{Maximize} \quad 25x_1 + 35x_2 + 30x_3 \qquad (8.6)$$

To allow for the limited capacity expansion possibilities, we introduce some 0-1 variables. Specifically, let

$$x_4 = \begin{cases} 1 & \text{if 50 machine-hours of A are added} \\ 0 & \text{otherwise} \end{cases}$$

and

$$x_5 = \begin{cases} 1 & \text{if 100 machine-hours of A are added} \\ 0 & \text{otherwise} \end{cases}$$

TABLE 8.6 Capital expansion possibilities for a company.

MACHINE	MACHINE-HOURS ADDED TO WEEKLY CAPACITY	COST ($ THOUSAND)	MACHINE-HOURS ADDED TO WEEKLY CAPACITY	COST ($ THOUSAND)
A	50	70	100	120
B	40	60	80	100
C	60	90		
D	45	80		

Then, $x_4 = 0$ and $x_5 = 0$ implies that machine A capacity will not be expanded. Also, if $x_4 = 1$ and $x_5 = 0$, the implication is that machine A capacity will be expanded by 50 machine-hours per week. Similarly, $x_4 = 0$ and $x_5 = 1$ corresponds to an expansion of 100 machine-hours per week. It is not, however, possible to increase capacity by both 50 and 100 machine-hours, so that x_4 and x_5 cannot both take the value 1. This restriction can be imposed by requiring

$$x_4 + x_5 \leq 1 \tag{8.7}$$

Similarly, for machine B expansion, define the 0-1 variables

$$x_6 = \begin{cases} 1 & \text{if 40 machine-hours of B are added} \\ 0 & \text{otherwise} \end{cases}$$

and

$$x_7 = \begin{cases} 1 & \text{if 80 machine-hours of B are added} \\ 0 & \text{otherwise} \end{cases}$$

together with the constraint

$$x_6 + x_7 \leq 1 \tag{8.8}$$

Finally, we must introduce two more 0-1 variables to allow the possibility of expanding machine C and machine D capacity. Define

$$x_8 = \begin{cases} 1 & \text{if 60 machine-hours of C are added} \\ 0 & \text{otherwise} \end{cases}$$

and

$$x_9 = \begin{cases} 1 & \text{if 45 machine-hours of D are added} \\ 0 & \text{otherwise} \end{cases}$$

Now, given our definitions of the 0-1 variables, $x_4, x_5, \ldots, x_9$, it follows from the information in Table 8.6 that the total cost of the capital expansion will be

$$\text{Total Cost} = 70x_4 + 120x_5 + 60x_6 + 100x_7 + 90x_8 + 80x_9$$

where cost is measured in thousands of dollars. It is required that this total cost not exceed $350 thousand, yielding the constraint

$$70x_4 + 120x_5 + 60x_6 + 100x_7 + 90x_8 + 80x_9 \leq 350 \tag{8.9}$$

In order to complete the problem specification, we must formulate the capacity constraints in light of the possibility of additional capital equipment. Initially, 700 machine-hours per week are available for machines type A. This capacity may remain unchanged, or be expanded by either 50 or 100 machine-hours per week. It follows from our definitions of the 0-1 variables that after capital expansion has been completed, a total of $700 + 50x_4 + 100x_5$ type A machine-hours per week will be available. Hence, from the information in Table 8.5, the machine A capacity constraint will be

$$2x_1 + x_2 + x_3 \leq 700 + 50x_4 + 100x_5$$

which can be written as

$$2x_1 + x_2 + x_3 - 50x_4 - 100x_5 \leq 700 \qquad (8.10)$$

By a similar argument, after expansion, the machine B capacity constraint will be

$$x_1 + x_2 + x_3 \leq 500 + 40x_6 + 80x_7$$

or

$$x_1 + x_2 + x_3 - 40x_6 - 80x_7 \leq 500 \qquad (8.11)$$

Finally, the capacity constraints for machine types C and D can be written

$$x_1 + 2x_2 + x_3 \leq 1000 + 60x_8$$

or

$$x_1 + 2x_2 + x_3 - 60x_8 \leq 1000 \qquad (8.12)$$

and

$$x_1 + 2x_2 + 2x_3 \leq 1300 + 45x_9$$

or

$$x_1 + 2x_2 + 2x_3 - 45x_9 \leq 1300 \qquad (8.13)$$

Collecting together equations (8.6)–(8.13), the constrained optimization problem that must be solved is

Maximize $\quad\quad\quad\quad\quad\quad\quad\quad\quad\quad 25x_1 + 35x_2 + 30x_3$

subject to $\quad\quad\quad\quad\quad\quad\quad\quad\quad\quad\quad\quad x_4 + x_5 \leq 1$

$$x_6 + x_7 \leq 1$$

$$70x_4 + 120x_5 + 60x_6 + 100x_7 + 90x_8 + 80x_9 \leq 350$$

$$2x_1 + x_2 + x_3 - 50x_4 - 100x_5 \leq 700$$

$$x_1 + x_2 + x_3 - 40x_6 - 80x_7 \leq 500$$

$$x_1 + 2x_2 + x_3 - 60x_8 \leq 1000$$

$$x_1 + 2x_2 + 2x_3 - 45x_9 \leq 1300$$

$$x_i \geq 0 \ (i = 1,2,3)$$

$$x_i = 0 \text{ or } 1 \ (i = 4,5, \ldots, 9)$$

The values of the 0-1 variables x_4, x_5, . . . , x_9 at the optimal solution to this problem provide the optimal capital budgeting strategy, while the values for x_1, x_2, x_3 provide the profit maximizing product mix when this strategy is employed.

LOCATION OF RETAIL OUTLETS: A MATCHING PROBLEM

A pure 0-1 integer linear programming problem arises from a class of applications where retail outlets or product distribution centers must be sited to serve customers in different locations. One variant of this class of problems is the **matching problem,** where distributors are concerned that different outlets not compete for the same customers.

To illustrate, a fast food chain is planning to move into a city and is considering seven possible sites for its outlets. After consulting with marketing experts, management believes that the city can be partitioned into ten areas, and that it is possible to estimate for each proposed site whether or not customers will be drawn. This information is set out in Table 8.7, where a 1 signifies that customers from an area will be drawn by a site, and a 0 that they will not. Also shown in this table are projected annual profits for location at each site. These profit projections are based on the assumption that no two establishments will compete for customers from the same area.

Suppose now that management of this chain does not wish to have any pair of outlets compete for customers from the same area. Subject to this constraint, outlets are to be sited so that total annual profit is a maximum.

This problem can be formulated by defining the 0-1 variables

$$x_i = \begin{bmatrix} 1 & \text{if an outlet is located at site } i \\ 0 & \text{otherwise} \end{bmatrix} (i = 1, 2, \ldots, 7)$$

TABLE 8.7 Possible sites for the location of fast food outlets [1 implies a site will attract customers from an area, 0 that it will not; profits are in thousands of dollars per year].

AREA	SITE 1	2	3	4	5	6	7
A	1	0	0	0	0	1	0
B	1	0	0	0	0	0	1
C	1	1	0	0	0	0	0
D	0	1	0	0	1	0	1
E	0	1	0	1	0	0	0
F	0	0	1	0	0	1	0
G	0	0	1	0	1	0	1
H	0	0	1	0	1	0	0
I	0	0	0	1	0	1	0
J	0	0	0	1	0	1	1
PROFIT	80	90	70	100	120	180	150

Given this definition, it follows that total expected annual profits, in thousands of dollars, will be

$$\text{Total Profit} = 80x_1 + 90x_2 + 70x_3 + 100x_4 + 120x_5 + 180x_6 + 150x_7 \tag{8.14}$$

The objective is to maximize this function.

It remains to formulate the constraints requiring that no two outlets should attract customers from the same area. Consider, for example, area A. From Table 8.7 it can be seen that potential customers from this area could be served by outlets at either site 1 or site 6. It is required, then, that outlets should not be simultaneously located at both these sites. In terms of our 0-1 variables, we cannot have both x_1 and x_6 equal to one. This implies the constraint

$$x_1 + x_6 \leq 1$$

As a further example, consider area J, whose potential customers could be served by outlets located at site 4, site 6, or site 7. Given management's constraint, it follows that an outlet can be located on, at most, one of these sites. Thus, at most, one of the variables x_4, x_6, and x_7 can take the value one. It follows that we must require

$$x_4 + x_6 + x_7 \leq 1$$

Continuing in this way, constraints can be derived by prohibiting multiple service for each of the other eight areas.

Together with the objective of maximizing the profit function (8.14), these constraints can be assembled to yield the problem formulation

Maximize $80x_1 + 90x_2 + 70x_3 + 100x_4 + 120x_5 + 180x_6 + 150x_7$

subject to

$$x_1 + x_6 \leq 1$$
$$x_1 + x_7 \leq 1$$
$$x_1 + x_2 \leq 1$$
$$x_2 + x_5 + x_7 \leq 1$$
$$x_2 + x_4 \leq 1$$
$$x_3 + x_6 \leq 1$$
$$x_3 + x_5 + x_7 \leq 1$$
$$x_3 + x_5 \leq 1$$
$$x_4 + x_6 \leq 1$$
$$x_4 + x_6 + x_7 \leq 1$$
$$x_i = 0 \text{ or } 1 \ (i = 1, 2, \ldots, 7)$$

LOCATION OF PLANTS IN A DISTRIBUTION SYSTEM: AN EXTENSION OF THE TRANSPORTATION PROBLEM

In Chapter 6 we discussed a class of problems in which a product was made at m different plants, and had to be shipped to n different customer service centers. Suppose that weekly supply capacity at the i-th plant is S_i, and that weekly demand at the j-th customer service center is D_j. Let x_{ij} denote the quantity of product shipped per week from the i-th plant to the j-th service center, and c_{ij} the total production and transportation cost per unit for this route. In the transportation problem the objective is to minimize total cost, subject to the requirements that plant supply capacities cannot be exceeded, and all demand must be met. Mathematically, the problem specification can be written

Minimize $\displaystyle\sum_{i=1}^{m} \sum_{j=1}^{n} c_{ij} x_{ij}$

subject to $\displaystyle\sum_{j=1}^{n} x_{ij} \leq S_i \ (i = 1, 2, \ldots, m)$ $\qquad$ (8.15)

$\displaystyle\sum_{i=1}^{m} x_{ij} = D_j \ (j = 1, 2, \ldots, n)$

$x_{ij} \geq 0 \qquad (i = 1, 2, \ldots, m; j = 1, 2, \ldots, n)$

Suppose now, however, that the production plants have not yet been built. The company is considering m different possible plant locations, and must decide how to proceed. As we have discussed so far, the transportation problem takes account only of **variable costs** which increase as a product is produced and shipped. However, in constructing new plants, **fixed costs** will also be incurred. These are costs, following from expenditures on construction and equipment, that must be paid however much is produced by a plant. We will denote by F_i the fixed costs of the i-th plant per week.

The parameters of our problem are set out in Table 8.8.

Suppose that the objective is to design a distribution system so that total costs—variable plus fixed—are as small as possible. Since we can choose whether or not to build any plant, and hence whether the associated fixed costs will actually be incurred, it is necessary to introduce 0-1 variables. Specifically, define the variables

$$z_i = \begin{bmatrix} 1 & \text{if plant } i \text{ is constructed} \\ 0 & \text{otherwise} \end{bmatrix} \quad (i = 1, 2, \ldots, m)$$

Then, since fixed costs will be incurred only if a plant is constructed, it follows that

$$\text{Total Fixed Cost} = \sum_{i=1}^{m} F_i z_i$$

The total variable cost associated with the distribution system will be precisely the same as in the basic version (8.15) of the transportation problem. Hence the objective is

$$\text{Minimize} \sum_{i=1}^{m} \sum_{j=1}^{n} c_{ij} x_{ij} + \sum_{i=1}^{m} F_i z_i$$

TABLE 8.8 Specifications for a transportation problem with fixed and variable costs.

FIXED COSTS	PLANT	CUSTOMER SERVICE CENTER			POTENTIAL SUPPLY
		1	2 .... n		
		VARIABLE COSTS PER UNIT			POTENTIAL SUPPLY
F_1	1	c_{11}	c_{12} .... c_{1n}		S_1
F_2	2	c_{21}	c_{22} .... c_{2n}		S_2
.	.	.	....		.
.	.	.	....		.
.	.	.	....		.
F_m	m	c_{m1}	c_{m2} .... c_{mn}		S_m
	DEMAND	D_1	D_2 .... D_n		

The requirement that demand at every customer service center should be met is formulated precisely as in (8.15). However, in formulating the supply constraints, we must take account of the fact that if a plant is not constructed, nothing can be supplied from it. If plant i is actually built with supply capacity S_i, then this is the most that can be shipped from it, so we have, exactly as in (8.15),

$$\sum_{j=1}^{n} x_{ij} \leq S_i$$

However, if the plant is not built, the most that can be shipped from it is zero, so that

$$\sum_{j=1}^{n} x_{ij} \leq 0$$

These considerations can be amalgamated into the single constraint

$$\sum_{j=1}^{n} x_{ij} \leq S_i z_i$$

since z_i takes the value 1 if plant i is built, and 0 if it is not.

The complete problem formulation, then, is

$$\text{Minimize} \quad \sum_{i=1}^{m} \sum_{j=1}^{n} c_{ij} x_{ij} + \sum_{i=1}^{m} F_i z_i$$

$$\text{subject to} \quad \sum_{j=1}^{n} x_{ij} - S_i z_i \leq 0 \quad (i = 1, 2, \ldots, m)$$

$$\sum_{i=1}^{m} x_{ij} = D_j \quad (j = 1, 2, \ldots, n)$$

$$x_{ij} \geq 0 \quad (i = 1, 2, \ldots, m; j = 1, 2, \ldots, n)$$

$$z_i = 0 \text{ or } 1 \quad (i = 1, 2, \ldots, m)$$

CHOOSING K OUT OF n DECISION VARIABLES: APPLICATION TO BLENDING

A further important class of problems, for which 0-1 variables are employed as solution aids, arises when there is some constraint on the number of decision variables that can take non-zero values in any solution. Thus, if there are n decision variables, it might be required, for example, that exactly K, or at most K, of these variables be nonzero, where K is some number less than n.

To illustrate this type of problem, consider the case where a diet blend containing four nutrients is to be made. The details are set out in Table 8.9. Six products are under consideration as potential ingredients, but due to costs associated with ordering and storage, management wants to use at most three products in the blend. Subject to this constraint, it is required to find the lowest cost blend satisfying the minimum nutrient standards.

TABLE 8.9 Specifications for a blending problem.

MINIMUM QUANTITIES REQUIRED (OUNCES)	NUTRIENT	NUTRIENTS PER UNIT (OUNCES)					
		PRODUCT 1	PRODUCT 2	PRODUCT 3	PRODUCT 4	PRODUCT 5	PRODUCT 6
10	A	0.2	0.1	0.3	0.1	0.2	0.3
12	B	0.2	0.3	0.3	0.1	0.1	0.1
15	C	0.3	0.3	0.2	0.2	0.2	0.4
20	D	0.4	0.3	0.4	0.2	0.5	0.3
COST PER UNIT (CENTS)		10	9	11	7	9	12

If we let

$$x_i = \text{Quantity of product } i \text{ used in the blend}$$

the objective is

$$\text{Minimize } 10x_1 + 9x_2 + 11x_3 + 7x_4 + 9x_5 + 12x_6 \qquad (8.16)$$

Directly from the data of Table 8.9 we obtain the following four constraints, which ensure that the minimum nutrient requirements will be met.

$$0.2x_1 + 0.1x_2 + 0.3x_3 + 0.1x_4 + 0.2x_5 + 0.3x_6 \geq 10$$
$$0.2x_1 + 0.3x_2 + 0.3x_3 + 0.1x_4 + 0.1x_5 + 0.1x_6 \geq 12$$
$$0.3x_1 + 0.3x_2 + 0.2x_3 + 0.2x_4 + 0.2x_5 + 0.4x_6 \geq 15 \qquad (8.17)$$
$$0.4x_1 + 0.3x_2 + 0.4x_3 + 0.2x_4 + 0.5x_5 + 0.3x_6 \geq 20$$

The standard blending problem requires minimization of the objective function (8.16), subject to the constraints (8.17), and nonnegativity constraints on the six decision variables. However, here we have the additional requirement that at most three products can be used in the blend. To allow for this further factor, we introduce the 0-1 variables

$$z_i = \begin{cases} 1 & \text{if product } i \text{ is used in the blend} \\ 0 & \text{otherwise} \end{cases}$$

Now, if at most three products are to be in the blend, then at most three of the z_i can take the value one, so that we require

$$z_1 + z_2 + z_3 + z_4 + z_5 + z_6 \leq 3 \qquad (8.18)$$

To complete the problem specification, we must ensure that no x_i can be positive when the corresponding z_i is zero, since product i cannot then be in the blend. This can be accomplished through the constraints

$$x_i \leq U_i z_i \quad (i = 1, 2, \ldots, 6)$$

or

$$x_i - U_i z_i \leq 0 \quad (i = 1, 2, \ldots, 6) \qquad (8.19)$$

where, in (8.19), U_i is a number chosen sufficiently large so that the constraint will be nonbinding when $z_i = 1$. Then, if $z_i = 0$, (8.19) ensures that x_i is also zero. When $z_i = 1$, (8.19) yields $x_i \leq U_i$, which we must ensure imposes no meaningful restriction. For example, consider product 1. We could not possibly want to use more than 60 units of this; that is, the maximum of (10/0.2, 12/0.2, 15/0.3, 20/0.4). This alone would be enough to satisfy all four nutrient requirements. Therefore, in (8.19) we can set $U_1 = 60$. Similarly, we can employ

$$U_2 = 100, \ U_3 = 75, \ U_4 = 120, \ U_5 = 120, \ U_6 = 120$$

Bringing together (8.16)–(8.19), the problem to be solved can be written

Minimize $\qquad 10x_1 + 9x_2 + 11x_3 + 7x_4 + 9x_5 + 12x_6$

subject to $\quad 0.2x_1 + 0.1x_2 + 0.3x_3 + 0.1x_4 + 0.2x_5 + 0.3x_6 \geq 10$

$\qquad\qquad 0.2x_1 + 0.3x_2 + 0.3x_3 + 0.1x_4 + 0.1x_5 + 0.1x_6 \geq 12$

$\qquad\qquad 0.3x_1 + 0.3x_2 + 0.2x_3 + 0.2x_4 + 0.2x_5 + 0.4x_6 \geq 15$

$\qquad\qquad 0.4x_1 + 0.3x_2 + 0.4x_3 + 0.2x_4 + 0.5x_5 + 0.3x_6 \geq 20$

$$z_1 + z_2 + z_3 + z_4 + z_5 + z_6 \leq 3$$

$$x_i - U_i z_i \leq 0 \quad (i = 1, 2, \ldots, 6)$$

$$x_i \geq 0 \quad (i = 1, 2, \ldots, 6)$$

$$z_i = 0 \text{ or } 1 \quad (i = 1, 2, \ldots, 6)$$

EXERCISES

8.1. For the integer linear programming problem

Maximize $\qquad x_1 + x_2$

subject to $\quad 2x_1 + 3x_2 \leq 20$

$\qquad\qquad 4x_1 + x_2 \leq 24$

$$x_1, x_2 \geq 0$$

$$x_1, x_2 \text{ integer}$$

(a) Draw a graph showing the feasible region.

(b) Write down the linear programming relaxation.

(c) Use the branch-and-bound method to derive an optimal solution.

8.2. For the integer linear programming problem

$$\text{Maximize} \quad 2x_1 + 3x_2$$

$$\text{subject to} \quad 3x_1 + 2x_2 \leq 30$$

$$x_1 + 2x_2 \leq 17$$

$$x_1, x_2 \geq 0$$

$$x_1, x_2 \text{ integer}$$

(a) Draw a graph showing the feasible region.

(b) Write down the linear programming relaxation.

(c) Use the branch-and-bound method to derive an optimal solution.

8.3. Consider the all-integer linear programming problem

$$\text{Maximize} \quad 3x_1 + 4x_2$$

$$\text{subject to} \quad 3x_1 + 2x_2 \leq 25$$

$$2x_1 + 3x_2 \leq 18$$

$$x_1, x_2 \geq 0$$

$$x_1, x_2 \text{ integer}$$

(a) Draw a graph showing the feasible region.

(b) Write down the linear programming relaxation.

(c) Use the branch-and-bound method to derive an optimal solution.

8.4. Consider the all-integer linear programming problem

$$\text{Maximize} \quad 4x_1 + 3x_2$$

$$\text{subject to} \quad 4x_1 + 2x_2 \leq 18$$

$$7x_1 + 5x_2 \leq 40$$

$$3x_1 + 4x_2 \leq 25$$

$$x_1, x_2 \geq 0$$

$$x_1, x_2 \text{ integer}$$

(a) Draw a graph showing the feasible region.

(b) Write down the linear programming relaxation.

(c) Use the branch-and-bound method to derive an optimal solution.

8.5. For the all-integer linear programming problem

$$\text{Maximize} \quad 5x_1 + 3x_2$$

$$\text{subject to} \quad 2x_1 + 3x_2 \leq 19$$

$$3x_1 + x_2 \leq 15$$

$$4x_1 + 3x_2 \leq 26$$

$$x_1, x_2 \geq 0$$

$$x_1, x_2 \text{ integer}$$

(a) Draw a graph showing the feasible region.
(b) Write down the linear programming relaxation.
(c) Use the branch-and-bound method to derive an optimal solution.

8.6. For the mixed-integer linear programming problem

$$\text{Maximize} \quad 4x_1 + 5x_2$$
$$\text{subject to} \quad 3x_1 + 5x_2 \leq 40$$
$$x_1 + x_2 \leq 9$$
$$x_1, x_2 \geq 0$$
$$x_1 \text{ integer}$$

(a) Draw a graph showing the feasible region.
(b) Write down the linear programming relaxation.
(c) Use the branch-and-bound method to derive an optimal solution.

8.7. Consider the mixed-integer linear programming problem

$$\text{Maximize} \quad 4x_1 + 5x_2$$
$$\text{subject to} \quad 5x_1 + 3x_2 \leq 62$$
$$x_1 + 2x_2 \leq 16$$
$$6x_1 + 5x_2 \leq 90$$
$$x_1, x_2 \geq 0$$
$$x_2 \text{ integer}$$

(a) Draw a graph showing the feasible region.
(b) Write down the linear programming relaxation.
(c) Use the branch-and-bound method to derive an optimal solution.

8.8. For the mixed-integer linear programming problem

$$\text{Maximize} \quad 2x_1 + x_2$$
$$\text{subject to} \quad x_1 + 2x_2 \leq 19$$
$$5x_1 + 2x_2 \leq 45$$
$$x_1 + 3x_2 \leq 23$$
$$3x_1 + 2x_2 \leq 28$$
$$x_1, x_2 \geq 0$$
$$x_1 \text{ integer}$$

(a) Draw a graph showing the feasible region.
(b) Write down the linear programming relaxation.
(c) Use the branch-and-bound method to derive an optimal solution.

8.9. For the mixed-integer linear programming problem

$$\text{Maximize} \quad x_1 + 2x_2 + x_3$$
$$\text{subject to} \quad x_1 + x_2 \leq 21$$
$$x_1 + x_2 + 2x_3 \leq 30$$
$$2x_1 + x_2 + x_3 \leq 32$$
$$x_1, x_2, x_3 \geq 0$$
$$x_1, x_2 \text{ integer}$$

(a) Write down the linear programming relaxation.
(b) Use the branch-and-bound method to find an optimal solution.

8.10. For the zero-one linear programming problem

$$\text{Maximize} \quad 5x_1 + 6x_2 + 4x_3 + 7x_4$$
$$\text{subject to} \quad 2x_1 + 3x_2 + 3x_3 + 4x_4 \leq 6$$
$$x_i = 0 \text{ or } 1 \ (i = 1, 2, 3, 4)$$

(a) Write down the linear programming relaxation.
(b) Use the branch-and-bound method to find an optimal solution.

8.11. For the all-integer linear programming problem

$$\text{Minimize} \quad x_1 + 2x_2$$
$$\text{subject to} \quad 2x_1 + 3x_2 \geq 30$$
$$2x_1 + 5x_2 \geq 41$$
$$x_1 \geq 4$$
$$x_2 \geq 5$$
$$x_1, x_2 \text{ integer}$$

(a) Draw a graph showing the feasible region.
(b) Write down the linear programming relaxation.
(c) Use the branch-and-bound method to find an optimal solution.

8.12. For the all-integer linear programming problem

$$\text{Minimize} \quad 2x_1 + 3x_2$$
$$\text{subject to} \quad x_1 + 2x_2 \leq 18$$
$$2x_1 + x_2 \leq 20$$
$$x_1 \geq 4$$
$$x_2 \geq 4$$
$$x_1, x_2 \text{ integer}$$

(a) Draw a graph showing the feasible region.

(b) Write down the linear programming relaxation.

(c) Use the branch-and-bound method to find an optimal solution.

8.13. Repeat Exercise 8.11, but now with only x_1 required to be integer.

8.14. Repeat Exercise 8.12, but now with only x_2 required to be integer.

8.15. Consider again the problem of the research laboratory discussed in the first two sections of this chapter. Suppose that this laboratory is able to employ, for the coming year, an additional 5000 hours of scientific manpower, with the remaining problem specifications remaining unchanged, as in Table 8.1. How many drugs and agricultural chemicals projects should now be undertaken?

8.16. A company manufactures two products, each of which requires time on four different machines. Only integer amounts of each can be made. The company wants to find the output mix that maximizes total profits, given the specifications shown in the following table.

TOTAL MACHINE-HOURS AVAILABLE	MACHINE	MACHINE-HOURS PER UNIT	
		PRODUCT I	PRODUCT II
3,400	A	200	500
1,450	B	100	200
2,000	C	200	300
2,400	D	400	100
PROFIT PER UNIT ($'000)		6	6

Find an optimal solution to this product mix problem and the maximum attainable total profit.

8.17. A manufacturing company produces two products, each of which must be processed through four departments. Only integer amounts of Product I can be produced. It is required to maximize total profits, given the specifications shown in the table below.

TOTAL MAN-HOURS AVAILABLE	DEPARTMENT	MAN-HOURS PER WEEK	
		PRODUCT I	PRODUCT II
3,700	A	400	200
3,000	B	300	200
1,700	C	100	200
4,100	D	200	500
PROFIT PER UNIT ($'000)		8	12

Find an optimal solution to the product mix problem and the maximum achievable total profit.

8.18. A corporation has a maximum of 4.8 million dollars to spend on research and development projects in the coming year. The table shows the costs and expected profits (both in millions of dollars) for these four projects.

PROJECT	1	2	3	4
COST	1.8	2.6	2.1	3.0
PROFIT	3.4	5.3	3.7	6.0

Which projects should be undertaken in order to maximize total expected profits?

8.19. A corporation is planning its research and development budget over the next three years. The table below shows the costs of each of the three possible projects, and the quantity of funds available (both in hundreds of thousands of dollars) in each of the three years.

PROJECT	PROJECT COSTS		
	YEAR 1	YEAR 2	YEAR 3
A	1.8	2.0	2.2
B	2.4	2.1	2.0
C	2.1	2.3	4.7
AVAILABLE FUNDS	4.6	4.6	4.7

The present values of expected future profits (taking into account development costs) from the three projects are, respectively, $800,000, $700,000, and $850,000.

(a) Show how this problem can be formulated as a zero-one integer linear programming problem.

(b) Write down the linear programming relaxation.

(c) Find the optimal solution to the zero-one programming problem.

8.20. An advertising manager has a total budget of $1 million to spend on promotion of a new project. He can spend parts of this total on television, radio, newspaper, and magazine campaigns. The table shows the costs (in hundreds of thousands of dollars) of each campaign and the expected numbers (in millions) of people reached.

	TELEVISION	RADIO	NEWSPAPERS	MAGAZINES
COST	4.7	3.4	2.5	2.8
NUMBER REACHED	2.5	1.8	1.3	1.4

If the objective is to maximize the total number of people reached, which campaigns should be mounted?

8.21. Consider the capital budgeting example of Section 8.5 in which a company was examining the possibility of adding capacity for four types of machines. Suppose that management imposes two further requirements

(i) Capacity for machine B will not be added unless capacity is added for machine A.

(ii) Capacity for machine C will be added if and only if capacity for machine D is added.

Leaving the other problem parameters unchanged, formulate the mathematical programming problem that must now be solved.

8.22. A fast food chain is planning to move into a city and has under consideration seven possible sites for its outlet. This city can be segmented into ten areas, and for each possible site an estimate is made as to whether or not customers will be attracted from any area. In the accompanying table, a 1 indicates that customers will be drawn from an area to a site, and a 0 that they will not. Also shown in the table are annual rental charges that must be paid for each site. (Figures are in thousands of dollars.) Management wants to locate its outlets in such a way that customers from each area will be attracted to at least one of the outlets. Subject to this constraint, sites must be chosen so that the total annual rent paid is as small as possible.

AREA	SITE						
	1	2	3	4	5	6	7
A	1	0	0	0	0	1	0
B	1	0	0	0	0	0	1
C	1	1	0	0	0	0	0
D	0	1	0	0	1	0	1
E	0	1	0	1	0	0	0
F	0	0	1	0	0	1	0
G	0	0	1	0	1	0	1
H	0	0	1	0	1	0	0
I	0	0	0	1	0	1	0
J	0	0	0	1	0	1	1
RENT	100	130	110	140	120	100	160

Formulate the mathematical programming problem that must be solved.
(In Section 8.5 we discussed location of outlets through the **matching problem**. This alternative approach is known as the **covering** problem, since outlets are located so that every area is covered.)

8.23. A corporation is planning to produce a new product, and is considering six possible sites for its manufacturing plants. The plants that are built must serve four customer service centers. The accompanying table shows expected monthly demand at each customer service center, and potential monthly capacity for each possible manufacturing plant. Also shown are unit production and transportation costs for each possible plant/service center route, together with fixed costs per month for each possible plant. These cost figures are all in dollars.

FIXED COSTS	PLANT	CUSTOMER SERVICE CENTER				POTENTIAL SUPPLY
		1	2	3	4	
		VARIABLE COSTS PER UNIT				
3,000	1	10	12	13	17	700
3,500	2	11	9	10	14	750
2,600	3	15	12	8	10	650
2,100	4	18	15	12	9	550
3,900	5	13	16	14	12	800
2,800	6	18	11	8	16	600
DEMAND		800	600	700	500	

This corporation wants to select plant sites and develop a transportation policy so that total monthly costs are as small as possible, subject to the requirement that all demand must be met. Formulate the mathematical programming problem that must be solved.

8.24. A company is planning to produce a diet blend containing four nutrients. A total of six products are under consideration as ingredients in this blend. The accompanying table shows minimum nutrient requirements and nutrient contents of the six products. Also shown are the costs per unit of these products. However, for each product there is also a fixed cost due to ordering expenses. These fixed costs, attributable to each batch of the blend, are also shown in the table. For example, if x_1 units of product 1 are used, the cost will be $15 + 10x_1$ cents, when x_1 is positive, and will be zero when x_1 is zero. The company wants to produce, at the lowest possible total cost, a blend satisfying all of the minimum nutrient requirements.

MINIMUM QUANTITIES REQUIRED (OUNCES)	NUTRIENT	NUTRIENTS PER UNIT (OUNCES)					
		PRODUCT 1	PRODUCT 2	PRODUCT 3	PRODUCT 4	PRODUCT 5	PRODUCT 6
10	A	0	0.1	0.3	0.1	0.2	0.3
12	B	0.2	0	0.3	0.1	0	0
15	C	0.3	0.3	0	0.2	0	0.4
20	D	0.4	0.3	0.4	0	0.5	0
COST PER UNIT (CENTS)		10	9	11	7	9	12
FIXED COST (CENTS)		15	18	20	20	16	15

Formulate the mathematical programming problem that must be solved.

8.25. A manufacturing company produces three products, each of which must be processed through four departments. The accompanying table gives the problem specifications. As a result of start-up difficulties, management additionally requires that if any of these products is to be produced in a given week, then at least 500 units of the product must be made. The aim is to find, subject to this and the departmental resource constraints, the profit maximizing product mix for the week

TOTAL MAN-HOURS AVAILABLE	DEPARTMENT	MAN-HOURS PER WEEK		
		PRODUCT 1	PRODUCT 2	PRODUCT 3
6000	A	4	1	1
4500	B	3	1	1
2000	C	1	2	1
2500	D	1	2	2
PROFIT PER UNIT ($)		3	2	2

Formulate the mathematical programming problem that must be solved.

8.26 A state government agency has received bids on four projects from four contractors. The bid amounts (in thousands of dollars) are shown in the accompanying table. One bid must be accepted on each project, and no contractor can work on more than one project. Projects 1 and 2 are large, while the other two are smaller.

Contractors 1 and 2 are from out of state, while the other two are from in-state. For political reasons, the state agency wants to assign at most one large project to an out-of-state contractor. Subject to these requirements, the aim is to accept those bids that will lead to the four projects being completed at the lowest possible total cost.

PROJECT	CONTRACTOR			
	1	2	3	4
1	600	630	650	690
2	550	520	530	560
3	120	140	150	140
4	170	180	190	180

Formulate the mathematical programming problem that must be solved.

Design of an Automated Assembly System: An Application of 0-1 Integer Programming[1]

An interesting application of integer programming is to the design of a fully automated computer-controlled assembly system in which individual tasks are performed by robots. A typical design problem for such a system would involve an assembly job consisting of some number N of distinct tasks which must be carried out in a specific sequence. A total of some number M of work stations could be made available for performing these tasks. For example, the authors of this study discuss the assembly of an automobile alternator for which 14 tasks must be carried out in sequence, and for which five work stations (each a computer-controlled robot) are available. (Not all robots are capable of performing all 14 tasks.)

This problem has two interesting features

1. The work stations will not be identical. Typically, the robots available will differ in terms of time taken and costs incurred in performing individual tasks.
2. The individual tasks must be performed in a specific sequence, and the tools required for each task may not be the same. Thus, if a robot performs one task, it may be necessary for it to retool, with consequent increase in cost and time, before performing its next task. Thus, in formulating the problem, we must know not only if task j is to be performed at work station i, but also what the next task is to be performed at that station. In formulating the problem then, the 0-1 variables

$$x_{ijk} = \begin{cases} 1 \text{ if task } j \text{ is carried out at work station } i \text{ and the next} \\ \quad \text{task performed at that station is task } k \\ 0 \text{ otherwise} \end{cases}$$

must be defined.

The objective is to design an assembly system that achieves a desired production rate at the lowest possible total costs. Both fixed and variable costs are incurred. Variable costs arise whenever a given task is carried out at a particular work station. As indicated, the size of these costs will depend on what the next task is to be performed at this station. Hence, in conformity with the above notation, costs c_{ijk} must be specified, and total variable costs of the system are the sum of $c_{ijk}x_{ijk}$ over all i, j, and k. Also, fixed costs are incurred for each work station that is actually employed in the system. It is therefore necessary to define the 0-1 variables

$$y_i = \begin{cases} 1 \text{ if station } i \text{ is in the system} \\ 0 \text{ otherwise} \end{cases}$$

---

[1] This discussion is based on S. C. Graves and B. W. Lamar, "An Integer Programming Procedure for Assembly System Design Problems," *Operations Research, 31* (1983), 522–545.

Then, total fixed cost is the sum of $F_i y_i$, where F_i is the fixed cost of work station i.

The total cost (variable plus fixed) can then be minimized for a given desired production rate. For the automobile alternator case, the authors found an optimal system in which just three of the available five robots were employed. At this solution, only one robot had to be retooled at any stage in the assembly cycle.

Scheduling Radioisotope Production at General Electric: An Application of Mixed Integer Programming[2]

Radioisotopes are produced in capsules of three sizes through irradiation of raw material in the core of a nuclear reactor. Depending on the level of irradiation, 16 grades of isotope can be made. The market for these isotopes has three segments—low-grade industrial use, medical teletherapy, and industrial radiography. Demand trends have been very stable, so that forecasts of future demand in these market segments are quite reliable. Production periods in this industry are six months long, and a desirable planning horizon is four years—the approximate time taken to produce the highest grade radioisotope under normal operating procedures.

The authors of this study describe a model aimed at finding the optimum production schedule, over this horizon, in terms of revenue maximization, subject to production, inventory, and demand constraints. The model involves a total of 1458 constraints and 2651 variables, 48 of which are required to be integers. The integer requirement arises because the numbers of capsules must be an integer. However, product demand is generally measured on a continuous scale, in curies. Thus, many variables in the model formulation will not be integers. The authors estimated in 1981 a computing cost of $460 for solving the model. This represented a very large savings compared with the manual decision-making process previously in use. Moreover, the model can generate further valuable information about the production process that otherwise would not be available.

---

[2] This discussion is based on S. C. Economides and W. T. Crawford, "Radioisotope Production Scheduling in a Nuclear Reactor," *Decision Sciences, 13*, (1982), 501–512.

dynamic programming

CHAPTER NINE

9.1. CONCEPTS OF DYNAMIC PROGRAMMING

The situations we have discussed so far have involved the making of **a single decision.** For example, a product mix has to be selected to maximize profits, or a set of transportation routes with smallest possible total cost must be determined. Such problems are essentially **static** in nature, the implicit assumption being that a corporation may look at an individual problem in isolation, and that any decision taken will not influence possibilities open in other areas of the organization. A broader view would encompass the potential for **interrelated decisions.** These might be sequential in time, so that for example, a series of monthly production schedules may need to be formulated. Production levels planned for one particular month will depend on plans for other months. Such problems are said to be **dynamic** in nature, and we refer to dynamic optimization problems as **dynamic programming** problems.

We have seen that dynamic programming addresses circumstances where a series of interrelated decisions, or combination of decisions, must be made. By contrast with our analysis in previous chapters of this text, there is no specific unique framework, leading to an optimal solution through a particular algorithm, in which all dynamic programming problems can be formulated. Rather, a certain amount of ingenuity is required in problem formulation. In the next three sections we will consider specific examples, which will provide some insight into the potential of dynamic programming and into this general approach to problem solving.

The broad line of attack on dynamic programming problems involves the breaking down of a large problem into smaller subproblems which are easier to solve. The solutions to the subproblems are employed to build up an optimal solution to the overall problem. The individual **stages** of the analysis, developed in this way, correspond to points at which decisions must be made.

9.2. A SHORTEST ROUTE PROBLEM

A freight dispatcher must plan a route for a shipment, by road, of a truck-load of parts. A road map is consulted, and several alternative routes found. The problem is set out in Figure 9.1, where node 1 represents the point of origin and node 10 the eventual destination. Nodes 2–9 are intermediate locations along feasible routes. Also shown are distances, in miles, between points along these routes. Thus, for example, one feasible route is 1-3-5-9-10, with total distance

$$120 + 140 + 160 + 190 = 610 \text{ miles}$$

The dispatcher's problem is to find the shortest possible route.

In common with many other problems which can be looked at in the dynamic programming framework, this particular problem admits other lines of attack. We will discuss an alternative approach to solving such problems in Chapter 13. However, our aim here is to illustrate the dynamic programming framework, so that we proceed, as shown in Figure 9.1, by breaking the problem down into stages. The strategy is to begin at the eventual objective, reach the final destination, and work backwards. We now proceed, by stages, to find an optimal solution to the freight dispatcher's problem.

STAGE 1

We begin at the right-hand side of Figure 9.1. The goal is to reach node 10 which can be accomplished only by passing through either node 7, node 8, or node 9. The shortest feasible distance from node 7 to node 10 is simply 180 miles, as this

FIGURE 9.1 Problem specifications for the freight dispatcher.

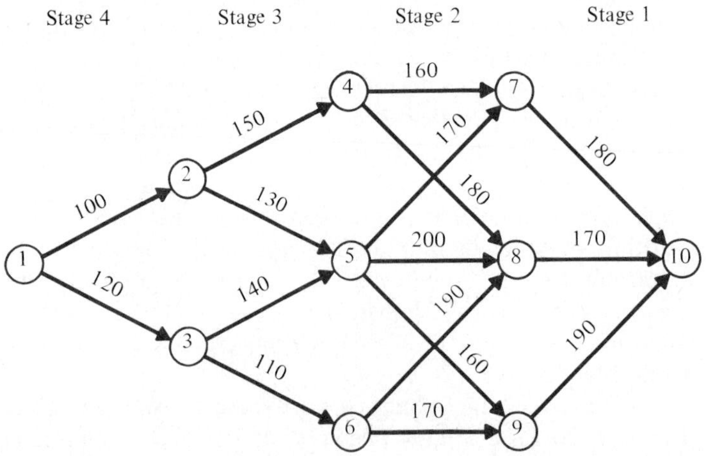

FIGURE 9.2 Stage 1 results for the freight dispatcher problem.

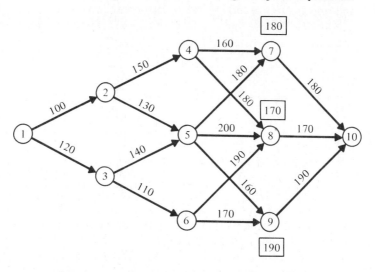

is the only possibility available. This information is incorporated in our schematic route map in Figure 9.2, in a box by node 7. The corresponding values for nodes 8 and 9 are similarly entered.

STAGE 2

It is now necessary to move back a step and consider, in turn, shipments passing through nodes 4, 5, and 6. Consider the first of these. To travel from node 4 to node 10, it is necessary to travel through either node 7 or node 8. In the former case, the total distance to the final destination is 160 + 180 = 340 miles, while in the latter it is 180 + 170 = 350 miles. We can therefore conclude that *if the shipment is to pass through node 4,* the optimum route thereafter passes through node 7. It follows that in our overall problem of finding the shortest route from node 1 to node 10, the only route out of node 4 that *can* enter any optimal solution passes through node 7. The argument we have just employed applies quite generally to dynamic programming problems and forms the basis of procedures for their solution. We state the general rule in the box.

Stage Solutions and Dynamic Programming Problems

A decision that is suboptimal at any stage of a dynamic programming problem remains suboptimal in the context of the overall problem. Thus, any such decision can be dropped from further consideration in solving the overall problem.

We can analyze possible routes passing through nodes 5 or 6 in precisely the same way. The second stage calculations are summarized in Table 9.1. The

TABLE 9.1 Stage 2 calculations for the freight dispatcher problem.

		DISTANCES		
ORIGIN NODE	INTERMEDIATE NODE	ORIGIN- INTERMEDIATE	INTERMEDIATE- DESTINATION	TOTAL
4	7	160	180	(340)
4	8	180	170	350
5	7	180	180	360
5	8	200	170	370
5	9	160	190	(350)
6	8	190	170	(360)
6	9	170	190	(360)

optimum total mileage figures for the three optimization problems are circled. Notice that from node 6, the total distance to the destination point is the same whichever of the two possible routes is followed. These two solutions, then, are jointly optimal. The minimum possible distances from nodes 4, 5, and 6 to node 10 are shown in Figure 9.3. In that figure, we have also eliminated those sub-routes that we now know will not be followed in any optimal solution to the overall problem.

STAGE 3

We now consider the problems of finding optimal routes for shipments passing, respectively, through node 2 or node 3, proceeding precisely as in the previous stage. Any shipment passing through node 2 must necessarily go on to either

FIGURE 9.4 Stage 2 results for the freight dispatcher problem.

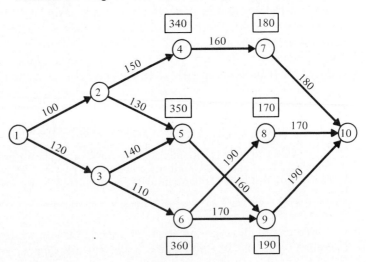

TABLE 9.2 Stage 3 calculations for the freight dispatcher problem.

| | | DISTANCES | | |
ORIGIN NODE	INTERMEDIATE NODE	ORIGIN-INTERMEDIATE	INTERMEDIATE-DESTINATION	TOTAL
2	4	150	340	490
2	5	130	350	⃝480
3	5	140	350	490
3	6	110	360	⃝470

node 4 or node 5. In the former case, the distance from node 2 to node 4 is 150 miles, while the shortest possible distance from node 4 to the final destination is 340 miles. Hence, for travel from node 2, via node 4, to node 10, the shortest possible distance is 490 miles. Similarly, we find that the shortest distance from node 2, via node 5, to node 10 is $130 + 350 = 480$ miles. It follows that if the truck-load of parts is to go through node 2, it should then proceed via node 5. These computations, together with those for shipments passing through node 3, are set out in Table 9.2. The minimum possible distances from nodes 2 or 3 to the final destination are indicated in Figure 9.4. Also in that figure we have eliminated those subroutes that we now know cannot constitute part of an optimal solution to the overall problem. Notice that since all routes entering node 4 can be eliminated, so of course can those subroutes leaving that node.

STAGE 4

Finally, we are in a position to derive the optimal solution to our shortest route problem. Any shipment from the origin, node 1, must pass through either node 2 or node 3. As shown in Table 9.3, the shortest possible complete routes in

FIGURE 9.3 Stage 3 results for the freight dispatcher problem.

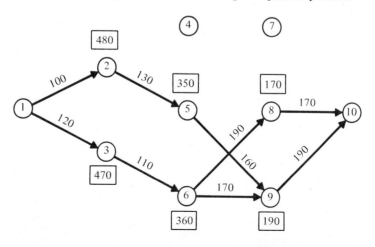

TABLE 9.3 Stage 4 calculations for the freight dispatcher problem.

		DISTANCES		
ORIGIN NODE	INTERMEDIATE NODE	ORIGIN-INTERMEDIATE	INTERMEDIATE-DESTINATION	TOTAL
1	2	100	480	580
1	3	120	470	590

these two cases are of respective distances 580 and 590 miles. It follows, then, that the best possible route is, as shown in Figure 9.5, 1–2–5–9–10, with a total distance of 580 miles.

This illustration of the application of dynamic programming to a shortest-route problem brings out some of the ingredients of the dynamic programming approach. We began at the eventual objective, reaching the destination, and worked back in stages. At each stage, relatively straightforward optimization subproblems were solved. This allowed us to eliminate many possible solutions to the overall problem when we found that they were suboptimal for the smaller constituent problems. Eventually, at the final stage, we had a small number of alternatives from which to choose, so that the overall problem was easily solved.

9.3. A JOB SCHEDULING PROBLEM

We turn now to a problem that is, on the surface, totally different in nature from that of Section 9.2. In fact, it will be seen, when viewed in the dynamic programming framework, that the structures of the two problems are rather similar.

A machine shop repair crew, beginning an 8-hour shift, is faced with machines of four different types needing repair. Table 9.4 shows the numbers of

FIGURE 9.5 Optimal solution for the freight dispatcher problem.

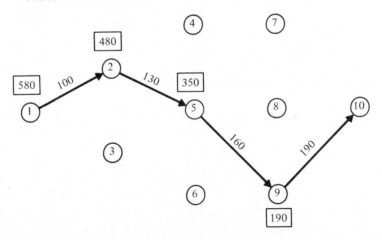

TABLE 9.4 Problem specifications for the machine shop repair crew working an 8-hour shift.

MACHINE TYPE	NUMBER NEEDING REPAIR	REPAIR TIMES PER MACHINE (HOURS)	VALUES (IN HUNDREDS OF $) OF REPAIRS
A	3	2	12, 10, 8
B	2	2	13, 11
C	2	3	9, 7
D	1	3	14

machines of each type requiring repair, estimated times taken to repair each type of machine, and the values to the company of having these machines repaired. Because of the effects on continuity of production it is typically more valuable to repair the first machine of any type than the second or third. Thus, for example, repair of one machine of type A is valued at $1200, while fixing the second and third machines of this type yields respectively additional value increments of $1000 and $800. Our problem is to find, subject to the constraint that only eight hours are available, which machines should be repaired in the shift. The position is such that any work begun must be completed during the shift, so that only integer solutions are feasible.[1]

In order to put the problem of the machine shop repair crew into a dynamic programming framework, we view the overall problem as involving a sequence of decisions made in the following order:

1. Decide how many machines of type A to repair.
2. Given the time remaining, decide how many machines of type B to repair.
3. Given the time remaining, decide how many machines of type C to repair.
4. Given the time remaining, decide how many machines of type D to repair.

This sequence is illustrated in Figure 9.6, which also shows the interdependence of the decisions. At any particular step, the decision made will determine the numbers of hours available, and hence what is possible to accomplish

---

[1] A special case of such job scheduling problems arises when values for jobs of each type are the same. Such problems can then be set in the integer programming framework. For example, suppose that the values are V_1 for machine type A, V_2 for type B, V_3 for type C, and V_4 for type D. Let x_1, x_2, x_3, and x_4 denote the numbers of machines of each type repaired in the 8-hour shift. Our problem could then be written as

$$\text{Maximize} \quad V_1 x_1 + V_2 x_2 + V_3 x_3 + V_4 x_4$$
$$\text{subject to} \quad 2x_1 + 2x_2 + 3x_3 + 3x_4 \leq 8$$
$$x_1 \leq 3$$
$$x_2 \leq 2$$
$$x_3 \leq 2$$
$$x_4 \leq 1$$
$$x_i \geq 0 \quad (i = 1, \ldots, 4)$$
$$x_i \text{ integer} \quad (i = 1, \ldots, 4)$$

Such problems can be solved using the methods of Chapter 8. Alternatively, the dynamic programming methodology, to be discussed in this section, can be employed.

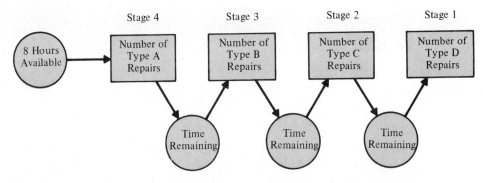

at subsequent steps. For example, for repair of type A machines a maximum of 8 hours is available. If it is decided to repair two of these machines, four of the available 8 hours will be required. Therefore, as an *input* to the decision on type B machines, the constraint that only 4 hours of the available total time remains must be incorporated. As we did for the shortest route problem of Section 9.2, we attack our job scheduling problem by working backward in stages. This, too, is shown in Figure 9.6. We begin, then, by examining the decision on the number of type D machines to repair.

STAGE 1

The difficulty faced when considering a decision on the number of machines of type D to repair is that we do not know how much time will be available. It is therefore necessary to consider all possibilities, from zero to 8 hours. Obviously, at this stage, the maximum possible number of machines should be repaired, that is, one machine if at least three hours are available, and none otherwise. This conclusion is set out in Table 9.5 which also shows the value of the repair work as $1400 if a machine is repaired, and zero otherwise.

TABLE 9.5 Stage 1 (machine D repairs) results for the machine shop repair crew problem.

AVAILABLE HOURS	OPTIMAL NUMBER OF MACHINES REPAIRED	VALUE OF WORK
0	0	0
1	0	0
2	0	0
3	1	14
4	1	14
5	1	14
6	1	14
7	1	14
8	1	14

TABLE 9.6 Stage 2 (machine C repairs) calculations for the machine shop repair crew problem.

AVAILABLE HOURS	MACHINES REPAIRED	VALUE OF WORK	HOURS USED	HOURS REMAINING	VALUE OF LATER STAGE WORK	TOTAL VALUE ($00's)
0	0	0	0	0	0	(0)
1	0	0	0	1	0	(0)
2	0	0	0	2	0	(0)
3	0	0	0	3	14	(14)
3	1	9	3	0	0	9
4	0	0	0	4	14	14
4	1	9	3	1	0	9
5	0	0	0	5	14	(14)
5	1	9	3	2	0	9
6	0	0	0	6	14	14
6	1	9	3	3	14	(23)
6	2	16	6	0	0	16
7	0	0	0	7	14	14
7	1	9	3	4	14	(23)
7	2	16	6	1	0	16
8	0	0	0	8	14	14
8	1	9	3	5	14	(23)
8	2	16	6	2	0	16

STAGE 2

Next, we consider the decision on the number of machines of type C to repair. This number must be either 0, 1, or 2, but what is feasible will again depend on how many hours are available. The calculations are set out in Table 9.6, where we must again consider all possibilities from zero to 8 for number of hours available. The table shows all the computations necessary to make optimal stage 2 decisions. For example, suppose that we enter with 6 hours available. This would allow the repair of up to two machines of type C. The value of the work done on these machines is either zero, $900, or $1600, depending on the number repaired. Next, we compute the amount of time spent on type C machine repairs, and, subtracting from the originally available 6 hours, the time remaining for repair of machines of type D. The highest value that can be achieved from repair of type D machines depends on the hours available, as shown in Table 9.5. These quantities (zero if no time is available, or $1400 if either 3 or 6 hours remain) are entered in the "value of later stage work" column of Table 9.6. The final column shows the total value of work on machines C and D for various possible decisions. These figures are obtained by summing those in the two constituent value columns. We can therefore conclude that *if 6 hours are available at stage 2,* the optimal decision is to repair one machine of type C, the total value of work on machines of types C and D then being $2300. This value is circled in Table 9.6. The principle employed in our analysis of Section 9.2 can again be invoked. It may be concluded that *if any optimal solution involves entering stage 2 with 6 hours available,* the best strategy thereafter is to repair one type C machine (and hence, also, one type D machine).

In exactly the same fashion, we can derive optimal solutions for any number of available hours entering stage 2. These are the figures circled in Table 9.6, and will be employed in our calculations at the next stage.

STAGE 3

The next step is to examine the decision as to how many machines of type B should be repaired during the shift. As at the previous two stages, we do not know how many hours will be available, and so must consider all possibilities. The computations are set out in Table 9.7 which has the same structure as Table 9.6. The "Value of Later Stage Work" column shows the highest possible values for repairs on machines of types C and D, given the number of hours remaining for such work. These figures, then, are obtained from the circled numbers in the final column of Table 9.6. For example, if stage 3 is entered with 5 hours available, and one type B machine is repaired, 3 hours are left for work on machines C and D. The final column of Table 9.6 shows that the best that can be achieved with these 3 hours is a value of $1400. Hence, the best total value for work on machines B, C, and D, given a total of 5 hours available and a decision to repair one machine of type B, is $2700. In fact, the final column of Table 9.7 shows that repair of one machine of type B is optimal if 5 hours remain at this stage. The optimal solutions to all the stage 3 problems are the values circled in the final column of this table.

TABLE 9.7 Stage 3 (machine B repairs) calculations for the machine shop repair crew problem.

AVAILABLE HOURS	MACHINES REPAIRED	VALUE OF WORK	HOURS USED	HOURS REMAINING	VALUE OF LATER STAGE WORK	TOTAL VALUE
0	0	0	0	0	0	⓪
1	0	0	0	1	0	⓪
2	0	0	0	2	0	0
2	1	13	2	0	0	⑬
3	0	0	0	3	14	⑭
3	1	13	2	1	0	13
4	0	0	0	4	14	14
4	1	13	2	2	0	13
4	2	24	4	0	0	㉔
5	0	0	0	5	14	14
5	1	13	2	3	14	㉗
5	2	24	4	1	0	24
6	0	0	0	6	23	23
6	1	13	2	4	14	㉗
6	2	24	4	2	0	24
7	0	0	0	7	23	23
7	1	13	2	5	14	27
7	2	24	4	3	14	㊳
8	0	0	0	8	23	23
8	1	13	2	6	23	36
8	2	24	4	4	14	㊳

TABLE 9.8 Stage 4 (machine A repairs) calculations for the machine shop repair crew problem.

AVAILABLE HOURS	MACHINES REPAIRED	VALUE OF WORK	HOURS USED	HOURS REMAINING	VALUE OF LATER STAGE WORK	TOTAL VALUE
8	0	0	0	8	38	38
8	1	12	2	6	27	39
8	2	22	4	4	24	㊻
8	3	30	6	2	13	43

STAGE 4

As indicated in Figure 9.6, we know at the outset that 8 hours are available, so that this is the only figure that has to be considered in the decision as to how many machines of type A to repair. Calculations for the four alternative strategies are set out in Table 9.8.

Suppose that it is decided to repair two type A machines. This work has a value of $2200 and uses up four of the available hours. From the final column of Table 9.7, we find that the best that can be achieved with the remaining four hours is a value of $2400. Hence, the total value resulting from this stage 4 choice is $4600. The final column of Table 9.8 shows that repair of two type A machines is the optimal strategy.

The complete optimal solution can now be read from the tables. First, we find from Table 9.8 that in the optimal solution, two type A machines should be repaired, leaving four hours for repair of other machines. Turning, now, to Table 9.7, with four hours available, we see that the best strategy is to repair two type B machines, a solution which leaves no further time for repair of machines of types C or D. The optimal solution is, then, repair of two machines each of types A and B, with a total value of $4600.

As we promised, our approach to the solution of this job scheduling problem does not differ radically in outline from the methodology used to attack the shortest route problem of Section 9.2. We again set up the problem as a sequence of interrelated decisions. Next, working backwards·in stages, optimal solutions are developed for subproblems, conditional on inputs from earlier decisions. This procedure allows us to eliminate many possible solutions as suboptimal, so that by the time the final stage is reached, we face the relatively simple question of how to choose from a fairly small number of alternative solutions that might be optimal.

9.4. AN INVENTORY CONTROL PROBLEM

In this section we will consider the problem of a manufacturer of specialized machine tools, planning a production schedule for the final three months of the year. The company enters this period with two units of a particular machine tool

TABLE 9.9 Problem specifications for the machine tools manufacturer.

MONTH	DEMAND FORECAST	PRODUCTION CAPACITY	UNIT PRODUCTION COST ($'00)	UNIT INVENTORY HOLDING COST ($'00)
October	3	4	45	4
November	4	3	50	8
December	3	4	54	10

Beginning Inventory: 2 units
Ending Inventory: 1 unit

in inventory, and wishes to end the year with an inventory of one unit. Production capacities and costs for each month, together with demand forecasts, are set out in Table 9.9. The aim is to manage production and inventory of these machine tools so that total production and inventory holding costs are minimized, subject to the company being able to meet anticipated demand in each month.

Once again we view the overall optimization problem in stages, which in this particular instance constitute a chronological sequence. Our approach, as previously, is to work backwards, so that stages 1, 2, and 3 involve, respectively, production decisions for December, November, and October. Before looking at these individual stages, we will introduce an algebraic formulation which is often useful in describing dynamic programming problems. As illustrated in Figure 9.7, the *input* at each decision stage is the inventory held at the beginning of the period. The decision made in any period will be based on this inventory level, and will in turn determine the amount of inventory carried forward to the next month. We will use d_1, d_2, and d_3 to denote the values of the decision variables—that is, the production levels—at each stage. Also, we denote by x_1, x_2, and x_3 the inputs to each decision stage; that is, the beginning period inventory levels. We know from our problem specifications that at the

FIGURE 9.7 Dynamic programming setup of the problem of the machine tools manufacturer.

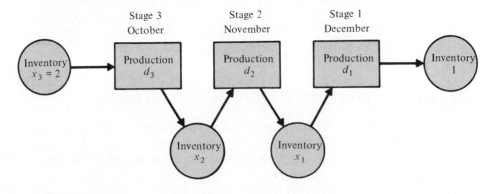

beginnning of October, two units are held in inventory. Therefore, in our notation, x_3 is equal to 2. This notation is

d_i = Output at stage i
x_i = Beginning period inventory at stage i $(i = 1, 2, 3)$

At each stage, for every feasible combination of decision and input variables, it
is possible to compute the total cost of production and inventory holding. This
will be represented as

$$C_i(x_i, d_i) = \text{Cost at stage } i$$

In the stage-by-stage dynamic programming solution approach, we attempt
to identify those decisions which are optimal, in this case in the sense of minimizing total costs, over all stages up to and including that presently under study.
We therefore need to define, for any input-decision combination

$$f_i(x_i, d_i) = \text{Total cost of all stages up to and including stage } i$$

From our definitions, it follows that

$$f_i(x_i, d_i) = f_{i-1}(x_{i-1}, d_{i-1}) + C_i(x_i, d_i) \qquad (9.1)$$

Now, the stage i problem can be viewed as finding, for each possible input x_i,
the value of the decision variable d_i for which the function (9.1) is a mininum,
subject to the satisfaction of the problem constraints. We saw in the two previous sections that this problem can be simplified by noting that any decisions
found to be suboptimal at one stage must also be suboptimal in the context of
the overall problem. To see how this conclusion affects the issue of minimizing
(9.1), consider any particular pair of feasible stage i values, x_i and d_i. These will
determine x_{i-1}, the inventory at the beginning of the next period (stage $i - 1$).
Now, correspondingly, the only value of the decision variable d_{i-1} that we need
look at is the optimal value found at stage $i - 1$. Therefore, if we define

$$d_i^* = \text{Optimal value of output at stage } i$$

the problem of minimizing (9.1) is simplified to that of minimizing

$$f_i(x_i, d_i) = f_{i-1}(x_{i-1}, d_{i-1}^*) + C_i(x_i, d_i) \qquad (9.2)$$

We are now in a position to formalize the solution procedure used for dynamic programming problems.

Consider a dynamic programming problem in which the objective is to minimize total costs. The problem is broken down into stages. At each stage we must choose the value d_i of a decision variable, given the value x_i of an input variable.[2] At the i-th stage, we proceed as follows:

(i) Each x_i, d_i combination yields a stage i cost $C_i(x_i, d_i)$

(ii) Given a specific pair x_i, d_i, the input x_{i-1} to the previous stage can be calculated

(iii) Associated with x_{i-1} is a value d_{i-1}^* for the decision variable, such that $f_{i-1}(x_{i-1}, d_{i-1})$, the total cost of all stages up to and including stage $i - 1$, is a minimum

(iv) For each x_i, we must now find d_i^* so that

$$f_i(x_i, d_i) = f_{i-1}(x_{i-1}, d_{i-1}^*) + C_i(x_i, d_i)$$

is as small as possible.

We now illustrate this formal framework by returning to the inventory control and production planning problem of the machine tools manufacturer.

STAGE 1

Our manufacturer enters December with x_1 machine tools in inventory. At this stage in our analysis we do not know precisely what this number will be, and so must take account of all possibilities. From Table 9.9, there is an initial inventory of two units, plus the capacity to produce a maximum of seven further units in October and November. Also, a total of seven units must be sold in these two months. It follows that at the beginning of December, inventory can be no higher than two units. We will therefore consider here the possible values of 0, 1, and 2 for x_1.

Using d_1 to denote the December production level, it follows since the production cost per unit is \$5400 that

$$\text{Stage 1 Production Cost} = 54d_1$$

The total number of machine tools available for sale in December is the sum of the beginning inventory and the December production; that is, $x_1 + d_1$. Since three of these units are to be sold in December, inventory at the end of that month will be

$$\text{Stage 1 Closing Inventory} = x_1 + d_1 - 3$$

It follows that the December inventory holding cost is (in hundreds of dollars)

$$\text{Stage 1 Inventory Holding Cost} = 10(x_1 + d_1 - 3)$$

---

[2] In more complex problems than that being studied here, there could be several input variables.

Total production and inventory holding costs for December are, therefore,

$$C_1(x_1, d_1) = 54d_1 + 10(x_1 + d_1 - 3)$$

Moreover, since there are no previous stages to take into account, in the notation just established,

$$f_1(x_1, d_1) = C_1(x_1, d_1)$$

The stage 1 decision problem is, then, to find for each possible x_1 the value of d_1 that minimizes the objective function

$$f_1(x_1, d_1) = 54d_1 + 10(x_1 + d_1 - 3) \qquad (9.3)$$

Next, we must consider the constraints on the possible solution values. These are:

$$
\begin{aligned}
&\text{Demand Satisfaction:} && x_1 + d_1 \geq 3 \\
&\text{Production Capacity:} && d_1 \leq 4 \qquad\qquad (9.4) \\
&\text{End of Period Inventory:} && x_1 + d_1 - 3 = 1
\end{aligned}
$$

The demand satisfaction constraint requires that at least three machine tools be available for sale in December, while the second equation in (9.4) indicates that no more than four units can be produced in that month. The end-of-period inventory constraint requires that at the end of December, there must be one unit in inventory.

The stage 1 optimization problem can now be stated as finding, for each possible x_1, the value d_1 that minimizes (9.3) subject to the constraints (9.4)[3], and a nonnegativity constraint on d_1.

The requirement that we end December with precisely one unit in inventory makes the optimization problem at this stage rather trivial. Given a particular value for beginning inventory, x_1, there can be at most one value of d_1 satisfying the third constraint of (9.4). For example, if $x_1 = 1$, then we must have $d_1 = 3$. The value of the objective function is, in that case, from (9.3),

$$f_1(1, 3) = 54d_1 + 10(x_1 + d_1 - 3)$$

$$= (54)(3) + (10)(1) = 172$$

where the units, here and elsewhere, are hundreds of dollars. The stage 1 results are set out in Table 9.10, where dashes are used to indicate infeasible solutions.

---

[3] In fact, in this particular instance, two of these constraints are redundant. If the end of period inventory constraint is satisfied, so must be the demand satisfaction constraint. Also, since x_1 cannot be negative, the production capacity constraint is satisfied as well.

TABLE 9.10 Stage 1 (December) results for the machine tools manufacturer.

		$f_1(x_1, d_1)$					OPTIMAL SOLUTIONS	
x_1	d_1:	0	1	2	3	4	d_1^*	$f_1(x_1, d_1^*)$
0		–	–	–	–	⑦226	4	226
1		–	–	–	⑦172	–	3	172
2		–	–	⑦118	–	–	2	118

Since there is just one feasible d_1 solution for each possible x_1 solution, this must necessarily be optimal, and is circled. The right-hand portion of the table records the values d_1^* of the decision variables at the optimal solutions, together with the optimal values $f_1(x_1, d_1^*)$ of the objective function.

STAGE 2

At the beginning of November, there are x_2 machine tools in inventory. This number can be at most three—the difference between pre-October inventory, plus October production capacity, and sales in that month. If d_2 denotes the level of production in November, then since unit cost of production is 50, we have

$$\text{Stage 2 Production Cost} = 50d_2$$

In November there will be $x_2 + d_2$ machine tools available for sale, of which four will actually be sold. The inventory at the end of November, which is, of course, also the inventory at the beginning of December must then be

$$\text{Stage 2 Closing Inventory} = x_2 + d_2 - 4 = x_1 \qquad (9.5)$$

Hence, November inventory holding costs will be

$$\text{Stage 2 Inventory Holding Cost} = 8(x_2 + d_2 - 4)$$

The sum of production and inventory holding costs for November is

$$C_2(x_2, d_2) = 50d_2 + 8(x_2 + d_2 - 4)$$

This cost must be added to the lowest achieveable costs at earlier stages, so that from (9.2) the function to be minimized at stage 2 is

$$\begin{aligned} f_2(x_2, d_2) &= f_1(x_1, d_1^*) + C_2(x_2, d_2) \\ &= f_1(x_1, d_1^*) + 50d_2 + 8(x_2 + d_2 - 4) \end{aligned} \qquad (9.6)$$

For any beginning inventory level x_2, we must find the value d_2 for November production that minimizes the objective function (9.6). Each possible (x_2, d_2) combination yields, from (9.5), a specific value x_1 for inventory at the beginning of December. For that x_1 value, we can read from Table 9.10 optimal December output d_1^*, and the corresponding cost $f_1(x_1, d_1^*)$.

At stage 2, the objective function (9.6) is minimized subject to the constraints

$$\begin{aligned}
\text{Demand Satisfaction:} \quad & x_2 + d_2 \geq 4 \\
\text{Production Capacity:} \quad & d_2 \leq 3 \qquad\qquad (9.7) \\
& d_2 \geq 0
\end{aligned}$$

We will illustrate the calculations involved for the case where there are two machine tools in inventory at the beginning of November; that is, $x_2 = 2$. In that case, the values zero and one for production level, d_2 are infeasible, as the demand satisfaction constraint of (9.7) will be violated. Taking next the case $d_2 = 2$, the outcome for end of period inventory is, from (9.5)

$$x_1 = x_2 + d_2 - 4 = 2 + 2 - 4 = 0$$

Turning to Table 9.10, we find for $x_1 = 0$ that optimal earlier stage costs are

$$f_1(x_1, d_1^*) = 226$$

The value of the stage 2 objective function is then obtained by substituting $x_2 = 2$ and $d_2 = 2$ in (9.6), giving

$$\begin{aligned}
f_2(x_2, d_2) &= f_1(x_1, d_1^*) + 50d_2 + 8(x_2 + d_2 - 4) \\
&= 226 + (50)(2) + (8)(0) = 326
\end{aligned}$$

Given $x_2 = 2$, consider next the solution $d_2 = 3$. In that case, using (9.5), the inventory at the beginning of Stage 1 is

$$x_1 = x_2 + d_2 - 4 = 2 + 3 - 4 = 1$$

Then, from Table 9.10, with $x_1 = 1$, we find

$$f_1(x_1, d_1^*) = 172$$

Hence, for $x_2 = 2$ and $d_2 = 3$, the objective function (9.6) has the value

$$f_2(x_2, d_2) = 172 + (50)(3) + (8)(1) = 330$$

Since this exceeds the figure found for the case $x_2 = 2$, it follows that, *if November is entered with two units in inventory*, the optimal strategy at that stage is the manufacture of two further units.

These findings, together with similar calculations for other possible beginning-of-November inventory levels, are set out in Table 9.11. Notice that if x_2

TABLE 9.11 Stage 2 (November) results for the machine tools manufacturer.

	$f_2(x_2, d_2)$				OPTIMAL SOLUTIONS	
x_2	d_2: 0	1	2	3	d_2^*	$f_2(x_2, d_2^*)$
0	–	–	–	–	Not feasible	
1	–	–	–	(376)	3	376
2	–	–	(326)	330	2	326
3	–	(276)	280	284	1	276

= 0, there is no feasible solution to the stage 2 problem. It follows that any solution which involves entering November with no inventory is infeasible in the context of our overall problem.

STAGE 3

We know that when entering October, there are two machine tools in inventory, so that two is necessarily the value of x_3. Using d_3 to represent the production level for October, production costs for that month are

$$\text{Stage 3 Production Cost} = 45d_3$$

Since three units are to be sold in October, it follows that

$$\text{Stage 3 Closing Inventory} = x_3 + d_3 - 3 = x_2 \qquad (9.8)$$

and hence that

$$\text{Stage 3 Inventory Holding Cost} = 4(x_3 + d_3 - 3)$$

The total stage 3 production and inventory holding cost is therefore

$$C_3(x_3, d_3) = 45d_3 + 4(x_3 + d_3 - 3)$$

We can therefore write the objective function to be minimized at this stage as

$$
\begin{aligned}
f_3(x_3, d_3) &= f_2(x_2, d_2^*) + C_3(x_3, d_3) \\
&= f_2(x_2, d_2^*) + 45d_3 + 4(x_3 + d_3 - 3)
\end{aligned} \qquad (9.9)
$$

where we know that x_3 is equal to two.

The Stage 3 problem, then, is to minimize the objective function (9.9), subject to the constraints

$$\begin{array}{rl} \text{Demand Satisfaction:} & x_3 + d_3 \geq 3 \\ \text{Production Capacity:} & d_3 \leq 4 \qquad\qquad (9.10) \\ & d_3 \geq 0 \end{array}$$

We know that x_3 is equal to two. Let us evaluate (9.9) for the production of three machine tools in October. Substituting $x_3 = 2$ and $d_3 = 3$ in (9.8) yields for the end-of-October inventory

$$x_2 = x_3 + d_3 - 3 = 2 + 3 - 3 = 2$$

From the final column of Table 9.11, we find that when entering November with two units in inventory, the lowest possible combined cost for stages 1 and 2 is

$$f_2(x_2, d_2^*) = 326$$

Hence, substituting in (9.9), the lowest achieveable total cost following from the choice of producing three machine tools in October is

$$\begin{aligned} f_3(x_3, d_3) &= f_2(x_2, d_2^*) + 45d_3 + 4(x_3 + d_3 - 3) \\ &= 326 + (45)(3) + (4)(2) = 469 \end{aligned}$$

Table 9.12 shows the results of the corresponding calculations for $d_3 = 2$ and $d_3 = 4$. Zero production in October would violate the demand satisfaction constraint of (9.10). Production of one unit in October is also infeasible in the context of our overall problem. This is so since it would lead to zero inventory entering November, a case for which, as we saw in Table 9.11, no feasible stage 2 solution exists.

Directly from Table 9.12 we can read that the optimal solution to the overall inventory control problem of the machine tools manufacturer has a total cost of $468 hundred and involves the production of four units in October. This implies that three units are held in inventory entering November, so that from Table 9.11, one unit should be produced in that month. Consequently, at the beginning of December there will be no inventory, and hence, as shown in Table 9.10, four units must be produced in that month.

The structure of the inventory control problem, through which we have worked in this section, is very similar to that of the job scheduling problem of

TABLE 9.12 Stage 3 (October) results for the machine tools manufacturer.

		$f_3(x_3, d_3)$					OPTIMAL SOLUTIONS	
x_3	d_3:	0	1	2	3	4	d_3^*	$f_3(x_3, d_3^*)$
2		–	–	470	469	(468)	4	468

Section 9.3. Moreover, essentially identical solution methods were applied to these two problems. However, in this section we have attempted to formalize this approach to solving dynamic programming problems of this type with the intention of providing a concise description of the general methodology of dynamic programming. An understanding of this formal framework should help the reader in the formulation and solution of a wide range of problems.

EXERCISES

9.1. A trucking company must ship a load of freight from an origin, which we label node 1, to a destination (node 10). The table shows distances, in miles, along various possible subroutes.

SUBROUTE	DISTANCE	SUBROUTE	DISTANCE
1–2	50	5–7	80
1–3	60	5–8	75
2–4	75	5–9	70
2–5	80	6–8	85
3–5	70	6–9	75
3–6	60	7–10	90
4–7	85	8–10	95
4–8	90	9–10	100

(a) If the objective is to find the shortest possible route, find an optimal solution.

(b) Find the length of the shortest possible route.

9.2. A company is planning to send, by road, a shipment of parts from a factory (node 1) to a warehouse (node 10). The table shows distances, in miles, for the possible subroutes from the factory to the warehouse. The objective is to find the route with the shortest possible total distance.

SUBROUTE	DISTANCE	SUBROUTE	DISTANCE
1–2	100	4–6	85
1–3	110	4–7	80
1–4	120	5–8	75
2–5	90	6–8	85
2–6	95	6–9	70
3–5	90	7–9	75
3–6	80	8–10	110
3–7	80	9–10	95

(a) Find an optimal solution to this problem.

(b) Find the length of the shortest possible route.

9.3. A family is planning a rural trip from home (node 1) to a resort (node 11). The accompanying table shows distances, in miles, along the various possible sub-routes. The aim is to find the route from home to the resort with the smallest possible total distance.

SUBROUTE	DISTANCE	SUBROUTE	DISTANCE
1–2	40	5–8	10
1–3	45	5–9	20
1–4	50	6–8	15
2–5	35	6–9	20
2–6	30	6–10	25
3–5	40	7–9	20
3–6	30	7–10	10
3–7	25	8–11	25
4–6	30	9–11	15
4–7	30	10–11	15

(a) Find an optimal solution to this problem.

(b) How long is the shortest possible route?

9.4. A dispatcher finds that due to heavy snow, the usual route taken for shipments to a customer is unavailable. Having consulted a road map, she finds several routes that are feasible from her plant (node 1) to this customer (node 11). The table shows distances along the various subroutes. The aim is to find that route with shortest possible total distance.

SUBROUTE	DISTANCE	SUBROUTE	DISTANCE
1–2	120	5–8	110
1–3	135	5–9	120
1–4	150	6–8	115
2–5	135	6–9	125
2–6	130	6–10	125
3–5	130	7–9	120
3–6	120	7–10	110
3–7	125	8–11	120
4–6	120	9–11	115
4–7	130	10–11	125

(a) Find an optimal solution.

(b) Find the shortest possible total distance for available routes from the plant to the customer.

9.5. Due to unanticipated heavy demand, one of a corporation's distribution centers finds its supply of parts almost exhausted and requests the shipment of a truck-load as soon as possible. The corporation finds that adequate supplies of these parts are available at two plants (nodes 1 and 2), and can be shipped from either to the distribution center (node 12). The objective is to find the shortest possible total route for the shipment of this truck-load of parts, based on the distances (in miles) of the various subroutes, shown in the accompanying table.

SUBROUTE	DISTANCE	SUBROUTE	DISTANCE
1–3	90	6–9	135
1–4	95	6–10	115
2–4	110	7–9	120
2–5	100	7–10	105
3–6	120	7–11	120
3–7	100	8–10	105
4–6	115	8–11	100
4–7	100	9–12	120
4–8	95	10–12	115
5–7	100	11–12	125
5–8	90		

(a) Find an optimal route for this truck-load of parts.

(b) What is the shortest possible achieveable distance from one of the plants to the distribution center?

9.6. A repair crew, beginning an 8-hour shift, has available work on four different types of machines. The accompanying table shows the numbers needing repair, times taken for repair work, and the value per unit to the company of these repairs.

MACHINE TYPE	NUMBER NEEDING REPAIR	REPAIR TIME PER MACHINE (HOURS)	VALUES PER UNIT (IN HUNDREDS OF $) OF REPAIRS
A	4	1	6
B	3	2	10
C	3	1	5
D	4	2	9

(a) If the objective is to schedule, in the available 8 hours, those repairs with the highest total value, use the dynamic programming approach to determine how many machines of each type should be repaired.

(b) Show how this problem can be set up within the integer linear programming framework, and indicate, without going into computational details, how an optimal solution can be obtained within that framework.

9.7. A repair crew works a shift of 10 hours, and has work on five types of machine. The accompanying table shows numbers requiring repair, estimated times taken, and the value of repairs to the firm.

MACHINE TYPE	NUMBER NEEDING REPAIR	REPAIR TIMES PER MACHINE (HOURS)	VALUES (IN HUNDREDS OF $) OF REPAIRS
A	3	3	5
B	5	4	7
C	3	2	4
D	3	3	8
E	4	2	3

If the aim is to schedule, in the 10 hours available, the repairs with the highest total value, how many machines of each type should be repaired?

9.8. Repeat Exercise 9.7, but now assume that the values of repairs for each machine of a particular type are not all equal, but rather are given by the figures in the table below.

MACHINE TYPE	VALUE (IN HUNDREDS OF $) OF REPAIRS
A	5, 4, 3
B	7, 6, 4, 2, 2
C	4, 3, 2
D	8, 7, 5
E	3, 2, 2, 1

9.9. An insurance salesman begins work on a day in which he has available a maximum of 10 hours for contacting potential clients. These clients have been identified as potential purchasers of either life, property, automobile, or business insurance. The table shows the numbers of clients of each type, together with estimates of contact time for, and expected profits from, each.

CLIENT TYPE	NUMBER	HOURS REQUIRED	EXPECTED PROFITS ($)
Life	2	2	50
Property	4	1	20
Automobile	4	1	15
Business	2	3	80

If the aim is to schedule, in the available 10 hours, those clients with the highest possible total expected profit, how many of each type should be contacted?

9.10. After a careful review of his preliminary information, the insurance salesman of the previous exercise concludes that expected profit from one of the life clients is $60, while that from the other is $40. For the two business clients he estimates profits of $95 and $65. If the remaining specifications of Exercise 9.9 are unchanged, how should the salesman now proceed?

9.11. At the beginning of the year, a manufacturer of aircraft engines faces for the next four months, the position shown in the accompanying table.

MONTH	DEMAND FORECAST	PRODUCTION CAPACITY	UNIT PRODUCTION COSTS ($ THOUSANDS)	UNIT INVENTORY HOLDING COSTS ($ THOUSANDS)
January	4	3	100	2
February	3	4	100	3
March	3	4	104	3
April	4	4	104	3

Beginning Inventory: 2 units
Desired Ending Inventory: 2 units

Find the lowest cost production schedule.

9.12. The manufacturer of the previous exercise has the possibility of raising production capacity in one single month, which the manufacturer may designate, by one unit. However, union negotiators are demanding a bonus for the overtime worked. What is the largest total bonus payment that should be offered?

9.13. A car dealer stocks luxury cars, which in January and February are purchased from the manufacturer for $20,000 each. At most 4 cars may be obtained in each of these months. In March, this price is to rise to $21,500, and 5 cars can be purchased. The dealer estimates a demand of 3 units in each of the first two months of the year, and 4 units in March. He estimates that these units can be sold for $22,000 in January and February and $23,000 in March. Inventory holding costs are calculated to be $500 per month. The dealer has no inventory at the beginning of the year, and wishes to have two units in inventory at the end of March. Given these constraints, how many cars should be purchased in each month if total profit is to be maximized?

9.14. A corporation has just hired 10 new sales representatives. The company has four territories to which representatives may be assigned. Estimates are made for the additional profit (in $ thousands) which will result from assigning various numbers of representatives to each territory, as shown in the accompanying table.

					NUMBERS OF REPRESENTATIVES					
TERRITORY	1	2	3	4	5	6	7	8	9	10
A	10	19	27	34	40	46	51	55	58	59
B	12	23	33	41	47	51	54	46	57	58
C	14	27	39	49	58	64	69	73	75	76
D	16	31	42	52	61	70	77	83	86	87

If the objective is to make the assignment yielding the highest possible total addition to profits, how many representatives should be assigned to each territory?

9.15. One of the new sales representatives of the previous exercise fails to report for work, and it is not possible at short notice to hire a replacement. How should the earlier assignment be modified?

9.16. A corporation is considering investments in four projects. Each project is such that investments at four different levels are possible, or no investment at all need be made. The present value of the expected return of investment in a project will depend on the size of the investment made. The table below shows, for each project, the costs of the investments that can be made and the present values of the associated expected returns, both in millions of dollars.

PROJECT 1		PROJECT 2		PROJECT 3		PROJECT 4	
INVEST-MENT COST	EXPECTED RETURN	INVEST-MENT COST	EXPECTED RETURN	INVEST-MENT COST	EXPECTED RETURN	INVEST-MENT COST	EXPECTED RETURN
2	0.50	1	0.30	2	0.55	1	0.28
4	1.08	3	0.86	5	1.30	4	1.12
6	1.59	6	1.72	8	2.10	8	2.12
8	2.02	9	2.54	9	2.50	10	2.88

The corporation has a total of $10 million to invest, and any amount not invested in these projects will be invested in government securities, with an expected present value of return equal to 0.2 million dollars for each million dollars invested. The aim is to find the investment mix with the highest possible expected total return. Use the dynamic programming approach to find the optimal strategy.

Oil Stockpiles: Planning for Disruptions in Supply[1]

The United States economy is heavily dependent on imported oil, and recent history suggests the possibility of disruptions in the supply of imports, with consequent negative effects on the performance of the national economy. One approach to this problem is to hold stockpiles of oil as insurance against future import reductions. However, like other forms of insurance, stockpiles are not costless. The additional demand for oil created in building up a stockpile may drive up its cost. Moreover, there will be physical storage costs in holding large quantities of oil as well as costs incurred through tying up resources in inventory holdings. A rough estimate of the total cost of holding a stockpile of oil would be in the neighborhood of $4 per barrel per year.

The benefits from holding a stockpile of oil follow from the ability to draw on that stockpile when imports are reduced, so that the price of oil is driven up. The expected benefit from stockpiling oil, then, will depend on the view that is taken of the likelihood of future severe reductions in imports.

If a stockpiling policy is in place, then each year decision-makers must determine the amount of oil to be added to or withdrawn from the stockpile. The position, then, is one in which *a sequence of decisions* must be taken, and the authors of this study show how dynamic programming methods can be applied to the solution of this problem. The optimal strategy in any year will depend on the level of the stockpile at the beginning of the year, and the size of the decrease, if any, in the availability of imported oil.

---

[1] This discussion is based on H. P. Chao and A. S. Manne, "Oil Stockpiles and Import Reductions: A Dynamic Programming Approach," *Operations Research, 31* (1983), 632–651.

probability and statistical distributions

CHAPTER TEN

10.1. UNCERTAINTY IN MANAGEMENT SCIENCE

In the previous eight chapters, we examined a range of programming problems. Many diverse illustrations were met, but all contained a common feature. It was assumed that such quantities as costs and profits were *known with certainty*. However, in reality, a great many important factors with which a manager must deal involve *uncertainty*. For example, it will typically not be the case that management can be sure about the future levels of product demand. Again, if a bid on a contract is to be submitted, it will be impossible to predict with perfect precision the levels of competitors' bids.

In subsequent chapters of this book, we must discuss various problems in which some element of uncertainty is present. Our objective in this chapter is to introduce a framework that allows us to analyze such problems. The first step is to provide a *language* for the discussion of uncertainty. This is the language of **probability.** Like all languages, it has a vocabulary and a set of "rules of grammar" which allow clear statements to be made. Therefore it is necessary to introduce some terminology and to become familiar with the manipulation of these terms in the production of probabilistic statements.

10.2. RANDOM EXPERIMENT, OUTCOMES, EVENTS

Suppose that a process which could lead to more than one outcome is to be observed and that there is uncertainty as to which outcome will arise. For example, in the early stages of the development of the Hibernia oil site in the

331

Atlantic Ocean, the Petroleum Directorate of Newfoundland was uncertain about the amount of economically recoverable reserves. The possibilities considered were:

O_1: Less than 500 million barrels
O_2: Between 500 million and 1 billion barrels
O_3: Between 1 billion and 2 billion barrels
O_4: More than 2 billion barrels

These possible outcomes are called **basic outcomes,** and the process giving rise to them is called a **random experiment.** Notice that the basic outcomes are defined in such a way that no two can occur simultaneously, and that the random experiment must necessarily lead to the occurrence of one of these outcomes. The set of these basic outcomes is called the **sample space** of the experiment, and denoted S, so that in our example we write

$$S = [O_1, O_2, O_3, O_4]$$

Definitions

A **random experiment** is a process leading to at least two possible outcomes, with uncertainty as to which will occur.
The possible outcomes of a random experiment are called the **basic outcomes,** and the set of all basic outcomes is called the **sample space** of the experiment.

Often, interest is not in the basic outcomes themselves but in some subset of all the basic outcomes in the sample space. For instance, we might be interested in the possibility that recoverable reserves in the Hibernia oil site exceed 1 billion barrels—a result that will occur if one of the basic outcomes O_3 or O_4 arises. Such sets of basic outcomes are called **events.**

Definition

An **event** is a set of basic outcomes from the sample space, and is said to *occur* if the random experiment gives rise to one of its constituent basic outcomes.

In many applications there is interest simultaneously in two or more events. In our example, consider the event A that recoverable reserves will exceed 1 billion barrels, that is

$$A = [O_3, O_4]$$

and the event B that recoverable reserves will be less than 2 billion barrels, that is

$$B = [O_1, O_2, O_3]$$

One possibility is that all of the events of interest will occur. This will be the case if the basic outcome arising from the random experiment belongs to all of these events. The set of basic outcomes belonging to all events in a group of events is called the **intersection** of these events.

Definition

Let A and B be two events contained in the sample space S of a random experiment. Their **intersection,** denoted $A \cap B$, is the event consisting of the set of all basic outcomes in S belonging to both A and B. Thus the intersection occurs if and only if both A and B occur.

More generally, given some number K of events, $E_1, E_2, \ldots E_K$, their intersection $E_1 \cap E_2 \cap \ldots \cap E_K$ is the set of all basic outcomes that belong to every E_i ($i = 1, 2, \ldots, K$).

In our example, the only basic outcome belonging to both A and B is O_3, so that

$$A \cap B = [O_3]$$

The intersection is thus the event that recoverable reserves will be between 1 and 2 billion barrels.

A useful pictorial representation for thinking about event relations is the **Venn diagram.** Figure 10.1 shows diagrams for pairs of events A and B. In part (a) of the figure, the rectangle S represents the sample space, and two closed figures represent the events A and B. Thus, for example, a basic outcome belonging to the event A will lie inside the corresponding closed figure. The shaded

FIGURE 10.1 Venn diagrams for the intersection of events A and B: (a) $A \cap B$ is the shaded area; (b) A and B are mutually exclusive.

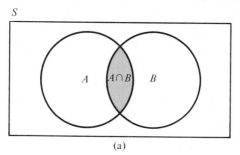

(a)

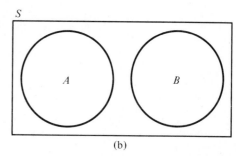

(b)

area, where the two closed figures intersect, is $A \cap B$. Obviously a basic outcome will be in this intersection if and only if it is in both A and B.

It can be the case that two events A and B have no basic outcomes in common. In that case, as in part (b) of Figure 10.1, the corresponding closed figures will not intersect. These events are then said to be **mutually exclusive.**

Definition

The events A and B are said to be **mutually exclusive** if they have no common basic outcomes.

More generally, the K events $E_1, E_2, \ldots, E_K$ are said to be mutually exclusive if every pair of them is a pair of mutually exclusive events.

A further possibility of interest when considering several events is that at least one of them will occur. This will be the case if the basic outcome arising from the random experiment belongs to at least one of these events. The set of outcomes belonging to at least one of a group of events is called their **union.**

Definition

Let A and B be two events contained in the sample space S of a random experiment. Their **union,** denoted $A \cup B$, is the event consisting of the set of all basic outcomes in S belonging to at least one of these two events. Thus the union occurs if and only if either A or B (or both) occurs.

More generally, given some number K of events, $E_1, E_2, \ldots, E_K$, their union $E_1 \cup E_2 \cup \ldots \cup E_K$ is the set of all basic outcomes that belong to at least one of the E_i $(i = 1, 2, \ldots, K)$.

The union of a pair of events is depicted in the Venn diagram of Figure 10.2. It can be seen that a basic outcome will be in $A \cup B$, if and only if, it is in at least one of A and B.

FIGURE 10.2 Venn diagram for the union of events A and B; $A \cup B$ is the shaded area.

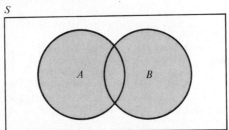

S

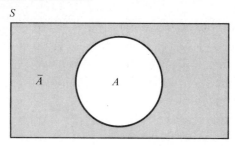

In our example of the Hibernia oil site, with

$$A = [O_3, O_4]; \ B = [O_1, O_2, O_3]$$

each of the four basic outcomes belongs to at least one of these two events, so that their union is

$$A \cup B = [O_1, O_2, O_3, O_4]$$

In a case such as this, where the union of events is the sample space, the events are said to be **collectively exhaustive.** It follows that at least one of these events must occur.

Definition

    Let $E_1, E_2, \ldots, E_K$ be K events in the sample space S. If the union of these K events is S, they are said to be **collectively exhaustive.**

    Next, let A be some event, and suppose that our interest is that this event not occur. This will happen if the basic outcome arising from the random experiment is in the sample space S (as it must be), but *not* in A. The set of basic outcomes belonging to the sample space, but not to event A, is called the **complement** of A, and denoted $\bar{A}$. The complement of the event A is illustrated in the Venn diagram of Figure 10.3.

    It is also possible to consider other unions or intersections, where event complements are involved. Figure 10.4 shows the intersection of the events $\bar{A}$ and B. This intersection contains all those basic outcomes that are both in B and not in A.

    We conclude this section by setting down three useful results involving intersections and unions of events.

1. Let A and B be a pair of events. Then the events $A \cap B$ and $\bar{A} \cap B$ are mutually exclusive, and their union is B. This is demonstrated graphically in Figure 10.5.
2. Let A and B be a pair of events. Then the events A and $\bar{A} \cap B$ are mutually exclusive, and their union is $A \cup B$. This can be seen from the Venn diagram of Figure 10.6.

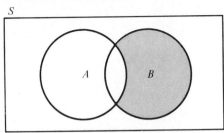

FIGURE 10.4 Venn diagram showing the intersection of $\overline{A}$ and B: $\overline{A} \cap B$ is the shaded area.

FIGURE 10.5 Venn diagram showing $A \cap B$ and $\overline{A} \cap B$.

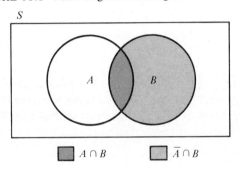

$A \cap B$ $\overline{A} \cap B$

FIGURE 10.6 Venn diagram showing A and $\overline{A} \cap B$.

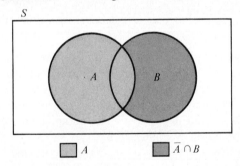

A $\overline{A} \cap B$

3. Let $E_1, E_2, \ldots, E_K$ be K mutually exclusive and collectively exhaustive events, and let A be some other event. Then the K events $E_1 \cap A, E_2 \cap A, \ldots, E_K \cap A$ are mutually exclusive and their union is A. To see this, consider the Venn diagram of Figure 10.7. The large rectangle denoting the complete sample space is subdivided into smaller rectangles depicting the K mutually exclusive and collectively exhaustive events $E_1, E_2, \ldots, E_K$. The event A is represented by a closed figure. Notice that the events comprised of the intersection of A and each E_i are mutually exclusive, and that the union of these events is A, so that

$$(E_1 \cap A) \cup (E_2 \cap A) \cup \ldots \cup (E_K \cap A) = A$$

FIGURE 10.7 Venn diagram showing $A \cap E_1$, $A \cap E_2$, $\ldots$, $A \cap E_K$.

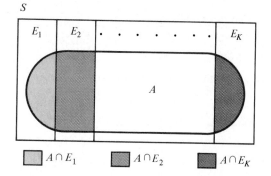

$$A \cap E_1 \qquad A \cap E_2 \qquad A \cap E_K$$

10.3. WHAT IS PROBABILITY?

A random experiment is to be observed, and interest is centered on some particular event. The notion of probability is intended to provide a numerical measure of the likelihood of that event's occurrence. Probability is measured on a continuum between 0 and 1. At the extremes, a probability of 0 signifies that the event certainly will not occur, while a probability of 1 represents its certain occurrence. Between these two extremes, the higher the probability, the more likely is the event to occur.

The concept of probability is most easily viewed through simple games of chance. For example, the statement "When a fair coin is thrown, the probability that a head results is $\frac{1}{2}$" can be interpreted through two distinct notions—**relative frequency** and **subjective probability.**

RELATIVE FREQUENCY

Suppose that a random experiment can be replicated in such a way that after each trial, it is possible to return to the initial conditions and repeat the experiment so that the resulting outcome is unaffected by earlier outcomes. A coin, for example, can be repeatedly thrown in this way.

Suppose that some number N of experiments are carried out in this way, and that the event A of interest occurs in N_A of these trials (where, of course, N_A depends on N). The proportion of occurrences of the event A is therefore

$$\text{Proportion of Occurrences of Event } A \text{ in } N \text{ Trials} = \frac{N_A}{N}$$

The **relative frequency** concept of probability is based on the conduct, at least conceptually, of a very large number of repeated trials. If N is very large, not much variation would be expected in the ratio N_A/N, with increasing N. This is the basis of the relative frequency definition of probability, as set out in the box below.

Definition

    Let N_A denote the number of occurrences of the event A in N trials. Then, according to the **relative frequency** concept, the probability that event A occurs is the limit of the ratio N_A/N, as N becomes infinitely large.

    According to this definition the statement, "The probability is $\frac{1}{2}$ that a head will result from the throw of a coin," means that if the coin is thrown repeatedly, the proportion of heads will become very close to $\frac{1}{2}$ as the number of trials gets very large.

    The relative frequency view of probability is intuitively much less satisfactory in those situations where it is difficult to conceive of replicated experiments. For example, the Hibernia oil site will only be developed once, so that it is hard to visualize in this manner the attachment of a probability to an event such as recoverable reserves being less than 500 million barrels.

SUBJECTIVE PROBABILITY

A different view, that does not depend on the notion of replicated trials, regards probability as a personal subjective concept, expressing a person's degree of belief about the likelihood of occurrence of a particular event. This idea can be understood in terms of **fair bets.**

    To illustrate, if it is asserted that the probability is $\frac{1}{2}$ that a head will result from the throw of a coin, the implication is that the coin appears to be fair and that the throw is just as likely to result in a head as a tail. The notion of repeated trials need not enter into this judgment; concern is only with the single throw. This subjective probability assessment implies that a wager in which \$1 would be won if a head resulted, and \$1 lost otherwise, would be seen as fair.

    Similarly, the assertion that the probability is 0.1 that recoverable reserves in the Hibernia oil site are less than 500 million barrels implies that a fair bet would be one in which \$9 were won if reserves turned out to be this low, and \$1 lost otherwise.

    It should be noted that subjective probabilities are personal; different people considering the same event will not necessarily arrive at the same conclusion about the probability of its occurrence. Of course, for simple games of chance such as the coin throw, sensible people will agree about the probabilities to be attached to events of interest. However, in the case of the assessment of the amount of recoverable reserves in the Hibernia oil site, the conclusion reached will depend on the information available to an individual, and his or her ability to interpret that information.

10.4. PROBABILITY POSTULATES AND THEIR CONSEQUENCES

We must now develop a framework for the assessment and manipulation of probabilities. As a first step, it is necessary to set out three rules (or postulates) that probabilities are required to obey.

PROBABILITY POSTULATES

Let S denote the sample space of a random experiment, O_i the basic outcomes, and A some event. Using the notation $P(A)$ to denote the probability of occurrence of A, the three postulates, on which probability statements are based, are set out below.

---

1. If A is any event in the sample space S

$$0 \leq P(A) \leq 1$$

2. If A is any event in S, and O_i are the basic outcomes

$$P(A) = \sum_A P(O_i)$$

where the notation implies that summation extends over all the basic outcomes in A.

3. $$P(S) = 1$$

The first postulate is merely a requirement that the probability of occurrence of any event is in the range 0 to 1. To motivate the second postulate, recall the relative frequency concept of probability. Suppose that a random experiment is repeated N times, and let N_i be the number of occurrences in N trials of the basic outcome O_i. Then, since the basic outcomes are mutually exclusive, the number of occurrences N_A of the event A is the sum of the N_i over all the basic outcomes belonging to A; that is

$$N_A = \sum_A N_i$$

Dividing through by the number of trials then yields

$$N_A/N = \frac{\sum_A N_i}{N}$$

Under the relative frequency concept, as the number N of trials becomes infinitely large, N_A/N approaches $P(A)$ and N_i/N approaches $P(O_i)$. Hence the second postulate can be viewed as a logical requirement under the relative frequency concept of probability.

The third postulate can be paraphrased as "When a random experiment is carried out, something must happen." Replacing event A by the sample space S in the second postulate, we have

$$P(S) = \sum_S P(O_i)$$

where the summation extends over all the basic outcomes in the sample space. Then, since $P(S)$ is equal to 1 by the third postulate, it follows that

$$\sum_S P(O_i) = 1 \qquad\qquad (10.1)$$

Thus the third postulate implies that the sum of the probabilities for all the basic outcomes in the sample space is 1.

CONSEQUENCES OF THE POSTULATES

We now list and illustrate some immediate consequences of the three probability postulates.

(i) If the sample space S contains a total of n basic outcomes $O_1, O_2, \ldots, O_n$, and these are equally likely to occur, then the probability of occurrence of each one of them is $1/n$; that is,

$$P(O_i) = \frac{1}{n} \quad (i = 1, 2, \ldots, n)$$

Suppose, for example, that a fair 6-sided die is thrown, so that the sample space is

$$S = [1, 2, 3, 4, 5, 6]$$

Then the probability that any one specific basic outcome arises is $\frac{1}{6}$. The result follows from (10.1). In general, if there are n possible basic outcomes, and the probabilities for each are the same, these probabilities must be $1/n$ in order that they sum to 1.

(ii) If the sample space S consists of n equally likely basic outcomes and the event A consists of n_A of these outcomes, then

$$P(A) = \frac{n_A}{n}$$

This conclusion follows immediately from consequence (i) and postulate 2. For example, in the die throw experiment, let A be the event "an even number results," so that

$$A = [2, 4, 6]$$

Then,

$$P(A) = \tfrac{3}{6} = \tfrac{1}{2}$$

(iii) Let A and B be **mutually exclusive** events in the sample space of a random experiment. Then the probability of their union is the sum of their individual probabilities, so that

$$P(A \cup B) = P(A) + P(B)$$

More generally, if $E_1, E_2, \ldots, E_K$ are K mutually exclusive events

$$P(E_1 \cup E_2 \cup \ldots \cup E_K) = P(E_1) + P(E_2) + \ldots + P(E_K)$$

This follows from the second postulate. The probability of the union is

$$P(A \cup B) = \sum_{A \cup B} P(O_i)$$

where summation extends over all the basic outcomes in $A \cup B$. Now, since A and B are mutually exclusive, the right-hand side of this expression can be broken into two parts, giving

$$\sum_{A \cup B} P(O_i) = \sum_{A} P(O_i) + \sum_{B} P(O_i)$$

The first term on the right-hand side of this equation is $P(A)$, and the second term is $P(B)$. In the next section, we will see how this result can be used to establish an expression for the probability of the union of *any* pair of events.

(iv) If $E_1, E_2, \ldots, E_K$ are collectively exhaustive events in the sample space of a random experiment, the probability of their union is 1; that is

$$P(E_1 \cup E_2 \cup \ldots \cup E_K) = 1$$

Since the events are collectively exhaustive, their union is the sample space S. The result then follows from postulate 3.

10.5. PROBABILITY RULES

Often interest is in some compound of events, such as their union or intersection. In this section, we derive expressions for the probabilities of such compound events.

First, consider the complement of an event. If A is some event, and $\overline{A}$ is its complement, then A and $\overline{A}$ are mutually exclusive and collectively exhaustive. Therefore, by consequences (iii) and (iv) of the previous section

$$P(A \cup \overline{A}) = P(A) + P(\overline{A}); \ P(A \cup \overline{A}) = 1$$

Combining these results, the required conclusion follows

Let A be an event, and $\overline{A}$ its complement. Then

$$P(A) + P(\overline{A}) = 1$$

so that

$$P(\overline{A}) = 1 - P(A)$$

For the Hibernia oil site, the Petroleum Directorate of Newfoundland established for the basic outcomes the subjective probabilities shown in Table 10.1. Let A be the event that recoverable reserves exceed 1 billion barrels, so that

$$A = [O_3, O_4]$$

Then, by the second probability postulate,

$$P(A) = P(O_3) + P(O_4) = 0.4 + 0.1 = 0.5$$

The complement of A is the event $\overline{A}$, that reserves do not exceed 1 billion barrels. Hence

$$P(\overline{A}) = 1 - P(A) = 1 - 0.5 = 0.5$$

Next, let A and B be two events in the sample space S. We require an expression for the probability of their union. We will employ two results given

---

TABLE 10.1 Probabilities for recoverable reserves in the Hibernia oil site.

RECOVERABLE RESERVES (BILLIONS OF BARRELS)	PROBABILITY
O_1: Less than 0.5	0.1
O_2: 0.5–1	0.4
O_3: 1–2	0.4
O_4: More than 2	0.1

in Section 10.2. First, the events $A \cap B$ and $\overline{A} \cap B$ are mutually exclusive, and their union is B. It follows from consequence (iii) of Section 10.4 that

$$P(B) = P(A \cap B) + P(\overline{A} \cap B) \qquad (10.2)$$

Second, the events A and $\overline{A} \cap B$ are mutually exclusive, and their union is $A \cup B$. Again, using consequence (iii) of Section 10.4, this implies

$$P(A \cup B) = P(A) + P(\overline{A} \cap B) \qquad (10.3)$$

Combining (10.2) and (10.3) by eliminating $P(\overline{A} \cap B)$ then yields the **addition rule of probability,** set out below

---

Addition Rule of Probability

Let A and B be two events. Then the probability of their union is

$$P(A \cup B) = P(A) + P(B) - P(A \cap B)$$

This result is easily verified for the Hibernia oil site. For the events

$$A = [O_3, O_4]; B = [O_1, O_2, O_3]$$

we have

$$A \cap B = [O_3]; A \cup B = [O_1, O_2, O_3, O_4]$$

Therefore, directly from Table 10.1, we find

$$P(A) = 0.5; P(B) = 0.9$$

$$P(A \cap B) = 0.4; P(A \cup B) = 1$$

It can be seen that these probabilities satisfy the addition rule.

CONDITIONAL PROBABILITY AND THE MULTIPLICATION RULE

Suppose now that our interest is in a pair of events A and B, and that we are given the information that event B has occurred. We might then ask, what is the probability that A will occur, *given that B has occurred?* The probability required here is called a **conditional probability.** The notion underlying this concept is that the likelihood of occurrence of a particular event may depend on whether or not other relevant events have occurred. For example, the price of oil next year is likely to be higher than otherwise if there is a serious war in the Middle East.

Definition

Let A and B be two events. The **conditional probability** of event A, given event B, denoted $P(A \mid B)$, is defined as

$$P(A \mid B) = \frac{P(A \cap B)}{P(B)}$$

provided that $P(B) > 0$. Similarly, the conditional probability of event B, given event A, is defined as

$$P(B \mid A) = \frac{P(A \cap B)}{P(A)}$$

provided that $P(A) > 0$.

This definition of conditional probability can be motivated through relative frequencies. Suppose a random experiment is repeated N times, with N_B occurrences of event B and $N_{A \cap B}$ occurrences of $A \cap B$. Then the proportion of times that A occurs, *when B has occurred*, is $N_{A \cap B}/N_B$. The conditional probability of A given B can be viewed as the limit of this proportion as the number of trials becomes infinitely large. We can write

$$\frac{N_{A \cap B}}{N_B} = \frac{N_{A \cap B}/N}{N_B/N}$$

Now, as N becomes infinitely large, the numerator and denominator of this expression approach, respectively, $P(A \cap B)$ and $P(B)$. Thus, our definition of conditional probability is compatible with the relative frequency concept.

As immediate consequence of the definition of conditional probability is the **multiplication rule of probability,** which relates the probability of an intersection to individual event probabilities and conditional probabilities.

Multiplication Rule of Probability

Let A and B be two events. Then the probability of their intersection is

$$P(A \cap B) = P(A \mid B)P(B)$$

Alternatively, this can be expressed as

$$P(A \cap B) = P(B \mid A)P(A)$$

To illustrate conditional probability calculations, consider a bank which classifies its borrowers as either high risk or low risk. Only 20% of the bank's loans are made to those in the high risk category. Of all its loans, 5% are in default, and 40% of those in default are to high risk borrowers. We want to find the probability that a high risk borrower will default. We know that

$$P(\text{High risk}) = 0.20; \; P(\text{Default}) = 0.05; \; P(\text{High risk} \mid \text{Default}) = 0.40$$

Using the multiplication rule, we find for the probability of the intersection

$$P(\text{High risk} \cap \text{Default}) = P(\text{High risk}|\text{Default})P(\text{Default})$$

$$= (0.40)(0.05) = 0.02$$

We require the conditional probability of default, given that a borrower is in the high risk category. This is

$$P(\text{Default}|\text{High risk}) = P(\text{High risk} \cap \text{Default})/P(\text{High risk})$$

$$= 0.02/0.20 = 0.10$$

Notice, from the multiplication rule, that in general, the probability of an intersection is not equal to the product of the individual event probabilities. However, in a special case, of much practical interest, this is in fact so. The events are then said to be **statistically independent.**

Definition

Let A and B be a pair of events. These events are said to be **statistically independent** if and only if

$$P(A \cap B) = P(A)P(B)$$

It follows from the multiplication rule of probability that equivalent conditions are:

    (i) $P(A|B) = P(A)$ (if $P(B) > 0$)

    (ii) $P(B|A) = P(B)$ (if $P(A) > 0$)

In general, the K events $E_1, E_2, \ldots, E_K$ are statistically independent if and only if

$$P(E_1 \cap E_2 \cap \ldots \cap E_K) = P(E_1)P(E_2) \ldots P(E_K)$$

This definition of statistical independence is best appreciated through conditional probabilities. For example, returning to the case of the bank, in the absence of any other information about a borrower, the probability of default is 0.05. However, if it is known that the borrower is in the high risk category, the probability of default increases to 0.10. Thus, the events "high risk" and "default" are related in the sense that they are not statistically independent. Where the sense is clear, the adjective "statistically" is often dropped, and we refer to "independent events."

10.6. BAYES' THEOREM

We now introduce a mechanism for the modification of probability assessments in the light of additional information. Let A and B be two events, with probabilities of occurrence $P(A)$ and $P(B)$. Then, by the multiplication rule of probabilities

$$P(A \cap B) = P(A|B)P(B)$$

and

$$P(A \cap B) = P(B|A)P(A)$$

Equating the right-hand sides of these two expressions yields

$$P(B|A)P(A) = P(A|B)P(B)$$

Dividing through this equation by $P(A)$ then gives Bayes' theorem

---

Bayes' Theorem

Let A and B be two events. Then

$$P(B|A) = \frac{P(A|B)P(B)}{P(A)} \qquad (10.4)$$

To illustrate, a life insurance salesman finds that of all the sales he makes, 70% are to people who already own policies. Also, 80% of all his contacts are with people who already own policies, and 40% of all contacts result in sales. We need the probability that a sale will result if the contact is a person who already owns a policy. We have

$$P(\text{Already Owns}|\text{Sale}) = 0.70; \ P(\text{Sale}) = 0.40; \ P(\text{Already Owns}) = 0.80$$

It is required to find the conditional probability of a sale, given that a policy is already owned. This is

$$P(\text{Sale}|\text{Already Owns}) = \frac{P(\text{Already Owns}|\text{Sale})P(\text{Sale})}{P(\text{Already Owns})}$$

$$= \frac{(0.70)(0.40)}{0.80} = 0.35$$

The most interesting interpretation of Bayes' theorem is through subjective probabilities. Suppose that the insurance agent meets a contact. In the absence of any other information, the agent will believe that the probability of making a sale is 0.40. This is known as a **prior** probability. However, if the agent is given the information that the contact already owns a policy, the probability of making a sale is reduced to 0.35. This modified, conditional, probability is called a **posterior** probability. Bayes' theorem can therefore be viewed as a mechanism for updating prior probability assessments to posterior probabilities, given additional relevant information.

Bayes' theorem is often written in a different, but equivalent, form. Let $E_1, E_2, \ldots, E_K$ be K mutually exclusive and collectively exhaustive events, and let A be some other event. We want an expression, in the form of Bayes' theorem, for the conditional probability of E_i, given A. This is easily achieved by substituting E_i for B in the formula (10.4) for Bayes' theorem. However, the information available is sometimes in the form of conditional probabilities $P(A|E_j)$ and $P(E_j)$. We now seek an expression for $P(A)$ involving these quantities. First, as was seen in Section 10.2, the events $E_1 \cap A$, $E_2 \cap A$, $\ldots$, $E_K \cap A$ are mutually exclusive, and their union is A. It therefore follows, from consequence (iii) of Section 10.4, that

$$P(A) = P(E_1 \cap A) + P(E_2 \cap A) + \ldots + P(E_K \cap A) \qquad (10.5)$$

Also, by the multiplication rule,

$$P(E_j \cap A) = P(A|E_j)P(E_j) \quad (j = 1, 2, \ldots, K)$$

Thus, on substitution in (10.5),

$$P(A) = P(A|E_1)P(E_1) + P(A|E_2)P(E_2) + \ldots + P(A|E_K)P(E_K) \qquad (10.6)$$

Finally, substitution of the right-hand side of (10.6) for $P(A)$ in (10.4) provides the alternative formulation of Bayes' theorem.

Bayes' Theorem (Alternative Statement)

Let $E_1, E_2, \ldots, E_K$ be K mutually exclusive and collectively exhaustive events, and A be some other event. Then the conditional probability of E_i given A can be written as

$$P(E_i|A) = \frac{P(A|E_i)P(E_i)}{P(A|E_1)P(E_1) + P(A|E_2)P(E_2) + \ldots + P(A|E_K)P(E_K)}$$

As an example of the use of this formula, consider the case of a psychologist who has developed a test designed to help predict whether production line workers in a large industry will perform well. The test was administered by a corporation to all new employees. At the end of their first year of work, these employees were rated by their supervisors: 20% were rated excellent, 40% satisfactory, and 40% poor. Fifty percent of the employees rated excellent passed the psychologist's test, as did 25% of those rated satisfactory, and 10% of those rated poor. We require the probability that an employee who passes the test will be rated poor. From the information given,

$$P(\text{Excellent}) = 0.20; \ P(\text{Satisfactory}) = 0.40; \ P(\text{Poor}) = 0.40$$

$$P(\text{Pass}|\text{Excellent}) = 0.50; \ P(\text{Pass}|\text{Satisfactory}) = 0.25; \ P(\text{Pass}|\text{Poor}) = 0.10$$

We then find the required conditional probability as

$P(\text{Poor}|\text{Pass})$

$$= \frac{P(\text{Pass}|\text{Poor})P(\text{Poor})}{P(\text{Pass}|\text{Excellent})P(\text{Excellent}) + P(\text{Pass}|\text{Satisfactory})P(\text{Satisfactory}) + P(\text{Pass}|\text{Poor})P(\text{Poor})}$$

$$= \frac{(0.10)(0.40)}{(0.50)(0.20) + (0.25)(0.40) + (0.10)(0.40)}$$

$$= \frac{0.04}{0.24} = 0.1667$$

10.7. RANDOM VARIABLES AND THEIR EXPECTATIONS

Suppose that a random experiment is to be carried out, and that numerical values can be attached to the potential outcomes. Before the experiment is conducted there will be uncertainty as to which outcome will arise, and this uncertainty can be characterized by probability statements. When the outcomes are numerical values, these probabilities may be conveniently summarized through the concept of a **random variable.**

Definition

    A **random variable** is a variable that takes on numerical values determined by the outcome of a random experiment.

    An important distinction is between a random variable and its possible values. Notationally we make this distinction by using capital letters, such as X, to denote the random variable, and the corresponding lower case x to represent its possible values. For example, suppose we observe the Dow-Jones Industrials average for five consecutive days and that the quantity of interest is the number of days on which this stock market index rises. Then X denotes the random variable representing the number of days the market rises, and $x = 0$, $x = 1$, . . . , $x = 5$ are its possible values.

A further distinction that must be made is between **discrete** and **continuous** random variables. Our stock market example provides a case of the former; there are just six possible outcomes, and a probability can be attached to each.

Definition

A random variable is **discrete** if it can take on at most countably many values, and a probability can be attached to each possible outcome.

From the definition, it follows that any random variable that can take only finitely many values is discrete. For instance, the number of heads resulting from ten throws of a coin is a discrete random variable. The random variable remains discrete if the number of possible outcomes is infinite but countable. One example is the number of throws of a coin needed before the first head results, where the possible outcomes are 1, 2, 3, . . . , and a probability can be associated with each. (A discrete random variable that can take a countably infinite number of values is the Poisson random variable, to be discussed in Section 10.10.) Other examples of discrete random variables are the following:

1. The number of defectives in a consignment of 20 parts.
2. The number of customers arriving at a supermarket check-out counter in a five-minute interval.
3. The number of material errors detected in a corporation's accounts receivable.
4. The number of claims on a medical insurance policy in a calendar year.

By contrast, suppose we are interested in the number of miles per gallon achieved on average by an automobile of a particular model. The random variable, distance per gallon, is measured on a continuum and is said to be **continuous.**

Definition

A random variable is **continuous** if it can take on any value in an interval.

One cannot attach probabilities to specific values of a continuous random variable. For example, the probability that average miles per gallon achieved by a certain model automobile is exactly 32.174 is 0. It will surely not be *precisely* that figure. However, probabilities can be determined for ranges, so that one could attach a probability to the event "On average the automobile will achieve between 32 and 33 miles per gallon." Other examples of continuous random variables are:

1. The income in a year for a family.
2. The amount of oil imported into the United States in a given week.
3. The change in the price of a share of General Motors stock in a month.
4. The time that elapses between successive arrivals at a supermarket check-out counter.

In a sense, the distinction that has been made between discrete and continuous random variables is somewhat artificial, for rarely is anything truly measured on a continuum. For example, the distance travelled by an automobile on a gallon of gasoline cannot be reported more precisely than the measuring instrument allows. Further, a family's income in a year will certainly be some integer number of cents. However, when measurements are made on a scale so finely graded that differences between adjacent values are of no practical significance, it is convenient to analyze them as if they had truly been made on a continuum. For instance, the difference between a family income of $35,276.21 and $35,276.22 is of virtually no practical importance, even to the family concerned, and the attachment of probabilities to each would be a tedious and worthless exercise. For practical purposes, we will treat as discrete those random variables for which probability statements about individual outcomes have worthwhile meaning, and treat other random variables as continuous.

An important way of summarizing the probability structure of a random variable is through the average value it would take over a very large number of independent trials. This notion of long run average is called the **expected value** of a random variable, and the expected value of the random variable X is denoted $E(X)$. The expectation of a random variable is called the **mean.** It is also of interest to inquire, for a single trial, how far from its mean a random variable is likely to be. One measure of this is the **variance,** which is the expectation of squared discrepancies about the mean. Since the variance is measured in squares of the original units of measurement, it is often convenient to compute its square root which is called the **standard deviation.**

Definitions

The expected value of a random variable is the average value it would take over a very large (essentially infinite) number of independent trials. The expected value of the random variable X is called its **mean,** and denoted μ_X, so that

$$\mu_X = E(X)$$

The **variance** of the random variable X, denoted σ_X^2, is the expectation of squared discrepancies about its mean, so that

$$\sigma_X^2 = E[(X - \mu_X)^2]$$

The **standard deviation** of a random variable is the square root of its variance.

10.8. DISCRETE RANDOM VARIABLES

Let X be a discrete random variable, and x denote one of its possible values. The probability that the random variable X takes the specific value x is written $P(X = x)$. The **probability function** of a discrete random variable provides a listing of the probabilities for all its possible values.

Definition

    The **probability function**, $P_X(x)$, of a discrete random variable X expresses the probability that X takes the value x, as a function of x. Thus,

$$P_X(x) = P(X = x)$$

where the function is evaluated at all possible values x.

Table 10.2 shows probabilities for numbers of breakdowns of a temperamental machine in a week, as estimated from company records. If we let X denote number of breakdowns, the probability function is:

$$P_X(0) = 0.10; \ P_X(1) = 0.30; \ P_X(2) = 0.40$$
$$P_X(3) = 0.15; \ P_X(4) = 0.05$$

Notice that these probabilities must sum to one; that is, for any probability function

$$\sum_x P_X(x) = 1.$$

The probability function can be graphed, as in Figure 10.8. Probabilities for 0, 1, 2, 3, 4 breakdowns are represented by spikes of the corresponding relative heights, while the probability for any other value is zero.

    Since the random variable X takes the specific value x with probability $P_X(x)$, the average value that it would take over a large number of repeated trials can be obtained by summing $xP_X(x)$ over all possible x. A similar argument leads to an expression for the variance.

Mean and Variance of Discrete Random Variables

    The **mean** of the random variable X is given by

$$\mu_X = E(X) = \sum_x xP_X(x)$$

where the notation indicates that summation extends over all possible values x.
    The **variance** of the random variable X is given by

$$\sigma_X^2 = E[(X - \mu_X)^2] = \sum_x (x - \mu_X)^2 P_X(x)$$

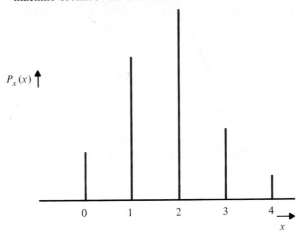

FIGURE 10.8 Probability function for the number of machine breakdowns in a week.

For the machine of Table 10.2, the mean, or expected number of weekly breakdowns is

$$\mu_X = \sum_x x\, P_X(x) = (0)(0.10) + (1)(0.30) + (2)(0.40) + (3)(0.15) + (4)(0.05)$$
$$= 1.75$$

Thus, over a long period of time, we would expect on average 1.75 breakdowns per week. The variance of the number of weekly breakdowns is

$$\sigma_X^2 = \sum_x (x - \mu_X)^2 P_X(x) = (0 - 1.75)^2(0.10) + (1 - 1.75)^2(0.30)$$
$$+ (2 - 1.75)^2(0.40) + (3 - 1.75)^2(0.15) + (4 - 1.75)^2(0.05) = 0.9875$$

so that the standard deviation is $\sqrt{(0.9875)} = 0.9937$ breakdown.

The standard deviation is useful in comparing variabilities about the mean of two or more **probability distributions.** For example, consider a second machine for which the probability function for the number of breakdowns in a week is

$$P_X(1) = 0.25; \; P_X(2) = 0.75$$

The mean of this distribution is also 1.75. However, here there is much less variability about the mean, as reflected by the standard deviation, which is

$$\sigma_X = \sqrt{(1 - 1.75)^2(0.25) + (2 - 1.75)^2(0.75)} = 0.4330$$

TABLE 10.2 Probabilities for the number of machine breakdowns in a week.

NUMBER OF BREAKDOWNS (x):	0	1	2	3	4
PROBABILITY ($P_X(x)$):	.10	.30	.40	.15	.05

In the next two sections, we will introduce two important discrete random variables.

10.9. THE BINOMIAL DISTRIBUTION

A class of problems that arises very frequently is where a single "experiment" can give rise to just two possible outcomes—for example a part may or may not be defective, a contact with a potential client may or may not result in a sale. The "experiment" is to be repeated several times, under identical conditions, and interest is centered on the number of outcomes arising of each possible type. The probability of a particular number of outcomes of a given type arising is described by the **binomial distribution.** We summarize in the box below the properties of this distribution.

The Binomial Distribution and Its Properties

Suppose that a random experiment can result in two possible mutually exclusive and collectively exhaustive outcomes, denoted "success" and "failure." Let p be the probability of a success resulting in a single trial. If n independent trials are carried out, each with probability of success p, the distribution of the number of successes resulting is called the **binomial distribution.** The probability function of this distribution is[1]

$$P_X(x) = \frac{n!}{x!(n - x)!} p^x (1 - p)^{n-x} \text{ for } x = 0, 1, 2, \ldots, n$$

The mean number of successes in n trials is

$$\mu_X = E(X) = np$$

and the variance is

$$\sigma_X^2 = E[(X - \mu_X)^2] = np(1 - p)$$

To illustrate the computation of binomial probabilities, a corporation which sells encyclopedias sends salespeople to those households which have indicated a preliminary interest. Records indicate that 25% of these household calls will result in sales. A salesperson is to make 5 calls. We can use the binomial distribution to find probabilities for different numbers of sales resulting from these calls. Let X denote the number of sales. Then, with

$$n = 5; p = 0.25$$

---

[1] In the factorial notation used here, $0! = 1$, and, for any positive integer x,

$$x! = x(x - 1)(x - 2) \ldots 2.1$$

we find

$$P(0 \text{ sales}) = P_X(0) = \frac{5!}{0!5!} (.25)^0(.75)^5 = (.75)^5 = .2373$$

$$P(1 \text{ sale}) = P_X(1) = \frac{5!}{1!5!} (.25)(.75)^4 = (5)(.25)(.75)^4 = .3955$$

$$P(2 \text{ sales}) = P_X(2) = \frac{5!}{2!3!} (.25)^2(.75)^3 = (10)(.25)^2(.75)^3 = .2637$$

$$P(3 \text{ sales}) = P_X(3) = \frac{5!}{3!2!} (.25)^3(.75)^2 = (10)(.25)^3(.75)^2 = .0879$$

$$P(4 \text{ sales}) = P_X(4) = \frac{5!}{4!1!} (.25)^4(.75) = (5)(.25)^4(.75) = .0146$$

$$P(5 \text{ sales}) = P_X(5) = \frac{5!}{5!0!} (.25)^5(.75)^0 = (.25)^5 = .0010$$

TABULATED PROBABILITIES FOR BINOMIAL DISTRIBUTION

If the number of trials n is not very small, the calculation of binomial probabilities is computationally very tedious. To facilitate problem solving, Table 1 in the Appendix at the back of this volume gives probabilities for values of n up to 20 and selected values of p up to and including 0.5. For higher values of p, binomial probabilities can be found using the rule:

$P[x$ successes in n trials when probability of success in a single trial is $p]$ $= P[(n - x)$ successes in n trials when probability of success in a single trial is $(1 - p)]$

To illustrate, the probability of 7 successes in 12 trials where $p = 0.6$ is the same as the probability of 5 successes in 12 trials with $p = 0.4$. Thus, setting $x = 7$, $n = 12$, and $p = 0.6$ in the above formula yields

$P[7$ successes in 12 trials when probability of success in a single trial is 0.6] $= P[5$ successes in 12 trials when probability of success in a single trial is 0.4]

This can be read directly from Table 1 by locating from the first two columns of the table the row corresponding to $n = 12$ and $x = 5$; we then see from the column corresponding to $p = 0.40$ that the required probability is 0.2270.

An important application of the binomial distribution is to **acceptance sampling.** When a company or distributor receives a very large shipment of goods from a supplier, it must decide, based on information about the quality of these goods, whether to accept delivery. If the consignment is very large, it would often be prohibitively expensive to thoroughly inspect every item, so a random

TABLE 10.3 Acceptance probabilities for sample size 20; the decision rule is to accept when at most 1 defective is found in the sample.

PROPORTION P OF DEFECTIVES IN SHIPMENT	0	.05	.10	.15	.20	.25	.30	.35	.40
PROBABILITY OF ACCEPTANCE	1	.7359	.3918	.1756	.0691	.0243	.0076	.0022	.0005

sample[2] is taken, and the sample members are inspected. Based on the findings from the sample a decision is made as to whether to accept the shipment. It is possible to calculate, for any decision rule of this kind, the probability of accepting a shipment with any given proportion of defectives. This is so, since if the proportion of defectives in the shipment is p, the distribution of the number X of defectives in a sample of n items is binomial.

We illustrate the calculations through the case of a company which, on receipt of a very large shipment of items, decides to accept delivery if, in a random sample of 20 items, not more than one is defective. The shipment is accepted, then, if the number of defectives in the sample is either 0 or 1. Thus, if $P_X(x)$ is the probability function for the number of defectives X in the sample, it follows that

$$P(\text{Shipment accepted}) = P_X(0) + P_X(1)$$

Suppose that the proportion of defectives in the shipment is in fact $p = .10$. Then, for $n = 20$, we read directly from Table 1 of the Appendix

$$P_X(0) = .1216; \; P_X(1) = .2702$$

Therefore, given this decision rule, the probability that the shipment will be accepted is

$$P(\text{Shipment accepted}) = P_X(0) + P_X(1) = .1216 + .2702 = .3918$$

Thus, the probability is .3918 that the company will accept a shipment when 10% of its items are defective. Table 10.3 shows acceptance probabilities, computed in the same manner, for different proportions p of defectives in the shipment. The probability of acceptance is graphed against the proportion of defectives in the shipment in Figure 10.9.

Any number of curves relating acceptance probabilities to proportion of defectives can be constructed by choosing different sample sizes and different rules for determining acceptance. Thus, a company is able to choose a scheme with the desired balance between the costs of accepting shipments with particular proportions of defectives, and of carrying out the sample checks on quality.

---

[2] By a random sample of n items we mean that the sample is chosen in such a way that every set of n items in the shipment is equally likely to be selected.

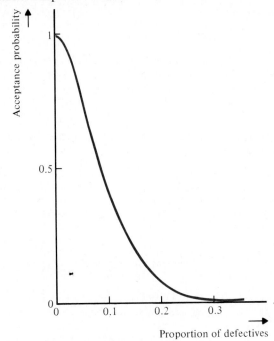

FIGURE 10.9 Acceptance probability as a function of the proportion of defectives in a shipment when the shipment is accepted if there is not more than one defective in a random sample of 20 items.

10.10. THE POISSON DISTRIBUTION

A random variable of considerable practical importance arises when we are interested in the number of occurrences of an event over a given interval of time, such as the number of arrivals in a minute of customers at a supermarket checkout counter. Experience suggests that for a wide range of situations of this sort, the **Poisson probability distribution** provides a good representation of the probabilities for numbers of occurrences.

Consider the situation illustrated in Figure 10.10. Time is measured along the horizontal axis, and we are interested in the period beginning at time 0 and ending at time t. Occurrences of the events of interest through time are indicated by . . . , so that in this illustration five events occur in the relevant time period. Suppose that the following assumptions can be made:

1. For any very small time interval, represented by a *small segment* of the time axis between zero and t in Figure 10.10, the probability that one event will occur in this small interval is proportional to its length.
2. The probability of two or more occurrences in such a small interval is negligibly small compared with the probability of one occurrence.
3. The numbers of occurrences in any nonoverlapping time intervals are independent of one another.

FIGURE 10.10 Illustration of random occurrences ● of an
event over time.

If these assumptions hold, it is possible to demonstrate that the probability of x
occurrences in the range from 0 to t is

$$P(x \text{ occurrences}) = \frac{e^{-\lambda}\lambda^x}{x!}$$

where λ is the expected, or mean, number of occurrences in the interval and
$e = 2.71828 \ldots$ is the base of the natural logarithms. Table 2 of the Appendix
at the end of this volume gives values of $e^{-\lambda}$ for $0 \le \lambda \le 10$. The statistical
distribution with these probabilities is called the **Poisson distribution.**

The Poisson Distribution

The random variable X follows the Poisson distribution if it has probability
function

$$P_X(x) = \frac{e^{-\lambda}\lambda^x}{x!} \text{ for } x = 0, 1, 2, \ldots$$

where λ is any positive number.
    This distribution has mean

$$\mu_X = E(X) = \lambda$$

and variance

$$\sigma_X^2 = E[(X - \mu_X)^2] = \lambda$$

Suppose, for example, that customers arrive at a supermarket check-out
counter at an average rate of $\lambda = 2$ per minute. We can then find probabilities
for the number X of arrivals in any given minute from

$$P_X(x) = \frac{e^{-2}(2)^x}{x!} \text{ for } x = 0, 1, 2, \ldots$$

From Table 2 of the Appendix, $e^{-2} = 0.135335$, so that

$$P(0 \text{ arrivals}) = P_X(0) = \frac{e^{-2}(2)^0}{0!} = \frac{(0.135335)(1)}{1} = 0.135335$$

$$P(1 \text{ arrival}) = P_X(1) = \frac{e^{-2}(2)^1}{1!} = \frac{(0.135335)(2)}{1} = 0.270670$$

$$P(2 \text{ arrivals}) = P_X(2) = \frac{e^{-2}(2)^2}{2!} = \frac{(0.135335)(4)}{2} = 0.270670$$

$$P(3 \text{ arrivals}) = P_X(3) = \frac{e^{-2}(2)^3}{3!} = \frac{(0.135335)(8)}{6} = 0.180447$$

$$P(4 \text{ arrivals}) = P_X(4) = \frac{e^{-2}(2)^4}{4!} = \frac{(0.135335)(16)}{24} = 0.090223$$

and so on. Since the probabilities for the different possible outcomes must sum to 1, it follows that the probability of more than 4 arrivals in a given minute is

$$P(X > 4) = 1 - P_X(0) - P_X(1) - P_X(2) - P_X(3) - P_X(4)$$

$$= 1 - 0.135335 - 0.270670 - 0.270670 - 0.180447 - 0.090223$$

$$= 0.052655$$

10.11. CONTINUOUS RANDOM VARIABLES

By definition, continuous random variables are such that it is meaningless to attach probabilities to specific values. However, it is meaningful to discuss the probability that such a variable falls in any given range. Probabilities of this sort, for any continuous random variable are fully described in either its **cumulative distribution function** or its **probability density function.**

Definitions

    The **cumulative distribution function,** $F_X(x)$, of a continuous random variable X expresses the probability that X does not exceed[3] the value x, as a function of x; that is

$$F_X(x) = P(X \leq x)$$

It follows that, if a and b are any pair of numbers, with $a < b$, the probability that the random variable X lies between them is

$$P(a < X < b) = F_X(b) - F_X(a)$$

    The **probability density function** $f_X(x)$ of the random variable X is a function with the following properties

(i) $f_X(x) \geq 0$ for all values of x
(ii) Suppose the density function is graphed. Let a and b be two possible values of the random variable X, with $a < b$. Then the probability that X lies between a and b is the area under the density function between these points. It follows that the total area under a probability density function is one.

---

[3] For continuous random variables, the probability of taking any specific value is zero. It therefore does not matter whether we write $P(X \leq x)$ or $P(X < x)$.

FIGURE 10.11 Probability density functions: (a) the shaded area is $P(a < X < b)$; (b) the shaded area is $F_X(a) = P(X < a)$.

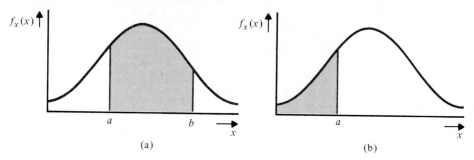

(a)

(b)

To illustrate the definition of a probability density function, part (a) of Figure 10.11 shows the plot of such a function for a continuous random variable. Two possible values, a and b, are shown, and the shaded area under the curve between these points is the probability that the random variable lies in the interval between them. It further follows from our definition that the cumulative distribution function, evaluated at the point a, is the area under the probability density function to the left of this point.[4] This is illustrated in part (b) of Figure 10.11.

In the following two sections we introduce two important continuous random variables.

10.12. THE NORMAL DISTRIBUTION

We now introduce a probability distribution which plays a very important role in statistical analysis. The **normal distribution** is defined in the box below.

Probability Density Function of the Normal Distribution

If the random variable X has probability density function

$$f_X(x) = \frac{1}{\sqrt{2\pi\sigma^2}} e^{-(x-\mu)^2/2\sigma^2} \text{ for } -\infty < x < \infty$$

---

[4] Readers with a knowledge of calculus will recognize that the probability that a random variable lies in a given range is the *integral* of the probability density function between the endpoints of that range; that is

$$P(a < X < b) = \int_a^b f_X(x)dx$$

and

$$F_X(a) = \int_{-\infty}^a f_X(x)dx$$

where μ and σ^2 are any numbers such that $-\infty < \mu < \infty$, $0 < \sigma^2 < \infty$, and $e =$ 2.71828 . . . , $\pi = 3.14159$ . . . are physical constants, then X is said to follow a **normal distribution.**

The distribution has the following properties:

(i) The mean of the random variable is μ; that is

$$E(X) = \mu$$

(ii) The variance of the random variable is σ^2; that is

$$E[(X - \mu)^2] = \sigma^2$$

(iii) The probability density function has the form of a bell-shaped curve, symmetric about the mean μ.

It can be seen from the definition that there is not just a single normal distribution, but a family of distributions. A specific member of that family is characterized by its mean, μ, and variance, σ^2. The mean of the distribution specifies its center, while the variance gives a measure of spread or dispersion about the mean. Thus, the values taken by μ and σ^2 have different effects on the probability density function of a normal random variable. Figure 10.12 (a) shows probability density functions for two normal distributions with a common variance, but different means. It can be seen that increasing the mean, while keeping the variance fixed, shifts the density function to the right but does not affect its shape. Figure 10.12 (b) shows the density functions of two normal random variables with the same mean but different variances. Each density function is symmetric about the common mean, but that with the larger variance is more disperse.

An important practical problem is to find the probability that a normal random variable X, with mean μ and variance σ^2, lies between two numbers, say a and b, with $a < b$. Thus we require

$$P(a < X < b) = F_X(b) - F_X(a)$$

where $F_X(x)$ is the cumulative distribution function of the normal random variable. Unfortunately, there does not exist a convenient algebraic expression allowing the evaluation of this cumulative distribution function. The difficulty is resolved by expressing probabilities for any normal distribution in terms of probabilities for a specific distribution, the **standard normal.**

The Standard Normal Distribution

Let Z be a normally distributed random variable with mean 0 and variance 1. Then Z is said to follow a **standard normal distribution.**

If the cumulative distribution function of this random variable is denoted $F_Z(z)$, and a^* and b^* are any two numbers, with $a^* < b^*$, then

$$P(a^* < Z < b^*) = F_Z(b^*) - F_Z(a^*)$$

FIGURE 10.12 (a) Normal distributions with means 5 and 9, and variance 1. (b) Normal distributions with mean 5, and variances 1 and 4.

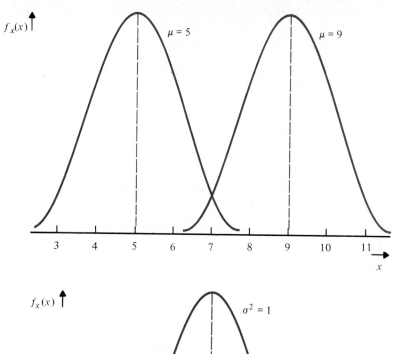

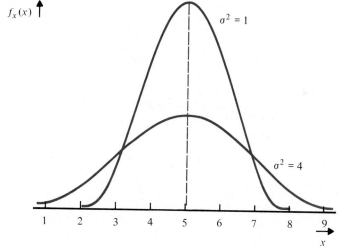

The cumulative distribution function of the standard normal is tabulated in Table 3 of the Appendix at the back of this volume. The table gives values of $F_Z(z)$ for nonnegative values of z. For example

$$P(Z < 1.20) = F_Z(1.20) = 0.8849$$

Values of the cumulative distribution function for negative z can be inferred from the symmetry of the probability density function, and the fact that since

$$P(-\infty < Z < \infty) = 1$$

the total area under the density function curve must be 1. As illustrated in Figure 10.13, because the density function of the standard normal random variable is symmetric about its mean, 0, it follows, for any positive number z that

$$P(Z < -z) = P(Z > z)$$

But, since the total area under the density function is 1,

$$P(Z > z) = 1 - P(Z < z) = 1 - F_Z(z)$$

It therefore follows, for positive z, that

$$P(Z < -z) = F_Z(-z) = 1 - F_Z(z)$$

Thus, for example, the probability that a standard normal random variable takes a value less than -1.20 is

$$P(Z < -1.20) = F_Z(-1.20) = 1 - F_Z(1.20) = 1 - 0.8849 = 0.1151$$

We now show how probabilities for any normal random variable can be expressed in terms of those for the standard normal random variable. Let the random variable X be normally distributed with mean μ and variance σ^2. It can then be shown that the random variable

$$Z = \frac{X - \mu}{\sigma}$$

FIGURE 10.13 For a standard normal random variable, $P(Z > 1.5) = P(Z < -1.5)$.

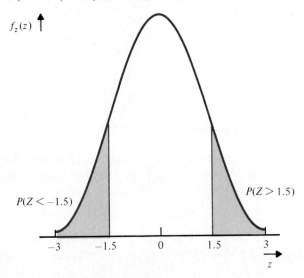

has a standard normal distribution. Suppose we require the probability that X lies between the numbers a and b. Then

$$P(a < X < b) = P\left(\frac{a - \mu}{\sigma} < \frac{X - \mu}{\sigma} < \frac{b - \mu}{\sigma}\right)$$

$$= P\left(\frac{a - \mu}{\sigma} < Z < \frac{b - \mu}{\sigma}\right)$$

Finding Range Probabilities for Normal Random Variables

Let X be a normal random variable with mean μ and variance σ^2. Then the random variable $Z = (X - \mu)/\sigma$ has a standard normal distribution. It therefore follows that

$$P(a < X < b) = P\left(\frac{a - \mu}{\sigma} < Z < \frac{b - \mu}{\sigma}\right)$$

$$= F_Z\left(\frac{b - \mu}{\sigma}\right) - F_Z\left(\frac{a - \mu}{\sigma}\right)$$

To illustrate, a company produces lightbulbs whose lifetimes follow a normal distribution with mean 1200 hours and standard deviation 250 hours. One lightbulb is to be randomly selected from the company's output. What is the probability that its lifetime will be between 1100 and 1400 hours? Letting X denote the lifetime of the bulb, we require $P(1100 < X < 1400)$. This probability is shown in Figure 10.14 (a). We have

$$P(1100 < X < 1400) = P\left(\frac{1100 - \mu}{\sigma} < Z < \frac{1400 - \mu}{\sigma}\right)$$

so that, with $\mu = 1200$ and $\sigma = 250$

$$P(1100 < X < 1400) = P(-0.4 < Z < 0.8)$$

Figure 10.14 (b) shows this probability in terms of the standard normal distribution.

Thus

$$P(1100 < X < 1400) = F_Z(0.8) - F_Z(-0.4)$$

$$= F_Z(0.8) - [1 - F_Z(0.4)]$$

$$= 0.7881 - (1 - 0.6554) = 0.4435$$

using Table 3 of the Appendix. We can interpret this as implying that 44.35% of all lightbulbs have lifetimes between 1100 and 1400 hours.

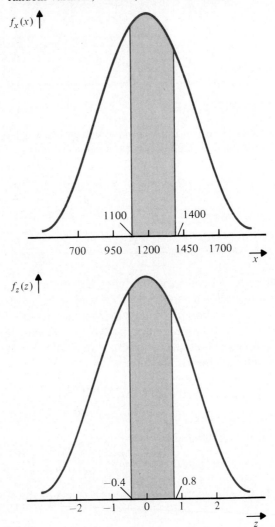

FIGURE 10.14 (a) Probability density function of normal random variable ($\mu = 1200$, $\sigma = 250$), with $P(1100 < X < 1400)$. (b) Probability density function of standard normal random variable, with $P(-0.4 < Z < 0.8)$.

Alternatively, we might require, for example, that lifetime such that 10% of all bulbs last more than this amount. This is the number b shown in Figure 10.15. Thus, we want to find the number b satisfying

$$0.10 = P(X > b)$$

so that

$$0.90 = P(X < b)$$

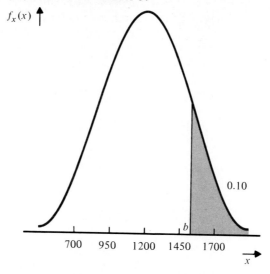

FIGURE 10.15 The probability is 0.10 that a normal random variable with mean 1200 and standard deviation 250 exceeds the number b.

In terms of the standard normal, then,

$$0.90 = P\left(Z < \frac{b - \mu}{\sigma}\right)$$

$$= P\left(Z < \frac{b - 1200}{250}\right)$$

$$= F_Z\left(\frac{b - 1200}{250}\right)$$

It therefore follows from Table 3 of the Appendix that

$$\frac{b - 1200}{250} = 1.28$$

so that

$$b = (1.28)(250) + 1200 = 1520$$

We therefore conclude that only 10% of all the lightbulbs have lifetimes of more than 1520 hours.

This example is readily generalized. Define z_α as that number exceeded with probability α by a standard normal random variable, so that

$$\alpha = P(Z > z_\alpha)$$

Then, if X is a normal random variable with mean μ and variance σ^2, it follows that

$$\alpha = P(X > \mu + \sigma z_\alpha)$$

Thus, the probability is α that this random variable exceeds $\mu + \sigma z_\alpha$.

The importance of the normal distribution in statistical analysis is a consequence of the **Central Limit Theorem**. This states that under very general conditions, the average of a large number of independent[5] random variables, whatever their own distribution, will have a distribution that is close to normal.

10.13. THE EXPONENTIAL DISTRIBUTION

Another class of continuous distributions of considerable practical interest is called the **exponential distribution.**

Definition

The random variable X is said to follow an **exponential distribution** if its probability density function is given by

$$f_X(x) = \lambda e^{-\lambda x} \quad \text{for } x \geq 0$$

for any positive number λ.
The cumulative distribution function is

$$F_X(x) = P(X \leq x) = 1 - e^{-\lambda x}$$

and the distribution has mean

$$E(X) = \frac{1}{\lambda}$$

This distribution is related to the Poisson distribution, in the sense that if the number of occurrences of an event in a given time interval follows a Poisson distribution with mean λ, the time between successive occurrences obeys an exponential distribution with parameter λ. In Section 10.10 we considered an example where customers arrived at a supermarket check-out counter at an average rate of 2 per minute. Now, let the random variable X denote the time in minutes between successive arrivals. This random variable has probability density function:

$$f_X(x) = 2e^{-2x} \quad \text{for } x \geq 0$$

The probability density function is graphed in Figure 10.16.
The mean of this distribution is

$$E(X) = \tfrac{1}{2} \text{ minute}$$

so that the average time between successive arrivals is 30 seconds.

---

[5] Random variables are independent if their falling in particular ranges are independent events.

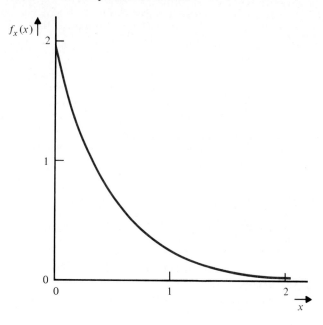

FIGURE 10.16 Probability density function of exponential distribution with parameter $\lambda = 2$.

The cumulative distribution function is

$$F_X(x) = 1 - e^{-2x}$$

We can thus find, for example, the probability that less than 15 seconds (0.25 minute) will elapse between successive arrivals. This is

$$F_X(0.25) = 1 - e^{-2(0.25)} = 1 - e^{-0.5}$$

$$= 1 - 0.606531 = 0.393469$$

from Table 2 of the Appendix. Thus the probability is approximately 0.39 that less than 15 seconds will elapse between successive arrivals at the check-out counter.

In Chapter 15 we will make extensive use of the Poisson and exponential distributions in analyzing the behavior of queues.

EXERCISES

10.1. A fair 6-sided die is thrown. Let A be the event "the result is an even number" and B be the event "the number resulting is at least 4."
   (a) Define the union and the intersection of the events A and B.
   (b) Find the probability of the union of A and B.
   (c) Find the probability of the intersection of A and B.

(d) Find the conditional probability of A given B.

(e) Are the events A and B statistically independent?

10.2. A card is drawn at random from a full deck of 52 cards. Let A be the event "the card drawn is a diamond" and B be the event "the card drawn is an ace."

(a) Find the probability of A.

(b) Find the probability of B.

(c) Find the probability of the intersection of A and B.

(d) Find the conditional probability of A given B.

(e) Are the events A and B statistically independent?

10.3. A contractor's probability assessment of the number of days in which a project will be completed is shown in the table. Let A be the event "the project will take at most 2 days to complete" and B the event "the project will take either 3 or 4 days to complete."

NUMBER OF DAYS	1	2	3	4	5
PROBABILITY	0.15	0.20	0.40	0.15	0.10

(a) Define the complement of event A and find its probability.

(b) Find the union of events A and B. Are these events collectively exhaustive?

(c) Find the intersection of events A and B. Are these events mutually exclusive?

(d) Find the probability of the union of A and B.

(e) Find the probability of the intersection of A and B.

10.4. Parts leaving an assembly line are independently examined by two inspectors. Each inspector detects 85% of the defective parts while both detect 75% of the defective parts.

(a) What is the probability that a defective part will be detected by at least one of the inspectors?

(b) What is the probability that a defective part not detected by the first inspector will be detected by the second?

10.5. State, with reasons, whether each of the following statements is true or false.

(a) The probability of the union of two events cannot be less than the probability of their intersection.

(b) The probability of the union of two events cannot be more than the sum of their individual probabilities.

(c) The probability of the intersection of two events cannot be more than either of their individual probabilities.

(d) If a pair of events are mutually exclusive they must also be collectively exhaustive.

(e) The conditional probability of A given B must be at least as big as the probability of A.

(f) The probability of the intersection of two events cannot exceed the product of their individual probabilities.

10.6. Show that the probability of the union of the events A and B can be written

$$P(A \cup B) = P(A) + P(B)[1 - P(A|B)]$$

10.7. A company places a "rush order" to a supplier for two sizes of paper. Consignments of each size of paper are to be sent immediately when they are available.

Experience suggests that the probability is 0.8 that at least one of these consignments will arrive within a week. It is estimated that if the consignment of smaller paper arrives within a week, the probability is 0.4 that the consignment of larger paper will arrive within a week. Also, if the larger paper arrives within a week, the probability is 0.6 that the smaller paper will arrive within a week.

(a) What is the probability that the smaller paper will arrive within a week?

(b) What is the probability that the larger paper will arrive within a week?

(c) What is the probability that both consignments will arrive within a week?

10.8. In a particular city, 70% of all households have color television and 60% of all households have stereos. If 50% of all households have both a color television and a stereo, what is the probability that a randomly chosen household will have at least one of these?

10.9. A survey of shoppers in a convenience grocery store shows that 75% purchase milk and 45% purchase bread. Also 35% of shoppers purchase both milk and bread.

(a) What is the probability that a randomly chosen shopper purchases at least one of these items?

(b) What is the probability that a shopper who purchases milk also purchases bread?

(c) What is the probability that a shopper who purchases bread also purchases milk?

(d) Are the events ''purchase bread'' and ''purchase milk'' statistically independent?

10.10. Candidates for employment in a large corporation are required to pass through two preliminary screening procedures—a written aptitude test and an oral interview. Corporation records indicate that 60% of the candidates are unsuccessful on the written test, 40% are unsuccessful in the interview, and 30% are unsuccessful in both. The corporation gives further consideration only to candidates who are successful in both screening procedures.

(a) What is the probability that a randomly chosen candidate will receive further consideration?

(b) What is the probability that a candidate who is successful in the written aptitude test will receive further consideration?

(c) What is the probability that a candidate who is successful in the oral interview will receive further consideration?

10.11. (a) Develop an example showing two events that are mutually exclusive but not statistically independent.

(b) Develop an example showing two events that are statistically independent but not mutually exclusive.

10.12. A conference began at noon with two parallel sessions. The session on Network Models was attended by 45% of the delegates, while the session on Simulation was attended by 50%. The single evening session, on Management Information Systems, was attended by 85% of the delegates.

(a) If attendance at the sessions on Network Models and Simulation are mutually exclusive, what is the probability a randomly chosen delegate attended at least one of them?

(b) If attendance at the sessions on Network Models and Management Information Systems are statistically independent, what is the probability a randomly chosen delegate attended at least one of them?

(c) Of those attending the simulation session, 95% also attended the Management Information Systems session. What is the probability that a randomly chosen delegate attended at least one of these sessions?

10.13. In examining past records of a corporation's account balances, an auditor finds that 15% of them have contained material errors. Of those balances with material errors, 60% were viewed as unusual values, based on historical figures. Of all the account balances, 20% were unusual values.

   (a) If the figure for a particular balance appears unusual on this basis, what is the probability that it contains a material error?

   (b) If the figure for a particular balance does not appear unusual on this basis, what is the probability that it contains a material error?

10.14. An inspector working on an assembly line has to make quick decisions about the acceptability of components as they pass his station. It was found that he rejected 10% of all the components. On detailed examination, it was found that of the rejected components, 80% were in fact defective. Also, 5% of the components accepted by this inspector turned out to be defective.

   (a) If a component is defective, what is the probability that it will be accepted by this inspector?

   (b) If a component is not defective, what is the probability it will be rejected by this inspector?

10.15. A stock market analyst examined the prospects of the shares of a large number of corporations. When the performance of these stocks was reviewed one year later, it was found that 25% performed much better than the market average, 25% much worse, and the other 50% about the same as the average. Of the stocks that did much better than the market average, 40% were rated "good buys" by this analyst, as were 20% of those that performed about the same as the average, and 10% of those that did much worse.

   (a) If a stock is rated "good buy" by this analyst, what is the probability that it will perform much better than the market average?

   (b) If a stock is rated "good buy" by this analyst, what is the probability that it will perform much worse than the market average?

   (c) If a stock is not rated "good buy" by this analyst, what is the probability that it will perform much better than the market average?

10.16. In assessing the prospects for inflation next year, a consultant concluded that the probabilities that inflation will be higher than in the current year are 0.15 if there is a small rise in energy prices, 0.65 if there is a moderate rise in energy prices, and 0.90 if there is a large rise in energy prices. The consultant also believes that the probabilities for small, moderate, and large rises in energy prices are, respectively, 0.4, 0.4, and 0.2.

   (a) According to this consultant, what is the probability that inflation next year will be higher than in the current year?

   (b) According to this consultant, if the inflation rate next year is higher than in the current year, what is the probability that the rise in the price of energy will have been large?

10.17. A publisher sends advertising material for an introductory business statistics text to 85% of all professors teaching the appropriate course. Of the professors who received the advertising material, 15% adopted the text, as did 5% of those professors who did not receive the advertising materials. What is the probability that a professor who adopts the text has not received the advertising material?

10.18. A manufacturer produces boxes of candy, each containing 10 pieces. Two machines are employed for this purpose. After a large batch has been made, one of the machines, which produces 30% of the total output, was found to have a fault which led to the introduction of an impurity into 10% of the pieces of candy it produces. From a single box of candy, one piece is chosen at random and tested. If that piece contains no impurity, what is the probability that the box from which it came is part of the output of the faulty machine?

10.19. In a large city, 5% of the inhabitants have contracted a particular disease. A test for this disease is positive for 80% of people who have the disease, and negative for 90% of people who do not have the disease.

(a) What is the probability that a person for whom the test result is positive has the disease?

(b) What is the probability that a person for whom the test result is negative does not have the disease?

10.20. A professor finds that she awards a course grade of A to 15% of the students in an introductory business course. Of those who obtain a course grade of A, 70% obtained an A on the midterm examination. Also, 10% of students who failed to obtain a course grade of A obtained an A on the midterm examination. What is the probability that a student who obtained an A on the midterm examination will obtain a course grade of A?

10.21. A review of textbooks in a segment of the business area found that 80% of all pages of text were error-free, 18% of all pages contained one error, and the remaining 2% of all pages contained two errors. A page from one of these books is chosen at random. Let the random variable X denote the number of errors on that page.

(a) Write down the probability function for X.

(b) Find the expected number of errors on this page.

(c) Find the standard deviation of the number of errors on this page.

10.22. An automobile dealer computes the proportion of new cars sold that have been returned various numbers of times for the correction of defects during the warranty period. The results are shown in the table

NUMBER OF RETURNS	0	1	2	3	4
PROPORTION	0.31	0.33	0.28	0.06	0.02

A new car is chosen at random. Let the random variable X denote the number of times it will be returned over the warranty period.

(a) Write down the probability function for X.

(b) Find the expected number of returns for this car.

(c) Find the standard deviation of the number of returns for this car.

10.23. In a study of energy use, the numbers of occupants in automobiles on an interstate highway were counted. The table shows proportions for all automobiles on this highway

NUMBER OF OCCUPANTS	1	2	3	4	5	6
PROPORTION	0.45	0.37	0.12	0.04	0.01	0.01

An automobile on this highway is chosen at random. Let the random variable X denote the number of occupants in this automobile.

(a) Write down the probability function for X.

(b) Find the expected number of occupants of this automobile.

(c) Find the standard deviation of the number of occupants of this automobile.

10.24. An insurance agent believes that for a particular contact, the probability of making a sale is 0.4. For the coming week, this agent has 5 contacts.

  (a) Find the probability that exactly two sales will result.

  (b) Find the probability that at least two sales will result.

  (c) Find the expected number of sales from these five contacts.

10.25. A corporation has a number of vacancies to fill in a particular department. Offers of employment are made to 20 candidates, and it is believed that for each candidate, the probability that the offer will be accepted is 0.8. If it is assumed that candidates' decisions are made independently, what is the probability that the number of acceptances will be between 15 and 17?

10.26. Company records suggest that in a given day, the probability of an assembly machine breaking down is 0.15. This company has 4 of these machines, operating independently.

  (a) What is the probability that exactly one of these machines will break down in a given day?

  (b) What is the probability that at least one of these machines will break down in a given day?

  (c) What is the expected number of these machines that will break down in a given day?

10.27. It is estimated that 20% of all new MBA graduates are women. A company advertises a position for a new MBA graduate and draws up a list of six candidates for a final interview. Assume that these six people can be regarded as a random sample of all new MBA graduates.

  (a) What is the probability that there will be exactly two women on the list?

  (b) What is the probability that there will be at least two women on the list?

  (c) What is the expected number of women on the list?

10.28. A company receives a very large shipment of parts. A random sample of 15 of these parts are checked and, if less than two are defective, the shipment is accepted.

  (a) What is the probability of accepting a shipment containing 5% defectives?

  (b) What is the probability of accepting a shipment containing 10% defectives?

  (c) What is the probability of accepting a shipment containing 20% defectives?

10.29. The following two acceptance rules are being considered for determining whether to take delivery of a large shipment of components:

  (i) A random sample of ten components is checked, and the shipment is accepted only if none of them are defective.

  (ii) A random sample of twenty components is checked, and the shipment is accepted only if not more than one of them is defective.

  Which of these acceptance rules has the smaller probability of accepting a shipment containing 15% defectives?

10.30. A company receives large shipments of parts from two sources: 75% of these come from a supplier whose shipments typically contain 10% defectives, and 25% from a supplier whose shipments typically contain 20% defectives. A shipment is received, but the source is unknown. A random sample of 20 items from this shipment is tested, and one of the sampled parts is found to be defective. What is the probability that this shipment came from the more reliable supplier?

10.31. Research suggests that for a typical plant in Britain with 2000 employees, the number of strikes in a year can be represented by a Poisson distribution with mean 0.4 strike per year.

  (a) For a randomly chosen plant, find the probability that there will be exactly two strikes in a given year.

(b) For a randomly chosen plant, find the probability that there will be at least two strikes in a given year.

10.32. On average, 4.5 telephone calls per minute are received at a corporation's switchboard in the mid-morning hours. If the distribution is Poisson, find the probability that in any given minute of this period there will be more than 3 calls.

10.33. The number of accidents in a manufacturing plant has a Poisson distribution with mean 1.2 per week.

(a) What is the probability of no accidents in a given week?

(b) What is the probability of more than 2 accidents in a given week?

10.34. The tread life of a certain brand of tire has a normal distribution with mean 35,000 miles and standard deviation 5000 miles. A tire of this brand is chosen at random. Find the probability that its tread life falls in each of the following ranges:

(a) Less than 40,000 miles

(b) More than 45,000 miles

(c) Less than 32,500 miles

(d) More than 27,500 miles

(e) Between 36,000 and 38,000 miles

(f) Between 29,000 and 41,000 miles

10.35. The weights of the contents of boxes of a brand of detergent follow a normal distribution with mean 30 ounces and standard deviation 0.5 ounce. A box of this detergent is chosen at random.

(a) What is the probability that its weight will be less than 29 ounces?

(b) What is the probability that its weight will be between 29.75 and 30.25 ounces?

(c) Without doing the calculations, state in which of the following ranges the weight is most likely to lie: 29.0 – 29.5 ounces, 29.25 – 29.75 ounces, 29.5 – 30.0 ounces, 29.75 – 30.25 ounces.

10.36. Seniors at a public school who take a placement test have scores that are normally distributed with a mean of 220 and a standard deviation of 40. Seniors at a private school who take the same test have scores that are normally distributed with mean 230 and standard deviation 50. A student qualifies for a state honorary society if his or her score exceeds 300. A senior from the public school is chosen at random, and a senior from the private school is independently chosen at random.

(a) Find the probability that the senior from the public school qualifies for the state honorary society.

(b) Find the probability that the senior from the private school qualifies for the state honorary society.

(c) Find the probability that at least one of these seniors qualifies for the state honorary society.

10.37. A company can purchase raw material from either of two suppliers and is concerned about the amount of impurity the material contains. A review of the records for each supplier finds that the percentage impurity levels in consignments of the raw material follow normal distributions with the means and standard deviations given in the accompanying table. The company is anxious that the impurity level in a consignment should not exceed 7.5%, and wants to purchase from the supplier more likely to meet that specification. Which supplier should be chosen?

	MEAN	STANDARD DEVIATION
Supplier A	6.9	0.4
Supplier B	6.7	0.6

10.38. Following an intensive employment interview, a personnel officer assigns to each candidate a score on a scale from 0 to 1000. The scores given follow a normal distribution with mean 620 and standard deviation 110. The top 15% of all candidates are invited to report back for further interviews, while the remaining candidates are immediately rejected. What score is needed to avoid an immediate rejection?

10.39. A management consultant found that the amount of time per day spent by executives performing tasks that could equally well be done by lower paid subordinates followed a normal distribution with mean 2.6 hours. It was also found that 10% of executives spent more than 3.5 hours per day on such tasks. Find the standard deviation of the distribution of daily time spent by executives on these tasks.

10.40. Customer service times at a bank follow an exponential distribution with mean 1.5 minutes.
   (a) For a randomly chosen customer, what is the probability that service will take less than 1.5 minutes?
   (b) For a randomly chosen customer, what is the probability that service will take more than 45 seconds?
   (c) For a randomly chosen customer, what is the probability that service will take between 3 and 4.5 minutes?

10.41. Customers arrive, according to a Poisson distribution, at a loading bay at an average rate of 4 per hour.
   (a) For any given hour, what is the probability that there will be less than 3 arrivals?
   (b) What is the probability that more than 45 minutes will elapse between successive arrivals?
   (c) What is the probability that less than 15 minutes will elapse between successive arrivals?

decision theory

CHAPTER ELEVEN

11.1. DECISION MAKING IN AN UNCERTAIN ENVIRONMENT

Every day managers must make decisions, choosing from a set of possible actions, or strategies. Very often, at the time the decision is to be made, it will be impossible to know with certainty which of these possible strategies will turn out to have been the best choice. This is so since quite typically, the degree of success of any particular strategy will depend on external factors which cannot be perfectly predicted. In this chapter we will discuss a class of problems where an individual, a group, or a corporation, has available several alternative feasible courses of action. The decision as to which action to take must be made in an environment in which there is uncertainty about the future behavior of those factors that will determine the consequences following from the possible courses of action.

In the business world, this type of problem often arises, as the following examples illustrate:

(i) The cost of drilling exploratory offshore oil wells is extremely high. In spite of the best geological advice, an oil company will not know, before a well is drilled, the size of deposits, or, indeed, whether commercially viable quantities of oil will be found. The decision as to whether and where to drill in a particular field must, then, be made in an uncertain environment.

(ii) An investor in the bond market would, if he or she believed that interest rates were currently at a peak, find the purchase of long term bonds a very attractive option. However, it is not possible to predict with certainty the future direction of interest rates, and, if rates continued to rise, the purchase of long term bonds would turn out to have been a very poor strategy.

(iii) Contractors must frequently submit competitive bids for projects, and a decision as to the level of the bid must be made. In this context there are two sources of uncertainty. First, it will not be known how low the bid must be in order to secure the contract. Second, it will generally not be possible to estimate precisely the cost of fulfilling the contract. Nevertheless, in spite of this uncertainty, some decision must be made.

(iv) When a new product is brought on to the market, management must decide on initial production levels, price, and advertising strategy. These decisions must be made at a time when the volume of demand at different price levels cannot be known with certainty, and the most promising sectors for market penetration can only be tentatively identified.

(v) A customer receiving a large consignment of goods must decide whether or not to accept delivery. It may be possible to check the quality of only a small sample of the whole consignment. In the previous chapter, we saw in our discussion of **acceptance sampling** how to compute probabilities that particular decision rules would lead to acceptance of consignments with specific proportions of defective goods.

Our aim in this chapter is to provide a framework for attacking decision-making problems of the type just discussed. We will illustrate the methodology by reference to the case of a perfumes manufacturer who is planning to introduce a new product. This manufacturer has available four alternative production processes, which we will label A, B, C, and D, ranging in scope from a relatively modest extension of existing facilities to a rather major plant expansion. The decision as to which of these four courses of action should be followed has to be taken at a time when eventual demand for the product cannot be known with certainty. We will consider here three possible demand levels, characterized as "low," "moderate," and "high." It will be assumed that for each of the twelve possible production process-level of demand combinations, it is possible to calculate the present values of the profits accruing from the product over the lifetime of the investment. Table 11.1 shows these profit levels.

This problem illustrates the general class of problems to be attacked in the present chapter. We will assume that a decision-maker is faced with a finite number, K, of possible **actions**, labelled $a_1, a_2, \ldots, a_K$, and from among which one must be selected. For the example of the perfume manufacturer these actions are the four possible production process adoptions. At the time that a decision must be made, there is uncertainty about some factor, or set of factors, that will influence the outcomes following from the possible actions. We will assume that the possibilities for these influential factors can be characterized by

TABLE 11.1 Estimated profits (in dollars) for the perfume manufacturer for the different production process-level of demand combinations.

PRODUCTION PROCESS	LEVEL OF DEMAND		
	LOW	MODERATE	HIGH
A	200,000	350,000	600,000
B	250,000	350,000	540,000
C	300,000	375,000	490,000
D	300,000	350,000	470,000

TABLE 11.2 The general form of a payoff table with K possible actions and H states of nature; M_{ij} is the payoff from action a_i under state of nature s_j.

ACTIONS	STATES OF NATURE			
	s_1	s_2	. . . .	s_H
a_1	M_{11}	M_{12}	. . . .	M_{1H}
a_2	M_{21}	M_{22}	. . . .	M_{2H}
.	.	.		.
.	.	.		.
.	.	.		.
a_K	M_{K1}	M_{K2}	. . . .	M_{KH}

a finite number, H, of **states of nature.** These states are denoted $s_1, s_2, . . ., s_H$. In our example, there are three possible states of nature, corresponding to the three possible demand levels. Finally, the decision-maker must be able to specify the monetary outcomes, or **payoffs,** resulting from each of the KH possible action-state of nature combinations. Let M_{ij} denote the payoff for action a_i when state of nature s_j occurs. As in Table 11.1, these payoffs can be displayed in a **payoff table.** The general form of the payoff table is shown in Table 11.2.

Framework for a Decision-Making Problem

(i) The decision-maker has K possible courses of **action:**

$$a_1, a_2, . . ., a_K$$

(ii) There are H possible uncertain **states of nature**

$$s_1, s_2, . . ., s_H$$

defined to be mutually exclusive and collectively exhaustive.

(iii) For each action-state of nature combination there is an associated **payoff,** M_{ij}, corresponding to action a_i and state of nature s_j.

As we have discussed it, the decision making problem is **discrete,** since we have assumed a finite number of available actions, and a finite number of possible states of nature. In practice, however, many real world problems are essentially **continuous** in character. State of nature, for example, may be more appropriately measured on a continuum rather than represented by a finite number of discrete possibilities. For the perfume manufacturer, it may be possible to consider a range of possible demand levels in place of three specific levels. Also, for some problems the available course of action is more appropriately represented on a continuum. Such a case might arise when a contractor has to decide the level of a bid for a contract. Nevertheless, in the remainder of this chapter, we will concentrate on the discrete case. The principles involved in the analysis of the continuous case are essentially the same, though the technical details are rather more difficult.

The appropriate choice of action in a decision problem will depend on the decision-maker's objectives which themselves may be rather complex. Here, we will describe a number of general lines of attack, though it must be kept in mind that each individual problem has its own special features. Whatever the approach eventually adopted, however, we can very easily specify one general rule. It is possible that some of the available actions can be eliminated from further consideration under any circumstances. Consider the payoff table for the perfume manufacturer, and, in particular, notice that whatever level of demand arises, the payoff from production process D cannot be higher than that from process C, though the payoff from the former could be lower than that from the latter. In these circumstances, it makes no sense at all to consider the adoption of process D. Since action C must be at least as rewarding as, and possibly be more rewarding than, action D, it is said that action C **dominates** action D. An action that is dominated by another available alternative action is called **inadmissible.** Such an action is removed from further consideration, since it could not possibly be preferable to adopt it rather than the dominating action.

Definitions

  If the payoff for action a_j is at least as high as that for action a_i for every state of nature, and if the payoff for a_j is higher than that for a_i for some state of nature, then a_j is said to **dominate** a_i.
  Any dominated action is said to be **inadmissible.** Such actions are deleted from the set of available actions prior to further analysis of decision making problems.
  If an action is not dominated by any other available action, it is said to be **admissible.**

We have seen, for the perfume manufacturer, that the adoption of production process D is an inadmissible action. Accordingly, in our subsequent analyses of this problem, we need consider only processes A, B, and C. Inspection of Table 11.1 reveals that all three of these actions are admissible.

11.2. SOLUTIONS NOT USING STATE OF NATURE PROBABILITIES

Before deciding on a course of action, a decision-maker would presumably want to form some judgment as to how likely each state of nature is to materialize. Indeed, since the decision-maker will almost certainly have some familiarity with the problem environment, it is natural to want to incorporate such expertise into the decision-making process. In the bulk of this chapter we will discuss, for decision problems, solution methods that require the specification of probabilities for the states of nature. However, in this section we will briefly discuss three action-choosing criteria that are not based on such probabilities. These approaches to decision-making problems depend exclusively on the structure of the payoff table. Such approaches may be appropriate when the decision-maker is so uncertain about the environment that he or she feels unable to estimate probabilities of occurrence of the states of nature.

The three approaches discussed in this section are called the **maximin criterion,** the **maximax criterion,** and the **minimax regret criterion.** Each will be illustrated through the problem of the perfume manufacturer, with the inadmissible action—adoption of production process D—eliminated.

(i) *MAXIMIN CRITERION*

The center of attention here is on the worst possible outcome for each action, whatever state of nature materializes. This worst outcome is just the lowest payoff that could possibly occur. For the problem of the perfume manufacturer, it can be seen from Table 11.1 that for each production process, the smallest payoff arises at the low level of demand. The **maximin criterion** selects that action for which the minimum payoff is highest. Thus we *maximize* the *minimum* payoff. As can be seen from Table 11.3, the highest value of these minimum payoffs is $300,000, which occurs when production process C is adopted. The maximin criterion, accordingly, selects this action.

The general form for the decision rule based on the maximin criterion is set out in the box below.

The Maximin Criterion Decision Rule

An action is to be chosen from among K admissible actions $a_1, a_2, \ldots, a_K$, given H possible states of nature. Let M_{ij} be the payoff resulting from action a_i in the j-th state.

For each action, find the smallest possible payoff. For example, for a_1 this is the smallest of $M_{11}, M_{12}, \ldots, M_{1H}$. Denote this minimum by M_1^*, so that

$$M_1^* = \text{Min}(M_{11}, M_{12}, \ldots, M_{1H})$$

In general, for action a_i, we have

$$M_i^* = \text{Min}(M_{i1}, M_{i2}, \ldots, M_{iH})$$

The **maximin criterion** selects that action a_i for which the corresponding M_i^* is largest.

TABLE 11.3 Choice of production process C by the maximin criterion for the problem of the perfume manufacturer.

PRODUCTION PROCESS	LEVEL OF DEMAND			MINIMUM PAYOFF
	LOW	MODERATE	HIGH	
A	200,000	350,000	600,000	200,000
B	250,000	350,000	540,000	250,000
C	300,000	375,000	490,000	300,000 ← Maximin

The maximin criterion, as our discussion has illustrated, produces the largest possible payoff *that can be guaranteed.* If production process C is used the perfume manufacturer is *assured* a payoff of *at least* $300,000, whatever level of demand actually arises. Neither of the available alternatives can *guarantee* as much. However, it is precisely within this guarantee that one finds reservations about the maximin criterion, as often a price must be paid for such an assurance. The price here is in the foregoing of opportunities to receive a very much higher payoff, through the choice of some other action, *however unlikely* the worst-case situation may be to arise. For example, suppose that the perfume manufacturer is virtually certain that demand for the new product will be high. In that case, production process C would be a poor choice, as it yields the lowest payoff at this demand level. The maximin criterion, then, can be viewed as a very cautious strategy. It may be appropriate in certain circumstances, but only an extreme pessimist would invariably employ it. For this reason, this rule is sometimes called the **Criterion of Pessimism.**

(ii) MAXIMAX CRITERION

By contrast with the maximin rule, the **maximax criterion,** or **Criterion of Optimism** selects that action for which the *maximum* possible payoff is highest. From Table 11.1, it can be seen that the highest possible payoffs from production processes A, B, and C are, respectively, $600,000, $540,000, and $490,000. The highest of these is for process A, which is therefore chosen according to this criterion.

In making this choice, the manufacturer runs the risk of a relatively low payoff if demand turns out to be low. Such considerations are ignored by the maximax criterion, which is therefore likely to suit an extreme optimist, or perhaps someone with a taste for gambling.

(iii) MINIMAX REGRET CRITERION

To understand the rationale for the minimax regret criterion, consider the position of a decision-maker who has chosen a particular action. One of the states of nature has occurred, and it is now possible to look back on the choice of action, either with satisfaction, or disappointment because, as it happened, some alternative action would have been preferable. Suppose, for the case of the perfume manufacturer, that the level of demand for the new product turns out to be high. In that case, the optimal strategy would have been to adopt production process A, giving a payoff of $600,000. If this choice had been made, the manufacturer would have had no **regret.** On the other hand, if process B had been chosen, the resulting profit would have been only $540,000, rather than the $600,000 that could have been obtained through what turned out to be the best choice. The amount of regret, then, is the difference

$$\$600,000 - \$540,000 = \$60,000$$

This amount can be thought of as the **opportunity loss** in choosing process B.

TABLE 11.4 Regret table for the perfume manufacturer.

PRODUCTION PROCESS	LEVEL OF DEMAND		
	LOW	MODERATE	HIGH
A	100,000	25,000	0
B	50,000	25,000	60,000
C	0	0	110,000

TABLE 11.5 Choice of production process B by the minimax regret criterion for the problem of the perfume manufacturer.

PRODUCTION PROCESS	LEVEL OF DEMAND			MAXIMUM REGRET
	LOW	MODERATE	HIGH	
A	100,000	25,000	0	100,000
B	50,000	25,000	60,000	60,000 ← Minimax Regret
C	0	0	110,000	110,000

Similarly, if process C had been chosen, and demand turned out to be high, the extent of the regret would be

$$\$600,000 - \$490,000 = \$110,000$$

In exactly the same way, we can calculate the regrets involved for low and moderate demand outcomes. In each case the regret is $0 for process C, since this would have been the best choice in both eventualities.

Proceeding in this way, we can construct a **regret table,** with an entry for each action-state of nature combination. Table 11.4 shows regrets (in dollars) for the decision problem of the perfume manufacturer.

The next step is to determine the largest amount of regret that can result for each possible choice of action. From Table 11.4 it emerges that these maxima are respectively $100,000, $60,000, and $110,000 for production processes A, B, and C. The **minimax regret criterion** chooses that action for which the maximum regret is smallest. It can be seen from Table 11.5 that for the problem of the perfume manufacturer, this would yield the choice of process B.

The general form of the decision rule based on the minimax regret criterion is set out in the box below.

The Minimax Regret Criterion Decision Rule

Consider a payoff table arranged in a rectangular array, with rows corresponding to actions and columns to states of nature. Then, if each payoff in the table is subtracted from the largest payoff in its column, the resulting array is called a **regret table.**

> Using the regret table, the action chosen by the **minimax regret criterion** is found as follows:
> **(i)** For each row (action) find the largest regret.
> **(ii)** Select that action corresponding to the minimum of these maximum regrets.

The minimax regret criterion yields that action with the smallest regret that can be *guaranteed*. However, two reservations about the practical use of this criterion should be noted. First, the logic behind this method of choice is not terribly compelling. There is certainly something to be said for not having to shed too many tears over missed opportunities. Nevertheless, in a rational world business decisions ought to be based on more substantial grounds. Second, in common with the maximin criterion, the minimax regret criterion does not allow the decision-maker to inject his or her views on the chances of occurrence of the states of nature into the decision-making process. Since for most practical business applications, the decision-maker will be working in an environment with which he or she is quite familiar, this represents a waste of valuable expertise.

11.3. THE EXPECTED MONETARY VALUE CRITERION

It has already been suggested that an important element in the analysis of many business decision-making problems should be the decision-maker's assessment of the chances of occurrence of the various states of nature relevant in the determination of the eventual payoff. For example, the perfume manufacturer will presumably have some experience in the market for the product and, based on that experience, could come to some view on the likelihood of occurrence of low, moderate, or heavy demand. In this section it is assumed that a *probability* of occurrence can be associated with each state of nature. These probabilities may be objective, but will more often be subjective, and we will see how they can be employed to suggest an appropriate decision.

Suppose that the perfume manufacturer knows that of all similar new introductions to this market, 10% have met low demand, 50% moderate demand, and 40% high demand. Given no further information about the chances of successful market penetration of the new product, it is then reasonable to postulate the following probabilities for the three states of nature:

Probability of low demand = 0.1

Probability of moderate demand = 0.5

Probability of high demand = 0.4

Since the states of nature are mutually exclusive and collectively exhaustive, that is, only one can occur, and one must occur, these probabilities necessarily sum to one.

TABLE 11.6 Payoffs and states of nature probabilities for the perfume manufacturer.

PRODUCTION PROCESS	LEVEL OF DEMAND		
	LOW	MODERATE	HIGH
PROBABILITIES	0.1	0.5	0.4
A	200,000	350,000	600,000
B	250,000	350,000	540,000
C	300,000	375,000	490,000

It is convenient to augment the payoff table through the addition of the states of nature probabilities, as in Table 11.6, since these probabilities will be used in conjunction with the payoffs in solving the decision problem.

In our general framework there are H possible states of nature to which probabilities must be attached. These probabilities will be denoted $p_1, p_2, \ldots, p_H$, so that p_j is the probability of occurrence of state of nature s_j. As before, these states of nature probabilities must sum to one, so that

$$\sum_{j=1}^{H} p_j = 1$$

The general setup of the decision making problem is conveniently tabulated as in Table 11.7.

At the time when an action is to be selected, the decision-maker has, for each possible choice of action, specific probabilities of receiving each of the associated payoffs. For example, if the perfume manufacturer were to adopt production process A, $200,000 would be received with probability 0.1, $350,000 with probability 0.5, and $600,000 with probability 0.4. The **expected payoff** arising from any particular action can then be computed by multiplying each payoff

TABLE 11.7 Payoffs, M_{ij}, and states of nature probabilities, p_j, for a decision problem with K admissible actions and H possible states of nature.

ACTIONS	STATES OF NATURE			
	s_1	s_2	$\cdots\cdots$	s_H
PROBABILITIES	p_1	p_2	$\cdots\cdots$	p_H
a_1	M_{11}	M_{12}	$\cdots\cdots$	M_{1H}
a_2	M_{21}	M_{22}	$\cdots\cdots$	M_{2H}
.	.	.		.
.	.	.	.	.
.	.	.		.
a_K	M_{K1}	M_{K2}	$\cdots\cdots$	M_{KH}

by its associated probability and summing over all states of nature. These expected payoffs, in the present context, are often referred to as the **expected monetary values** of the actions. For the perfume manufacturer, the expected monetary values for the three admissible actions are:

$$\text{EMV(A)} = (0.1)(200{,}000) + (0.5)(350{,}000) + (0.4)(600{,}000) = \$435{,}000$$

$$\text{EMV(B)} = (0.1)(250{,}000) + (0.5)(350{,}000) + (0.4)(540{,}000) = \$416{,}000$$

$$\text{EMV(C)} = (0.1)(300{,}000) + (0.5)(375{,}000) + (0.4)(490{,}000) = \$413{,}500$$

In the box below we set out the procedure for computing expected monetary values in the general discrete decision problem.

Expected Monetary Values

Suppose that a decision-maker, faced with H possible states of nature, has available K admissible actions, $a_1, a_2, \ldots, a_K$. Let M_{ij} denote the payoff from action a_i under the j-th state of nature, and p_j the probability of occurrence of that state, with

$$\sum_{j=1}^{H} p_j = 1$$

Then, the **expected monetary value** of action a_i is

$$\text{EMV}(a_i) = p_1 M_{i1} + p_2 M_{i2} + \ldots + p_H M_{iH}$$

$$= \sum_{j=1}^{H} p_j M_{ij}$$

The expected monetary values represent, for each action, the expected returns to the decision maker. Therefore, an attractive criterion for choosing among alternative actions involves the selection of that action for which expected monetary value is highest. Following this rule, the perfume manufacturer would opt to employ production process A. It is interesting to recall that neither the maximin criterion nor the minimax regret criterion yielded this solution. However, we have now incorporated into our analysis the additional piece of information that a high level of demand is much more likely to arise than a low level. From the structure of the payoff table it is clear that this factor renders process A relatively attractive.

Expected Monetary Value Criterion

The expected monetary value criterion dictates the choice of that action for which expected monetary value is highest.

ANALYSIS THROUGH DECISION TREES

A convenient way to analyze decision making problems is through the construction of a **decision tree,** as illustrated in Figure 11.1 for the case of the perfume manufacturer. The tree is constructed, beginning at the left-hand side of the figure with a **square junction,** which is used to indicate a *point at which a decision must be taken.* Emerging from this junction are three branches, one for each of the admissible actions. Proceeding to the right, we reach **circular junctions.** Emerging from these are branches, each representing a **possible state of nature,** with the associated probabilities indicated. Finally, at the end of these branches, the payoffs corresponding to each action-state of nature combination are indicated. The numerical calculations proceed from right to left, beginning with these payoffs. For each circular junction we compute the sum of probability times payoff for the emerging branches. This yields the expected monetary value of each action. Finally, the largest of these expected monetary values is shown at the square junction. As we have already found, this results from adoption of process A, which is thus selected by the expected monetary value criterion. The expected payoff from this optimal choice of action is $435,000.

SENSITIVITY ANALYSIS

We have concluded that according to the expected monetary value criterion, production process A should be employed. However, this decision was based on a reliance on the subjective probability assessments for different levels of

FIGURE 11.1 Decision tree for the perfume manufacturer.

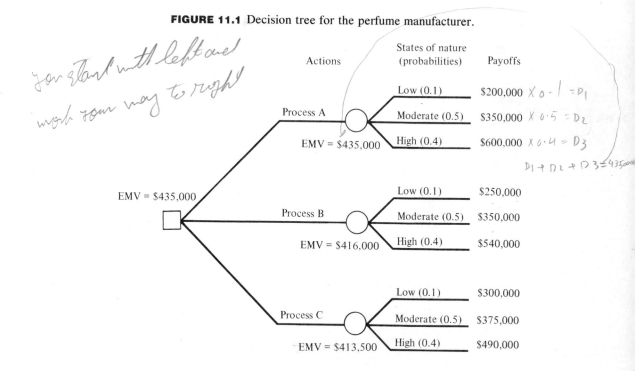

demand and estimates of the profits that would result in each case. In many applications a decision-maker may not have complete faith in his or her ability to make such probability assessments or to accurately estimate future payoffs. It is therefore useful to ask under what range of specifications a decision chosen by the EMV criterion will remain optimal.

Suppose that the perfume manufacturer is comfortable with the assessment that the probability of high demand is 0.4, but is less sure of the assessments for the other two states of nature. Let p denote the probability of low demand, and $(0.6 - p)$ the probability of moderate demand. We now ask under what range of p values would adoption of process A be optimal according to the expected monetary value criterion. We now find

$$EMV(A) = (p)(200,000) + (0.6 - p)(350,000) + (0.4)(600,000)$$
$$= \$(450,000 - 150,000p)$$

$$EMV(B) = (p)(250,000) + (0.6 - p)(350,000) + (0.4)(540,000)$$
$$= \$(426,000 - 100,000p)$$

$$EMV(C) = (p)(300,000) + (0.6 - p)(375,000) + (0.4)(490,000)$$
$$= \$(421,000 - 75,000p)$$

Choice of process A will remain optimal provided the associated EMV is higher than that of each of the other two processes. Thus, for choice of process A to be preferable to that of process B we require

$$450,000 - 150,000\,p \geq 426,000 - 100,000\,p$$

or

$$24,000 \geq 50,000\,p$$

so that

$$p \leq 0.48$$

Similarly, for process A to be preferred to process C, we must have

$$450,000 - 150,000\,p \geq 421,000 - 75,000\,p$$

or

$$29,000 \geq 75,000\,p$$

so that

$$p \leq 0.387$$

We have thus established that if the payoffs are as postulated and the probability of high demand is 0.4, process A will be chosen by the expected monetary value criterion provided the probability of low demand is at most 0.387.

The perfume manufacturer is also concerned that the estimate of $600,000 profit for process A under high demand may be too optimistic. We now explore under what range of payoffs process A will be the optimal choice, when all other problem specifications are kept at their original levels. If we denote by M the payoff for process A under high demand, the expected monetary value for this process is

$$\text{EMV}(A) = (0.1)(200,000) + (0.5)(350,000) + (0.4)(M) = \$(195,000 + 0.4M)$$

The expected monetary values for processes B and C are, as before, $416,000 and $413,500. Therefore process A will be the optimal choice provided

$$195,000 + 0.4M \geq 416,000$$

or

$$0.4M \geq 221,000$$

so that

$$M \geq 552,500$$

We have therefore shown that if the states of nature probabilities and the other payoffs are as originally postulated, process A will be chosen by the expected monetary value criterion provided that the payoff from that process under high demand is at least $552,500.

11.4. USING SAMPLE INFORMATION: BAYESIAN ANALYSIS

In our analysis of the decision-making problem of the perfume manufacturer in the previous section, we employed, as probabilities for the states of nature, the proportions of the times that previous new introductions to this market had met low, moderate, and high levels of demand. This is a reasonable strategy in the absence of any other relevant information, though the analyst is also free to inject his or her own subjective probabilities in place of these values. One way of forming a more firm judgment about the environment of a decision problem is to obtain some additional information about that environment. In this section we will investigate how such information can be incorporated into the decision-making process. For example, in the context of our new product introduction problem, useful information about potential demand might be obtained through a market research study. Of course, there will typically be some cost involved in acquiring this information, but in many decision-making problems the cost of a suboptimal choice of action can be substantial, so that the benefits, in terms of better decisions, from the acquisition of further information, may well out-weigh its cost. In this section, we will concentrate on the use of additional information in decision-making, postponing until Section 11.5, the question as to whether the cost of obtaining the information can be justified.

In Section 11.3, the perfume manufacturer, using only records of past market introductions, assessed the probabilities for low, moderate, and high levels of demand for the new product as 0.1, 0.5, and 0.4, respectively. Suppose, now, that market research is to be carried out on the prospects for this product. On the basis of such research, these initial or **prior probabilities** will typically be modified, yielding updated probabilities, which we call **posterior probabilities** for the three possible levels of demand. The new information (in this case, the results of the market research) inducing the modification of the probabilities for the states of nature is referred to as **sample information.** As we saw in Chapter 10, **Bayes' theorem** provides a mechanism for modifying prior probabilities to yield posterior probabilities. For convenience, we restate this theorem in the box below.

Bayes' Theorem in Decision Making

Let $s_1, s_2, \ldots, s_H$ be H mutually exclusive and collectively exhaustive events, which correspond to the H states of nature of a decision problem. Let A be some other event, denoting the **sample information.** Write the conditional probability that state s_i will occur, given that A occurs, as $P(s_i|A)$, and the probability of A given s_i as $P(A|s_i)$.

Then, the conditional probability of s_i given A is

$$P(s_i|A) = \frac{P(A|s_i)P(s_i)}{P(A)}$$

$$= \frac{P(A|s_i)P(s_i)}{P(A|s_1)P(s_1) + P(A|s_2)P(s_2) + \ldots + P(A|s_H)P(s_H)}$$

In the present context, $P(s_i)$ is the **prior probability** of state of nature s_i, and is modified to the **posterior probability,** $P(s_i|A)$, given the **sample information** A.

Suppose now that the perfume manufacturer employs a market research organization to predict the level of demand for the new product. On the basis of its research, this organization provides a rating of either "poor," "fair," or "good" for the market prospects of the product. A review of the market research organization's past performance is set out in Table 11.8, which shows, for each level of demand outcome, the proportion of poor, fair, and good assessments that were made. Thus, for example, on 10% of those occasions when demand was high, the assessment was "poor." Therefore, in the notation of conditional probability, denoting low, moderate, and high demand levels by s_1, s_2, and s_3 respectively, we can write

$$P(\text{Poor}|s_1) = 0.6; \; P(\text{Poor}|s_2) = 0.3; \; P(\text{Poor}|s_3) = 0.1$$

and similarly for the other two possible assessments.

TABLE 11.8 Proportion of assessments of each type given by the market research organization for perfumes achieving given levels of demand.

ASSESSMENT	LEVEL OF DEMAND		
	LOW(s_1)	MODERATE(s_2)	HIGH(s_3)
POOR	0.6	0.3	0.1
FAIR	0.2	0.3	0.2
GOOD	0.2	0.4	0.7

Let us assume that the market research organization has been consulted, and that it has assessed prospects for the new perfume as poor. On the basis of this new information, the prior probabilities

$$P(s_1) = 0.1; P(s_2) = 0.5; P(s_3) = 0.4$$

for the three possible demand levels are modified through Bayes' theorem. For low level of demand, the posterior probability is

$$P(s_1|\text{Poor}) = \frac{P(\text{Poor}|s_1)P(s_1)}{P(\text{Poor}|s_1)P(s_1) + P(\text{Poor}|s_2)P(s_2) + P(\text{Poor}|s_3)P(s_3)}$$

$$= \frac{(0.6)(0.1)}{(0.6)(0.1) + (0.3)(0.5) + (0.1)(0.4)} = \frac{0.06}{0.25} = 0.24$$

In the same way, for the other two demand levels, we find

$$P(s_2|\text{Poor}) = \frac{(0.3)(0.5)}{0.25} = 0.60$$

$$P(s_3|\text{Poor}) = \frac{(0.1)(0.4)}{0.25} = 0.16$$

These posterior probabilities can now be used to compute expected monetary values for the three admissible actions, given the market research organization's assessment that prospects for the new product are poor. Table 11.9 sets out the payoffs, together with the posterior probabilities for the three states of nature. This table is merely a modification of Table 11.6, with the posterior probabilities for the demand levels replacing the prior probabilities of that table.

The expected monetary values of the three actions are found in exactly the same way as in the previous section. These are now:

EMV(A) = (0.24)(200,000) + (0.60)(350,000) + (0.16)(600,000) = \$354,000

EMV(B) = (0.24)(250,000) + (0.60)(350,000) + (0.16)(540,000) = \$356,400

EMV(C) = (0.24)(300,000) + (0.60)(375,000) + (0.16)(490,000) = \$375,400

TABLE 11.9 Payoffs for the perfume manufacturer and posterior probabilities for states of nature, given an assessment of "poor" prospects by the market research organization.

PRODUCTION PROCESS	LEVEL OF DEMAND		
	LOW	MODERATE	HIGH
POSTERIOR PROBABILITIES	0.24	0.60	0.16
A	200,000	350,000	600,000
B	250,000	350,000	540,000
C	300,000	375,000	490,000

TABLE 11.10 Expected monetary values (in dollars) for the perfume manufacturer for each of three possible assessments by the market research organization.

PRODUCTION PROCESS	ASSESSMENT		
	POOR	FAIR	GOOD
A	354,000	418,000	484,000
B	356,400	402,800	452,400
C	375,400	405,800	436,400

It follows that if an assessment of "poor" is provided by the market research organization then according to the expected monetary value criterion, production process C should be used. Notice that this decision differs from that of the previous section, when only prior probabilities for the states of nature were employed, leading to a preference for process A. However, the market research organization's assessment renders a high level of demand much less likely now, leading to a preference for process C if the decision is to be based on expected dollar payoff.

In exactly the same manner, it is possible to determine the decisions that would be optimal if the market research organization's assessment had been "fair" or "good." Appealing to Bayes' theorem, the posterior probabilities of the three states of nature given a "fair" assessment for market prospects are:

$$P(s_1|\text{Fair}) = 0.08; \; P(s_2|\text{Fair}) = 0.60; \; P(s_3|\text{Fair}) = 0.32$$

Similarly, for a "good" assessment

$$P(s_1|\text{Good}) = 0.04; \; P(s_2|\text{Good}) = 0.40; \; P(s_3|\text{Good}) = 0.56$$

Given these posterior probabilities, the expected monetary values for each production process, for each assessment, can be computed. The results of these calculations are set out in Table 11.10.

As already noted, we see from Table 11.10 that production process C is preferred, according to the expected monetary value criterion, if the assessment is "poor." On the other hand, for either of the other two possible assessments the optimal choice of action is to use process A. Recall that when the prior probabilities for the states of nature were employed, the optimal decision, according to the expected monetary value criterion, was to employ process A. We now find that it can be the case (if the market research organization's assessment is "poor") that a different decision will be made when these prior probabilities are modified in the light of sample information. It therefore emerges that consulting the market research organization could be fruitful for the perfume manufacturer. Of course, if the choice of process A had proved to be optimal, whatever the assessment, the sample information could not possibly be of value. In the next section we examine in more detail the value of sample information.

11.5. THE VALUE OF SAMPLE INFORMATION

In the previous section we saw how sample information can be injected into the decision-making process. On the basis of such information, initial beliefs about the chances of occurrence of the states of nature are modified to give posterior probabilities. These posterior probabilities then form the appropriate weights for the payoffs in the computation of expected monetary values given the sample information. The potential value of sample information in decision-making, of course, lies in its provision of a better feel for the likelihood of occurrence of the various states of nature. This, in turn, can provide a sounder basis for decision-making. In this section we will see how a *monetary* value can be attached to sample information. This is necessary since there will generally be some cost in acquiring that information, and the decision-maker will wish to assess whether the expected value of the sample information is greater than its cost.

As noted at the end of the previous section, sample information can only be of value if the sample result could lead to a different choice of action than would otherwise have been taken. Accordingly, in this section we need only consider those situations in which such is the case. Our analysis will be illustrated through the problem of the perfume manufacturer planning to introduce a new product. In Section 11.3 we saw that in the absence of sample information, the optimal strategy for this manufacturer was to use production process A, with an expected monetary value of $435,000. However, before making a final decision, the option of consulting a market research organization is available. As we saw in the previous section, it is possible, on the basis of this information, that the manufacturer will prefer a different action.

EXPECTED VALUE OF PERFECT INFORMATION

In reality it is very unlikely that a decision-maker will ever be able to know for sure which state of nature will arise. However good the sample information, some uncertainty will almost surely remain. Nevertheless, as a preview to our consideration of the value of sample information in general, it is worthwhile to consider the extreme case of **perfect information;** that is, the case where a decision-maker is able to learn with certainty which state of nature will occur. We now analyze the value to the decision-maker of having such perfect information.

For the manufacturer of perfume, perfect information corresponds to knowing which of the three demand levels for the new product will materialize. In the absence of any sample information, and using just the prior probabilities, production process A will be used. Turning to Table 11.6, we can see what would be the best choices if perfect information were available. If it were known that demand would be low, then process C would be chosen. The payoff, $300,000, is $100,000 higher than that from process A which would have been used in the absence of this knowledge. Hence, the value of knowing that demand will be low is $100,000. Similarly, if it were known that demand would be moderate, process C is again the best choice. Its payoff exceeds that of process A by $25,000, which is therefore the value of knowing that demand will be moderate. Knowledge that demand will be high is of no value, since in that event process A would in any case be the optimal choice. We see, then, that the value of perfect information will depend on what that information is. Using the prior probabilities of the states of nature, the **expected value of perfect information** can be found.

For the perfume manufacturer, the prior probabilities are 0.1 for low, 0.5 for moderate, and 0.4 for high demand. Therefore, to this manufacturer, perfect information is worth $100,000 with probability 0.1, $25,000 with probability 0.5, and nothing with probability 0.4. The expected value of perfect information is thus:

$$\text{EVPI} = (0.1)(100,000) + (0.5)(25,000) + (0.4)(0) = \$22,500$$

We therefore conclude that the expected value to the perfume manufacturer of knowing which demand level will result is $22,500.

The general procedure for computing the expected value of perfect information is set out in the box below.

Expected Value of Perfect Information

Suppose a decision-maker has to choose from among K possible actions, and is faced with H states of nature, $s_1, s_2, \ldots, s_H$. **Perfect information** is the certain knowledge of which state of nature will occur. The expected value of perfect information is found as follows:

(i) Determine which action will be selected if only the prior probabilities $P(s_1)$, $P(s_2), \ldots, P(s_H)$ are used.

(ii) For each possible state of nature, s_i, find the difference, W_i, between the payoff for the best choice of action if it were known that state would occur, and the payoff for the action chosen using only the prior probabilities. This is the value of perfect information when it is known that s_i will occur.

(iii) The **expected value of perfect information** is then calculated from

$$\text{EVPI} = P(s_1)W_1 + P(s_2)W_2 + \ldots + P(s_H)W_H$$

As we have already suggested, it will generally be unrealistic to believe that perfect information can be obtained. Nevertheless, the expected value of perfect information is a useful concept. Since no sample information can be better than perfect, it cannot possibly have more value than perfect information. Therefore the expected value of perfect information provides an *upper bound* for the expected value of any sample information. Suppose, for example, that a market research group offered to carry out, at a cost of $25,000, an evaluation for the perfume manufacturer. It is not even necessary to enquire how reliable this evaluation might be. It is already known that whatever its quality, its expected value to the manufacturer cannot be more than $22,500. Since this expected value is less than its cost, the sample information should not, according to the expected monetary value criterion, be purchased.

EXPECTED VALUE OF SAMPLE INFORMATION

Next we turn to the more general problem of assessing the value to a decision-maker of sample information that may be less than perfect. The market research organization which can supply assessments to the perfume manufacturer has a track record, as shown in Table 11.8. This allows us to determine the quality of the information provided by this organization, and hence its value. The market research group rates the prospects for the new product as either "poor," "fair," or "good." We saw in Section 11.4 that in both of these last two cases, process A, the original choice based on only the prior probabilities, will still be chosen. Therefore, if a "fair" or "good" rating is provided, the initial choice of action will remain unchanged, so that the sample information will have no monetary value to the decision maker. It will simply confirm the appropriateness of a decision that in any case would have been taken.

The position is different, however, if the rating provided for the prospects of the new product is "poor." From Table 11.10, we now see that the optimal decision is to use production process C. This optimal choice would give an expected monetary value of $375,400, compared with $354,000 for process A which would have been chosen in the absence of the sample information. The difference in these amounts, $21,400, is the value of the sample information, *if the assessment is "poor."* Thus, the sample information has no value for assessments of "fair" or "good," and a value of $21,400 if the assessment is "poor."

In order to find the expected value of the sample information, we must determine the probabilities of these three assessments. In general, if A denotes a piece of sample information and $s_1, s_2, \ldots, s_H$ are the H possible states of nature, the probability of obtaining this specific sample information can be expressed as

$$P(A) = P(A|s_1)P(s_1) + P(A|s_2)P(s_2) + \ldots + P(A|s_H)P(s_H)$$

For the perfume manufacturer, with s_1, s_2, s_3 denoting respectively low, moderate, and high demand, the prior probabilities are

$$P(s_1) = 0.1; P(s_2) = 0.5; P(s_3) = 0.4$$

Also, from Table 11.8 we can extract the conditional probabilities

$$P(\text{Poor}|s_1) = 0.6; P(\text{Poor}|s_2) = 0.3; P(\text{Poor}|s_3) = 0.1$$

It follows therefore that the probability of a "poor" assessment is

$$P(\text{Poor}) = P(\text{Poor}|s_1)P(s_1) + P(\text{Poor}|s_2)P(s_2) + P(\text{Poor}|s_3)P(s_3)$$

$$= (0.6)(0.1) + (0.3)(0.5) + (0.1)(0.4) = 0.25$$

In the same manner, using the prior probabilities in conjunction with the conditional probabilities of Table 11.8, we find for the other two possible assessments

$$P(\text{Fair}) = 0.25; P(\text{Good}) = 0.50$$

It can be seen that the value of the sample information is $21,400 with probability 0.25, $0 with probability 0.25, and $0 with probability 0.50. Therefore, the **expected value of this sample information** is

$$\text{EVSI} = (0.25)(21,400) + (0.25)(0) + (0.50)(0) = \$5350$$

This amount represents the expected worth to the decision-maker of the sample information. Following the expected monetary value criterion, the sample information will be worth acquiring provided its cost is less than its expected value. The **expected net value of sample information** is defined as the difference between expected value and cost.

If the market research organization requires a fee of $2500 for assessing the prospects of the new product, the expected net value of this assessment to the perfume manufacturer is $(5350 - 2500) = \$2850$. We can therefore conclude that if the sample information is purchased, the manufacturer's expected payoff will be $2850 higher than if it is not. This amount represents the expected worth of acquiring that information taking into account its cost. It follows, of course, that the overall optimal strategy for the perfume manufacturer is to first consult the market research group, and then to use process C if the assessment is "poor" and process A otherwise. The expected monetary value of this strategy is the sum of two parts—$435,000 which would be expected if the decision were based exclusively on prior probabilities for the states of nature—plus an additional $2850 which is the expected net gain from consulting the market reserach group. The optimal strategy therefore has a total expected monetary value of $437,850.

The general procedure for computing the expected value of sample information is set out in the box below.

Expected Value of Sample Information

Suppose a decision maker has to choose from among K possible actions, and is faced with H states of nature, $s_1, s_2, \ldots, s_H$. The opportunity is available to acquire sample information, with M possible sample results, $A_1, A_2, \ldots, A_M$. The expected value of sample information is computed as follows:

(i) Determine which action would be selected if only the prior probabilities were used.

(ii) Find the probabilities of obtaining each sample result

$$P(A_i) = P(A_i|s_1)P(s_1) + P(A_i|s_2)P(s_2) + \ldots + P(A_i|s_H)P(s_H)$$

for $i = 1, 2, \ldots, M$.

(iii) For each possible sample outcome, A_i, find the difference, V_i, between the expected monetary value for the optimal action and that for the action chosen when only the prior probabilities are used. This is the value of the sample information given that the sample outcome A_i has occurred.

(iv) The **expected value of sample information** is then computed as

$$\text{EVSI} = P(A_1)V_1 + P(A_2)V_2 + \ldots + P(A_M)V_M$$

The **expected net value of sample information** is the difference between EVSI and the cost of the information.

By the expected monetary value criterion, sample information should be purchased if and only if its expected net value is positive.

DECISION TREES AND THE VALUE OF SAMPLE INFORMATION

The expected value of sample information can be calculated in an alternative, but equivalent way, which, although it is arithmetically somewhat more lengthy, allows the problem to be seen through the construction of decision trees.

We can look at the problem as one in which a *sequence* of decisions must be taken. First, it must be decided whether or not to purchase the sample information. Next, an action must be chosen. In sequential decision-making problems, analysis proceeds in the reverse order to that in which the decisions must be taken. Accordingly, we first examine the choice of production process, given specific evaluations from the market research group. (Later we will discuss the problem of whether or not to purchase such an evaluation.)

Figure 11.2 shows the decision trees following from the three possible market research appraisals. These trees have the same general structure as that of Figure 11.1. The essential difference is that the probabilities associated with the three states of nature are the appropriate **posterior probabilities,** based on the specific sample information. These posterior probabilities were found in the previous section. The payoffs are now weighted by the posterior probabilities, giving the expected monetary value of each action, given each possible sample result. These are the expected monetary values of Table 11.10. Finally, at the left of each part of Figure 11.2, we show the highest achievable expected monetary value for each possible sample outcome.

This information is transferred to Figure 11.3, in which the decision as to whether or not to purchase the market research study is analyzed. If this information is not bought, then we see in the bottom half of the figure an expected monetary value of $435,000. This results from using the prior probabilities, and is taken from Figure 11.1.

Turning now to the upper half of Figure 11.3, the expected monetary value that results will depend on the sample outcome. The probabilities are 0.25 for "poor," 0.25 for "fair," and 0.50 for "good," as we have already seen. Thus, since $375,400 can be expected with probability 0.25, $418,000 with probability 0.25, and $484,000 with probability 0.50, the expected payoff if the sample information is purchased is

$$(0.25)(375,400) + (0.25)(418,000) + (0.50)(484,000) = \$440,350$$

However, it is necessary to subtract from this figure the $2500 cost of the sample information, leaving $437,850. Since this exceeds the expected payoff when no

FIGURE 11.2 Decision trees for the perfume manufacturer, given the market research organization assessments of (a) "poor," (b) "fair," and (c) "good."

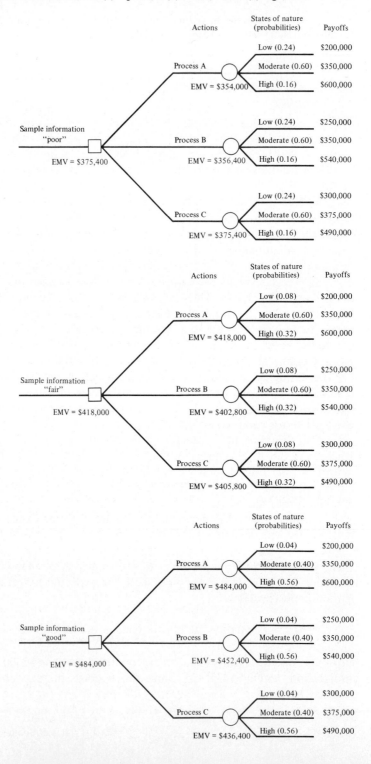

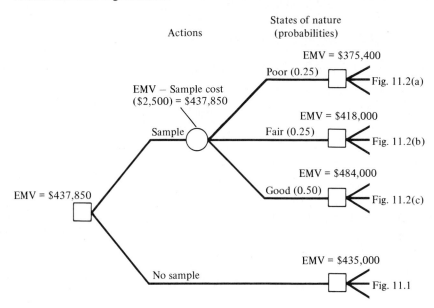

sample information is obtained, the optimal strategy is to purchase the services of the market research group. The optimal decision has, as indicated at the left of Figure 11.3, an expected monetary value of $437,850.

11.6. A FURTHER EXAMPLE

To further illustrate the ideas of the previous sections, consider the problem of a consultant who is thinking of the possibility of submitting detailed bids for two contracts. The bid for the first contract will cost $1000 to prepare, while that for the second contract will cost $1500. If the bid for the first contract is accepted and the work is carried out, the consultant will earn a profit of $8000. If the bid for the second contract is accepted and the work is carried out, the profit on this contract will be $12,000. Costs of bid preparation must be subtracted from these profits. The consultant can, if she chooses, submit bids on both contracts. However, she does not have the resources to carry out both pieces of work simultaneously. In the event that both bids are accepted, she must then decline to work on one of the contracts. This consultant estimates that through such an action, she will incur a goodwill loss of $2000.

The consultant has four possible actions from which to choose:

a_1: Bid on neither contract

a_2: Bid on first contract, but not on second

a_3: Bid on second contract, but not on first

a_4: Bid on both contracts

Also, there are four possible states of nature:

s_1: Both bids would be rejected

s_2: Bid on first contract would be accepted, and that on the second rejected

s_3: Bid on second contract would be accepted, and that on the first rejected

s_4: Both bids would be accepted

The payoffs for the sixteen action-state of nature combinations are then calculated by subtracting from profit for work done, costs of bid preparation and goodwill loss (if any). Table 11.11 displays these payoffs. Notice that if both bids are prepared and accepted, work can only proceed on one contract. This will be the second, as it is the more profitable. Also, in this case we must subtract $2000 goodwill loss as well as the costs of preparing the two bids. The payoff for action a_4, under state of nature s_4, is therefore

$$\text{Payoff} = 12,000 - 1000 - 1500 - 2000 = \$7500$$

Examination of Table 11.11 reveals that all four actions are admissible. We will now consider the application of the expected monetary value criterion to the solution of this decision problem. To do so, it is necessary to specify probabilities for the four states of nature. In fact, the consultant believes that the probability is 0.8 that a bid for the first contract would be accepted, and the probability is 0.5 that a bid for the second contract would be accepted. Moreover, the acceptance of one bid is believed to be statistically independent of the acceptance of the other. In these circumstances, the probabilities for the four states of nature are:

$P(s_1) = P(\text{First Rejected} \cap \text{Second Rejected}) = (1 - 0.8)(1 - 0.5) = 0.1$

$P(s_2) = P(\text{First Accepted} \cap \text{Second Rejected}) = 0.8(1 - 0.5) = 0.4$

$P(s_3) = P(\text{First Rejected} \cap \text{Second Accepted}) = (1 - 0.8)0.5 = 0.1$

$P(s_4) = P(\text{First Accepted} \cap \text{Second Accepted}) = (0.8)(0.5) = 0.4$

These probabilities can then be used to weight the payoffs of Table 11.11 in the calculation of expected monetary values for the four actions. We find:

$\text{EMV}(a_1) = (0.1)(0) + (0.4)(0) + (0.1)(0) + (0.4)(0) = \$0$

$\text{EMV}(a_2) = (0.1)(-1000) + (0.4)(7000) + (0.1)(-1000) + (0.4)(7000) = \$5400$

$\text{EMV}(a_3) = (0.1)(-1500) + (0.4)(-1500) + (0.1)(10,500)$
$$+ (0.4)(10,500) = \$4500$$

$\text{EMV}(a_4) = (0.1)(-2500) + (0.4)(5500) + (0.1)(9500) + (0.4)(7500) = \$5900$

TABLE 11.11 Payoff table for the consultant (in dollars).

ACTIONS	STATES OF NATURE			
	s_1	s_2	s_3	s_4
a_1	0	0	0	0
a_2	−1,000	7,000	−1,000	7,000
a_3	−1,500	−1,500	10,500	10,500
a_4	−2,500	5,500	9,500	7,500

It can be seen that by the expected monetary value criterion, action a_4, with an expected payoff of $5900, should be chosen. The consultant's best strategy, if expected payoff is to be maximized, is to submit bids for both contracts. This conclusion is illustrated in the decision tree of Figure 11.4.

Suppose now that the consultant has the opportunity to purchase "inside information" on the prospects of the bid for the first contract. (No such infor-

FIGURE 11.4 Decision tree for the consultant.

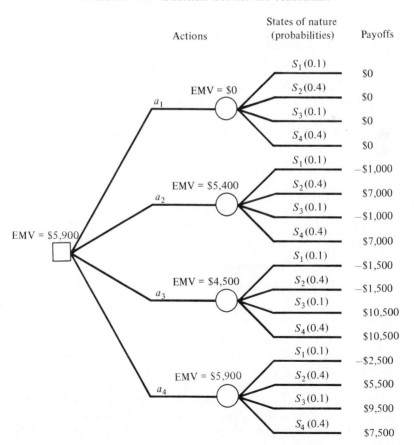

mation is available for the second contract.) The informant is thought to be 99% reliable, in the sense that whatever the eventual outcome, that outcome will be correctly predicted 99% of the time. In terms of conditional probabilities, then,

$$P(\text{Predict Accepted}|\text{Accepted}) = 0.99; \ P(\text{Predict Rejected}|\text{Rejected}) = 0.99$$

We can now find the posterior probabilities that *the bid for the first contract* will be accepted, given the two possible predictions from the informant. This is achieved through Bayes' theorem, using the prior probabilities

$$P(\text{Accepted}) = 0.8; \ P(\text{Rejected}) = 0.2$$

We find, then,

$P(\text{Accepted}|\text{Predict Accepted})$

$$= \frac{P(\text{Predict Accepted}|\text{Accepted})P(\text{Accepted})}{P(\text{Predict Accepted}|\text{Accepted})P(\text{Accepted}) + P(\text{Predict Accepted}|\text{Rejected})P(\text{Rejected})}$$

$$= \frac{(0.99)(0.8)}{(0.99)(0.8) + (0.01)(0.2)} = 0.9975$$

and

$P(\text{Accepted}|\text{Predict Rejected})$

$$= \frac{P(\text{Predict Rejected}|\text{Accepted})P(\text{Accepted})}{P(\text{Predict Rejected}|\text{Accepted})P(\text{Accepted}) + P(\text{Predict Rejected}|\text{Rejected})P(\text{Rejected})}$$

$$= \frac{(0.01)(0.8)}{(0.01)(0.8) + (0.99)(0.2)} = 0.3883$$

We now apply the expected monetary value criterion to the consultant's decision problem for the two possible predictions from the informant.

(i) *Prediction that bid for first contract will be accepted:* Given such a prediction, the posterior probability for acceptance of the bid for the first contract is 0.9975. Since no additional information is available on the bid for the second contract, the probability of its acceptance remains 0.5. The probabilities for the four states of nature, given the sample information, are therefore

$$P(s_1) = P(\text{First Rejected} \cap \text{Second Rejected}) = (0.0025)(0.5) = 0.00125$$

$$P(s_2) = P(\text{First Accepted} \cap \text{Second Rejected}) = (0.9975)(0.5) = 0.49875$$

$$P(s_3) = P(\text{First Rejected} \cap \text{Second Accepted}) = (0.0025)(0.5) = 0.00125$$

$$P(s_4) = P(\text{First Accepted} \cap \text{Second Accepted}) = (0.9975)(0.5) = 0.49875$$

The expected monetary values for the four actions are now:

$$\text{EMV}(a_1) = (0.00125)(0) + (0.49875)(0) + (0.00125)(0) + (0.49875)(0) = \$0$$

$$\text{EMV}(a_2) = (0.00125)(-1000) + (0.49875)(7000) + (0.00125)(-1000)$$
$$+ (0.49875)(7000) = \$6980$$

$$\text{EMV}(a_3) = (0.00125)(-1500) + (0.49875)(-1500) + (0.00125)(10,500)$$
$$+ (0.49875)(10,500) = \$4500$$

$$\text{EMV}(a_4) = (0.00125)(-2500) + (0.49875)(5500) + (0.00125)(9500)$$
$$+ (0.49875)(7500) = \$6492.50$$

It can be concluded, then, that if the prediction is that the bid for the first contract will be accepted, the optimal action is now a_2—bid on the first contract, but not on the second—with expected payoff $6980.

(ii) *Prediction that bid for first contract will be rejected:* Since, in the event of this prediction, the posterior probability that the first project bid will be accepted is 0.3883, it follows that the posterior probabilities for the states of nature are:

$$P(s_1) = P(\text{First Rejected} \cap \text{Second Rejected}) = (0.6117)(0.5) = 0.30585$$

$$P(s_2) = P(\text{First Accepted} \cap \text{Second Rejected}) = (0.3883)(0.5) = 0.19415$$

$$P(s_3) = P(\text{First Rejected} \cap \text{Second Accepted}) = (0.6117)(0.5) = 0.30585$$

$$P(s_4) = P(\text{First Accepted} \cap \text{Second Accepted}) = (0.3883)(0.5) = 0.19415$$

Hence, the expected monetary values for the four actions are:

$$\text{EMV}(a_1) = (0.30585)(0) + (0.19415)(0) + (0.30585)(0) + (0.19415)(0) = \$0$$

$$\text{EMV}(a_2) = (0.30585)(-1000) + (0.19415)(7000) + (0.30585)(-1000)$$
$$+ (0.19415)(7000) = \$2106.40$$

$$\text{EMV}(a_3) = (0.30585)(-1500) + (0.19415)(-1500) + (0.30585)(10,500)$$
$$+ (0.19415)(10,500) = \$4500$$

$$\text{EMV}(a_4) = (0.30585)(-2500) + (0.19415)(5500) + (0.30585)(9500)$$
$$+ (0.19415)(7500) = \$4664.90$$

Here it emerges that as in the case where only the prior probabilities are used, the optimal decision is to submit bids for both contracts. Given the prediction that the bid for the first contract will be rejected, this action now has an expected payoff of $4664.90.

EXPECTED VALUE OF THE SAMPLE INFORMATION

In the absence of inside information, the consultant will submit bids for both contracts, and this will remain the optimal course of action even if the prediction is that the bid for the first contract will be rejected. Therefore, the sample information only has positive value when the prediction is that the bid will be accepted. In that case, a bid should only be made on the first contract. The gain from the sample information is then $6980 − \$6,492.50 = \$487.50$, the difference between the expected value of the optimal action and that of the action that would have been chosen in the absence of sample information.

To compute the expected value of the sample information we need the probabilities of occurrence of the sample outcomes. The probability of a prediction that the bid will be accepted is

$$P(\text{Predict Accepted}) = P(\text{Predict Accepted}|\text{Accepted})P(\text{Accepted}) + P(\text{Predict Accepted}|\text{Rejected})P(\text{Rejected})$$

$$= (0.99)(0.8) + (0.01)(0.2) = 0.794$$

Therefore, the sample information has value $487.50 with probability 0.794 and value $0 with probability 0.206. Hence its expected value is

$$\text{EVSI} = (0.794)(487.50) + (0.206)(0) = \$387.075$$

Thus, according to the expected monetary value criterion, it follows that the inside information on the prospects of the bid for the first contract should only be purchased by the consultant if its cost is less than $387.075.

EXPECTED VALUE OF PERFECT INFORMATION

In the context of decision-making problems, perfect information is knowledge of which state of nature will occur. For the consultant this is equivalent to knowing whether or not each of the two prospective bids would be accepted. To find the expected value of such information, we refer to Table 11.11, and recall that in the absence of sample information a_4 is the optimal action.

If s_1 results, a_1 is the best choice, and its payoff exceeds by $2500 that of a_4. Given state s_2, action a_2 would be best, and has a payoff $1500 above that of a_4. Under state s_3, the best course is a_3, with a payoff $1000 higher than that of a_4. Finally, the optimal action in state s_4 is also a_3, with a payoff of $3000 more than a_4. Weighting these gains by their probabilities of occurrence, that is, by the prior probabilities, gives the expected value of perfect information

$$\text{EVPI} = (0.1)(2500) + (0.4)(1500) + (0.1)(1000) + (0.4)(3,000) = \$2150$$

This is the most, according to the expected monetary value criterion, that the consultant should pay for any sample information, however reliable.

11.7. RISK AND EXPECTED UTILITY

The expected monetary value criterion is a widely applicable tool for the analysis of decision-making problems. In many practical situations the decision-maker will feel it is appropriate to adopt that course of action for which expected monetary value is highest. This, however, is not invariably the case. The following two examples illustrate circumstances in which a rational individual may prefer some action other than that with the highest expected monetary value.

Consider the position of a family member who has to decide whether or not to purchase term life insurance. The two available actions are to purchase or not to purchase. Now, if no purchase is made, the expected payoff is zero. On the other hand, for the purchase of such a policy, the expected payoff is negative. This must be the case, since on the average, insurance companies set the prices of policies sufficiently high to cover operating costs and provide a margin of profit as well as covering expected payments on claims. It can be seen, then, that if expected monetary value is used as the criterion for decision making, term life insurance will not be purchased. Nevertheless, many rational people do buy this insurance coverage. They are prepared to sacrifice something in expected return in order to provide some financial security for other family members in the event of death.

An investor may consider investment in several mutual funds. Generally, these will not all have the same expected rates of return. However, it is not invariably appropriate to invest in that fund with the highest expected return. It is typically the case that those funds with the highest expected returns also have the greatest uncertainty about such expectations. Thus, the chances of sustaining a large capital loss are relatively high for these funds. Many investors will be prepared to make tradeoffs in expected return, preferring a more conservative investment with more security. Hence, this too is a situation in which a rational decision-maker may choose an action which does not have the highest possible expected monetary value.

In our two examples, the decision-maker has exhibited a preference for a criterion of choice other than expected monetary value, and in both cases this preference appears quite reasonable. Both examples involve a common ingredient, in addition to expected monetary value, that influences the decision-maker. In each case, the decision-maker is taking into account **risk.** The purchaser of term life insurance is prepared to accept a negative expected payoff as the price to be paid for the chance of a large positive payoff in the event of death. In so doing, he is expressing a **preference** for risk. On the other hand, the investor who sacrifices something in expected return by purchasing stock in a less risky mutual fund is exhibiting an **aversion** to risk.

The expected monetary value criterion is inappropriate for decision makers who have either a preference for, or an aversion to, risk. However, it is possible to modify this criterion to allow for attitude to risk. In the present section we will see how this can be accomplished.

THE CONCEPT OF UTILITY

To illustrate the ideas involved, consider an investor who wishes to choose between investing $10,000 for one year at a fixed, assured, interest rate of 12%, and investing the same amount over that period in a portfolio of common stocks. If the fixed interest choice is made, the investor will receive with certainty a payoff of $1200. However, if the stock portfolio is chosen, the return achieved will depend on the performance over the year of the stock market. If the market is buoyant, a profit of $2500 is expected; if the market is steady expected profit is $500, and if the market is depressed a loss of $1000 is expected. The investor believes that the probabilities for a buoyant, steady, and depressed stock market are, respectively, 0.6, 0.2, and 0.2. This information is summarized in Table 11.12.

We will begin our analysis of this problem by applying the expected monetary value criterion. Since the fixed interest investment will yield $1200 whatever state of nature arises, that is the expected monetary value of this action. For investment in the portfolio of stocks, the expected monetary value is

$$\text{EMV(Stock Portfolio)} = (0.6)(2500) + (0.2)(500) + (0.2)(-1000) = \$1400$$

TABLE 11.12 Payoffs and states of nature probabilities for the investor.

INVESTMENT	STATE OF MARKET		
	BUOYANT	STEADY	DEPRESSED
PROBABILITIES	0.6	0.2	0.2
FIXED INTEREST	1,200	1,200	1,200
STOCK PORTFOLIO	2,500	500	−1,000

Therefore, according to the expected monetary value criterion, the stock portfolio should be chosen.

We now need to ask, for a particular investor, whether the higher expected return from the stock portfolio merits the risk of losing $1000, which would occur if the market turned out to be depressed. For a very wealthy investor, who could easily sustain such a loss, this would almost certainly be the case. However, the position could be quite different for a relatively poor person, to whom the loss of $1000 would be a serious financial blow. For such an investor, it is necessary to substitute for the dollar payoffs quantities which more adequately reflect the serious nature of a loss of $1000. These quantities need to measure the value, or **utility,** to the investor of a loss of $1000 as compared with, for example, gains of $1200 or $2500.

The notion of utility, which plays a fundamental part in micro-economic theory, provides a basis for the solution of decision-making problems when there is either aversion to, or preference for risk. To employ it, only fairly mild and generally reasonable, assumptions need to be made. Suppose that an individual is faced with several alternative payoffs which need not be monetary in nature. We assume that the individual can rank in order (possibly with ties) the satisfaction, or utility, derived from each of these payoffs. Then, if payoff A is preferred to B, and B is preferred to C, it must be the case that A is preferred to C.

Also it is necessary to assume that if payoff A is preferred to B, and B is preferred to C, there exists a wager in which A is offered with probability p and C is offered with probability $1 - p$, such that the decision-maker is indifferent between the wager and receiving B with certainty. Given these, and certain other generally reasonable assumptions, it can be proved that a rational decision-maker will choose that course of action for which expected utility is as high as possible. Therefore, decision problems can be analyzed exactly as in the previous four sections, *but with utilities in place of payoffs.* Thus, we build a utility table rather than a payoff table, and employ states of nature probabilities to compute expected utilities.

We will now see how utilities can be determined, illustrating through the case of the investor whose four possible payoffs are −$1000, $500, $1200, and $2500. The steps involved are set out in the box below.

Suppose that a decision-maker could receive several different payoffs. The corresponding utilities are obtained as follows:

(i) The scale of measurement of utilities is arbitrary. Any choice that is convenient can be made. Let L be the lowest and H the highest of all the payoffs. We can assign utility zero to payoff L and utility 100 to payoff H.

(ii) Denote by I any payoff intermediate between L and H. It is necessary to find the probability p such that the decision-maker is indifferent between the following two alternatives:
   (a) Receive payoff H with probability p and payoff L with probability $1 - p$.
   (b) Receive payoff I with certainty.

(iii) The utility to this decision-maker of payoff I is then $100p$. The curve which describes the relationship between utility and payoff is called a **utility function.**

The first step is straightforward and simply provides a convenient scale for measuring utility. Any other would do; for example, we could assign utility zero to the lowest payoff and one to the highest.

In practice, the second step is the most difficult. The probability p is found by trial and error, through asking the decision maker questions of the type:

Q. "Would you prefer to receive I with certainty, or a wager in which you received H with probability 0.9 and L with probability 0.1?"

Q. "Would you prefer to receive I with certainty, or a wager in which you received H with probability 0.8 and L with probability 0.2?"

We continue in this way until the point of indifference is reached.

The rationale behind the final step is easily seen. Since H has utility 100 and L has utility zero, the **expected** utility from receiving H with probability p and L with utility $1 - p$ is $100p$. Since the decision-maker is indifferent between this wager and receiving I with certainty, utility $100p$ is attached to the intermediate payoff.

We return now to the problem of the investor, for whom the possible payoffs are $-\$1000$, $\$500$, $\$1200$, and $\$2500$. Utility zero is attached to a loss of $\$1000$ and utility 100 to a gain of $\$2500$. To obtain utilities for the two intermediate payoffs, the investor must be asked series of questions of the form:

Q. "Would you prefer to receive $\$500$ with certainty, or a wager in which you gained $\$2500$ with probability p and lost $\$1000$ with probability $1 - p$?"

Different values of the probability p are tried until the point of indifference is found. The process is repeated for the payoff of $\$1200$.

Assume that this investor is indifferent between an assured payoff of $500 and a wager in which $2500 is gained with probability 0.6 and $1000 lost with probability 0.4. The investor is also indifferent between the certain receipt of $1200 and a wager in which $2500 is gained with probability 0.8 and $1000 lost with probability 0.2. Then, the utilities for the two intermediate payoffs are:

Payoff $500 : Utility = (100)(0.6) = 60
Payoff $1200: Utility = (100)(0.8) = 80

In Figure 11.5 we have plotted the four utilities against the corresponding payoffs for this investor, and joined the points with a smooth curve. The shape of this curve characterizes the investor's attitude to risk. Of necessity, utility increases as the payoff increases. Notice, however, that it does so at a decreasing rate. This implies a distaste for the lowest payoffs that is more than commensurate with their dollar amounts, and hence an **aversion** to risk. This aversion can be seen from the decision-maker's attitudes to the wagers offered. For instance, the investor is indifferent between an assured payoff of $1200 and a wager in which $2500 is gained with probability 0.8 and $1000 lost with probability 0.2. The expected monetary value of this wager is

$$(0.8)(2500) + (0.2)(-1000) = \$1800$$

which is well above the equally preferred certain payoff of $1200. The extent of this difference gives a measure of the degree of aversion to risk.

FIGURE 11.5 Utility function for an investor.

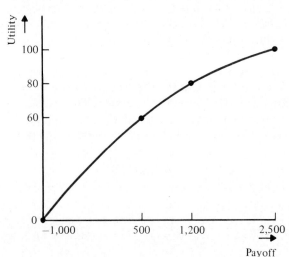

FIGURE 11.6 Utility functions.

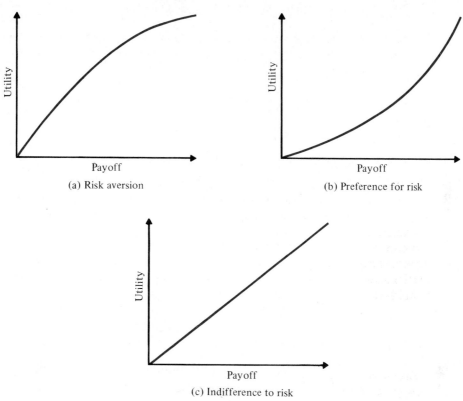

FIGURE 11.6 Utility functions.

(a) Risk aversion

(b) Preference for risk

(c) Indifference to risk

The shape of Figure 11.5 is characteristic of aversion to risk. Figure 11.6 shows three types of utility functions. That in part (a) of the figure, where the rate of increase of utility is greatest at the lowest payoffs, has the same shape as Figure 11.5, again showing an **aversion** to risk. In part (b) of Figure 11.6 the rate of increase of utility is greatest at the highest payoffs. This implies a taste for these payoffs that is more than commensurate with their dollar values; and hence a **preference** for risk. Part (c) of the figure depicts the intermediate case. The relationship between utility and payoff is linear, so that utility increases at a constant rate over the whole range of payoffs. In this case the monetary values of the payoffs provide a true measure of the utility of these payoffs to the decision-maker. In this case, then, the decision-maker is **indifferent** to risk.

THE EXPECTED UTILITY CRITERION

Once the decision-maker's utilities for the different possible payoffs have been determined, expected utilities for each action can be found using the probabilities for the states of nature. The expected utility criterion then dictates the choice of that action for which expected utility is highest.

Consider a decision-maker with K possible actions, $a_1, a_2, \ldots, a_K$, and faced with H states of nature. Denote by U_{ij} the utility of the i-th action in the j-th state, and let p_j be the probability of occurrence of the j-th state. Then, the **expected utility** of action a_i is

$$EU(a_i) = p_1\, U_{i1} + p_2\, U_{i2} + \ldots + p_H\, U_{iH}$$

$$= \sum_{j=1}^{H} p_j\, U_{ij}$$

Under the **expected utility criterion**, the action with highest expected utility is chosen. Given generally realistic assumptions, it can be shown that this criterion should be adopted by a rational decision-maker.

If the decision-maker is indifferent to risk, the expected utility criterion and the expected monetary value criterion are identical.

Table 11.13 shows utilities and states of nature probabilities for the investor considering a stock portfolio and fixed interest investment. It differs from Table 11.13 only in the replacement of dollar payoffs by their utilities to this investor. For investment in the fixed interest securities the expected utility is 80, as this utility will be derived whatever state of nature arises. The expected utility from the common stock portfolio is

$$EU(\text{Stock Portfolio}) = (0.6)(100) + (0.2)(60) + (0.2)(0) = 72$$

Since this is less than 80, the investor should, according to the expected utility criterion, choose the fixed interest investment. Based on the expected monetary value criterion, the portfolio of stocks was preferred. However, the incorporation into the analysis of the extent of this investor's aversion to risk now leads us to see that the fixed interest investment is a better choice. This example shows that when risk is an important consideration, the expected monetary value criterion can be inappropriate for the solution of decision-making problems.

As we illustrate in Figure 11.7, a decision tree can be employed to represent the application of the expected utility criterion to decision-making problems.

TABLE 11.13 Utilities and states of nature probabilities for the investor.

INVESTMENT	STATE OF MARKET		
	BUOYANT	STEADY	DEPRESSED
PROBABILITIES	0.6	0.2	0.2
FIXED INTEREST	80	80	80
STOCK PORTFOLIO	100	60	0

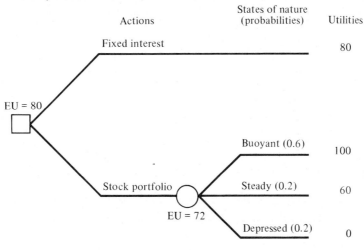

FIGURE 11.7 Decision tree for an investor using the expected utility criterion.

The expected utility criterion is the most broadly applicable and intellectually justifiable of the criteria we have discussed for analyzing decision-making problems. Its main drawback in practical application lies in the difficulty of eliciting information about which wagers are seen as equally attractive to particular assured payoffs. This type of information is essential for the determination of utilities. For a wide range of problems, where indifference to risk can reasonably be assumed, the expected monetary value criterion can still be employed. This would generally be the case, for example, in decision-making in a mature corporation, when the payoffs would represent only a very small fraction of the corporation's turnover. On the other hand, if (as may be the case in the development of new high technology products, for example) possible losses from a project could threaten a corporation with bankruptcy, the appropriate utilities should reflect an aversion to risk.

EXERCISES

11.1. A manufacturer of candy bars is preparing to introduce a new product, and is considering four possible production processes. Three possible levels of demand—low, moderate, and high—are contemplated. The payoff table (where figures are given in dollars) is shown below

PRODUCTION PROCESS	LEVEL OF DEMAND		
	LOW	MODERATE	HIGH
A	70,000	120,000	200,000
B	80,000	120,000	180,000
C	100,000	125,000	160,000
D	100,000	120,000	150,000

(a) Are any of these actions inadmissible?

(b) Which action is selected by the maximin criterion?

(c) Which action is selected by the maximax criterion?

(d) Which action is selected by the minimax regret criterion?

(e) This manufacturer knows that 10% of new introductions to this market have met low demand, 50% moderate demand, and 40% high demand. On the basis of this information, which production process should be employed according to the expected monetary value criterion?

(f) Draw a decision tree illustrating your solution in (d).

11.2. The manufacturer of Exercise 11.1 has the opportunity to consult a market research organization, which will provide an assessment of either "poor," "fair," or "good" for the market prospects of the new candy bar. The table below shows the historical proportions of assessments of each type for candy bars achieving given levels of demand.

ASSESSMENT	LEVEL OF DEMAND		
	LOW	MODERATE	HIGH
POOR	0.6	0.3	0.1
FAIR	0.2	0.4	0.2
GOOD	0.2	0.3	0.7

(a) What are the posterior probabilities of the three states of nature, given an assessment of "poor"?

(b) If the assessment is "poor," which production process should be used?

(c) What are the posterior probabilities of the three states of nature, given an assessment of "fair"?

(d) If the assessment is "fair," which production process should be used?

(e) What are the posterior probabilities of the three states of nature, given an assessment of "good"?

(f) If the assessment is "good," which production process should be used?

(g) What is the expected value to the candy bar manufacturer of a report from the market research organization?

(h) If the market research organization charges a fee of $750 for its assessment, should this be purchased according to the expected monetary value criterion?

(i) What is the expected value of perfect information to the candy bar manufacturer?

11.3. An investor wants to choose among three alternatives—a savings account, a high-risk stock, and a low-risk stock—for a $20,000 investment. The following possible states of nature are contemplated:

s_1: Stock market rises
s_2: Stock market remains flat
s_3: Stock market falls

The payoff table (in dollars) is as follows.

ACTIONS	STATES OF NATURE		
	s_1	s_2	s_3
SAVINGS	1200	1200	1200
HIGH-RISK STOCK	3500	250	−1500
LOW-RISK STOCK	2250	500	−250

(a) Are any of these actions inadmissible?

(b) Which action is selected by the maximin criterion?

(c) Which action is selected by the maximax criterion?

(d) Which action is selected by the minimax regret criterion?

(e) The investor believes that the probability is 0.5 that the stock market will rise, 0.3 that it will remain flat, and 0.2 that it will fall. According to the expected monetary value criterion, which investment should be chosen?

(f) Draw a decision tree illustrating your solution in (d).

(g) This investor is confident of the assessment that the probability is 0.5 that the stock market will rise, but is less sure of the probability assessments for the other two states of nature. In these circumstances, for what range of values for the probability that the market will fall does the action chosen in (e) remain optimal, according to the expected monetary value criterion?

11.4. A manufacturer of earth-moving equipment has to decide if, and when, to introduce a new product line. There are four possible actions:

a_1: Begin production immediately

a_2: Delay production one year

a_3: Delay production two years

a_4: Cancel the product line

The future profitability of the new product depends on the level of road construction activity over the next five years. There are three possible states of nature:

s_1: Low activity level

s_2: Medium activity level

s_3: High activity level

The table below shows payoffs in millions of dollars.

ACTIONS	STATES OF NATURE		
	s_1	s_2	s_3
a_1	−10	1	18
a_2	−7	4	8
a_3	−7	−2	6
a_4	0	0	0

(a) Are any of the actions inadmissible?

(b) Which action is chosen by the maximin criterion?

(c) Which action is chosen by the maximax criterion?

(d) Which action is chosen by the minimax regret criterion?

(e) Historically, 20% of the time construction activity has been low, 40% of the time it has been medium, and 40% of the time it has been high. Given only this information, which action should be chosen according to the expected monetary value criterion?

(f) Draw a decision tree to illustrate your solution to (d).

(g) This manufacturer is uncertain about the estimated payoff for action a_1 under state of nature s_3. Under what range of values for this payoff does the action chosen in (e) remain optimal, according to the expected monetary value criterion, if the states of nature probabilities and the other payoffs are held at their original levels?

11.5. The manufacturer of Exercise 11.4 has the opportunity to purchase from a forecasting group a prediction of the future level of road construction activity. The following table shows the proportions of "weak," "steady," and "buoyant" forecasts, given the level of activity actually resulting:

FORECAST	ACTIVITY LEVEL		
	LOW	MEDIUM	HIGH
WEAK	0.6	0.3	0.2
STEADY	0.3	0.4	0.3
BUOYANT	0.1	0.3	0.5

(a) What are the posterior probabilities of the three states of nature, given a forecast of "weak"?

(b) If the assessment is "weak," which action should be taken?

(c) What are the posterior probabilities of the three states of nature, given a forecast of "steady?"

(d) If the forecast is "steady," which action should be taken?

(e) What are the posterior probabilities of the three states of nature, given a forecast of "buoyant?"

(f) If the forecast is "buoyant," which action should be taken?

(g) What is the expected value to the manufacturer of earth-moving equipment of a prediction from the forecasting group?

(h) What is the expected value of perfect information to the manufacturer of earth-moving equipment?

11.6. Consider a decision problem with two possible actions and two states of nature.

(a) Provide an example of a payoff table such that both actions are admissible, and the same action is chosen by the maximin criterion and the minimax regret criterion.

(b) Provide an example of a payoff table such that different actions are chosen by the maximin criterion and the minimax regret criterion.

(c) Formulate a description of the form the payoff table must take if the same action is chosen by the maximin criterion and the minimax regret criterion.

11.7. The prospective operator of a toy store has the opportunity to locate either in an established and successful shopping center, or, at a lower cost, in a new, recently completed center. If the new center turns out to be very successful, annual store profits from location in it are expected to be $125,000. If the center is only moderately successful, annual profit would be $50,000, while if the center is unsuccessful an annual loss of $15,000 would be expected for the toy store. The profits expected from location in the established center will also depend somewhat on the level of success of the new center, since the two centers will compete for customers. If the new center were to be unsuccessful, expected annual profit from location of the toy store in the established center would be $90,000. This expected profit would be $60,000 if the new center were moderately successful, and $30,000 if it were very successful.

(a) Set up the payoff table for the decision-making problem of the toy store operator.

(b) Where should the toy store operator locate according to the maximin criterion?

(c) Where should the toy store operator locate according to the minimax regret criterion?

(d) Historically, 40% of new shopping centers are very successful, 30% are moderately successful, and 30% unsuccessful. Based on this information, where should the toy store operator locate according to the expected monetary value criterion?

(e) Draw a decision tree to illustrate your solution in (d).

11.8. The toy store operator of Exercise 11.7 has the opportunity to purchase from a consulting group an assessment of the prospects of the new shopping center. The table shows the proportions of "good," "fair," and "poor" assessments, given the particular outcome actually materializing.

ASSESSMENT	LEVEL OF SUCCESS		
	VERY SUCCESSFUL	MODERATELY SUCCESSFUL	UNSUCCESSFUL
GOOD	0.6	0.3	0.2
FAIR	0.3	0.4	0.3
POOR	0.1	0.3	0.5

(a) What are the posterior probabilities of the three states of nature, given an assessment of "good"?

(b) Where should the toy store operator locate, given an assessment of "good"?

(c) What are the posterior probabilities of the three states of nature, given an assessment of "fair"?

(d) Where should the toy store operator locate, given an assessment of "fair"?

(e) What are the posterior probabilities of the three states of nature, given an assessment of "poor"?

(f) Where should the toy store operator locate, given an assessment of "poor"?

(g) What is the expected value to the toy store operator of an assessment from the consulting group?

(h) What is the expected value to the toy store operator of perfect information?

11.9. A company must decide how to heat a new facility. The following three alternative actions are being contemplated?

a_1: Complete solar system
a_2: Oil and natural gas
a_3: Combination of solar energy and oil and natural gas

Heating costs will depend on future energy price growth. Three states of nature are considered:

s_1: Low increases in energy prices
s_2: Moderate increases in energy prices
s_3: Large increases in energy prices

The table shows heating *costs* (in hundreds of thousands of dollars), for every year over the expected life of the facility.

ACTIONS	STATES OF NATURE		
	s_1	s_2	s_3
a_1	5	5	5
a_2	2	6	10
a_3	4	5	8

(a) Set up the payoff table.
(b) Are any of the actions inadmissible?
(c) Which action is chosen according to the maximin criterion?
(d) Which action is chosen according to the minimax regret criterion?
(e) Management believes that the probabilities for low, moderate, and large increases in energy prices are, respectively, 0.1, 0.3, and 0.6. According to the expected monetary value criterion, which action should be taken?
(f) Draw a decision tree to illustrate your solution to (d).

11.10. Consider a decision-making problem with K possible actions and H potential states of nature. Show that for such a problem, an inadmissible action cannot be selected by the expected monetary value criterion.

11.11. Consider a decision-making problem with two possible actions and two potential states of nature, each of which is equally likely to occur.
(a) Will the action chosen by the expected monetary value criterion always be the same as that chosen by the maximin criterion?
(b) Will the action chosen by the expected monetary value criterion always be the same as that chosen by the minimiax regret criterion?
(c) Will the action chosen by the expected monetary value criterion always be that for which the average of the payoffs is highest?
(d) Would your answer to (c) be the same if the two states of nature were not equally likely to occur?

11.12. A manufacturer must decide whether to mount, at a cost of $150,000, a new advertising campaign. It is estimated that if the campaign is very successful, profits will increase by $500,000 (excluding the cost of the advertising campaign). If the campaign is moderately successful, profits will increase by $200,000 while if the campaign is unsuccessful profits will be unchanged. It is estimated that the probabilities for very successful, moderately successful, and unsuccessful advertising campaigns are, respectively, 0.2, 0.4, and 0.4.
(a) Set up the payoff table.

(b) Which action should be selected according to the expected monetary value criterion?

(c) Draw a decision tree illustrating your answer in (b).

11.13. On Friday evening, the manager of a small branch of a car rental agency finds that she has available six cars for rental for the weekend. However, she is able to request delivery of additional cars, at a cost of $25 each, from the regional depot. Each car that is rented produces an expected profit of $50. (The cost of delivery of the car must be subtracted from this profit.) Each potential customer requesting a car when none is available is counted a $10 loss in goodwill. On reviewing her records for previous weekends, the manger finds that the numbers of cars requested have ranged from six to ten, with the percentages shown in the accompanying table. The manager has to decide how many cars, if any, to order from the regional depot.

NUMBER OF REQUESTS	6	7	8	9	10
PERCENT	15	25	30	20	10

(a) Set up the payoff table.

(b) According to the expected monetary value criterion, how many cars should be ordered from the regional depot?

11.14. A contractor has decided to place a bid for a project. Bids are to be set in multiples of $25,000. It is estimated that the probability that a bid of $475,000 will secure the contract is 0.3, the probability that a bid of $450,000 will be successful is 0.6, while the probability that a bid of $425,000 will be accepted is 0.8. It is believed that any bid below $425,000 is certain to succeed, while any bid over $475,000 is sure to fail. If the contractor secures the contract, it will be necessary to solve a design problem. There are two possible options. Outside consultants, who for a price of $100,000 will guarantee a solution, can be hired. Alternatively, at a cost of $30,000, an attempt can be made to solve the problem internally; if this effort fails, the consultants must then be engaged. It is estimated that the probability of successfully solving the problem internally is 0.6. When this problem has been solved, the additional cost of fulfilling the contract is $360,000.

(a) The contractor has two potential decisions to make. What are they?

(b) Draw the decision tree.

(c) According to the expected monetary value criterion, how should the contractor proceed?

11.15. A publisher intends to sign a contract for an introductory marketing text with one of three authors, Lloyd, Richards, or Gomes. If the text turns out to be very successful, then profits (excluding extraordinary advertising costs) will be $400,000, while if the book is only moderately successful these profits will be $100,000. In the event that the text fails, a loss of $75,000 will result. The following table shows probabilities, conjectured by an editor, for these states of nature for books written by the three authors.

	VERY SUCCESSFUL	MODERATELY SUCCESSFUL	FAILURE
LLOYD	0.2	0.6	0.2
RICHARDS	0.1	0.7	0.2
GOMES	0.3	0.3	0.4

The publisher also has the opportunity to mount, at a cost of $70,000, an extraordinary advertising campaign for the text, once it has been published. The editor estimates that, if this were done, the probabilities for the states of nature would be those shown in the table below.

	VERY SUCCESSFUL	MODERATELY SUCCESSFUL	FAILURE
LLOYD	0.4	0.4	0.2
RICHARDS	0.3	0.6	0.1
GOMES	0.4	0.5	0.1

(a) The publisher has two decisions to make. What are they?

(b) Draw the decision tree.

(c) According to the expected monetary value criterion, how should the publisher proceed?

(d) Following the calculations in part (c), the publisher has signed a contract with the selected author. It is then discovered that an error has been made in the publicity department, and that the actual cost of the extraordinary advertising campaign is in fact $90,000. According to the expected monetary value criterion, should the publisher offer to pay the chosen author to withdraw from the contract, and, if so, what is the largest sum that should be offered?

11.16. Consider a decision-making problem with two actions, a_1 and a_2, and two states of nature, s_1 and s_2. Let M_{ij} denote the payoff for action a_i in state s_j, and p denote the probability of occurrence of state of nature s_1.

(a) Show that action a_1 is chosen by the expected monetary value criterion if

$$p(M_{11} - M_{21}) > (1 - p)(M_{22} - M_{12}) \quad .$$

(b) Show that, if a_1 is an admissible action, there is some probability, p, for which it will be selected by the expected monetary value criterion. However, if a_1 is inadmissible, it will not be chosen, whatever the value of p.

11.17. A manufacturer makes precision instruments which have two potential faults. It is possible to check for these faults before instruments are shipped to customers. The cost of checking for the first fault is $30 and for the second, $40. If a fault is found, it can be repaired at negligible cost. Records indicate that 10% of all the instruments have the first fault, and 10% have the second fault. Also, 5% of all instruments have both faults. The manufacturer estimates the damage done, through goodwill loss by the shipment of each faulty instrument, at $400. There are three possible actions:

(i) All instruments can be shipped without checking for faults.

(ii) The check for the first fault can be made, but not for the second.

(iii) The check for the first fault can be made, and if an instrument passes this check, a check can be made for the second fault.

According to the expected monetary value criterion, which of these actions should be taken?

11.18. A manufacturer must decide whether to mount, at a cost of $150,000, an advertising campaign for a brand whose sales have been flat. It is estimated that a highly successful campaign would add $500,000 (from which the campaign's cost must be deducted) to profits. A moderately successful campaign would similarly add $200,000, while an unsuccessful campaign would add nothing. Historically, 50% of all similar campaigns have been very successful, 30% moderately successful, and 20% unsuccessful. The manufacturer can consult a media consultant for an assessment of the potential effectiveness of the advertising campaign. This consultant's record is such that she had reported favorably on 80% of campaigns that turned out to be highly successful, 40% of those that were moderately successful, and 10% of unsuccessful campaigns.

(a) What are the prior probabilities for the three states of nature?

(b) If no report from the media consultant is available, should the advertising campaign be mounted according to the expected monetary value criterion?

(c) What are the posterior probabilities for the three states of nature, given a favorable report from the media consultant?

(d) Given a favorable report from the media consultant, should the advertising campaign be mounted?

(e) What are the posterior probabilities for the three states of nature, given that the report from the media consultant is not favorable?

(f) Given that the report from the media consultant is not favorable, should the advertising campaign be mounted?

(g) According to the expected monetary value criterion, what is the most that the manufacturer should pay for a report from the media consultant?

(h) What is the expected value of perfect information to this manufacturer?

11.19. The Watts On Lightbulb Corporation ships large consignments of lightbulbs to big industrial users. When the production process is operating correctly (which occurs 90% of the time), 10% of all bulbs produced are defective. However, the production process is susceptible to a malfunction, leading to a defective rate of 20%. The Watts On Corporation views the shipment of a consignment with the higher defective rate to an industrial user as a goodwill loss of $5000. If a consignment is suspected to contain this higher proportion of defectives, it can instead be sold to a chain of discount stores. This involves a reduction of $600 in profits, whether or not the consignment does in fact contain a large proportion of defective lightbulbs. Decisions in this corporation are made according to the expected monetary value criterion.

(a) A consignment is produced. Given no further information, should it be shipped to an industrial user or to the discount chain?

(b) A single bulb from the consignment is checked. Determine where the consignment should be shipped in each of the following cases.

   (i) This bulb is defective.
   (ii) This bulb is not defective.

(c) Two bulbs from a consignment are checked. Determine where the consignment should be shipped in each of the following cases.

   (i) Both bulbs are defective.
   (ii) Only one bulb is defective.
   (iii) Neither bulb is defective.

(d) What is the expected value to the corporation of checking a single lightbulb?

(e) What is the expected value to the corporation of checking two lightbulbs?

(f) What is the difference between the expected values of checking two and one bulbs?

(g) If the first bulb checked is defective, what is the expected value of checking the second?

(h) If the first bulb is not defective, what is the expected value of checking the second?

(i) Reconcile your answer to part (f) with those to parts (g) and (h).

11.20. A manufacturer receives regular contracts for large consignments of parts for the automobile industry. This manufacturer's production process is such that when it is functioning correctly, 10% of all parts produced do not meet industry specifications. However, the process is prone to an occasional malfunction, whose presence can be checked at the beginning of a production run. When the process is operated with this malfunction, 30% of all parts produced fail to meet specifications. The manufacturer supplies these parts under a contract which yields a profit of $20,000 if only 10% of the parts are defective, and a profit of $12,000 if 30% of the parts are defective. The cost of checking for the malfunction is $1000 and, if it emerges that repair is needed, this costs an additional $2000. If these costs are incurred they must be subtracted from the profits of the contract. Historically, it has been found that the process functions correctly 80% of the time. The manufacturer must decide whether or not to check the process at the beginning of a production run, and the decision is to be based on the expected monetary value criterion.

(a) Set up the payoff table.

(b) According to the expected monetary value criterion, should the production process be checked?

(c) Draw a decision tree illustrating your answer in (b).

(d) Before commencing the full production run, it is possible to produce a single part and check whether it meets the specifications. This involves a cost of $25.

    (i) Suppose that a single part is produced, and that it turns out to be defective. Should the production process then be checked?

    (ii) Suppose that a single part is produced, and that it turns out not to be defective. Should the production process then be checked?

    (iii) Should a single part be produced and checked before deciding whether or not to examine the production process?

    (iv) Draw a decision tree illustrating your answer in (iii).

11.21. A drug manufacturer holds the patent rights to a new formula for arthritic pain relief. The manufacturer is able to sell the patent for $100,000 or to proceed with intensive tests of the drug's efficacy. The cost of carrying out these tests is $20,000. If the drug is found to be ineffective, it will not be marketed and the cost of the tests is written off as a loss. In the past, tests of drugs of a broadly similar type have shown 60% to be effective and 40% ineffective. If the manufacturer carries out the tests, and the drug is found to be effective, two options are available. The patent rights and test results could be sold for $240,000. Alternatively, the manufacturer can market the drug. In that event, if the sales campaign is highly successful, it is estimated that profits on sales (exclusive of the cost of the tests) will amount to $360,000. If the sales campaign is only moderately successful, a profit of $180,000 would be expected. The probability that the campaign will be highly successful is 0.5. This manufacturer bases decisions on the expected monetary value criterion.

(a) Potentially the drug manufacturer has two decisions to make. What are they?

(b) Draw the decision tree.

(c) How should the manufacturer proceed?

(d) What is the expected monetary value of the optimal course of action?

11.22. The drug manufacturer of Exercise 11.21 has the option of carrying out, at modest cost, an initial test on the arthritic pain drug, before deciding whether to sell the patent or proceed with intensive tests. The initial test is not infallible. For drugs that have subsequently proved effective, the initial test result was "positive" on 60% of occasions and negative on the remainder. For ineffective drugs, a "positive" initial test result was obtained 30% of the time, the other results being "negative." It is still possible to sell the patent for $100,000 if the intial test result is "negative."

(a) If the initial test result is "positive," how should the manufacturer proceed?

(b) If the initial test result is "negative," how should the manufacturer proceed?

(c) What is the expected value to the manufacturer of the initial test?

11.23. The investor of Exercise 11.3 has the following seven possible payoffs (in dollars)

$$-1500; \ -250; \ 250; \ 500; \ 1200; \ 2250; \ 3500$$

Assign utility zero to the payoff $-\$1500$ and utility 100 to the payoff $\$3500$. For each of the other five possible payoffs, the investor is asked the question:

Q. "Would you prefer to receive payoff I with certainty, or a wager in which you gain $3500 with probability p and lose $1500 with probability $(1-p)$?"

The probability p, at which the investor is indifferent between these alternatives, is then recorded. The results obtained are shown in the following table:

PAYOFF	-250	250	500	1,200	2,250
p	0.25	0.35	0.50	0.70	0.95

(a) What are the utilities for the five intermediate payoffs?

(b) If the probabilities for the three states of nature are

$$P(s_1) = 0.5; \ P(s_2) = 0.3; \ P(s_3) = 0.2$$

which investment should be selected to maximize expected utility?

11.24. A decision-maker is faced with a problem in which the possible payoffs (in dollars) are:

$$300; \ 400; \ 700; \ 1200; \ 2200; \ 4000$$

Utility zero is assigned to a payoff of $300, and utility 100 to a payoff of $4000. This decision-maker is indifferent to risk for payoffs in this range.

(a) What are the utilities for the four intermediate payoffs?

(b) For each intermediate payoff, I, find the probability, p, such that the decision maker is indifferent between I with certainty and a wager in which $4000 is obtained with probability p and $300 with probability $(1-p)$.

11.25. Refer to Exercise 11.4. After the inadmissible action is eliminated, the manufacturer of earth-moving equipment has the following seven possible payoffs (in millions of dollars):

$$-10; \ -7; \ 0; \ 1; \ 4; \ 8; \ 18$$

Utility zero is assigned to a loss of $10 million and utility 100 to a gain of $18 million. For each intermediate payoff, I, the probabilities p such that this manufacturer is indifferent between receiving I with certainty, and a wager in which $18 million is gained with probability p and \$10 million lost with probability $(1 - p)$, are:

PAYOFF	-7	0	1	4	8
p	0.10	0.35	0.45	0.60	0.75

(a) What are the utilities for the five intermediate payoffs?
(b) If the probabilities for the three states of nature are

$$P(s_1) = 0.2; \ P(s_2) = 0.4; \ P(s_3) = 0.4$$

which action should be selected according to the expected utility criterion?

Choosing an Auxiliary Device for Icebreakers: Decision Making by the U.S. Coast Guard[1]

The Ice Operations Program Plan of the United States Coast Guard is responsible for aiding maritime transportation in ice-laden domestic and arctic waters, and for the prevention of flooding resulting from the accumulation of ice. The Coast Guard employs ice-breaking ships, or icebreakers, on its missions. Several auxiliary devices have been developed for possible installation on conventional icebreakers to increase their effectiveness. The authors of this study consider 18 such auxiliary devices and discuss the problem of deciding which of these should be employed in a particular geographic region of the Coast Guard's activity.

Fourteen desirable attributes, including thickness of ice that can be broken, fuel consumption, and maneuverability, were identified, and probability density functions assessed for each over the different types of mission the icebreakers would be required to carry out. Utilities were assessed for each possible attribute combination, based on information provided by icebreaker operators. Depending on the geographic region, weights were assessed for the relative importance of different mission types, such as clearing a channel for shipping, breaking free a vessel trapped by ice, or speed of response to a call for help.

The expected utility was then computed for each of the 18 auxiliary devices that could be employed. Because the relative importance of different types of mission differs from one geographic region to another, the optimal choice of auxiliary device will not necessarily be the same in each region. However, it was found that one particular device, pitching systems, was generally preferred by the expected utility criterion. These systems have now become quite widely used as auxiliary icebreaking devices by the U.S. Coast Guard.

Newspaper Advertising Rates: When to Raise Prices[2]

At the time of this study a company owned two British national Sunday newspapers, which competed for readers in a market segment with a third newspaper recently taken over by new owners. Company management was certain that the

---

[1] This discussion is based on E. L. Hannan, J. A. Smith and G. R. Gilbert, "A Multiattribute Decision-making Approach to the Selection of an Auxiliary Device for Icebreakers," *Decision Sciences, 14* (1983), 240–252.

[2] This discussion is based on J. C. Higgins, "Decision-making at Board Level Using Decision Analysis: Two Case Studies," *Journal of Operational Research Society, 33* (1982), 319–326.

new owners of their competitor would raise advertising rates by about 10% in an attempt to increase profitability, and that this increase would be put into effect in either spring or fall, as was traditional in this market. There was, however, uncertainty as to which of these times the rate increase would occur.

In consequence, the company wanted to consider an increase in the advertising rates of its own newspapers and in particular, to decide on the timing of an increase. The effects on revenues of different strategies were estimated, given the two assumptions about the timing of the competitor's increase. In this way it was possible to estimate utilities for each action (company raises rates in spring or fall) under each state of nature (competitor raises rates in spring or fall). The expected utilities for each action were then computed as a function of p, where

$$p = \text{probability competitor's rate increase occurs in spring}$$

The decision-makers—in this case the board of directors of the company—were then presented with a recommendation that said, in effect, "If you believe that the probability, p, of competitor's rate increasing in spring is in a particular range, then the optimal decision is to raise your rates in spring. Otherwise delay the increase until fall." Members of the board felt able, from their experience with the behavior of the competing paper's ownership, to reach a consensus on an appropriate choice for the probability p, and based their decision on this model.

forecasting

CHAPTER TWELVE

12.1. INTRODUCTION

In the previous chapter we stressed that very often business decisions must be made in an uncertain environment. Now, it is assuredly the case that managers will often be uncertain about future trends in the environment in which they must operate. However, that is not to say that management will, or can, know *nothing* about the future. Indeed, considerable effort is made to *forecast* future developments, in order to minimize as far as possible the degree of uncertainty about their course, and hence provide a sounder basis for decision-making.

Because access to reliable forecasts can yield a substantial contribution to profits through improved decision-making, forecasting has become an integral part of modern management. However, because of the range of types of problems that might arise, it is not appropriate to view forecasting as a homogeneous activity where a single methodology can be applied in every situation. To see this, consider two examples. Many corporations produce a vast array of mature products, for which month by month demand will vary somewhat. Production schedules must be set so that on the one hand, customer relations are not impaired by frequent product unavailability, while, on the other hand, excessive output does not lead to high inventory holding costs. Obviously reliable forecasts of future demand levels can provide an important input to the production scheduling decision. Corporations in this position require the routine production of monthly demand forecasts, often for hundreds of product lines. A very different example of the need for reliable forecasts arises when a corporation is considering costly investment in a foreign country. One important consideration here is the future political stability of that country. There may be some concern that an abrupt change in government policy could lead to exchange controls, unfavorable tax treatment, or even the expropriation of assets. Difficult as the task may be, it is important to form some judgment about the likelihood of occurrence of such developments. Of course, it is foolish to expect that a sensible approach to the prediction of political change in a foreign country would bear much resemblance to the methodology one might employ to forecast monthly demand for mature products. The two problems call for different types of expertise, and different types of information on which to base their solution will be available. A political scientist, with knowledge of the country in question, may have much of value to contribute to a discussion on its likely future attitude to the investments of multinational corporations. It is likely that such an analysis would be based on *judgment,* rather than the application of some formal model. On the other hand, the corporation's marketing department may have valuable insight into the future sales prospects of mature products. Moreover, the availability of data on past monthly sales, and perhaps other relevant information, suggests the possibility of building a **quantitative model** to generate the required forecasts.

We will not, in the space available, be able to provide a full discussion of the wide array of approaches that have been successfully employed in business forecasting. Rather, in subsequent sections of this chapter, we will concentrate on some useful quantitative models. Before doing so, however, it is important to consider some general questions that might arise in a practical forecasting exercise. These can be characterized as:

1. Why are forecasts required?
2. Precisely what quantities or factors must be predicted?
3. How important to the business function are more accurate forecasts?
4. Should forecasts be produced inhouse, or purchased from consultants?
5. What relevant information and expertise are available for forecast production?
6. How should this information and expertise be employed to produce forecasts?

The first of these questions is perhaps the most important, as the answer to it will influence the manner in which one approaches the other questions. Excluding idle curiosity as a motivation for forecasting, the major application of all predictions is as an aid to decision-making. Once this is realized, a number of practical consequences follow. For instance, we can specify the **time horizon** for forecasting. For example, if sales forecasts are wanted for inventory control, it will typically be necessary to look only a few months ahead. Production plans can be modified rather frequently, and forecasts of sales levels many years hence are of little relevance for this purpose. On the other hand, if a substantial investment is to be made in a foreign country, the relevant horizon is the lifetime of that investment, which could be many years.

Given a thorough understanding of the motivation for forecasting, it should be clear just what variables need to be predicted. However, care is needed. I was once asked to predict the demand for color television sets over several years in Great Britain. My client was a manufacturer of wooden cabinets into which television chasis were mounted. In fact, the future market for color televisions looked to be, and in the event turned out to be, very strong. However, the future turned out to be much less bright for this manufacturer, as the market came to be dominated by less expensive preassembled units.

The answer to the question of the importance to the business of very accurate forecasts will help to determine the amount of effort put into, and the cost expended on, a forecasting exercise. If predictions of future sales are required for hundreds of product lines for inventory control purposes, it is doubtful that it will be worth going to the expense of carrying out a very detailed analysis of each product line. Rather, a quickly implemented procedure that generally performs quite well over a wide range of products should prove satisfactory in terms of value for money.

For some forecasting problems, inhouse expertise may not be available to produce answers in a reasonable amount of time, so that it may be preferable to purchase a report from a specialist consulting group. As an example, a corporation's prospects will depend to some extent on the future levels of national and international economic activity. Several consulting organizations specialize in the production of macroeconomic forecasts, and it might well be preferable to subscribe to such a service, rather than maintain a substantial body of inhouse expertise in this area.

The final two questions are related. Ideally, forecasts should be based on all relevant information that is available, or can be collected at reasonable cost. Often this information is quantitative, and can readily be incorporated into a formal forecasting model. However, such nonquantifiable factors, as the judgments of those with expertise and experience in the field, will also be important ingredients in the forecast-generating mechanism. The perceived relative values of quantitative and judgmental factors will have much to do with the choice of approach to a forecasting problem. The choice of forecasting approach that is made for any problem need not mean irrevocable commitment. Forecast accuracy can be monitored, and if this proves to be inadequate, it may be possible to secure some improvement through an alternative approach.

In the remaining sections of this chapter we will concentrate on quantitative forecasting models. However, before doing so, we mention one judgmental approach, the **Delphi method,** that is frequently employed as an aid to long term planning, particularly when it is important to anticipate technological developments. In Delphi, which was developed by RAND Corporation in the 1960s, a panel of experts is assembled. A questionnaire is given to each panel member, and, on the basis of the answers received, a further questionnaire is prepared. The aim is that in this way, each panel member will have access to the information available to others, without being influenced by their opinions. It is hoped that through the careful design of a sequence of questionnaires, some consensus can be reached.

12.2. SIMPLE EXPONENTIAL SMOOTHING

In this section, we introduce a procedure which forms the basis of many commonly applied approaches to routine short-term forecasting. This group of methods is often called **exponential smoothing,** and is particularly useful when routine sales forecasts, for inventory control purposes, are required for many product lines.

Suppose that we observe n equally spaced observations through time, X_1, X_2, . . . , X_n, on the process of interest, and want to predict the unknown future values, X_{n+1}, X_{n+2}, ... We will develop and illustrate here the **simple exponential smoothing** method, which can be appropriate when the process under study is not substantially influenced by seasonal factors, and shows no consistent upward or downward trend.

Given the assumption of no trend or seasonality, the objective of simple exponential smoothing is to estimate, at any point in time, the current *level* of the process. This estimate is then used as the forecast of all future values. The position, then, is that standing at the present time (time n), we are looking back at the series of past observations, X_n, X_{n-1}, X_{n-2}, . . . , and want to assess the current level. Consider the following two possibilities:

(i) Use as the estimate of level the most recent observation, X_n. Then, the forecast of all future values would simply be the most recent observation. For some important business processes, including prices in speculative markets, this is close to optimal if predictions are to be based exclusively on the history of the process. However, it is often suboptimal to base forecasts on just one observation. Rather, it is preferable to give some weight also to earlier observations.

(ii) Use as the estimate of level the simple average of *all* the available observations. This is generally not a sensible approach, for, in forming the simple average, equal weight is given to every observation. For example, if future product sales were to be predicted in this manner, the same weight would be given to sales many years in the past as to the most recent sales figures. However, it is almost inevitably the case that distant experience will be less informative than the more recent observations about future behavior.

Simple exponential smoothing provides a compromise between these extremes, giving a forecast that is a **weighted average** of current and past observations. In computing this average, most weight is given to the most recent observation, somewhat less weight to the immediately preceding value, less weight to the one before that, and so on. A simple procedure for obtaining such a weighted average is to estimate the level of the process in the current time period n by $\overline{X}_n$, where

$$\overline{X}_n = (1 - \alpha)X_n + \alpha(1 - \alpha)X_{n-1} + \alpha^2(1 - \alpha)X_{n-2} + \ . \ . \ . \qquad (12.1)$$

In equation (12.1), α is any number between zero and one. For example, if α is set at 0.6, future values of the series are predicted by

$$\overline{X}_n = 0.4\,X_n + 0.24\,X_{n-1} + 0.144\,X_{n-2} + \ . \ . \ .$$

so that a weighted average, with exponentially declining weights, is applied to current and past observations in calculating the forecasts.

We now show how, given a series of observations on the process of interest, the exponential smoothing predictor can be efficiently computed. Let X_t denote the observed value of the process at time t. Then, by analogy with (12.1), the level of the series at time t is estimated by

$$\overline{X}_t = (1 - \alpha)X_t + \alpha(1 - \alpha)X_{t-1} + \alpha^2(1 - \alpha)X_{t-2} + \ldots \qquad (12.2)$$

Similarly, the level at the previous time period would be estimated by

$$\overline{X}_{t-1} = (1 - \alpha)X_{t-1} + \alpha(1 - \alpha)X_{t-2} + \alpha^2(1 - \alpha)X_{t-3} + \ldots$$

Multiplying through this last equation by α yields

$$\alpha\overline{X}_{t-1} = \alpha(1 - \alpha)X_{t-1} + \alpha^2(1 - \alpha)X_{t-2} + \ldots \qquad (12.3)$$

Then, on subtracting (12.3) from (12.2), we find

$$\overline{X}_t - \alpha\overline{X}_{t-1} = (1 - \alpha)X_t$$

which can be rewritten as

$$\overline{X}_t = \alpha\overline{X}_{t-1} + (1 - \alpha)X_t \qquad (0 < \alpha < 1) \qquad (12.4)$$

In the simple exponential smoothing approach, standing at time t, $\overline{X}_t$ is used as the forecast of all future values of the series.

Equation (12.4) yields a computationally convenient recursive algorithm for calculating the estimates of level. It expresses the level $\overline{X}_t$, at time t, as a weighted average of the level, $\overline{X}_{t-1}$, at the previous time period, and the current observation, X_t. The weights given to each depend on the choice of α, which is called the **smoothing constant.** The calculations are initiated by setting

$$\overline{X}_1 = X_1$$

Equation (12.4) is then applied in turn for $t = 2, 3, 4, \ldots, n$.

To illustrate, consider a series of 30 annual observations on product sales. These observations[1] are set out in the second column of Table 12.1.

---

[1] The data are taken from K. S. Palda, *The Measurement of Cumulative Advertising Effects* (Englewood Cliffs, N.J.: Prentice-Hall, Inc.; 1964).

TABLE 12.1 Simple exponential smoothing ($\alpha = 0.4$) of sales data.

t	X_t	$\overline{X}_t$	t	X_t	$\overline{X}_t$
1	1,806	1,806.0	16	2,177	2,336.5
2	1,644	1,708.8	17	1,920	2,086.6
3	1,814	1,771.9	18	1,910	1,980.6
4	1,770	1,770.8	19	1,984	1,982.6
5	1,518	1,619.1	20	1,787	1,865.2
6	1,103	1,309.4	21	1,689	1,759.5
7	1,266	1,283.4	22	1,866	1,823.4
8	1,473	1,397.2	23	1,896	1,867.0
9	1,423	1,412.7	24	1,684	1,757.2
10	1,767	1,625.3	25	1,633	1,682.7
11	2,161	1,946.7	26	1,657	1,667.3
12	2,336	2,180.3	27	1,569	1,608.3
13	2,602	2,433.3	28	1,390	1,477.3
14	2,518	2,484.1	29	1,387	1,423.1
15	2,637	2,575.8	30	1,289	1,342.6

The calculations are started off by setting

$$\overline{X}_1 = X_1 = 1806$$

We will base our forecasts on the smoothing constant $\alpha = 0.4$. Then, using equation (12.4), with $t = 2$, we have

$$\overline{X}_2 = 0.4\,\overline{X}_1 + 0.6\,X_2$$

$$= (0.4)(1,806) + (0.6)(1,644) = 1708.8$$

Setting $t = 3$ in (12.4) then yields

$$\overline{X}_3 = 0.4\,\overline{X}_2 + 0.6\,X_3$$

$$= (0.4)(1,708.8) + (0.6)(1,814) = 1771.9$$

Continuing in this way, setting in turn $t = 4, 5, \ldots, 30$ in (12.4), yields the values $\overline{X}_t$ shown in the final column of Table 12.1.

From Table 12.1, it can be seen that the most recent estimate of level is given by

$$\overline{X}_n = \overline{X}_{30} = 1342.6$$

Thus, our prediction of sales in all future years is 1342.6 units. This series of observations, together with the forecasts, is shown in Figure 12.1. This procedure is appropriate for forecasting over relatively short time horizons.

Forecasting Through Simple Exponential Smoothing

Let $X_1, X_2, \ldots, X_n$ be n consecutive observations through time on a process. The **simple exponential smoothing** forecasting procedure proceeds as follows:

(i) Compute the estimates of level

$$\overline{X}_1 = X_1$$

$$\overline{X}_t = \alpha \overline{X}_{t-1} + (1 - \alpha)X_t \qquad (0 < \alpha < 1;\ t = 2, 3, \ldots, n)$$

(ii) Standing at time n, use as forecasts of all future values X_{n+h},

$$\hat{X}_{n+h} = \overline{X}_n \qquad (h = 1, 2, 3, \ldots)$$

Up to this point, we have not discussed the choice of the smoothing constant, α, to be used in the simple exponential smoothing algorithm. One possibility is to make the choice subjectively. For example, we could select a value that experience has suggested has yielded satisfactory forecasts of similar processes. Often the same constant is used for the prediction of future sales of

FIGURE 12.1 Annual sales and forecasts based on simple exponential smoothing.

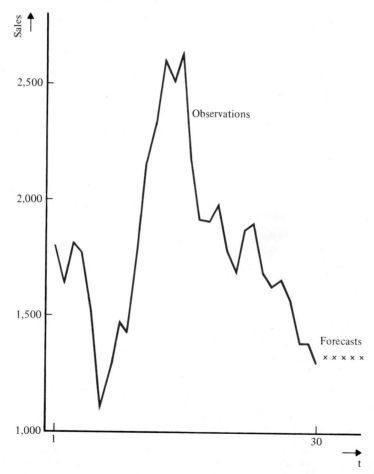

related product lines. Alternatively, a choice of smoothing constant might be suggested by visual inspection of a graph of the observed data. If the picture is of very choppy, eratic, behavior through time, we would not want to give a lot of weight to the most recent observation, suggesting a high value for α in (12.1). On the other hand, if the progression through time of the process is quite smooth, as for example where product sales have been relatively stable, a lower value of α would be appropriate.

A more objective approach is to experiment with several possible values of the smoothing constant, and pick that value that yields the best forecasts of the observations. Using simple exponential smoothing, the forecast of X_t, made at time $t - 1$, is $\overline{X}_{t-1}$. The error made in this forecast is

$$e_t = X_t - \overline{X}_{t-1}$$

In some applications it is possible to assign a *cost*, $C(e_t)$, to an error of size e_t. Often, in practice, simple cost of error functions are assumed. The most common examples are

(i) The cost of error is proportional to the absolute value of the error. The constant of proportionality is irrelevant, and we can write

$$C(e_t) = |e_t|$$

(ii) The cost of error is proportional to the square of the error, so that we can write

$$C(e_t) = e_t^2$$

The particular cost of error function used will depend on the problem at hand. The smoothing constant is chosen by picking a grid of values, say $\alpha = 0.2, 0.4, 0.6, 0.8$, and for each value computing the forecasts $\overline{X}_{t-1}$ of the observed X_t, and the errors e_t. We then choose to proceed with that value of the smoothing constant for which

$$\text{Total Cost of Error} = \sum_{t=2}^{n} C(e_t)$$

is smallest. This procedure gives some assurance that the smoothing constant chosen will be appropriate for the given data set. Its disadvantage is that it is computationally more expensive than subjective choice of α.

12.3. THE HOLT-WINTERS EXPONENTIAL SMOOTHING PROCEDURE

Many models in wide use in business that attempt to extrapolate a process from its own past are elaborations of simple exponential smoothing. In this section we introduce one such approach, the **Holt-Winters procedure**, which is designed to take into account trend, and possibly also seasonal variation, in the process. We will concentrate here on the nonseasonal case, only briefly discussing an elaboration appropriate for forecasting seasonal processes.

The Holt-Winters approach involves the estimation, at each point in time, of the level and the trend of a process. We will again use X_t to denote the observed value at time t, and $\overline{X}_t$ the estimate of level at that time. The trend estimate is denoted T_t. The principle behind the estimation of level and trend in the Holt-Winters algorithm is essentially the same as that followed in simple exponential smoothing. The estimating equations are

$$\overline{X}_t = A(\overline{X}_{t-1} + T_{t-1}) + (1 - A)X_t \qquad (0 < A < 1) \qquad (12.5)$$

and

$$T_t = B\,T_{t-1} + (1 - B)(\overline{X}_t - \overline{X}_{t-1}) \qquad (0 < B < 1) \qquad (12.6)$$

where A and B are smoothing constants, whose choice depends on the characteristics of the data. Equations (12.5) and (12.6) can be regarded as **updating formulas,** where estimates made in the previous time period are modified after the acquisition of a new piece of data. The estimate of level, $\overline{X}_{t-1}$, made at time $t - 1$, together with the trend estimate T_{t-1}, suggests a level $(\overline{X}_{t-1} + T_{t-1})$ for time t. Given the new observation, X_t, the original estimate is modified by (12.5) to yield $\overline{X}_t$, a weighted average of $(\overline{X}_{t-1} + T_{t-1})$ and X_t. Similarly, at time $t - 1$ the trend estimate is T_{t-1}. Given the new observation, X_t, we can compute an alternative estimate of trend as the difference, $(\overline{X}_t - \overline{X}_{t-1})$, between the two most recent levels. In (12.6) a weighted average of these two estimates is employed to form T_t.

The Holt-Winters algorithm is initiated by using the first two observations to give the trend and level estimates

$$T_2 = X_2 - X_1, \overline{X}_2 = X_2$$

The calculations then proceed by setting in turn $t = 3, 4, \ldots, n$ in (12.5) and (12.6).

To illustrate, we will apply the Holt-Winters algorithm to a series of 24 annual observations[2] on car ownership in Great Britain. The observed data are shown in the second column of Table 12.2. The estimates of trend and level in the second year are

$$T_2 = X_2 - X_1 = 0.051 - 0.049 = 0.002$$

and

$$\overline{X}_2 = X_2 = 0.051$$

---

[2] The data are taken from R. J. Brooks, et al., "A Note on Forecasting Car Ownership," *Journal of Royal Statistical Society A, 141* (1978), 64–68.

TABLE 12.2 The Holt-Winters algorithm applied to the number of cars per capita in Great Britain.

t	X_t	$\overline{X}_t$	T_t	t	X_t	$\overline{X}_t$	T_t
1	0.049			13	0.142	0.1409	0.0135
2	0.051	0.0510	0.0020	14	0.157	0.1565	0.0151
3	0.056	0.0554	0.0039	15	0.169	0.1696	0.0135
4	0.063	0.0623	0.0063	16	0.180	0.1806	0.0115
5	0.071	0.0705	0.0079	17	0.194	0.1936	0.0127
6	0.078	0.0781	0.0076	18	0.202	0.2029	0.0099
7	0.084	0.0843	0.0065	19	0.209	0.2098	0.0075
8	0.091	0.0910	0.0066	20	0.214	0.2147	0.0054
9	0.098	0.0979	0.0069	21	0.223	0.2224	0.0073
10	0.108	0.1074	0.0089	22	0.234	0.2331	0.0100
11	0.116	0.1161	0.0087	23	0.248	0.2470	0.0131
12	0.127	0.1266	0.0102	24	0.251	0.2528	0.0073

We will use as smoothing constants

$$A = 0.2; B = 0.2$$

The algorithm then proceeds by substituting in turn $t = 3, 4, \ldots$ in equations (12.5) and (12.6). From (12.5), with $t = 3$, we have

$$\overline{X}_3 = 0.2(\overline{X}_2 + T_2) + 0.8X_3$$

$$= (0.2)(0.051 + 0.002) + (0.8)(0.056) = 0.0554$$

Then, using (12.6), we find

$$T_3 = 0.2T_2 + 0.8(\overline{X}_3 - \overline{X}_2)$$

$$= (0.2)(0.002) + (0.8)(0.0554 - 0.051) = 0.00392$$

Next, setting $t = 4$ in equations (12.5) and (12.6), we find

$$\overline{X}_4 = 0.2(\overline{X}_3 + T_3) + 0.8X_4$$

$$= (0.2)(0.0554 + 0.00392) + (0.8)(0.063) = 0.062264$$

and

$$T_4 = (0.2)(0.00392) + (0.8)(0.062264 - 0.0554) = 0.0062752$$

The remaining calculations are carried out in exactly the same way, and the results are set out in the final two columns of Table 12.2.

These estimates of level and trend can now be used to forecast future values of the process. Given a series X_t, $t = 1, 2, \ldots, n$, the most recent estimates of level and trend are $\overline{X}_n$ and T_n. In forecasting, we assume that this latest trend will continue into the future, from the most recent level. Hence, the next observation is predicted to be

$$\hat{X}_{n+1} = \overline{X}_n + T_n$$

The forecast of X_{n+2} is

$$\hat{X}_{n+2} = \overline{X}_n + 2T_n$$

and, in general, forecasting h time periods into the future, we have

$$\hat{X}_{n+h} = \overline{X}_n + hT_n$$

For the series on car registrations in Great Britain, the latest estimates of level and trend are, from Table 12.2,

$$\overline{X}_{24} = 0.2528; \quad T_{24} = 0.0073$$

Then, the forecast of the next year is

$$\hat{X}_{25} = 0.2528 + 0.0073 = 0.2601$$

Continuing, the forecasts for two to five years ahead are

$$\hat{X}_{26} = 0.2528 + 2(0.0073) = 0.2674$$

$$\hat{X}_{27} = 0.2528 + 3(0.0073) = 0.2747$$

$$\hat{X}_{28} = 0.2528 + 4(0.0073) = 0.2820$$

$$\hat{X}_{29} = 0.2528 + 5(0.0073) = 0.2893$$

The observed data, together with these forecasts, are graphed in Figure 12.2.

The Holt-Winters Method for Nonseasonal Processes

Let $X_1, X_2, \ldots, X_n$ be n consecutive observations through time on a process. The Holt-Winters method of forecasting nonseasonal processes proceeds as follows:

(i) Compute estimates of level $\overline{X}_t$ and trend T_t as

$$\overline{X}_2 = X_2; \quad T_2 = X_2 - X_1$$

$$\overline{X}_t = A(\overline{X}_{t-1} + T_{t-1}) + (1 - A)X_t \quad (0 < A < 1; t = 3, 4, \ldots, n)$$

$$T_t = BT_{t-1} + (1 - B)(\overline{X}_t - \overline{X}_{t-1}) \quad (0 < B < 1; t = 3, 4, \ldots, n)$$

where A and B are fixed smoothing constants.

(ii) Forecast future values X_{n+h} by

$$\hat{X}_{n+h} = \overline{X}_n + hT_n \quad (h = 1, 2, 3, \ldots)$$

Many processes met in the real world exhibit seasonality. For example, for many products sales are regularly higher in particular months of the year than others. The Holt-Winters procedure can be extended to yield forecasts of such

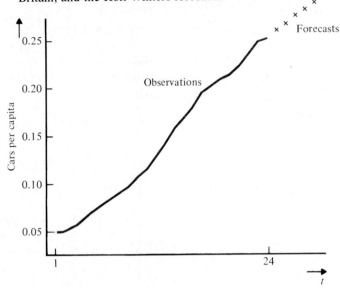

FIGURE 12.2 Annual number of cars per capita in Great Britain, and the Holt-Winters forecasts.

processes. The aim is to estimate, for each period of the year, a **seasonal factor**, together with level and trend. Suppose, for example that monthly seasonal data, X_t, are available. The seasonal factor is generally taken to be multiplicative, in the sense that in any month actual sales are assumed to be a multiple of what they would have been in the absence of seasonality. We will denote the level, trend, and seasonal factor at time t by $\overline{X}_t$, T_t, and F_t, respectively. These elements are then updated from one time period to the next through the following three equations:

$$\overline{X}_t = A(\overline{X}_{t-1} + T_{t-1}) + (1 - A)\left(\frac{X_t}{F_{t-12}}\right) \qquad (0 < A < 1) \qquad (12.7)$$

$$T_t = BT_{t-1} + (1 - B)(\overline{X}_t - \overline{X}_{t-1}) \qquad (0 < B < 1) \qquad (12.8)$$

$$F_t = CF_{t-12} + (1 - C)\left(\frac{X_t}{\overline{X}_t}\right) \qquad (0 < C < 1) \qquad (12.9)$$

In equation (12.7), the term $(\overline{X}_{t-1} + T_{t-1})$ is an estimate of the level of the process at time t, formed at time $t - 1$. Given the new observation X_t, an alternative estimate of current level can be formed. This is achieved by deflating this observation by F_{t-12}, the last availabile estimated seasonal factor for this month of the year. The updated level estimate $\overline{X}_t$ is then a weighted average of these two components. Equation (12.8), through which the trend estimate is updated, is precisely the same as equation (12.6), used in the nonseasonal Holt-Winters algorithm. Finally, in equation (12.9), the previous seasonal factor, F_{t-12}, for this month is updated, given the new measure of seasonality $X_t/\overline{X}_t$. Manual computation through this algorithm is somewhat tedious. However, the repetitive nature of the calculations makes them ideally suited for programming on an electronic computer, and software based on this method is quite widely available.

Once the most recent estimates of level, trend, and seasonal factors have been calculated, forecasts of future values of the process are obtained from

$$\hat{X}_{n+h} = (\overline{X}_n + hT_n)F_{n+h-12} \qquad (h = 1, 2, \ldots, 12)$$

$$= (\overline{X}_n + hT_n)F_{n+h-24} \qquad (h = 13, 14, \ldots, 24)$$

and so on. Thus, the most recent trend estimate is projected forward from the latest estimate of level, and the result multiplied by the last available seasonal factor for the month of interest.

As in the case of simple exponential smoothing, the choice of smoothing constants for use in the Holt-Winters algorithm can be made subjectively or objectively. One possibility is to use smoothing constants that have been known to yield satisfactory forecasts of similar processes. Alternatively, a grid of possible values can be tried, and that set which performs best in predicting the observed data can be employed to forecast the future.

12.4. FORECASTING FROM REGRESSION MODELS

In the previous two sections of this chapter, we considered procedures for forecasting future values of a process, based exclusively on past observations of that process. Now, in practice, we want to base forecasts on *all* relevant information. For example, it may be felt that information that is not readily quantifiable is of relevance to future trends in a process. In that event, forecasts that may have been based, for example, on an exponential smoothing procedure can be modified judgmentally, taking account of this additional information.

A further possibility is that useful information on quantitative variables may be available. In that case an approach to forecasting based on the construction of **regression models** may be appropriate. In the simplest variant of this model, suppose that observations Y_t on the process of interest are available, and that we also have access to observations X_t on a related process, so that the value Y_t is thought to depend on the value X_t. In many applications, to a good approximation, the relationship between these variables is **linear.** For example,

TABLE 12.3 Annual observations on U.S. disposable income per household (X_t) and retail sales per household (Y_t), in 1972 dollars.

YEAR	X_t	Y_t	YEAR	X_t	Y_t
1	9,098	5,492	12	11,307	5,907
2	9,138	5,540	13	11,432	6,124
3	9,094	5,305	14	11,449	6,186
4	9,282	5,507	15	11,697	6,224
5	9,229	5,418	16	11,871	6,496
6	9,347	5,320	17	12,018	6,718
7	9,525	5,538	18	12,523	6,921
8	9,756	5,692	19	12,053	6,471
9	10,282	5,871	20	12,088	6,394
10	10,662	6,157	21	12,215	6,555
11	11,019	6,342	22	12,494	6,755

Table 12.3 shows 22 annual observations[3] on retail sales per household (Y_t) and disposable income per household (X_t). The aim is to exploit the dependence of retail sales on disposable income in an attempt to predict future values of the former. Figure 12.3 shows a plot of these data, and inspection of that graph suggests that a linear relationship may be appropriate.

Given a plot such as Figure 12.3, we want to find a line to fit through the data. The general equation for a line is

$$Y = a + bX$$

and, in regression analysis, the numbers a and b are most often found by the method of **least squares,** choosing those values for which the sum of squared discrepancies

$$S = \sum_{t=1}^{n} (Y_t - a - bX_t)^2$$

is a minimum, where n is the number of pairs of observations. It can be shown that the least squares line is given by

$$b = \frac{\sum\limits_{t=1}^{n} X_t Y_t - \frac{1}{n} \sum\limits_{t=1}^{n} X_t \sum\limits_{t=1}^{n} Y_t}{\sum\limits_{t=1}^{n} X_t^2 - \frac{1}{n} \left(\sum\limits_{t=1}^{n} X_t \right)^2}$$

and

$$a = \frac{\sum\limits_{t=1}^{n} Y_t - b \sum\limits_{t=1}^{n} X_t}{n}$$

---

[3] The data are taken from N. K. Dhalla, "Short-term Forecasts of Advertising Expenditures," *Journal of Advertising Research, 19,* no. 1, (1979), 7–14. Reprinted from the Journal of Advertising Research © Copyright 1979, by the Advertising Research Foundation.

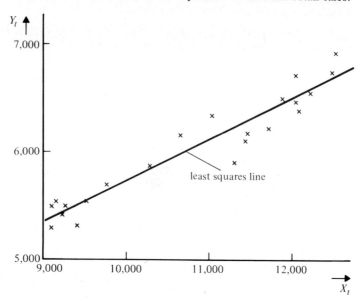

FIGURE 12.3 Plot of data on disposable income and retail sales.

The calculations for the data on disposable incomes and retail sales are set out in Table 12.4. From that table, we find

$$\sum_{t=1}^{22} X_t = 237,579; \quad \sum_{t=1}^{22} Y_t = 132,933;$$

$$\sum_{t=1}^{22} X_t Y_t = 1,488,555,000; \quad \sum_{t=1}^{22} X_t^2 = 2,599,715,000$$

Then, we find

$$b = \frac{\sum X_t Y_t - \dfrac{1}{n} \sum X_t \sum Y_t}{\sum X_t^2 - \dfrac{1}{n} (\sum X_t)^2}$$

$$= \frac{1,448,555,000 - \dfrac{1}{22}(237,579)(132,933)}{2,599,715,000 - \dfrac{1}{22}(237,579)^2} = 0.3815$$

and

$$a = \frac{\sum Y_t - b \sum X_t}{22} = \frac{132,933 - (0.3815)(237,579)}{22} = 1923$$

TABLE 12.4 Calculations for the least squares regression of retail sales on disposable income (X_tY_t and X_t^2, rounded to the nearest thousand).

X_t	Y_t	X_tY_t	X_t^2
9,098	5,492	49,966,000	82,774,000
9,138	5,540	50,625,000	83,503,000
9,094	5,305	48,244,000	82,701,000
9,282	5,507	51,116,000	86,156,000
9,229	5,418	50,003,000	85,174,000
9,347	5,320	49,726,000	87,366,000
9,525	5,538	52,749,000	90,726,000
9,756	5,692	55,531,000	95,180,000
10,282	5,871	60,366,000	105,720,000
10,662	6,157	65,646,000	113,678,000
11,019	6,342	69,882,000	121,418,000
11,307	5,907	66,790,000	127,848,000
11,432	6,124	70,010,000	130,691,000
11,449	6,186	70,824,000	131,080,000
11,697	6,224	72,802,000	136,820,000
11,871	6,496	77,114,000	140,921,000
12,018	6,718	80,737,000	144,432,000
12,523	6,921	86,672,000	156,826,000
12,053	6,471	77,995,000	145,275,000
12,088	6,394	77,291,000	146,120,000
12,215	6,555	80,069,000	149,206,000
12,494	6,755	84,397,000	156,100,000
Sums 237,579	132,933	1,448,555,000	2,599,715,000

The least squares line is therefore given by

$$Y = 1923 + 0.3815\,X$$

This line is drawn in on Figure 12.3. Visual inspection suggests that it fits these data quite well.

Having estimated a regression model, in which a **dependent variable, Y_t** is related to an **independent variable, X_t,** the model can then be employed to produce **conditional forecasts** of the dependent variable. By this we mean that it is possible to predict future values of the dependent variable, given an estimate of future values of the independent variable. Suppose that in some future time period, the independent variable is expected to take the value X_{next}. Then, the forecast of the dependent variable is

$$\hat{Y}_{next} = a + bX_{next}$$

To illustrate, suppose that in a future year, disposable income per household is expected to be $12,500. Then for that year predicted retail sales per household would be

$$\hat{Y}_{next} = a + bX_{next}$$

$$= 1923 + (0.3815)(12,500) = \$6692$$

Linear Regression Models for Forecasting

Suppose that we have n pairs of observations through time, (X_1, Y_1), (X_2, Y_2), . . . , (X_n, Y_n) on a dependent variable Y and an independent variable X. Then the least squares estimated regression of Y on X is

$$Y = a + bX$$

where

$$b = \frac{\sum X_t Y_t - \dfrac{1}{n} \sum X_t \sum Y_t}{\sum X_t^2 - \dfrac{1}{n} (\sum X_t)^2}$$

and

$$a = \frac{\sum Y_t - b \sum X_t}{n}$$

If, in a future year, the independent variable is expected to take the value X_{next}, the dependent variable in that year is predicted by

$$\hat{Y}_{\text{next}} = a + bX_{\text{next}}$$

MULTIPLE REGRESSION MODELS

The linear regression model just discussed is appropriate when a dependent variable is to be related to a single independent variable. Very often it happens that several independent variables may be useful in explaining the behavior of a dependent variable. For example, suppose that the dependent variable Y is to be related to K independent variables, $X_1, X_2, . . . , X_K$. The **multiple regression model** is an extension of the linear model in which the estimated relationship is expressed as

$$Y = a + b_1 X_1 + b_2 X_2 + . . . + b_K X_K$$

Given data, the constants a, b_1, b_2, . . . , b_K are found by the method of least squares. Thus, given n sets of observations $(Y_1, X_{11}, X_{21}, . . . , X_{K1})$, $(Y_2, X_{12}, X_{22}, . . . , X_{K2})$, . . . , $(Y_n, X_{1n}, X_{2n}, . . . , X_{Kn})$, these constants are the values for which the sum of squares

$$S = \sum_{t=1}^{n} (Y_t - b_1 X_{1t} - b_2 X_{2t} - . . . - b_K X_{Kt})^2$$

is a minimum.

Manual computation of the least squares estimates can be extremely tedious unless the number of independent variables is very small. However, computer packages, such as the Statistical Analysis System (SAS) and the Statistical Package for the Social Sciences (SPSS), are very widely available for performing these calculations.

TABLE 12.5 Data on the percentage of net revenues per deposit dollar (X_{1t}), the number of offices (X_{2t}), and the percentage of profit margin (Y_t) for U.S. savings and loan associations.

YEAR	X_{1t}	X_{2t}	Y_t	YEAR	X_{1t}	X_{2t}	Y_t
1	3.92	7,298	0.75	14	3.78	6,672	0.84
2	3.61	6,855	0.71	15	3.82	6,890	0.79
3	3.32	6,636	0.66	16	3.97	7,115	0.70
4	3.07	6,506	0.61	17	4.07	7,327	0.68
5	3.06	6,450	0.70	18	4.25	7,546	0.72
6	3.11	6,402	0.72	19	4.41	7,931	0.55
7	3.21	6,368	0.77	20	4.49	8,097	0.63
8	3.26	6,340	0.74	21	4.70	8,468	0.56
9	3.42	6,349	0.90	22	4.58	8,717	0.41
10	3.42	6,352	0.82	23	4.69	8,991	0.51
11	3.45	6,361	0.75	24	4.71	9,179	0.47
12	3.58	6,369	0.77	25	4.78	9,318	0.32
13	3.66	6,546	0.78				

To illustrate the application of multiple regression, Table 12.5 shows 25 annual observations[4] on savings and loan association profit margins (Y_t), net revenues per deposit dollar (X_{1t}) and number of offices (X_{2t}). The estimated multiple regression is therefore of the form

$$Y = a + b_1 X_1 + b_2 X_2$$

and, using the SAS program, we found

$$a = 1.565; \quad b_1 = 0.237; \quad b_2 = -0.000249$$

Assuming that projections of future values of the independent variables are available, a fitted multiple regression model can be used to derive conditional forecasts of future values of the dependent variable. If, in some future time period, the dependent variables are expected to take the values $X_{1,next}$, $X_{2,next}$, . . . , $X_{K,next}$, the forecast of the dependent variable for that time period is

$$\hat{Y}_{next} = a + b_1 X_{1,next} + b_2 X_{2,next} + \ldots + b_K X_{K,next}$$

To illustrate, if savings and loan association net revenues per deposit dollar are expected to be 4.8%, and the number of offices is expected to be 9200, then the predicted profit margin is

$$\hat{Y}_{next} = 1.565 + 0.237 X_{1,next} - 0.000249 X_{2,next}$$

$$= 1.565 + (0.237)(4.8) - (0.000249)(9,200) = 0.41\%$$

The reader should be cautioned that the regression analysis we have described is based on certain statistical assumptions about the process generating

---

[4] The data are taken from L. J. Spellman, "Entry and Profitability in a Rate-free Savings and Loan Market," *Quarterly Review of Economics and Business, 18,* No. 2, (1978), 87–95.

the data. When these assumptions hold, this approach can yield a valuable forecasting tool. However, in the event that key assumptions break down, this analysis can give misleading results, and very poor forecast performance. In such circumstances, it may be possible to modify the standard regression model to produce useful forecasts.[5]

just read though

12.5. FORECASTING FROM ARIMA MODELS: BOX-JENKINS METHODS

Finally, we turn to a brief discussion of a class of quantitative forecasting models that offer the user a considerable amount of flexibility in tailoring the forecast generating mechanism to the characteristics displayed by the available data. As a first step, suppose that we have available a series of observations through time; $X_1, X_2, \ldots, X_n$, on a process of interest. It is intended to base the forecast $\hat{X}_{n+1}$ of the next value X_{n+1} on these observations, the assumption being that a satisfactory forecast can be obtained as a linear combination of the p most recent observations. The forecast is then of the form

$$\hat{X}_{n+1} = \gamma + \phi_1 X_n + \phi_2 X_{n-1} + \ldots + \phi_p X_{n-p+1} \qquad (12.10)$$

Equation (12.10) is called an **autoregressive** forecasting model. The fixed coefficients $\gamma, \phi_1, \phi_2, \ldots, \phi_p$ of this model can be estimated by the method of least squares, as those values for which

$$S = \sum_{t=p}^{n-1} (X_{t+1} - \gamma - \phi_1 X_t - \phi_2 X_{t-1} - \ldots - \phi_p X_{t-p+1})^2$$

is smallest. To illustrate, an autoregressive model of order four (that is, $p = 4$ in (12.10)) was fitted to the sales data of Table 12.1 by the method of least squares, yielding the estimates

$$\gamma = 446.22; \ \phi_1 = 1.194; \ \phi_2 = -0.439; \ \phi_3 = 0.286; \ \phi_4 = -0.291$$

The forecast of the next value in this series is then

$$\hat{X}_{31} = 446.22 + 1.194X_{30} - 0.439X_{29} + 0.286X_{28} - 0.291X_{27}$$

$$= 446.22 + (1.194)(1289) - (0.439)(1387) + (0.286)(1390) - (0.291)(1569)$$

$$= 1317$$

---

[5] Regression analysis is discussed in considerably more detail in Chapters 12–14 of Paul Newbold, *Statistics for Business and Economics* (Englewood Cliffs, N.J.: Prentice-Hall, Inc.; 1984).

We can continue in this way to forecast further ahead. Thus X_{32} is predicted by

$$\hat{X}_{32} = 446.22 + 1.194\hat{X}_{31} - 0.439X_{30} + 0.286X_{29} - 0.291X_{28}$$

$$= 446.22 + (1.194)(1317) - (0.439)(1289) + (0.286)(1387) - (0.291)(1390)$$

$$= 1445$$

Similarly,

$$\hat{X}_{33} = 446.22 + 1.94\hat{X}_{32} - 0.439\hat{X}_{31} + 0.286X_{30} - 0.291X_{29}$$

$$= 446.22 + (1.194)(1445) - (0.439)(1317) + (0.286)(1289) - (0.291)(1387)$$

$$= 1558$$

Continuing in this way, the model can be projected forward to derive forecasts as far ahead as desired.

Now, autoregressive models have been found to be very useful in practical business forecasting. However, there is one potential drawback to their use. For the autoregressive model of order p, forecasts of all future values of a series are based on just its p most recent values. It may often be the case that for satisfactory forecasts, relatively many past observations need to be incorporated into the forecast function; that is, a high value of p in (12.10) will be required. However, typically, with only moderate amounts of data available, the estimates of a large number of parameters ϕ_i will not be very accurate. A forecast function that allows weight to be given to all past observations through the use of just three parameters—γ, ϕ, and θ—is

$$\hat{X}_{n+1} = \gamma + (\phi - \theta)X_n + \theta(\phi - \theta)X_{n-1}$$
$$+ \theta^2(\phi - \theta)X_{n-2} + \theta^3(\phi - \theta)X_{n-3} + \ldots \qquad (12.11)$$

With $0 < \theta < \phi < 1$ this gives declining positive weights to all past observations. The forecast function (12.11) is one member of the class of **autoregressive integrated moving average (ARIMA)** models.

The popularity of ARIMA models in forecasting was stimulated by the work of Box and Jenkins.[6] These authors developed a methodology for fitting to data a model of the ARIMA class. Their approach involves a three step cycle of model selection, parameter estimation, and model checking. At the first step, based on the characteristics of the data, a specific model is selected from the general ARIMA class. Next, the unknown parameters of the model are estimated, and finally the adequacy of the model is checked. This approach allows

---

[6] See G. E. P. Box and G. M. Jenkins, *Time Series Analysis, Forecasting and Control* (San Francisco: Holden-Day, 1970). An excellent introduction to the Box-Jenkins methodology is provided by C. R. Nelson, *Applied Time Series for Managerial Forecasting* (San Francisco: Holden-Day, 1973).

a wide variety of possible forecast functions—for example, the simple exponential smoothing and Holt-Winters predictors are members of the ARIMA class. Moreover, the approach can be extended to allow, through elaborations of the regression model, for the incorporation of information on other relevant variables.

The Box-Jenkins approach to forecasting is more time consuming than the other quantitative approaches discussed in this chapter. However, its versatility often makes it a sensible choice for many practical problems. Unfortunately, in the space available, it is not possible to discuss the details of this methodology.

EXERCISES

12.1. The accompanying table shows an index of annual product sales over a period of twelve years.

YEAR	SALES	YEAR	SALES
1	100.0	7	101.4
2	92.7	8	115.3
3	90.3	9	110.6
4	98.4	10	104.5
5	106.3	11	116.8
6	112.5	12	119.2

Using simple exponential smoothing, with a smoothing constant $\alpha = 0.3$, forecast sales for the next three years.

12.2. The accompanying table shows earnings per share, in dollars, for a corporation over a period of fourteen years.

YEAR	EARNINGS	YEAR	EARNINGS
1	3.10	8	7.02
2	3.16	9	6.51
3	3.61	10	5.83
4	3.69	11	4.99
5	5.10	12	3.51
6	6.11	13	3.40
7	6.31	14	3.55

Using simple exponential smoothing, with a smoothing constant $\alpha = 0.5$, forecast sales for the next five years.

12.3. If forecasts are based on simple exponential smoothing, with X_t denoting the actual value of a series, and $\overline{X}_t$ the smoothed value at time t, the error that is made in forecasting X_t, standing at time $(t - 1)$, is

$$e_t = X_t - \overline{X}_{t-1}$$

Show that

$$\bar{X}_t = X_t - \alpha e_t$$

where α is the smoothing constant. Hence, the most recent observation and the most recent forecast error are used to compute the next forecast.

12.4. "Annual product sales vary widely from year to year, yet simple exponential smoothing yields the same forecast of sales for every future year. Hence this method is obviously inappropriate for sales forecasting." Comment on this statement.

12.5. The accompanying table shows annual sales of a line of clothing over a period of eleven years.

YEAR	SALES	YEAR	SALES
1	1,025	7	1,045
2	1,278	8	1,108
3	1,291	9	1,207
4	1,103	10	1,185
5	1,062	11	1,130
6	983		

Using simple exponential smoothing, with a smoothing constant $\alpha = 0.4$, forecast sales for the next four years.

12.6. The accompanying table shows quarterly sales over a period of three years for a product. It is known that sales are unaffected by seasonal factors.

QUARTER	SALES	QUARTER	SALES
1	437	7	479
2	465	8	470
3	492	9	488
4	508	10	499
5	502	11	506
6	483	12	520

Use the Holt-Winters procedure, with smoothing constants $A = 0.3$, $B = 0.4$, to forecast sales for the next four quarters.

12.7. The accompanying table shows monthly figures for new applications for credit for a department store chain over a period of fourteen months.

MONTH	APPLICATIONS	MONTH	APPLICATIONS
1	237	8	218
2	249	9	227
3	260	10	241
4	258	11	269
5	236	12	278
6	225	13	279
7	215	14	270

Use the Holt-Winters procedure, with smoothing constants $A = 0.4$, $B = 0.2$, to forecast new applications for credit for the next three months.

12.8. If forecasts are based on the Holt-Winters procedure, with X_t denoting the actual value of a series, $\bar{X}_t$ the level estimate, and T_t the trend estimate at time t, the error that is made in forecasting X_t, standing at time $(t - 1)$, is

$$e_t = X_t - \bar{X}_{t-1} - T_{t-1}$$

Show that

$$\bar{X}_t = X_t - Ae_t$$

and

$$T_t = X_t - X_{t-1} - A(e_t - e_{t-1}) - B(1 - A)e_t$$

12.9. Repeat Exercise 12.7, but using the smoothing constants $A = 0.5$, $B = 0.5$. Which of these two pairs of smoothing constants would you prefer to use for forecasting this series?

12.10. Forecasts are to be based on the Holt-Winters procedure. Let $f_{n,h}$ be the forecast of X_{n+h} made at time n, and $f_{n-1,h+1}$ the forecast of the same quantity made at time $(n - 1)$. Show that

$$f_{n,h} = f_{n-1,h+1} + (1 - A)[1 + h(1 - B)]e_n$$

where

$$e_n = X_n - \bar{X}_{n-1} - T_{n-1}$$

Interpret this result.

12.11. The accompanying table shows motor vehicle death rates per 100,000 population and the percentage of vehicles on highways exceeding 60 miles per hour over a period of 10 years.

DEATH RATE	% EXCEEDING 60 MPH	DEATH RATE	% EXCEEDING 60 MPH
22.0	18	28.3	40
23.1	21	27.8	44
24.3	29	28.8	45
26.1	32	27.6	46
26.5	34	25.3	47

Estimate the regression of death rate on percent of vehicles exceeding 60 m.p.h., and predict the death rate in a year in which 50% of vehicles exceed this speed.

12.12. The following table shows percentage change in sales volume and percentage change in price for a product over a period of eight years.

% CHANGE IN PRICE	% CHANGE IN SALES	% CHANGE IN PRICE	% CHANGE IN SALES
6.0	5.2	7.0	5.3
5.0	7.3	6.0	5.0
4.0	7.4	10.0	-1.0
7.0	4.6	8.0	2.7

Estimate the regression of percentage change in sales on percentage change in price, and predict the percentage change in sales for a year in which price increases by 7.5%.

12.13. A second order autoregressive model was fitted to monthly sales data. The estimated model was

$$\hat{X}_{n+1} = 1.38X_n - 0.38X_{n-1}$$

The last two monthly observations were

$$X_{n-1} = 725; \; X_n = 702$$

Forecast X_{n+1}, X_{n+2}, and X_{n+3}.

Extrapolation of Past Experience: Forecasting Emergency Workload for the British Gas Corporation[1]

The British Gas Corporation is organized into twelve local regions, of which one, North Thames Gas, is the focus of this study. North Thames Gas maintains five pools of emergency workers, geographically spread over the region. These workers are available to answer as soon as possible emergency calls for assistance in the event of gas escapes. The numbers of emergency calls fluctuate quite widely day by day, and, since a large emergency staff is maintained to facilitate response in times of heavy demand, it is often the case that many of the emergency staff are unoccupied. If it were possible to anticipate a day ahead the level of emergency calls, then work would be found for unassigned emergency staff. The author of this study, then, faces the problem of forecasting, one day ahead, the number of emergency calls that will be received.

Data on past numbers of daily emergency calls were available, and it was decided to attempt to use a forecasting model that extrapolated past experience. The simplest possibility of this sort might be to predict tomorrow's demand as a multiple of today's. Alternatively, more weight could be given to other past observations, for example by relating future demand to demand in the previous week. The author opted for a combination of these two possibilities, using a forecast that was a linear combination of emergency calls on the previous day, and emergency calls in the previous week. Finally, it was noted that there was a very distinct day-of-week pattern to the emergency calls, so that demand was almost invariably higher on certain days of the week than others. This can be taken into account by computing a "day-of-week factor" for each of the seven days, giving the proportion of calls received on that particular day.

The forecasting model eventually employed, after a number of alternative extrapolation formulations had been compared, was

$$\begin{matrix} \text{Predicted} \\ \text{Number} \\ \text{of Calls} \end{matrix} = \begin{pmatrix} \text{Day of} \\ \text{Week} \\ \text{Factor} \end{pmatrix} \left[\begin{matrix} \text{Previous} \\ \text{Day's} \\ \text{Demand} \end{matrix} + k \begin{pmatrix} \text{Previous} \\ \text{Week's} \\ \text{Demand} \end{pmatrix} \right]$$

Various values of the parameter k were employed to see which best explained past behavior of the series of emergency calls. The author chose on this basis $k = \frac{1}{5}$, which yielded a procedure giving satisfactory forecasts of emergency calls one day ahead.

---

[1] This discussion is based on H. Sutlieff, "Forecasting Emergency Workload for Day Ahead," *Journal of Operational Research Society*, 33 (1982), 129–136.

network models

CHAPTER THIRTEEN

13.1. INTRODUCTION

Many important practical management problems of a highly complex nature can be attacked through a graphical representation known as a **network.** In Chapter 6 we met one class of cases of this sort—the transportation problem. Our object in the present chapter is to review a broader range of questions that can be approached through representation as networks.

We will begin by looking at two well-known network analysis techniques, the Program Evaluation and Review Technique (PERT) and the Critical Path Method (CPM). These two techniques were both designed for the management of large scale projects involving many constituent interdependent activities. In order to meet project completion deadlines, it may be critically important that some of the constituent activities be completed on schedule, while for others some overrun may not be detrimental. In certain circumstances, if the costs of doing so are not too high, management may be able to assign additional resources to the most critical activities, and so bring forward the completion date of the whole project. As a basis for such a decision, it is essential to have information about the effects of individual activities on the entire project.

PERT was developed in the late 1950s, through the U.S. Navy Special Projects Office, specifically for planning and controlling the Polaris missile program. This project, involving thousands of contractors and subcontractors, depended on much technological work that had never previously been attempted. This being the case, there was a good deal of uncertainty about the time that would be needed to complete many of the constituent activities. Thus, from the outset, *uncertainty* about activity completion times was incorporated into the PERT analysis.

On the other hand, CPM, which was developed at about the same time as PERT by DuPont and Remington Rand, was initially aimed at industrial projects where constituent activity times were known with near-certainty. It also differed from PERT in concentrating on the *costs* incurred when the times of individual activities were reduced through the addition of extra resources.

In more recent years the distinction between PERT and CPM has largely disappeared. Computer programs designed for the analysis of scheduling and control problems in large projects typically incorporate features which allow both for uncertain activity times and the possibility of activity time/cost trade-offs. The analysis of networks by such methods is known as the PERT/CPM approach.

13.2. PERT/CPM NETWORKS

As discussed in the previous section, our aim is to analyze projects involving several constituent parts, or **activities.** The focus of interest is on the timing of these activities. In particular, we will be concerned with the following questions:

1. When is the project expected to be finished?
2. What are the scheduled start and finish times of the constituent activities involved in the project?
3. Which of the constituent activities are *critical,* in the sense that they must be completed on time in order that the entire project remain on schedule?
4. For *noncritical* activities, how much delay is possible without affecting the completion time of the whole project?
5. Is it possible to allocate additional resources to critical activities to shorten the completion time of the project?

We will illustrate the construction of PERT/CPM networks, which are used to answer questions of this sort, through the case of a manufacturer of detergent. Recently sales of one brand of detergent have been rather flat, and the manufacturer has decided to mount a promotional campaign. The campaign is to involve a new package, incorporating a coupon which customers can redeem to provide a discount on the next purchase of the product. The campaign launch will involve also radio, television, newspaper, and magazine advertisements. The first step in organizing this campaign is to set out an **activity list,** as shown in Table 13.1.

Table 13.1 shows the complete project broken down into 10 constituent activities, labelled A–J. Once an overall budget for the project has been determined, resources must be allocated to production, radio and television advertising, and newspaper and magazine advertising. Details of the repeat purchase offer, such as the size of the discounts offered, must be determined, and new

TABLE 13.1 Activity list for the detergent promotional campaign.

ACTIVITY	DESCRIPTION OF ACTIVITY	IMMEDIATE PREDECESSORS
A	Determine total available budget	—
B	Determine allocation of total budget resources	A
C	Schedule radio and television time	B
D	Work out details of repeat purchase offer	B
E	Schedule newspaper and magazine advertisements	B
F	Produce new packages	D
G	Prepare radio and television advertisements	C, D
H	Prepare advertising copy for newspapers and magazines	D, E
I	Distribute new packages to supermarkets	F
J	Run promotional campaign	G, H, I

packages incorporating this information produced. Advertising time and space must be purchased, and the advertisements prepared. The new packages have to be distributed to those supermarkets involved in the campaign. Finally, when all is ready, the campaign can be run.

An activity list involves more than a simple listing of the constituent activities of a project. It also contains essential information about the scheduling of individual activities. This information is displayed in the final column of Table 13.1. For example, the promotional campaign cannot be run until advertisements have been prepared for radio and television, and for newspapers and magazines, and the new packages have been distributed to supermarkets. Accordingly, activities G, H, and I are shown as **immediate predecessors** of activity J. The immediate precedessors of any activity are those activities that must be completed directly before the activity of interest is started.

A **PERT/CPM network** involves a graphical representation of the activity list. We will see how to build up such a network for the detergent promotional campaign. To begin, suppose that the activity list involves just the four activities A, B, C, and D. The network, which is sometimes called an **activities on arcs** representation, is shown in Figure 13.1. A PERT/CPM network consists of numbered circles, or **nodes**, joined by **branches** or **arcs**, with arrows. Each branch represents the carrying out of a constituent activity. Node 1 depicts the start of

FIGURE 13.1 PERT/CPM network for activities A, B, C, D of Table 13.1.

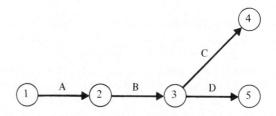

FIGURE 13.2 PERT/CPM network for activities A, B, C, D, F, G of Table 13.1.

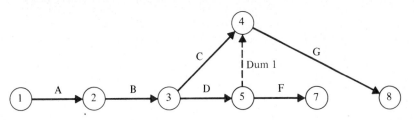

activity A, while the other nodes depict **events,** representing the completion of an activity or group of activities. These are the events that must occur before other activities can be started. Thus, a numbered node represents a point at which one or more activities have been completed, and one or more activities can be started.

We will continue to build up the network by now assuming an activity list consisting just of A, B, C, D, F, and G. This presents a certain difficulty since, while F can be started immediately, when D is completed, both C and D must be completed before starting G. The problem is resolved in Figure 13.2 by introducing a **dummy activity,** represented by a dashed line, connecting nodes 5 and 4. Dummy activities are activities which are not in fact carried out, but are introduced as a graphical convenience in order to properly represent immediate predecessor relationships. It is now clear from Figure 13.2 that in order to begin G, both C and the dummy activity (labelled dum 1) must be completed. In turn, dum 1 requires the completion of D. In subsequent sections, dummy activities will have no influence on our calculations of project completion times, as we will assume that such activities take no time to carry out.

To see why dummy activities may be needed in the proper construction of PERT/CPM networks, we attempt in Figure 13.3 to depict the set of activities A, B, C, D, F, and G without recourse to a dummy activity. The event depicted by node 4 in Figure 13.3 is the completion of both activities C and D. This is precisely the event that must occur before activity G can be started. However, Figure 13.3 also implies, incorrectly, that C as well as D must be finished before

FIGURE 13.3 Incorrect PERT/CPM network for activities A, B, C, D, F, G of Table 13.1.

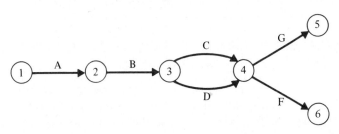

FIGURE 13.4 PERT/CPM network for the detergent promotional campaign.

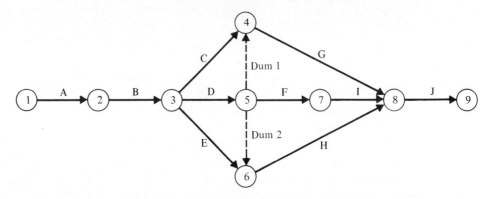

F can be started. In circumstances such as this the only way to avoid an incorrect network representation is to use a dummy activity, as in Figure 13.2.

The complete network for the detergent promotional campaign example of Table 13.1 is shown in Figure 13.4, which is an extension of Figure 13.2. Two features of the PERT/CPM network should be noted. First, leading from node 5 to node 6 is a second dummy activity, dum 2. This is required since, although H has immediate predecessors both D and E, only activity D need be completed before F is started. Also, notice that the event represented by node 8 is the completion of the three activities G, H, and I. This, as can be seen from Table 13.1, is precisely the event that is required before the final activity, running the promotional campaign, can be started.

Definitions

A **project** is made up of several interrelated constituent **activities.**

The **activity list** for a project defines the activities and shows immediate predecessor relationships.

Immediate predecessors of an activity are those activities that must be completed directly before the activity of interest is started.

A **PERT/CPM network** is a graphical representation of the activity list, in which nodes are linked by arcs, or branches.

The **branches** of a network depict activities, while the **nodes** represent **events** involving the completion of one or more activities.

Dummy activities are fictitious activities that may have to be introduced into the network in order to provide a correct representation of immediate predecessor relationships.

13.3. PROJECT SCHEDULING WITH UNCERTAIN ACTIVITY TIMES: STOCHASTIC PERT

Our interest now is in the overall time taken to complete a project, and in the influence of the individual activities on the whole schedule. In some problems, managers will be pretty certain about constituent activity times. However, this

TABLE 13.2 Activity times for the detergent promotional campaign.

	ACTIVITY TIMES (IN WEEKS)		
ACTIVITY	OPTIMISTIC	MOST LIKELY	PESSIMISTIC
A	0.5	1	1.5
B	0.5	1	3
C	2	3	4
D	0.5	1	1.5
E	0.5	1	3
F	4	5	9
G	2	4	9
H	2	3	7
I	1.5	3	4.5
J	4	4	4

will not invariably be the case, and allowance will be made here for uncertainty about these times. Each activity time is then represented, not by a fixed number, but rather by a random variable to reflect this uncertainty. It has been found that one way to elicit from managers information about the uncertain distribution of activity times is to request three pieces of information for each activity; these are

1. the most likely activity time
2. an optimistic activity time
3. a pessimistic activity time

The most likely time is management's best guess as to how long the activity will take to complete, while the optimistic and pessimistic times are estimates for the outcomes in best-case and worst-case circumstances.

Table 13.2 shows management estimates of optimistic, most likely, and pessimistic activity times for the detergent promotional campaign. It was determined at the outset that the campaign would run for exactly four weeks. Therefore, for activity J, optimistic, most likely, and pessimistic times are the same. However, for the other nine activities, these times differ, reflecting management uncertainty about the actual outcomes. When such uncertainty is involved, the algorithm employed for the analysis of the problem is sometimes called **stochastic PERT**.[1]

Experience in this area has suggested that a very satisfactory way to represent uncertain activity times is through a continuous probability distribution called the **beta distribution**. In the box below we set out the relevant properties of this distribution in the present context.

---

[1] *Deterministic PERT* is a special case of this algorithm, employed when all activity times are assumed to be known with certainty.

The Beta Distribution for Uncertain Activity Times

Suppose that optimistic, most likely, and pessimistic times are given for an activity. Then uncertainty about completion time for that activity can generally be well represented by the **beta distribution.** The mean (or expected value) and variance of this distribution are given by

$$\text{Mean Activity Time} = \frac{\text{Optimistic} + 4(\text{Most Likely}) + \text{Pessimistic}}{6}$$

and

$$\text{Variance of Activity Time} = \left(\frac{\text{Pessimistic} - \text{Optimistic}}{6}\right)^2$$

Figure 13.5 shows a typical probability density function for the beta distribution. The graph shows the most likely value, at the point where the density function is highest, and the mean of the distribution.

In Table 13.3 we have computed the means and variances of the individual activity times for the detergent promotional campaign, using the information in Table 13.2. For example, for activity G, preparation of radio and television advertisements, the mean, or expected, time is

$$\text{Mean Activity Time} = \frac{\text{Optimistic} + 4(\text{Most Likely}) + \text{Pessimistic}}{6}$$

$$= \frac{2 + (4)(4) + 9}{6} = 4.5 \text{ weeks}$$

FIGURE 13.5 Beta distribution representing uncertain activity time.

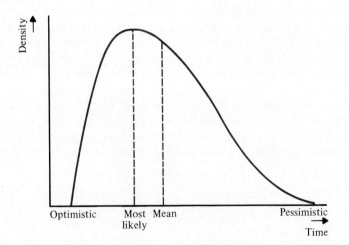

TABLE 13.3 Mean and variance of activity times for the detergent promotional campaign.

	ACTIVITY TIMES (IN WEEKS)	
ACTIVITY	MEAN	VARIANCE
A	1	0.0277
B	1.25	0.1736
C	3	0.1111
D	1	0.0277
E	1.25	0.1736
F	5.5	0.6944
G	4.5	1.3611
H	3.5	0.6944
I	3	0.2500
J	4	0

and the variance is

$$\text{Variance of Activity Times} = \left(\frac{\text{Pessimistic} - \text{Optimistic}}{6}\right)^2$$

$$= \left(\frac{9 - 2}{6}\right)^2 = 1.3611$$

In our subsequent analysis of this problem, we will ignore for the time being uncertainty about activity times, and, for each activity, work with the mean time for completion. Figure 13.6 shows the PERT/CPM network for the detergent promotional campaign with these expected activity times added. The variance of activity J is zero, since the campaign will definitely last 4 weeks. Also, since the dummy activities are fictitious, the associated activity times are zero.

FIGURE 13.6 PERT/CPM network for the detergent promotional campaign, with expected activity times.

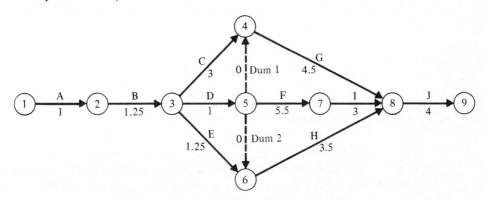

EARLIEST AND LATEST STARTING AND FINISHING TIMES FOR ACTIVITIES

In order to complete the entire promotional project, the detergent manufacturer must move from node 1 to node 9 in Figure 13.6. Our aim here is to determine the expected amount of time that this will take. One way to gain insight into the problem is to find the earliest possible time at which each activity can start and finish, taking the expected activity times as being the actual times. Measuring time in weeks, and beginning at time zero, activity A can start at the earliest at time zero. Also, since the time for this activity is one week, the earliest possible finishing time for activity A is one week into the project. Continuing in this way, activity B cannot be started until A has been finished, so that the earliest possible starting date for this activity is one week into the project, and so, of course, the earliest possible finishing time for the activity is 2.25 weeks into the project. Continuing in this manner, we can obtain earliest starting and finishing times for each activity. These are displayed on the PERT/CPM network in Figure 13.7.

The results shown in Figure 13.7 follow from the fact that an activity cannot start until *all* of its immediate predecessor activities have finished. For example, consider the position at node 8. Activity J has as immediate predecessors activities G, I, and H, with respective earliest finishing times 9.75, 11.75, and 7 weeks. It follows that the earliest possible starting time for activity J is 11.75 weeks into the project. Once the earliest starting time for any activity has been found, the earliest finishing time is obtained by adding the expected time taken by that activity.

Determination of Earliest Starting and Finishing Times

Given a PERT/CPM network, with expected activity times, the earliest starting and finishing times for the activities are found as follows:

(i) The earliest starting time for any activity is the highest of the earliest finishing times for all its immediate predecessors. If there are no immediate predecessors, the earliest starting time is zero.

(ii) For any activity, let

$$EF = \text{Earliest finishing time}$$

$$ES = \text{Earliest starting time}$$

$$t = \text{Expected activity time}$$

Then

$$EF = ES + t$$

Now, a project is completed when and only when all its constituent activities are finished. The highest of the earliest finishing times for these activities therefore determines the soonest achieveable expected completion time date for

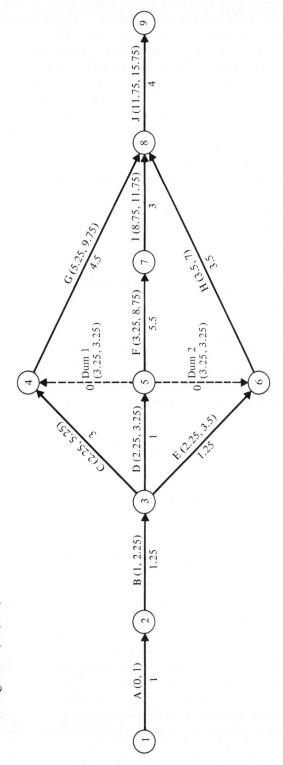

FIGURE 13.7 PERT/CPM network for the detergent promotional campaign, with expected activity times and earliest starting and finishing times (ES, EF).

the project. Referring to Figure 13.7, it can be seen that the best that can be done is an expected end of the project 15.75 weeks after its start.

The next step in our analysis is to determine how *late* individual activities can start and finish without extending the expected completion date of the project. Beginning at node 9, activity J must be finished after 15.75 weeks. Since this activity takes 4 weeks, its latest possible starting date must be 11.75 weeks into the project. Moving now to node 8, activities G, I, and H must be finished 11.75 weeks into the project in order that J be started at that time. Given that G, I, and H have respective expected activity times of 4.5, 3, and 3.5 weeks, it follows that their latest starting times are 7.25, 8.75, and 8.25 weeks into the project. Continuing to argue in this way, the latest starting and finishing times displayed in Figure 13.8 can be found.

Determination of Latest Starting and Finishing Times

The latest starting and finishing times for an activity are the latest times that will preserve the earliest possible end of project date. These times are found as follows:

(i) The latest finishing time for an activity is the latest starting time for an activity for which the activity of interest is an immediate predecessor in the PERT/CPM network. If the activity of interest is not an immediate predecessor of any other activity, its latest finishing time is the earliest possible end of project date.

(ii) For any activity, let

$$LF = \text{Latest finishing time}$$

$$LS = \text{Latest starting time}$$

$$t = \text{Expected activity time}$$

Then

$$LS = LF - t$$

THE CRITICAL PATH

For our example of the detergent promotional campaign, we have seen that an expected project completion time of 15.75 weeks is attainable. However, in order for this goal to be met, certain of the constituent activities must be started and finished at specific times. These activities can be identified from the earliest and latest starting and finishing times, given in Figure 13.8 and also displayed in Table 13.4, which is known as an **activity schedule**.

To illustrate again the interpretation of earliest and latest starting and finishing times, consider activity C, scheduling of radio and television time. The earliest this can be started, if actual activity times are the same as expected

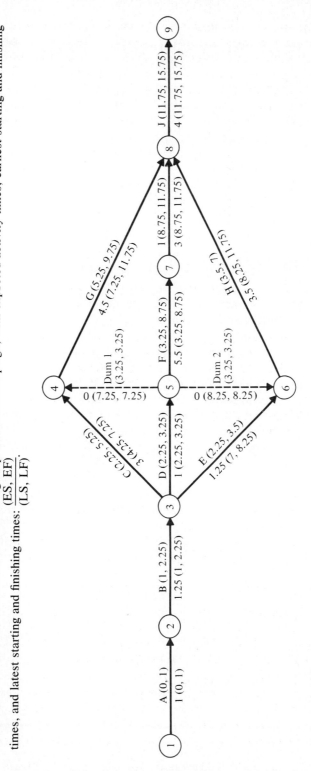

FIGURE 13.8 PERT/CPM network for the detergent promotional campaign, with expected activity times, earliest starting and finishing times, and latest starting and finishing times: $\dfrac{(ES, EF)}{(LS, LF)}$.

TABLE 13.4 Activity schedule for the detergent promotional campaign.

	TIMES (WEEKS)					
ACTIVITY	ES	LS	EF	LF	SLACK	ON CRITICAL PATH?
A	0	0	1.00	1.00	0	Yes
B	1.00	1.00	2.25	2.25	0	Yes
C	2.25	4.25	5.25	7.25	2.00	No
D	2.25	2.25	3.25	3.25	0	Yes
E	2.25	7.00	3.50	8.25	4.75	No
F	3.25	3.25	8.75	8.75	0	Yes
G	5.25	7.25	9.75	11.75	2.00	No
H	3.50	8.25	7.00	11.75	4.75	No
I	8.75	8.75	11.75	11.75	0	Yes
J	11.75	11.75	15.75	15.75	0	Yes

times, is 2.25 weeks into the project, and the corresponding earliest finishing date is 3 weeks later. However, the expected completion date of the whole project will be unchanged if this activity is started after 4.25 weeks, and completed 7.25 weeks into the project. We therefore infer that there is some leeway, or **slack,** available in the timing of activity C. The amount of this slack is 2 weeks—the difference between the earliest possible start and the latest possible start that will leave the project completion date unaltered.

The penultimate column of Table 13.4 shows the amount of slack for each activity, calculated as just described. Notice that for six of the activities slack is zero. The implication is that these activities must commence at their earliest starting times if the expected project completion date is not to extend beyond 15.75 weeks. Such activities are said to be **critical.**

Notice from Figure 13.8 that the six critical activities form a path A–B–D–F–I–J through the PERT/CPM network; that is, project completion at node 9 can be reached from the starting point at node 1 by following a path along the arcs A, B, D, F, I, J. Any path through a network made up entirely of critical activities is called a **critical path.** The total time taken for the critical path activities is 15.75 weeks. By contrast, consider the alternative path A–B–E–H–J. The total time taken for these activities is 11 weeks, so that this path is not critical. A critical path is one for which the sum of expected activity times is highest.

Definitions

The **slack** time associated with any activity is given by

$$Slack = LS - ES = LF - EF$$

Any activity with zero slack is said to be **critical.**
A path, made up entirely of critical activities, through a PERT/CPM network is called a **critical path.**

Knowledge of which activities are critical is important to management. In monitoring the progress of a project it will generally be preferable to pay relatively more attention to the prompt carrying out of such activities if there is concern about slippage in the project completion date.

UNCERTAINTY ABOUT THE PROJECT COMPLETION DATE

Up to this point we have worked exclusively with the mean activity times, finding for the detergent promotional campaign an expected completion date of 15.75 weeks. In deterministic PERT, where actual times are assumed equal to the mean activity times with probability one, this would be the end of the story. However, when there is uncertainty about individual activity times, this will induce uncertainty in the completion date. We now analyze this factor.

It has already been seen that the expected completion date depends on the activities along the critical path. Similarly, uncertainty about the project completion date also depends on these activities. In Table 13.5 we reproduce, from Table 13.3, the means and variances of the critical path activities for the detergent promotional campaign.

Now, the total project completion time is the sum of the times for the critical path activities. In order to find the mean and variance for project completion time, we will use the fact that the mean of the sum of random variables is the sum of their means, and, provided the random variables are independent, the variance of their sum is the sum of their variances.[2] Further, we will make use of the fact that by virtue of the Central Limit Theorem, the sum of a moderately large number of random variables has a distribution that is close to normal.

Statistical Distribution for the Project Completion Date

In Stochastic PERT the project completion date is a random variable whose distribution is normal, with mean, μ, equal to the sum of the means of the critical path activities, and whose variance, σ^2, is equal to the sum of the variances of the critical path activities.

From the final row of Table 13.5 we find for the detergent promotional campaign that the mean and variance of project completion time are

$$\mu = 15.75; \sigma^2 = 1.1734$$

so that the standard deviation is

$$\sigma = \sqrt{1.1734} = 1.0832 \text{ weeks}$$

---

[2] This conclusion depends on the independence of the random variables. In what follows we will assume that the individual activity times are independent of one another.

TABLE 13.5 Mean and variance of critical path activity times for the detergent promotional campaign.

| ACTIVITY | ACTIVITY TIMES (IN WEEKS) | |
	MEAN	VARIANCE
A	1	0.0277
B	1.25	0.1736
D	1	0.0277
F	5.5	0.6944
I	3	0.2500
J	4	0
Sums	15.75	1.1734

Since the distribution is taken to be normal, it is possible to calculate the probability that the overall project completion time lies in any given range, using the methods of Chapter 10.

Management is anxious to complete the detergent promotional campaign within 18 weeks. We now find the probability that this goal will be achieved. Let the random variable X denote total project completion time. Figure 13.9 shows the probability density function of a normal distribution with mean 15.75 and standard deviation 1.0832, with the required probability indicated.

We have

$$P(X < 18) = P\left(Z < \frac{18 - \mu}{\sigma}\right)$$

FIGURE 13.9 Shaded area shows the probability that a normal random variable with mean 15.75 and standard deviation 1.0832 does not exceed 18.

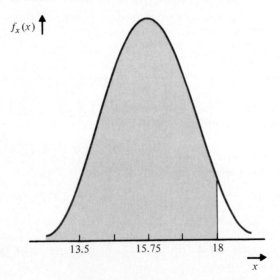

where Z is a standard normal random variable. Therefore

$$P(X < 18) = P\left(Z < \frac{18 - 15.75}{1.0832}\right)$$
$$= P(Z < 2.08)$$
$$= 0.9812$$

from Table 3 of the Appendix. There is, therefore, an excellent chance that management's target will be met.[3]

WHAT CAN BE LEARNED FROM STOCHASTIC PERT?

We are now in a position to review the contributions of stochastic PERT to project scheduling. Let us see what information management has acquired from the analysis of the detergent promotional campaign case.

1. It has been established that the expected completion time for the whole project is 15.75 weeks.
2. Start and finish dates for each activity have been found. These are the earliest possible values, *ES* and *EF,* shown in Table 13.4 and Figure 13.7.
3. The critical activities—those that must be started and finished on time—have been identified.
4. The amount of delay possible for noncritical activities, such that the expected completion date is maintained, has been found. These are the slack times given in Table 13.4.
5. It has been found that the probability is 0.9812 that management's target of completing the project within 18 weeks will be attained.

In fact, for the example of this section, all of this information was relatively easily obtained through straightforward hand calculations. However, many projects involve very large numbers of interrelated activities, making hand calculations prohibitively tedious. Computer programs for the analysis of such networks are readily available and produce the kind of information we have found here in the simple example of the detergent promotional campaign.

---

[3] Our calculation here has involved a simplifying assumption. Strictly speaking, what we have found is that the probability is 0.9812 *that the critical path* will be completed within 18 weeks. However, the whole project is completed only when *every* path through the network is completed. Thus, for example, A–B–C–G–J in Figure 13.8 is not critical. The probability that such a path will be completed before the target date is not necessarily negligibly different from one, even if the critical path is completed on time. Typically, the paths through a PERT/CPM network are not independent of one another, which makes it difficult to find analytically the probability that every path will be completed by a particular time. In that event, simulation methods can be employed to find the required probability.

Up to this point we have taken individual activity times as quantities over which management has little control. In fact, in many projects, it will be possible to reduce these times, though at some cost. In this section we allow for this possibility, regarding individual activity times as a function of their cost—the shorter an activity time is to be made, the greater will be the cost of that activity. For any particular cost, activity time will be taken to be a fixed number rather than a random variable. This is the original CPM formulation.

To illustrate, we will consider the case of a machine shop, which has just taken delivery of three machines that are to be employed together as a system. The machines must be installed, their operating characteristics checked and adjusted, and the whole system tested. Table 13.6 shows the activity list for this project, under normal machine shop working conditions.

Figure 13.10 shows the network for this problem and incorporates the calculations of the earliest and lastest starting and finishing times under normal

TABLE 13.6 Activity list, with normal times, for the machine shop problem.

ACTIVITY	DESCRIPTION OF ACTIVITY	IMMEDIATE PREDECESSORS	NORMAL TIME (DAYS)
A	Install Machine I	—	7
B	Install Machine II	—	5
C	Install Machine III	—	8
D	Check Machine I	A	2
E	Check Machine II	B	3
F	Check Machine III	C	3
G	Test Complete System	D, E, F	4

FIGURE 13.10 PERT/CPM network for the machine shop problem, with normal activity times, and earliest and latest normal starting and finishing times:
(ES, EF)
(LS, LF).

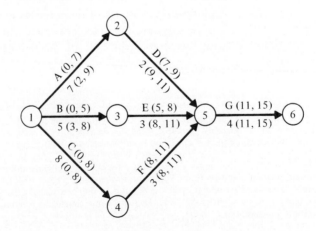

TABLE 13.7 Activity schedule for the machine shop problem given normal working conditions.

ACTIVITY	TIMES (DAYS)					ON CRITICAL PATH?
	ES	LS	EF	LF	SLACK	
A	0	2	7	9	2	No
B	0	3	5	8	3	No
C	0	0	8	8	0	Yes
D	7	9	9	11	2	No
E	5	8	8	11	3	No
F	8	8	11	11	0	Yes
G	11	11	15	15	0	Yes

working conditions. The information in this graph is reproduced in Table 13.7, where the activity slack times are computed.

From this deterministic PERT analysis, it can be seen that under normal working conditions, the quickest possible time to complete the project is 15 working days, and that if this is to be achieved, activities C, F, and G are critical.

Machine shop mangagement is unhappy with the finding that it will be 15 working days before this system is fully operational and regards as essential that the whole project be completed within 10 working days. In order to achieve this target management is prepared to commit, where necessary, additional resources to the project. This will involve overtime working, so that if an activity time is to be shortened the cost of that activity will increase. The addition of resources to shorten normal activity times is generally referred to as **crashing**. Resource constraints will limit the amount of crashing that is possible, and the shortest possible time that can be achieved for an activity in this manner is called its **crash time.**

Definitions

Crashing is the reduction of an activity time below its normal level through the addition of extra resources to that activity.

The **crash time** of an activity is the time required for it under maximum crashing.

The CPM analysis requires management to provide the following estimates for each activity:

1. The normal time
2. The crash time
3. The cost under normal time
4. The cost under crash time

For the machine shop problem, these data are shown in Table 13.8.

TABLE 13.8 Normal and crash activity times and costs for the machine shop problem.

ACTIVITY	TIME (DAYS) NORMAL	CRASH	COST ($) NORMAL	CRASH	CRASH COST ($) PER DAY
A	7	4	2,100	3,000	300
B	5	3	1,400	1,800	200
C	8	5	2,700	3,900	400
D	2	1	900	1,000	100
E	3	1.5	1,200	1,500	200
F	3	1.5	1,000	1,300	200
G	4	2	1,200	1,700	250
Totals			10,500	14,200	

From Table 13.8 we see immediately that under normal working conditions (where the project will take 15 days to complete) the total cost of setting up the system will be $10,500. On the other hand, if there is maximum crashing of each activity, this total cost rises to $14,200. In fact, it is easily seen that,[4] under maximum crashing, it is possible to complete the project in 8.5 days, which is well within management's target of 10 days.

The reader will have realized that this target could be met more cheaply if not all activities are crashed to the maximum possible. It is necessary, therefore, to consider the costs of crashing below the maximum possible level. The assumption that will be made is of **linearity** of cost; that is, it will be assumed that up to the maximum possible, the cost of any crashing for an activity is directly proportional to the reduction in time below the normal time. Given this assumption, the crash costs per unit of time for each activity can be found.

Unit Crashing Costs

For any activity the crash cost per unit of time is given by

$$\text{Unit Crash Cost} = \frac{\text{Crash Cost} - \text{Normal Cost}}{\text{Normal Time} - \text{Crash Time}}$$

To illustrate, in our machine shop problem, for activity A, the installation of machine I, we find

$$\text{Unit Crash Cost} = \frac{3000 - 2100}{7 - 4} = \$300 \text{ per day}$$

---

[4] This result follows from a routine application of deterministic PERT, in precisely the same form as employed in Figure 13.10, and is left as an exercise to the reader.

The interpretation is that under normal working conditions, installation of machine I requires 7 days and costs $2100. This activity time can be reduced to as little as 4 days, with each day of reduced time costing $300.

We have now reached the point where a target completion date, which cannot be achieved under normal working conditions, has been set for a project. It is, however, possible to meet the target by committing, at a cost, additional resources to some or all of the constituent activities. An interesting question, to which we now turn, is how to meet the target *at the lowest possible cost*. It will be recognized that our problem involves constrained optimization. Total project cost is to be minimized, subject to the target completion date being met and subject, also, to the limitations imposed by the availability of resources for each activity. Our assumption that unit crashing costs are constant for each activity ensures, as we will now see, that this problem can be set in a linear programming framework.

LINEAR PROGRAMMING SOLUTION FOR CPM COST/TIME TRADE-OFF PROBLEMS

Our task now is to set up algebraically the problem of completing a project by a set target date at the smallest possible cost. Two types of decision variables are needed:

(a) The time at which each event (represented by a node in the PERT/CPM network) is to occur.
(b) The amount of crashing time for each activity.

For notational convenience, we denote the former by x_i and the latter by y_j. Thus, for the machine shop problem, where, as can be seen from Figure 13.10, there are 6 events and 7 activities, we have:

x_1 = Time event 1 occurs
x_2 = Time event 2 occurs
x_3 = Time event 3 occurs
x_4 = Time event 4 occurs
x_5 = Time event 5 occurs
x_6 = Time event 6 occurs

and

y_A = Crash time used for activity A
y_B = Crash time used for activity B
y_C = Crash time used for activity C
y_D = Crash time used for activity D
y_E = Crash time used for activity E
y_F = Crash time used for activity F
y_G = Crash time used for activity G

We continue to measure time in working days.

Now, the normal time costs will certainly be incurred, so that we can concentrate on the costs of crashing. The total cost of crashing is simply the sum of the crashing costs for each individual activity. Table 13.8 shows the daily crash cost for each activity, from which it follows that the total crashing cost for the project is (in dollars).

$$\text{Total Crash Cost} = 300\, y_A + 200\, y_B + 400\, y_C + 100\, y_D + 200\, y_E + 200\, y_F + 250\, y_G$$

Notice that this objective function does not involve the decision variables x_1, x_2, . . ., x_6.

The aim is to set the values of the decision variables so that total crash cost is as small as possible. There are three types of constraints that must be met. These are:

(i) MEETING PROJECT COMPLETION TARGET DATE

For the machine shop problem, the target is to complete the entire project within 10 working days. As can be seen from Figure 13.10, project completion corresponds to event 6. Therefore, if the target is to be met, we must have

$$x_6 \leq 10$$

(ii) MAXIMUM FEASIBLE CRASHING

The amount of crashing possible for each activity can be found from Table 13.8 as the difference between the normal time and the time taken under maximum crashing. For example, for activity A, the most crashing that is possible is a reduction of $(7 - 4) = 3$ days below the normal time. We therefore have

$$y_A \leq 3$$

Similarly, for the other activities,

$$y_B \leq 2$$
$$y_C \leq 3$$
$$y_D \leq 1$$
$$y_E \leq 1.5$$
$$y_F \leq 1.5$$
$$y_G \leq 2$$

(iii) FEASIBLE TIMING OF EVENTS

Event 1 is simply the start of the project, so that, since work is begun at time zero, we have

$$x_1 = 0$$

and the decision variable x_1 can be ignored in the further development of this problem.

From Figure 13.10, it can be seen that event 2 is the completion of activity A, which starts at time zero. Under normal working conditions, this activity takes 7 days, so that if the amount of crashing is y_A, the time for activity A will be $7 - y_A$ days. It therefore follows, for the occurrence of event 2, that

$$x_2 \geq 7 - y_A$$

or

$$x_2 + y_A \geq 7$$

Arguing in exactly the same way, we find for events 3 and 4

$$x_3 + y_B \geq 5$$

$$x_4 + y_C \geq 8$$

Turning now to event 5, this occurs when and only when 3 activities—D, E, and F—have been completed. A separate constraint is required for each. Now, activity D can be started only after event 2, so that its earliest starting time is x_2. The time taken for activity D is the normal time, 2 days, less the amount of crashing, y_D; that is, $(2 - y_D)$ days. Thus, the earliest time that activity D can be completed is $x_2 + (2 - y_D)$. It therefore follows that

$$x_5 \geq x_2 + (2 - y_D)$$

or

$$-x_2 + x_5 + y_D \geq 2$$

Similarly, for the completion of events E and F, we find

$$x_5 \geq x_3 + (3 - y_E)$$

and

$$x_5 \geq x_4 + (3 - y_F)$$

or

$$-x_3 + x_5 + y_E \geq 3$$

and

$$-x_4 + x_5 + y_F \geq 3$$

Finally, for event 6, completion of the project, activity G must be carried out. This activity can only be started after the occurrence of event 5, at time x_5. The time taken for activity G will be $(4 - y_G)$ days, so that

$$x_6 \geq x_5 + (4 - y_G)$$

or

$$-x_5 + x_6 + y_G \geq 4$$

We can now put together these individual elements, and write the constrained cost minimization problem of the machine shop as

Minimize $300\,y_A + 200\,y_B + 400\,y_C + 100\,y_D + 200\,y_E + 200\,y_F + 250\,y_G$

subject to
$$x_6 \leq 10$$
$$y_A \leq 3$$
$$y_B \leq 2$$
$$y_C \leq 3$$
$$y_D \leq 1$$
$$y_E \leq 1.5$$
$$y_F \leq 1.5$$
$$y_G \leq 2$$
$$x_2 + y_A \geq 7$$
$$x_3 + y_B \geq 5$$
$$x_4 + y_C \geq 8$$
$$-x_2 + x_5 + y_D \geq 2$$
$$-x_3 + x_5 + y_E \geq 3$$
$$-x_4 + x_5 + y_F \geq 3$$
$$-x_5 + x_6 + y_G \geq 4$$
$$x_i \geq 0 \quad (i = 2, 3, \ldots, 6)$$
$$y_j \geq 0 \quad (j = A, B, \ldots, G)$$

Using a computer program for solving the linear programming problem, it is found that the optimum solution is:

$$y_A = 0, \, y_B = 0, \, y_C = 1.5, \, y_D = 1, \, y_E = 0, \, y_F = 1.5, \, y_G = 2$$
$$x_2 = 7, \, x_3 = 5, \, x_4 = 6.5, \, x_5 = 8, \, x_6 = 10$$

Recalling that the y_j are the crash times used for the activities, it can be seen that the minimum cost solution for completing the project in 10 days requires no crashing of activities A, B, and E. For activities, C, D, F, and G, crashing amounts respectively to 1.5, 1, 1.5, and 2 days. The x_i provide the timing of the events in Figure 13.10. Notice that the value $x_6 = 10$ implies that the project will be finished in 10 days. The value of the objective function at the optimum solution was found to be 1500. Hence $1500 is the smallest possible additional cost that can be incurred if the project completion time is to be reduced to 10 days. Recall that under normal working, the entire project takes 15 days, at a total cost of $10,500. We have now learned that it is possible to complete all of the work in 10 days, at a total cost of $12,000.

TABLE 13.9 Activity schedule for the machine shop problem when the project completion time is reduced to 10 days at the lowest possible cost.

	TIMES (DAYS)						
ACTIVITY	TIME TAKEN	ES	LS	EF	LF	SLACK	ON CRITICAL PATH?
A	7	0	0	7	7	0	Yes
B	5	0	0	5	5	0	Yes
C	6.5	0	0	6.5	6.5	0	Yes
D	1	7	7	8	8	0	Yes
E	3	5	5	8	8	0	Yes
F	1.5	6.5	6.5	8	8	0	Yes
G	2	8	8	10	10	0	Yes

The new activity schedule is set out in Table 13.9. First, the time taken for each activity is calculated as the difference between the normal time (given in Table 13.6) and the amount of crash time that is to be used. The earliest and latest starting and finishing times for the new schedule can then be computed using familiar procedures. The calculations are precisely the same as those of Figure 13.10, but now with the new activity times replacing the normal working times. Notice that for this particular problem, it turns out that if the project is to be completed on schedule, every activity is now critical.

We have seen, then, how the CPM analysis provides management with important information on the trade-offs between project cost and completion date. In our machine shop example, we were able to show that total completion time could be reduced from 15 to 10 days, but only if an additional $1500 were spent on the project. It is not possible, given management estimates of crashing costs, to more cheaply meet the target of installing this system within 10 working days.

13.5. CONTROL OF PROJECT COSTS: PERT/Cost

So far our discussion of PERT/CPM networks has concentrated on the scheduling of activities and its effect on the timetable for completion of a project. A second issue, which is often of equal importance is the *cost* of a project. For a large project with many constituent activities, management will find it of great value to implement a formal mechanism for planning and monitoring expenditures as the project proceeds. In practice, many projects are so complex that monitoring costs for each individual activity is prohibitively expensive. In such cases, it is generally possible to group together related activities into **activity packages.** Attention is then concentrated on the costs of the packages as a whole.

The technique known as PERT/Cost is employed in the planning and controlling of project expenditures. To illustrate the elements of this technique, we will consider a research and development project of a drug company whose ac-

ACTIVITY PACKAGE	IMMEDIATE PREDECESSORS
A	—
B	—
C	A
D	B
E	A
F	C, D
G	B
H	F
I	F
J	E, I
K	H
L	G

tivity list is shown in Table 13.10. The PERT/CPM network is drawn in Figure 13.11 which also shows the estimated times for each activity package. These times are employed to calculate earliest and latest starting and finishing times for the 12 activity packages. This information is reproduced in the activity schedule of Table 13.11. The slack times are computed in this table, and it can be seen that the critical path for the drug company research and development project network is A–C–F–H–K. It also follows from Table 13.11 that if the activity schedule is met, the completion of the project, which is represented by node 9 in Figure 13.11, will occur after 12 months.

Our analysis to date of the drug company research and development project network has been along the lines of Sections 13.2 and 13.3. We now proceed further by considering the estimated costs of the activity packages. These are set out in Table 13.12, where we have also calculated the costs per month for

FIGURE 13.11 PERT/CPM network for the drug company research and development project, with activity times, and earliest and latest starting and finishing times: $\dfrac{(ES,\ EF)}{(LS,\ LF)}$.

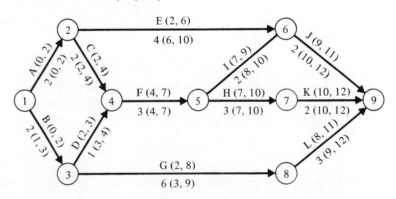

TABLE 13.11 Activity schedule for the drug company research and development project.

ACTIVITY PACKAGE	EST. TIME	TIMES (MONTHS)					ON CRITICAL PATH?
		ES	LS	EF	LF	SLACK	
A	2	0	0	2	2	0	Yes
B	2	0	1	2	3	1	No
C	2	2	2	4	4	0	Yes
D	1	2	3	3	4	1	No
E	4	2	6	6	10	4	No
F	3	4	4	7	7	0	Yes
G	6	2	3	8	9	1	No
H	3	7	7	10	10	0	Yes
I	2	7	8	9	10	1	No
J	2	9	10	11	12	1	No
K	2	10	10	12	12	0	Yes
L	3	8	9	11	12	1	No

TABLE 13.12 Budget for the drug company research and development project.

ACTIVITY PACKAGE	ESTIMATED TIME (MONTHS)	ESTIMATED COST ($)	BUDGET IN $ PER MONTH
A	2	20,000	10,000
B	2	24,000	12,000
C	2	30,000	15,000
D	1	18,000	18,000
E	4	28,000	7,000
F	3	33,000	11,000
G	6	54,000	9,000
H	3	21,000	7,000
I	2	10,000	5,000
J	2	28,000	14,000
K	2	42,000	21,000
L	3	51,000	17,000
Total		359,000	

each activity package.[5] The total estimated cost for the project is $359,000, and our aim now is to examine *when* this money will be spent.

We begin the study of this question in Table 13.13, which shows, month by month for the project, the amounts that are budgeted to be spent if each activity begins at its earliest starting time. Consider, for example, activity E. From Table 13.11, it can be seen that this activity has an earliest starting time 2 months after the beginning of the project, and is expected to take 4 months to

---

[5] It will be assumed, for each activity package, that costs are incurred *uniformly*—that is, once work on a package has started—expenditure per month will be constant up to its conclusion.

TABLE 13.13 Budgeted costs (in thousands of dollars) for the drug company research and development project with the earliest starting times schedule.

ACTIVITY PACKAGE	MONTH											
	1	2	3	4	5	6	7	8	9	10	11	12
A	10	10										
B	12	12										
C			15	15								
D			18									
E			7	7	7	7						
F					11	11	11					
G			9	9	9	9	9	9				
H								7	7	7		
I								5	5			
J										14	14	
K											21	21
L									17	17	17	
Monthly Cost	22	22	49	31	27	27	20	21	29	38	52	21
Accumulated Project Cost	22	44	93	124	151	178	198	219	248	286	338	359

complete. Activity E will therefore be carried out in the third, fourth, fifth, and sixth months of the project. Given our assumption of a constant expenditure rate on activity packages, it can be seen from Table 13.12 that $7000 is budgeted to be spent on this activity in each of these four months.

In the penultimate row of Table 13.13 we have calculated the total month by month expenditures for the whole project. The final row of the table shows the accumulated expenditures. For example, we see that under the earliest starting time schedule, a total of $198,000 is budgeted to be spent by the end of the seventh month. Notice that since the earliest starting times yield the earliest times at which expenditures can be incurred, it follows that if actual costs are the same as those budgeted, the accumulated project costs in Table 13.13 are the *highest* total costs that can be incurred at the corresponding time points.

Table 13.14 is in the same format as Table 13.13, but is based on the *latest* starting times for each activity package. For example, for activity package I, it can be seen from Table 13.11 that if the activity schedule is to be followed, the latest possible starting time is 8 months into the project. Since this activity takes 2 months, at a cost of $5000 per month, this expenditure is incurred in the ninth and tenth months of the project. The final two rows of Table 13.14 show the month by month total expenditures and accumulated expenditures for the project if every activity starts at the latest time compatible with project completion in 12 months. If actual costs are equal to those budgeted, the accumulated project costs of Table 13.14 will be the *lowest* total costs that can have been incurred at the corresponding time points if progress is within the activity schedule. For example, from Tables 13.13 and 13.14 it can be concluded that if, after 7 months,

TABLE 13.14 Budgeted costs (in thousands of dollars) for the drug company research and development project with the latest starting times schedule.

ACTIVITY PACKAGE	MONTH											
	1	2	3	4	5	6	7	8	9	10	11	12
A	10	10										
B		12	12									
C			15	15								
D				18								
E							7	7	7	7		
F					11	11	11					
G				9	9	9	9	9	9			
H								7	7	7		
I									5	5		
J											14	14
K											21	21
L										17	17	17
Monthly Cost	10	22	27	42	20	20	27	23	28	36	52	52
Accumulated Project Cost	10	32	59	101	121	141	168	191	219	255	307	359

the project has been running to schedule, total budgeted expenditure is between $168,000 and $198,000.

The information in the bottom rows of Tables 13.13 and 13.14 is presented graphically in Figure 13.12. The lower set of points depict accumulated costs over 12 months if the latest starting times schedule is followed. These points are connected by straight lines, as would be appropriate if, in any given month, costs accrued at a uniform rate. The upper set of points in Figure 13.12 show the accumulated costs through the year assuming that the earliest starting times schedule is followed. It therefore follows that if the project is proceeding according to schedule, the total costs incurred at any point in time should lie in the shaded area of Figure 13.12. If actual cost is above this region, then management is immediately alerted to the cost overrun problem, and a fuller investigation to detect its causes can be carried out.

Managers will generally want, from time to time as a project progresses, up-to-date information about both the scheduling and cost status for individual activity packages, and for the project as a whole.

The necessary information can be readily provided in tabular form, provided that the corporation's accounting practices allow the provision of costs accrued for activity packages. To illustrate, suppose that a cost status report is required 6 months into the drug company research and development project. For each activity package, two pieces of information are required:

(a) The actual costs that have been incurred
(b) The percentage of the work that has been completed

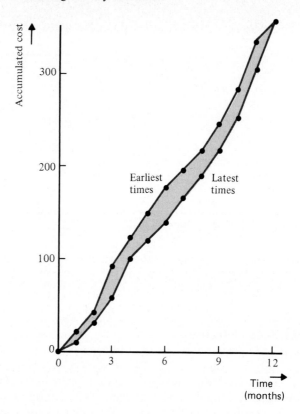

FIGURE 13.12 Accumulated budgeted costs for the drug company research and development project following activity schedule.

These are set out in the second and third columns of Table 13.15.

In order to determine the extent of any overruns, the costs actually incurred must be compared with the *budgeted value* of the work that has been done. This is obtained for each activity package as

$$\text{Budgeted Value} = \frac{(\text{Percent Completion})(\text{Budgeted Cost})}{100}$$

For example, from Table 13.12, the budgeted cost of activity package E is $28,000. Since 75% of the work on this package has been completed, the budgeted value of completed work is 75% of $28,000, or $21,000. The penultimate column of Table 13.15 shows the budgeted values of the work done on every activity package after 6 months.

Finally, for each package, the cost overrun is obtained as the difference between actual cost and budgeted value; that is

$$\text{Cost Overrun} = \text{Actual Cost} - \text{Budgeted Value}$$

Thus, it can be seen that for activity package E, costs so far incurred are $500

TABLE 13.15 Status report after six months of costs of the drug company research and development project.

ACTIVITY PACKAGE	ACTUAL COST ($)	PERCENT COMPLETION	BUDGETED VALUE ($)	COST OVERRUN ($)
A	22,000	100	20,000	2,000
B	23,000	100	24,000	−1,000
C	31,500	100	30,000	1,500
D	18,750	100	18,000	750
E	20,500	75	21,000	−500
F	23,750	$66\frac{2}{3}$	22,000	1,750
G	33,750	60	32,400	1,350
H	0	0	0	0
I	0	0	0	0
J	0	0	0	0
K	0	0	0	0
L	0	0	0	0
Totals	173,250		167,400	5,850

below the budgeted value of the work done. This is shown in the final column of Table 13.15 as a negative overrun.

The cost overruns for the individual activity packages are summed to give the total cost overrun for the project. It can be seen from Table 13.15 that after 6 months, the total overspend is $5850. This can best be interpreted by expressing it as a percentage of the total budgeted value of the work done. We find

$$\text{Percentage Cost Overrun} = 100 \, \frac{\text{Total Cost Overrun}}{\text{Total Budgeted Value}}$$

$$= 100 \, \frac{5850}{167,400} = 3.49\%$$

It emerges, then, that 6 months into the project, costs incurred exceed by 3.49% the amount budgeted for the work that has been done. Such a modest overrun will typically not arouse too much alarm to management. However, it might be noted from Table 13.15 that a substantial proportion of the overrun arises from 2 packages, F and G, on which work is still in progress. It may well pay to investigate further what problems have arisen in carrying out these activities, and determine whether action can be taken to minimize further overruns.

13.6. THE SHORTEST ROUTE PROBLEM

In this and the following two sections we will introduce three special network problems and algorithms for their solution. The first of these, the shortest route problem, was discussed in Section 9.2, where we saw how the dynamic programming approach could be employed in its solution. Here, an alternative algorithm will be presented. The general problem arises when it is required to move from an initial starting point to a final destination, and a number of alternative feasible routes exist. The aim is to find that route with the shortest distance, or, perhaps, the lowest cost.

As an illustration, consider the problem of a freight dispatcher who has to plan a route for the shipment by road of a consignment of parts. A road map is examined, and it emerges that there are several possible routes which are represented schematically in Figure 13.13. The consignment leaves from node 1 and must reach node 9. Intermediate points on possible routes are represented by nodes 2–8. Lines, or arcs, are used to connect any pair of nodes between which it is possible to travel directly, without passing through some other node. For example, it is not possible to travel directly from node 6 to node 9. Rather, any route from the former to the latter must pass through either node 7 or node 8. Also shown on each arc in Figure 13.13 are the distances, in miles, between the connected nodes. The freight dispatcher's problem is to find the shortest route between nodes 1 and 9. In fact, the reader may feel confident of being able to solve this problem quite quickly through inspection of Figure 13.13 and a little mental arithmetic. However, many shortest route problems are a good deal more complex than that illustrated here, which is presented only as a convenient tool for the exposition of the general solution algorithm.

The algorithm we will employ is based on the **labeling of nodes,** the general objective being to find iteratively in a systematic way the shortest route from node 1 to each other node, until, at the final step, the shortest route to the destination is discovered.

ITERATION 1

We begin at the starting point, node 1, and consider all those nodes that can be reached directly from that point; that is, nodes 2, 3, and 4. The labeling procedure employed in the algorithm for solving the shortest route problem requires us to attach two numbers to each node considered. The first is the shortest total

FIGURE 13.13 Shortest route problem for the freight dispatcher.

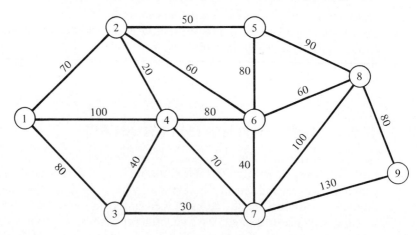

distance found to date from the starting point to the node of interest; the second is the number of the immediately previous node—the predecessor—along the corresponding route. The distances from node 1 to nodes 2, 3, and 4, along the direct routes, are, respectively, 70, 80, and 100 miles. Accordingly, in Figure 13.14, these nodes are labeled (70, 1), (80, 1), and (100, 1).

Now, the lowest distance from the starting point to any labeled node is 70 miles to node 2. It is therefore impossible to find any shorter route from node 1 to node 2. The problem of finding the shortest route to node 2 is therefore solved, so that this node can be **permanently labeled.** By contrast, we have at this stage no assurance that the routes so far examined to nodes 3 and 4 will turn out to be the shortest possible. Accordingly, these nodes are only **temporarily labeled,** their labels can be **updated** if shorter routes from the starting point are discovered at a subsequent iteration.

To distinguish between permanently and temporarily labeled nodes, the former are shaded. Hence, in Figure 13.14, node 2 is shaded. We have also shaded node 1, which is the starting point, and labeled it S.

Labeling of Nodes in Shortest Route Algorithm

Each node examined is labeled (x, y), where x is the distance of the shortest route found to date from the starting point to the node of interest, and y is the number of the predecessor node on that route.

A label is **permanent** if it has been ascertained that no shorter route from the starting point to the node of interest can be found. Otherwise the label is **temporary,** and may subsequently be **updated.**

FIGURE 13.14 Solution of the shortest route problem for the freight dispatcher: Iteration 1.

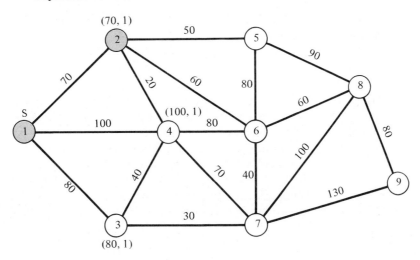

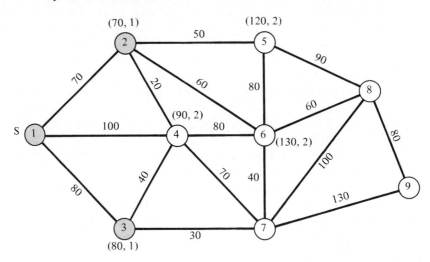

FIGURE 13.15 Solution of the shortest route problem for the freight dispatcher: Iteration 2.

ITERATION 2

At each interation of the solution algorithm, arcs originating at the most recently permanently labeled node are considered. Accordingly, in Figure 13.15, we concentrate on arcs 2–4, 2–5, and 2–6.

Since the shortest distance from node 1 to node 2 is 70 miles, it follows that the shortest distance from node 1 to node 4, passing through node 2, is 70 + 20 = 90 miles. This is shorter than the best route found previously. Accordingly, the labeling of node 4 is updated to (90, 2). Similarly, we label nodes 5 and 6 (120, 2) and (130, 2).

At this stage there are four temporarily labeled nodes—3, 4, 5, and 6. The minimal shortest route so far found from the starting point to any of these is 80 miles to node 3. It follows that there can be no shorter route to that node, so that it can be permanently labeled.

ITERATION 3

Next, in Figure 13.16, we consider those nodes that can be reached directly from node 3; that is, nodes 4 and 7. Since the shortest distance from node 1 to node 3 is 80 miles, the shortest distance from node 1 to node 4, passing through node 3, is 80 + 40 = 120 miles. However, this is longer than the best route found to date, so that the labeling of node 4 is unchanged.

Reasoning as before, node 7 is labeled (110, 3). The minimal shortest route from the starting point to a temporarily labeled node is now 90 miles to node 4, which is therefore permanently labeled.

FIGURE 13.16 Solution of the shortest route problem for the freight dispatcher: Iteration 3.

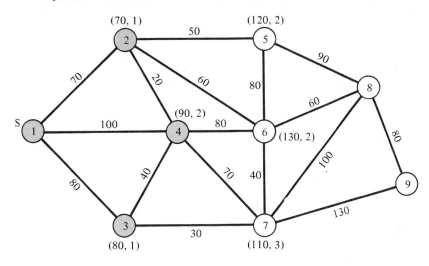

FIGURE 13.17 Solution of the shortest route problem for the freight dispatcher: Iteration 4.

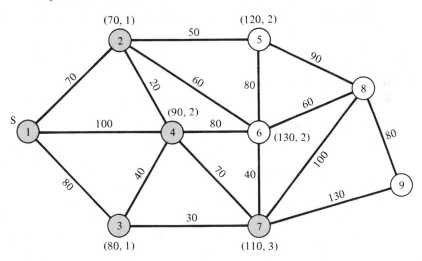

ITERATION 4

In Figure 13.17, we consider arcs 4–6 and 4–7. It is found that the labels on nodes 6 and 7 should not be updated, and that node 7 can now be permanently labeled.

FIGURE 13.18 Solution of the shortest route problem for the freight dispatcher: Iteration 5.

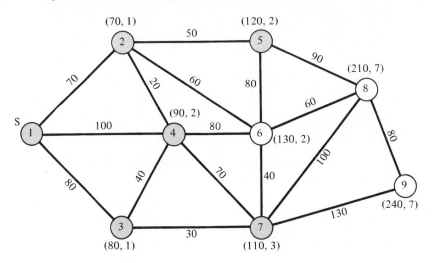

ITERATION 5

Figure 13.18 analyzes arcs 7–6, 7–8, and 7–9. The conclusion is that the label on node 6 should not be updated, while nodes 8 and 9 are labeled (210, 7) and (240, 7). The label on node 5 can now be made permanent.

ITERATION 6

Arcs 5–6 and 5–8 are examined in Figure 13.19. It emerges that the temporary labels on nodes 6 and 8 should not be updated, and that on node 6 can now be made permanent.

ITERATION 7

The only arc to be examined in Figure 13.20 is 6–8. It can be seen that a route which is only 190 miles long from the starting point to node 8 is possible. That node is now labeled (190, 6), a label which is permanent, since the shortest route so far found to the only other temporarily labeled node is longer than 190 miles.

ITERATION 8

Turning, finally to Figure 13.21, we see that the label (240, 7), attached to node 9 can be made permanent. This follows since the shortest possible route from the starting point to node 9, passing through node 8, is 190 + 80 = 270 miles.

We have now established that the shortest possible route for this consignment from the origin (node 1) to the final destination (node 9) is 240 miles long. It remains only to determine that route.

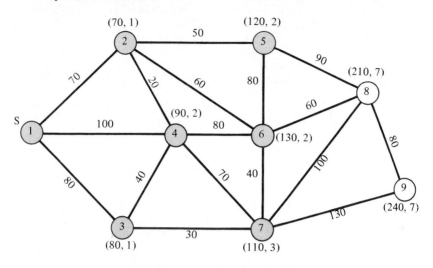

FIGURE 13.19 Solution of the shortest route problem for the freight dispatcher: Iteration 6.

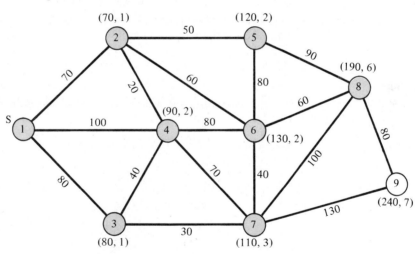

FIGURE 13.20 Solution of the shortest route problem for the freight dispatcher: Iteration 7.

Determination of Node Labels in Shortest Route Algorithm

The algorithm proceeds in the following steps:

STEP 1 ☐ Permanently label the starting point node.

STEP 2 ☐ Consider all nodes which have the most recently permanently labeled node as a predecessor, and analyze the arcs to these from the permanently labeled node. Let (x_p, y_p) denote the label on the permanently labeled node, and d the distance from that node to the node of interest. If that node is unlabeled, label it $(x_p + d, y^*)$, where y^* is the number of the permanently labeled node. If the node of interest is temporarily labeled (x_t, y_t), leave that label unchanged unless $x_p + d < x_t$, in which case it is updated to $(x_p + d, y^*)$.

STEP 3 ☐ Now, let (x_t, y_t) denote the labels of all temporarily labeled nodes. Make permanent the labeling of that node for which x_t is smallest.

STEP 4 ☐ If all nodes are permanently labeled, the algorithm terminates: otherwise, return to Step 2.

USING BACKTRACKING TO FIND THE SHORTEST ROUTE

Figure 13.21, obtained at the final iteration of the labeling algorithm, can now be employed to determine the shortest route. The procedure employed is known as **backtracking**, since we begin at the destination and work back to the origin, using the predecessor labels.

From Figure 13.21, it can be seen that for the optimal route, the predecessor of node 9 is node 7. Continuing to backtrack, the predecessor of node 7 is node 3, and the predecessor of node 3 is the starting point, node 1. We now have a complete solution to the problem: the shortest route from the origin to the final destination is 1–3–7–9, and that route is 240 miles long.

Notice that in Figure 13.21, we have effectively solved not just one, but eight, shortest route problems. Since every node is permanently labeled, the

FIGURE 13.21 Solution of the shortest route problem for the freight dispatcher: Final iteration.

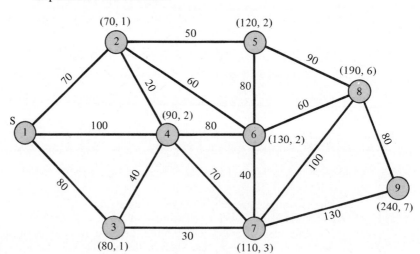

shortest route from the starting point to each of the other eight nodes has been found. For example, suppose at some later date the freight dispatcher has to send a shipment to node 8. It can be seen from Figure 13.21 that the shortest possible route is 190 miles long, and, by backtracking, it emerges that this route is 1–2–6–8.

13.7. THE MINIMAL SPANNING TREE PROBLEM

We now consider a problem in which arcs must be selected in such a way that any node in a network can be reached from any other, and the total length of the connecting arcs should be as small as possible. This is known as the **minimal spanning tree problem,** and arises when a system of highways or pipelines, for example, is to be designed. A further application, which we illustrate here, is to the design of teleprocessing systems.

Consider a data processing center that services terminals at seven remote sites. Communications lines must be installed so that the center is directly or indirectly connected to each site. The problem is illustrated in Figure 13.22, where node 1 represents the center, and nodes 2–8 depict the remote sites. Only certain direct connections are possible, and these are shown by arcs in Figure 13.22, together with the corresponding distances, in miles.

To see the problem that is to be solved, suppose that in fact, node 1 has been connected directly to nodes 2 and 4. Then there is nothing to be gained by connecting nodes 2 and 4, so the corresponding arc can be eliminated. Our objective is to produce a solution in which the remaining arcs allow the data processing center to be reached from every terminal, and, subject to this constraint, the total length of the communications lines should be as small as possible.

FIGURE 13.22 Minimal spanning tree problem for the data processing center.

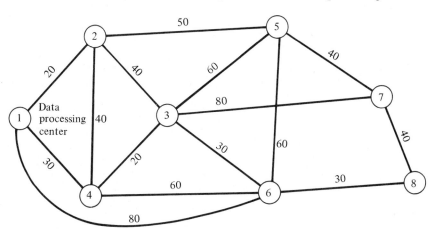

The algorithm employed to solve the minimal spanning tree problem is particularly simple. Beginning with any node, we make that connection with the shortest distance. The algorithm then progresses, step by step, making the shortest possible connection from any unconnected to any connected node. The details are set out in the box below.

Algorithm for Solution of Minimal Spanning Tree Problem

STEP 1 □ Arbitrarily pick any node and designate that node as being connected.

STEP 2 □ Find the shortest distance from any connected node to any unconnected node. The corresponding arc then enters the problem solution, and the unconnected node is now designated as connected.

STEP 3 □ Check to see if all nodes have been connected. If this is the case, the algorithm terminates; otherwise, return to Step 2.

The minimal spanning tree solution algorithm can be followed in either graphical or tabular form. Here we adopt the latter approach. The information in Figure 13.22 is reproduced in Table 13.16, which shows the distances from any node to any other to which it is directly connected. The symbol M is used when direct connection is infeasible: M is taken to be a very large positive number. This ensures that infeasible arcs will not enter the final solution.

The details of the solution algorithm are set out in Table 13.17. We begin by choosing node 1 to be connected. Since we have no further interest in moving to a node that has already been connected, the columns of these nodes are deleted. Thus, in part (i) of Table 13.17, the node 1 column is deleted. A node that has been connected is denoted by √. We require, now, the shortest distance from any connected node to any unconnected node. Thus, in part (i) of Table

TABLE 13.16 Minimal spanning tree problem for the data processing center (distances between nodes are in miles).

FROM NODE	TO NODE							
	1	2	3	4	5	6	7	8
1	0	20	M	30	M	80	M	M
2	20	0	40	40	50	M	M	M
3	M	40	0	20	60	30	80	M
4	30	40	20	0	M	60	M	M
5	M	50	60	M	0	60	40	M
6	80	M	30	60	60	0	M	30
7	M	M	80	M	40	M	0	40
8	M	M	M	M	M	30	40	0

13.17, we must find the smallest number in the node 1 row. This is 20 miles, the distance from node 1 to node 2. Accordingly, as indicated by the circle, arc 1–2 enters the solution, and node 2 is now connected.

TABLE 13.17 Solution of the minimal spanning tree problem for the data processing center.

CONNECTED	FROM NODE	TO NODE							
		1	2	3	4	5	6	7	8
(i) ✓	1		(20)	M	30	M	80	M	M
	2		0	40	40	50	M	M	M
	3		40	0	20	60	30	80	M
	4		40	20	0	M	60	M	M
	5		50	60	M	0	60	40	M
	6		M	30	60	60	0	M	30
	7		M	80	M	40	M	0	40
	8		M	M	M	M	30	40	0
(ii) ✓	1			M	(30)	M	80	M	M
✓	2			40	40	50	M	M	M
	3			0	20	60	30	80	M
	4			20	0	M	60	M	M
	5			60	M	0	60	40	M
	6			30	60	60	0	M	30
	7			80	M	40	M	0	40
	8			M	M	M	30	40	0
(iii) ✓	1			M		M	80	M	M
✓	2			40		50	M	M	M
	3			0		60	30	80	M
✓	4			(20)		M	60	M	M
	5			60		0	60	40	M
	6			30		60	0	M	30
	7			80		40	M	0	40
	8			M		M	30	40	0
(iv) ✓	1					M	80	M	M
✓	2					50	M	M	M
✓	3					60	(30)	80	M
✓	4					M	60	M	M
	5					0	60	40	M
	6					60	0	M	30
	7					40	M	0	40
	8					M	30	40	0
(v) ✓	1					M		M	M
✓	2					50		M	M
✓	3					60		80	M
✓	4					M		M	M
	5					0		40	M
✓	6					60		M	(30)
	7					40		0	40
	8					M		40	0

TABLE 13.17 *(Continued)*

CONNECTED		FROM NODE	TO NODE							
			1	2	3	4	5	6	7	8
(vi)	√	1					*M*		*M*	
	√	2					50		*M*	
	√	3					60		80	
	√	4					*M*		*M*	
		5					0		40	
	√	6					60		*M*	
		7					40		0	
	√	8					*M*		ⓐ40	
(vii)	√	1					*M*			
	√	2					50			
	√	3					60			
	√	4					*M*			
		5					0			
	√	6					60			
	√	7					ⓐ40			
	√	8					*M*			
(viii)	√	1								
	√	2								
	√	3								
	√	4								
	√	5								
	√	6								
	√	7								
	√	8								

In part (ii) of Table 13.17, we have indicated by √ that nodes 1 and 2 are connected, and the corresponding columns have been deleted. We now need the smallest number in either the node 1 or node 2 row. This is the 30 miles from node 1 to node 4, as indicated by the circle.

Moving to part (iii) of Table 13.17, nodes 1, 2, and 4 are now connected, and the corresponding columns have been deleted. The smallest number in rows 1, 2, or 4 is the 20 miles from node 4 to node 3. Hence, this arc enters the solution, and node 3 is connected.

Continuing in this manner through the stages of Table 13.17, it is finally found at stage (viii) that all nodes have been connected. Our problem is now essentially solved. We need only look in Table 13.17 at the circled figures to see which arcs enter the optimal solution. These are set out in Table 13.18, from which it can be seen that the data processing center can be connected to all terminals with a total of only 210 miles of communication lines. The optimal minimal spanning tree network is graphed in Figure 13.23.

TABLE 13.18 Arcs entering the optimal solution of the minimal spanning tree problem of the data processing center.

STAGE	ARC	LENGTH (IN MILES)
(i)	1–2	20
(ii)	1–4	30
(iii)	4–3	20
(iv)	3–6	30
(v)	6–8	30
(vi)	8–7	40
(vii)	7–5	40
	Total	210

FIGURE 13.23 Optimal solution of the minimal spanning tree problem for the data processing center.

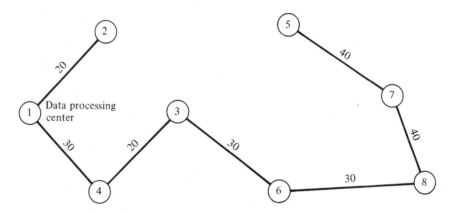

13.8. THE MAXIMAL FLOW PROBLEM

We now study a network model that is widely used when the objective is to maximize the **flow** of some quantity, such as traffic over a network of roads, or oil through a network of pipelines, from an origin to a final destination. In the terminology of the maximal flow problem, the origin node is called the **source,** and the destination node the **sink.** The arcs of the network, which would represent, for example, sections of highway or stretches of pipeline, have limited capacities, thus imposing constraints on the total volume of flow. The aim is to discover the maximum possible flow from the source to the sink, and the volume in each arc that leads to this optimal solution.

To illustrate the maximal flow problem, consider an oil refinery connected by pipelines to six distribution centers. Management has noticed that from time to time, shortages have occurred at one of these distribution centers, and is

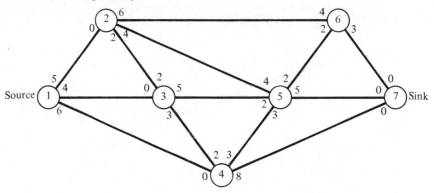

FIGURE 13.24 Maximal flow problem of the oil refinery (capacities are in thousands of gallons per hour).

anxious to find, when such an eventuality is threatened, how much oil can be sent to that center in a short amount of time. The distribution network is graphed in Figure 13.24. The refinery is located at node 1—the source—and the distribution center of interest at node 7—the sink. Also shown in Figure 13.24 are the capacities, in thousands of gallons per hour, of the segments of pipelines in each of the two possible directions. The number on an arc by a node represents the capacity of an arc on a route *out of* that node. For example, for the arc 3–5, we find

This implies that at most 5000 gallons per hour can be shipped from node 3 to node 5, while a maximum of 2000 gallons per hour can be shipped in the other direction.

The algorithm for the solution of the maximal flow problem proceeds by searching for routes along which positive quantities can be shipped from the source to the sink, adding to the total volume of flow until all such possibilities are exhausted. This may seem rather haphazard. However, the algorithm is structured so that an initial setup, involving some quantity of flow along a particular arc, can be modified if an alternative arrangement can be shown to yield a higher total flow from the source to the sink. The details of the solution algorithm are set out in the box below.

Algorithm for Solution of Maximal Flow Problem

STEP 1 ☐ Find any route from the source to the sink along which a positive flow is possible. This requires a positive output capacity, in the source to sink direction, of each arc on the route. If no such route can be found, the algorithm terminates.

STEP 2 ☐ The flow along this route is increased by the maximum amount possible, which is the smallest outflow capacity, in the source to sink direction, of all arcs on the route. Denote by F this amount. Add F to the quantity so far determined that can be shipped from source to sink.

STEP 3 ☐ For each arc on the route from source to sink, reduce by F the outflow capacity in the source-sink direction, and increase by F the capacity in the reverse direction. Return to Step 1.

We now apply this algorithm to the solution of the oil refinery problem.

ITERATION 1 ☐ We choose first to look at route 1–2–6–7. From Figure 13.24 it can be seen that the most that can be shipped along this route is 3000 gallons per hour, as this will exhaust the capacity of arc 6–7. Accordingly, in Figure 13.25 we show that at this stage, we are able to ship 3000 gallons from source to sink. The outflow capacities in the directions 1–2, 2–6, and 6–7 must be reduced by 3000 gallons to 2000, 3000, and zero gallons. Also, capacities in the directions 7–6, 6–2, and 2–1 are increased by 3000 gallons, as shown in Figure 13.25. This calls for some explanation. We do not intend to imply that oil will physically be shipped from node 2 to the source. However, it is conceivable that to achieve an optimal solution, it may be desirable to reduce the current level of shipment from node 1 to node 2 by up to 3000 gallons per hour. Adjusting the flow capacities as we have done allows this option.

ITERATION 2 ☐ Next, consider route 1–3–5–7. From Figure 13.25, it follows that at most 4000 gallons per hour can be shipped along this route. In Figure 13.26 we have added this to the 3000 gallons that can be shipped from source to sink, and adjusted by 4000 gallons the capacities along the route.

ITERATION 3 ☐ We now look at route 1–4–7 for which, as can be seen from Figure 13.26, a flow of 6000 gallons per hour is possible. Figure 13.27 shows the adjusted arc capacities and indicates that we are now able to ship 13,000 gallons from source to sink.

ITERATION 4 ☐ From Figure 13.27 it emerges that 2000 gallons can be shipped along route 1–2–3–4–7. Figure 13.28 shows the adjusted flows when this is done, and indicates that it is now possible to ship 15,000 gallons per hour from source to sink.

FIGURE 13.25 Solution of the maximal flow problem of the oil refinery: Iteration 1.

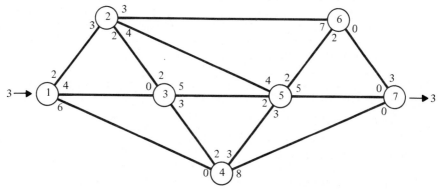

FIGURE 13.26 Solution of the maximal flow problem of the oil refinery: Iteration 2.

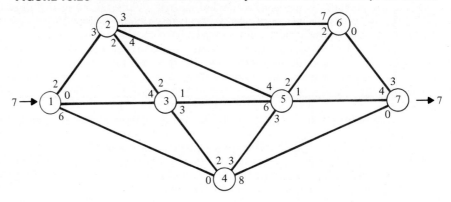

FIGURE 13.27 Solution of the maximal flow problem of the oil refinery: Iteration 3.

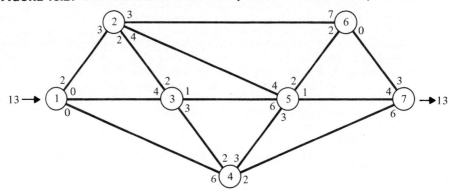

ITERATION 5 □ Looking now at Figure 13.28, we find that there now exists no route from source to sink along which further positive flow is possible. The optimal solution to our problem has therefore been found, and it can be concluded that a maximum of 15,000 gallons of oil per hour can be shipped from the refinery to the distribution center represented by node 7.

We must now determine the volume carried by each arc in the optimal solution. This is done by finding the outflow reductions in the network shown for the final iteration (Figure 13.28) as compared with the original capacities in Figure 13.24. Table 13.19 shows those directions in which capacity has been reduced. To illustrate the reasoning behind Table 13.19, consider the flow from node 3 to node 5. From Figure 13.24 it can be seen that the initial capacity is 5000 gallons per hour. As can be seen from Figure 13.28, at the optimal solution this capacity has been reduced to 1000 gallons per hour. It follows that the optimal solution requires the shipment of 4000 gallons of oil per hour from node 3 to node 5.

Figure 13.29 displays the optimal solution to the oil refinery maximal flow problem. The numbers on each arc represent the volume of flow at that solution, and, where there is positive flow, its direction is indicated by an arrow.

FIGURE 13.28 Solution of the maximal flow problem of the oil refinery: Iteration 4.

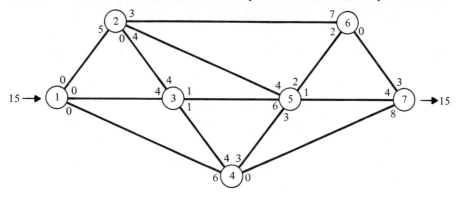

TABLE 13.19 Positive flows along arcs in the optimal solution of the maximal flow problem of the oil refinery.

DIRECTION OF FLOW	FLOW CAPACITIES (THOUSANDS OF GALLONS PER HOUR)		
	INITIAL	FINAL	DIFFERENCE
1–2	5	0	5
1–3	4	0	4
1–4	6	0	6
2–3	2	0	2
2–6	6	3	3
3–4	3	1	2
3–5	5	1	4
4–7	8	0	8
5–7	5	1	4
6–7	3	0	3

FIGURE 13.29 Optimal solution of the maximal flow problem of the oil refinery.

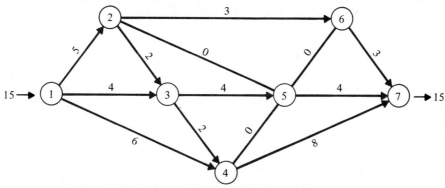

13.1. A research and development project has twelve activities. The activity list below shows immediate predecessors, and optimistic, most likely, and pessimistic activity times (measured in weeks).

ACTIVITY	IMMEDIATE PREDECESSORS	ACTIVITY TIMES (IN WEEKS)		
		OPTIMISTIC	MOST LIKELY	PESSIMISTIC
A	–	1.5	3	5
B	–	1	2	3.5
C	A	3	4	5
D	B	2	3	5
E	A, B	4	5	6
F	C	5	7	8.5
G	C, D	3	4	5
H	E	2	3	3.5
I	F, G	4.5	6	8
J	H	4.5	5	5.5
K	J	2	2	2
L	I, K	2	2	2

(a) Assuming a beta distribution, find the means and variances for the twelve individual activity times.

(b) Using a PERT/CPM network and the mean activity times, find the earliest starting and finishing times for each activity, and the latest starting and finishing times that will preserve the earliest possible end of project date.

(c) Find the critical path for this project.

(d) Assuming a normal distribution, find the probability that the critical path activities can all be completed within 30 weeks.

13.2. A construction project has eleven activities. The immediate predecessors, and optimistic, most likely and pessimistic activity times (in months) are shown in the activity list below.

ACTIVITY	IMMEDIATE PREDECESSORS	ACTIVITY TIMES (IN MONTHS)		
		OPTIMISTIC	MOST LIKELY	PESSIMISTIC
A	—	1	1	1
B	A	0.5	1	3
C	A	1	2	6
D	B, C	1.5	2	4
E	D	1.5	3	4.5
F	D	1.5	2	4
G	D	2	4	9
H	E, F	2	3	4
I	E, G	4	5	9
J	F, G	4	4	4
K	H, I, J	1	2	4.5

(a) Assuming a beta distribution, find the means and variances for the eleven individual activity times.

(b) Using a PERT/CPM network and the mean activity times, find the earliest starting and finishing times for each activity, and the latest starting and finishing times that will preserve the earliest possible end of project date.

(c) Find the critical path for this construction project.

(d) Assuming a normal distribution, find the probability that the critical path activities can all be completed within 18 months.

13.3. A campaign is being developed for the market introduction of a new product. The campaign involves twelve activities. The table below shows immediate predecessors, and optimistic, pessimistic, and most likely activity times (in weeks).

ACTIVITY	IMMEDIATE PREDECESSORS	ACTIVITY TIMES (IN WEEKS)		
		OPTIMISTIC	MOST LIKELY	PESSIMISTIC
A	–	1	1	1
B	A	0.5	1	3
C	B	1.5	3	4.5
D	B	2	3	7
E	C, D	0.5	1	3
F	C, D	2	3	4
G	E	3	4	6.5
H	E, F	2	4	9
I	H	3	3	3
J	G, I	1	1	1
K	I	4	5	9
L	J	4	4	4

(a) Assuming a beta distribution, find the means and variances for the twelve individual activity times.

(b) Using the mean activity times, construct an activity schedule showing the earliest and latest starting and finishing times, and the amounts of slack for each activity.

(c) Find the critical path for this campaign.

(d) Assuming a normal distribution, find the probability that the critical path activities can be completed within 20 weeks.

13.4. A company is retooling a machine shop. This project involves fourteen activities, whose immediate predecessors and times (in days) are set out in the activity list below.

ACTIVITY	IMMEDIATE PREDECESSORS	ACTIVITY TIMES (IN DAYS)		
		OPTIMISTIC	MOST LIKELY	PESSIMISTIC
A	–	1	2	4.5
B	–	1	2	3
C	A	2	3	4
D	B	1	2	6

ACTIVITY	IMMEDIATE PREDECESSORS	ACTIVITY TIMES (IN DAYS)		
		OPTIMISTIC	MOST LIKELY	PESSIMISTIC
E	A, B	2	4	9
F	B, C	2	4	7.5
G	D	2	3	7
H	D, E	4	5	9
I	F	1	2	3
J	G	3	5	7
K	G, H	2	3	4
L	I, J	4.5	5	8
M	K	3	4	6.5
N	L	4	5	6

(a) Assuming a beta distribution, find the means and variances for the fourteen individual activity times.

(b) Using the mean activity times, construct an activity schedule showing the earliest and latest starting and finishing times, and the amounts of slack for each activity.

(c) Find the critical path for this project.

(d) Assuming a normal distribution, find the probability that the critical path activities can be completed within 30 days.

13.5. The probability that a project can be completed within a given period of time differs somewhat from the probability that the critical path activities can be completed within that time. Carefully explain why this is so, referring for illustration to the machine shop retooling problem of Exercise 13.4. What difficulties would you encounter in trying to work out the probability that this project will be completed within 30 days?

13.6. A student is planning to write a term paper for a business class. The instructor has left the choice of topic to the student, but insists that the project should involve the collection and analysis of data. The student has set out the activity list shown below.

ACTIVITY	DESCRIPTION OF ACTIVITY	IMMEDIATE PREDECESSORS
A	Conduct preliminary research to decide on a topic	–
B	Write outline proposal for the professor	A
C	Submit outline proposal to professor, discuss, and obtain approval	B
D	Review previous research in this area	C
E	Collect data for analysis	C
F	Obtain access to computer programs to analyze data	C
G	Analyze the data	D, E, F
H	Write literature survey portion of project report	D
I	Write up the data analysis	G
J	Write a concluding section in which results of the data analysis are related to previous work	H, I

The student estimates optimistic, pessimistic, and most likely activity times (in weeks), as shown below.

ACTIVITY	TIMES (IN WEEKS)		
	OPTIMISTIC	MOST LIKELY	PESSIMISTIC
A	0.5	1	1.5
B	1.5	2	2.5
C	0.5	1	1.5
D	2	4	9
E	2	3	7
F	1	2	3
G	2	3	4
H	2.5	3	3.5
I	1.5	2	2.5
J	1	2	3

(a) Assuming a beta distribution, find the means and variances for the ten individual activity times.

(b) Using the mean activity times, construct an activity schedule showing the earliest and latest starting and finishing times, and the amounts of slack for each activity.

(c) Find the critical path.

(d) Assuming a normal distribution, what is the probability that the critical path activities can be completed in 15 weeks?

13.7. A company is retooling a machine shop, and is anxious to avoid too much lost production as a result of this project. The table below shows, for each activity, immediate predecessors, normal and crash times, and normal and crash costs.

ACTIVITY	IMMEDIATE PREDECESSORS	TIME (DAYS)		COST ($)	
		NORMAL	CRASH	NORMAL	CRASH
A	–	7	5	2,400	2,800
B	A	8	4	3,200	4,000
C	A	6	4	2,900	3,100
D	B	8	3	5,100	7,100
E	C	7	4	3,600	4,500
F	D, E	6	5	2,700	3,100
G	F	4	3	1,500	1,600

(a) Find the crash cost per day for each activity.

(b) The company wants to complete the entire project within 25 days at the lowest possible total cost. Set out the algebraic form of the linear programming problem that must be solved.

(c) Use a computer program to solve this problem and provide a full discussion of the results.

13.8. A company is working on a new promotional campaign for a product in a highly competitive market. Management is very anxious to mount the campaign quickly, as there is concern that at least one rival is planning additional promotional activity. The following table shows, for each activity in the campaign, immediate predecessors, normal and crash times, and normal and crash costs.

ACTIVITY	IMMEDIATE PREDECESSORS	TIME (WEEKS)		COST ($)	
		NORMAL	CRASH	NORMAL	CRASH
A	–	2	1	1,000	1,200
B	A	3	2	3,000	3,600
C	A	4	2	5,000	6,000
D	A	3	2	3,400	3,600
E	B, C	5	2	6,200	8,000
F	C, D	4	2	3,400	4,000
G	E, F	2	1	2,500	2,600

(a) Find the crash cost per week for each activity.

(b) Management insists that the whole project must be completed within 10 weeks at the lowest possible cost. Set out the algebraic form of the linear programming problem that must be solved.

(c) Use a computer program to solve this problem and discuss fully the results of your analysis.

13.9. A repair crew is to work on some sensitive equipment, the quick repair of which is important to an electronics manufacturer. By paying overtime rates to critical employees, it is possible to speed up the constituent activities. The table shows, for each activity, immediate predecessors, normal and crash times, and normal and crash costs.

ACTIVITY	IMMEDIATE PREDECESSORS	TIME (DAYS)		COST ($)	
		NORMAL	CRASH	NORMAL	CRASH
A	–	6	4	4,000	4,800
B	A	8	6	5,800	6,400
C	A	5	2	4,600	5,800
D	B	7	3	8,200	9,000
E	C	7	5	6,900	7,500
F	D, E	9	6	8,800	10,300
G	E	4	3	3,900	4,000
H	F, G	5	3	5,800	6,000

(a) Find the crash cost per day for each activity.

(b) The manufacturer's aim is to complete the repairs within 30 days at the lowest possible total cost. Set out the algebraic form of the linear programming problem that must be solved.

(c) Use a computer program to solve this problem and provide a full discussion of the results.

13.10. A firm is planning the installation of some new machinery and is concerned about the amount of time involved in this project. The table shows, for the eight constituent activities, immediate predecessors, normal and crash times, and normal and crash costs.

ACTIVITY	IMMEDIATE PREDECESSORS	TIME (DAYS)		COST ($)	
		NORMAL	CRASH	NORMAL	CRASH
A	–	6	4	3,100	3,500
B	A	7	3	2,500	2,900
C	A	5	4	3,600	3,900
D	B	6	2	5,200	6,800
E	B, C	3	2	2,100	2,300
F	D	4	2	3,500	4,500
G	E	8	4	4,900	6,100
H	F	6	4	5,100	5,900

(a) Find the crash cost per day for each of the eight activities.

(b) The firm wants to complete the project in eighteen days at the lowest possible total cost. Write down the algebraic form of the constrained optimization problem that must be solved.

(c) Use a computer program to solve this problem and give a full discussion of the results.

13.11. A research and development project involves twelve activity packages. For each package, the accompanying table shows immediate predecessors, estimated times, and estimated costs.

ACTIVITY PACKAGE	IMMEDIATE PREDECESSORS	ESTIMATED TIME (MONTHS)	ESTIMATED COST ($)
A	–	2	20,000
B	–	2	26,000
C	A	1	15,000
D	B	3	24,000
E	A, B	2	18,000
F	C	4	32,000
G	D	3	27,000
H	D, E	2	14,000
I	F	1	8,000
J	G, H	3	30,000
K	I	4	28,000
L	J	2	16,000

(a) Given the estimated times, find the earliest possible completion date.

(b) For the tightest possible schedule, find the earliest and latest starting and finishing times for the twelve activity packages.

(c) Find the accumulated monthly budgeted costs for the project with the earliest starting times schedule.

(d) Find the accumulated monthly budgeted costs for the project with the latest starting times schedule.

13.12. Refer to Exercise 13.11. The table below shows a status report six months into the project.

ACTIVITY PACKAGE	ACTUAL COST ($)	PERCENT COMPLETION
A	22,000	100
B	25,500	100
C	25,000	100
D	25,500	100
E	17,500	100
F	26,000	75
G	7,500	25
H	7,500	50
I	0	0
J	0	0
K	0	0
L	0	0

(a) Find the cost overrun for each activity package.

(b) Find the percentage cost overrun for the work completed to date on this project.

13.13. A construction project has fourteen activity packages. The accompanying table shows immediate predecessors, estimated times, and estimated costs.

ACTIVITY PACKAGE	IMMEDIATE PREDECESSORS	ESTIMATED TIME (MONTHS)	ESTIMATED COST ($)
A	–	2	30,000
B	A	3	42,000
C	A	3	45,000
D	B	2	26,000
E	B, C	4	60,000
F	C, D	1	15,000
G	D	4	48,000
H	E, F	3	30,000
I	G	3	54,000
J	H	2	27,000
K	I, J	1	18,000
L	J	4	56,000
M	J	3	36,000
N	K, L, M	2	25,000

(a) Based on these estimated times, find the earliest possible project completion date.

(b) Given the completion date in (a), find the earliest and latest starting and finishing times for the activity packages.

(c) Find the accumulated monthly budgeted costs for the project with the earliest starting times schedule.

(d) Find the accumulated monthly budgeted costs for the project with the latest starting times schedule.

13.14. Refer to Exercise 13.13. The accompanying table shows a status report eight months into the project.

ACTIVITY PACKAGE	ACTUAL COST ($)	PERCENT COMPLETION
A	29,500	100
B	43,500	100
C	48,000	100
D	25,000	100
E	49,000	75
F	17,500	100
G	13,000	25
H	0	0
I	0	0
J	0	0
K	0	0
L	0	0
M	0	0
N	0	0

(a) Find the cost overrun for each activity package.

(b) Find the percentage cost overrun for the work completed to date on this project.

13.15. A corporation is planning a major extension to its production plant. The project has been planned in a set of activity packages which have the immediate predecessors, and estimated times and costs shown in the accompanying table.

ACTIVITY PACKAGE	IMMEDIATE PREDECESSORS	ESTIMATED TIME (MONTHS)	ESTIMATED COST ($)
A	–	3	75,000
B	A	4	80,000
C	B	2	42,000
D	B	5	85,000
E	C, D	3	54,000
F	E	4	72,000
G	E	3	51,000
H	E	5	80,000
I	F	2	40,000
J	F, G	4	64,000
K	G, H	3	39,000
L	I, J	4	56,000

(a) Based on the estimated times, find the earliest possible project completion date.

(b) Given the completion date in (a), find the earliest and latest starting and finishing times for the activity packages.

(c) Find the accumulated monthly budgeted costs for the project with the earliest starting times schedule.

(d) Find the accumulated monthly budgeted costs for the project with the latest starting times schedule.

(e) Draw a graph to illustrate your answers to (c) and (d).

13.16. A research and development project has thirteen activity packages, for which the accompanying table shows immediate predecessors and estimated times and costs.

ACTIVITY PACKAGE	IMMEDIATE PREDECESSORS	ESTIMATED TIME (MONTHS)	ESTIMATED COST ($)
A	–	3	21,000
B	–	2	16,000
C	A	4	34,000
D	B	2	14,000
E	A, B	2	15,000
F	C	4	36,000
G	C, D	3	33,000
H	C, D	2	18,000
I	F	5	30,000
J	G	4	34,000
K	F, H	2	20,000
L	I, J	2	22,000
M	K	4	36,000

(a) Based on the estimated times, find the earliest possible project completion date.

(b) Given the completion date in (a), find the earliest and latest starting and finishing times for the activity packages.

(c) Find the accumulated monthly budgeted costs for the project with the earliest starting times schedule.

(d) Find the accumulated monthly budgeted costs for the project with the latest starting times schedule.

13.17. Refer to Exercise 13.16. The accompanying table shows a status report eight months into the project.

ACTIVITY PACKAGE	ACTUAL COST ($)	PERCENT COMPLETION
A	22,500	100
B	17,000	100
C	38,500	100
D	13,000	100
E	15,500	100
F	10,500	25
G	9,500	75
H	10,500	50
I	0	0
J	0	0
K	0	0
L	0	0
M	0	0

(a) Find the cost overrun for each activity package.

(b) Find the percentage cost overrun for the work completed after eight months.

13.18. A salesman is planning a trip by road. The journey is to begin at node 1 in the accompanying figure, and end at node 10. Distances (in miles) between adjacent nodes between which direct travel is possible, are shown on the corresponding arcs.

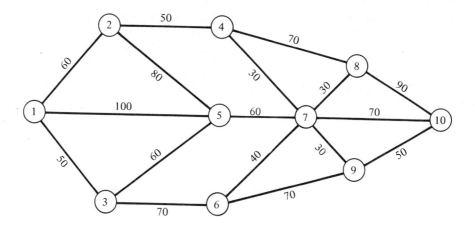

(a) What is the shortest possible distance from node 1 to node 10?

(b) Find the shortest route for this salesman.

13.19. A shipment must be sent from node 1 to node 12 on the road network depicted in the accompanying figure. The figures on the arcs represent distances in miles between the corresponding nodes.

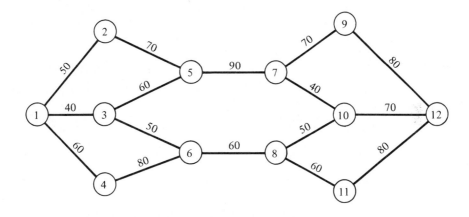

(a) What is the shortest possible distance from node 1 to node 12?

(b) Find the shortest route for this shipment.

13.20. A journey is planned from an origin (node 1) to a final destination (node 10). The table below lists distances in miles between nodes where direct travel is possible.

ROUTE	DISTANCE	ROUTE	DISTANCE	ROUTE	DISTANCE
1–2	50	3–6	50	6–9	40
1–3	70	4–6	30	7–8	30
1–4	40	5–7	70	7–9	80
2–5	60	5–8	90	8–10	70
3–5	80	6–7	60	9–10	60

(a) What is the shortest possible distance from the origin to the destination?

(b) Find the shortest route for this journey.

13.21. A shipment is to be sent from an origin (node 1) to a destination (node 10). After consulting a map, a freight dispatcher has compiled a list of distances between possible nodes along feasible routes. These distances, in miles, are shown in the accompanying table.

ROUTE	DISTANCE	ROUTE	DISTANCE	ROUTE	DISTANCE
1–2	50	3–4	20	5–8	40
1–3	40	3–6	50	6–8	80
1–4	70	4–5	70	6–9	70
2–4	60	4–6	60	7–10	70
2–5	80	5–7	60	8–10	60
				9–10	50

(a) What is the shortest possible distance from the origin to the destination?

(b) Find the shortest route for this shipment.

13.22. Having solved the problem of Exercise 13.21, the freight dispatcher regularly sends shipments along the shortest route. However, the road linking nodes 9 and 10 is to be closed for extensive repairs. What is the minimum additional distance that must now be covered by shipments from the origin to the destination?

13.23. The freight dispatcher of Exercise 13.21 needs to send a shipment of goods from node 1 to node 7. Refer to the algorithm used in the solution of Exercise 13.21 and determine the shortest possible route, and the distance of that route.

13.24. A company wishes to lease a piece of equipment for a period of 4 years. At the beginning of each year, it is possible to replace the currently leased equipment, and lease a new piece. Thus, for example, the company may lease equipment at the beginning of the period, and hold this equipment for four years. At the other extreme, a new piece of equipment could be leased at the beginning of each year. Also, intermediate strategies, where a piece of leased equipment can be held for 2 or 3 years are possible. The optimal decision will depend on expected leasing and maintenance costs. The following table shows estimated costs (in thousands of dollars, and expressed in terms of present values) for each year leased equipment is held for each possible leasing time.

EQUIPMENT LEASED AT BEGINNING OF YEAR	ESTIMATED COST ($ THOUSAND)			
	FIRST YEAR	SECOND YEAR	THIRD YEAR	FOURTH YEAR
1	12	10	11	14
2	13	11.5	12.5	–
3	13.5	12.5	–	–
4	14	–	–	–

The company wishes to devise the strategy that will allow the equipment to be leased for 4 years at the lowest possible estimated total cost. Formulate this problem as a shortest route problem.

(a) What is the lowest possible total estimated cost for leasing this equipment over 4 years?

(b) Find the optimal leasing strategy.

13.25. A system of pipelines, in which a refinery (node 1) must be connected to eight remote sites (nodes 2–9) is to be constructed. The accompanying table shows distances (in miles) between nodes.

FROM NODE	TO NODE								
	1	2	3	4	5	6	7	8	9
1	0	30	20	40	M	50	M	M	M
2	30	0	40	20	50	60	M	M	M
3	20	20	0	30	40	40	60	M	M
4	40	20	30	0	30	60	70	80	M
5	M	50	40	30	0	20	40	60	70
6	50	60	40	60	20	0	30	30	50
7	M	M	60	70	40	30	0	20	40
8	M	M	M	80	60	30	20	0	30
9	M	M	M	M	70	50	40	30	0

The symbol M indicates that one node cannot be reached directly from another. Find the network which allows the refinery to be connected to the remote sites with the shortest possible total length of pipeline.

13.26. A state park has a large system of hiking trails, all of which are quite rugged. However, park management now believes that some of these trails should be upgraded in quality to allow their use by less physically active hikers. In this park there are eight points of great natural beauty, and it is felt that it should be possible to reach any of these from any other along upgraded trails. The accompanying table shows the distances, in miles, of trails linking the eight beauty spots (nodes). The symbol M indicates that there is no trail connecting the corresponding nodes.

FROM NODE	TO NODE							
	1	2	3	4	5	6	7	8
1	0	0.5	1.1	1.4	1.9	M	M	M
2	0.5	0	0.8	1.0	1.3	1.6	M	M
3	1.1	0.8	0	0.6	1.2	1.5	1.9	M
4	1.4	1.0	0.6	0	0.5	0.8	1.3	2.2
5	1.9	1.3	1.2	0.5	0	0.8	1.1	2.0
6	M	1.6	1.5	0.8	0.8	0	0.7	1.3
7	M	M	1.9	1.3	1.1	0.7	0	0.9
8	M	M	M	2.2	2.0	1.3	0.9	0

Which trails should be upgraded if the total number of trail miles to be upgraded is to be kept to a minimum, subject to the requirement that any node can be reached from any other on upgraded trails?

13.27. A college campus has ten major clusters of buildings connected by a system of roads. The campus is in an area that frequently experiences heavy snowfalls, and, in the event of a severe overnight storm, it is not possible to clear the entire road system before morning classes begin. Campus administration is attempting to devise a system where enough roads are cleared so that it is possible to get from any cluster of buildings to any other on snow-free roads. The accompanying table shows distances, in miles, between building clusters (nodes). The symbol M indicates that the corresponding nodes are not directly connected by roads.

FROM NODE	TO NODE									
	1	2	3	4	5	6	7	8	9	10
1	0	0.2	0.3	0.5	0.5	0.6	M	M	M	M
2	0.2	0	0.4	0.6	0.7	0.7	1.0	1.2	M	M
3	0.3	0.4	0	0.2	0.5	0.8	0.9	0.9	1.4	M
4	0.5	0.6	0.2	0	0.2	0.5	0.8	0.8	1.0	M
5	0.5	0.7	0.5	0.2	0	0.3	0.5	0.5	0.9	1.2
6	0.6	0.7	0.8	0.5	0.3	0	0.2	0.4	0.6	0.9
7	M	1.0	0.9	0.8	0.5	0.2	0	0.3	0.5	0.8
8	M	1.2	0.9	0.8	0.5	0.4	0.3	0	0.3	0.8
9	M	M	1.4	1.0	0.9	0.6	0.5	0.3	0	0.6
10	M	M	M	M	1.2	0.9	0.8	0.8	0.6	0

Which roads should be cleared, if the total number of miles cleared is to be minimized, subject to the requirement that it must be possible to reach any node from any other on cleared roads?

13.28. The accompanying figure shows a data processing center (node 1) and eight remote terminal sites (nodes 2–9). The arcs of the figure represent possible direct connections between nodes. It is required to install telecommunications lines in such a way that each site is connected to the terminal, and the total length of lines is as small as possible. The figures on the arcs in the graph are distances in miles between nodes. Find the optimal installation of communications lines.

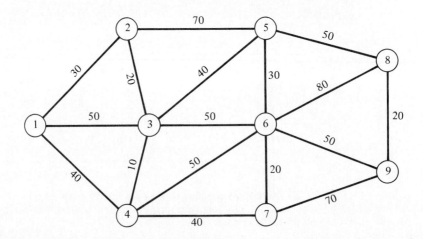

13.29. Refer to Exercise 13.28. Management of the data processing center wants to provide a superior service to the remote terminals, and requires that in order to guard against breakdowns, communications lines should be installed so that each site can be reached from the center by two distinct routes. Under such an arrangement, failure in any single stretch of line will not cause interruption in service to any site. Design a system that meets this objective using the smallest possible total length of communications lines.

13.30. The accompanying figure represents a traffic flow network for vehicles entering a city at its western boundary (node 1) and leaving at its eastern boundary (node 8). Figures along the arcs are in thousands of vehicles per hour.

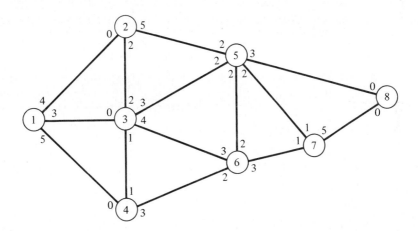

(a) What is the largest volume of traffic that can pass through this city in a west to east direction?

(b) Find a solution giving the flow on each arc so that the maximal flow is achieved.

13.31. Refer to Exercise 13.30. The road linking nodes 4 and 6 is to be closed for repairs. What is the effect of this closure on the maximal flow of traffic in a west to east direction in this city?

13.32. The accompanying figure represents a traffic flow network over a system of highways linking the western suburbs (node 1) of a city with the downtown district (node 10). Figures along the arcs are in thousands of vehicles per hour.

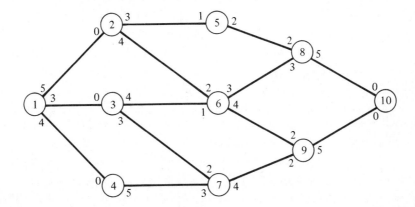

(a) What is the largest volume of traffic that can be handled by this network?

(b) Find a solution giving the flow on each arc so that maximal flow is achieved.

13.33. Refer to Exercise 13.32. The city engineer is planning to build a new highway directly linking node 7 and the downtown district. However, construction will only be undertaken if this highway leads to an improvement in maximal traffic flow. Moreover, since the cost of the new highway will be directly proportional to the traffic flow that it can handle, and since no further construction is planned for the foreseeable future, the engineer is anxious not to build in redundant capacity. Thus, if the highway is to be constructed, it should be of a size to be precisely fully utilized during peak traffic flows. How would you advise the city engineer to proceed?

13.34. An oil company has a system of pipelines linking a refinery (node 1) to an important distribution center (node 8). The accompanying table shows all positive flow capacities (in thousands of gallons per hour) between points on the distribution network.

FLOW DIRECTION	CAPACITY	FLOW DIRECTION	CAPACITY	FLOW DIRECTION	CAPACITY
1–2	8	4–5	3	6–4	2
1–3	7	4–6	2	6–7	3
2–4	3	4–7	5	6–8	2
2–5	4	5–2	2	7–4	2
3–4	5	5–4	2	7–5	3
3–6	4	5–7	3	7–6	2
4–2	1	5–8	4	7–8	6
4–3	2	6–3	3		

(a) What is the largest volume of oil that can be sent from the refinery to the distribution center at node 8?

(b) Find a solution giving the flow along each stretch of pipeline so that the maximal flow is achieved.

A Network for Product Distribution: The Problem of a Chemical Firm[1]

The authors of this study describe a problem faced by a large chemical firm in transporting its goods throughout the continental United States and parts of Canada. In meeting demand, this firm has two shipment options: either to engage a common carrier or to use a vehicle from its own leased fleet. The leased vehicles were tractor trailers. A tractor could transport a single trailer from an origin to a destination, and the trailer load could not be split. These vehicles could be housed at one of three depots, and could remain on the road for up to 120 continuous hours. Costs for any trip made by the leased trucks could be computed, and the charges of the alternative common carrier were readily available. Demand patterns for different routes each week were known, and did not fluctuate greatly over time.

The chemical firm required answers to three related questions:

1. How large should be the fleet of leased trucks?
2. Which parts of the total demand should be met by using the leased fleet, and which by using the common carrier?
3. Which routes should be used by the vehicles in the leased fleet?

The authors of this study show how this complex problem can be analyzed as a network and discuss algorithms that were implemented in its solution.

---

[1] This discussion is based on M. O. Ball, B. L. Golden, A. A. Assad and L. D. Bodin, "Planning for Truck Fleet Size in the Presence of a Common Carrier Option," *Decision Sciences, 14* (1983), 103–120.

inventory models

CHAPTER FOURTEEN

14.1. INVENTORY HOLDING: BENEFITS AND COSTS

Manufacturers and distributors invariably carry stocks of finished products and materials, and parts required in the production process. This **inventory** of items not for immediate use may tie up a large amount of a corporation's resources, so that effective inventory management can have a sizeable impact on the company's overall financial position. Our objective in this chapter is to discuss various procedures that might profitably be applied to inventory management. Before doing so, however, we pause to consider both the motivations for, and the costs associated with, inventory holding.

There are several reasons why stocks of products and parts might be held in inventory. These include:

1. A manufacturer or distributor will be eager to avoid being in a position of not having available sufficient quantities of a product to meet customer demand. Failure to meet demand will, of course, entail foregone profits. This loss could also be compounded by a negative impact on customer goodwill, leading to a reduced level of future demand. The chances of failure to meet demand can be considerably reduced through carrying a sufficiently large inventory.

2. If a manufacturer's stocks of vital material or parts are exhausted, the consequence could be a costly interruption in the production process. Expensive labor and capital resources may be idled until these stocks can be replenished. To minimize the duration of such delays, the manufacturer may have to pay a higher price than would otherwise be necessary to ensure rapid delivery of additional quantities of the material or parts needed to resume production.

3. For many products, demand fluctuates quite sharply over time. Demand for a wide range of goods, for example, is seasonal, regularly peaking at the same time each

year. However, the adjustment of production schedules to match these demand fluctuations can be very expensive. If sufficient capital equipment is acquired to produce at peak demand levels, much of this valuable equipment will lie idle when demand is low. Moreover, a manufacturer will be discouraged by the high rates that must be paid to induce employees to work overtime hours when demand is high. For these reasons, companies will generally prefer a smoother production schedule, with amounts in excess of immediate requirements produced during low demand periods held in inventory in anticipation of an upturn in demand.

4. A distributor may not be able to fully rely on the supply of products immediately when they are needed. Similarly, a manufacturer may suspect the possibility of delays in the delivery of vital materials and parts. Inventory holding can then be viewed as insurance against such delays.

5. It is often the case that distributors are able to obtain substantial discounts on bulk purchases. Manufacturers, too, may be able to secure a lower unit price on large orders of materials and parts. These discounts could be sufficiently generous to induce the placement of bulk orders, the excess over short-term needs then being placed in inventory.

For the reasons just discussed, manufacturers and distributors will generally want to hold inventories. However, inventory holding is not without cost. We will be concerned here with the following two types of cost.

1. The **holding costs** of inventory are costs incurred through keeping stocks of goods and materials that are surplus to immediate requirements. Suppose, for example, that the total value of inventory held by a distributor is $1 million. The distributor may have to borrow the money to finance this inventory holding, in which case interest must be paid on the loan. If this million dollars is part of the distributor's own capital, the position is similar, for that money might otherwise be employed to produce profit. Thus, in holding inventory, the distributor may forego the opportunity to make profitable investments. In addition the distributor will have to pay costs associated with storage, insurance, damage, and theft of the inventory. In total these holding costs are likely to amount to a nonnegligible fraction of the total value of the inventory.

2. **Ordering costs** arise whenever new orders must be placed to replenish inventory holdings. These chiefly involve the time of employees in the purchasing and accounting departments of a company. These employees must process the paper work whenever a new order is placed. The time and effort involved are likely to be the same, whatever the size of the order.

In some of our subsequent analyses we will find it convenient to introduce a third type of cost. These are the costs associated with the exhaustion of inventory and consequent failure to meet product demand, and are sometimes referred to as **shortage costs,** or **backorder costs.** Properly speaking, of course, these should be viewed as the costs of *not* holding sufficient inventory.

The size of inventory holdings of many manufacturers and distributors is generally such that an optimal inventory holding policy, as opposed to an ill-conceived strategy, can produce a substantial improvement in the corporate balance sheet. In the remainder of this chapter we will analyze some inventory problems and show how optimal solutions can be derived. Because manufacturers and distributors face different environments, there is no unique formulation of the problem, and hence no unique solution algorithm. Rather, we will present a number of different models aimed at capturing the essence of a range of practical inventory holding problems. One important distinction we will make is between models which assume **deterministic demand** and those that allow for **probabilistic,** or **stochastic,** demand. In the former case, it is assumed that future demand levels are known with certainty, while the latter class of models allows for uncertainty about future demand levels. These models require forecasts (developed, for example, through methods discussed in Chapter 12) of future demand levels, but recognize the probability of discrepancies between forecasts and actual outcomes. In most practical problems this latter specification is the more realistic.

14.2. THE ECONOMIC ORDER QUANTITY (EOQ) MODEL

In this section we develop an inventory management model, variants of which are widely used in practice. We will begin with the basic version of this model, illustrating by reference to a distributor of automobile tires, and we will concentrate on a single type of a given size. Provided that the model assumptions hold, the subsequent analysis can be applied to every type/size combination.

The EOQ model is not universally applicable; it can be used provided that certain assumptions are satisfied. These assumptions are stated in the box below.

Assumptions for the Basic EOQ Model

1. Demand is known in advance, *and will occur at a constant rate through time.*
2. Orders are placed at fixed points in time, and the total amount of any order will be delivered after some **delay,** or **lead time,** whose duration is known and fixed.
3. Orders are placed so that *no shortages* will occur; that is, stocks will be replenished immediately when they are exhausted.
4. Holding costs of inventory, over any period of time, are a fixed proportion of the total value of the inventory.
5. The cost of placing an order is the same whatever the size of the order.
6. There are no discounts for larger-sized orders.

The tire distributor finds that demand for the type/size tire of interest has, in the past, been approximately constant at 500 per week, or, since a 5-day week is worked with demand spread evenly over the week, 100 tires per day. Of course, in practice, product demand will never be *precisely* constant through time. However, for some products, variability in demand is sufficiently slight that our assumption of a constant rate will prove adequate in practice. The usual formulation of the EOQ model is couched in terms of annual demand, denoted by D. We therefore have, with fifty-two weeks per year

$$D = (500)(52) = 26,000$$

Since demand occurs at a steady rate through time, a natural strategy is to place orders of a fixed amount at equally spaced intervals of time. We will denote by Q the quantity of tires in each order.

The accountants employed by the tire distributor compute that the combined effects of finance charges and other associated costs lead to annual inventory holding costs of 20% of the value of the inventory. Each tire is valued at $50. Hence, denoting by C_H unit annual inventory holding cost, it follows that the cost of holding a tire in inventory for a year is

$$C_H = (0.20)(50) = \$10$$

Finally, we must allow for the cost of placing an order. In general this is denoted C_O. The tire distributor calculates that for each order, employee time expended is valued at $50. We therefore have

$$C_O = \$50$$

The notation employed in the EOQ model is summarized below:

Notation for the EOQ Model

Q = Number of Units per Order
D = Number of Units Demanded per Annum
C_H = Inventory Holding Cost per Unit per Annum
C_O = Cost per Order

Our problem now is to determine the optimum value of Q, the number of units that should be ordered each time. This optimum is known as the **economic order quantity**, from which our model is named.

We attack this problem by considering the total annual inventory cost. This total cost is the sum of two components—holding costs and ordering costs—so that we can write

$$\text{Total Cost} = \text{Holding Cost} + \text{Ordering Cost}$$

Each element of this total cost will depend on the quantity Q of units per order. The higher is Q, the higher on average will be inventory levels throughout the year, and hence the higher will be holding costs. On the other hand, a relatively high value of Q implies that relatively few orders will have to be placed during the year. Hence, the higher is Q, the lower will be ordering costs. Combining these two factors suggests the possibility that we may be able to find a value of Q for which the sum of holding and ordering costs is a minimum. Any departure from this optimum would lead to an increase of one of these costs which exceeds any savings in the other. We now seek this optimum solution.

FIGURE 14.1 Progression through time of inventory level under the EOQ model.

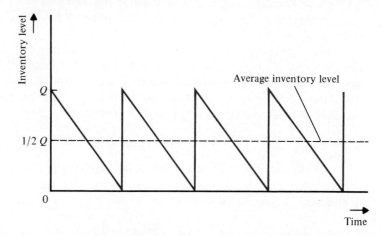

Let us first consider holding cost. Figure 14.1 depicts the inventory exhaustion and replenishment position through time implied by the assumptions of the EOQ model. Orders are timed so that each consignment of Q units arrives precisely at the time that stocks are exhausted. Then, since demand is at a constant rate through time, the inventory depletion follows a linear path, down to zero, at which point a new consignment is received. Visual inspection of the path through time followed by inventory levels suggests that the average amount of inventory over time is $\frac{1}{2}Q$. Then, since annual inventory holding costs per unit are C_H, it follows that the total annual inventory holding cost will be

$$\text{Annual Holding Cost} = \frac{1}{2}QC_H$$

Hence, since C_H is $10 for the tire distributor, it can be seen that

$$\text{Annual Holding Cost} = 5Q$$

Thus, annual holding costs amount to $5 for each unit in a consignment order.

Next, we must deal with the second element of inventory costs—ordering cost. Since total annual demand is D units, and each order is for Q units, it follows that if this total demand is to be met, the number of orders that must be placed in a year is D/Q. Since the cost of each order is C_O, it follows that the total cost of placing orders for the year will be

$$\text{Annual Ordering Cost} = \frac{D}{Q}C_O$$

For the tire distributor, annual demand is 26,000 and ordering cost is $50 per order. We thus see that

$$\text{Annual Ordering Cost} = \left(\frac{26,000}{Q}\right)50 = \frac{1,300,000}{Q}$$

Summing these two components, it can be seen that an algebraic expression for total annual inventory cost (TC) is given by

$$TC = \frac{1}{2}QC_H + \frac{D}{Q}C_O \qquad (14.1)$$

Specifically, for the tire distributor, this total cost is

$$TC = 5Q + \frac{1,300,000}{Q} \qquad (14.2)$$

In Table 14.1, we have computed annual holding costs, ordering costs, and total inventory costs, as given by equation (14.2), for the tire distributor for several possible order quantities. As anticipated, holding costs increase, and ordering costs decrease, with increasing Q. As the order quantity increases, total inventory cost first falls, and then rises. It appears that total cost is at a minimum somewhere in the neighborhood of orders of 500 tires.

Figure 14.2 shows plots of total inventory costs and its two components against order quantity. From this graph it is possible to read that minimum total cost is achieved at an order quantity slightly in excess of 500 tires. Notice also that *this minimum occurs at the value of Q at which the holding cost and order cost curves intersect;* that is, where holding and ordering costs are equal. This is no accident; the result always holds for the EOQ model.

To see that this is so, let Q_{opt} denote the order quantity at which holding and ordering costs are equal, so that

$$\frac{1}{2}Q_{opt}C_H = \frac{D}{Q_{opt}}C_O$$

TABLE 14.1 Inventory costs of the tire distributor for various order quantities (figures are rounded to the nearest dollar).

ORDER QUANTITY	HOLDING COST ($)	ORDERING COST ($)	TOTAL COST ($)
Q	$5Q$	$1,300,000/Q$	
200	1,000	6,500	7,500
300	1,500	4,333	5,833
400	2,000	3,250	5,250
500	2,500	2,600	5,100
600	3,000	2,167	5,167
700	3,500	1,857	5,357
800	4,000	1,625	5,625

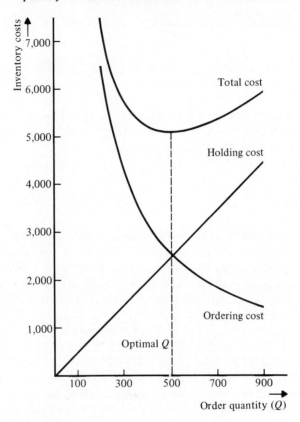

FIGURE 14.2 Inventory costs as function of order quantity for the tire distributor.

Now suppose that order quantity is increased by 1 unit, from Q_{opt} to $Q_{opt} + 1$. Then, the change in holding cost is

$$\frac{1}{2}(Q_{opt} + 1)C_H - \frac{1}{2}Q_{opt}C_H = \frac{1}{2}C_H$$

The change in order cost is

$$\frac{D}{Q_{opt} + 1}C_O - \frac{D}{Q_{opt}}C_O = -\frac{D}{Q_{opt}(Q_{opt} + 1)}C_O = -\frac{1}{2}C_H\left(\frac{Q_{opt}}{Q_{opt} + 1}\right)$$

Hence, the increase in holding cost is greater than the decrease in order cost, so that total cost increases.

Similarly, suppose order quantity is reduced from Q_{opt} to $Q_{opt} - 1$. Then, the change in holding cost is

$$\frac{1}{2}(Q_{opt} - 1)C_H - \frac{1}{2}Q_{opt}C_H = -\frac{1}{2}C_H$$

The change in order cost is

$$\frac{D}{Q_{opt}-1}C_O - \frac{D}{Q_{opt}}C_O = \frac{D}{Q_{opt}(Q_{opt}-1)}C_O = \frac{1}{2}C_H\left(\frac{Q_{opt}}{Q_{opt}-1}\right)$$

Thus, the increase in order costs is greater than the decrease in holding costs, so that again total cost increases.

We see then, given the shapes of the holding cost and order cost functions, that any movement in order quantity away from the level at which holding and order costs are the same, leads to higher total cost.

Now, in principle, we could solve any EOQ model problem by graphing the total inventory cost curve and visually locating the order quantity at its minimum. Alternatively, but equivalently, the holding and ordering cost curves can be plotted and the value of Q at which they intersect read from the graph. However, as we will now see, such an exercise is unnecessary as a straightforward algebraic expression is available for optimal order quantity.

OPTIMAL ORDER QUANTITY

Using differential calculus, it is possible to derive the value Q for which total annual inventory cost (14.1) is a minimum. Denoting by Q_{opt} the order quantity for which total cost is smallest, it can be shown[1] using calculus that

$$Q_{opt} = \sqrt{\frac{2DC_O}{C_H}} \qquad (14.3)$$

---

[1] Differentiating total cost in (14.1) with respect to Q yields.

$$\frac{dTC}{dQ} = \frac{1}{2}C_H - \frac{D}{Q^2}C_O$$

The optimal Q is then that value for which this derivative is zero. Hence

$$\frac{1}{2}C_H - \frac{D}{Q_{opt}^2}C_O = 0$$

so that

$$Q_{opt}^2 = \frac{2\,DC_O}{C_H}$$

and

$$Q_{opt} = \sqrt{\frac{2\,DC_O}{C_H}}$$

Optimal Order Quantity in the EOQ Model

    If the assumptions of the EOQ model hold, then in order to minimize total inventory costs, the number of units per order should be

$$Q_{opt} = \sqrt{\frac{2DC_O}{C_H}}$$

    We can also establish (14.3) by recalling that optimal order quantity is that level for which holding and order costs are the same. Thus

$$\frac{1}{2}Q_{opt}C_H = \frac{D}{Q_{opt}}C_O$$

so that

$$Q_{opt}^2 = \frac{2DC_O}{C_H}$$

from which (14.3) follows.

    Let us apply the result (14.3) to the problem of the tire distributor. Substituting the values

$$D = 26{,}000; \ C_O = 50; \ C_H = 10$$

into this expression yields

$$Q_{opt} = \sqrt{\frac{(2)(26{,}000)(50)}{10}} \simeq 510$$

where we have rounded to the nearest integer since it is not possible to order a fraction of a tire. It is seen, then, that if the tire distributor is to keep total inventory costs as low as possible, each order should be for 510 tires.

    The minimum achievable annual total inventory cost can now be obtained by substituting the optimal value for Q in (14.1). For the tire distributor we find from (14.2)

$$TC = (5)(510) + \frac{1{,}300{,}000}{510} \simeq 5{,}099$$

The best that can be done then is a total annual cost of $5,099.

OPTIMAL ORDER CYCLE

Continuing to explore the consequences of the optimal solution to the EOQ model, if total annual demand is D, and orders of size Q_{opt} are to be placed, then the number of orders per year must be

$$\text{Optimal Order Frequency} = \frac{D}{Q_{opt}}$$

Therefore, for the tire distributor, we find

$$\text{Optimal Order Frequency} = 26,000/510 = 51$$

Thus, as a corollary to our optimal solution, it follows that the distributor must place 51 orders per year.

Alternatively, we can compute the optimal order cycle, or time between orders, as

$$\text{Optimal Order Cycle} = \frac{Q_{opt}}{D}$$

Thus, for the tire distributor

$$\text{Optimal Order Cycle} = \frac{510}{26,000} = 0.019615 \text{ year}$$

Since there are 260 working days in a year, orders should optimally be placed every $(0.019615)(260) = 5.1$ working days.

OPTIMAL TIMING OF ORDERS

To this point we have not dealt with the possibility of delay between the placement of an order and its delivery. Suppose, in the case of the tire distributor, this delay, known as the **lead time,** is two days. We know that over a 5-day working week demand is 500 tires, so that 100 tires per day are needed. Hence, if inventory is not to be exhausted, it follows that a new order must be placed when the number of tires in the inventory falls to 200. This is known as the **optimal reorder point,** and generalizing the above argument, it can be seen that

$$\text{Optimal Reorder Point} = dt$$

where

$d = $ daily demand
$t = $ delay time in days

SENSITIVITY ANALYSIS

It can be seen that provided the assumptions of the EOQ model hold, use of the optimal order quantity in preference to some arbitrarily chosen level has the potential to yield substantial cost savings. For example, from Table 14.1 we note that had the tire distributor ordered in units of 200, the inventory cost of $7500 per year would substantially exceed the $5099 that can be achieved through ordering the optimal quantity of 510 tires. However, referring to Figure 14.2, notice that in the neighborhood of its minimum, the total inventory cost curve is fairly flat. This suggests that it should be possible to move some distance from the optimal order quantity without substantially increasing total cost. The same conclusion emerges from the data of Table 14.1, from which it is found, for example, that if the order quantity is 600 tires, inventory cost rises only to $5167. This observation leads to the conjecture that the optimal EOQ model

it follows, on substitution in (14.7), that the optimal production lot size is

$$Q_{opt} = \sqrt{\frac{(2)(6000)(500)}{(1 - 0.4)5}} \simeq 1414$$

where we have rounded to the nearest integer. Therefore, if total inventory costs are to be minimized, 1414 watches per run should be made.

Substituting this optimal value for Q in (14.6) then yields the minimum attainable total annual inventory cost as

$$TC = \left(\frac{1}{2}\right)(1414)\left(1 - \frac{6000}{15000}\right)(5) + \left(\frac{6000}{1414}\right)(500) \simeq 4243$$

Hence, the optimal solution yields a total cost of $4243 per year.

OPTIMAL PRODUCTION CYCLE

Let us assume that the watch manufacturer operates over 250 working days per year, so that daily production capability is $15,000/250 = 60$. Since 1414 watches per run are to be made, the production period extends over $1414/60 \simeq 24$ working days. At the end of this period, inventory will have built up to its maximum level

$$I_{max} = Q_{opt}\left(1 - \frac{D}{P}\right) = 1414\,(1 - 0.4) \simeq 848$$

Daily demand is $6000/250 = 24$, so that inventory will be exhausted after $848/24 \simeq 35$ days. The optimal solution, then, calls for production over 24 working days, followed by 35 days of nonproduction. This cycle repeats as long as the problem specifications remain unchanged.

14.4. ALLOWING FOR STOCK-OUTS

In our analysis of the inventory management problem to this point, it has been assumed that inventory will be replenished immediately when it is exhausted. For most practical applications this is precisely what is required, as it will generally be poor strategy to keep customers waiting for their orders to be filled. However, in circumstances where inventory holding costs are high, generally for high-priced goods, it may pay to plan for periods where no products are on hand to meet demand; that is, for inventory **stock-outs.** During such periods orders will accumulate, and only when a new consignment of goods is received will these **backorders** be filled.

We will consider the possibility of allowing for stock-outs in the context of the EOQ model of Section 14.2. Our assumptions are identical to those made previously for that model, with one exception. Assumption 3 is now replaced by allowing, after the exhaustion of inventory, a period of time over which backorders accumulate to some level which we denote S. At that point a new consignment of Q units is received. The inventory cycle is best seen graphically and

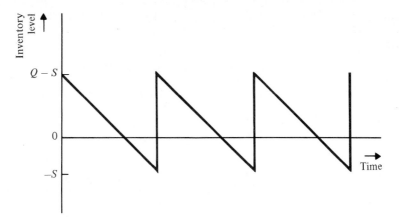

FIGURE 14.4 Progression through time of inventory and stockout.

is shown in Figure 14.4. When a shipment of Q goods is received, S of these go to filling backorders, and the remaining $Q - S$ are placed in inventory. From this maximum point inventory declines at a steady rate, eventually reaching zero. Then backorders accumulate, eventually reaching level S. At this stage a new consignment of goods arrives, and the cycle is then repeated.

To complete the specification of the problem, it is necessary to consider the costs to a distributor of being unable to meet all orders immediately when they are placed. These costs may include the extra expense of having to expedite shipments, or of having to purchase more expensive items to meet demand and goodwill losses through delays in filling orders. Such goodwill losses are hard to quantify, but in many businesses will certainly be nonnegligible. We will use the symbol C_B to denote the cost per year of each backordered item. The total annual inventory cost is now the sum of three components, so that

$$\text{Total Cost} = \text{Holding Cost} + \text{Ordering Cost} + \text{Backorder Cost}$$

We will consider these three elements individually in deriving an expression relating total cost to order quantity, Q, and maximum backorder level, S. Beginning with holding costs, it is necessary to find the average inventory level throughout the year. To see how this is accomplished, refer to Figure 14.5, which depicts a single cycle of the inventory holding process.

Over the time period from zero to t_1, while inventory is being run down to zero, the average level of inventory is half its maximum level, that is $\frac{1}{2}(Q - S)$. Between time t_1 and time t_2, while backorders build up, inventory is zero. What proportion of the time is inventory held? Looking at the two triangles in Figure 14.5, it can be seen that the length of the time segment $0 - t_1$, as a proportion of the time period $0 - t_2$, is the same as $(Q - S)/[(Q - S) + S] = (Q - S)/Q$. We therefore conclude that for a proportion $(Q - S)/Q$ of the time, average inventory level is $\frac{1}{2}(Q - S)$, while for the remaining proportion S/Q of the time average inventory level is zero. It therefore follows that over the whole time period,

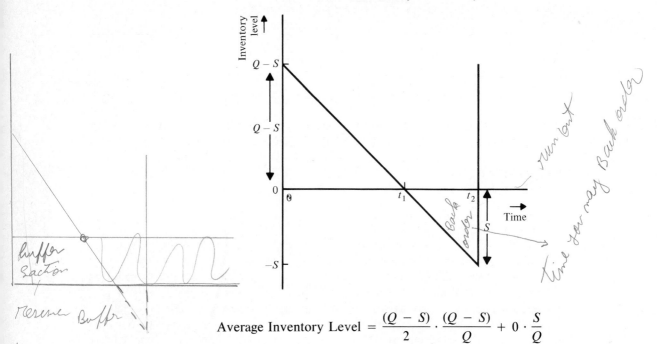

FIGURE 14.5 An inventory–stockout cycle.

(handwritten margin notes: buffer saaction, reserve buffer, two Bin order, Back order, S, number out, time you may Back order)

$$\text{Average Inventory Level} = \frac{(Q-S)}{2} \cdot \frac{(Q-S)}{Q} + 0 \cdot \frac{S}{Q}$$
$$= \frac{(Q-S)^2}{2Q}$$

Since the inventory holding cost per unit per year is C_H, it follows that

$$\text{Annual Holding Cost} = \frac{(Q-S)^2}{2Q}C_H$$

A similar argument allows us to find annual backorder costs. Referring again to Figure 14.5, backorder level is zero over the period 0 to t_1, that is a proportion $(Q-S)/Q$ of the time. Over the period t_1 to t_2, such periods occupying a proportion S/Q of the time, average backorder level is $\frac{1}{2}S$. Therefore, over the whole time period

$$\text{Average Backorder Level} = 0 \cdot \frac{(Q-S)}{Q} + \frac{S}{2} \cdot \frac{S}{Q} = \frac{S^2}{2Q}$$

Since the annual backorder cost per unit is C_B, we then have

$$\text{Annual Backorder Cost} = \frac{S^2}{2Q}C_B$$

Finally, exactly as in our analysis of the EOQ model in Section 14.2, for ordering costs we have

$$\text{Annual Ordering Cost} = \frac{D}{Q}C_O$$

Putting these three elements together, it emerges that for the EOQ model with stock-outs, total annual inventory cost is given by

$$TC = \frac{(Q - S)^2}{2Q}C_H + \frac{D}{Q}C_O + \frac{S^2}{2Q}C_B \qquad (14.8)$$

If stock-outs are permitted, management can choose the values of two decision variables—the order level Q, and the maximum backorder level S. We now find how to select these values so that total annual inventory cost (14.8) is as small as possible

OPTIMAL ORDER QUANTITY AND MAXIMUM BACKORDER LEVEL

Through differential calculus it can be shown[3] that to minimize total annual inventory cost, the optimal order quantity is

$$Q_{opt} = \sqrt{\frac{2DC_O(C_H + C_B)}{C_HC_B}} \qquad (14.9)$$

---

[3] From (14.8), the partial derivatives of total cost with respect to Q and S are

$$\frac{\delta\, TC}{\delta\, Q} = \frac{Q^2 - S^2}{2Q^2}C_H - \frac{D}{Q^2}C_O - \frac{S^2}{2\,Q^2}C_B$$

and

$$\frac{\delta\, TC}{\delta\, S} = \frac{S}{Q}C_B - \frac{Q - S}{Q}C_H$$

The optimal values of Q and S are, then, those values for which these partial derivatives are zero, so that

$$\frac{1}{2}(Q_{opt}^2 - S_{opt}^2)C_H - DC_O - \frac{1}{2}S_{opt}^2\, C_B = 0 \qquad (*)$$

and

$$S_{opt}\, C_B - (Q_{opt} - S_{opt})\, C_H = 0 \qquad (**)$$

From equation (**) it follows that

$$S_{opt} = \frac{Q_{opt}C_H}{(C_H + C_B)}$$

which establishes (14.10). Finally, on substituting this optimal value of S in (*), we find, after a little algebraic rearrangement,

$$2\, DC_O = \frac{Q_{opt}^2 C_H\, C_B}{(C_H + C_B)}$$

from which (14.9) follows.

and the maximum backorder level should be

$$S_{opt} = \frac{Q_{opt}C_H}{(C_H + C_B)} \tag{14.10}$$

To illustrate these formulae, suppose that the tire distributor of Section 14.2 is considering the possibility of allowing for stock-outs. Now, since they involve such intangible concepts as goodwill loss, backorder costs are difficult to estimate with any great precision. This distributor feels that a figure of $30 per tire per year might be reasonable. Combining this with the other problem specifications, we have

$$D = 26,000; \; C_O = 50; \; C_H = 10; \; C_B = 30$$

Substitution in (14.9) then yields

$$Q_{opt} = \sqrt{\frac{2(26,000)(50)(40)}{(10)(30)}} \approx 589$$

Then, from (14.10), we obtain

$$S_{opt} = \frac{(589)(10)}{40} \approx 147$$

This solution implies that if the model assumptions and cost estimates are correct, the distributor should place orders of 589 tires, planning to replenish inventory when backorders reach a level of 147 tires. Under this solution, the maximum inventory level will be the difference between Q_{opt} and S_{opt}; that is, 442 tires. Also, since total annual demand is 26,000 tires, the number of orders placed per year should be $26,000/589 \approx 44$.

14.5. ALLOWING FOR QUANTITY DISCOUNTS

Our analysis of the inventory management problem in previous sections of this chapter has depended on the assumption that whatever the size of an order, the unit purchase price is the same. However, in practice, the costs per unit to a manufacturer of filling a large order are often smaller than the corresponding costs for orders of lesser amounts. Accordingly, manufacturers may offer discounts for bulk purchases. These quantity discounts are aimed at inducing the placement of larger orders. In this section we will see how quantity discounts can be incorporated into the analysis of the EOQ model.

We return again to the problem of the tire distributor. In the analysis of Section 14.2, it was assumed that whatever the size of the order, each tire cost the distributor $50. Let us now consider a more elaborate problem specification where the distributor is offered four price schedules, depending on order quan-

EOQ is the best one to order

tities, for another type of tire for which demand is relatively low, and ordering costs quite high. For this tire annual demand is 2000 units, and the cost of placing each order is $100, so that

$$D = 2000; \; C_O = 100$$

Annual inventory holding costs are again estimated to be 20% of the value of inventory holdings. Table 14.3 shows the price per tire that the distributor must pay for orders of different sizes, these prices declining with increasing order size. The final column of the table shows the inventory holding cost per unit per year as 20% of the price paid per tire.

We begin by computing the economic order quantities for different price levels, using the result (14.3); that is

$$Q_{opt} = \sqrt{\frac{2DC_O}{C_H}}$$

For the four different price levels we find:

(i) $Q_{opt}^{(i)} = \sqrt{\dfrac{(2)(2,000)(100)}{12.2}} \simeq 181$

(ii) $Q_{opt}^{(ii)} = \sqrt{\dfrac{(2)(2,000)(100)}{12}} \simeq 183$

(iii) $Q_{opt}^{(iii)} = \sqrt{\dfrac{(2)(2,000)(100)}{11.8}} \simeq 184$

(iv) $Q_{opt}^{(iv)} = \sqrt{\dfrac{(2)(2,000)(100)}{11.6}} \simeq 186$

if you order more then what you need you get more discount but you have to remember the price goes down by inv holding cost may go up. They are usually in a block, 1000 – 2000; 2001 – 4000 always work it on in a smaller amount like 1000 or 2001

Now, if a price of $61 per tire were to be paid, total inventory holding costs would be minimized for orders of 181 tires. However, for orders of this size it is only necessary to pay $60 per tire. Therefore, it follows that ordering under price schedule (i) cannot be an optimal solution to the inventory management problem. For a price of $60 per tire, the optimal strategy would be to order 183 tires, which is a feasible solution to the problem. If the price of tires were $59 each and the distributor were completely free to choose order quantity, the best solution would be orders of 184 tires. However, the $59 price is not available for

TABLE 14.3 Price schedule faced by the tire distributor.

PRICE SCHEDULE	ORDER QUANTITY	PRICE PER UNIT (C_U)	ANNUAL HOLDING COST PER UNIT (C_H)
(i)	less than 100	$61	$12.20
(ii)	100– 599	$60	$12.00
(iii)	600–1,199	$59	$11.80
(iv)	1,200 or more	$58	$11.60

TABLE 14.4 Solution to the tire distributor problem with quantity discounts.

PRICE SCHEDULE	Q_{opt}	HOLDING COST	ORDERING COST	TOTAL PRICE PAID	TOTAL COST
(ii)	183	1,098	1,093	120,000	122,191
(iii)	600	3,540	333	118,000	121,873
(iv)	1,200	6,960	167	116,000	123,127

such small orders. The best that can be done within schedule (iii) is to keep order quantity as small as possible, at 600 tires. By the same argument, if orders are placed in price schedule (iv), the best that can be done is to place orders for 1200 tires. Hence, in place of the two solutions above, we must use

$$Q_{opt}^{(iii)} = 600; \ Q_{opt}^{(iv)} = 1200$$

We have now reduced the problem to the point at which it can be concluded that one of three strategies must be optimal—order quantities of 183, 600, or 1200 tires. The total cost to the distributor is the sum of three components—holding cost, ordering cost, and the total price that must be paid for the tires. This last component has not been included in our earlier analyses, as it has not depended on the order quantity. If we let C_U denote the price per unit paid, then the cost of meeting an entire year's demand is $C_U D$. Therefore, augmenting equation (14.1), the total annual cost is given by

$$TC = \frac{1}{2} Q C_H + \frac{D}{Q} C_O + D C_U$$

Table 14.4 shows these components and the total cost for the three solutions in which we remain interested.

The final column of the table, which is the sum of the previous three, shows total costs for the three solutions. We see that the best strategy is to place orders of 600 tires. It emerges, then, that the quantity discount has induced the distributor to place larger orders than would have been the case in its absence. Had the price per tire been $60, whatever the size of the order, then only 183 tires would be required in each order. In solving this problem, the distributor must balance the value of the quantity discounts against the additional costs that must be incurred from holding inventory for longer periods. In the present problem we see that it is worthwhile to increase order size to 600 tires, but that it does not pay to go beyond this point.

14.6. THE MATERIAL REQUIREMENTS PLANNING (MRP) APPROACH

The inventory management models discussed in the previous sections of this chapter are primarily applicable to cases where a distributor must place orders for final produced goods, or, as for the economic production lot size model of Section 14.3, to relatively simple production problems. In the typical corpora-

FIGURE 14.6 Part of the bill of materials for the MRP system.

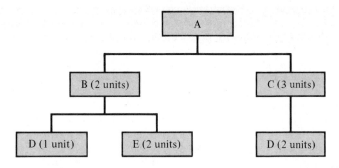

tion, however, a wide array of products are made. These products in turn will require components which must either be manufactured in-house or ordered from suppliers. Allowance must be made for the time taken to manufacture these components, or for delays in their delivery. If there are not to be costly delays in the production schedule it is important that materials be available as required at various stages in the production processes.

The **Material Requirements Planning** (MRP) approach was designed to provide a mechanism for allowing appropriate scheduling of orders for components and material, so that they will be on hand when needed. In practice the typical corporate production/material requirements model is so complex that it must be computerized in order to allow the necessary calculations to be readily carried out. It is possible here only to provide, through a small example, a flavor of the MRP approach—space limitations preclude a fuller discussion.[4]

To illustrate the considerations involved in MRP, consider a company which, to meet an order, must produce 60 units of product A in 6 weeks. This requirement forms part of the company's **master production schedule,** which provides a listing of what quantities of finished products are to be produced at what times. Given a master production schedule, the next requirement, for each finished product, is a **bill of materials** which shows what materials are needed in the production process, and at what stages in the process these materials are required. The bill of materials, then, is not merely a list but a description of the production process, showing how the product is put together. For product A, it is known that each unit requires 2 units of component B, and 3 units of component C, and that the fabrication process for orders of this size takes one week.

The components B and C are both made in-house. Each unit of B requires one unit of component D and 2 units of E, the process taking 3 weeks from start to completion. Production of C takes 2 weeks, each unit requiring 2 units of D. Components D and E are ordered from outside suppliers, the respective delivery delays being one and 2 weeks.

Figure 14.6 illustrates graphically the structure of the production process,

---

[4] The reader interested in more detail is referred to J. Orlicky, *Materials Requirements Planning,* (New York: McGraw Hill, 1975).

TABLE 14.5 Some specifications for the MRP system.

PRODUCT/ COMPONENT	FABRICATION TIME/ ORDER DELAYS (WEEKS)	INITIAL INVENTORY HOLDING
A	1	0
B	3	20
C	2	30
D	1	50
E	2	40

while Table 14.5 contains other relevant information. In that table we show, at the outset, inventory holdings of 20 units of B, 30 units of C, 50 units of D, and 40 units of E. The problem we must solve is when to place orders for D and E, and to begin production of B, C, and A so that 60 units of A are available at the end of 6 weeks. It will be assumed that desired inventory holdings of the intermediate components at the end of this period are zero. In practice, it may be preferable to maintain a small inventory in case of unanticipated demand, and, as will be seen, our analysis is easily modified to allow for this.

To attack problems of this sort, it is necessary to work back from the final output requirements. We do so in stages:

1. Since 60 units of A are needed at the end of week 6, it will be necessary to have to hand 120 units of B and 180 units of C at the beginning of that week. Some of these can be taken from inventory, leaving 100 units of B and 150 units of C to be made.
2. It will be necessary to begin production of 100 units of B at the beginning of week 3, which requires that 100 units of D and 200 units of E be available at that time. Some of these can be taken from inventory, leaving the remainder to be ordered.
3. Production of 150 units of C commences at the beginning of week 4. This requires 300 units of D.
4. As a result of (2) it is necessary to order 50 units of D at the beginning of week 2, and 160 units of E at the beginning of week 1.
5. Following from (3), 300 units of D must be ordered at the beginning of week 3.

The solution is set out schematically in Figure 14.7, and the points at which actions must be taken indicated in Table 14.6, where it is understood that the time refers to the beginning of the weeks.

Of course, the example we have just discussed is sufficiently straightforward so that the burden of storing the required information and carrying out the calculations presented no great difficulty. However, material requirements planning problems faced by corporations in practice are far more complex than this. With many products, several intermediate production stages, and hundreds of materials and components requirements, it is not possible to store all of the necessary details in an easily understood chart. In that case, the MRP system must be computerized. Such computerized systems can then be employed to plan the production and ordering schedule to avoid vital shortages. Moreover, through such an approach it is possible to allow for eventualities such as breakdowns in the production of intermediate components. It may be possible to order

FIGURE 14.7 Solution to an MRP problem.

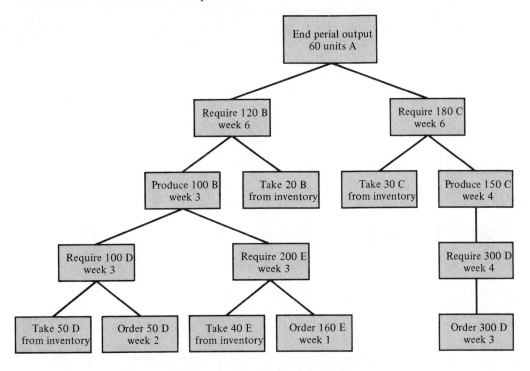

TABLE 14.6 Actions required in the solution of the MRP problem.

WEEK	ACTION
1	Order 160 units of E
2	Order 50 units of D
3	Order 300 units of D
	Begin production of 100 units of B
4	Begin production of 150 units of C
6	Begin production of 60 units of A

the components from suppliers, and the system can be programmed to cost the expenses and delays involved, and examine alternative strategies.

14.7. REORDER POINT MODELS: ALLOWING FOR STOCHASTIC DEMAND

The assumption made in much of our analysis—that product demand is known with precision in advance—is generally unrealistic. For the typical consumer product, demand fluctuates over time in a manner that cannot be precisely predicted. In such circumstances, when there is a delay between the placement of an order and its receipt, there will be some chance of stock-outs due to unusually high demand, before inventory can be replenished.

To illustrate the issues involved, consider the case of a regional distributor of canned food. For one product—baked beans—the distributor estimates that *average* demand will be 13,000 cases per year, or 250 cases per week. However, this estimate does not imply that demand will be exactly at that level every week. Rather, it is believed that over time, actual demand will *fluctuate* around this level in a manner that is not predictable in advance. Each case of baked beans is valued at $12, and the distributor estimates annual holding costs at 20% of the value of inventory, so that annual inventory holding cost per case is $2.40. It is further estimated that for this product, ordering costs are $20 per order.

We might approach this distributor's inventory management problem by ignoring the uncertain, or **stochastic,** element in demand, temporarily assuming a constant rate of 13,000 cases per year. The EOQ model can then be applied, and with

$$D = 13,000; \; C_H = 2.40; \; C_O = 20$$

the optimal order quantity, using (14.3), is

$$Q_{opt} = \sqrt{\frac{2DC_O}{C_H}} = \sqrt{\frac{(2)(13,000)(20)}{2.40}} \approx 465$$

This analysis suggests, then, that orders of 465 cases should be placed.

The distributor works a 5-day week, so that average daily demand for baked beans is 50 cases. Once an order is placed, the *lead time* before it is filled is 3 days. Therefore, if demand were at a constant level over time, the distributor would place a new order when inventory was down to 150 cases. As before, we refer to this level as the **reorder point.** Now, if demand really were at a constant rate, all would be well. Inventory would steadily decline and would be replenished precisely at the time it reached zero, so that there will be no stock-outs. However, if demand is stochastic, then there will be some chance that it will exceed 150 cases over the lead time period, so that stock-outs would then occur. This is the important factor which must be considered once the possibility of stochastic demand is recognized.

If the distributor of canned beans opts to order more stock when inventory reaches 150 cases, the *average* demand level over the 3-day lead time, then we might expect the probability of stock-out during the period to be quite high since demand will often exceed the average. In this sense the distributor would be providing pretty poor service to those customers whose orders could not be immediately filled. A higher **service level** could be provided by following a strategy that lowered the probability of stock-outs. It is fairly clear how this can be achieved. Suppose that rather than waiting until there were only 150 cases in stock, the distributor set the reorder point at 170 cases. The associated decline in the chances of stock-outs would lead to higher levels of customer goodwill, and, in the terminology of Section 14.4, reduce backorder costs. However, this benefit does not accrue without cost. The increase of 20 cases in the reorder point implies that annual inventory will, on average, be 20 cases higher. This additional inventory, which provides some protection against the chance of stock-outs, is called **safety stock,** and must be paid for through increased holding costs.

In this section we will discuss three approaches to the determination of an appropriate reorder point. These approaches vary in complexity, and the strategy adopted in practice will depend on individual problem specifications—particularly on what is known or assumed about backorder costs.

Terminology for Reorder Point Models

Lead time: time between the placement and filling of an order
Reorder point: level of inventory at which a new order is placed
Service level: measured by the chances of stock-outs; the lower the probability of stock-out, the higher the service level
Safety stock: additional inventory carried to reduce the probability of stock-out

---

DETERMINING THE REORDER POINT TO ACHIEVE A GIVEN SERVICE LEVEL

In many practical applications backorder costs are extremely difficult to estimate, and management will prefer to work with a more tangible concept. An approach to our problem that is often useful in such circumstances is to find the reorder point needed to achieve some desired service level. It is possible to measure service level in a number of ways. Here we will consider two:

(a) The most straightforward approach is to fix the probability of a stock-out during any given lead time period.
(b) An alternative is to fix the average number of stock-outs per year.

The difficulty with the first approach is that fixing the probability of stock-out in any lead time period leaves the frequency of stock-outs dependent on the number of orders per year. It is therefore more realistic to set the expected number of stock-outs per year. The two concepts are related, since

$$\begin{pmatrix} \text{Expected} \\ \text{Stock-outs} \\ \text{per Year} \end{pmatrix} = \begin{pmatrix} \text{Probability} \\ \text{of} \\ \text{Stock-out} \end{pmatrix} \begin{pmatrix} \text{Number} \\ \text{of Orders} \\ \text{per Year)} \end{pmatrix}$$

Now, let

D = Annual demand

Q_{opt} = Optimal Order Size (under EOQ model)

α = Probability of stock-out in any lead time period

E = Expected number of stock-outs per year

Then, since the number of orders per year is D/Q_{opt}, it follows that

$$\alpha = \frac{E}{D/Q_{opt}} \qquad (14.11)$$

Suppose that the distributor of baked beans wants to set the average number of stock-outs at one per year. Then, setting

$$E = 1; D = 13,000; Q_{opt} = 465$$

in (14.11) yields

$$\alpha = \frac{1}{13,000/465} = 0.0358$$

It is therefore required that the probability be 0.0358 that any lead time period involves a stock-out.

In order to find the reorder point that will ensure a desired service level, it is necessary to know how likely particular levels of demand are within the lead time period. This can generally be estimated from past records. In practice, it is often convenient to assume that demand varies according to some specific probability distribution, and the **normal distribution** is frequently employed for this purpose. The assumption of normality of demand can be checked from historical sales records, and some other distribution may be used if necessary. We will proceed here with a normal distribution, assuming over the reorder period that demand is normally distributed with mean μ and variance σ^2. The situation is illustrated in Figure 14.8, where demand, r, is shown to vary about its mean μ. Recalling our discussion of Chapter 10, the probability that a continuous random variable lies in an interval is given by the area under the probability density function for that interval. Therefore, in the figure, r_α is the lead-time period demand that is exceeded with probability α. It follows that a reorder point, r_α, will produce the service level corresponding to stock-out probability α.

FIGURE 14.8 Normally distributed demand over lead-time period.

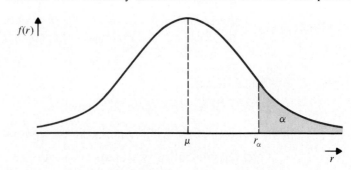

Given the mean μ and variance σ^2, the normal distribution for lead time period demand is fully specified, and, for any stock-out probability α, the corresponding reorder point α can be found using the procedure discussed in Chapter 10. We know that

normal transfor (handwritten)

$$r_\alpha = \mu + z_\alpha \sigma \qquad (14.12)$$

where z_α is such that

$$P(Z > z_\alpha) = \alpha$$

with the random variable Z obeying a standard normal distribution. For any given α, the value of z_α can be read from Table 3 of the appendix at the back of this volume.

Reorder Point for a Given Service Level

Suppose that over the lead-time period, demand is normally distributed with mean μ and variance σ^2. If the probability of stock-out during any lead time period is to be α, then the reorder point must be

$$r_\alpha = \mu + z_\alpha \sigma$$

where z_α is the number exceeded with probability α by a standard normal random variable.

Returning to the problem of the distributor of baked beans, suppose that over a 3-day lead-time period, demand is normally distributed with mean 150 cases and standard deviation 20 cases (so that the variance is 400).[5] If the expected number of stock-outs is to be held to one per year, we have seen that the probability of a stock-out in any single lead time period must be $\alpha = 0.0358$. From Table 3 of the appendix we find

$$z_\alpha = z_{0.0358} = 1.80$$

Therefore, using (14.12), we have

$$r_\alpha = \mu + z_\alpha \sigma = 150 + (1.80)(20) = 186$$

---

[5] In practice demand might be expressed in daily terms. Suppose that daily demand is normally distributed with mean μ_d and variance σ_d^2. Then, over a lead time of K days, demand will be normally distributed with mean $K\mu_d$ and variance $K\sigma_d^2$. This is so since the demand over K days will be the sum of the demands for each day. Then, taking demand to be independent from day to day, we use the facts that the mean of the sum of random variables is the sum of their means, and the variance of the sum of independent random variables is the sum of their variances.

The conclusion, then, is that to achieve an expected number of stock-outs of one per year, a new order should be placed when inventory falls to 186 cases.

This reorder point exceeds the mean demand over the lead time period by 36 cases, this amount being the safety stock, held to provide protection against stock-outs. It follows that with this policy, the distributor's average inventory level will be 36 cases higher than if safety stock were not held. The additional inventory cost of carrying this safety stock is, then, the annual holding cost of 36 cases. Therefore

$$\text{Safety Stock Holding Cost} = C_H \text{ (Safety Stock)}$$

$$= (2.40)(36) = 86.40$$

Hence, the carrying of sufficient safety stock to ensure a service level, such that the expected number of stock-outs per year is one, entails an additional $86.40 in inventory costs per annum.

It should be intuitively quite clear that the level of safety stock, and hence the cost of holding this stock, will depend on the service level. The better the service level, the higher will be the associated additional inventory costs. This conclusion is illustrated for the distributor of baked beans in Table 14.7, where we have calculated for this distributor annual safety stock holding costs for different probabilities of stock-out in a lead-time period.

DETERMINING THE REORDER POINT WHEN BACKORDER COSTS ARE KNOWN

So far we have treated service level as a parameter stipulated, somewhat arbitrarily, by management. But, how in fact would a manager arrive at such a value? One temptation, of course, is to assert that the chance of stock-out should be made as small as possible. However, as we saw in Table 14.7, stock-out probability can only be decreased at the expense of incurring additional holding costs for safety stock. It seems then that at some point, it might be desirable to strike a balance between service level and holding costs. Anyone attempting to analyze where this balance point should be will have to confront

TABLE 14.7 Safety stock holding costs corresponding to various service levels for the distributor of canned beans.

STOCK-OUT PROBABILITY α	EXPECTED STOCK-OUTS PER YEAR	z_α	REORDER POINT	SAFETY STOCK	ANNUAL HOLDING COST OF SAFETY STOCK
0.01	0.28	2.33	197	47	112.80
0.025	0.70	1.96	189	39	93.60
0.0358	1	1.80	186	36	84.40
0.05	1.40	1.645	183	33	79.20
0.10	2.80	1.28	176	26	62.40
0.25	6.99	0.675	164	14	33.60
0.50	13.98	0	150	0	0

the difficult problem of trying to estimate the goodwill lost from backorders. All other things equal, it is clear that the greater this goodwill loss is thought to be, the better the level of service it will be desirable to provide. We now see how, if backorder costs can be specified, the reorder point can be chosen when demand is uncertain. The development of our results is more straightforward when a discrete rather than a continuous probability distribution is specified for demand.

Consider again the distributor of canned beans, assuming the same problem specifications as previously, except that demand over a 3-day period can be represented by the discrete probability distribution set out in Table 14.8. In practice, these probabilities could be estimated as the proportion of 3-day stretches in the past where demand has been at the corresponding levels. To keep the computations manageable, we have assumed that demand arises only in multiples of ten cases. This simplification is merely a convenience and is not essential in solving problems of this type.

Denoting the eleven possible demand levels by $d_i(i = 1, 2, \ldots, 11)$, and the corresponding probabilities by $P(d_i)$, then expected demand over lead time periods is

$$E(D) = \sum_{i=1}^{11} d_i P(d_i)$$

$$= (100)(0.02) + (110)(0.04) + \ldots + (200)(0.02) = 150$$

As we have already seen, if annual demand were constant at this rate, then according to the EOQ model, consignments of 465 cases should be ordered.

The distributor counts a goodwill cost of 50 cents for each backordered case of beans. Given this information our task is to determine the best possible reorder point. In fact it can be shown that the only values that need be considered are those with nonzero demand probabilities. We must therefore look at eleven possible reorder points, our strategy being to find shortage costs and holding costs for each.

To begin, we find for each reorder point, the expected number of cases short in any lead time period. We must therefore find

$$E(\text{Shortages/Lead Time Period}) = \Sigma s_i P(s_i)$$

TABLE 14.8 Demand probabilities over the lead-time period for the distributor of canned beans.

DEMAND	PROBABILITY	DEMAND	PROBABILITY
100	0.02	160	0.16
110	0.04	170	0.10
120	0.08	180	0.08
130	0.10	190	0.04
140	0.16	200	0.02
150	0.20		

where the s_i are the possible shortage levels, $P(s_i)$ their probabilities, and summation is over all possible shortage levels. As an illustration, suppose that a reorder point of 130 cases is chosen. Then, if lead-time demand is no more than 130 cases there will be no shortages. If demand is 140 cases, which will occur with probability 0.16, there will be a shortage of 10 cases. Continuing to argue in this way, we find for a reorder point of 130 cases,

$$E(\text{Shortages/Lead Time Period}) = (0)(0.02) + (0)(0.04) + (0)(0.08) + (0)(0.10)$$
$$+ (10)(0.16) + (20)(0.20) + (30)(0.16) + (40)(0.10)$$
$$+ (50)(0.08) + (60)(0.04) + (70)(0.02) = 22.2$$

The corresponding results for other possible reorder points are shown in the second column of Table 14.9.

Now, to compute the total expected annual shortage costs, we must multiply the expected shortages per period by the unit shortage cost (50 cents in this case), and by the number of orders placed per year. Here, total demand per annum is, on average, 13,000 cases, so that with orders of 465 cases, the number of orders placed is 13,000/465. Hence we have

$$\begin{array}{c}\text{Expected Annual} \\ \text{Shortage Cost}\end{array} = \left(\frac{\text{Expected Shortages}}{\text{Lead Time Period}}\right)\left(\begin{array}{c}\text{Unit Shortage} \\ \text{Cost}\end{array}\right)\left(\begin{array}{c}\text{Orders} \\ \text{per Year}\end{array}\right)$$

so that, for a reorder point of 130 cases, we find

$$\text{Expected Annual Shortage Cost} = (22.2)(0.50)(13,000/465) = \$310$$

Expected annual shortage costs for each possible reorder point are shown in the third column of Table 14.9.

Next, we consider inventory holding costs for different reorder points. The lowest holding cost will be achieved when orders for 100 cases are placed. For each other possible reorder point, we find the excess holding costs over this

TABLE 14.9 Determining the optimal reorder point for the distributor of canned beans, given data of Table 14.8.

REORDER POINT	EXPECTED SHORTAGES PER LEAD TIME PERIOD	EXPECTED ANNUAL SHORTAGE COSTS ($)	EXCESS ANNUAL HOLDING COSTS ($)	TOTAL COST
100	50.0	699	0	699
110	40.2	562	24	586
120	30.8	481	48	529
130	22.2	310	72	382
140	14.6	204	96	300
150	8.6	120	120	240
160	4.6	64	144	208
170	2.2	31	168	199
180	0.8	11	192	203
190	0.2	3	216	219
200	0	0	240	240

get a lest cost from this table

minimum level. To a reasonable approximation, any excess over 100 in order size will result in an excess of the same amount in average inventory levels. This excess amount is then multiplied by annual unit holding costs of $2.40 to obtain the figures in the penultimate column of Table 14.9. For example, for a reorder point of 130 cases we find that

$$\text{Excess Annual Holding Cost} = (30)(2.40) = \$72$$

The final column of Table 14.9 shows the sum of shortage and holding costs for each possible reorder point. It emerges that the lowest total cost is for a reorder point of 170 cases. We therefore conclude, given the distributor's estimate of goodwill losses from shortages, that orders should be placed when inventory level falls to 170 cases. Of course, a higher estimated figure for goodwill loss could lead to a higher reorder point.

ORDER QUANTITY AND THE REORDER POINT DECISION

We began our analysis by finding the reorder point needed to achieve any particular service level. Next, we showed how, if the costs of shortages could be estimated, the reorder point could be chosen so as to make the sum of annual shortage and holding costs as small as possible. It might seem that under these conditions, such a solution is the best that can be achieved. However, this is not the case. Our previous solution was based on the assumption that the order quantity would be set *at that level that would be optimal if demand were at a constant rate,* equal to the average rate for the stochastic demand model. In fact, it may be advantageous to order larger quantities than those suggested by this solution to the EOQ model. The reason is that increasing the order quantity will result in having to place fewer orders per year. In consequence, for any given reorder point, this leads to lower expected shortage costs.

The foregoing argument suggests that our previous solution to the reorder point problem is not completely optimal. Rather it will be necessary to consider reorder point and order quantity jointly, and determine the pair of values for which total inventory cost is a minimum. This entails an analysis of a complexity beyond the scope of this book. We note, however, that, although the solutions presented here are not fully optimal, they nevertheless will be sufficiently close to the optimum to render them very useful for many practical problems.

14.8. ALLOWING FOR DECLINING VALUE OF ITEMS IN INVENTORY

The inventory management models of the previous sections embodied an array of assumptions. However, one constant running through the analyses was the assumption that although holding costs were incurred in keeping an item in inventory, its value remained constant, in the sense that at some time in the future it could eventually be sold at a price equal to its original value. There are in fact many goods for which such an assumption is clearly inappropriate. The quality of freshly baked bread, or of many fresh fruits and vegetables, for example, quickly deteriorates over time, as, therefore, does the price that consumers are prepared to pay for such perishable commodities. A similar phenomenon applies to many physically nonperishable commodities. Yesterday's news is not in very great demand, so that a distributor who orders too many copies of a daily newspaper may quickly be in the position of holding surplus stock that cannot be sold at any price. The sales of many clothing goods, such as down-filled jackets and swim suits, are highly seasonal. Premium prices can be commanded during the peak demand season, but, at the end of that season, any unsold stock must be offered at sale prices in order to clear inventory.

In this section a problem involving deteriorating inventory value will be examined. Rather than looking at a continuing process of building up and running down inventory over time, we will consider a model in which an order for a single shipment is to be placed. Over a peak demand period, each item in the shipment can be sold at a fixed price. However, once the peak season is over, it is necessary to reduce this price in order to sell any remaining items. Such models are sometimes called **single period inventory models.**

To illustrate the kind of situation we have in mind, consider the problem of a local chain store manager who must place an order for a line of swim suits. The shipment of suits will cost the store $25 each, and, over the peak demand period, the suits can be sold for $40 each. However, at the end of the season, a sale is to be held to clear the remaining stock, the original selling price being cut in half. The store manager must decide how many swim suits to order. This decision will naturally be based on the view that is taken of upcoming peak season demand. Of course, if this demand were known precisely there would be no problem—an order of that amount would be placed. However, it is almost invariably unrealistic to believe that future demand levels will be known with precision. It will therefore be necessary to attempt to characterize uncertainty about peak season demand through a probability distribution.

We summarize below the assumptions on which our subsequent analysis of single period inventory models is based.

Assumptions for Single Period Inventory Models

1. Only one consignment of a product can be ordered, and the price per unit paid is the same whatever the size of the consignment.
2. During a peak demand period, items are sold at a fixed price per unit.
3. At the end of the peak demand period, each unsold item is sold at a lower price, called the **salvage value.**
4. A probability distribution for peak period demand can be established.

If the store manager were clairvoyant, she would make the perfect decision and order precisely the number of swim suits that could be sold in the peak demand season. However, in practice, the occurrence of such a happy solution would be entirely fortuitous. It is to be expected that the quantity ordered will, in the event, turn out to be either somewhat higher or somewhat lower than the actual demand level. We must therefore consider the costs involved in these two types of departure of demand from order quantity. First suppose that order quantity exceeds peak season demand, so that there will be an overstock of swim suits. Each unit overstocked results in a loss to the store amounting to the difference between its purchase cost and its salvage value. Hence we can write

$$\text{Unit Overstock Cost} = C_O = \text{Purchase Cost} - \text{Salvage Value}$$

For the swim suits, then,

$$C_O = 25 - 20 = \$5$$

If the order quantity falls short of the peak season demand level, we must allow for two possible "costs." First, for each unit that could have been sold, had it been available, there is a foregone profit equal to the difference between the peak season selling price and the purchase cost. Second, it might be desirable to account for loss in customer goodwill through not having the product available for sale. Therefore, we have

$$\begin{array}{l}\text{Unit} \\ \text{Understock} = C_U = (\text{Selling Price} - \text{Purchase Cost}) + \text{Goodwill Loss} \\ \text{Cost} \end{array}$$

The store manager counts each swim suit demanded when stock is unavailable as a 50 cents goodwill loss, so that

$$C_U = (40 - 25) + 0.50 = \$15.50$$

To see how the optimal order quantity can be found, let us assume that order quantity Q is at some specific level Q_O, and ask what would be the consequences of either increasing or decreasing this quantity by a single unit. Consider first the increase of order quantity from Q_O to $Q_O + 1$. The effect of this change on costs will depend on the demand level. We must consider two possibilities:

1. Suppose that demand is at most Q_O units. Then, increasing order quantity to $Q_O + 1$ will yield an additional unit of overstock, and hence an additional cost C_O. The probability that this additional cost actually materializes is simply the probability that demand does not exceed Q_O, which we write $P(D \leq Q_O)$.
2. If demand is more than Q_O units, increasing order quantity to $Q_O + 1$ results in one unit less of understock, and therefore reduction of C_U in cost. The probability that this cost reduction occurs is the probability that demand exceeds Q_O, that is $P(D > Q_O)$, or, equivalently $1 - P(D \leq Q_O)$.

We have seen then that if order quantity is at Q_O, an increase of one unit in this quantity results in increased cost of C_O with probability $P(D \leq Q_O)$ and decreased cost of C_U with probability $1 - P(D \leq Q_O)$. It follows therefore that the expected change in cost is

$$E(\text{Cost of Ordering one more Unit}) = C_O P(D \leq Q_O) \\ \qquad\qquad - C_U[1 - P(D \leq Q_O)] \qquad (14.13)$$

Therefore, if (14.13) is negative, expected costs can be reduced by ordering an additional unit.

Now consider the reduction of order quantity from Q_O to $Q_O - 1$. The two possible impacts on costs are:

1. If demand exceeds $Q_O - 1$ units, decreasing order quantity to $Q_O - 1$ involves an additional cost C_U. This occurs with probability $P(D > Q_O - 1)$, or $1 - P(D \leq Q_O - 1)$.
2. If demand does not exceed $Q_O - 1$ units, decreasing order quantity to $Q_O - 1$ involves a reduction in cost of C_O. This occurs with probability $P(D \leq Q_O - 1)$.

It follows that the expected change in cost when order quantity is lowered from Q_O to $Q_O - 1$ is

$$E(\text{Cost of Ordering one less Unit}) = C_U[1 - P(D \leq Q_O - 1)] \\ \qquad\qquad - C_O P(D \leq Q_O - 1) \qquad (14.14)$$

For products where demand is moderately high, the probability that demand will be *precisely* equal to any specific number is negligbly small. We can therefore write

$$P(D \leq Q_O - 1) \simeq P(D \leq Q_O)$$

and so, on substitution in (14.14),

$$E(\text{Cost of Ordering one less Unit}) = C_U[1 - P(D \leq Q_O)] \\ \qquad\qquad - C_O P(D \leq Q_O) \qquad (14.15)$$

It follows that if (14.15) is negative, or equivalently (14.13) is positive, expected costs can be reduced by ordering one less unit.

We have seen that expected costs can be reduced by ordering one more unit if (14.13) is negative, or by ordering one less unit if (14.13) is positive. However, in the intermediate case, where that expression is zero, no such improvements are possible. We therefore conclude that the optimal order quantity, Q_{opt}, is that number for which

$$C_O P(D \leq Q_{opt}) = C_U[1 - P(D \leq Q_{opt})]$$

from which it follows that

$$P(D \leq Q_{opt}) = \frac{C_U}{C_U + C_O} \qquad (14.16)$$

For the store purchasing swim suits, we have found

$$C_O = 5; C_U = 15.50$$

and therefore, using (14.16), it follows that

$$P(D \leq Q_{opt}) = \frac{15.50}{(15.50 + 5)} = 0.7561$$

We conclude, then, that the order quantity that minimizes expected costs is such that the probability that demand does not exceed that quantity is 0.7561.

Optimal Solution for Single Period Inventory Model

Suppose that the assumptions of the single period inventory model are satisfied, with C_O and C_U denoting respectively unit overstock and understock costs. Then the minimum expected cost order quantity, Q_{opt}, is that number for which the probability that demand does not exceed Q_{opt} is given by

$$P(D \leq Q_{opt}) = \frac{C_U}{(C_U + C_O)}$$

To proceed further, it is necessary to specify a probability distribution for peak period demand. In practice, this is by no means a trivial matter, and this difficulty constitutes a drawback to the use of single period inventory models. For purposes of illustration, let us assume that management's uncertainty about demand can be represented by a normal distribution with mean μ and standard deviation σ. Figure 14.9 shows the probability density function, together with

FIGURE 14.9 Distribution of demand, and optimal order quantity.

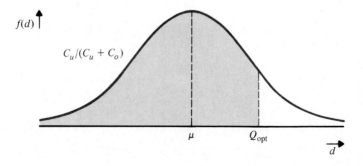

optimal order quantity, Q_{opt}. As indicated in the figure, the probability is $C_U/(C_U + C_O)$ that demand is below this level.

Setting

$$1 - \alpha = \frac{C_U}{(C_U + C_O)}$$

we have

$$1 - \alpha = P(D \le Q_{opt})$$

from which it follows that

$$1 - \alpha = P\left[Z \le \frac{Q_{opt} - \mu}{\sigma} \right]$$

where Z follows a standard normal distribution. Then, again denoting by z_α that number exceeded with probability α by a standard normal random variable, we have

$$1 - \alpha = P(Z \le z_\alpha)$$

so that

$$\frac{(Q_{opt} - \mu)}{\sigma} = z_\alpha$$

It therefore follows that the optimal order quantity is

$$Q_{opt} = \mu + z_\alpha \sigma \qquad (14.17)$$

Optimal Solution for Single Period Inventory Models with Normally Distributed Demand

Suppose that the assumptions of the single period inventory model are satisfied, and that peak period demand is normally distributed with mean μ and standard deviation σ. Then the minimum cost order quantity is given by

$$Q_{opt} = \mu + z_\alpha \sigma$$

where z_α is the number exceeded with probability α by a standard normal random variable, and

$$1 - \alpha = \frac{C_U}{(C_U + C_O)}$$

For the store ordering swim suits, we have already found that

$$1 - \alpha = 0.7561$$

Hence, from Table 3 of the appendix we find

$$z_\alpha = z_{.2439} = 0.69$$

If peak period demand for swim suits is thought to be normally distributed with mean 1000 and standard deviation 200, we find, using (14.17)

$$Q_{opt} = 1000 + (0.69)(200) = 1138$$

Therefore, if expected costs are to be minimized, 1138 swim suits should be ordered.

EXERCISES

14.1. A distributor stocks portable radios, for which annual demand is 6500, and is constant over a working year of 52 five-day weeks. These radios cost the distributor $20 each. It is estimated that inventory holding costs are 20% per annum of the value of inventory, and it costs $100 to place an order. The delay between the placement of an order and its receipt is 3 working days. The distributor wants to minimize total inventory costs, with no stock-outs.

(a) What is the optimal order quantity?

(b) How many orders per year should be placed?

(c) What is the average level of inventory holdings?

(d) Find the reorder point.

14.2. A distributor of wine faces, for a brand of California red, an annual demand at a constant rate of 5000 cases. The distributor works 50 weeks a year, 5 days per week. Each case of wine is valued at $30. Inventory holding costs are estimated at 25% per annum of the value of inventory, and it costs $75 to place an order. Each order is received 4 working days after placement. The distributor wishes to avoid stock-outs, and, subject to this constraint, to minimize total inventory costs.

(a) What is the optimal order quantity?

(b) How many orders per year should be placed?

(c) What is the average level of inventory holdings?

(d) Find the reorder point.

250 days

14.3. A manufacturer of two-wheel bicycles produces, over a working year of 50 five-day weeks, at a constant rate of 100 bicycles per week. Tires for these bicycles are ordered from an outside supplier, at a cost of $5 per tire. The manufacturer estimates that it costs $80 to place an order, and that holding costs are 18% per annum of the value of inventory. Delivery of tires is guaranteed three days after an order is placed. The manufacturer wants to minimize total inventory costs but insists that production should not be held up through a shortage of tires.

(a) How many tires per order should be purchased?

(b) How many orders per year should be placed?

(c) What is the average number of tires held in inventory?

(d) Find the reorder point.

(e) What is the minimum achievable annual inventory cost?

14.4. Under the assumptions of the EOQ model, a distributor is currently placing orders of optimal quantity Q_{opt}. By how much will total cost increase if order quantity is doubled?

14.5. A distributor faces a constant rate of demand for a product, the other assumptions of the EOQ model also being satisfied. Order quantities are determined so that total inventory costs are as small as possible. This distributor intends to expand his territory and anticipates that this will yield a 25% increase in demand, which will continue to be at a constant rate. Ordering costs and unit inventory holding costs are expected to be unchanged. The distributor asserts that his best strategy now is to increase order quantities by 25%. Do you agree? Without using algebra, present for the distributor an explanation of your conclusion.

14.6. Given the assumptions of the EOQ model, show that the lowest possible total annual inventory cost is given by

$$TC_{opt} = \sqrt{2DC_OC_H}$$

14.7. Refer to Exercise 14.1. The distributor of portable radios is not completely certain about estimated ordering costs and holding costs. Consider the possible values $80, $100, and $120 for placing an order, and possible holding costs of 15%, 20%, and 25% per year of the value of inventory. For these nine possible cost combinations, compute the economic order quantities and find the largest percentage increase in total inventory costs that can result from using the solution to Exercise 14.1 in place of the optimal order quantity. Comment on your results.

14.8. A distributor finds that by automating part of the process, ordering costs can be reduced by 25%. What effect does this have on the minimum achievable total annual inventory costs, given that the assumptions of the EOQ model are satisfied?

14.9. Refer to Exercise 14.2. The wine distributor wants to consider nine possible combinations of values for ordering costs and holding costs. These involve possible ordering costs of $50, $75, and $100, and holding costs of 20%, 25%, and 30% per annum of the value of inventory. Find the economic order quantities. What is the largest increase in total inventory costs that arises from using the solution to Exercise 14.2 in place of these optimal quantities? Comment on your findings.

14.10. A company, operating over 250 working days per year manufactures desk lamps. Annual demand for these lamps is 10,000 and occurs at a constant rate. Each lamp is valued at $15. The company has the capacity to manufacture 24,000 lamps per year, if the process is in operation every day. It is estimated that holding costs amount to 20% per annum of the value of inventory, and that to start up a production run costs $1000. The company intends to produce lot sizes such that total inventory costs are as small as possible, with the constraint that there be no shortages.

(a) What is the optimal production lot size?

(b) What is the average level of inventory holdings?

(c) How many working days are taken up by a single production run?

(d) How many working days are there in a single nonproduction period?

(e) What is the mininum attainable total annual inventory cost?

14.11. A manufacturer produces several types of lawnmowers, requiring different sized engines which are made in-house. Demand for one type of engine is constant at 20 per day, over a year of 250 working days. It is possible to produce 40 engines per day, with those not immediately required held in inventory. Each engine is valued at $40. It is estimated that annual holding cost is 15% of the value of inventory, and that it costs $750 to set up a production run for these engines. The manufacturer wants to avoid stock-outs, and, subject to this constraint, to minimize total inventory costs.

(a) What is the optimal production lot size?

(b) What is the highest level that inventory holdings will reach?

(c) How many working days are occupied by a single production run?

(d) How many working days make up a single nonproduction period?

(e) What is the minimum possible total annual inventory cost?

14.12. Consider again the bicycle manufacturer of Exercise 14.3. The manufacturer is considering producing tires in-house, rather than from an outside supplier. It is estimated that each tire will cost $4.50 to produce, and that available capacity allows the production of 100 tires per day. Inventory holding costs are still estimated at 18% per annum of the value of inventory. Also, in addition to the production costs, it costs $500 to set up a production run. There are to be no stock-outs.

(a) What is the optimal production lot size?

(b) What is the average level of inventory holdings?

(c) How many working days are taken up by a single production run?

(d) How many working days constitute a single nonproduction period?

(e) What is the minimum possible total annual inventory cost?

(f) Will it pay the bicycle manufacturer to produce the tires in-house, rather than ordering from the outside supplier, as in Exercise 14.3?

14.13. (a) Given the assumptions of the economic production lot size model, the optimal production lot size is given by equation (14.7). Show that under this solution, annual holding costs will be equal to annual start-up costs.

(b) Verify the result of (a) by drawing, for the manufacturer of desk lamps of Exercise 14.10, a graph showing annual holding costs, start-up costs, and total costs as functions of production lot size.

14.14. Given the assumptions of the economic production lot size model, show that the lowest possible total annual inventory cost is given by

$$TC_{opt} = \sqrt{2DC_OC_H(1 - D/P)}$$

14.15. A manufacturer, operating under the conditions assumed by the economic production lot size model, anticipates a 20% increase in demand, and plans a 20% increase in production capacity. Start-up and holding costs are expected to remain unchanged. Should production lot size also be increased by 20%? Justify your answer algebraically and verbally.

14.16. Under the assumptions of the economic production lot size model, optimal production lot size is given by equation (14.7). Show that as production capacity increases, this expression eventually approaches

$$Q_{opt} = \sqrt{\frac{2DC_O}{C_H}}$$

Interpret this finding.

14.17. The optimal solution to the economic production lot size model involves a cycle of production periods followed by nonproduction periods. Show that the production and nonproduction periods will be of the same length if, and only if, daily production capacity is equal to twice daily demand level.

14.18. A distributor is given the alternative of receiving, at the same cost, entire orders in single consignments, or of receiving the items ordered at a steady rate over time until the entire quantity ordered has been delivered. Ordering costs and holding costs as a percentage of inventory value are unaffected by the option chosen. Using the results of Exercises 14.6 and 14.14, determine which alternative should be chosen. Provide a verbal justification for your answer.

14.19. Refer to Exercise 14.10. The manufacturer of desk lamps is not certain about estimated holding costs or start-up costs. Consider the possible values $800, $1000 and $1200 for starting up a production run, and possible holding costs of 15%, 20%, and 25% per annum of the value of inventory. For these nine possible cost combinations, compute the economic production lot sizes and find the largest percentage increase in total inventory costs that can result from using the solution to Exercise 14.10 in place of the optimal production lot size. Comment on your findings.

14.20. Refer to Exercise 14.1. Suppose, now, that the distributor of portable radios permits stock-outs. Backorder costs are estimated at $15 per unit per year. The other problem specifications remain unchanged. The objective is to minimize total inventory costs.

 (a) What is the optimal order quantity?

 (b) What will be the maximum backorder level?

 (c) How many orders per year should be placed?

 (d) What is the maximum inventory level?

 (e) What is the lowest achievable total annual inventory cost?

 (f) By comparison with the answer to Exercise 14.1, how much per annum is saved by allowing backorders?

14.21. Refer to Exercise 14.2. Suppose that the wine distributor allows stock-outs. The distributor estimates backorder costs at $30 per case per annum. The other problem specifications are as in Exercise 14.2. The distributor's objective remains the minimization of total inventory costs.

 (a) What is the optimal order quantity?

 (b) Find the maximum backorder level.

 (c) How many orders per year should be placed?

 (d) Find the maximum level of inventory.

 (e) Find the average inventory level.

 (f) Find the average backorder level.

 (g) Over what proportion of the time is there zero inventory?

 (h) What is the lowest achievable total annual inventory cost?

 (i) By comparison with the answer to Exercise 14.2, how much per annum is saved by allowing backorders?

14.22. For the EOQ model with stock-outs permitted, show that under the mininum total inventory cost solution, there will be zero inventory a proportion $C_H/(C_H + C_B)$ of the time, where C_H and C_B denote, respectively, annual unit holding and backorder costs.

14.23. For the EOQ model with stock-outs optimal order quantity, and maximum backorder level are given, respectively, by equations (14.9) and (14.10). Examine the behavior of these solutions as unit annual backorder cost, C_B, becomes increasingly large. Comment on your findings.

14.24. For the EOQ model with stock-outs, the optimal solution is given by equations (14.9) and (14.10). Show that under this solution, annual ordering costs will be equal to the sum of annual holding and backorder costs.

14.25. Given the assumptions of the EOQ model with stock-outs, show that the lowest possible total annual inventory cost is given by

$$TC_{opt} = \sqrt{\frac{2DC_oC_HC_B}{(C_H + C_B)}}$$

By comparison with the result of Exercise 14.6, show that under the EOQ model, total inventory costs are reduced by permitting stock-outs for any finite level of backorder costs.

14.26. The distributor of Exercise 14.20 is fairly sure of the parameters of the inventory management problem, with the exception of backorder costs. Consider possible backorder costs of $5, $10, $20, and $25 per unit per year. For each of these backorder cost levels, compute the optimal order quantities and maximum backorder levels, and compare the resulting total annual inventory costs with those that would follow from using the solution to Exercise 14.20. Comment on your results.

14.27. A distributor of beer, over a year of 50 working weeks, faces a constant demand for a particular brand of 500 cases per week. Whatever its size, it costs $30 to place an order for this beer, and inventory holding costs are estimated at 20% of the value of inventory per annum. No stock-outs are to be permitted. The distributor is offered four price schedules, depending on the size of orders, as shown in the table below:

PRICE SCHEDULE	ORDER QUANTITY (CASES)	PRICE PER CASE
(i)	less than 1000	$6.10
(ii)	1000–1499	$6.00
(iii)	1500–1999	$5.90
(iv)	2000 or more	$5.80

This is the ANS

The objective is to minimize the sum of total price paid for the beer and inventory costs over a year.

(a) What is the optimal order quantity?

(b) How many orders per year should be placed?

(c) What is the average level of inventory holdings?

(d) What is the minimum achievable level for the sum of annual price paid and inventory costs?

14.28. The beer distributor of Exercise 14.27 stocks a second brand of beer, for which weekly demand is 400 cases. Again, it costs $30 to place an order, and holding costs are 20% per annum of the value of inventory. This beer is purchased from the manufacturer at $6 per case. The distributor's aim is to minimize total costs, subject to there being no stock-outs. What price must the manufacturer offer in order to persuade this distributor to double order sizes?

14.29. A distributor carries a brand of portable radio for which annual demand is 6500 units. The cost of placing an order, whatever its size, is $100, and holding costs are estimated at 20% per annum of the value of inventory. The distributor permits stock-outs, backorder costs being estimated at $15 per unit per year. The distributor is offered five price schedules, depending on order quantities, as shown in the accompanying table:

PRICE SCHEDULE	ORDER QUANTITY	PRICE PER UNIT
(i)	less than 500	$20.25
(ii)	500– 749	$20.00
(iii)	750– 999	$19.75
(iv)	1000–1249	$19.50
(v)	1250 or more	$19.25

The distributor wants to minimize the sum of total price paid and inventory costs.

(a) What is the optimal order quantity?

(b) What will be the maximum backorder level?

(c) How many orders per year should be placed?

(d) What is the maximum inventory level?

(e) What is the average inventory level?

(f) What is the average backorder level?

(g) What is the minimum achievable level for the sum of annual price paid and inventory costs?

14.30. In six weeks time, a corporation must produce 80 units of product A. Each unit of this product requires 3 units each of components B and C, both of which are made in-house. The production process requires 2 weeks. It takes 2 weeks to produce component B, each unit of output requiring 2 units of component D and 3 units of component E. Production of component C takes one week, and for each unit of output 2 units of D and one unit of E are needed. Components D and E are ordered from outside suppliers, the delay times being respectively one and 2 weeks. Initial inventory holdings are 50 units each of B and C, and 100 units each of D and E. At the end of the 6-week period, the corporation wants to hold an inventory of 20 units each of B, C, D, and E. Use the MRP approach to develop an ordering and production schedule.

14.31. In 8 weeks time, a corporation must fill an order for 100 units of product A. Each unit of this product requires 2 units of component B and 3 units each of components C and D, with the production process taking 2 weeks. Components B, C, and D are all manufactured in-house. Production of component B takes one week, and, for each unit of output, 2 units each of components E, F, and G are required. Each unit of component C requires one unit of component E and 3 units of component F, with a production time of 2 weeks. Each unit of component D requires one unit of F and 3 units of G, with a production time of 3 weeks. Components E, F, and G must all be ordered from outside suppliers, the delay times being respectively one, 2, and 3 weeks. There are no initial inventory holdings, and no inventory is required at the end of the period. Use the MRP approach to develop an ordering and production schedule.

14.32. When the manufacturer of Exercise 14.31 first places an order for component G, it is learned that supplies will not be available for several months. However, a second supplier promises delivery in 4 weeks. Obtain a modified ordering and production schedule so that 100 units of product A can be manufactured as quickly as possible. (Assume that supplies of E and F will be available with the usual delivery times.)

14.33. A distributor with a working year of 52 five-day weeks stocks portable radios for which daily demand is normally distributed with mean 25 and standard deviation 4 units. The radios cost the distributor $20 each. Holding costs are 20% per annum of the value of inventory, and it costs $100 to place an order. The lead time for an order is 3 working days. The distributor sets order quantity at the EOQ optimal solution for demand at its mean rate. (Refer to Exercise 14.1.) It is required that the expected number of stock-outs be one per year.

(a) What is the probability of a stock-out during any given lead time period?

(b) What should be the reorder point?

(c) Find the annual safety stock holding cost.

14.34. Refer to Exercise 14.33. What would be the expected number of stock-outs per year for the following reorder points?

(a) 75 radios

(b) 100 radios

14.35. A distributor, with a working year of 50 five-day weeks carries a brand of California red wine for which daily demand is normally distributed with mean 20 and standard deviation 2 cases. Each case costs the distributor $30. Holding costs are 25% per annum of the value of inventory, and ordering costs are $75 per order. The lead time for an order is 4 working days. Order quantity is set at the EOQ optimal solution for demand at its mean rate. (Refer to Exercise 14.2.) The distributor wants an expected number of stock-outs of two per year.

(a) What is the probability of a stock-out during any given lead time period?

(b) What should be the reorder point?

(c) Find the annual safety stock holding cost.

(d) By how much would annual safety stock holding cost increase if the expected number of stock-outs was reduced to one per year?

14.36. Refer to Exercise 14.35. What would be the expected number of stock-outs per year for the following reorder points?

(a) 80 cases of wine

(b) 100 cases of wine

14.37. A distributor of canned soup with a working year of 50 five-day weeks faces, for vegetable soup, a daily demand that is normally distributed with mean 80 and standard deviation 15 cases. Each case costs the distributor $10. Holding costs are 20% per annum of the value of inventory, and it cost $50 to place an order, whatever its size. The lead time for an order is 3 working days. The distributor sets order quantity at the EOQ optimal solution for demand at its mean rate. It is required that the expected number of stock-outs be 1.5 per year.

(a) What is the order quantity?

(b) Find the probability of a stock-out during any given lead time period.

(c) What should be the reorder point?

(d) Find the annual safety stock holding cost.

(e) By how much would annual safety stock holding cost increase if the expected number of stock-outs were reduced to one per year?

(f) What would be the expected number of stock-outs per year for a reorder point of 320 cases?

14.38. A distributor of canned cat food pays $12 per case for this product. It costs $60 to place an order, and inventory holding costs are 20% per annum of the value of inventory. The distributor works a year of 50 five-day weeks, and lead time for an order is 4 working days. The distributor sets order quantity at the EOQ optimal solution for demand at its mean rate. The accompanying table shows probabilities for different demand levels over periods of 4 working days.

DEMAND	PROBABILITY	DEMAND	PROBABILITY
55	0.10	75	0.20
60	0.10	80	0.10
65	0.15	85	0.05
70	0.30		

Shortage costs are estimated at 75 cents per case.

(a) Find the expected demand over periods of 4 working days.

(b) Find the expected annual demand.

(c) Find the order quantity.

(d) For each possible reorder point, find the expected number of shortages per lead time period.

(e) For each possible reorder point, find expected annual shortage costs.

(f) For each possible reorder point, find annual holding costs in excess of those that would result from a reorder point of 55 cases.

(g) Find the optimal reorder point.

14.39. Refer to Exercise 14.38. For what range of values of shortage costs does your solution to part (g) of that exercise remain the optimal reorder point?

14.40. The distributor of the previous two exercises also handles canned dog food which costs $15 per case. Order costs are $70 per order, and holding cost is again 20% per annum of the value of inventory. Lead time for an order is 2 days. Order quantity is set at the EOQ optimal solution for demand at the expected rate, and shortage costs are estimated at 75 cents per case. For any given day, the distributor anticipates 3 possible demand levels—20, 25, and 30 cases, with respective probabilities of 0.2, 0.5, 0.3. Demand on any day is independent of that on any other.

(a) Find the expected demand per day.

(b) Find the expected annual demand.

(c) Find the order quantity.

(d) Find the possible demand levels for 2-day periods and their associated probabilities.

(e) For each possible reorder point find the expected number of shortages per lead time period.

(f) For each possible reorder point find expected annual shortage costs.

(g) For each possible reorder point find annual holding costs in excess of those that would result from a reorder point of 40 cases.

(h) Find the optimal reorder point.

(i) For what range of values of shortage costs does the solution to part (h) remain the optimal reorder point?

14.41. A drug store chain stocks copies of an out-of-town newspaper. These papers are purchased for 25 cents per copy and sold for 30 cents each. Any papers that are unsold at the end of the day are thrown away. Daily demand for this paper is believed to be normally distributed with mean 1000 and standard deviation 150 copies. Each customer requesting a copy of this paper when none is available is counted as a goodwill loss of 6 cents. Find the optimal number of newspapers to be ordered by the drug store chain.

14.42. A retailer is operating in a situation in which the assumptions of the single period inventory model are satisfied. What is the effect on optimal order quantity of:

(a) An increase in salvage value, with everything else remaining fixed?

(b) An increase in unit goodwill loss, with all else fixed?

14.43. A retailer operates in a situation in which the assumptions of the single period inventory model are satisfied. Demand is normally distributed with mean μ. Show that the optimal order quantity is equal to μ, if and only if, unit overstock cost is equal to unit understock cost.

14.44. A bakery makes cream cakes. Each cake costs 35 cents to make and can be sold on the day it is made, for 50 cents. Any unsold cakes will be sold the following day for 25 cents each. Each unsatisfied order for a fresh cream cake is counted as a goodwill loss of 5 cents. Find the optimal number of cakes that should be baked in any day if demand for fresh cakes is normally distributed with mean 500 and standard deviation 50.

14.45. A chain store manager must decide how many overcoats to purchase to meet the coming peak season demand. The store purchases these coats for $60 and sells them for $75 each. At the end of the peak season, a sale will be held, and it is anticipated that the remaining stock can be sold for $35 per coat. Each customer unable to purchase a coat during the peak season is counted as a $5 goodwill loss. Management uncertainty about peak season demand can be represented by a normal distribution with mean 1000 and standard deviation 250 coats.

(a) What is the optimal order quantity?
(b) Given that the optimal order quantity is chosen, what is the probability that inventory will be exhausted by the end of the peak season?

Management of Spare Parts: The U.S. Army Wholesale Supply System[1]

The U.S. Army formerly had a policy of not holding stocks of certain spare parts, but simply purchasing the amount requested at the time a requisition was received. This policy led to high ordering costs through the need to frequently place orders for small quantities, and to high imputed backorder costs due to delivery delays. Dissatisfaction with this procedure led to the introduction of a **minimum buy** policy for nonstocked parts. Under this policy, if an order was received for an item not in stock, the size of the purchase actually made was at least some specified mininum, say $100. Any excess amount over immediate requirements was then held in inventory, so that holding costs were incurred.

Based on records of past requisition patterns, the authors of this study evaluated four alternative inventory management procedures for 2392 aviation parts. The four procedures examined were:

1. No minimum buy: purchase only the amount requisitioned.
2. Minimum buy: different dollar levels for the minimum purchase size were examined.
3. Buy an additional dollar amount in addition to the amount requisitioned. (Again different levels for this additional purchase were evaluated.)
4. Buy the economic order quantity in addition to the amount demanded.

The authors estimated, given past demand patterns, the various costs incurred for each of these approaches. For approaches 2 and 3 dollar levels of $100 were found to be superior to the other alternatives tested. The estimated total costs per requisition were $356.91 for the no minimum buy policy, $274.22 for the minimum buy approach, $260.69 for the additional purchase policy, and $252.08 for the policy of purchasing the economic order quantity in addition to the amount demanded. This study serves to demonstrate the impressive savings that can be generated by a more scientific approach to inventory management.

---

[1] This discussion is based on A. Kaplan and S. Frazza, "Empirical Inventory Simulation: A Case Study," *Decision Sciences, 14* (1983), 62–75.

queueing

CHAPTER FIFTEEN

15.1. THE WAITING LINE PROBLEM

The subject of this chapter is one with which we are all familiar from frustrating experience. We have all waited in lines at supermarket checkout counters, hairdressers, or tollbooths. In this kind of situation we accept that some delay, though tedious, is almost inevitable. However, we are likely to react unfavorably to an excessively long wait. How often have you stood in a supermarket checkout line and cursed management for not providing more clerks to speed things up? In such circumstances, customers may feel sufficiently aggrieved to try another store next time. Obviously, management wants to provide good service, so as not to discourage customers from returning, and will therefore also be concerned about the amount of time customers spend waiting in line. The importance of studying the waiting line problem in the service industries, then, is clear.

However, the applicability of **waiting line,** or **queueing,** models extends further. For example, at various stages in a manufacturing process, partly finished or finished products will be examined for defects. Products leaving an assembly line will be checked by one or more inspectors. If there are too few inspectors and the inspection process is slow, the result could be costly hold-ups in the production process, while the employment of more inspectors than is really necessary will result in labor costs that are higher than they need be. A thorough study of the system through which products arrive at an inspection station and are checked should shed some light on the problem.

In subsequent sections of this chapter we will study the characteristics of queueing systems by reference to a corporate department that generates a good deal of photocopying work. At the present time management in this department has noticed increasing demand for the one photocopier that is currently owned. The system that is currently in operation involves individual secretaries bringing work to the copier, waiting in line until the machine is free, and then carrying out their own photocopying. Historically this arrangement has caused no great concern, but, as a result of increased demand, it is suspected that too much valuable employee time is expended in unproductive queueing. There are a number of possible solutions to this dilemma, including the purchase of an additional photocopier, or the lease or purchase of a more efficient machine to replace the existing copier. As a first step, however, it is deemed desirable to carry out a thorough investigation of the current position.

The characteristics of a general waiting line problem can be examined under three main headings, as follows:

(i) *The Arrival Process.* We can think of the people or objects arriving at a waiting line as coming from a population of potential customers. Obviously, a critical factor in determining the features of the queue is the timing of these arrivals. Rarely will it be realistic to view this timing in a deterministic framework. Customers for the photocopying machine, for example, will not arrive precisely three minutes apart. Rather, the arrival process will almost inevitably involve a chance, or random, element. Thus, while it would be useful to know that, *on average,* one customer per three minutes comes to the copying machine, we must go further and consider the likelihood of periods of differing intensities of demand.

(ii) *Waiting Line Discipline.* If service is immediately available when a customer arrives, then all is well. However, if others are waiting, then some criteria are required to determine service priorities for waiting customers. The system with which we are most familiar, and on which we will concentrate most of our attention here, is **first-in-first-out (FIFO)**. Here, customers are served in the order in which they arrive at the queue. The FIFO discipline is certainly widely applicable but not invariably appropriate. For example, a machine shop repair crew will almost certainly not work on malfunctioning equipment in this way. Some pieces of equipment will be more critical to the production process than others, and will have to be given a higher priority than less important equipment that has been waiting longer for service.

(iii) *The Service Process.* Finally it is necessary to characterize the process by which customers are served. Two factors are of particular importance. In our photocopying example, just a single machine is available to carry out the work. We refer to this as **single-channel** service. By contrast, the typical supermarket has several checkout counters available for arriving customers, a situation called **multiple-channel** service. The second factor that must be considered is the time taken to complete the service of a customer. This time will vary from customer to customer, and must be characterized by a random variable whose distribution depicts the distribution of service times.

The position we have just described is outlined schematically in Figure 15.1. A member of the population of customers arrives at the service facility and joins a waiting line. A procedure for determining which of the waiting customers will be served next is in place. Often this is simply first-in-first-out, but a more complex system for assigning priorities may be employed. Once selected for service, a customer enters a service channel, departing from the facility once service has been completed.

In the remainder of this chapter we will discuss specific queueing models and show how the characteristics of the waiting line process can be found.

FIGURE 15.2 Part of a probability function for the number of arrivals in a fifteen-minute period at the photocopier.

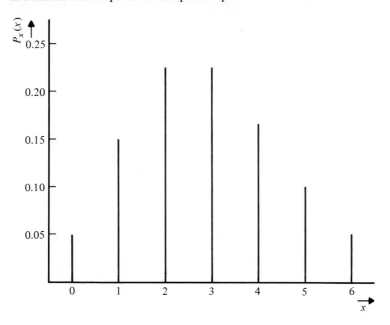

We now note two properties of the Poisson distribution that will be useful in our analysis of this queueing problem:

(i) As we noted in Chapter 10, if the random variable X obeys a Poisson distribution, then, *over a very small fraction of the time interval,* the probability it takes any value greater than one is negligibly small. Let h be a very small fraction of our arrival time interval. Then, the expected number of arrivals in this small space of time is λh. Hence, since we need consider the possibilities only of zero or one arrivals, it follows that

$$P(1 \text{ arrival}) = \lambda h; \ P(0 \text{ arrivals}) = 1 - \lambda h$$

To illustrate, suppose we consider a time segment of 6 seconds, which is a fraction 1/150 of the fifteen minute time interval. Then, to a good approximation, we have

$$P(1 \text{ arrival}) = \lambda h = \frac{3}{150} = 0.02$$

$$P(0 \text{ arrivals}) = 1 - \lambda h = 0.98$$

(ii) Again, following our discussion of Chapter 10, we know that if the number of occurrences of an event in a time period follows a Poisson distribution, the time between occurrences obeys an **exponential distribution.** Specifically, if the number of arrivals at a service facility follows a Poisson distribution with mean λ per time period, then the random variable Y, representing the time (in terms of that period) between successive arrivals, has probability density function

$$f_Y(y) = \lambda e^{-\lambda y} \qquad \text{for } y \geq 0$$

This distribution has mean $1/\lambda$. Thus, for the photocopier example, since $\lambda = 3$, the mean, or expected, time that elapses between successive arrivals is $\frac{1}{3}$ of fifteen minutes, or five minutes. The cumulative distribution function of the exponential distribution is given by

$$F_Y(y) = P(Y \le y) = 1 - e^{-\lambda y}$$

Thus, for example, we find for our problem that the probability that no more than 6 minutes (that is, 40% of 15 minutes) elapses between successive arrivals is

$$F_Y(0.4) = P(Y \le 0.4) = 1 - e^{-(3)(0.4)} = 1 - e^{-1.2}$$
$$= 1 - 0.301194 = 0.698806$$

Hence 69.88% of the time no more than 6 minutes will elapse between successive arrivals. Similarly, the probability that at most 30 minutes elapses between successive arrivals is (since 30 is twice 15)

$$P\left(Y \le \frac{30}{15}\right) = F_Y(2) = 1 - e^{-(3)(2)} = 1 - e^{-6}$$
$$= 1 - 0.002479 = 0.997521$$

The Poisson Arrival Distribution

(a) If the number of arrivals X in any given time interval obeys a Poisson distribution with mean λ, its probability function is given by

$$P_X(x) = e^{-\lambda} \frac{\lambda^x}{x!} \quad \text{for } x = 0, 1, 2, \ldots$$

(b) If h is a very small fraction of the given time interval, the probabilities for zero and one arrivals in this space of time are well approximated by $(1 - \lambda h)$ and λh, respectively, with probabilities for more than one arrival negligibly small.

(c) If number of arrivals in a time interval follows a Poisson distribution, the time Y between successive arrivals has an exponential distribution, with
  (i) Expected time between arrivals equal to $1/\lambda$
  (ii) Probability that time between successive arrivals does not exceed y given by

$$F_Y(y) = 1 - e^{-\lambda y}$$

where y is measured in terms of the original time interval.

SERVICE TIME DISTRIBUTION

We will not usually want to assume that each customer service takes the same amount of time. It is more realistic to represent service times by a continuous random variable. The most commonly applied distribution for this purpose is the **exponential distribution.** This has been found to well represent service time over a wide range of practical applications, and also has considerable theoretical advantages in the study of the characteristics of a queueing problem. The exponential distribution will not yield an adequate description of service times in all practical applications, and it is advisable to collect data to verify its suitability.

Although in some circumstances another continuous probability distribution, such as the normal, may be preferable, we will assume here that the exponential distribution is to be used to represent service times.

Let the random variable Y denote the time taken to complete a single service, where time is measured in some convenient unit (In fact, we will use the same units to describe the service distribution as the arrival distribution). Then, if Y obeys an exponential distribution, its probability density function is given by

$$f_Y(y) = \mu e^{-\mu y} \qquad \text{for } y \geq 0$$

where μ denotes the average number of customers that can be served per unit time interval, so that the mean service time is $1/\mu$. The cumulative distribution function, which gives the probability that a service time will not exceed the specific value y, is

$$F_Y(y) = 1 - e^{-\mu y}$$

The average time spent by users of the photocopying machine is three minutes, so that, on average, five customers per 15 minute period can be served. Substituting $\mu = 5$ then yields the cumulative distribution function as

$$F_Y(y) = 1 - e^{-5y} \qquad\qquad (15.3)$$

Table 15.1 shows probabilities computed from equation (15.3) using Table 2 of the Appendix, and the cumulative distribution is drawn in Figure 15.3. We see, then, for example, for the probability that a single service will take less than a minute and a half, with $y = 1.5/15 = 0.1$,

$$F_Y(0.1) = 1 - e^{-0.5} = 1 - 0.606531 = 0.393469$$

TABLE 15.1 Cumulative probabilities for the photocopier service times.

SERVICE TIME (MINUTES)	y	$F_Y(y) = 1 - e^{-5y}$
0	0	0
0.3	0.02	0.095163
0.6	0.04	0.181269
0.9	0.06	0.259182
1.2	0.08	0.329680
1.5	0.10	0.393469
1.8	0.12	0.451188
2.4	0.16	0.550671
3.0	0.20	0.632121
3.6	0.24	0.698806
4.8	0.32	0.798103
6.0	0.40	0.864665
9.0	0.60	0.950213

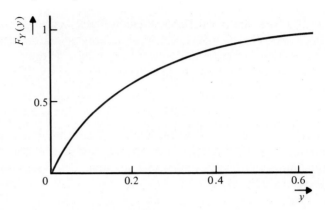

Therefore, 39.35% of all users occupy the machine for less than a minute and a half.

We have already noted the duality between the exponential and Poisson distributions. Thus, a consequence of our assumption of an exponential distribution for service times is that the number of customers that can be served over the unit time period has a Poisson distribution with mean μ. It follows, then, that for a very small fraction of this time period, to a close approximation,

$P(1 \text{ customer can be served}) = \mu h; P(0 \text{ customers can be served}) = 1 - \mu h$

and the probability that more than one customer can be served is negligibly small.

The Exponential Service Distribution

(a) If the mean number of customers per time period that can be served is μ, and service time Y follows an exponential distribution, then:
   (i) Mean service time is $1/\mu$
   (ii) The probability that for a single customer, service time is at most y is

$$F_Y(y) = 1 - e^{-\mu y}$$

(b) If h is a very small fraction of the time interval, the probabilities that zero and one customers can be served in this space of time are approximately $(1 - \mu h)$ and μh, respectively, with probabilities for higher numbers negligibly small.

CHARACTERIZATION OF THE STEADY STATE

Having specified arrival and service time distributions, it is possible to provide a fairly full description of queue behavior. We set down below the assumptions required for our results.

The last of these assumptions is necessary unless there is to be, on the average, a steady build up over time of customers waiting for service, so that the queue will tend to grow longer as time goes on. If this assumption does hold, we can imagine a situation where, after an initial starting up span of time, the queueing system settles into a **steady state**, where its characteristics remain constant over time. To illustrate, consider our photocopying machine example. At the beginning of the day, when the service facility is first opened, there will be no customers. Then customers will arrive and be served, according to the arrival and service distributions. The characteristics of the queue will then evolve from the initial point at the opening time of the facility. In fact, given the assumptions made above, it can be demonstrated that the system eventually reaches a steady state, in the sense that the probability distribution for the number of customers in the service facility becomes constant over time. It is this steady state that we are able to describe, in relatively straightforward terms, as a function of the mean potential service rate and mean arrival rate of customers.

Given the five assumptions made above, it is possible to set down the characteristics of a queueing system. The derivations of these results, which are somewhat involved, are provided in Appendix A15.1 at the end of this chapter.[1] The conclusions are set out in the box below.

Some Characteristics of the Steady State for a Single-Channel Queueing Model

1. The probability that there are no customers in the service facility is

$$P_0 = 1 - \frac{\lambda}{\mu}$$

2. For any nonnegative integer n, the probability of n customers in the service facility is

$$P_n = \left(\frac{\lambda}{\mu}\right)^n P_0 = \left(\frac{\lambda}{\mu}\right)^n \left(1 - \frac{\lambda}{\mu}\right)$$

---

[1] Readers may skip the material in this appendix without loss of continuity.

3. The probability that an arriving customer will have to wait for service is

$$1 - P_0 = \frac{\lambda}{\mu}$$

This is therefore the proportion of the time that the server is in use, and is referred to as the **utilization rate,** for which the symbol ρ is employed. Hence

$$\rho = \frac{\lambda}{\mu}$$

4. The average number of customers in the service facility is

$$L_S = \frac{\lambda}{\mu - \lambda}$$

5. The average time spent by a customer in the service facility is

$$W_S = \frac{1}{\mu - \lambda}$$

6. The average number of customers waiting in line for service is

$$L_Q = \frac{\lambda}{\mu - \lambda} - \frac{\lambda}{\mu} = \frac{\lambda^2}{\mu(\mu - \lambda)}$$

7. The average time spent by customers waiting in line for service is

$$W_Q = \frac{1}{\mu - \lambda} - \frac{1}{\mu} = \frac{\lambda}{\mu(\mu - \lambda)}$$

8. For any nonnegative integer K, the probability that there are more than K customers in the service facility is

$$P_{n>K} = \left(\frac{\lambda}{\mu}\right)^{K+1}$$

In this notation, the distinction between L_S and W_S on the one hand and L_Q and W_Q on the other is that the latter refer only to time spent and number of customers waiting for service, while the former include also time spent and number of customers being served.

It can be seen that given a Poisson distribution for arrivals and an exponential distribution for service times, a very full characterization of the queueing system can be achieved in terms of just two parameters—the mean potential service rate and the mean arrival rate. We will illustrate these formulae for the photocopying machine example, where customers arrive at an average rate of three per 15 minute period and, on average, five customers can be served in periods of this length, so that

$$\lambda = 3; \mu = 5$$

We can then set out the characteristics of the queue. It should be emphasized that our results refer to the steady state, so that the start-up period, before this state is reached, is ignored. Using the above formulae, we find:

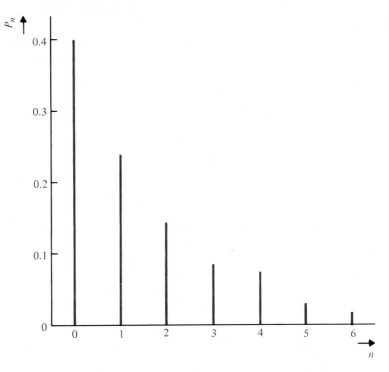

FIGURE 15.4 Probabilities P_n for numbers n of customers in service facility for the photocopier.

1.
$$P_0 = 1 - \frac{\lambda}{\mu} = 1 - \frac{3}{5} = 0.4$$

Therefore, the probability is 0.4 that there will be no customers in the service facility.

2. The probability of n customers in the facility is
$$P_n = \left(\frac{\lambda}{\mu}\right)^n P_0 = (0.6)^n(0.4)$$

Therefore, for example, the probability that there will be two customers in the facility is
$$P_2 = (0.6)^2(0.4) = 0.144$$

This set of probabilities is conveniently described graphically, as in Figure 15.4.

3. The utilization rate of the photocopier is
$$\rho = 1 - P_0 = 1 - 0.4 = 0.6$$

implying that the machine is in use 60% of the time.

4. The average number of customers in the facility is
$$L_S = \frac{\lambda}{\mu - \lambda} = \frac{3}{5 - 3} = 1.5$$

Therefore, on average over time, we would find 1.5 customers in the facility.

5. The average time spent in the facility is

$$W_S = \frac{1}{\mu - \lambda} = \frac{1}{5 - 3} = 0.5$$

Since we are measuring time in units of 15 minutes, it follows that on average, customers will spend 7.5 minutes in the photocopying facility.

6. The average number of customers waiting in line is

$$L_Q = \frac{\lambda}{\mu - \lambda} - \frac{\lambda}{\mu} = 1.5 - 0.6 = 0.9$$

so that the average number, over time, of customers waiting for service is 0.9.

7. The average time spent waiting in line is

$$W_Q = \frac{1}{\mu - \lambda} - \frac{1}{\mu} = 0.5 - 0.2 = 0.3$$

Hence, since we are dealing with 15-minute time intervals, customers will spend, on average, 4.5 minutes waiting in line.

8. The probability of more than K customers in the facility is

$$P_{n>K} = \left(\frac{\lambda}{\mu}\right)^{K+1} = (0.6)^{K+1}$$

Hence, for example, the probability that there will be more than two customers in the facility is

$$P_{n>2} = (0.6)^3 = 0.216$$

Some of these probabilities are graphed in Figure 15.5.

One application of this analysis is to the comparison of alternative systems. For example, by varying λ, we could study the effects of changing demand rates, as reflected by varying average rates of arrival, on the characteristics of the queue. Alternatively, suppose that the photocopier in current use is leased, and the company is considering, at the end of the lease period, three alternative machines. One of these is similar to the current copier, while the other two can serve respectively four and six customers per 15-minute period, on average. Table 15.2 summarizes some of the queue characteristics for values of $\mu = 4, 5, 6$, with λ set at three arrivals per 15 minutes.

From Table 15.2 we can read, for example, that the fastest of these machines would be in use just half the time, while the slowest would be employed three-quarters of the time. The values for W_S imply that customers of the fastest machine can expect to spend 5 minutes in the service facility, while those of the slowest machine would spend three times as much. Such considerations would, of course, have to be balanced against machine costs in deciding which unit to acquire.

FIGURE 15.5 Probabilities $P_{n>K}$ that the number of customers in the service center exceeds K for the photocopier example.

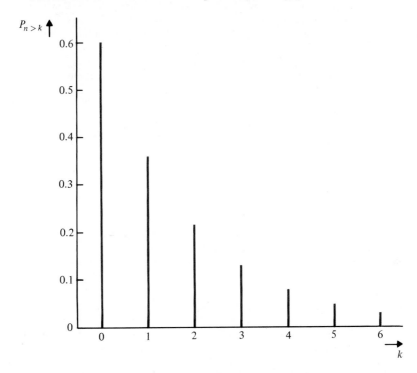

TABLE 15.2 Queue characteristics of three photocopiers ($\lambda = 3$).

CHARACTERISTIC	$\mu = 4$	$\mu = 5$	$\mu = 6$
ρ	0.75	0.60	0.50
L_S	3.00	1.50	1.00
W_S	1.00	0.50	0.33
L_Q	2.25	0.90	0.50
W_Q	0.75	0.30	0.17

15.3. A MULTIPLE-CHANNEL QUEUEING MODEL

In this section we will examine a queueing model that generalizes the analysis of the previous section to the case where waiting customers can be channeled to one of several servers. For example, an office photocopying center may have several machines. Our assumptions, which are stated in the box below, are similar to those of Section 15.2, with the servers taken to be essentially identical in their capacities to process customers.

1. Customers enter a service facility, with arrivals following a Poisson distribution having mean λ per unit time period.
2. Waiting line discipline is FIFO.
3. There are s servers available, and the next customer in line moves to the first unoccupied service channel. Service times are independent of one another, and, for each server, follow an exponential distribution such that μ customers per unit time period can be served on average.
4. Service times are independent of the number of arrivals.
5. The number of servers, s, exceeds the ratio, λ/μ, of mean arrival rate to mean potential service rate per server.

The final assumption assures that on the average, there will not be a continual build-up of customers waiting in the service facility. Rather, after an initial start-up period, the system eventually reaches a steady state. We now proceed to describe the characteristics of the steady state.[2]

Some Characteristics of the Steady State for a Multiple-Channel Queueing Model

1. The probability that there are no customers in the service facility is

$$P_0 = \frac{1}{\sum_{n=0}^{s-1} \frac{(\lambda/\mu)^n}{n!} + \frac{(\lambda/\mu)^s}{s!} \cdot \frac{s\mu}{s\mu - \lambda}}$$

2. The probability of n customers in the service facility is

$$P_n = \frac{(\lambda/\mu)^n}{n!} P_0 \qquad \text{for } 0 \le n \le s$$

and

$$P_n = \frac{(\lambda/\mu)^n}{s! \, s^{n-s}} P_0 \qquad \text{for } n > s$$

3. The probability that an arriving customer will have to wait for service is

$$P_W = \frac{(\lambda/\mu)^s}{s!} \cdot \frac{s\mu}{s\mu - \lambda} P_0$$

Of course, this is also the probability that all servers are in use.

---

[2] In essence, the method of derivation of these results is similar to that for the single-channel model of Section 15.2. The details, however, are rather tedious, and will be omitted.

4. The average number of customers in the service facility is

$$L_S = \frac{\lambda\mu(\lambda/\mu)^s}{(s-1)!\,(s\mu-\lambda)^2}\,P_0 + \frac{\lambda}{\mu}$$

5. The average time spent by a customer in the service facility is

$$W_S = \frac{\mu(\lambda/\mu)^s}{(s-1)!\,(s\mu-\lambda)^2}\,P_0 + \frac{1}{\mu} = \frac{L_S}{\lambda}$$

6. The average number of customers waiting in line for service is

$$L_Q = L_S - \frac{\lambda}{\mu}$$

7. The average time spent by customers waiting in line for service is

$$W_Q = W_S - \frac{1}{\mu}$$

It can be seen from these formulae that once the probability, P_0, that there are no units in the system has been computed, the other steady state characteristics are relatively easily derived. However, the expression for P_0 can involve tedious arithmetic, unless the number of servers, s, is very small. In Table 4 of the Appendix at the back of this volume we provide values of P_0 for different numbers of servers and for particular values of the **system utilization ratio**, $\lambda/s\mu$.

We now illustrate the formulae by considering a photocopying center which has three machines. Each machine is able to serve, on average, five customers per 15-minute period, and service times follow an exponential distribution. Customers of this facility arrive according to a Poisson distribution at an average rate of nine per 15-minute period. Therefore, in our notation,

$$s = 3; \mu = 5; \lambda = 9$$

We then find:

1.
$$\sum_{n=0}^{s-1} \frac{(\lambda/\mu)^n}{n!} = \sum_{n=0}^{2} \frac{(1.8)^n}{n!} = 1 + 1.8 + \frac{(1.8)^2}{2} = 4.42$$

Thus, the probability that there are no customers in the facility is

$$P_0 = \frac{1}{4.42 + [(1.8)^3/6](15/6)} = \frac{1}{6.85} = 0.1460$$

We can verify this result in Table 4 of the Appendix at the back of this volume, since here $s = 3$ and $\lambda/s\mu = 0.60$.

2. For values of n less than or equal to s, the probability of n customers in the facility is

$$P_n = \frac{(\lambda/\mu)^n}{n!}\,P_0 = \frac{(1.8)^n}{n!}\,(0.1460)$$

TABLE 15.3 Probabilities for differing numbers of customers in the photocopying center with three machines.

n	0	1	2	3	4	5	6
P_n	.1460	.2628	.2365	.1419	.0851	.0511	.0307

Thus, for example, the probability there will be two customers in the facility is

$$P_2 = \frac{(1.8)^2}{2}(0.1460) = 0.2365$$

For values of n bigger than s, the probability of n customers in the facility is

$$P_n = \frac{(\lambda/\mu)^n}{s! \, s^{n-s}} P_0 = \frac{(1.8)^n}{6(3^{n-3})}(0.1460)$$

For example, the probability there will be four customers in the service facility is

$$P_4 = \frac{(1.8)^4}{18}(0.1460) = 0.0851$$

Probabilities for up to six customers in the facility are shown in Table 15.3, and graphed in Figure 15.6.

We can compute the probability that there will be more than six customers in the service facility as

$$P_{n>6} = 1 - (P_0 + P_1 + \ldots + P_6)$$
$$= 1 - (0.1460 + 0.2628 + \ldots + 0.0307) = 0.0459$$

3. The probability that a new arrival will have to wait for service is

$$P_W = \frac{(\lambda/\mu)^s}{s!} \frac{s\mu}{s\mu - \lambda} P_0$$

$$= [(1.8)^3/6](15/6)(0.1460) = 0.3548$$

Hence, 35.48% of customers have to wait for service, or equivalently, all three copiers are simultaneously in use 35.48% of the time.[3]

4. The average number of customers in the facility over time is

$$L_S = \frac{\lambda\mu(\lambda/\mu)^s}{(s-1)! \, (s\mu - \lambda)^2} P_0 + \frac{\lambda}{\mu}$$

$$= \frac{(9)(5)(1.8)^3}{(2)(6)^2}(0.1460) + 1.8 = 2.332$$

5. The average time spent by a customer in the facility is

$$W_S = \frac{L_S}{\lambda} = \frac{2.332}{9} = 0.259$$

---

[3] We could also calculate the probability as $1 - P_0 - P_1 - P_2$.

FIGURE 15.6 Probabilities P_n for the numbers n of customers in the photocopying center with three machines.

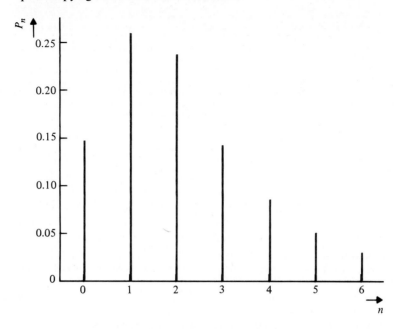

Since we are working with time intervals of 15 minutes, it can be seen that, on average, customers spend $(0.259)(15) = 3.885$ minutes in the photocopying facility.

6. The average number of customers waiting in line is

$$L_Q = L_S - \frac{\lambda}{\mu} = 2.332 - 1.8 = 0.532$$

7. The average time spent waiting in line is

$$W_Q = W_S - \frac{1}{\mu} = 0.259 - 0.2 = 0.059$$

Thus, on average, a customer spends $(0.059)(15) = 0.885$ minute waiting in line for service.

The model can be used to analyze the impact on customers of any changes in the system. Management has noticed that this particular photocopying center is often not very busy, and is considering moving one of the machines to another department where work has been heavier. Our formulae can be used to study the consequences of such a move. We now have just two machines, so that

$$s = 2; \mu = 5; \lambda = 9$$

Then, either directly from the formula, or from Table 4 of the Appendix, with $s = 2$ and $\lambda/s\mu = 0.9$, it is found that the probability that there will be no customers in the facility is

$$P_0 = 0.0526$$

TABLE 15.4 Queue characteristics for the facility with two and three photocopying machines ($\lambda = 3$, $\mu = 5$).

CHARACTERISTIC	$s = 2$	$s = 3$
P_W	0.8521	0.3548
L_S	9.469	2.332
W_S	1.052	0.259
L_Q	7.669	0.532
W_Q	0.852	0.059

We can then calculate other characteristics of the modified system. The results, together with those for the original system, are set out in Table 15.4. It can seen, for example, that removal of one photocopying machine raises the probability that a customer will have to wait for service from 0.3548 to 0.8521. Also, the average time spent by a customer in the facility increases from 3.885 minutes to $(1.052)(15) = 15.780$ minutes. Obviously this change can result in a serious loss of efficiency, which must be weighed against the benefits of moving the machine before any decision is made.

15.4. SOME OTHER QUEUEING MODELS

In our analysis to this point, it has been assumed that customers arrive at a service center according to a Poisson distribution, wait in line with FIFO discipline, and are served by one or more servers with exponentially distributed service times. Many queueing systems met in practice will depart in some respect from these assumptions, and other models have been developed to represent such systems. In this section we will look at three of these models.

A LIMITED WAITING CAPACITY MODEL

It often happens that a service facility is incapable of accommodating all arriving potential customers. When the facility is full, new arrivals will not join the waiting line, but rather will leave, perhaps to return at a later time. We will consider here a single-channel queueing model, for which all of the assumptions of Section 15.2 are satisfied, except that the maximum number of customers in the system (including the one being served) must be some finite number M. If at some time there are M customers in the system, then new arrivals will not be admitted.

The following characteristics of such a model have been derived:

1. The probability that there are no customers in the service facility is

$$P_0 = \frac{1 - (\lambda/\mu)}{1 - (\lambda/\mu)^{M+1}}$$

2. The probability that there are n customers in the service facility is

$$P_n = \left(\frac{\lambda}{\mu}\right)^n P_0 \qquad \text{for } n = 0, 1, 2, \ldots, M$$

3. The probability that an arriving customer will not be served immediately is $1 - P_0$, and the probability an arrival will not be able to enter the facility is

$$P_M = \left(\frac{\lambda}{\mu}\right)^M P_0$$

4. The average number of customers in the service facility is

$$L_S = \frac{\lambda/\mu}{1 - (\lambda/\mu)} - \frac{(M+1)(\lambda/\mu)^{M+1}}{1 - (\lambda/\mu)^{M+1}}$$

5. The average time spent by a customer in the service facility is

$$W_S = \frac{L_S}{\lambda(1 - P_M)}$$

6. The average number of customers waiting in line for service is

$$L_Q = L_S - 1 + P_0$$

7. The average time spent by customers waiting in line for service is

$$W_Q = W_S - \frac{1}{\mu}$$

To illustrate these formulae, consider a small automobile repair shop. It has been found that customer requests for service arrive according to a Poisson distribution at an average rate of eight per day. Service times follow an exponential distribution, and on average it has been found that ten automobiles per day can be serviced. However, the repair shop has a very limited amount of space available, so that no more than six cars at any one time can be accommodated on the premises. When this space is full, any additional customers asking for service must be turned away, or asked to return at a later time. Service is assumed to be first-in–first-out. In the above notation, then, we have

$$\lambda = 8; \mu = 10; M = 6 \quad \text{should be } 7$$

We then find the probability that there are no customers in the facility to be

$$P_0 = \frac{1 - (\lambda/\mu)}{1 - (\lambda/\mu)^{M+1}} = \frac{1 - 0.8}{1 - (0.8)^7} = 0.2531$$

so that 25.31% of the time this repair shop is idle. The probability that an arriving potential customer will have to be turned away is

$$P_M = \left(\frac{\lambda}{\mu}\right)^M P_0 = (0.8)^6(0.2531) = 0.0663$$

so that 6.63% of potential customers cannot be accommodated. Obviously it will be frustrating to management that so many customers cannot be taken while, at other times, the repair shop is completely idle. One use of this model is to study the effect of increasing facility capacity M on these and other characteristics of the queueing system.

The average number of customers in the repair shop will be

$$L_S = \frac{\lambda/\mu}{1 - (\lambda/\mu)} - \frac{(M + 1)\,(\lambda/\mu)^{M+1}}{1 - (\lambda/\mu)^{M+1}}$$

$$= \frac{0.8}{1 - 0.8} - \frac{7(0.8)^7}{1 - (0.8)^7} = 2.142$$

while the average time spent by each customer in the shop is

$$W_S = \frac{L_S}{\lambda(1 - P_M)} = \frac{2.142}{(8)(0.9337)} = 0.287 \text{ day}$$

The average number of customers waiting in line for service is

$$L_Q = L_S - 1 + P_0 = 2.142 - 1 + 0.2531 = 1.395$$

with average waiting time

$$W_Q = W_S - \frac{1}{\mu} = 0.287 - 0.1 = 0.187 \text{ day}$$

A FINITE SOURCE POPULATION MODEL

Up to this point we have implicitly assumed that customers arriving at a service facility are drawn from a very large (essentially infinite) source population of potential customers. A somewhat different queueing problem arises when the number of potential customers is limited. For example, a repair crew may be responsible for dealing with breakdowns in four computing systems operated by a corporation. In these circumstances the rate at which new systems require service will depend on the number already being serviced or waiting for service. In analyzing problems of this sort it is convenient to consider the mean arrival rate for a single customer. We will denote this rate by λ, and assume that it is the same for each customer. Therefore $1/\lambda$ is the average time between a service completion and the need for a new service. It will further be assumed that individual arrival rates follow a Poisson distribution. We will consider a system with s servers, for each of which service time follows an exponential distribution with mean $1/\mu$.

The following steady state characteristics of a model satisfying these assumptions have been found:

1. The probability that there are no customers in the service facility is

$$P_0 = \frac{1}{\displaystyle\sum_{n=s}^{N} \frac{N!}{(N-n)!\,s!\,s^{n-s}} \left(\frac{\lambda}{\mu}\right)^n + \sum_{n=0}^{s-1} \frac{N!}{(N-n)!\,n!} \left(\frac{\lambda}{\mu}\right)^n}$$

where N is the number of members of the source population.

2. The probability that there are n customers in the service facility is

$$P_n = \frac{N!}{(N-n)!\, n!} \left(\frac{\lambda}{\mu}\right)^n P_0 \quad \text{for } 0 \leq n \leq s$$

and

$$P_n = \frac{N!}{(N-n)!\, s!\, s^{n-s}} \left(\frac{\lambda}{\mu}\right)^n P_0 \qquad \text{for } s \leq n \leq N$$

Of course, there cannot be more than N customers in the facility.

3. The average number of customers in the service facility is

$$L_S = \sum_{n=1}^{N} n P_n$$

4. The average time spent by a customer in the service facility is

$$W_S = \frac{L_S}{\lambda(N - L_S)}$$

5. The average number of customers waiting for service is

$$L_Q = L_S - (N - L_S)\left(\frac{\lambda}{\mu}\right)$$

6. The average time spent by customers waiting in line for service is

$$W_Q = W_S - \frac{1}{\mu}$$

To illustrate these formulae, suppose that a corporation has four computing systems, each of which breaks down once a week on average. The corporation employs two service crews, working a five-day week. Repair times are exponentially distributed, with mean two days. Therefore, taking a unit time interval of one week, we have in the above notation,

$$\lambda = 1; \; \mu = 2.5; \; N = 4; \; s = 2$$

Then, the probability that there are no computing systems either being repaired or waiting for repair is P_0, which we can find from

$$\sum_{n=s}^{N} \frac{N!}{(N-n)!\, s!\, s^{n-s}} \left(\frac{\lambda}{\mu}\right)^n = \frac{4!}{2!\, 2!}(0.4)^2 + \frac{4!}{(2!)\,(2)}(0.4)^3 + \frac{4!}{(2!)\,(4)}(0.4)^4$$

$$= 1.4208$$

and

$$\sum_{n=0}^{s-1} \frac{N!}{(N-n)!\, n!} \left(\frac{\lambda}{\mu}\right)^n = 1 + \frac{4!}{3!}(0.4) = 2.6$$

Hence we find

$$P_0 = \frac{1}{(1.4208 + 2.6)} = 0.2487$$

We see then that 24.87% of the time all the computing systems are functioning. The probability that one system is under repair is

$$P_1 = \frac{4!}{3!}(0.4)(0.2487) = 0.3979$$

and similarly

$$P_2 = \frac{4!}{2!\,2!}(0.4)^2(0.2487) = 0.2388$$

The probability that three of these systems are being repaired or waiting for repair is

$$P_3 = \frac{4!}{(2!)\,(2)}(0.4)^3(0.2487) = 0.0955$$

The probability that all four systems are under repair or waiting for repair can then either be found directly, or more simply from

$$P_4 = 1 - P_0 - P_1 - P_2 = 1 - 0.2487 - 0.3979 - 0.2388 - 0.0955 = 0.0191$$

We can therefore calculate the probability that, at any time, both service crews will be busy as

$$P_2 + P_3 + P_4 = 0.2388 + 0.0955 + 0.0191 = 0.3534$$

The average number of systems being serviced, or waiting for service is

$$L_S = \sum_{n=1}^{N} nP_n = 0.3979 + (2)(0.2388) + (3)(0.0955) + (4)(0.0191) = 1.2384$$

The average time between the breakdown of a system and its return to functioning is

$$W_S = \frac{L_S}{\lambda(N - L_S)} = \frac{1.2384}{(1)(2.7616)} = 0.4484 \text{ week}$$

which, since a five-day week is worked, implies an average down time of duration $(5)(0.4484) = 2.242$ working days.

The average number of systems waiting for service is

$$L_Q = L_S - (N - L_S)\left(\frac{\lambda}{\mu}\right) = 1.2384 - (2.7616)(0.4) = 0.1338$$

while the average time between a system breakdown and the beginning of repairs is

$$W_Q = W_S - \frac{1}{\mu} = 0.4484 - 0.4 = 0.0484 \text{ week}$$

A PRIORITY QUEUEING MODEL

The assumption that waiting line discipline is first-in-first-out is frequently appropriate. However, in certain circumstances it will be desirable to give higher priority to some customers than to others. We will assume that any customer can be placed in one of m priority classes, labeled $1, 2, \ldots, m$, with 1 the highest and m the lowest priority. Within each priority class line discipline is FIFO. However, no waiting customer is served if a customer from a higher priority class is also waiting for service. We will assume essentially infinite populations of potential customers in each class. For the ith class, arrivals have a Poisson distribution with mean rate λ_i, and service times are taken to follow an exponential distribution, with mean $1/\mu_i$. We will restrict attention to the case where there is a single server.

Provided that the condition

$$\sum_{i=1}^{m} \frac{\lambda_i}{\mu_i} < 1$$

is satisfied, it can be shown that this queueing model will move to a steady state, having the following characteristics:

1. The average number of customers of priority class j in the service facility is

$$L_S^{(j)} = \frac{\lambda_j \sum_{i=1}^{m} \lambda_i/\mu_i^2}{(1 - C_{j-1})(1 - C_j)} + \frac{\lambda_j}{\mu_j}$$

where

$$C_0 = 0$$

and

$$C_j = \sum_{i=1}^{j} \frac{\lambda_i}{\mu_i} \qquad \text{for } j = 1, 2, \ldots, m$$

2. The average time spent by a customer from priority class j in the service facility is

$$W_S^{(j)} = \frac{L_S^{(j)}}{\lambda_j}$$

3. The average number of customers of priority class j waiting for service is

$$L_Q^{(j)} = L_S^{(j)} - \frac{\lambda_j}{\mu_j}$$

4. The average time spent waiting for service by a customer of priority class j is

$$W_Q^{(j)} = W_S^{(j)} - \frac{1}{\mu_j}$$

5. The average time spent by *all* customers in the facility is

$$W_S = \frac{\sum_{j=1}^{m} \lambda_j W_S^{(j)}}{\sum_{j=1}^{m} \lambda_j}$$

6. The average time spent waiting for service by *all* customers is

$$W_Q = \frac{\sum_{j=1}^{m} \lambda_j W_Q^{(j)}}{\sum_{j=1}^{m} \lambda_j}$$

To see how these results can be employed, consider a small hospital out-patient clinic, staffed by a single doctor. Patients arrive without appointments, and are assigned to one of three priority classes. Highest priority is given to emergency cases, which arrive at an average rate of one every 2 hours, and require, on average, 30 minutes of the doctor's time. For nonemergency patients, a higher priority is assigned to those who have a health maintenance contract with the hospital than to those who do not. The former group arrive at an average rate of one every half hour, and the latter at an average rate of one per hour. For both groups, average time per patient spent with the doctor is 10 minutes. We will assume that arrival rates are Poisson, and service times exponential. Then, in our notation, with a one hour unit time interval, we have

$$m = 3; \ \lambda_1 = 0.5; \ \mu_1 = 2; \ \lambda_2 = 2; \ \mu_2 = 6; \ \lambda_3 = 1; \ \mu_3 = 6$$

We begin by finding

$$C_1 = \frac{\lambda_1}{\mu_1} = \frac{1}{4}$$

$$C_2 = C_1 + \frac{\lambda_2}{\mu_2} = \frac{7}{12}$$

$$C_3 = C_2 + \frac{\lambda_3}{\mu_3} = \frac{3}{4}$$

The average numbers of patients of each priority class in the clinic at any one time are then

$$L_S^{(1)} = \frac{\lambda_1 \sum_{i=1}^{3} \lambda_i/\mu_i^2}{(1 - C_0)(1 - C_1)} + \frac{\lambda_1}{\mu_1}$$

$$= \frac{0.5(1/8 + 1/18 + 1/36)}{3/4} + \frac{1}{4}$$

$$= \frac{(0.5)(15/72)}{3/4} + \frac{1}{4} = 0.389$$

$$L_S^{(2)} = \frac{(2)(15/72)}{(3/4)(5/12)} + \frac{1}{3} = 1.667$$

and

$$L_S^{(3)} = \frac{(1)(15/72)}{(5/12)(1/4)} + \frac{1}{6} = 2.167$$

The average times spent by patients of the three priority classes in the clinic are

$$W_S^{(1)} = \frac{L_S^{(1)}}{\lambda_1} = \frac{0.389}{0.5} = 0.778 \text{ hour}$$

$$W_S^{(2)} = \frac{L_S^{(2)}}{\lambda_2} = \frac{1.667}{2} = 0.833 \text{ hour}$$

$$W_S^{(3)} = \frac{L_S^{(3)}}{\lambda_3} = \frac{2.167}{1} = 2.167 \text{ hours}$$

Therefore, emergency patients spend an average of $(0.778)(60) = 46.7$ minutes in the clinic, nonemergency health maintenance contract patients are in the clinic for an average of 50.0 minutes, while other nonemergency patients can expect to spend 2 hours and 10 minutes in the clinic.

The average numbers of patients from the three classes waiting to see the doctor are

$$L_Q^{(1)} = L_S^{(1)} - \frac{\lambda_1}{\mu_1} = 0.389 - 0.25 = 0.139$$

$$L_Q^{(2)} = L_S^{(2)} - \frac{\lambda_2}{\mu_2} = 1.667 - 0.333 = 1.334$$

$$L_Q^{(3)} = L_S^{(3)} - \frac{\lambda_3}{\mu_3} = 2.167 - 0.167 = 2$$

The average times spent waiting to see the doctor are

$$W_Q^{(1)} = W_S^{(1)} - \frac{1}{\mu_1} = 0.778 - 0.5 = 0.278 \text{ hour}$$

$$W_Q^{(2)} = W_S^{(2)} - \frac{1}{\mu_2} = 0.833 - 0.167 = 0.666 \text{ hour}$$

$$W_Q^{(3)} = W_S^{(3)} - \frac{1}{\mu_3} = 2.167 - 0.167 = 2 \text{ hours}$$

Therefore, emergency patients have an average wait of $(0.278)(60) = 16.7$ minutes, while average waits for patients in the other two classes are 40 minutes and 2 hours.

The average time spent by all patients in the clinic is

$$W_S = \frac{\sum_{j=1}^{m} \lambda_j W_S^{(j)}}{\sum_{j=1}^{m} \lambda_j} = \frac{(0.5)(0.778) + (2)(0.833) + (1)(2.167)}{0.5 + 2 + 1} = 1.206 \text{ hours}$$

and the average time spent waiting to see the doctor for all patients is

$$W_Q = \frac{\sum_{j=1}^{m} \lambda_j W_Q^{(j)}}{\sum_{j=1}^{m} \lambda_j} = \frac{(0.5)(0.278) + (2)(0.666) + (1)(2)}{0.5 + 2 + 1} = 0.992 \text{ hour}$$

so that the mean waiting time is fractionally under one hour.

In this section we have considered a number of departures from the assumptions of the basic queueing models of the previous two sections. In particular, the possibilities of limited waiting capacity, a finite source population, and priority queueing discipline have been examined. The models studied here certainly do not exhaust the practically important possibilities. For example, it will on occasion be desirable to relax the assumption that service times follow an exponential distribution. In addition, two or more discrepancies from the basic model assumptions may occur simultaneously. For instance, we may have a finite source population and priority queueing discipline, as would occur if maintenance of one of the four computing systems were especially critical to operation of the business. Our aim here has been to provide for the reader a flavor of the wide range of problems that can be handled by variants of the basic queueing models. Formulae for evaluating queue characteristics have been developed for a multitude of such variants and are widely employed in industry.

SIMULATION OF QUEUEING MODELS

We have shown that relatively easily employed formulae can be used to describe the characteristics of waiting line problems, where specific sets of assumptions are satisfied. There is, however, an alternative line of attack, which is particularly valuable in approaching more complex problems, where the development of elegant formulae may be considerably more difficult than for the models discussed in this chapter. Computer **simulation** methods can be used to quickly describe queue behavior and to estimate the characteristics of queues under a wide range of arrival processes, waiting line discipline, and serving process specifications. We will discuss simulation methods in Chapter 16.

15.5. THE ECONOMIC ANALYSIS OF WAITING LINE PROBLEMS

We have seen how the characteristics of a queue can be determined. Next, it will be shown how this analysis can provide useful input for decision-making. In Sections 15.2 and 15.3 we met two examples where improved *service,* in terms of shorter waiting periods, could be provided to customers. In the context of our photocopying case, this could be achieved either by adding more machines or by replacing the existing machine with a more efficient one. Certainly such an improvement in customer service would be beneficial, but these benefits must be weighed against the additional cost of the improved provision before determining whether to upgrade service. We can think of two kinds of costs associated with waiting lines; these are

(a) The cost of customer waiting time, C_1.
(b) The cost of service provision, C_2.

The total waiting line cost, which will be expressed in convenient time units, such as dollars per hour, is then the sum of these components

$$C = C_1 + C_2$$

Now, the greater the level of service provided, the higher will be its cost, C_2. On the other hand, better service will lead to shorter average waiting times, and hence a decrease in the cost C_1. In these circumstances, it is generally the case that a level of service can be found such that total cost C is a mininum. The position is illustrated graphically in Figure 15.7, which shows a total cost function having a mininum. In fact, in the typical real world example, only a discrete number of levels of service are feasible. For example, we may have to decide how many servers to provide. In theory, at least, such problems can be solved by computing waiting and service costs, and hence total costs, for each possible level of service provision, and then selecting that service level for which total cost is smallest. In practice, however, it may be difficult to specify all of the parameters involved. Consider, for example, the problem of a supermarket manager who is trying to decide whether to add a further check-out clerk during

FIGURE 15.7 Relation between the queue costs and the service provision.

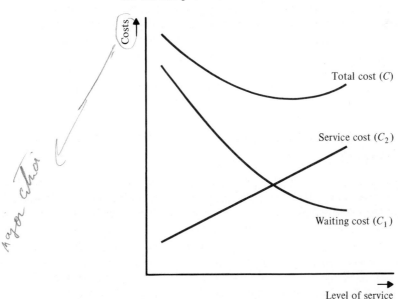

a busy period. The cost of providing this improved level of service is easy enough to calculate. It should also be possible to assess the benefits to customers in terms of average waiting times. However, the benefit to the supermarket will accrue from improved customer goodwill, on which it is very difficult to set a specific dollar value.

We will illustrate the economic analysis of waiting line problems through an example where cost assessments are quite straightforward. A large corporation has recently become concerned about the sizable amounts of money spent on trips by junior managers. In an attempt to control these expenditures, a system has been instituted whereby any junior manager planning a trip must first meet with a member of the financial staff to discuss the proposed budget. Junior managers are paid an average of $20 per hour, while the corresponding figure for financial staff members to be assigned to this task is $15. It is estimated that on average, two junior managers per hour must be interviewed, and that a financial staff member could conduct, on average, 2.5 interviews per hour. The question at issue is the number of financial staff members to be assigned to this task.

Using the values

$$\lambda = 2; \mu = 2.5$$

together with assumptions of Poisson arrival rates and exponential serving times, the procedures of Section 15.3 can be used to compute queue characteristics for different numbers of servers (financial staff). Some results[4] are summarized in Table 15.5.

Next, in Table 15.6, we compute the costs per hour of each level of service. The cost of the junior manager's waiting time is $20 per manager per hour. Thus, the average hourly cost is simply the product of $20 and the average number of managers in the system. Therefore, if there are two servers, we find

$$C_1 = (0.9524)(20) = \$19.048$$

The hourly cost of service provision is simply $15 for each financial staff member employed in this capacity. Hence, if there are two servers, hourly service cost is $30, so that total cost is

$$C = C_1 + C_2$$

$$= 19.048 + 30 = \$49.048$$

TABLE 15.5 Levels of service for different numbers of servers for the trip planning example.

NUMBER OF SERVERS	P_0	AVERAGE NUMBER IN SYSTEM (L_S)
1	0.2000	4.0000
2	0.4286	0.9524
3	0.4472	0.8189

[4] We leave the verification of these results as an exercise to the reader.

TABLE 15.6 Hourly costs (in dollars) for different numbers of servers for the trip planning example.

NUMBER OF SERVERS	CUSTOMER WAITING COST (C_1)	SERVICE COST (C_2)	TOTAL COST ($C = C_1 + C_2$)
1	(4.000)(20) = 80.000	(1)(15) = 15	95.000
2	(0.9524)(20) = 19.048	(2)(15) = 30	49.048
3	(0.8189)(20) = 16.378	(3)(15) = 45	61.378

From Table 15.6 it emerges that the solution with the lowest possible total cost is to assign two financial staff to this task. (It is clear that we do not need to carry out the computations for more than three servers. Each additional server will increase C_2 by \$15, but yield relatively little decrease in C_1.) The analysis can be taken a little further. Our optimal solution costs \$49.048 per hour. Since requests for trips arrive at the rate of two per hour, the cost is \$24.524 per trip. Management may at some time want to review this scheme to determine whether it is yielding average savings per trip in excess of this amount. If it is not, then a good case can be made for its abandonment.

As we have indicated, this example was chosen because cost assessments were easy to make. In many cases where such intangible quantities as goodwill must be taken into account in assessing costs, it may be desirable to carry out a sensitivity analysis, performing the calculations for a range of values around the best cost estimates.

EXERCISES

15.1. Customers arrive at a supermarket checkout, according to a Poisson distribution, at an average rate of four per minute.

(a) Find the probability, in any given minute, that there will be no arrivals.

(b) Find the probability, in any given minute, that there will be more than three arrivals.

(c) What is the average time between successive arrivals?

(d) Find the probability that there is less than 30 seconds between successive arrivals.

15.2. During the early afternoon hours, automobiles arrive at an expressway toll booth at an average rate of six per minute, according to a Poisson distribution.

(a) Find the probability, in any given minute, that there will be less than two arrivals.

(b) Find the probability, in any given minute, that there will be more than three arrivals.

(c) What is the average time between successive arrivals?

(d) Find the probability there is more than 20 seconds between successive arrivals.

15.3. Customers arrive at a barbershop at an average rate of five per hour, according to a Poisson distribution.

(a) Find the probability, in any hour, that less than two customers will arrive.

(b) Find the probability, in any hour, that more than four customers will arrive.

(c) Draw the probability function for the number of arrivals in an hour.

(d) What is the average time between successive arrivals?

(e) Find the probability there is more than 30 minutes between successive arrivals.

15.4. Service of customers at a library information desk follows an exponential distribution, with mean service time 10 minutes.

(a) Find the probability that service of a single customer takes less than 15 minutes.

(b) Find the probability that service of a single customer takes more than 20 minutes.

(c) Draw the cumulative distribution function for service times.

15.5. A professor sees students during regular office hours. Time spent with students follows an exponential distribution with mean 15 minutes.

(a) Find the probability that a particular student spends less than 30 minutes with the professor.

(b) Find the probability that a particular student spends more than 15 minutes with the professor.

(c) Draw the cumulative distribution function for time spent with the professor.

15.6. Customers arrive, according to a Poisson distribution, at the checkout counter of a small grocery store at an average rate of one every 10 minutes. Service times follow an exponential distribution, with mean 5 minutes. Waiting line discipline is FIFO. In the steady state:

(a) What is the probability that there are no customers at the service facility; that is, either being served or waiting for service?

(b) What is the probability that there are more than two customers at the service facility?

(c) What proportion of the time is the checkout clerk serving a customer?

(d) What is the average number of customers in the service facility?

(e) What is the average time spent by a customer in the service facility?

(f) What is the average number of customers waiting in line for service?

(g) What is the average time spent by customers waiting in line for service?

15.7. Customers arrive at a barbershop, with a single barber, according to a Poisson distribution, at an average rate of two per hour. Service times follow an exponential distribution, with mean 20 minutes. Waiting line discipline is FIFO. In the steady state:

(a) What is the probability that there are no customers in the barbershop?

(b) What is the probability that there are exactly two customers in the barbershop?

(c) What is the probability that there are more than three customers in the barbershop?

(d) What is the probability, at any given time, that the barber will be serving a customer?

(e) What is the average number of customers in the barbershop?

(f) What is the average time spent by a customer in the barbershop?

(g) What is the average number of customers waiting for service?

(h) What is the average time spent by customers waiting for service?

15.8. Suppose that the assumptions of the single-channel queueing model of Section 15.2 are satisfied.

(a) Let n_1 and n_2 be any nonnegative integers, with $n_1 < n_2$. Show that the probability that there are exactly n_2 customers in the facility is less than the probability that there are exactly n_1 customers in the facility, in the steady state.

(b) Let n_1 and n_2 be any nonnegative integers, with $n_1 < n_2$. Show that the probability that there are more than n_2 customers in the facility as a proportion of the probability that there are more than n_1 customers in the facility depends only on the utilization rate and the difference between n_2 and n_1, in the steady state.

15.9. Given the assumptions of Section 15.2 for the single-channel queueing model, show that in the steady state, if the utilization rate is ρ:

(a) The average number of customers waiting in the service facility is

$$L_S = \frac{\rho}{1 - \rho}$$

(b) The average number of customers waiting in line for service is

$$L_Q = \frac{\rho^2}{1 - \rho}$$

15.10. Trucks arrive at a loading bay at an average rate of four per hour, according to a Poisson distribution. If the bay is busy, these trucks must wait in line for service, line discipline being on a first-in–first-out basis. Service times follow an exponential distribution, with mean 12 minutes. For the steady state:

(a) What is the probability that there are no trucks in the service facility?

(b) What is the probability that there are more than three trucks in the service facility?

(c) What proportion of the time is the loading bay in use?

(d) What is the average number of trucks in the service facility?

(e) What is the average time spent by a truck in the service facility?

(f) What is the average number of trucks waiting in line for service?

(g) What is the average time spent by trucks waiting in line for service?

15.11. Refer to Exercise 15.10. Due to increased business, it is expected that over the coming months, the arrival rate of trucks at the loading bay will increase to five per hour. In anticipation of this heavier demand, management is planning capital investments to speed up service. To what level must average service time be reduced in order that trucks spend, on average, no more time in the service facility than previously?

15.12. For a single-channel queueing model, for which the assumptions of Section 15.2 are satisfied, mean arrival rate is λ and mean service rate is μ. Suppose now that both mean arrival rate and mean service rate are increased by 10 %. For the steady state solution, state whether the following are true or false:

(a) The utilization rate remains unchanged.

(b) The average number of customers in the service facility remains unchanged.

(c) The average time spent by a customer in the service facility remains unchanged.

(d) The average number of customers waiting in line for service remains unchanged.

(e) The average time spent by a customer waiting in line for service remains unchanged.

15.13. For a single-channel queueing model, satisfying the assumptions of Section 15.2, average service rate is μ. Over the years, demand at this facility has grown, so that mean arrival rate has become bigger. If this trend continues, mean arrival rate will soon be equal to mean service rate. Discuss the behavior of the average time spent waiting by customers in the steady state as this point is reached. Can you provide a verbal interpretation of your answer?

15.14. A small gas station has a single pump for lead-free gas. Motorists arrive at an average rate of one every 6 minutes, according to a Poisson distribution. Service times follow an exponential distribution, with mean 3 minutes, and waiting line discipline is FIFO. For the steady state:

(a) What is the probability that there are no customers in the gas station?

(b) What is the probability that there are less than three customers in the gas station?

(c) What proportion of the time is the pump busy?

(d) What is the average number of customers in the gas station?

(e) What is the average time spent by a customer in the gas station?

(f) What is the average number of drivers waiting in line for service?

(g) What is the average time spent by a driver waiting in line for service?

15.15. In Section 15.5, we discussed a problem where junior managers arrived at an average rate of two per hour to discuss their proposed budgets for trips with a member of the financial staff. On average, a financial staff member can conduct 2.5 of these interviews per hour. We considered the number of financial staff members employed for this purpose as either (i) one, (ii) two, or (iii) three. For each of these three possibilities, in the steady state:

(a) Verify the values for the average number of junior managers in the system, given in Table 15.5.

(b) Find the probability that an arriving junior manager will have to wait before seeing a member of the financial staff.

(c) Find the average time spent by a junior manager in the system.

(d) Find the average number of junior managers waiting in line to see a member of the financial staff.

(e) Find the average time spent by a junior manager waiting in line to see a member of the financial staff.

15.16. In Section 15.3 we considered a company with a photocopying facility for which customers arrived at an average rate of nine per 15-minute period. At the present time the company has three copiers, each capable of serving an average of five customers per 15-minute period. Management has noticed that often this system is not fully utilized, and is considering two cheaper alternatives: (i) two copiers, each capable of serving an average of six customers in 15 minutes, or (ii) three copiers, each capable of serving an average of four customers in 15 minutes. For each of these systems in the steady state:

(a) Find the probability that there are no customers in the service facility.

(b) Find the probability that an arriving customer will have to wait for service.

(c) Find the average number of customers in the service facility.

(d) Find the average time spent by a customer in the service facility.

(e) Find the average number of customers waiting in line for service.

(f) Find the average time spent by customers waiting in line for service.

15.17. In Section 15.3, we give formulae for the characteristics, in the steady state, of a multiple-channel queueing model with s servers.

(a) Show that, when $s = 1$, the formula for the probability that there are no customers in the service facility reduces to

$$P_0 = 1 - \frac{\lambda}{\mu}$$

(b) Hence show that, when $s = 1$, the formulae for the probability that an arriving customer must wait for service, average numbers of customers in the facility and waiting for service, and average times spent by customers in the facility and waiting for service reduce to the corresponding formulae given in Section 15.2 for the single-channel queueing model.

15.18. Consider the multiple-channel queueing model, for which the assumptions of Section 15.3 are satisfied. Let μ denote the average potential service rate per server, λ the average arrival rate, and s the number of servers. Denote by P_n the probability that there are n customers in the service facility.

(a) Show that, for all $n \geq s - 1$,

$$P_{n+1} < P_n$$

(b) Show that, if $n < s - 1$

$$P_{n+1} < P_n$$

if and only if

$$\lambda < (n + 1)\mu$$

15.19. Customers arrive at a supermarket checkout, according to a Poisson distribution, at an average rate of one every 30 seconds. There are five checkout clerks, and for each customer service times follow an exponential distribution, with mean 2 minutes. For the steady state:

(a) Find the probability that there are no customers in the system.

(b) Find the probability that an arriving customer must wait for service.

(c) Find the average number of customers in the system.

(d) Find the average time spent by a customer in the system.

(e) Find the average number of customers waiting for service.

(f) Find the average time spent by customers waiting for service.

15.20. Refer to Exercise 15.19. The supermarket manager wants to know how many checkout clerks must be added in order to cut in half the average time spent by customers waiting for service. What is the smallest number of additional clerks necessary to achieve this objective?

15.21. Automobiles arrive at an expressway toll at an average rate of one every 10 seconds. There are four booths, and average service time at each is 20 seconds. Assume that arrival rates follow a Poisson distribution and that service times are exponentially distributed. For the steady state:

(a) What is the probability that there are no automobiles in the system?

(b) What is the probability that an arriving automobile will have to wait for service?

(c) Find the average number of customers in the system.

(d) Find the average time spent by a customer in the system.

(e) What is the average time spent by a customer waiting for service?

(f) Find the average number of automobiles waiting for service.

15.22. A bank is planning to set up a drive-in facility. Management expects that during the busiest periods, customers will arrive at an average rate of one every 2 minutes. Average service time is expected to be 4 minutes for each teller. Bank management wants to install enough tellers so that at the busiest periods, the average time spent by a customer waiting in line for service should be no more than 5 minutes. What is the smallest number of tellers needed to attain this objective?

15.23. For a multiple-channel queueing model, in the steady state, we give in Section 15.3 formulae for the probabilities $P_n (n = 0, 1, 2, \ldots)$ for n customers in the service facility. Use these formulae to show that the probability that an arriving customer must wait for service is given by

$$P_W = \frac{(\lambda/\mu)^s}{s!} \frac{s\mu}{s\mu - \lambda} P_0$$

15.24. Trucks arrive at a loading bay with three docks at an average rate of twelve per hour, according to a Poisson distribution. Service times at each dock follow an exponential distribution with mean 12 minutes. For the steady state:

(a) What is the probability that none of these docks is busy?

(b) What is the probability that at least two of the docks are busy?

(c) What is the probability that an arriving truck will have to wait for service?

(d) What is the probability that an arriving truck will find at least one other truck waiting in line for service?

(e) A company sends three trucks a week to this loading bay. What is the probability that at least one of these three trucks will have to wait for service?

(f) What is the average number of trucks in the service area?

(g) What is the average time spent by a truck in the service area?

(h) What is the average number of trucks waiting in line for service?

(i) What is the average time spent by a truck waiting in line for service?

15.25. Refer to Exercise 15.24. A freight manager is considering the use of an alternative loading bay, which has four docks, for each of which average service time is 15 minutes. The average arrival rate at this bay is also twelve trucks per hour. Will the average time spent by a truck in this facility be less than that in the facility of Exercise 15.24?

15.26. Consider the single-server, limited-waiting capacity model of Section 15.4, for a mean arrival rate λ, mean potential service rate μ, and facility customer capacity M.

(a) Let P_0 denote the probability that there are no customers in the facility. Show that, as facility capacity M is increased, to become infinitely large, this probability approaches

$$P_0 = 1 - \frac{\lambda}{\mu}$$

(b) Hence show that, as M becomes infinitely large, the formulae for determining average numbers in the facility and waiting for service, and average times in the facility and waiting for service, reduce to the corresponding formulae for the single-channel queueing model of Section 15.2.

15.27. Consider the single-channel, limited-waiting capacity model of Section 15.4. Show that if customer capacity, M, is increased, and the arrival and service distributions remain unchanged, the probability that the facility is idle will decrease, and that the probability that an arriving customer will not be able to enter the facility will also decrease.

15.28. Consider the single-channel, limited-waiting capacity model of Section 15.4. Show that the average number of customers waiting in line for service, L_Q, can be expressed as

$$L_Q = L_S - \frac{\lambda(1 - P_M)}{\mu}$$

where L_S is the average number of customers in the facility, λ and μ are the mean arrival and mean potential service rates, and P_M is the probability that a new arrival will not be able to enter the facility.

15.29. A barbershop, with a single barber, has six chairs available for customers waiting in line for service. Arriving customers will take a chair and wait, if one is available, but will leave the shop if all of these chairs are taken. Customers arrive, according to a Poisson distribution, at an average rate of 2.5 per hour. Service times follow an exponential distribution, with mean 20 minutes. In the steady state:

(a) What is the probability that there are no customers in the barbershop?

(b) What is the probability that there are at least two customers in the barbershop?

(c) What is the probability an arriving customer will have to wait for service?

(d) What is the probability that no chair will be available for an arriving customer?

(e) Find the average number of customers in the barbershop.

(f) Find the average time spent by a customer in the barbershop.

(g) Find the average number of customers waiting in line for service.

(h) Find the average time spent by customers waiting in line for service.

15.30. A professor holds office hours the day before a test. He believes that if three students are waiting in line to see him, any further arrivals will be discouraged and leave. Students arrive, according to a Poisson distribution, at an average rate of five per hour. Times spent with the professor follow an exponential distribution with mean 10 minutes. In the steady state:

(a) What is the probability that there is no student with the professor?

(b) What is the probability that an arriving student will find three other students waiting in line to see the professor?

(c) What is the average number of students waiting in line to see the professor?

(d) What is the average time spent by a student waiting in line to see the professor?

15.31. Refer to Exercise 15.30. The professor is concerned about the number of students who leave because three others are waiting in line. He would like to speed up his discussions with students, so that they take on average only $7\frac{1}{2}$ minutes. In that case, what proportion of arriving students will find three others waiting in line?

15.32. Consider the finite source population model with s channels of Section 15.4. Show that if there is just a single server so that s is equal to one:

(a) The probability that there are no customers in the service facility is

$$P_0 = \frac{1}{\displaystyle\sum_{n=0}^{N} \frac{N!}{(N-n)!}\left(\frac{\lambda}{\mu}\right)^n}$$

(b) The probability that there are n customers in the facility is

$$P_n = \frac{N!}{(N-n)!}\left(\frac{\lambda}{\mu}\right)^n P_0 \quad \text{for } n = 0, 1, 2, \ldots, N$$

15.33. In Section 15.4, we studied the case of a corporation with four computing systems and two repair crews. This corporation is planning to acquire a fifth system, with the same characteristics as the other four, but not to add a further repair crew. In the steady state:

(a) Find the probability that there are no computing systems either being repaired or waiting for repair.

(b) Find the probability that at least one of the repair crews is unoccupied.

(c) Find the average number of computing systems either being serviced or waiting for service.

(d) Find the average time between system breakdown and the completion of its repair.

(e) Find the average number of systems waiting for service.

(f) Find the average time between system breakdown and the start of its repair.

15.34. A consultant works a year of 50 weeks. She handles contracts to perform specific tasks and also receives invitations to bid for contracts. However, she will only prepare bids when all work for clients is completed. This consultant obtains contracts at an average rate of six per year, according to a Poisson distribution, and spends, on average, 5 weeks on each contract. The times taken follow an exponential distribution. She also gets an average of five requests per year to prepare bids. On average it takes one week to prepare a bid. Both the times between requests for bids and the times for bid preparation follow exponential distributions. In the steady state:

(a) What is the average number of contracts either being worked on or waiting for this consultant to work on?

(b) What is the average number of bids that the consultant is working on or has available to work on?

(c) What is the average time between receipt of a contract and completion of the work?

(d) What is the average time between receipt of request for a bid and the completion of the bid preparation?

(e) What is the average number of contracts awaiting the consultant's attention?

(f) What is the average number of bid preparation requests awaiting the consultant's attention?

15.35. Consider a priority queueing model with two priority classes, of which class 1 has the highest priority. Let λ_1 and λ_2 denote the mean arrival rates, and μ_1 and μ_2 the mean potential service rates. Show that the average number of customers of priority class 1 waiting for service exceeds that of priority class 2 if and only if

$$\frac{\lambda_2}{\lambda_1} < 1 - \frac{\lambda_1}{\mu_1} - \frac{\lambda_2}{\mu_2}$$

15.36. Refer to the example of the hospital outpatient clinic of Section 15.4. Hospital management is concerned about the large waiting times for nonemergency patients who do not have a health maintenance contract with the hospital. It is considering giving all nonemergency patients equal priority, with emergency patients retaining a higher priority. Discuss the effects of this proposed change on:

(a) Emergency patients.

(b) Nonemergency patients with health maintenance contracts.

(c) Nonemergency patients without health maintance contracts.

15.37. In Section 15.5, we studied a problem where junior managers had to discuss proposed budgets for trips with a member of the financial staff. Concern has been expressed about the cost of this arrangement, and an effort is to be made to reduce costs by streamlining the interviews.

(a) To what level would average interview times have to be reduced in order to lower total hourly cost over the system to $40?

(b) To what level would average interview time have to be reduced for the optimum solution to involve the assignment of only one member of the financial staff to this task?

15.38. Customers arrive at an airport rental car desk, according to a Poisson distribution, at an average rate of twenty per hour. Service times are exponentially distributed, with mean 10 minutes. Each service clerk is paid $10 per hour. The rental car company counts each minute that a customer spends waiting in line for service as a one cent loss in goodwill. How many clerks should be employed to staff this desk?

15.39. An automobile repair shop employs six mechanics, each of whom is paid $12 per hour. When a mechanic needs a part, he or she must obtain this part from a clerk who is paid $6 per hour. Service times for these transactions are exponentially distributed and average 5 minutes. For each mechanic, arrival rates follow a Poisson distribution, with mean two per hour. How many clerks should be employed in order to minimize the total cost of this system?

APPENDIX A15.1

In this appendix we establish the results of Section 15.2 for the single-channel queueing model in the steady state. We begin by deriving probabilities for numbers of customers in the system at any time, using the notation $P_n(t)$ to represent the probability that n customers are in the system at time t. Our strategy is to consider the evolution of the queue over a very small interval of time, of length h. We therefore relate the probabilities for numbers in the system at time $t + h$ to the corresponding probabilities at time t. The interval h is taken to be sufficiently small that at most one arrival and one service completion is possible in this time span.

We want to find the probability that there are exactly n units in the system at time $t + h$. In Figure A15.1, the only ways in which this outcome can arise are set out. The possibilities are as follows:

(i) If there are $n - 1$ units in the system at time t, then there will be n units at time $t + h$ if there is one arrival and no service completed in this short time span. (We are here assuming that n is greater than zero—the case where n is zero must be treated separately.) This conjunction of events occurs with probability $\lambda h(1 - \mu h)$. Hence, the probability of both $n - 1$ units at time t and n units at time $t + h$ is $\lambda h(1 - \mu h)P_{n-1}(t)$.

(ii) If there are n units in the system at time t, there will be n units at time $t + h$ if there are no arrivals and no completed services, which will occur with probability $(1 - \lambda h)(1 - \mu h)$. There will also be n units at time $t + h$ with one arrival and one

FIGURE A15.1 Generation of n units in the system at the time $t + h$.

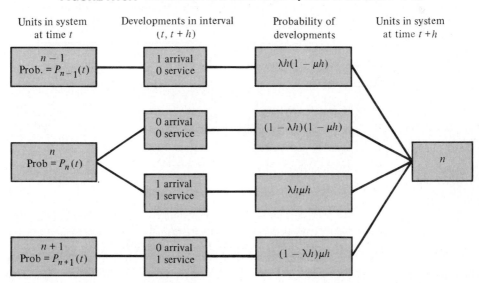

completed service, for which the probability is $\lambda h \mu h$. It follows that the probability of both n units at time t and n units at time $t + h$ is $[(1 - \lambda h)(1 - \mu h) + \lambda h \mu h]P_n(t)$.

(iii) If there are $n + 1$ units in the system at time t, there will be n units at time $t + h$ if there are no arrivals and one completed service in this time span. This occurs with probability $(1 - \lambda h)\mu h$. Therefore, the probability of both $n + 1$ units at time t and n units at time $t + h$ is $(1 - \lambda h)\mu h P_{n+1}(t)$.

Putting these three terms together, we see that the probability that there will be n customers in the service center at time $t + h$ is given by

$$P_n(t + h) = \lambda h(1 - \mu h)P_{n-1}(t) + [(1 - \lambda h)(1 - \mu h) + \lambda h \mu h]P_n(t) \\ + (1 - \lambda h)\mu h P_{n+1}(t) \qquad \text{for } n > 0 \qquad \text{(A15.1)}$$

We must now find the probability that there are no units in the system at time $t + h$. There are only two possible ways that this can occur:

1. If there are no units in the system at time t, there will be none at time $t + h$ if there are no arrivals in this time interval. This occurs with probability $1 - \lambda h$. There will also be no units at time $t + h$ if there is one arrival and one completed service, for which the probability is $\lambda h \mu h$. Thus, the probability that there are both no units at time t and none at time $t + h$ is $[(1 - \lambda h) + \lambda h \mu h]P_0(t)$.
2. If there is one unit in the system at time t, there will be none at time $t + h$ if there are no arrivals and one completed service, which occurs with probability $(1 - \lambda h)\mu h$. Hence the probability of both one unit at time t and one at time $t + h$ is $(1 - \lambda h)\mu h P_1(t)$.

Combining these two terms, it can be seen that the probability of no units in the system at time $t + h$ is

$$P_0(t + h) = [(1 - \lambda h) + \lambda h \mu h]P_0(t) + (1 - \lambda h)\mu h P_1(t) \qquad \text{(A15.2)}$$

We must now consider the rate of change over time of these probabilities. From equations (A15.1) and (A15.2), it follows that

$$\frac{P_n(t+h) - P_n(t)}{h} = \lambda(1 - \mu h)P_{n-1}(t) - (\lambda + \mu - 2\lambda\mu h)P_n(t) \\ + (1 - \lambda h)\mu P_{n+1}(t) \qquad \text{for } n > 0$$

and

$$\frac{P_0(t + h) - P_0(t)}{h} = -(\lambda - \lambda\mu h)P_0(t) + (1 - \lambda h)\mu P_1(t)$$

Setting h to zero in these two expressions, the rates of change can be expressed as derivatives of the probabilities with respect to time. This yields

$$\frac{dP_n(t)}{dt} = \lambda P_{n-1}(t) - (\lambda + \mu)P_n(t) + \mu P_{n+1}(t) \qquad \text{for } n > 0 \qquad \text{(A15.3)}$$

and

$$\frac{dP_0(t)}{dt} = -\lambda P_0(t) + \mu P_1(t) \qquad\qquad\qquad \text{(A15.4)}$$

Now, if the queueing system is in the steady state, the probabilities for numbers of customers will not change over time, so that these two derivatives must be zero. Since the probabilities are fixed through time in the steady state, we can write P_n for $P_n(t)$, and setting the expressions (A15.3) and (A15.4) to zero then gives

$$\lambda P_{n-1} - (\lambda + \mu)P_n + \mu P_{n+1} = 0 \qquad \text{for } n > 0 \qquad \text{(A15.5)}$$

and

$$-\lambda P_0 + \mu P_1 = 0 \qquad\qquad\qquad \text{(A15.6)}$$

It follows from (A15.6) that

$$P_1 = \frac{\lambda}{\mu} P_0$$

Setting n equal to one and substituting for P_1 in (A15.5) then gives

$$P_2 = \left(\frac{\lambda}{\mu}\right)^2 P_0$$

Continuing in this fashion, setting in turn $n = 2, 3, 4, \ldots$ in (A15.5) gives

$$P_n = \left(\frac{\lambda}{\mu}\right)^n P_0$$

Now, the probabilities P_n, for $n = 0, 1, 2, \ldots$, must sum to one, so that we have

$$1 = \sum_{n=0}^{\infty} P_n = \sum_{n=0}^{\infty} \left(\frac{\lambda}{\mu}\right)^n P_0 = \frac{1}{1 - \lambda/\mu} P_0 \qquad (\text{A15.7})$$

where we have used the fact that, if $|x| < 1$,

$$\sum_{n=0}^{\infty} x^n = \frac{1}{(1 - x)}$$

It follows from (A15.7) that

$$P_0 = 1 - \frac{\lambda}{\mu}$$

Thus, we have established results 1 and 2 of Section 15.2.

The probability that there is at least one unit in the system—that is, that the server is in use—is

$$\rho = 1 - P_0 = \frac{\lambda}{\mu}$$

establishing result 3. Also, the probability of more than K units in the system is

$$\begin{aligned}
P_{n>K} &= \sum_{n=K+1}^{\infty} P_n = \left(1 - \frac{\lambda}{\mu}\right) \sum_{n=K+1}^{\infty} \left(\frac{\lambda}{\mu}\right)^n \\
&= \left(1 - \frac{\lambda}{\mu}\right)\left(\frac{\lambda}{\mu}\right)^{K+1} \sum_{n=0}^{\infty} \left(\frac{\lambda}{\mu}\right)^n \\
&= \left(1 - \frac{\lambda}{\mu}\right)\left(\frac{\lambda}{\mu}\right)^{K+1} \left[\frac{1}{1 - \lambda/\mu}\right] \\
&= \left(\frac{\lambda}{\mu}\right)^{K+1}
\end{aligned}$$

which establishes result 8.

Now, since the probability of n customers in the system is P_n, it follows that the average, or expected, number of customers in the system is

$$L_S = \sum_{n=0}^{\infty} n P_n = \left(1 - \frac{\lambda}{\mu}\right) \sum_{n=0}^{\infty} n \left(\frac{\lambda}{\mu}\right)^n$$

Then, using the fact that, if $0 < x < 1$,

$$\sum_{n=0}^{\infty} n x^n = \frac{x}{(1 - x)^2}$$

we have

$$L_S = \left(1 - \frac{\lambda}{\mu}\right) \frac{\lambda/\mu}{(1 - \lambda/\mu)^2} = \frac{\lambda}{\mu - \lambda}$$

which is result 4 of Section 15.2.

If, when a customer arrives at a service facility, there are already n customers in the facility, the new customer will be the $(n + 1)^{st}$ to be served. Since each service takes up expected time $1/\mu$, the service of $(n + 1)$ customers takes, on average, time $(n + 1)/\mu$. Therefore the average amount of time spent by customers in the facility is

$$W_S = \sum_{n=0}^{\infty} (n + 1)\mu^{-1}P_n = \frac{\sum_{n=0}^{\infty} nP_n}{\mu} + \frac{\sum_{n=0}^{\infty} P_n}{\mu}$$

$$= \frac{\lambda}{\mu(\mu - \lambda)} + \frac{1}{\mu} = \frac{1}{\mu - \lambda}$$

This is result 5.

The number of customers waiting in line for service is zero if there are no customers in the facility, and otherwise one less than the number of customers. Therefore, the average number of customers waiting in line is

$$L_Q = \sum_{n=1}^{\infty} (n - 1)P_n = \sum_{n=0}^{\infty} nP_n - (1 - P_0)$$

$$= \frac{\lambda}{\mu - \lambda} - \frac{\lambda}{\mu}$$

yielding result 6.

Finally, the average amount of time spent waiting in line is simply the average total time in the facility, less the average time for service, so that

$$W_Q = W_S - \frac{1}{\mu} = \frac{1}{\mu - \lambda} - \frac{1}{\mu}$$

This is result 7 of Section 15.2.

Police Patrol Operations: A Complex Queueing System[1]

A number of studies have been devoted to building queueing models for the dispatch of police patrol vehicles. The problem is an important one, as it is estimated that at least half the costs of urban police departments are due to patrol car operations. Calls for assistance are received, and patrol cars must be assigned, if and when available, to respond to these calls. The delays involved are of concern to police departments, and the lengths of such delays are taken as an indicator of department efficiency. Because of concern over this problem, many urban police departments have employed queueing models to determine the numbers of patrol cars that should be assigned to different precincts at various times of the day or week.

The problem of modeling and analyzing the queueing system for an urban police department is by no means simple, and we will not discuss here the technical details. It is, however, interesting to examine qualitatively some of the elements of the problem in the light of our analyses of queueing models in this chapter.

The major features of the queueing problem for police patrol cars appear to be:

1. The queueing system has a number of identical servers—patrol cars.
2. Calls for service arrive at random.
3. These calls are not of equal priority, but rather can be grouped into priority classes. Within each class, calls will be answered on a first-in-first-out basis.
4. Different numbers of servers need to be assigned to different calls. Thus, a significant proportion of calls for help will require the dispatch of two or more patrol cars. The number of cars required for a call is regarded as a random variable.
5. When a call reaches the head of a queue, patrol cars are assigned to it as they become available, but service begins only when the number of cars required is available. It is thus possible for customers to be waiting and for servers to be idle simultaneously.
6. The lengths of time required for servers to complete the service of a call are independent random variables.

This problem is certainly not straightforward to model. In particular, it has the interesting element that different customers will require different numbers of servers—a possibility not discussed in the simpler models of this chapter. The author discusses the statistical properties of this queueing model and its application in the New York City police department.

---

[1] This discussion is based on L. Green, "A Multiple Dispatch Queueing Model of Police Patrol Operations," *Management Science, 30* (1984), 653–670.

simulation

CHAPTER SIXTEEN

16.1. INTRODUCTION

In the previous chapters of this book, we have used **mathematical models** to describe and analyze the characteristics of business systems. These models could be solved analytically to yield optimal decisions or to describe system behavior. However, despite the fact that mathematical model building can be, and has been, successfully applied to a wide range of management problems, it often happens that a problem is so complex that this approach is not viable. In these circumstances, it is often possible to use an electronic computer to **simulate** the system of interest. Simulation of management systems is also often employed to estimate the impact of system changes when it is infeasible to experiment physically with the system itself.

Simulation is a general technique, widely used by managers, aimed at building a model which can be analyzed by the computer, and which describes the essential characteristics of a real-world system. If the model provides a faithful description of the real system, then it should be possible, in a few minutes of computer time, to analyze the behavior of the model, and hence make inferences about the behavior of the system over a period of many months, or even years.

One can think of a management simulation model as serving a similar function to laboratory experimentation in the physical sciences. Experimentation with a real system may be costly, time consuming, or undesirably risky. On the other hand, it is often relatively straightforward to adjust specifications of a simulation model and to use the computer to analyze the behavior of the modified model. If the model provides a good description of the real-world system, it

601

should be possible to make reliable inference about the characteristics of the system, based on the analysis of the model.

Management simulation models are often employed in the analysis of systems in which there is an element of uncertainty. For example, in Chapter 15 we studied the characteristics of waiting lines, for which both arrival times and service times are uncertain. When specific distributional assumptions about these times are made, it can, as we have seen, be relatively straightforward to formulate and analyze a mathematical model of queue behavior. However, this can be extremely difficult if arrival time and service time distributions differ markedly from the forms assumed in Chapter 15. In that event, it may be possible to construct a model that simulates actual arrival and service behavior, and hence obtain a description of the real system. The simulation of uncertain behavior in this manner is often referred to as the **Monte Carlo method.** It is important to emphasize that this approach is designed to provide a characterization of system behavior. It is not a methodology for the derivation of optimal decisions, as for example is a linear programming algorithm. Moreover, the approach is not *precise,* in the sense that it only yields estimates, which are subject to error, of system characteristics.

Despite these drawbacks, managers frequently employ simulation methods as the only viable means of analyzing problems. Such methods are valuable when the system under study is too complex to allow the formulation and analysis of a mathematical model, and when experimentation with the real-world system is not feasible. In this chapter we aim to provide a flavor of the general technique of simulation, through its application to familiar problems.

As a first example of the methodology of simulation, consider a small PERT/CPM network of the type discussed in Section 13.2. A project consists of four activities, A, B, C, and D. Activities B and C cannot be started until A is completed, and activity D cannot be started until both B and C have been completed. Thus, in the terminology of Chapter 13, activity A is an immediate predecessor of both activities B and C, while B and C are immediate predecessors of activity D. The network is graphed in Figure 16.1.

Management is uncertain about the times required to carry out the four constituent activities of the project and believes this uncertainty can be characterized as follows:

ACTIVITY A ☐ 3 days with probability 0.25, 4 days with probability 0.60, 5 days with probability 0.15

ACTIVITY B ☐ 2 days with probability 0.18, 3 days with probability 0.58, 4 days with probability 0.24

FIGURE 16.1 PERT/CPM network for the simulation example.

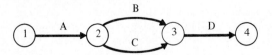

Activity C □ 3 days with probability 0.20, 4 days with probability 0.63, 5 days with probability 0.17

Activity D □ 4 days with probability 0.16, 5 days with probability 0.62, 6 days with probability 0.22

Our aim is to assess how much time will be required to complete this project. The total time needed is:

$$\begin{matrix} \text{Total} \\ \text{Time} \end{matrix} = \begin{matrix} \text{Time for} \\ \text{Activity A} \end{matrix} + \begin{matrix} \text{Time for} \\ \text{Activity D} \end{matrix} + \begin{matrix} \text{Larger of Times} \\ \text{for Activities B and C} \end{matrix}$$

We will estimate this time using the Monte Carlo approach. In order to do so, it is necessary to devise a chance mechanism that faithfully duplicates the assumed structure of the real-world process. For example, consider the question of how many days will be required to carry out activity A. We cannot know with certainty the answer to this question. However, we do know that the chances for completion in 3 days are 25 in 100, while the chances for completion in 4 and 5 days are, respectively, 60 in 100 and 15 in 100. Suppose, then, that we wrote down on pieces of paper 100 2-digit numbers, 00, 01, 02, . . . , 99. We can associate the first 25 of these, 00–24, with completion in 3 days, the next 60, 25–84, with completion in 4 days, and the last 15, 85–99, with completion in 5 days. Then, having thoroughly mixed these 100 pieces of paper, one can be chosen at random, the outcome determining actual time required for activity A in a simulation of this system. This procedure will ensure that in the simulation experiment, the probability of occurrence of any event will match that for the real-world system. Now, the approach just described, though effective, is rather crude and unnecessarily time consuming. In its place, we can substitute the use of **uniformly distributed random numbers.** These numbers are generated in such a way as to mimic the successive independent random choices of a single number from the set 0, 1, 2, . . . , 9. Table 5 in the Appendix at the back of this volume lists some five–digit random numbers. These are constructed so that each of the 100,000 numbers from 00000 to 99999 is equally likely to occur, and successive occurrences are independent of one another.

We can therefore devise a simulation experiment in which the whole project is depicted by drawing four 2–digit random numbers—one for each of the four activities. Random numbers drawn can be associated with event occurrences as shown in Table 16.1. We can begin to draw random numbers from any place in Table 5 of the Appendix. Suppose we start at the top of the first column. The first four numbers are

$$85387 \qquad 84176 \qquad 27258 \qquad 99398$$

Since only 2-digit random numbers are needed, we will use the last two digits of these numbers; that is,

$$87 \qquad 76 \qquad 58 \qquad 98$$

Using these in turn to determine times for activities A, B, C, and D, we find, from Table 16.1, 5 days for activity A, 4 days for activity B, 4 days for activity

TABLE 16.1 Association of random numbers with activity times for the simulation of the project completion time.

ACTIVITY	DAYS FOR COMPLETION	PROBABILITY	RANDOM NUMBERS
A	3	0.25	00–24
	4	0.60	25–84
	5	0.15	85–99
B	2	0.18	00–17
	3	0.58	18–75
	4	0.24	76–99
C	3	0.20	00–19
	4	0.63	20–82
	5	0.17	83–99
D	4	0.16	00–15
	5	0.62	16–77
	6	0.22	78–99

C, and 6 days for activity D. Given these individual activity times, the whole project would take 15 days to complete.

To get a surer grasp on what is likely to happen in practice, we must *replicate* this experiment. Thus, continuing to draw random numbers, we again find individual activity times, and hence project completion times. The results from carrying out 10 simulation experiments, drawing in turn random numbers from the first column of Table 5 of the Appendix, are set out in Table 16.2. Uncertainty about the time required for the whole project is reflected in the times found in the final column of this table.

One way to summarize this information is to find the average time required over these 10 trials. This yields an estimate of the *expected* time required for the

TABLE 16.2 Simulation, over 10 replications, of a project duration.

REPLICATION	RANDOM NUMBER	DAYS FOR A	RANDOM NUMBER	DAYS FOR B	RANDOM NUMBER	DAYS FOR C	RANDOM NUMBER	DAYS FOR D	DAYS FOR PROJECT
1	87	5	76	4	58	4	98	6	15
2	52	4	90	4	20	4	25	5	13
3	68	4	30	3	25	4	53	5	13
4	30	4	80	4	78	4	87	6	14
5	65	4	89	4	58	4	56	5	13
6	16	3	84	4	35	4	01	4	11
7	36	4	76	4	79	4	55	5	13
8	58	4	73	3	78	4	69	5	13
9	19	3	44	3	36	4	58	5	12
10	38	4	38	3	64	4	00	4	12
							TOTAL		129

project. Thus, from Table 16.2 we find that estimated expected time for project completion is $\frac{129}{10}$ = 12.9 days. We might also want to estimate the probability that the project will take more than 13 days to complete. From Table 16.2, we find that in 10 trials, project completion time exceeds 13 days twice. Hence, we estimate that the probability is $\frac{2}{10}$ = 0.2 that it will require more than 13 days to finish this project.

Now, the estimates that we have computed are based on only 10 replications of the simulation experiment, and so are subject to substantial error. In practice, using an electronic computer, computations for a very large number of trials can be quite quickly carried out, thus yielding more reliable estimates of the characteristics of the system.

16.2. SIMULATION OF A QUEUEING SYSTEM

In Chapter 15 we considered the mathematical modeling and analysis of waiting lines, and were able to obtain the characteristics of such systems when arrivals were at a Poisson rate and service times followed an exponential distribution. Now, although such assumptions are often appropriate for real-world queueing systems, they are not invariably so. For alternative characterizations of arrival and service behavior, formal mathematical analysis can be extremely difficult and often is impossible. In such circumstances, simulation provides an attractive alternative approach.

We will illustrate the use of simulation in the study of queues through a problem where there is a finite source population, similar to that discussed in Section 15.4. A corporation has four computing networks, and two repair crews to service these networks. Experience has indicated that the Poisson distribution does not well represent the rate at which networks need service, and the exponential distribution does not well represent service times. Instead, experience suggests that if a network is operational at the beginning of a day, the probability is 0.1 that it will break down at some stage during the day. Also, management has estimated probabilities for numbers of days required to repair a malfunctioning network. These probabilities are shown in Table 16.3.

If a network breaks down, and a repair crew is unoccupied, it can be serviced immediately. Otherwise, it will be necessary for the malfunctioning network to wait in line for service.

TABLE 16.3 Repair time probabilities for malfunctioning computer networks.

DAYS NEEDED FOR REPAIR	PROBABILITY
1	0.52
2	0.39
3	0.07
4	0.02

MANUAL SIMULATION OF THE SYSTEM

Our aim is to devise a mechanism that provides hypothetical day to day behavior of the queueing system. To do so, we must depict the possible status of each of the four computer networks, and of the repair crews, each day. Obviously we cannot be certain of these factors, or about whether a network will require repair and about how long that repair will take.

To see how the possible course of events can be simulated, consider a single computer network that is functioning at the beginning of a day. Will that network break down during the day? Of course, the answer to this question cannot be known with certainty. The probability is 0.1 that the network will break down, and therefore 0.9 that it will not.

To simulate the possibility of breakdown, then, we can employ single-digit random numbers, associating the event "break down" with the number zero, and the event "not break down" with the numbers one through 9. Suppose that we draw random numbers from the second column of Table 5 of the Appendix. The first six numbers in the second column are:

51571   03311   51746   46950   89364   93551

In the present context, we need only single-digit numbers, so that we can concentrate on the final digit of each of these five-digit random numbers; that is,

1   1   6   0   4   1

Then, the first six events encountered will be:

Not break down, Not break down, Not break down,
Break down, Not break down, Not break down

Next, we need to represent in our simulation model the lengths of time needed for repairs of malfunctioning networks. It is required that the probabilities for 1, 2, 3, and 4 days necessary for repair be, respectively, 0.52, 0.39, 0.07, and 0.02. For this purpose, then, we will require uniformly distributed random digits from 00 to 99. Then, if the first 52 of these are associated with repairs requiring one day, the next 39 with repairs requiring 2 days, and so on, the assumed real world probabilities will be accurately duplicated in the simulations. Hence, we associate days needed for repair with random numbers as in Table 16.4.

TABLE 16.4 Association of random numbers with repair times in the computer networks simulation.

DAYS NEEDED FOR REPAIR	PROBABILITY	RANDOM NUMBERS
1	0.52	00–51
2	0.39	52–90
3	0.07	91–97
4	0.02	98–99

We will begin to select random numbers at the top of the third column of Table 5 of the Appendix. The first six entries in this column are:

$$57714 \quad 16955 \quad 67223 \quad 19399 \quad 02150 \quad 11649$$

We use the last two digits of these numbers to determine time needed to repair malfunctioning computer networks; that is,

$$14 \quad 55 \quad 23 \quad 99 \quad 50 \quad 49$$

Hence, from Table 16.4, the times needed for repairs of the first six network breakdowns in the simulations are:

$$1 \text{ day} \quad 2 \text{ days} \quad 1 \text{ day} \quad 4 \text{ days} \quad 1 \text{ day} \quad 1 \text{ day}$$

We have now seen how random numbers can be employed to generate in a simulation model occurrences of uncertain events in a real-world system. The procedure just described ensures that such events occur with the same relative frequencies in the simulation experiments as they are expected to occur in the real system.

Using this technique, it is now possible to develop a simulation model to represent the queueing system for malfunctioning computer networks. We will follow the possible development of this process day by day, using a construction known as a **fixed-time simulation model,** to keep track of important characteristics of the system. Specifically, management is interested in two features of the waiting line:

(a) The amount of computer network down-time that develops
(b) The amount of time malfunctioning computer networks must wait for service

In order to generate the required information, it is convenient to establish some notation, as set out in Table 16.5.

In this notation, if a network, say A, is functioning at the beginning of day i, then $A(i)$ is set to zero. A positive value for $A(i)$ indicates the number of days before the network will be functioning again. We will look at time in discrete steps of one day, assuming for the sake of simplicity that breakdowns can only

TABLE 16.5 Notation for the simulation of the queueing model for computer networks.

COMPUTER NETWORK	NUMBER OF DAYS BEFORE NETWORK BACK IN USE AT START OF DAY i	NUMBER OF DAYS SERVICE TIME GENERATED BY NETWORK ON DAY i	NUMBER OF DAYS DOWN-TIME GENERATED BY NETWORK ON DAY i	NUMBER OF DAYS WAITING TIME GENERATED BY NETWORK ON DAY i
A	$A(i)$	$AS(i)$	$AD(i)$	$AW(i)$
B	$B(i)$	$BS(i)$	$BD(i)$	$BW(i)$
C	$C(i)$	$CS(i)$	$CD(i)$	$CW(i)$
D	$D(i)$	$DS(i)$	$DD(i)$	$DW(i)$

occur in those systems that are operating at the beginning of the day. (Thus, the possibility that a network is returned to use during a day, and subsequently malfunctions again on that day, is ignored. This will have negligible impact on the validity of our calculations, though somewhat more accuracy could be obtained by following the process hour by hour rather than day by day. Effectively, our assumption is that a network becomes operational at the beginning of the day after service is completed.)

For each network operating at the beginning of a day, a random number is drawn, the outcome indicating whether or not the network will break down during that day. If the outcome is a network malfunction, a second random number is drawn to determine the number of days repair time service needed. Thus, for example, if network A is operating at the beginning of day i, but breaks down on that day, generating d days of service time, $AS(i)$ is set equal to d. Otherwise this variable is set to zero. If more than one network breaks down in a day, it will be assumed that the order of breakdowns is A, B, C, D. This implies no loss of generality since breakdown probabilities and service time need distributions are identical for the four networks.

Next, if a computer network breaks down, it is necessary to determine whether it can be serviced immediately, and, if not, how long it must wait for service. Suppose that Network A breaks down on day i. It can be serviced immediately if at least one of the two service crews is unoccupied—that is, if at least two of $[B(i), C(i), D(i)]$ are equal to zero. However, if two of the other networks are being serviced (while the third remains operational), network A will have to wait for the first service completion. In that case, waiting time for service will be the smaller of the two positive numbers in $[B(i), C(i), D(i)]$, which is, of course, the second largest number of that set. Finally, if all three other networks are malfunctioning, network A will have to wait for two service completions, so that waiting time will be the second largest of $[B(i), C(i), D(i)]$. We have thus established that, if network A breaks down on day i, the waiting time generated is

$$AW(i) = \text{Second largest of } [B(i), C(i), D(i)]$$

The total number of days down-time is then the sum of waiting time and service time, so that

$$AD(i) = AS(i) + AW(i)$$

Then, if network A breaks down on day i, it follows that at the beginning of the next day, this network will be $AD(i)$ days away from service, so that

$$A(i + 1) = AD(i)$$

Of course, if network A is not operating at the beginning of day i, it will be one day closer to return to service at the beginning of day $(i + 1)$, so that

$$A(i + 1) = A(i) - 1$$

We can argue in exactly the same way for the other networks, except that we must consider the possibility that another network has previously broken down in the day. For example, if network B breaks down, it is possible that the queue for service will have been lengthened by a prior breakdown of network A, which will be reflected in the value of $AD(i)$. Hence the waiting time will be

$$BW(i) = \text{Second largest of } [AL(i), C(i), D(i)]$$

where $AL(i)$ is the larger of $A(i)$ and $AD(i)$. Similarly, for breakdowns in networks C and D, waiting times will be

$$CW(i) = \text{Second largest of } [AL(i), BL(i), D(i)]$$

and

$$DW(i) = \text{Second largest of } [AL(i), BL(i), CL(i)]$$

where $BL(i)$ is the larger of $B(i)$ and $BD(i)$, and $CL(i)$ is the larger of $C(i)$ and $CD(i)$.

We can now set up the complete model for a single iteration of the simulations. Suppose we begin the day with values $A(i)$, $B(i)$, $C(i)$ and $D(i)$. We then proceed as follows.

FOR NETWORK A

1. If $A(i) > 0$, set $A(i + 1) = A(i) - 1$; $AS(i) = AD(i) = AW(i) = 0$
2. If $A(i) = 0$, draw random number to determine whether breakdown occurs
   (a) If no breakdown occurs, set $A(i + 1) = AS(i) = AD(i) = AW(i) = 0$
   (b) If breakdown occurs, draw random number to determine number of days service needed. Denote this by $AS(i)$. Set

   $$AW(i) = \text{Second largest of } [B(i), C(i), D(i)]$$
   $$AD(i) = AS(i) + AW(i)$$
   $$A(i + 1) = AD(i)$$

3. Set $AL(i)$ equal to larger of $A(i)$ and $AD(i)$

FOR NETWORK B

1. If $B(i) > 0$, set $B(i + 1) = B(i) - 1$; $BS(i) = BD(i) = BW(i) = 0$
2. If $B(i) = 0$, draw random number to determine whether breakdown occurs
   (a) If no breakdown occurs, set $B(i + 1) = BS(i) = BD(i) = BW(i) = 0$
   (b) If breakdown occurs, draw random number to determine number of days service needed. Denote this by $BS(i)$. Set

   $$BW(i) = \text{Second largest of } [AL(i), C(i), D(i)]$$
   $$BD(i) = BS(i) + BW(i)$$
   $$B(i + 1) = BD(i)$$

3. Set $BL(i)$ equal to larger of $B(i)$ and $BD(i)$

FOR NETWORK C

1. If $C(i) > 0$, set $C(i + 1) = C(i) - 1$; $CS(i) = CD(i) = CW(i) = 0$
2. If $C(i) = 0$, draw random number to determine whether breakdown occurs
   (a) If no breakdown occurs, set $C(i + 1) = CS(i) = CD(i) = CW(i) = 0$
   (b) If breakdown occurs, draw random number to determine number of days service needed. Denote this by $CS(i)$. Set

$$CW(i) = \text{Second largest of } [AL(i), BL(i), D(i)]$$
$$CD(i) = CS(i) + CW(i)$$
$$C(i + 1) = CD(i)$$

3. Set $CL(i)$ equal to larger of $C(i)$ and $CD(i)$

FOR NETWORK D

1. If $D(i) > 0$, set $D(i + 1) = D(i) - 1$; $DS(i) = DD(i) = DW(i) = 0$
2. If $D(i) = 0$. draw random number to determine whether breakdown occurs
   (a) If no breakdown occurs, set $D(i + 1) = DS(i) = DD(i) = DW(i) = 0$
   (b) If breakdown occurs, draw random number to determine number of days service needed. Denote this by $DS(i)$. Set

$$DW(i) = \text{Second largest of } [AL(i), BL(i), CL(i)]$$
$$DD(i) = DS(i) + DW(i)$$
$$D(i + 1) = DD(i)$$

Using the notation and simulation process outlined, we will simulate 10 days of this queueing system. It will be assumed that at the beginning of the first day, networks A, B, and C are operating, but that 2 days service work on network D is required before it will become operational. Hence, in our notation

$$A(1) = 0; \ B(1) = 0; \ C(1) = 0; \ D(1) = 2$$

Events will be simulated by drawing random numbers from the seventh column of Table 5 of the Appendix. These are reproduced in Table 16.6, where we have set out just the final two digits of each number, since that is the most that will be needed. In determining whether a network will malfunction during the day, only the last digit is employed: a zero indicates malfunction, while any other

TABLE 16.6 Random numbers used in the manual simulation of the computer networks repair system (drawn from column 7 of Table 5 of Appendix).

81	33	40	93
85	45	80	57
30	71	24	17
23	49	30	11
95	32	51	30
01	93	07	48
26	22	35	47
26	05	81	04
50	61	90	53

number implies that the network will remain operational throughout the day. In the event of a network malfunction, a two-digit random number is drawn and the outcome determined according to Table 16.4. Proceeding one day at a time, we find:

DAY 1 □ With the starting values $A(1) = 0$; $B(1) = 0$; $C(1) = 0$; $D(1) = 2$; the first random number is examined. Its final digit is 1, so that network A does not breakdown, and we can set $A(2) = AS(1) = AD(1) = AW(1) = AL(1) = 0$. The final digit of the second random number is 5, so that network B does not breakdown. Hence we set $B(2) = BS(1) = BD(1) = BW(1) = BL(1) = 0$. The final digit of the next random number is 0, implying a malfunction in network C. The next random number is 23, so that, from Table 16.4, repair of this malfunction will require 1 day of work. Hence, we set $CS(1) = 1$. Then $CW(1)$ is the second largest of $[0,0,2]$. Thus, $CW(1) = 0$, implying that network C will not have to wait for service. Next $CD(1) = CS(1) + CW(1) = 1$, and $C(2) = CD(1) = 1$. Finally, since a day's service on network D will have been completed, we set $D(2) = D(1) - 1 = 1$.

DAY 2 □ From the day 1 calculations, we have found for the starting conditions of day 2, $A(2) = 0$, $B(2) = 0$, $C(2) = 1$, $D(2) = 1$. The final digit of the next random number in Table 16.6 is 5, so that network A does not breakdown. Hence $A(3) = AS(2) = AD(2) = AW(2) = AL(2) = 0$. The next random number has final digit 1, so that network B does not breakdown, and hence $B(3) = BS(2) = BD(2) = BW(2) = BL(2) = 0$. Finally, we see that $C(3)$ and $D(3)$ are both zero.

DAY 3 □ At the beginning of the third day, we have $A(3) = B(3) = C(3) = D(3) = 0$; that is, all four networks are operational. The final digit of each of the next two random numbers is 6, so that neither network A nor network B breaks down. Hence, $A(4) = AS(3) = AD(3) = AW(3) = AL(3) = 0$, and $B(4) = BS(3) = BD(3) = BW(3) = BL(3) = 0$. Since the final digit of the next random number is 0, network C develops a malfunction this day. Looking at the next random number, 33, it emerges that one day of repair time will be required, so that $CS(3) = 1$. Obviously, since $AL(3) = BL(3) = D(3) = 0$, there will be no wait for service. Thus, $CW(3) = 0$, $CD(3) = 1$, and $C(4) = 1 = CL(3)$. Since the final digit of the next random number is 5, network D does not breakdown, so that all associated variables are set to zero.

We can continue in this way to simulate the behavior of the system for as many days as required. Table 16.7 summarizes the results for the first 10 days. (The reader is invited to verify these findings, using the random numbers of Table 16.6.)

The results of this small simulation experiment can now be summarized, concentrating on the amounts of network down-time and service waiting time generated. The total amount of network down-time generated over 10 days of operations is obtained by summing $[AD(i) + BD(i) + CD(i) + DD(i)]$ over the 10 days. As can be seen from Table 16.7, total down-time is 9 days. Hence 0.9 day of down-time is generated per day of operations. The total amount of service waiting time is the sum of $[AW(i) + BW(i) + CW(i) + DW(i)]$ over the 10 days. In fact, as can be seen from Table 16.7, no waiting time is generated during the 10 simulated days of operation. In one sense, this is encouraging. It certainly appears quite likely that it will be possible to commence repairs immediately if a network malfunctions. However, management may be uneasy about the apparent underutilization of the repair crews' time. It may be possible to find other

TABLE 16.7 Manual simulation of 10 days of the computer networks repair system.

DAY i	RANDOM NUMBERS USED	A(i)	B(i)	C(i)	D(i)	AS(i) AD(i)	AW(i) AL(i)	BS(i) BD(i)	BW(i) BL(i)	CS(i) CD(i)	CW(i) CL(i)	DS(i) DD(i)	DW(i)
1	1, 5, 0, 23	0	0	0	2	0 0	0 0	0 0	0 0	1 1	0 1	0 0	0
2	5, 1	0	0	1	1	0 0	0 0	0 0	0 0	0 0	0 1	0 0	0
3	6, 6, 0, 33, 5	0	0	0	0	0 0	0 0	0 0	0 0	1 1	0 1	0 0	0
4	1, 9, 2	0	0	1	0	0 0	0 0	0 0	0 0	0 0	0 1	0 0	0
5	3, 2, 5, 1	0	0	0	0	0 0	0 0	0 0	0 0	0 0	0 0	0 0	0
6	0, 80, 4, 0, 51,7	0	0	0	0	2 2	0 2	0 0	0 0	1 1	0 1	0 0	0
7	5, 1	2	0	1	0	0 0	0 2	0 0	0 0	0 0	0 1	0 0	0
8	0, 93, 7, 7	1	0	0	0	0 0	0 1	3 3	0 3	0 0	0 0	0 0	0
9	1, 0, 48, 7	0	3	0	0	0 0	0 0	0 0	0 3	1 1	0 1	0 0	0
10	4, 3	0	2	1	0	0 0	0 0	0 0	0 2	0 0	0 1	0 0	0

$$\sum_{i=1}^{10} [AD(i) + BD(i) + CD(i) + DD(i)] = 9;\ \sum_{i=1}^{10} [AW(i) + BW(i) + CW(i) + DW(i)] = 0$$

productive tasks for the crew members when they are not required for computer network service.

The reader should be cautioned, however, that estimates based on just 10 time periods of simulation experiments are not usually very reliable. In order to obtain reasonably accurate estimates of system characteristics, a much larger simulation study is required.

COMPUTER SIMULATION OF THE SYSTEM

The manual computations that we carried out in simulating 10 days of the computer networks repair queue were quite tedious. Yet, 10 time periods of simulation experiments are woefully inadequate to obtain reliable estimates of system parameters—to obtain results in which much confidence could be placed, many times this number of experiments would be required. Therefore, in practice, simulation is an activity that requires use of a computer. Computer simulation is

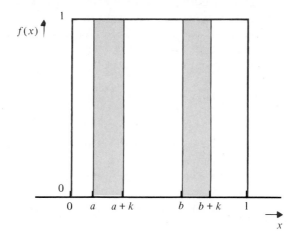

FIGURE 16.2 Probability density function of the random variable X that is uniformly distributed between 0 and 1. The shaded areas, which are equal, show $P(a < X < a + k)$ and $P(b < X < b + k)$.

now widely used by managers, facilitated by the development of special purpose simulation languages, such as GPSS and SIMSCRIPT.[1] These languages are considerably more efficient for generating simulation experiments than general purpose languages such as FORTRAN.

The availability of special simulation languages, and of prewritten subroutines for the simulation of important management models explains much of the recent popularity of computer simulation. However, recourse to the computer is, in any case, a necessity in this field. It simply is not feasible, in an acceptable amount of time, to achieve sufficiently accurate estimates in even the simplest of models through manual simulation.

Most modern computer systems have built-in software for the generation of random numbers. Invariably these numbers are generated from a statistical distribution that is uniform in a range from zero to one.[2] The uniform distribution has the particularly simple probability density function shown in Figure 16.2. This distribution has the property that the probability that an observation drawn from it lies in any interval in the range (0, 1) is the same as the probability for any other interval of the same width in that range. To illustrate, let a, b, $a + k$ and $b + k$ be four numbers between zero and one. Then, the probability that an observation falls between a and $a + k$ is the same as the probability that it falls between b and $b + k$. This is shown graphically in Figure 16.2.

---

[1] For a description of one of these languages, see T. J. Schriber, *Simulation Using GPSS,* (New York: John Wiley and Sons, Inc.; 1974).

[2] The capacity to generate random numbers from other statistical distributions, particularly the normal, may also be available. Otherwise, there exist procedures to allow the transformation of uniformly distributed random numbers to random observations from other distributions.

We now turn to our computer networks queueing problem, and see how uniformly distributed random numbers can be employed in the simulations to generate events with the required probabilities of occurrence. First, we know that the probability is 0.1 that a network that is operational at the beginning of a day will breakdown during the day. Now, it can be seen that the probability is 0.1 that an observation from a uniform distribution will lie between 0 and 0.1, and the probability is 0.9 that it will lie between 0.1 and 1. Hence, the required occurrence probabilities will result if we associate the event "breakdown" with a random number in the former interval, and "not breakdown" with one in the latter.

In the same way we can faithfully duplicate the probabilities for the numbers of days required to repair a malfunctioning system. Recall that the probabilities are 0.52, 0.39, 0.07, and 0.02 for one, 2, 3, and 4 days of repair time. The scheme set out in Table 16.8 ensures that these probabilities are replicated in the simulation experiments.

A computer program was written to simulate the computer networks repair system, and 1000 consecutive days of operation were simulated, taking as starting conditions all networks to be operational at the beginning of the first day. Thus, the simulation experiment is initiated by setting

$$A(1) = B(1) = C(1) = D(1) = 0$$

Over the thousand days, we found

$$\sum_{i=1}^{1000} [AD(i) + BD(i) + CD(i) + DD(i)] = 536$$

and

$$\sum_{i=1}^{1000} [AW(i) + BW(i) + CW(i) + DW(i)] = 27$$

It can be seen, then, that a total of 536 network-days of down-time are generated over 1000 days of operation—that is, 0.536 network-day of down-time per day of operation. It therefore follows that the average number of networks operating per day is $4 - 0.536 = 3.464$. Judging by these simulation results, no great problem seems likely to arise through malfunctioning networks waiting for ser-

TABLE 16.8 Association of random numbers from uniform distribution with repair times in the computer networks simulation.

DAYS NEEDED FOR REPAIR	PROBABILITY	RANDOM NUMBER, x, FROM UNIFORM DISTRIBUTION
1	0.52	$0 \leq x < 0.52$
2	0.39	$0.52 \leq x < 0.91$
3	0.07	$0.91 \leq x < 0.98$
4	0.02	$0.98 \leq x < 1$

TABLE 16.9 One thousand days of computer networks simulation for different breakdown probabilities.

Daily Breakdown Probability	0.1	0.2	0.3	0.4
Days of Down-time Generated	536	1080	1656	2079
Days of Waiting Time Generated	27	212	563	872

vice. Only 27 network-days of waiting time are generated over the 1000 days of simulated operations.

Since they were based on a much larger simulated period, these results are likely to be far more reliable than those reported earlier on the basis of 10 days of manually simulated operations.

EXPERIMENTATION WITH A SIMULATED MODEL

Computer simulation models are particularly valuable when information is required about hypothetical variants of real-world systems. For example, it is straightforward to modify our model to deal with computer networks with higher probabilities of malfunction. In Table 16.9, we show simulation results for downtime and service waiting-time totals over 1000 days of operations when each network has daily malfunction probabilities 0.2, 0.3, and 0.4, and the other problem specifications are unchanged. As is to be expected, these totals increase as the networks become less reliable.

Other variants of the model could also be simulated. For example, we could assess the impact of a reduction of the number of repair crews from two to one, or of an increase in the number of networks from four to five. We leave it as an exercise to the reader to discuss how the simulation program should be modified to run these experiments.

16.3. **VALIDATION OF A SIMULATION MODEL**

As we have just seen, the speed with which modern electronic computers can carry out routine arithmetic manipulations allows managers to rapidly carry out very large simulation experiments. However, these experiments will only be useful if the simulation model provides a good representation of the actual system of interest. Indeed, if the simulation model is seriously deficient in this respect, the simulation results could be badly misleading, and may persuade management to make poor decisions about the real-world system. For this reason, an important component of any simulation exercise is an attempt to validate the adequacy of representation of the simulation model to the real-world system. Depending on the nature of the system being simulated, a number of validation options may be available.

First, it is important to discuss the characteristics of a proposed simulation model with experts who have a good understanding of the real-world system.

These deliberations are necessarily subjective, but may well lead to the discovery of influential features of the system that have been overlooked by the model builders. Any model is bound to be a simplification of complex real-world behavior. However, it is important that the system not be oversimplified to the point where the model fails to incorporate vital features of the system. The advice of experts can be extremely valuable in trying to assess which factors can safely be ignored and which cannot.

One obvious source of possible unreliability in a computer simulation exercise arises from errors in the computer program. It is important that the program be thoroughly checked and tested. For example, intermediate calculations at various stages of the program can be printed out to assess whether different segments of the program are operating as expected; some of these calculations can be verified manually.

The two stages of simulation model validation just discussed represent part of sound standard practice. Nevertheless, it is quite conceivable that a simulation program could be error-free, and yet inadequately represent the real-world system, due to some factor with an importance insufficiently appreciated by the experts whose judgments were solicitied. If the system being simulated is one that is actually in operation rather than one being contemplated or planned, it may be possible, provided that adequate records have been kept, to validate at least parts of the simulation output through comparison with these historical records. Any serious discrepancies that are found may suggest, to the model builders, elaborations that will allow the model to more faithfully represent the real system.

If historical records are available, one feature of the model that can be checked is the assumed probability distribution for event occurrences. For example, in the previous section we simulated a queueing system for computer network repairs, in which it was assumed that the probabilities were 0.52, 0.39, 0.07, and 0.02 for 1, 2, 3, and 4 days required for repair of malfunctioning systems. These probabilities were based on management estimates. However, repair crew work records are available, covering the last 80 network breakdowns. Inspection of these records shows that 46 of these malfunctions required one day of repair work, 27 required 2 days, 4 needed 3 days, and 3 needed 4 days. We must now ask whether these observations provide strong evidence against the assumed probabilities. This question can be attacked through a statistical hypothesis test. The particular procedure used here is known as the **chi-square goodness of fit test.**

The information required to carry out this test is set out in Table 16.10. The first row of this table shows the numbers of occurrences of breakdowns requiring 1, 2, 3, and 4 days for repair. In general, let us suppose that occurrences are classified into K categories (so that $K = 4$ in this particular example), and that the observed numbers of occurrences in the categories are denoted O_1, O_2, . . . , O_K. Let n denote the total number of occurrences so that

$$n = \sum_{i=1}^{K} O_i$$

TABLE 16.10 Comparison of observed and expected numbers of occurrences for computer networks repair times.

	DAYS FOR REPAIR				
	1	2	3	4	TOTAL
Observed Number of Occurrences	46	27	4	3	80
Probability (under H_0)	0.52	0.39	0.07	0.02	1
Expected Number of Occurrences (under H_0)	41.6	31.2	5.6	1.6	80

The second row of Table 16.10 shows the postulated probabilities for numbers of days needed for repair. These probabilities will be denoted $p_1, p_2, \ldots, p_K$, and, in general, since one of these K outcomes must occur, it is required that

$$\sum_{i=1}^{K} p_i = 1$$

Our aim is to use the available data to test the hypothesis that repair times follow the assumed probability structure. In the parlance of statistical hypothesis testing, this is known as a **null hypothesis**—a hypothesis that will be assumed to be true unless, or until, sufficient contrary evidence is found. The test of this hypothesis is based on the comparison of the *observed* numbers of occurrences in each category with the numbers that would be *expected* if the null hypothesis were true. In our example, we have a total of 80 breakdowns, and if, indeed, 52% of all breakdowns took one day to repair, we would expect to find $(0.52)(80)$ $= 41.6$ occurrences in this category. In general, the expected numbers, E_i, are given by

$$E_i = p_i n \qquad (i = 1, 2, \ldots, K)$$

The complete set of expected values is shown in the final row of Table 16.10.

Looking at Table 16.10, the numbers of observed occurrences in each category certainly seem quite close to those that would be expected if the assumed probability distribution held. We will denote this null hypothesis H_0. Then, the test of H_0 is based on the statistic

$$\chi^2 = \sum_{i=1}^{K} \frac{(O_i - E_i)^2}{E_i} \qquad (16.1)$$

The statistic (16.1) provides a measure of the closeness of the observed and expected numbers of occurrences. It can be shown that a valid test is based on the comparison of this test statistic with tabulated values of the **chi-square distribution with $K - 1$ degrees of freedom.** Values of this distribution are given in

Table 6 of the appendix at the back of this volume. The test procedure is set out in the box below.

A Goodness of Fit Test

A null hypothesis, H_0, specifies occurrence probabilities $p_1, p_2, \ldots, p_K$ for K categories (with $\sum_{i=1}^{K} p_i = 1$). From a sample of n occurrences, numbers observed in each category are $O_1, O_2, \ldots, O_K$. The numbers expected, if H_0 were true, would be

$$E_i = p_i n \qquad (i = 1, 2, \ldots, K)$$

The hypothesis test decision rule is

$$\text{Reject } H_0 \text{ if } \sum_{i=1}^{K} \frac{(O_i - E_i)^2}{E_i} > \chi^2_{K-1, \alpha}$$

where $\chi^2_{K-1, \alpha}$ is the tabulated value of the chi-square distribution with $K - 1$ degrees of freedom, for a test of significance level[3] α.

For the data of Table 16.10, we find

$$\sum_{i=1}^{K} \frac{(O_i - E_i)^2}{E_i} = \frac{(46 - 41.6)^2}{41.6} + \frac{(27 - 31.2)^2}{31.2} + \frac{(4 - 5.6)^2}{5.6} + \frac{(3 - 1.6)^2}{1.6} = 2.7129$$

Since there are $K = 4$ categories, we need to compare the test statistic with values of the chi-square distribution with $K - 1 = 3$ degrees of freedom. Suppose we are prepared to allow a probability of 0.1 of rejecting the null hypothesis if it is in fact true. Then, with $\alpha = 0.1$, we find from Table 6 of the appendix

$$\chi^2_{K-1, \alpha} = \chi^2_{3, 0.1} = 6.25$$

Since the test statistic 2.7129 is less than 6.25, the null hypothesis is not rejected by a test with significance level 0.1. These data, then, provide little evidence against our conjecture that the probabilities are 0.52, 0.39, 0.07, and 0.02 for 1, 2, 3, and 4 days of needed service time.

A further check on the validity of a simulation study requires a test that the random numbers generated by the computer do in fact follow the statistical distribution that they should follow. A chi-squared goodness of fit test can also be employed for this hypothesis.

---

[3] The significance level of a test is that probability that an analyst is prepared to allow of rejecting a null hypothesis that is in fact true.

16.4. GENERATION OF RANDOM NUMBERS FOR COMPUTER SIMULATION[4]

dor. Tread

In order to carry out simulation experiments of adequate size, we require access to software that generates random numbers. Such software, for the generation of uniformly distributed random numbers, is now very widely available. Moreover, given uniformly distributed random numbers, there exist several procedures for their transformation to random numbers from other important statistical distributions.

Many uniform random number generators are based on the **multiplicative congruential generator**, which can be expressed as

$$x_{i+1} = ax_i \;(\text{mod } m)$$

$$u_{i+1} = \frac{x_{i+1}}{m} \tag{16.2}$$

In (16.2), u_i is the i-th uniform random number in the sequence, and a and m are nonnegative integers. The sequence is started by picking a starting value, or **seed**, x_0, and the **modulus** notation implies that x_{i+1} is the remainder when ax_i is divided by m. For example, suppose we set

$$a = 43; \; m = 99; \; x_0 = 50$$

Then $ax_0 = 2150$. Dividing 2150 by 99 yields 21, with a remainder of 71, so that

$$x_1 = 71$$

and

$$u_1 = \frac{71}{99} = 0.72$$

Continuing, $ax_1 = (43)(71) = 3053$. Dividing this number by 99, gives 30, with a remainder of 83, so that

$$x_2 = 83$$

and

$$u_2 = \frac{83}{99} = 0.84$$

---

[4] This section can be skipped with no loss of continuity. We are here able only to give a very brief account of randon number generation. A detailed discussion is provided by R. Y. Rubinstein, *Simulation and the Monte Carlo Method*, (New York: John Wiley and Sons, Inc., 1981), on which the present discussion is based.

This iterative generation procedure continues until the requisite number of random numbers has been generated.

In fact, some choices of *a, m,* and x_0 are far more satisfactory than others in the production of sequences with the desirable randomness properties, and much research has gone into this question. However, these issues are beyond the scope of our present discussion. One particular choice that has proved successful is $a = 7^5 = 16,807$, $m = 2^{31} - 1$, with x_0 any positive integer. This yields the **IBM System/360 Uniform Random Number Generator.** Versions of this generator form the basis of several widely available random number generation packages.

Now, many probability distributions other than the uniform, are employed to represent chance occurrences in management science problems. It is therefore important to be able to generate random observations from other distributions. One procedure for accomplishing this is set out in the box below.

Generation of Random Numbers by the Inverse Transformation Method

Suppose that we want to generate random numbers from a probability distribution whose cumulative distribution function is $F_X(x)$, given random numbers *u* from a distribution that is uniform in the interval (0, 1). The required random numbers are obtained from [5]

$$x = F_X^{-1}(u)$$

that is, *x* is that number for which $F_X(x) = u$.

To illustrate, in Chapters 10 and 15 we introduced the exponential distribution, which is often useful in describing service times, and the times between successive event occurrences. This distribution has cumulative distribution function

$$F_X(x) = 1 - e^{-\lambda x} \tag{16.3}$$

where λ is a positive number, and λ^{-1} is the mean of the distribution. Suppose that we want to generate random numbers *x* from this distribution, and have

---

[5] This result follows since, if the random variable *U* is uniformly distributed on (0, 1), then the random variable $X = F_X^{-1}(U)$ has cumulative distribution function $F_X(x)$, as

$$P(X \leq x) = P[F_X^{-1}(U) \leq x] = P[U \leq F_X(x)].$$

Then, this probability is the area under the uniform density function between 0 and $F_X(x)$, which is simply $F_X(x)$.

available random numbers u from the uniform distribution on $(0, 1)$. Then, from (16.3), this is achieved by setting

$$u = 1 - e^{-\lambda x}$$

Thus, we have

$$e^{-\lambda x} = 1 - u$$

or

$$-\lambda x = \log(1 - u)$$

Hence, the exponentially distributed random numbers are obtained as

$$x = \frac{-\log(1 - u)}{\lambda} \qquad (16.4)$$

For example, suppose that we want to simulate observations from a service time distribution, which is assumed to be exponential, with a mean of 5 minutes. Then, given uniformly distributed random numbers, u, we have, on setting $\lambda = \frac{1}{5}$ in (16.4)

$$x = -5 \log(1 - u)$$

where the service times, x, are measured in minutes.

The application of the inverse transformation method is quite straightforward if a closed form algebraic expression is available for the cumulative distribution function of the probability distribution from which we want to simulate observations. However, many important probability distributions do not have this property, and alternative methods must be employed. A case of this sort of special interest is the normal distribution.

One procedure for generating observations from a standard normal distribution is the **Box-Muller method.** Given a pair of random numbers, u_1 and u_2, from a distribution uniform on $(0, 1)$, we can obtain a pair, z_1 and z_2, from a standard normal distribution through

$$z_1 = (-2 \log u_1)^{1/2} \cos(2\pi u_2)$$
$$z_2 = (-2 \log u_1)^{1/2} \sin(2\pi u_2)$$

Proceeding in this way, standard normal random numbers can be generated two at a time. Then, if we require random numbers x_i from a normal distribution with mean μ and standard deviation σ, those are found from

$$x_i = \mu + \sigma z_i$$

In fact, because the normal distribution plays such an important role in statistical analysis, software for the generation of random numbers from this distribution is widely available.

16.5. SIMULATION OF AN INVENTORY SYSTEM

In this section we will show how simulation can be employed to model an inventory system, through an example similar to that discussed in Section 14.7. Consider a regional distributor of canned food, concentrating on a single product—baked beans. This distributor has found, on the basis of past experience, that daily demand for this product can be well represented by a normal distribution with mean 50 cases and standard deviation 12 cases. The distributor holds inventory to meet projected demand, and, when this falls to a certain level—the **reorder point**—an order is placed to the supplier for further stock. The size of those orders is called the **order quantity.** The cost of placing an order, whatever its size, is $20. Inventory holding costs for this product are estimated at $0.01 per case per day. There is a delay between the placement of an order and its receipt. All orders are delivered at the beginning of a working day that is 3 complete days, plus a fraction of a day, after the order was placed. Thus, if an order is placed at any time on day i, it will be received at the beginning of day $i+4$.

Our distributor is anxious to learn, for specific reorder points and order quantities, what will be the total inventory costs (made up of ordering costs and holding costs), and how many orders cannot be met as a result of stock-outs. We will approach this problem by constructing a fixed-time simulation model, tracking day by day a possible path of the system. In order to accomplish this, we employ the notation set out in Table 16.11.

If an order has been placed, but not yet received, then $L(i)$ will be equal to 1, 2, or 3, depending on when the order was placed. A value of zero for $L(i)$ implies that a new order is to be received at the beginning of day i. If no unfilled orders are outstanding, we can set $L(i)$ at some arbitrary high value, say 100.

We now show how to follow this system through a day, for which $S(i)$ and $L(i)$ are given.

If $L(i) = 0$, then an order of size OQ is to be received at the beginning of day i, so that $S(i)$ is increased to $S(i) + OQ$; otherwise, $S(i)$ is left unaltered. Next, a random number is drawn from a normal distribution with mean 50 and standard deviation 12. This gives us $D(i)$, the demand for this day.

TABLE 16.11 Notation for simulation of inventory system of the canned food distributor.

OQ =	Order quantity; the size of an order
RP =	Reorder point; the inventory level at which a new order is placed
$S(i)$ =	Number of cases in stock at beginning of day i
$L(i)$ =	Number of days, at beginning of day i, before a new order is received
$D(i)$ =	Number of cases demanded on day i
$UD(i)$ =	Unmet demand (in cases) on day i
$HC(i)$ =	Cost of inventory holding on day i (in $)
$OC(i)$ =	Cost of orders placed on day i (in $)

We must now consider the following three mutually exclusive possibilities:

1. If $D(i) > S(i)$ the implication is that the quantity demanded exceeds the available stock, and there will be unmet demand of

$$UD(i) = D(i) - S(i)$$

There will be no stock available at the end of the day, so we can set

$$S(i + 1) = 0$$

Also, since there is no inventory at the end of the day, holding costs will be zero; that is

$$HC(i) = 0$$

At this stage, the computations depend on whether or not an order, for which the distributor is awaiting delivery, has already been placed. There are two possibilities:

(a) If an order has already been placed,[6] so that $L(i) \leq 3$, no further order is placed. Thus, there is no order cost, and

$$OC(i) = 0$$

Also, since a day of delivery lag will have elapsed, we set

$$L(i + 1) = L(i) - 1$$

(b) If $L(i) > 3$, an order must be placed, at a cost of \$20; thus

$$OC(i) = 20$$

Further, since three more days must elapse before delivery is made, we must set

$$L(i + 1) = 3$$

2. If $0 \leq S(i) - D(i) \leq RP$, demand will not have been sufficient to exhaust stocks. However, inventory will fall below the reorder point, so that a new order must be placed, unless the distributor is already waiting for delivery of a previously placed order. Since there is no unmet demand, we have

$$UD(i) = 0$$

At the end of the day, the remaining stock is

$$S(i + 1) = S(i) - D(i)$$

and since daily unit holding cost is \$0.01, the cost incurred through carrying inventory in excess of demand is

$$HC(i) = 0.01[S(i) - D(i)]$$

The remaining calculations depend, as in (1), on whether an order has already been placed. Thus:

(a) If $L(i) \leq 3$, set

$$OC(i) = 0; L(i + 1) = L(i) - 1$$

---

[6] In these simulations, OQ is set sufficiently large that there is no possibility that stocks will be exhausted on a day on which a new shipment is received.

(b) If $L(i) > 3$, set

$$OC(i) = 20; L(i + 1) = 3$$

3. The final possibility is that $S(i) - D(i) > RP$. All demand will be satisfied, and, at the end of the day, inventories will still exceed the level at which a new order must be placed. Since there is no unsatisfied demand, and no new order is to be placed, we have

$$UD(i) = 0; OC(i) = 0$$

Also, since at day's end stocks will be the difference between initial stocks and demand, it follows that

$$S(i + 1) = S(i) - D(i)$$

and

$$HC(i) = 0.01[S(i) - D(i)]$$

Finally, since there will be no outstanding order, we set

$$L(i + 1) = 100$$

This simulation scheme is shown diagramatically in Figure 16.3.

Nine experiments, each of 5000 days, were carried out with the simulation model of the canned food distributor's inventory system. In these experiments, three different order quantities—400, 450, and 500 cases—and three different reorder points—150, 175, and 200 cases—were used in combination. The simulation runs were begun by assuming that at the beginning of the first day, the number of cases in stock was equal to the order quantity, and no new order had been placed. Thus, we set

$$S(1) = OQ; L(1) = 100$$

Over the 5000-day simulation period we measured inventory costs and the amount of unmet demand. The average order cost per day is

$$\text{Average Order Cost} = \sum_{i=1}^{5000} \frac{OC(i)}{5000}$$

Similarly, the average inventory holding cost per day

$$\text{Average Holding Cost} = \sum_{i=1}^{5000} \frac{HC(i)}{5000}$$

The total average inventory cost is the sum of average order and holding costs. The average amount of unmet demand per day is

$$\text{Average Unmet Demand} = \sum_{i=1}^{5000} \frac{UD(i)}{5000}$$

Thus, since average daily demand is 50 cases, the percentage of demand that is unmet is

$$\% \text{ Demand Unmet} = \frac{\text{Average Unmet Demand}}{50} \times 100$$

$$= \sum_{i=1}^{5000} \frac{UD(i)}{2500}$$

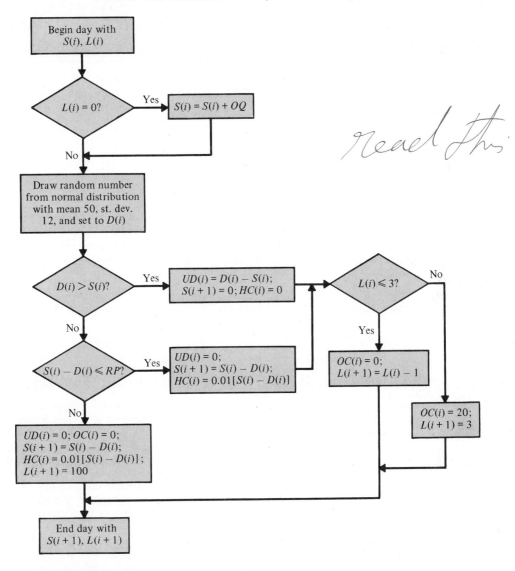

FIGURE 16.3 Simulation of a day of an inventory process.

The results of these simulation experiments are set out in Table 16.12. The final two columns of this table compare inventory costs with service level, as measured by the level of unmet demand. Generally speaking, the better the service level, the greater the cost of its provision. However, in the terminology of decision theory, it does emerge that some of these actions are inadmissible. For example ($OQ = 400$, $RP = 175$) is dominated by ($OQ = 450$, $RP = 175$) since the latter provides a better service level at a lower cost. Similarly ($OQ = 400$, $RP = 200$) is dominated by ($OQ = 450$, $RP = 200$), and ($OQ = 500$, $RP = 200$) is also dominated by ($OQ = 450$, $RP = 200$).

TABLE 16.12 Results of the simulation experiments for the inventory system of the canned foods distributor.

OQ	RP	AVERAGE DAILY ORDER COST ($)	AVERAGE DAILY HOLDING COST ($)	AVERAGE TOTAL INVENTORY COST ($)	% DEMAND UNMET
400	150	2.34	1.67	4.01	6.66
400	175	2.44	1.81	4.25	2.82
400	200	2.49	2.00	4.49	0.63
450	150	2.10	1.92	4.02	5.98
450	175	2.18	2.06	4.24	2.40
450	200	2.22	2.26	4.48	0.58
500	150	1.90	2.16	4.06	5.46
500	175	1.96	2.30	4.26	2.34
500	200	1.99	2.50	4.49	0.61

Which particular admissible choices of order quantity and reorder point are attractive to this distributor will depend on how important the provision of a high service level is. The value of simulation experiments like this is that at relatively modest cost, it is possible to estimate both the costs and service level provisions resulting from possible choices. Obviously, if the simulation model provides a good description of the actual system, this strategy is much to be preferred, in terms of both cost and time, to experimentation with the system itself.

EXERCISES

16.1. When I drive to my office, I must pass four gas stations. I have noticed that for each of these stations, the probabilities of finding 0, 1, 2, 3, and 4 other vehicles waiting for service are 0.2, 0.3, 0.25, 0.15, and 0.1, respectively. Also, the number waiting at one station appears to be independent of the number waiting at any other. If, at the beginning of my journey, I decide that I must get gas before reaching the office, I adopt the following procedure. Stop at the first gas station only if no vehicles are waiting for service. Otherwise, proceed on the journey, only stopping at a gas station if it has less waiting vehicles than the first station. However, if neither the second nor third stations have less waiting customers than the first, stop at the fourth station however many vehicles are waiting there.

(a) I intend to simulate this system through a simulation model. As one element of that model, it is necessary to employ random numbers to generate occurrences of different numbers of vehicles waiting for service at the first gas station. Carefully explain how to accomplish this, using for illustration the first five numbers in the final column of Table 5 of the Appendix.

(b) Develop a simulation model to estimate

  (i) the probability that I will stop at a station where there are no vehicles waiting for service.

  (ii) the expected number of vehicles waiting for service at the station at which I stop.

(c) Drawing, in order, random numbers from the first column of Table 5 of the Appendix, simulate this process 10 times, and obtain the estimates required in (b).

16.2. A service depot for electronic equipment faces uncertain demand over the first 6 months of the year for a particular part. For each of these months, demand probabilities are:

QUANTITY DEMANDED:	0	1	2	3	4	5	6
PROBABILITY:	0.10	0.15	0.20	0.25	0.15	0.10	0.05

This depot must order these parts from a distributor who can only deliver at the beginning of each month, and who insists that all orders for the first 6 months of the year must be placed immediately. The service depot manager, who currently has none of these parts in stock, has noted that expected monthly demand is 2.7 parts. Prompted by this information, he decides to place an order for 3 parts to be delivered at the beginning of each month. At the end of any month, unwanted parts will be held in inventory.

(a) If this system is to be simulated, random numbers must be used to generate occurrences of different demand levels in any given month. Carefully explain how this can be done, using for illustration, the first 6 numbers in the second column of Table 5 of the Appendix.

(b) Develop a simulation model to estimate

   (i) the expected amount of unmet demand over this period of 6 months.

   (ii) the expected number of parts that will be held in inventory at the end of the 6-month period.

   (iii) the probability that end of month inventory will reach at least 6 parts at some time during this period.

(c) Drawing, in order, random numbers from the second column of Table 5 of the Appendix, simulate this process 8 times, and obtain the estimates required in (b).

16.3. Refer to the simulation of the queueing system for malfunctioning computer networks, discussed in Section 16.2. Carefully explain how to modify the simulation model to estimate waiting time if the corporation has only one repair crew to service the four networks.

16.4. Refer to the simulation of the manlfunctioning computer networks queueing system of Section 16.2. Carefully explain how the simulation model should be modified to estimate waiting time if the corporation has two repair crews to service five networks.

16.5. A bank has a branch with a single server for drive-in customers. The system has been studied closely, with the following findings:

   (i) During any period of 30 seconds, the probability is 0.9 that no customers will arrive, 0.1 that one customer will arrive, and zero that more than one customer will arrive.

   (ii) If a customer is being served at the beginning of a 30 seconds period, the probability is 0.12 that service will be completed at the end of that period.

   (iii) The probability is zero that more than one service can be completed in any period of 30 seconds.

   (iv) The probability is zero that a customer can arrive and be served within 30 seconds.

   (v) If more than three customers are being served or waiting in line for service, arriving customers will depart rather than wait in line for service. However, if the line is shorter than this it will be joined by an arriving customer.

(a) If this system is to be simulated, random numbers must be used to generate occurrences of the event "no customers arrive in a 30 seconds period." Explain how this can be done, using for illustration the first ten numbers in the third column of Table 5 of the Appendix.

(b) Develop a simulation model to estimate

    (i) The proportion of time the server is idle.

    (ii) The proportion of potential customers who depart because more than three customers are being served or waiting for service.

16.6. A company receives a shipment of 20 components, for which it is expensive to test that all specifications are met. The experience of this company is that 36% of all shipments contain no defectives, 38% contain one defective, 19% contain two defectives, 6% contain three defectives, and 1% contain four defectives. The company policy is to test two of these components, and refuse to accept delivery if either one of the tested components is defective. However, if the first tested component is defective, the test on the second need not be carried out. It is required to simulate this system.

(a) Random numbers must be used to generate occurrences of different numbers of defectives in a shipment. Explain how this can be achieved, using for illustration the first five numbers of Table 5 of the Appendix.

(b) Develop a simulation model to estimate

    (i) The proportion of all shipments for which delivery is refused.

    (ii) The proportion of those shipments for which delivery is refused that contain one, two, and three defectives.

    (iii) The expected number of components tested per shipment.

16.7. In August, demand for a financial analysis program to be used on micro computers was 200 copies. It has been predicted that for the final 4 months of the year, change in demand (September–August, October–September, and so on) will have the following probability distribution:

CHANGE IN DEMAND	−20	−10	0	10	20
PROBABILITY	.15	.20	.30	.20	.15

It is believed that monthly changes in demand will be independent of one another.

(a) To simulate this system, it is necessary to use random numbers to generate occurrences of different monthly changes in demand. Explain how this can be accomplished, illustrating with the first five numbers in the fifth column of Table 5 of the Appendix.

(b) Develop a simulation model to estimate the probability that average monthly sales over the last 4 months of the year will exceed 210 copies.

(c) Drawing in order random numbers from the fifth column of Table 5 of the Appendix, simulate this process 10 times, and obtain the estimate required in (b).

16.8. At the beginning of each working day, a department store manager must decide whether additional help is needed to restock the shelves. Experience has indicated that if extra help is needed one day, the probability is 0.4 that it will be needed the next. On the other hand, if extra help is not needed one day, the probability is 0.1 that it will be needed the next.

(a) Develop a simulation model to estimate the proportion of days on which extra help is needed, assuming that extra help was not needed on the day before the simulation run starts.

(b) Using the random numbers from the seventh column of Table 5 of the Appendix, run the simulation model for 20 days, and estimate the proportion of days on which extra help is needed.

16.9. A branch of a car rental agency receives each day requests for rentals according to the following probability distribution.

NUMBER OF REQUESTS	0	1	2	3	4	5	6
PROBABILITY	.07	.12	.20	.29	.18	.10	.04

The numbers of cars returned to this agency in a day have the probability distribution shown below.

NUMBER OF RETURNS	0	1	2	3	4	5	6
PROBABILITY	.04	.15	.22	.25	.20	.11	.03

A car that is returned one day must be checked and cleaned, and will not be available for rental until the following day. Assume that the number of rental requests in a day is independent of the number of returns.

(a) To simulate this system, random numbers must be used to generate occurrences of daily requests for rentals. Explain how this can be done, using for illustration the first five numbers in the eighth column of Table 5 of the Appendix.

(b) Assume that the agency begins with five cars available at the start of the first day. Develop a simulation model to estimate

  (i) The number of requests for rental per day, on average, that cannot be met.

  (ii) The proportion of days ending with at least eight cars in stock.

(c) Drawing random numbers from the ninth column of Table 5 of the Appendix, simulate this process for 20 days, and obtain the estimates required in (b).

16.10. An insurance company executive asserts that in any given year, there will be no claims on 10% of all medical policies, one claim on 15% of all policies, two claims on 25% of all policies, three claims on 20% of policies, four claims on 15% of policies, five claims on 10% of policies, and more than five claims on the other policies. A hundred policies were chosen at random, and the numbers of claims checked for a year, yielding the results shown below:

NUMBER OF CLAIMS	0	1	2	3	4	5	more than 5
NUMBER OF POLICIES	7	12	29	23	18	7	4

What do you think of this executive's assertion?

16.11. A manager of a small commuter airline that runs several daily flights between two cities estimates that 28% of these flights are full, 31% have one empty seat, 17% have two empty seats, 10% have three empty seats, 8% have four empty seats, and the remaining flights have more than four empty seats. A random sample of 200 flights found the following results:

NUMBER OF EMPTY SEATS	0	1	2	3	4	more than 4
NUMBER OF FLIGHTS	64	81	40	6	5	4

What do you think of the manager's estimate?

16.12. Consider the multiplicative congruential generator

$$x_{i+1} = 4x_i \pmod{10}, \; x_0 = 7$$

$$u_{i+1} = \frac{x_{i+1}}{10}$$

(a) Find $u_i(i = 1, 2, \ldots, 6)$.

(b) Comment on the suitability of this procedure as a generator of uniformly distributed random numbers.

16.13. A distribution which has been found to represent well the life length of many mechanical components is the **Weibull distribution.** Its cumulative distribution function is

$$F_X(x) = 1 - e^{-x^m/\alpha}, \; x \geq 0$$

where m and α are positive constants whose values are determined by the characteristics of the component. Suppose you have available random numbers uniformly distributed on (0, 1). Show how these can be used to generate random numbers from a Weibull distribution for which m and α are specified.

16.14. In Section 16.4 we discussed the generation of random numbers from a continuous distribution, given uniformly distributed random numbers, through the inverse transformation method. This approach can also be employed to generate observations from discrete probability distributions. A company has six machines of a particular type. For any one of these, the probability of breakdown in a given week is 0.20, and the performance of any machine is independent of that of any other. Given random numbers independent on (0, 1), show how to generate observations on the number of machines that breakdown in a week (Hint: the number of machines that breakdown has a binomial distribution. Use the probabilities in Table 1 of the Appendix.).

16.15. In Section 3 of Chapter 13, we discussed, through a Stochastic PERT analysis, a detergent promotional campaign project. Management of the detergent manufacturer was concerned that this project be completed within 18 weeks. In Chapter 13 we estimated the probability of this occurring by computing the probability that the critical path activities would all be finished within 18 weeks. However, project completion requires that *all* activities, whether or not they are on the critical path, be finished. Taking this into account, design a simulation model to estimate the probability that the project will be completed within 18 weeks. Assume that you have available random numbers generated from the relevant beta distributions.

16.16. A research and development project has five activities. The activity list below shows immediate predecessors.

ACTIVITY	A	B	C	D	E
IMMEDIATE PREDECESSORS	–	A	A	B, C	D

Activity times (in weeks) for the component activities are independent of one another, with the probability distributions shown below:

ACTIVITY	WEEKS					
	1	2	3	4	5	6
A	0.6	0.3	0.1	0	0	0
B	0.1	0.4	0.4	0.1	0	0
C	0.2	0.2	0.3	0.2	0.1	0
D	0	0	0.2	0.3	0.3	0.2
E	0	0	0	0.2	0.5	0.3

(a) Develop a simulation model to estimate the probability that this project can be completed in 15 weeks.

(b) Drawing, in turn, random numbers from the final column of Table 5 of the Appendix, estimate the probability in (a) through simulating the model 10 times.

Simulation of a Queueing System: The Reproduction Unit of an Aerospace Manufacturer[1]

The author of this study discusses a queueing problem of a reproduction unit in a division of an aerospace manufacturer in southern California. This unit houses two machines—a copying machine and a ditto machine—the latter yielding less expensive but lower quality reproductions. On average the unit has approximately 135 jobs per day, 55–70% of which require the more expensive copying machine. The reproduction unit has a single operator, who takes jobs from the reception window, at which they arrive, to the appropriate machine and carries out the work. In the terminology of queueing, then, the unit has a single server and two service facilities. One aspect of this problem is that the operator will not be aware of arrivals at the reception window until returning there from the machines.

The author studied actual arrival and service time distributions for this reproduction unit, and used these as the basis for a simulation study of different possible operating procedures. Since the facility experiences a relatively busy period each day, simulations were carried out to estimate queue characteristics separately for that period and for the day as a whole. Five different possible operating procedures were simulated:

1. A first-come-first-served system, in which the earliest arriving job at the reception window is taken to the appropriate machine and processed, the operator then returning to the service window. This rule closely approximated the procedure actually practiced in the reproduction unit.

2. To avoid delays caused by the operator making frequent trips between machines and service desk, all available jobs requiring the machine needed for the earliest arriving job are taken to that machine and processed. Only when this work has been completed does the operator return to the service window.

3. The job at the reception window with the shortest process time is taken to the appropriate machine and processed, the operator then returning the service window.

4. All available jobs requiring the machine needed for the job with shortest process time are taken to that machine and processed. The operator returns to the service window when this work has been completed.

5. The final rule employed is a more complicated one in which rule 4 is modified by requiring the operator to return to the service window if the probability is sufficiently high that a shorter job for the other machine will be waiting. The operating characteristics of this rule can be computed so as to minimize mean job flow time.

---

[1] This discussion is based on R. E. Gunther, "Dual-resource Parallel Queues with Server Transfer and Information Access Delays," *Decision Sciences, 12* (1981), 97–111.

FIGURE 17.1 Tree diagram for the university computing system.

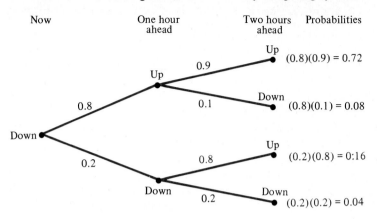

Suppose we know, initially, that the system is down. Denoting this initial condition as time zero, then since the system is certainly in state 2 at that time, it follows that

$$\pi(0) = [\pi_1(0) \qquad \pi_2(0)] = [0 \qquad 1]$$

We now show how, given the state probabilities $\pi(t)$, and the matrix of transition probabilities, the state probabilities $\pi(t + 1)$ for the next time period can be determined. For the case of two states, the probability that the system will be in state 1 at time $t + 1$ is

$P(\text{State 1 time } t + 1) = P(\text{State 1 time } t + 1 \cap \text{State 1 time } t)$
$\qquad\qquad\qquad\qquad + P(\text{State 1 time } t + 1 \cap \text{State 2 time } t)$
$\qquad\qquad = P(\text{State 1 time } t + 1|\text{State 1 time } t)P(\text{State 1 time } t)$
$\qquad\qquad\quad + P(\text{State 1 time } t + 1|\text{State 2 time } t)P(\text{State 2 time } t)$

In our notation, then, we can write

$$\pi_1(t + 1) = p_{11}\pi_1(t) + p_{21}\pi_2(t) \qquad\qquad (17.1)$$

A similar argument establishes that the probability that the system is in state 2 at time $t + 1$ is

$$\pi_2(t + 1) = p_{12}\pi_1(t) + p_{22}\pi_2(t) \qquad\qquad (17.2)$$

The results (17.1) and (17.2) can be efficiently summarized using matrix multiplication.[1] We have

$$[\pi_1(t+1) \quad \pi_2(t+1)] = [p_{11}\pi_1(t) + p_{21}\pi_2(t) \quad p_{12}\pi_1(t) + p_{22}\pi_2(t)]$$

$$= [\pi_1(t) \quad \pi_2(t)] \begin{bmatrix} p_{11} & p_{12} \\ p_{21} & p_{22} \end{bmatrix}$$

Therefore, we can write

$$\pi(t+1) = \pi(t)P \tag{17.3}$$

Equation (17.3) allows us to compute probabilities for each state at any point in time, starting with the initial condition at time zero. Thus, we have

$$\pi(1) = \pi(0)P$$

$$= [0 \quad 1] \begin{bmatrix} 0.9 & 0.1 \\ 0.8 & 0.2 \end{bmatrix}$$

$$= [0.8 \quad 0.2]$$

The state probabilities at the second time period are then found as

$$\pi(2) = \pi(1)P$$

$$= [0.8 \quad 0.2] \begin{bmatrix} 0.9 & 0.1 \\ 0.8 & 0.2 \end{bmatrix}$$

$$= [0.88 \quad 0.12]$$

This confirms our earlier findings on the tree diagram of Figure 17.1. Continuing in this fashion we can find, for any number of hours ahead, the probabilities for the two states, given the initial condition that the system is down. These results are set out in Table 17.2.

Notice, from Table 17.2, that as time moves on from the initial condition, the state probabilities begin to settle down, eventually changing very little from one hour to the next. This observation suggests that, looking sufficiently far

TABLE 17.2 State probabilities for the university computing system that is down at time zero.

TIME t	0	1	2	3	4	5
$\pi_1(t)$	0	.8	.88	.888	.8888	.88888
$\pi_2(t)$	1	.2	.12	.112	.1112	.11112

[1] In the appendix at the end of this chapter we summarize some useful results in matrix algebra.

TABLE 17.3 State probabilities for the university computing system that is up at time zero.

TIME t	0	1	2	3	4	5
$\pi_1(t)$	1	.9	.89	.889	.8889	.88889
$\pi_2(t)$	0	.1	.11	.111	.1111	.11111

ahead, a point will be reached where these probabilities remain effectively constant.

We can also compute, using the same methodology as before, the state probabilities when initially the system is up. Beginning with

$$\pi(0) = [1 \quad 0]$$

we can again employ equation (17.3). This yields the results shown in Table 17.3.

Again, it appears from Table 17.3 that, after some time, the state probabilities settle down. Moreover, comparing the results in Tables 17.2 and 17.3, it seems that the system eventually converges to *the same* state probabilities, whatever its initial condition. In these circumstances the system is said to move toward a **steady state.** It is no accident that this phenomenon arises in our example; indeed, under very general conditions, it will do so.

Homogeneous Markov Chains and the Steady State

A homogeneous Markov chain will converge through time to a **steady state,** where the state probabilities remain fixed at levels which do not depend on the initial conditions, provided that for some positive integer t, no elements in P^t are zero. The vector of steady state probabilities is denoted

$$\pi = [\pi_1 \quad \pi_2 \ldots \pi_N]$$

FINDING THE STEADY STATE PROBABILITIES

We have seen that the progression through time of the state probabilities is given by

$$\pi(t + 1) = \pi(t)P$$

Now, in the steady state, where probabilities do not change over time, we have

$$\pi(t) = \pi(t + 1) = \pi$$

so that we may write

$$\pi = \pi P \tag{17.4}$$

Equation (17.4) can be used to find the steady state probabilities. For the university computing center example, this gives

$$[\pi_1 \quad \pi_2] = [\pi_1 \quad \pi_2] \begin{bmatrix} 0.9 & 0.1 \\ 0.8 & 0.2 \end{bmatrix}$$

so that

$$\pi_1 = 0.9\pi_1 + 0.8\pi_2 \tag{17.5}$$

$$\pi_2 = 0.1\pi_1 + 0.2\pi_2 \tag{17.6}$$

Notice that both equation (17.5) and (17.6) imply, using some mathematical manipulation, that

$$0.1\pi_1 = 0.8\pi_2$$

so that one of this pair of equations is redundant, and they cannot be solved to uniquely determine π_1 and π_2. However, we also know that the probabilities for the individual states must sum to one, so that

$$\pi_1 + \pi_2 = 1 \tag{17.7}$$

The steady state probabilities are then found by solving (17.7) in conjunction with either (17.5) or (17.6).

From (17.7), we have

$$\pi_2 = 1 - \pi_1$$

so that, on substitution in (17.5),

$$\pi_1 = 0.9\pi_1 + 0.8(1 - \pi_1)$$

which yields

$$0.9\pi_1 = 0.8$$

Therefore

$$\pi_1 = \tfrac{8}{9}$$

and

$$\pi_2 = 1 - \tfrac{8}{9} = \tfrac{1}{9}$$

We can interpret the steady state probabilities as implying that, over the long run, regardless of the initial condition, the university computing system will be up $\frac{8}{9}$ of the time and down $\frac{1}{9}$ of the time.

ANALYSIS OF ALTERNATIVE TRANSITION PROBABILITY MATRIX

The university computing center is considering replacement of the current system with a new, more reliable system. One element in this decision is an assessment of the reduced cost of down time. The transition probabilities for the hour to hour state of the new system are shown in Table 17.4.

Denoting again by P the matrix of transition probabilities and by π the vector of steady state probabilities, then equation (17.4) yields

$$[\pi_1 \quad \pi_2] = [\pi_1 \quad \pi_2] \begin{bmatrix} 0.95 & 0.05 \\ 0.85 & 0.15 \end{bmatrix}$$

Therefore we find

$$\pi_1 = 0.95\pi_1 + 0.85\pi_2 \qquad (17.8)$$

$$\pi_2 = 0.05\pi_1 + 0.15\pi_2$$

TABLE 17.4 Transition probabilities for the new university computing system.

TIME t	TIME $t + 1$	
	1. SYSTEM UP	2. SYSTEM DOWN
1. System Up	0.95	0.05
2. System Down	0.85	0.15

[2] Note that one of this first set of equations will be redundant. Any one of these equations can be dropped, leaving us with a total of N equations in the N unknowns, $\pi_1, \pi_2, \ldots, \pi_N$.

Again, the individual steady state probabilities must sum to one, so that substituting

$$\pi_2 = 1 - \pi_1$$

in (17.8), we have

$$\pi_1 = 0.95\pi_1 + 0.85(1 - \pi_1)$$

Therefore

$$0.9\pi_1 = 0.85$$

so that

$$\pi_1 = \frac{17}{18}$$

and

$$\pi_2 = 1 - \frac{17}{18} = \frac{1}{18}$$

It can therefore be concluded, over the long run, that the new system will be up $\frac{17}{18}$ of the time and down $\frac{1}{18}$ of the time. Suppose that the computing center operates 720 hours per month, and that each hour of down time is assessed at cost of \$500. This cost involves both maintenance expense and an element measuring the inconvenience to users of down time. The original system is down $\frac{1}{9}$ of the time; that is, $\frac{720}{9} = 80$ hours per month. Thus monthly down time cost is $(80)(500) = \$40,000$. For the new system, expected down time per month is $\frac{720}{18} = 40$ hours, at a cost of $(40)(500) = \$20,000$. We therefore conclude that the installation of the new system should result in monthly savings of \$20,000 in down time costs.

17.2. APPLICATION TO BRAND SHARES

One common application of Markov processes is to the study of markets for a product of which there are two or more brands. Consumers may switch from purchase to purchase among brands, and it is the examination of the switching mechanism, or **brand loyalty** characteristics, to which we now turn.

In a certain market for light beer, three brands—Blitz, Schlusch, and Lindwall—are available. We will study the behavior, week by week, through time of this market. A market research survey has estimated current transition probabilities in this market. Specifically, it was estimated that of all purchasers of Blitz in one week, 80% would stay with that brand in the following week, while 10% would switch to Schlusch and 10% to Lindwall. Seventy percent of Schlusch purchasers were expected to stay with that brand next week, while it was estimated that 20% would switch to Blitz and 10% to Lindwall. For all purchasers of Lindwall in the current week, it is estimated that next week 60% will remain with that brand, while 20% will switch to each of the other two brands. These transition probabilities are set out in Table 17.5, and represent, for each brand

TABLE 17.5 Transition probabilities for the light beer market.

TIME t	TIME $t + 1$		
	1. BLITZ	2. SCHLUSCH	3. LINDWALL
1. Blitz	0.80	0.10	0.10
2. Schlusch	0.20	0.70	0.10
3. Lindwall	0.20	0.20	0.60

in week t, the probabilities that a randomly chosen purchaser will stay with that brand or move to one of the other brands in the following week.

Our objective is to examine the behavior over time of this market, *provided the transition probabilities remain constant* at the values shown in Table 17.5, and the other assumptions for a homogeneous Markov chain hold.

STATE PROBABILITIES FOR A CONSUMER OF ONE BRAND

Denoting the current week as time zero, we consider a randomly chosen current purchaser of Lindwall light beer. In the notation of the previous section, then, the initial state probabilities for such a consumer are

$$\pi(0) = [\pi_1(0) \quad \pi_2(0) \quad \pi_3(0)] = [0 \quad 0 \quad 1]$$

We will again denote by P the matrix of transition probabilities, so that

$$P = \begin{bmatrix} 0.8 & 0.1 & 0.1 \\ 0.2 & 0.7 & 0.1 \\ 0.2 & 0.2 & 0.6 \end{bmatrix}$$

In Section 17.1, we derived a formula to describe the evolution through time of state probabilities for a homogeneous Markov chain with two states. In fact, it can be shown that this relationship holds for any finite number of states, so that if $\pi(t)$ is the vector of state probabilities at time t, we have

$$\pi(t + 1) = \pi(t)P$$

For a current consumer of Lindwall, the purchase probabilities next week are[3]

$$\pi(1) = \pi(0)P$$

$$= [0 \quad 0 \quad 1] \begin{bmatrix} 0.8 & 0.1 & 0.1 \\ 0.2 & 0.7 & 0.1 \\ 0.2 & 0.2 & 0.6 \end{bmatrix}$$

$$= [0.2 \quad 0.2 \quad 0.6]$$

---

[3] Here and subsequently we will exploit the rules of matrix multiplication given in the appendix at the end of this chapter.

TABLE 17.6 State probabilities for the randomly chosen initial Lindwall purchaser.

TIME t	$\pi_1(t)$	$\pi_2(t)$	$\pi_3(t)$
0	0	0	1
1	0.2	0.2	0.6
2	0.32	0.28	0.40
3	0.392	0.308	0.300
4	0.4352	0.3148	0.2500
5	0.46112	0.31388	0.22500
6	0.476672	0.310828	0.212500
7	0.4860032	0.3077468	0.2062500

Continuing in this way, we find

$$\pi(2) = \pi(1)P$$

$$= [0.2 \quad 0.2 \quad 0.6] \begin{bmatrix} 0.8 & 0.1 & 0.1 \\ 0.2 & 0.7 & 0.1 \\ 0.2 & 0.2 & 0.6 \end{bmatrix}$$

$$= [0.32 \quad 0.28 \quad 0.40]$$

These results imply that of all current purchasers of Lindwall, in two weeks time 32% will be buying Blitz, 28% Schlusch, and 40% Lindwall.

In similar fashion, state probabilities for a randomly chosen current Lindwall purchaser can be determined as far ahead as required. Some results are summarized in Table 17.6. Notice that as time goes on, these probabilities appear to be stabilizing.

Precisely the same methodology can be used to determine week by week state probabilities for randomly chosen initial purchasers of Blitz or Schlusch. Here we would begin with respective initial state probability vectors $\pi(0)$ at [1 0 0] and [0 1 0].

PROGRESSION THROUGH TIME OF MARKET SHARES

The market research survey that produced the matrix of estimated transition probabilities for this light beer market also showed that at the present time, 40% of all consumers purchase Blitz, 35% Schlusch, and 25% Lindwall. Therefore, for a randomly chosen consumer, the initial state probabilities are

$$\pi(0) = [\pi_1(0) \quad \pi_2(0) \quad \pi_3(0)] = [0.40 \quad 0.35 \quad 0.25]$$

It then follows that the purchase probabilities next week for a randomly chosen consumer are

$$\pi(1) = \pi(0)P$$

$$= [0.40 \quad 0.35 \quad 0.25] \begin{bmatrix} 0.8 & 0.1 & 0.1 \\ 0.2 & 0.7 & 0.1 \\ 0.2 & 0.2 & 0.6 \end{bmatrix}$$

$$= [0.440 \quad 0.335 \quad 0.225]$$

TABLE 17.7 State probabilities for the randomly chosen consumer when initially 40% purchase Blitz, 35% purchase Schlusch, and 25% purchase Lindwall.

TIME t	$\pi_1(t)$	$\pi_2(t)$	$\pi_3(t)$
0	0.40	0.35	0.25
1	0.440	0.335	0.225
2	0.4640	0.3235	0.2125
3	0.47840	0.31535	0.20625
4	0.487040	0.309835	0.203125
5	0.4922240	0.3062135	0.2015625

Similarly, we find

$$\pi(2) = \pi(1)P$$

$$= [0.440 \quad 0.335 \quad 0.225] \begin{bmatrix} 0.8 & 0.1 & 0.1 \\ 0.2 & 0.7 & 0.1 \\ 0.2 & 0.2 & 0.6 \end{bmatrix}$$

$$= [0.4640 \quad 0.3235 \quad 0.2125]$$

These findings imply that, in two weeks time, 46.40% of consumers will purchase Blitz, 32.35% will purchase Schlusch, and 21.25% will purchase Lindwall.

Table 17.7 shows state probabilities further ahead, calculated in the same way. Again these probabilities appear to be stabilizing, and, indeed, the limiting states here and in Table 17.6 seem to be the same. This suggests the existence of a steady state solution.

THE STEADY STATE

Since the matrix of transition probabilities for the light beer brand shares model has no zeros, we know that the system converges, through time, to a steady state where the market shares for each brand remain fixed. Denoting by π the vector of steady state probabilities, we have

$$\pi = \pi P$$

so that

$$[\pi_1 \quad \pi_2 \quad \pi_3] = [\pi_1 \quad \pi_2 \quad \pi_3] \begin{bmatrix} 0.8 & 0.1 & 0.1 \\ 0.2 & 0.7 & 0.1 \\ 0.2 & 0.2 & 0.6 \end{bmatrix}$$

Writing out this system of equations yields

$$\pi_1 = 0.8\pi_1 + 0.2\pi_2 + 0.2\pi_3 \qquad (17.9)$$

$$\pi_2 = 0.1\pi_1 + 0.7\pi_2 + 0.2\pi_3 \qquad (17.10)$$

$$\pi_3 = 0.1\pi_1 + 0.1\pi_2 + 0.6\pi_3 \qquad (17.11)$$

Now, as in our previous discussion, one of these equations is redundant, in the sense that if any two of them hold, so must the third. Therefore, there is not a unique set of probabilities π_1, π_2, π_3 satisfying this set of equations. However, we can obtain a unique solution by considering any two of them in conjunction with the requirement that the probabilities must sum to one,

$$\pi_1 + \pi_2 + \pi_3 = 1 \qquad (17.12)$$

It can be shown[4] that the solution of the system of equations (17.9), (17.10), (17.12) is

$$\pi_1 = 0.5; \; \pi_2 = 0.3; \; \pi_3 = 0.2$$

from which it follows that if the matrix of transition probabilities remains fixed over time, this market will move toward the point where 50% of consumers purchase Blitz, 30% purchase Schlusch, and 20% purchase Lindwall. Given our findings in Tables 17.6 and 17.7, this result is not surprising; we have seen for two different initial state probabilities that after a few weeks, the state probabilities are already very close to these steady state solutions.

ANALYSIS OF AN ALTERNATIVE TRANSITION PROBABILITY MATRIX

The findings of the market research survey should cause concern to the management of Schlusch. Currently, this brand has 35% of the market. However, as we have just shown, if brand switching over time occurs in the manner predicted by the survey, the market share of Schlusch will fall to 30%. As we have seen, the brand that is expected to gain strength in this market is Blitz. Suppose, now, the Schlusch management decides to react to these predictions by mounting an advertising campaign, aimed at convincing Blitz drinkers of the virtues of Schlusch. This campaign has the goal of increasing from 10% to 15% the percentage of Blitz purchasers who will switch to Schlusch in the following week. The campaign is intended to run for several weeks, with the intention of establishing the transition probability matrix shown in Table 17.8.

The new steady state probabilities are again obtained from

$$\pi = \pi P$$

so that, with the revised transition probabilities matrix, we have

$$[\pi_1 \quad \pi_2 \quad \pi_3] = [\pi_1 \quad \pi_2 \quad \pi_3] \begin{bmatrix} 0.75 & 0.15 & 0.10 \\ 0.20 & 0.70 & 0.10 \\ 0.20 & 0.20 & 0.60 \end{bmatrix}$$

[4] In the appendix at the end of this chapter we describe and illustrate a procedure for solving systems of linear equations.

TABLE 17.8 Transition probabilities for the light beer market after the Schlusch advertising campaign.

TIME t	TIME $t+1$		
	1. BLITZ	2. SCHLUSCH	3. LINDWALL
1. Blitz	0.75	0.15	0.10
2. Schlusch	0.20	0.70	0.10
3. Lindwall	0.20	0.20	0.60

This yields the set of equations

$$\pi_1 = 0.75\pi_1 + 0.20\pi_2 + 0.20\pi_3$$

$$\pi_2 = 0.15\pi_1 + 0.70\pi_2 + 0.20\pi_3$$

$$\pi_3 = 0.10\pi_1 + 0.10\pi_2 + 0.60\pi_3$$

Taking any pair of these equations in conjunction with the requirement (17.12) that the steady state probabilities must sum to one, yields the solution

$$\pi_1 = \frac{4}{9}; \ \pi_2 = \frac{16}{45}; \ \pi_3 = \frac{1}{5}$$

It therefore follows that if the advertising campaign meets its objective of establishing the transition probabilities matrix of Table 17.8, the market share of Schlusch should stabilize at $\frac{16}{45}$, or 35.56%. This is slightly in excess of the current share, and a good deal better than the 30% share projected in the absence of the advertising campaign.

17.3. MARKOV CHAINS WITH ABSORBING STATES

In this section we will show how to analyze a special kind of Markov process. To see how processes of the type we have in mind can arise, consider the accounts receivable of a department store. Each account is put into one of five categories:

1. Fully paid
2. Bad debt
3. 0–30 days old
4. 31–60 days old
5. 61–90 days old

If an account is more than 90 days old, it is classified as a bad debt. This store uses the **total balance** method for classifying accounts receivable; the whole of a customer's account is classified according to the oldest unpaid bill in that account. Thus, for example, if the customer has a 70-days old bill and a 50-days old bill, and pays the former, the new balance is put into category 4, moving this amount of dollars out of category 5.

Management of the department store has tracked the behavior of accounts receivable over a period of several weeks, and has established the matrix of transition probabilities, for week to week movements of a single dollar, shown in Table 17.9. For example, for each dollar in a 61–90 days old account, the probability it will be paid in a week is 0.3, and the probability of lapsing into bad debt is 0.2. The probability that such a dollar will be in a 0–30 days old account in a week's time is 0.1, while 20% of these dollars move to 31–60 days old accounts and the remaining 20% stay in 61–90 days old accounts. A dollar that is currently in either a 0–30 days old or a 31–60 days old account cannot become a bad debt in only one week, so that the corresponding transition probabilities are zero. Similarly, it is not possible for a dollar in a 0–30 days old account to move in one week to a 61–90 days old account.

The matrix of transition probabilities in Table 17.9 has a very special feature. For two states—fully paid and bad debt—once a dollar is in that state it will remain there. Thus the probability is one that a dollar currently in one of these states will be in the same state next week. A bill that is paid remains paid, and it is assumed that once an account becomes a bad debt it is not collectible. Now, it is clear that every dollar that is currently in the system must eventually find its way to one of these two states, which are therefore referred to as **absorbing states.**

For a Markov chain with absorbing states, we do not find steady state probabilities, as in the previous two sections, since the eventual location of any dollar in the system will depend on its initial location. It is, however, important to ask what the probabilities are that a dollar, initially located in one of the nonabsorbing states, will eventually end in each of the absorbing states. Thus, for example, management of the department store will want to be able to estimate what proportion of money in the 0–30 days old accounts will eventually be paid.

We approach problems of this sort by **partitioning** the matrix P of transition probabilities, separating the absorbing from the nonabsorbing states. For the matrix of transition probabilities for department store accounts receivable, we therefore partition as

$$
P = \begin{bmatrix} 1 & 0 & 0 & 0 & 0 \\ 0 & 1 & 0 & 0 & 0 \\ 0.4 & 0 & 0.4 & 0.2 & 0 \\ 0.4 & 0 & 0.2 & 0.3 & 0.1 \\ 0.3 & 0.2 & 0.1 & 0.2 & 0.2 \end{bmatrix} = \left[\begin{array}{cc|ccc} 1 & 0 & 0 & 0 & 0 \\ 0 & 1 & 0 & 0 & 0 \\ \hline 0.4 & 0 & 0.4 & 0.2 & 0 \\ 0.4 & 0 & 0.2 & 0.3 & 0.1 \\ 0.3 & 0.2 & 0.1 & 0.2 & 0.2 \end{array} \right]
$$

In general, we will write the matrix of transition probabilities as

$$
P = \left[\begin{array}{c|c} I & 0 \\ \hline C & D \end{array} \right] \tag{17.13}
$$

TABLE 17.9 Transition probabilities for the department store's accounts receivable.

TIME t	TIME $t + 1$				
	1. FULLY PAID	2. BAD DEBT	3. 0–30 DAYS	4. 31–60 DAYS	5. 61–90 DAYS
1. Fully Paid	1	0	0	0	0
2. Bad Debt	0	1	0	0	0
3. 0–30 Days	0.4	0	0.4	0.2	0
4. 31–60 Days	0.4	0	0.2	0.3	0.1
5. 61–90 Days	0.3	0.2	0.1	0.2	0.2

where I is an identity matrix (whose dimension is the same as the number of absorbing states), and 0 is a matrix of zeros.

Given this notation, it is possible to find the required probabilities. It can be shown that this may be accomplished through the following steps:

1. Find the matrix

$$Q = I - D$$

where I is an identity matrix whose dimension is the same as that of D. For the department store accounts receivable problem, we find

$$
Q = \begin{bmatrix} 1 & 0 & 0 \\ 0 & 1 & 0 \\ 0 & 0 & 1 \end{bmatrix} - \begin{bmatrix} 0.4 & 0.2 & 0 \\ 0.2 & 0.3 & 0.1 \\ 0.1 & 0.2 & 0.2 \end{bmatrix}
$$

$$
= \begin{bmatrix} 0.6 & -0.2 & 0 \\ -0.2 & 0.7 & -0.1 \\ -0.1 & -0.2 & 0.8 \end{bmatrix}
$$

(17.14)

2. Find the inverse[5] of the matrix Q. It can be shown, for our example, that

$$
Q^{-1} = (I - D)^{-1} = \begin{bmatrix} 1.86207 & 0.55172 & 0.06897 \\ 0.58621 & 1.65517 & 0.20690 \\ 0.37931 & 0.48276 & 1.31034 \end{bmatrix}
$$

where elements are rounded to five decimal places.

3. Compute the matrix

$$R = Q^{-1}C = (I - D)^{-1}C$$

---

[5] One procedure for finding the inverse of a square matrix is given in the appendix at the end of this chapter.

where C is defined in (17.13). We therefore have

$$
R = \begin{bmatrix} 1.86207 & 0.55172 & 0.06897 \\ 0.58621 & 1.65517 & 0.20690 \\ 0.37931 & 0.48276 & 1.31034 \end{bmatrix} \begin{bmatrix} 0.4 & 0 \\ 0.4 & 0 \\ 0.3 & 0.2 \end{bmatrix}
$$
(17.15)
$$
= \begin{bmatrix} 0.9862 & 0.0138 \\ 0.9586 & 0.0414 \\ 0.7379 & 0.2621 \end{bmatrix}
$$

This matrix contains the required probabilities, the rows relating to the three non-absorbing states, and the columns to the two absorbing states. Specifically, then, given the assumptions of a homogeneous Markov chain, it follows that 98.62% of the dollars in 0–30 days old accounts will be paid, while 1.38% will become bad debts. Similarly, 4.14% of dollars in 31–60 days old accounts, and 26.21% of dollars in 61–90 days old accounts will eventually become bad debts.

Movements to Absorbing States

Consider a homogeneous Markov chain. If a state is such that the probability is 1 that the system is in that state at time $t + 1$, given it is in the state at time t, this is said to be an **absorbing state.** Whatever the initial condition, the system will move through time to a point where only absorbing states have nonzero probabilities.

Suppose that a homogeneous Markov chain has n absorbing and m nonabsorbing states. Let P denote the matrix of transition probabilities, arranged so that the first n rows and columns denote the absorbing states. This matrix can then be partitioned as

$$
P = \left[\begin{array}{c|c} I & 0 \\ \hline C & D \end{array} \right]
$$

where I is the $n \times n$ identity matrix. Define the $m \times n$ matrix R as

$$
R = (I_m - D)^{-1}C
$$

where I_m is the $m \times m$ identity matrix. Then the (i, j) element of the matrix R is the probability the system will move to the j-th absorbing state, given that it is initially in the i-th nonabsorbing state.

ESTIMATION OF FUTURE BAD DEBTS IN ACCOUNTS RECEIVABLE

The department store management is fully aware that not all of the dollar face value of its accounts receivable will eventually be paid, and it would be imprudent accounting practice to ignore this consideration. Rather, in attaching a value to these accounts, it is more realistic to try to estimate how much money will eventually be realized. Currently, this store has a total of $70,000 in active accounts, made up of $35,000 in 0 – 30-days-old accounts, $25,000 in 31 – 60-days-old accounts, and $10,000 in 61 – 90-days-old accounts.

We can compute the *expected* amount of bad debt by using the probabilities in (17.15) for each account category. It follows that

$$E(\text{Bad Debt}) = (0.0138)(35,000) + (0.0414)(25,000) + (0.2621)(10,000)$$

$$= \$4139$$

Thus, since it is expected that $4139 of those $70,000 in accounts receivable will lapse into bad debt, it follows that the expected amount collectible is $65,861.

EXERCISES

17.1. At the beginning of each working day, a department manager decides whether or not to request additional help from the company's secretarial pool, based on the number of absences among the department's permanent secretarial staff and the size of the day's work load. This manager finds that if a pool secretary is needed today, the probability is 0.7 that one will be needed tomorrow, while if a secretary is not needed today, the probability is 0.1 that one will be needed tomorrow. The system can be taken to satisfy the assumptions for a homogeneous Markov chain.

    (a) If a secretary from the pool is needed today, what is the probability that one will be needed in 2 days' time?

    (b) If a secretary from the pool is not needed today, what is the probability that one will not be needed in 3 days' time?

    (c) On what proportion of working days does this department need help from the secretarial pool?

17.2. A certain baseball player is a noted "streak hitter." It has been observed that if he gets a hit in one game, the probability is 0.7 that he will get a hit in the next, whereas if he does not get a hit in a game, the probability is 0.4 that he will get a hit in the following game. The assumptions of a homogeneous Markov chain are satisfied.

    (a) If the player gets a hit in the first game of the season, what is the probability he will get a hit in the third game?

    (b) If the player does not get a hit in the first game of the season, what is the probability he will get a hit in the fourth game?

    (c) If the player does not get a hit in the first game of the season, what is the probability he will get a hit in at least one of the next two games?

    (d) If the player gets a hit in the first game of the season, what is the probability he will begin the season with a three game hitting streak?

    (e) In what proportion of games does this player fail to get a hit?

17.3. A meteorologist in a particular town notices that if there is rain one day, then the probability of rain the following day is 0.3, while the probability is 0.1 that a day without rain will be followed by a day with rain. It was found that the system obeys the assumptions of a homogeneous Markov chain.

    (a) If there is no rain today, what is the probability there will be rain in 2 days' time?

    (b) If there is rain today, what is the probability there will be no rain in 3 days' time?

(c) If there is no rain today, what is the probability there will be rain on at least one of the next 2 days?

(d) What is the probability that there will be rain in this town on September 23 in the year 2000?

(e) What is the probability that there will be rain on each of three consecutive days in September of the year 2000?

17.4. A homogeneous Markov chain has two states. If the system is in the first state in the current time period, the probability is p_{11} that it will be in the first state in the next time period. If the system is in the second state in the current time period, the probability is p_{22} that it will be in the second state in the next time period.

(a) Show that the steady state probability for the first state is

$$\pi_1 = \frac{(1 - p_{22})}{(1 - p_{11}) + (1 - p_{22})}$$

(b) Show that $\pi_1 = 0.5$ if and only if $p_{11} = p_{22}$.

(c) Discuss the behavior of π_1 when $p_{11} = 1$, with $p_{22} < 1$. Provide a verbal explanation of your finding.

(d) Discuss the behavior of the expression π_1 of part (a) when $p_{11} = p_{22} = 1$. Provide a verbal explanation.

17.5. A homogeneous Markov chain has two states. If the system is in the first state in the current time period, the probability is p_{11} that it will be in the first state in the next time period. If the system is in the second state in the current time period, the probability is p_{22} that it will be in the second state in the next time period. Suppose initially (time $t = 0$) the system is in the first state.

(a) Show that the probability that the system is in the first state at time $t = 2$ is

$$\pi_1(2) = p_{11}^2 + (1 - p_{11})(1 - p_{22})$$

(b) Show that the probability that the system is in the first state at time $t = 3$ is

$$\pi_1(3) = p_{11}[p_{11}^2 + (1 - p_{22})^2] + (p_{11} + p_{22})(1 - p_{11})(1 - p_{22})$$

17.6. Refer to the company department of Exercise 17.1. Suppose you observe that today this department has help from the secretarial pool. Assess the probability that the department also required such help yesterday.

17.7. You watch a baseball game in which the player of Exercise 17.2 fails to get a hit. Assess the probability that this player got a hit in his previous game.

17.8. A stock market analyst characterizes 10% of all trading days as having heavy volume, and asserts that if volume is heavy one trading day the probability is 0.5 that it will be heavy the next. Trading volume over time is known to exhibit homogeneous Markov chain behavior. What proportion of days without heavy trading volume are followed by days in which trading volume is heavy?

17.9. A financial analyst monitoring the tire industry has noticed that if Goodstone Corporation reports, in one quarter, a profit rate higher than the industry average, then the probability that it will do so again in the following quarter is 0.65. On the other hand, if Goodstone's profit rate is currently not higher than the industry average, the probability that it will be higher next quarter is only 0.4. The process satisfies the assumptions of a homogeneous Markov chain.

(a) If Goodstone's profits in the current quarter are higher than the industry average, what is the probability they will also be higher in 2 quarters' time?

(b) If Goodstone's profits in the current quarter are higher than the industry average, what is the probability they will be higher in both of the next 2 quarters?

(c) In what proportion of all quarters are Goodstone's profits higher than the industry average?

17.10. A town has three supermarkets—Supersaver, Value Plus, and Fresh Foods. A market research study has estimated the transition probabilities below for week to week shopping of a randomly chosen consumer.

TIME t	TIME $t + 1$		
	SUPERSAVER	VALUE PLUS	FRESH FOODS
Supersaver	0.85	0.05	0.10
Value Plus	0.10	0.80	0.10
Fresh Foods	0.15	0.10	0.75

Suppose that these transition probabilities continue to hold in the future, and that the other assumptions for a homogeneous Markov chain hold.

(a) What is the probability that a randomly chosen consumer who shops at Supersaver in the current week will also shop at that store in 2 weeks' time?

(b) What is the probability that a randomly chosen consumer who shops at Value Plus in the current week will shop at Supersaver in 2 weeks' time?

(c) What is the probability that a randomly chosen consumer who shops at Fresh Foods in the current week will shop at Supersaver in at least one of the next 2 weeks?

(d) Find and interpret the steady state probabilities.

17.11. Refer to Exercise 17.10. Fresh Foods mounts a promotion to encourage customers to return to the store by giving coupons which can be redeemed on the following visit. The objective is to increase to 0.85 the probability that a current Fresh Foods customer will return to that store next week. It is expected that the probabilities that such a customer will shop at Supersaver and Value Plus will fall to 0.10 and 0.05, respectively, and that the other transition probabilities will remain unchanged. If this is the case, find and interpret the new steady state probabilities.

17.12. Refer to Exercise 17.10. The market research survey results indicate that currently, 40% of all consumers do their weekly shopping at Supersaver, while 30% shop at each of the other two supermarkets. Find the market shares of these three supermarkets in 2 weeks' time, given the transition probabilities of Exercise 17.10.

17.13. A homogeneous Markov chain has three states. The probability is p_{ij} that the system will be in state j at time $t + 1$, given that it is in state i at time t. Let π_i ($i = 1, 2, 3$) denote the steady state probability for the i-th state. Show that

$$(1 - p_{11} + p_{31})\pi_1 + (p_{31} - p_{21})\pi_2 = p_{31}$$

and

$$(p_{32} - p_{12})\pi_1 + (1 - p_{22} + p_{32})\pi_2 = p_{32}$$

17.14. A homogeneous Markov chain has three states. The probability is p_{ij} that the system will be in state j at time $t + 1$, given that it is in state i at time t. The system is currently in the first state.

(a) Show that the probability is p_{11} that the system will be in the first state in the next time period.

(b) Show that the probability is p_{11}^2 that the system will be in the first state in both of the next 2 time periods.

(c) Show that the probability is $p_{11}^2 + p_{12}p_{21} + p_{13}p_{31}$ that the system will be in the first state 2 time periods in the future.

(d) Use the results (a)–(c) to find the probability that the system will be in the first state in at least one of the next 2 time periods.

17.15. A town has two newspapers. Households are classified as purchasers of one or other of these papers—the Bugle or the Globe—or as nonpurchasers. (Assume that no household purchases both newspapers.) A recent survey has led to the following transition probabilities for month to month purchases

TIME t	TIME $t + 1$		
	BUGLE	GLOBE	NONPURCHASE
Bugle	0.80	0.05	0.15
Globe	0.15	0.75	0.10
Nonpurchase	0.25	0.25	0.50

Suppose that these transition probabilities continue to hold in the future, and that the other assumptions for a homogeneous Markov chain are satisfied.

(a) What is the probability that a randomly chosen consumer who currently purchases the Bugle will continue to do so in 2 months' time?

(b) What is the probability that a randomly chosen consumer who currently purchases the Globe will be a Bugle purchaser in 2 months' time?

(c) What is the probability that a randomly chosen consumer who does not currently purchase a newspaper will be a newspaper purchaser in 2 months' time?

17.16. Refer to Exercise 17.15. Suppose that these transition probabilities have in fact held over a considerable period of time. What proportion of households in this town purchase a newspaper?

17.17. Refer to Exercise 17.15, and consider a randomly chosen current purchaser of the Bugle.

(a) What is the probability this household will purchase the Globe next month?

(b) What is the probability this household will purchase the Globe in both of the next 2 months?

(c) What is the probability this household will purchase the Globe in 2 months' time?

(d) What is the probability this household will purchase the Globe in at least one of the next 2 months?

17.18. During a prime time hour on Thursday evenings, the three main television networks run, in competition, the shows Houston, Fantasy Boat, and SMASH. An audience research organization classifies households as viewers of one or other of these shows, or nonviewers. The following table gives the week to week transition probabilities.

TIME t	TIME $t + 1$			
	HOUSTON	FANTASY BOAT	SMASH	NONVIEWER
Houston	0.85	0	0.05	0.10
Fantasy Boat	0	0.90	0.05	0.05
SMASH	0.05	0	0.85	0.10
Nonviewer	0.10	0.20	0.20	0.50

(a) Find the probability that a randomly chosen household that watches Fantasy Boat in the current week will watch SMASH in 2 weeks' time.

(b) Find the probability that a randomly chosen household that does not watch any of these shows in the current week will watch one of them in 2 weeks' time.

(c) Find the probability that a randomly chosen household that watches Houston in the current week will also watch that show in at least one of the next 2 weeks.

(d) Find and interpret the steady state probabilities.

17.19. Refer to Exercise 17.18, and assume that this system is currently in the steady state. Beginning next week, the network showing Houston intends to fill the previous 30 minutes of air time with a stronger lead-in show. The marketing department believes that after this change, the transition probabilities will be as shown in the following table.

TIME t	TIME $t + 1$			
	HOUSTON	FANTASY BOAT	SMASH	NONVIEWER
Houston	0.90	0	0.05	0.05
Fantasy Boat	0.05	0.85	0.05	0.05
SMASH	0.10	0	0.80	0.10
Nonviewer	0.15	0.20	0.20	0.45

Trace out the effect, over time, of this change on the percentage of households watching Houston.

17.20. Table 17.9 shows week to week transition probabilities for a department store's accounts receivable.

(a) Find the probability that an account that is currently 61–90 days old will be fully paid within the next 2 weeks.

(b) Find the probability that an account that is currently 0–30 days old will remain in that category in both of the next 2 weeks.

17.21. The department store of Section 17.3 institutes a tougher debt collection policy by sending strongly worded letters to customers whose accounts are more than 30 days old. It is hoped that this measure will produce the transition probabilities shown in the following table.

TIME t	TIME $t + 1$				
	FULLY PAID	BAD DEBT	0–30 DAYS	31–60 DAYS	61–90 DAYS
Fully Paid	1	0	0	0	0
Bad Debt	0	1	0	0	0
0–30 Days	0.4	0	0.4	0.2	0
31–60 Days	0.6	0	0.2	0.1	0.1
61–90 Days	0.4	0.2	0.1	0.1	0.2

(a) What proportion of the money, currently in 0–30 days old accounts, will eventually become bad debt?

(b) What proportion of the money, currently in 31–60 days old accounts, will eventually become bad debt?

(c) What proportion of the money, currently in 61–90 days old accounts, will eventually become bad debt?

(d) Currently, this store has a total of $70,000 in active accounts, consisting of $35,000 in 0–30 days old accounts, $25,000 in 31–60 days old accounts, and $10,000 in 61–90 days old accounts. How much of this money should the store expect to eventually be repaid?

17.22. A store classifies its accounts receivable into one of just three categories—"fully paid," "bad debt," and "unpaid." The first two are absorbing states. It has been found that, of all the money in the unpaid category, a proportion p_1 will be fully paid, a proportion p_2 will become bad debt, and the remainder will still be in the unpaid category the following week. Show that a proportion $p_2/(p_1 + p_2)$ of the money currently in the unpaid category will eventually become bad debt.

17.23. A stock market analyst has recommended several stocks to clients. Each month she sends a report to these clients in which each stock is assigned to one of four categories.

1. Sell at a profit
2. Sell at a loss
3. Performance is so far good, but continue to hold the stock
4. Performance is so far poor, but continue to hold the stock

The following table shows the month to month transition probabilities.

TIME t	TIME $t + 1$			
	1	2	3	4
1	1	0	0	0
2	0	1	0	0
3	0.3	0	0.6	0.1
4	0	0.2	0.3	0.5

(a) What is the probability that a stock currently in the "performance so far good, but continue to hold" category will eventually be sold for a profit?

(b) What is the probability that a stock currently in the "performance so far poor, but continue to hold" category will eventually be sold at a loss?

(c) The active portfolio currently consists of fifteen stocks—ten in the "performance so far good, but continue to hold" category, and five in the "performance so far poor, but continue to hold" category. Find the expected number of these stocks that will eventually be sold for a profit.

APPENDIX A17.1

MATRIX ALGEBRA AND THE SOLUTION OF SETS OF LINEAR EQUATIONS

Matrices provide a very convenient way of storing and manipulating certain types of numerical information. In particular, they yield a valuable framework for describing and solving systems of simultaneous linear equations. In this appendix, we will review arithmetic rules for matrices and show how these rules can be exploited in the solution of linear equations.

DEFINITIONS

A **matrix** is a rectangular array of numbers. If the matrix has m rows and n columns, it will be called an **$m \times n$ matrix.** In general, it will be convenient to denote by a capital, such as A, a matrix, and by the corresponding lower case, a_{ij}, the element in the i-th row and j-th column of that matrix. Thus, if A is an $m \times n$ matrix, we write

$$A = \begin{bmatrix} a_{11} & a_{12} & \cdots & a_{1n} \\ a_{21} & a_{22} & \cdots & a_{2n} \\ \cdot & \cdot & \cdot & \cdot \\ a_{m1} & a_{m2} & \cdots & a_{mn} \end{bmatrix}$$

A matrix with the same number of rows as columns is called a **square matrix.**

A matrix with a single row is often referred to as a **row vector,** while a matrix with a single column is called a **column vector.**

ADDITION AND SUBTRACTION OF MATRICES

The application of matrices to a wide range of practical problems is facilitated by the definition of arithmetic operations, such as addition and subtraction. Provided two matrices have the same dimension—that is, both are $m \times n$, for positive integers m and n—their sum and difference can be defined:

(i) Let A be an $m \times n$ matrix whose (i, j)-th element is a_{ij}, and B an $m \times n$ matrix whose (i, j)-th element is b_{ij}. Then their sum, $A + B$, is the $m \times n$ matrix C, whose (i, j)-th element is

$$c_{ij} = a_{ij} + b_{ij}$$

For example,

$$\begin{bmatrix} 1 & 3 \\ 4 & 1 \\ 3 & 7 \end{bmatrix} + \begin{bmatrix} 3 & 6 \\ 4 & 11 \\ 9 & 2 \end{bmatrix} = \begin{bmatrix} 1+3 & 3+6 \\ 4+4 & 1+11 \\ 3+9 & 7+2 \end{bmatrix} = \begin{bmatrix} 4 & 9 \\ 8 & 12 \\ 12 & 9 \end{bmatrix}$$

Notice that it follows that

$$A + B = B + A$$

(ii) Let A and B be defined as before. Then their difference, $A - B$, is the $m \times n$ matrix D, whose (i, j)-th element is

$$d_{ij} = a_{ij} - b_{ij}$$

For example,

$$\begin{bmatrix} 1 & 3 \\ 4 & 1 \\ 3 & 7 \end{bmatrix} - \begin{bmatrix} 3 & 6 \\ 4 & 11 \\ 9 & 2 \end{bmatrix} = \begin{bmatrix} 1-3 & 3-6 \\ 4-4 & 1-11 \\ 3-9 & 7-2 \end{bmatrix} = \begin{bmatrix} -2 & -3 \\ 0 & -10 \\ -6 & 5 \end{bmatrix}$$

MULTIPLICATION OF MATRICES

If the number of columns in the matrix A is the same as the number of rows in the matrix B, the product AB can be defined. Let A be an $m \times p$ matrix whose (i, j)-th element is a_{ij}, and B a $p \times n$ matrix, whose (i, j)-th elements is b_{ij}. Then, their product AB is the $m \times n$ matrix C, whose (i, j)-th element is

$$c_{ij} = \sum_{k=1}^{P} a_{ik} b_{kj}$$

In words, the (i, j)-th element of AB is obtained by multiplying each element of the i-th row of A by the corresponding element of the j-th column of B, and summing.

For example,

$$\begin{bmatrix} 1 & 2 & 5 \\ 3 & 6 & 2 \end{bmatrix} \begin{bmatrix} 3 & 2 \\ 1 & 0 \\ 7 & -1 \end{bmatrix}$$

$$= \begin{bmatrix} (1)(3) + (2)(1) + (5)(7) & (1)(2) + (2)(0) + (5)(-1) \\ (3)(3) + (6)(1) + (2)(7) & (3)(2) + (6)(0) + (2)(-1) \end{bmatrix}$$

$$= \begin{bmatrix} 40 & -3 \\ 29 & 4 \end{bmatrix}$$

Notice that in general, BA is *not* the same as AB. Indeed, as in the above example, these products need not be of the same dimension. Moreover, one of these products may be defined while the other is not. Thus, if A is $m \times p$ and B is $p \times n$, AB is defined, but BA is not unless m and n are equal.

MATRIX REPRESENTATION OF A SYSTEM OF LINEAR EQUATIONS

Let $x_1, x_2, \ldots, x_n$ be a set of n variables, related by the system of equations

$$a_{11}x_1 + a_{12}x_2 + \ldots + a_{1n}x_n = b_1$$

$$a_{21}x_1 + a_{22}x_2 + \ldots + a_{2n}x_n = b_2$$

$$a_{n1}x_1 + a_{n2}x_2 + \ldots + a_{nn}x_n = b_n$$

where the a_{ij} and b_j are fixed numbers. Then, it follows from the matrix multiplication rule that we can write this set of linear equations as

$$\begin{bmatrix} a_{11} & a_{12} & \cdots & a_{1n} \\ a_{21} & a_{22} & \cdots & a_{2n} \\ \vdots & \vdots & & \vdots \\ a_{n1} & a_{n2} & \cdots & a_{nn} \end{bmatrix} \begin{bmatrix} x_1 \\ x_2 \\ \vdots \\ x_n \end{bmatrix} = \begin{bmatrix} b_1 \\ b_2 \\ \vdots \\ b_n \end{bmatrix}$$

or, more compactly

$$Ax = b$$

where A is the $n \times n$ matrix whose (i, j)-th element is a_{ij}, and x and b are the n dimensional column vectors

$$x = \begin{bmatrix} x_1 \\ x_2 \\ \vdots \\ x_n \end{bmatrix}; \; b = \begin{bmatrix} b_1 \\ b_2 \\ \vdots \\ b_n \end{bmatrix}$$

For example, the set of three equations

$$x_1 + 2x_2 - 3x_3 = 4$$

$$2x_1 + x_2 + 4x_3 = 7$$

$$3x_1 + 4x_2 - 2x_3 = 0$$

is written

$$\begin{bmatrix} 1 & 2 & -3 \\ 2 & 1 & 4 \\ 3 & 4 & -2 \end{bmatrix} \begin{bmatrix} x_1 \\ x_2 \\ x_3 \end{bmatrix} = \begin{bmatrix} 4 \\ 7 \\ 0 \end{bmatrix}$$

THE IDENTITY MATRIX

A square matrix whose elements consist of ones along the main diagonal—that is, in the (i, i) positions—and zeros elsewhere is called an **identity matrix**. The symbol I is invariably used to denote such a matrix, with a subscript sometimes added to specify the dimension, so that the $n \times n$ identity matrix may be denoted I_n. Thus, for example,

$$I_3 = \begin{bmatrix} 1 & 0 & 0 \\ 0 & 1 & 0 \\ 0 & 0 & 1 \end{bmatrix}$$

It follows from the rule of matrix multiplication that premultiplication or postmultiplication of a matrix by an identity matrix leaves that matrix unchanged. Thus, if A is an $m \times n$ matrix,

$$AI_n = A; \; I_m A = A$$

To illustrate, we see that

$$\begin{bmatrix} 1 & 2 & 5 \\ 3 & 6 & 2 \end{bmatrix}\begin{bmatrix} 1 & 0 & 0 \\ 0 & 1 & 0 \\ 0 & 0 & 1 \end{bmatrix}$$

$$= \begin{bmatrix} (1)(1) + (2)(0) + (5)(0) & (1)(0) + (2)(1) + (5)(0) & (1)(0) + (2)(0) + (5)(1) \\ (3)(1) + (6)(0) + (2)(0) & (3)(0) + (6)(1) + (2)(0) & (3)(0) + (6)(0) + (2)(1) \end{bmatrix}$$

$$= \begin{bmatrix} 1 & 2 & 5 \\ 3 & 6 & 2 \end{bmatrix}$$

We can think of the identity matrix as playing the same role in matrix arithmetic operations as does the number one in the arithmetic of ordinary numbers.

THE INVERSE OF A SQUARE MATRIX

The reciprocal, or inverse, of any nonzero number a is

$$a^{-1} = \frac{1}{a}$$

so that

$$a^{-1}a = 1$$

Now, in matrix multiplication, the identity matrix plays the role of the number one. With this in mind, we can define the **inverse** of a square matrix. Let A be an $n \times n$ matrix. Then, its inverse is the $n \times n$ matrix A^{-1}, which is such that

$$A^{-1}A = I \qquad\qquad\qquad\qquad \text{(A17.1)}$$

For example, if

$$A = \begin{bmatrix} 2 & 1 \\ 3 & 2 \end{bmatrix} \qquad\qquad\qquad\qquad \text{(A17.2)}$$

then its inverse is

$$A^{-1} = \begin{bmatrix} 2 & -1 \\ -3 & 2 \end{bmatrix}$$

as can be checked by verifying directly that (A17.1) holds.

Not every square matrix possesses an inverse; that is, it is not invariably possible to find a matrix A^{-1} satisfying (A17.1). A square matrix possessing an inverse is said to be **nonsingular.** A square matrix such as

$$B = \begin{bmatrix} 1 & 1 \\ 2 & 2 \end{bmatrix}$$

that does not possess an inverse is said to be **singular.**

If the square matrix A is nonsingular, so that (A17.1) holds, it also follows that[6]

$$AA^{-1} = I$$

Suppose that we have a system of n linear equations in n variables x, given by

$$Ax = b \tag{A17.3}$$

If the matrix A is nonsingular, we can premultiply through (A17.3) by A^{-1}, yielding

$$A^{-1}Ax = A^{-1}b$$

so that, using (A17.1)

$$x = A^{-1}b$$

We thus see that the inverse of a matrix plays an important part in the solution of systems of equations.

A PROCEDURE FOR FINDING THE INVERSE OF A MATRIX

A number of algorithms exist for determining the inverse of a nonsingular matrix. We will illustrate by finding the inverse of the matrix A of (A17.2). This is accomplished by setting out, side by side, the matrix to be inverted and an identity matrix of the same dimension. Thus, we write

$$\begin{bmatrix} 2 & 1 \\ 3 & 2 \end{bmatrix} \quad \begin{bmatrix} 1 & 0 \\ 0 & 1 \end{bmatrix}$$

We now proceed with a sequence of **row operations,** in which either each row is multiplied by a constant, or a row is replaced by the sum of itself and a constant

---

[6] Premultiply both sides (A17.1) by A, so that

$$(AA^{-1})A = A$$

and hence, since AA^{-1} must therefore be the identity matrix,

$$AA^{-1} = I$$

multiple of any other row. In such an operation we are, in effect, premultiplying each of our matrices by another matrix. The final object is to achieve, in the place of the first matrix, the identity matrix; the second matrix will be the required inverse.

We proceed, in steps as follows:

1. Multiply the first rows by $\frac{1}{2}$, giving

$$\begin{bmatrix} 1 & \frac{1}{2} \\ 3 & 2 \end{bmatrix} \quad \begin{bmatrix} \frac{1}{2} & 0 \\ 0 & 1 \end{bmatrix}$$

2. Subtract 3 times the first rows from the second rows, and put the results in the second rows. This gives

$$\begin{bmatrix} 1 & \frac{1}{2} \\ 0 & \frac{1}{2} \end{bmatrix} \quad \begin{bmatrix} \frac{1}{2} & 0 \\ -\frac{3}{2} & 1 \end{bmatrix}$$

3. Subtract the second rows from the first rows, and put the results in the first rows. This gives

$$\begin{bmatrix} 1 & 0 \\ 0 & \frac{1}{2} \end{bmatrix} \quad \begin{bmatrix} 2 & -1 \\ -\frac{3}{2} & 1 \end{bmatrix}$$

4. Finally, multiply the second rows by 2, giving

$$\begin{bmatrix} 1 & 0 \\ 0 & 1 \end{bmatrix} \quad \begin{bmatrix} 2 & -1 \\ -3 & 2 \end{bmatrix}$$

The second of these matrices is the required inverse.

A PROCEDURE FOR SOLVING A SET OF LINEAR EQUATIONS

Given a set of n linear equations

$$Ax = b$$

in the n variables x, we can write

$$x = A^{-1}b$$

Thus, the equations can be solved by first finding the inverse of the matrix A, and then computing the product $A^{-1}b$. However, a more direct approach utilizes the same technique as just described for matrix inversion, but now operating on the matrix A and the column vector b.

To illustrate, in Section 17.2 we required the solution of the set of equations (17.9), (17.10), and (17.12), which can be written

$$\begin{bmatrix} 0.2 & -0.2 & -0.2 \\ -0.1 & 0.3 & -0.2 \\ 1 & 1 & 1 \end{bmatrix} \begin{bmatrix} \pi_1 \\ \pi_2 \\ \pi_3 \end{bmatrix} = \begin{bmatrix} 0 \\ 0 \\ 1 \end{bmatrix}$$

We therefore operate on

$$\begin{bmatrix} 0.2 & -0.2 & -0.2 \\ -0.1 & 0.3 & -0.2 \\ 1 & 1 & 1 \end{bmatrix} \quad \begin{bmatrix} 0 \\ 0 \\ 1 \end{bmatrix}$$

through the following steps:

1. Multiply the first rows by 5, giving

$$
\begin{bmatrix} 1 & -1 & -1 \\ -0.1 & 0.3 & -0.2 \\ 1 & 1 & 1 \end{bmatrix}
\begin{bmatrix} 0 \\ 0 \\ 1 \end{bmatrix}
$$

2. Add 0.1 times the first rows to the second rows, and put the results in the second rows. This yields

$$
\begin{bmatrix} 1 & -1 & -1 \\ 0 & 0.2 & -0.3 \\ 1 & 1 & 1 \end{bmatrix}
\begin{bmatrix} 0 \\ 0 \\ 1 \end{bmatrix}
$$

3. Subtract the first rows from the third rows, and put the results in the third rows, yielding

$$
\begin{bmatrix} 1 & -1 & -1 \\ 0 & 0.2 & -0.3 \\ 0 & 2 & 2 \end{bmatrix}
\begin{bmatrix} 0 \\ 0 \\ 1 \end{bmatrix}
$$

4. Multiply the second rows by 5, giving

$$
\begin{bmatrix} 1 & -1 & -1 \\ 0 & 1 & -1.5 \\ 0 & 2 & 2 \end{bmatrix}
\begin{bmatrix} 0 \\ 0 \\ 1 \end{bmatrix}
$$

5. Add the second rows to the first rows, and put the results in the first rows, giving

$$
\begin{bmatrix} 1 & 0 & -2.5 \\ 0 & 1 & -1.5 \\ 0 & 2 & 2 \end{bmatrix}
\begin{bmatrix} 0 \\ 0 \\ 1 \end{bmatrix}
$$

6. Subtract twice the second rows from the third rows, and put the results in the third rows, giving

$$
\begin{bmatrix} 1 & 0 & -2.5 \\ 0 & 1 & -1.5 \\ 0 & 0 & 5 \end{bmatrix}
\begin{bmatrix} 0 \\ 0 \\ 1 \end{bmatrix}
$$

7. Multiply the third rows by 0.2, yielding

$$
\begin{bmatrix} 1 & 0 & -2.5 \\ 0 & 1 & -1.5 \\ 0 & 0 & 1 \end{bmatrix}
\begin{bmatrix} 0 \\ 0 \\ 0.2 \end{bmatrix}
$$

8. Add 2.5 times the third rows to the first rows, and put the results in the first rows. This gives

$$
\begin{bmatrix} 1 & 0 & 0 \\ 0 & 1 & -1.5 \\ 0 & 0 & 1 \end{bmatrix}
\begin{bmatrix} 0.5 \\ 0 \\ 0.2 \end{bmatrix}
$$

9. Finally, add 1.5 times the third rows to the second rows, and put the results in the second rows. This produces

$$
\begin{bmatrix} 1 & 0 & 0 \\ 0 & 1 & 0 \\ 0 & 0 & 1 \end{bmatrix}
\begin{bmatrix} 0.5 \\ 0.3 \\ 0.2 \end{bmatrix}
$$

As a result of these manipulations, we know that

$$\begin{bmatrix} 1 & 0 & 0 \\ 0 & 1 & 0 \\ 0 & 0 & 1 \end{bmatrix} \begin{bmatrix} \pi_1 \\ \pi_2 \\ \pi_3 \end{bmatrix} = \begin{bmatrix} 0.5 \\ 0.3 \\ 0.2 \end{bmatrix}$$

so that the solution to the original set of equations is

$$\pi_1 = 0.5; \pi_2 = 0.3; \pi_3 = 0.2$$

For larger systems, the procedures we have just described for matrix inversion and the solution of sets of linear equations become arithmetically tedious. However, because of their importance, computer programs are very widely available for carrying out these tasks. These programs allow the ready solution of much larger Markov chain problems than those that have been illustrated in this chapter.

Faculty Flow: Manpower Planning in Universities[1]

The author of this study describes a model for use in forecasting or decision-making by university administrators concerned about the future size and composition of the faculty. This model is intended to provide estimates of the size and composition, by age, rank, and appointment type, of the faculty in future years, both under current policies and alternative policy options (such as institution of an early retirement plan or a tightening of the standards required for tenure).

Broadly speaking, faculty members can be grouped into four types:

1. Tenured faculty
2. Tenure track faculty. These are faculty members not yet tenured but eligible for consideration for tenure. Thus, from year to year there are movements from this category to the tenured category.
3. Faculty on fixed-term appointments. These faculty members are not eligible for consideration for tenure: they may, however, in a subsequent year be appointed to a tenure track position.
4. Part-time faculty. These faculty members will generally not move to one of the other categories.

Faculty members may move out of any of these categories also through death, retirement, termination, or resignation.

The author discusses a Markov chain model with 26 states, which can be classified as follows:

(a) Part-time faculty
(b) Two states for fixed-term contract faculty, depending on whether or not an ending date is specified in the contract.
(c) Seven states for tenure track faculty, corresponding to seven possible years in this grade.
(d) Twelve states for tenured faculty, based on crossclassification by three ranks (assistant, associate, or full professor) and four age ranges.
(e) Four absorbing states: resignation, termination, retirement, and death

---

[1] This discussion is based on B. L. Bleau, "The Academic Flow Model: A Markov-chain Model for Faculty Planning," *Decision Sciences,* Vol. *12* (1981), 294–309.

Transition probabilities for movements from one state to another can be estimated from historical data. Administrators can also employ the model to assess the impact of policy options that will alter some of these probabilities. The model is completed by allowing for new hires to each of the 22 appointment states. Again, it is possible to employ the model to project the consequence of continuing current hiring patterns, or to assess the impact of modifying those patterns. The study discusses the application of this Markov chain model of faculty flow to the Altoona campus and the Capitol campus of Pennsylvania State University.

management information and decision support systems

CHAPTER EIGHTEEN

18.1. INTRODUCTION

In the previous chapters of this book, we have discussed a range of quantitative techniques to which the labels **management science** or **operations research** are generally attached. Although there exists a diversity of models that fall in these categories, they have a common objective—to aid management decision-making. Their development and practical implementation in the solution of many business problems was, of course, enhanced and facilitated by the power of the electronic computer. A parallel development, also based on the capabilities of the computer, has been the evolution of **management information systems.** This field, too, grew as an aid to management decision-making.

In the modern business environment, managers must make decisions on an increasingly complex array of problems. Many of these problems are much less well-defined than those discussed in the earlier chapters of this book, and issues arising in different areas of corporate activity are, of necessity, interconnected. Very often their formalization into a relatively simple mathematical model is infeasible, and answers to such questions require judgment, insight, and intuition. Nevertheless, it has become increasingly well-recognized that these informal approaches to decision-making will be most sound when based on the timely availability of relevant *information*. The capacity of modern computers to store and process vast amounts of information has allowed the development of management information systems as an extremely valuable tool in decision-making.

In this chapter, we will very briefly[1] discuss management information systems, and their relationship with management science methods.

As the name suggests, management information systems were originally developed to store and process information. However, in the last few years, management science models and algorithms for their solution, have increasingly come to be incorporated into such systems. The resulting entities are often called **decision support systems.**

A simplified schematic view of a management information system is depicted in Figure 18.1. The necessary prerequisite for the system is the acquisition of relevant *data*. These data constitute the raw factual description of corporate operations and environment, and will include records of sales, inventories, production, and financial variables. Such data are routinely collected and stored on computer tapes. The data collection process is tedious and time-consuming. However, the availability of a comprehensive and accurate data bank is essential if timely and reliable information is to be at hand for management decision-making. When a particular problem arises, time may not permit the acquisition of much new data: decisions must often be based on information derived from data currently in the bank. It is thus important that coverage be as comprehensive as possible. Moreover, the desire for accuracy is also clear. However sophisticated are the tools brought to bear on its analysis, very little of value can be derived from the interpretation of seriously inaccurate data.

In the present context, we need to distinguish between data and *information*. The raw data provide the basis for the derivation of information that is in a relevant form for the management task at hand. This information can be ob-

FIGURE 18.1 Schematic view of a Management Information System.

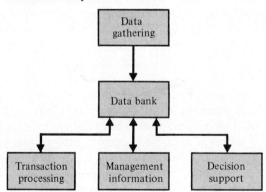

---

[1] Management information systems are discussed in far more detail in G. B. Davis, *Management Information Systems: Conceptual Foundations, Structure and Development,* (New York: McGraw-Hill Book Co., 1974), and R. G. Murdick, *M.I.S: Concepts and Design,* (Englewood Cliffs, N.J.: Prentice-Hall, Inc., 1980).

tained through more or less complex manipulations of the data. For example, the publisher will accumulate data on the sales of this book. These data will include numbers of books shipped and cash received from named college bookstores, and can be transferred to computer tapes as orders are sent out and payments are received. Much useful information can be derived from such data. For example, the cash receipts will be amalgamated with other receipts in the production of periodic income statements of the publisher's operations. More specifically, an editor will be able to quickly learn on which types of campuses a book is selling well, and on which it is not. This information will provide important ingredients into decisions on when and how many further copies should be printed, and whether a further edition should be contemplated.

In Figure 18.1, we have distinguished three separate potential outputs from the data bank. These are:

1. Transaction Processing
2. Management Information
3. Decision Support

In subsequent sections of this chapter, these will be discussed in some detail.

18.2. TRANSACTION PROCESSING SYSTEMS

The earliest computerized management systems were employed for the processing of transactions. Transaction processing systems may include programs for the collection, storage, and retrieval of information on

1. Orders and sales
2. Customer billing
3. Inventories
4. Payroll
5. Accounts receivable
6. Stockholding

In modern transaction processing systems, data are gathered on line, so that the shipment of goods, or receipt of payment, for example, is routinely entered into the data bank. Information on production and sales, processed in this manner, allows inventory holdings to be routinely updated.

Transaction processing systems thus contribute immensely to business efficiency, allowing large savings in labor costs, as well as the storage of far more data than would be possible without the computer. Much of the work carried out by computer processing systems is of this nature. However, the distinguishing feature of transactions processing is that it does not directly provide managers with information for decision-making. In this sense, transaction processing is not a true management information system, but simply a data processing system.

18.3. INFORMATION SYSTEMS

A transaction processing system can be viewed as providing support for the *operations* of a business. By contrast, a true management information system provides aid for management *decision-making*. The uses of such systems can be broadly categorized into four classes:

1. Preparation of standard reports
2. Preparation of exception reports
3. Preparation of special reports
4. Answering specific queries

In each case, programs are written so that information is derived from the data and presented in a format that is most useful to management.

Standard reports are generally prepared on a regular basis, the reporting period depending on the aspect of the business under study. These might include income statements, inventory holdings, and a summary of product quality. Typically standard reports provide a basis for routine decision-making, and for the production of externally required information, say, for accounting purposes. For example, a publisher may produce semi-annual reports on the sales of different titles and on inventories held in stock.

At a less routine level, exception reports are generally produced to signal a situation in which some prompt management action may need to be taken. For example, our book publisher will want to be alerted when inventory holdings of any title are low in relation to projected sales. Again, a corporation requires information about seriously delinquent accounts receivable. Much exception reporting, then, can be thought of as the production of selective information from that which is routinely reported. An example of exception reporting arises in routine sales forecasting. For corporations with many product lines, monthly sales forecasts are often generated routinely, generally using an exponential smoothing procedure such as those discussed in Chapter 12. When forecasts of sales of hundreds of product lines are required, it is economically suboptimal to devote a great deal of effort to the development of individual forecast models, tailored to the characteristics of each data series. Rather, a relatively straight-forward approach, that is expected to generally perform quite well, will typically be applied to each series. However, there will almost inevitably be some product lines for which this approach does not work well. A program which signals those series, where sales have differed substantially from projections, can alert management to the need to devote special attention to developing adequate forecasts for these product lines.

Special reports are generally prepared in response to specific management requests for information, typically to support a one-off decision. For example, suppose that a new edition of a textbook is to be prepared. An editor may wish to commission reviews from professors who are using the current edition in their classrooms, and also from professors at those types of institutions where the current edition has met with little success. The data bank can be accessed to produce a list of professors controlling large adoptions of the book, and also to indicate the type of institutions where the book has been successful and those where it has not.

Special requests may also be made for specific pieces of information. Perhaps the most commonly met example of this sort can be found in the offices of travel agents. Customer demand for air travel is greatly facilitated by computer access to information on flights along different routes and the availability of seats on these flights. As a further example, a customer service representative of a book distributor may receive a call on the availability of a specific title. Ready access to information on inventory holdings will allow a speedy response to this request.

18.4. DECISION SUPPORT SYSTEMS[2]

In the previous two sections, we have seen how management information systems are used for transactions processing, and how they can be employed in the preparation of reports as aids in management decision-making. A more recent development in the management information systems field has seen the incorporation of the models of management science and operations research into these systems. This new type of information system is called a **decision support system.**

A decision support system is an integrated collection of models and associated solution algorithms, together with a data base. The aim of such a system is to provide decision support for the analysis of those problems for which there is sufficient formal structure to permit some analytical modeling. However, the decision support system rationale differs from that of the earlier chapters of this book in that the injection of managers' judgment into the decision-making process is an important input, and attention can be focussed on the complete system, rather than on optimization within a segment of the whole corporate system.

Decision support systems are designed with the capability of analyzing a wide range of decision problems. They are intended to provide aid for the decision-maker faced with problems that are not fully structured: thus, such a system does not merely provide optimal solutions for constrained maximization or minimization problems, but contemplates multiple possible solutions. An important element of such systems, then, is interaction between the computer and the manager in the evaluation of alternative problem solutions and decision options.

---

[2] This topic is discussed in considerably more detail in P. G. W. Keen and M. S. Scott Merton, *Decision Support Systems: An Organizational Perspective,* (Reading, Mass.: Addison-Wesley Publishing Co., Inc., 1978), and S. Alter, *Decision Support Systems: Current Practice and Continuing Challenges,* (Reading, Mass: Addison-Wesley Publishing Co., Inc., 1980).

Decision support systems are designed to evolve through the incorporation of both relevant new data, and of useful models. Using interactive computing techniques, managers can have fast access to the data and models of the system. It is to be expected that such systems, incorporating modern developments in both management information systems and operations research, will broaden the applicability of both disciplines, and come to play an increasingly important part in modern management decision-making.

Academic Resource Planning: A Decision Support System Based on Goal Programming[1]

The authors of this study describe a decision support system aimed at facilitating decision making by university administrators. Specifically, the system provides support for decisions on the allocation of resources.

The decision support system employed was based on the goal programming algorithm, and involved three subsystems. These were:

1. A subsystem whose purpose was to elicit from the decision-maker information about his or her priorities.
2. A subsystem whose purpose was, through the goal programming algorithm, to determine satisfactory allocations based on the established priorities.
3. A subsystem designed to allow the decision-maker to evaluate the solution. Specifically, probabilities of attainments of goals are computed, and the possibilities of tradeoffs analyzed.

The decision-maker may interact with the decision support system by modifying priority assignments or by requesting the analysis of alternative solutions. The decision-making process then iterates until a solution satisfying the decision-maker's preferences is found.

The decision support system was employed to analyze allocations in the sociology department of a large midwestern university. Four decision makers—the Assistant Dean of the College of Liberal Arts, the Chairman of the Sociology Department, the Assistant Director of Operations Analysis for the University, and a Professor of Sociology—interacted separately with the decision support system. The resource allocation problem for this department involved twelve decision variables, twenty-nine goal constraints, and nine goals. The decision variables were of two types:

(a) Numbers of people to be employed in eight different categories: graduate research assistants, graduate teaching assistants, instructors, assistant professors, associate professors, full professors, technical and professional support staff, and secretarial support staff.
(b) Dollars to be allocated to total payroll budget, operating budget, faculty development fund, and salary increases.

---

[1] This discussion is based on L. S. Franz, S. M. Lee, and J. C. Van Horn, "An Adaptive Decision Support System for Academic Resource Planning," *Decision Sciences, 12,* (1981), 276–293.

Each of the four decision-makers, using the decision support system, arrived at what he or she regarded as a satisfactory working solution to the problem of allocating resources in the sociology department. The numbers of iterations required ranged from four to seven. As would be expected, there were differences among the four final decisions, reflecting differences in the priorities of the decision-makers. The most significant differences concerned the number of graduate teaching assistants to be hired. This can be seen as a reflection of the different philosophies of the four people on this issue.

tables

TABLE 1 Probability function of the binomial distribution.

The table shows the probability of x successes in n independent trials, each with probability of success p. For example, the probability of 4 successes in 8 independent trials, each with probability of success 0.35, is 0.1875.

n	x	p									
		.05	.10	.15	.20	.25	.30	.35	.40	.45	.50
1	0	.9500	.9000	.8500	.8000	.7500	.7000	.6500	.6000	.5500	.5000
	1	.0500	.1000	.1500	.2000	.2500	.3000	.3500	.4000	.4500	.5000
2	0	.9025	.8100	.7225	.6400	.5625	.4900	.4225	.3600	.3025	.2500
	1	.0950	.1800	.2550	.3200	.3750	.4200	.4550	.4800	.4950	.5000
	2	.0025	.0100	.0225	.0400	.0625	.0900	.1225	.1600	.2025	.2500
3	0	.8574	.7290	.6141	.5120	.4219	.3430	.2746	.2160	.1664	.1250
	1	.1354	.2430	.3251	.3840	.4219	.4410	.4436	.4320	.4084	.3750
	2	.0071	.0270	.0574	.0960	.1406	.1890	.2389	.2880	.3341	.3750
	3	.0001	.0010	.0034	.0080	.0156	.0270	.0429	.0640	.0911	.1250
4	0	.8145	.6561	.5220	.4096	.3164	.2401	.1785	.1296	.0915	.0625
	1	.1715	.2916	.3685	.4096	.4219	.4116	.3845	.3456	.2995	.2500
	2	.0135	.0486	.0975	.1536	.2109	.2646	.3105	.3456	.3675	.3750
	3	.0005	.0036	.0115	.0256	.0469	.0756	.1115	.1536	.2005	.2500
	4	.0000	.0001	.0005	.0016	.0039	.0081	.0150	.0256	.0410	.0625
5	0	.7738	.5905	.4437	.3277	.2373	.1681	.1160	.0778	.0503	.0312
	1	.2036	.3280	.3915	.4096	.3955	.3602	.3124	.2592	.2059	.1562
	2	.0214	.0729	.1382	.2048	.2637	.3087	.3364	.3456	.3369	.3125
	3	.0011	.0081	.0244	.0512	.0879	.1323	.1811	.2304	.2757	.3125
	4	.0000	.0004	.0022	.0064	.0146	.0284	.0488	.0768	.1128	.1562
	5	.0000	.0000	.0001	.0003	.0010	.0024	.0053	.0102	.0185	.0312

TABLE 1 *(Continued)*

n	x	.05	.10	.15	.20	.25	.30	.35	.40	.45	.50
							p				
6	0	.7351	.5314	.3771	.2621	.1780	.1176	.0754	.0467	.0277	.0156
	1	.2321	.3543	.3993	.3932	.3560	.3025	.2437	.1866	.1359	.0938
	2	.0305	.0984	.1762	.2458	.2966	.3241	.3280	.3110	.2780	.2344
	3	.0021	.0146	.0415	.0819	.1318	.1852	.2355	.2765	.3032	.3125
	4	.0001	.0012	.0055	.0154	.0330	.0595	.0951	.1382	.1861	.2344
	5	.0000	.0001	.0004	.0015	.0044	.0102	.0205	.0369	.0609	.0938
	6	.0000	.0000	.0000	.0001	.0002	.0007	.0018	.0041	.0083	.0156
7	0	.6983	.4783	.3206	.2097	.1335	.0824	.0490	.0280	.0152	.0078
	1	.2573	.3720	.3960	.3670	.3115	.2471	.1848	.1306	.0872	.0547
	2	.0406	.1240	.2097	.2753	.3115	.3177	.2985	.2613	.2140	.1641
	3	.0036	.0230	.0617	.1147	.1730	.2269	.2679	.2903	.2918	.2734
	4	.0002	.0026	.0109	.0287	.0577	.0972	.1442	.1935	.2388	.2734
	5	.0000	.0002	.0012	.0043	.0115	.0250	.0466	.0774	.1172	.1641
	6	.0000	.0000	.0001	.0004	.0013	.0036	.0084	.0172	.0320	.0547
	7	.0000	.0000	.0000	.0000	.0001	.0002	.0006	.0016	.0037	.0078
8	0	.6634	.4305	.2725	.1678	.1001	.0576	.0319	.0168	.0084	.0039
	1	.2793	.3826	.3847	.3355	.2670	.1977	.1373	.0896	.0548	.0312
	2	.0515	.1488	.2376	.2936	.3115	.2965	.2587	.2090	.1569	.1094
	3	.0054	.0331	.0839	.1468	.2076	.2541	.2786	.2787	.2568	.2188
	4	.0004	.0046	.0815	.0459	.0865	.1361	.1875	.2322	.2627	.2734
	5	.0000	.0004	.0026	.0092	.0231	.0467	.0808	.1239	.1719	.2188
	6	.0000	.0000	.0002	.0011	.0038	.0100	.0217	.0413	.0703	.1094
	7	.0000	.0000	.0000	.0001	.0004	.0012	.0033	.0079	.0164	.0312
	8	.0000	.0000	.0000	.0000	.0000	.0001	.0002	.0007	.0017	.0039
9	0	.6302	.3874	.2316	.1342	.0751	.0404	.0207	.0101	.0046	.0020
	1	.2985	.3874	.3679	.3020	.2253	.1556	.1004	.0605	.0339	.0176
	2	.0629	.1722	.2597	.3020	.3003	.2668	.2162	.1612	.1110	.0703
	3	.0077	.0446	.1069	.1762	.2336	.2668	.2716	.2508	.2119	.1641
	4	.0006	.0074	.0283	.0661	.1168	.1715	.2194	.2508	.2600	.2461
	5	.0000	.0008	.0050	.0165	.0389	.0735	.1181	.1672	.2128	.2461
	6	.0000	.0001	.0006	.0028	.0087	.0210	.0424	.0743	.1160	.1641
	7	.0000	.0000	.0000	.0003	.0012	.0039	.0098	.0212	.0407	.0703
	8	.0000	.0000	.0000	.0000	.0001	.0004	.0013	.0035	.0083	.0176
	9	.0000	.0000	.0000	.0000	.0000	.0000	.0001	.0003	.0008	.0020
10	0	.5987	.3487	.1969	.1074	.0563	.0282	.0135	.0060	.0025	.0010
	1	.3151	.3874	.3474	.2684	.1877	.1211	.0725	.0403	.0207	.0098
	2	.0746	.1937	.2759	.3020	.2816	.2335	.1757	.1209	.0763	.0439
	3	.0105	.0574	.1298	.2013	.2503	.2668	.2522	.2150	.1665	.1172
	4	.0010	.0112	.0401	.0881	.1460	.2001	.2377	.2508	.2384	.2051
	5	.0001	.0015	.0085	.0264	.0584	.1029	.1536	.2007	.2340	.2461
	6	.0000	.0001	.0012	.0055	.0162	.0368	.0689	.1115	.1596	.2051
	7	.0000	.0000	.0001	.0008	.0031	.0090	.0212	.0425	.0746	.1172
	8	.0000	.0000	.0000	.0001	.0004	.0014	.0043	.0106	.0229	.0439
	9	.0000	.0000	.0000	.0000	.0000	.0001	.0005	.0016	.0042	.0098
	10	.0000	.0000	.0000	.0000	.0000	.0000	.0000	.0001	.0003	.0010
11	0	.5688	.3138	.1673	.0859	.0422	.0198	.0088	.0036	.0014	.0005
	1	.3293	.3835	.3248	.2362	.1549	.0932	.0518	.0266	.0125	.0054
	2	.0867	.2131	.2866	.2953	.2581	.1998	.1395	.0887	.0513	.0269
	3	.0137	.0710	.1517	.2215	.2581	.2568	.2254	.1774	.1259	.0806
	4	.0014	.0158	.0536	.1107	.1721	.2201	.2428	.2365	.2060	.1611
	5	.0001	.0025	.0132	.0388	.0803	.1321	.1830	.2207	.2360	.2256

TABLE 1 *(Continued)*

n	x	.05	.10	.15	.20	.25	.30	.35	.40	.45	.50
	6	.0000	.0003	.0023	.0097	.0268	.0566	.0985	.1471	.1931	.2256
	7	.0000	.0000	.0003	.0017	.0064	.0173	.0379	.0701	.1128	.1611
	8	.0000	.0000	.0000	.0002	.0011	.0037	.0102	.0234	.0462	.0806
	9	.0000	.0000	.0000	.0000	.0001	.0005	.0018	.0052	.0126	.0269
	10	.0000	.0000	.0000	.0000	.0000	.0000	.0002	.0007	.0021	.0054
	11	.0000	.0000	.0000	.0000	.0000	.0000	.0000	.0000	.0002	.0005
12	0	.5404	.2824	.1422	.0687	.0317	.0138	.0057	.0022	.0008	.0002
	1	.3413	.3766	.3012	.2062	.1267	.0712	.0368	.0174	.0075	.0029
	2	.0988	.2301	.2924	.2835	.2323	.1678	.1088	.0639	.0339	.0161
	3	.0173	.0852	.1720	.2362	.2581	.2397	.1954	.1419	.0923	.0537
	4	.0021	.0213	.0683	.1329	.1936	.2311	.2367	.2128	.1700	.1208
	5	.0002	.0038	.0193	.0532	.1032	.1585	.2039	.2270	.2225	.1934
	6	.0000	.0005	.0040	.0155	.0401	.0792	.1281	.1766	.2124	.2256
	7	.0000	.0000	.0006	.0033	.0115	.0291	.0591	.1009	.1489	.1934
	8	.0000	.0000	.0001	.0005	.0024	.0078	.0199	.0420	.0762	.1208
	9	.0000	.0000	.0000	.0001	.0004	.0015	.0048	.0125	.0277	.0537
	10	.0000	.0000	.0000	.0000	.0000	.0002	.0008	.0025	.0068	.0161
	11	.0000	.0000	.0000	.0000	.0000	.0000	.0001	.0003	.0010	.0029
	12	.0000	.0000	.0000	.0000	.0000	.0000	.0000	.0000	.0001	.0002
13	0	.5133	.2542	.1209	.0550	.0238	.0097	.0037	.0013	.0004	.0001
	1	.3512	.3672	.2774	.1787	.1029	.0540	.0259	.0113	.0045	.0016
	2	.1109	.2448	.2937	.2680	.2059	.1388	.0836	.0453	.0220	.0095
	3	.0214	.0997	.1900	.2457	.2517	.2181	.1651	.1107	.0660	.0349
	4	.0028	.0277	.0838	.1535	.2097	.2337	.2222	.1845	.1350	.0873
	5	.0003	.0055	.0266	.0691	.1258	.1803	.2154	.2214	.1989	.1571
	6	.0000	.0008	.0063	.0230	.0559	.1030	.1546	.1968	.2169	.2095
	7	.0000	.0001	.0011	.0058	.0186	.0442	.0833	.1312	.1775	.2095
	8	.0000	.0000	.0001	.0011	.0047	.0142	.0336	.0656	.1089	.1571
	9	.0000	.0000	.0000	.0001	.0009	.0034	.0101	.0243	.0495	.0873
	10	.0000	.0000	.0000	.0000	.0001	.0006	.0022	.0065	.0162	.0349
	11	.0000	.0000	.0000	.0000	.0000	.0001	.0003	.0012	.0036	.0095
	12	.0000	.0000	.0000	.0000	.0000	.0000	.0000	.0001	.0005	.0016
	13	.0000	.0000	.0000	.0000	.0000	.0000	.0000	.0000	.0000	.0001
14	0	.4877	.2288	.1028	.0440	.0178	.0068	.0024	.0008	.0002	.0001
	1	.3593	.3559	.2539	.1539	.0832	.0407	.0181	.0073	.0027	.0009
	2	.1229	.2570	.2912	.2501	.1802	.1134	.0634	.0317	.0141	.0056
	3	.0259	.1142	.2056	.2501	.2402	.1943	.1366	.0845	.0462	.0222
	4	.0037	.0348	.0998	.1720	.2202	.2290	.2022	.1549	.1040	.0611
	5	.0004	.0078	.0352	.0860	.1468	.1963	.2178	.2066	.1701	.1222
	6	.0000	.0013	.0093	.0322	.0734	.1262	.1759	.2066	.2088	.1833
	7	.0000	.0002	.0019	.0092	.0280	.0618	.1082	.1574	.1952	.2095
	8	.0000	.0000	.0003	.0020	.0082	.0232	.0510	.0918	.1398	.1833
	9	.0000	.0000	.0000	.0003	.0018	.0066	.0183	.0408	.0762	.1222
	10	.0000	.0000	.0000	.0000	.0003	.0014	.0049	.0136	.0312	.0611
	11	.0000	.0000	.0000	.0000	.0000	.0002	.0010	.0033	.0093	.0222
	12	.0000	.0000	.0000	.0000	.0000	.0000	.0001	.0005	.0019	.0056
	13	.0000	.0000	.0000	.0000	.0000	.0000	.0000	.0001	.0002	.0009
	14	.0000	.0000	.0000	.0000	.0000	.0000	.0000	.0000	.0000	.0001
15	0	.4633	.2059	.0874	.0352	.0134	.0047	.0016	.0005	.0001	.0000
	1	.3658	.3432	.2312	.1319	.0668	.0305	.0126	.0047	.0016	.0005
	2	.1348	.2669	.2856	.2309	.1559	.0916	.0476	.0219	.0090	.0032

TABLE 1 *(Continued)*

n	x	.05	.10	.15	.20	.25	.30	.35	.40	.45	.50
	3	.0307	.1285	.2184	.2501	.2252	.1700	.1110	.0634	.0318	.0139
	4	.0049	.0428	.1156	.1876	.2252	.2186	.1792	.1268	.0780	.0417
	5	.0006	.0105	.0449	.1032	.1651	.2061	.2123	.1859	.1404	.0916
	6	.0000	.0019	.0132	.0430	.0917	.1472	.1906	.2066	.1914	.1527
	7	.0000	.0003	.0030	.0138	.0393	.0811	.1319	.1771	.2013	.1964
	8	.0000	.0000	.0005	.0035	.0131	.0348	.0710	.1181	.1647	.1964
	9	.0000	.0000	.0001	.0007	.0034	.0116	.0298	.0612	.1048	.1527
	10	.0000	.0000	.0000	.0001	.0007	.0030	.0096	.0245	.0515	.0916
	11	.0000	.0000	.0000	.0000	.0001	.0006	.0024	.0074	.0191	.0417
	12	.0000	.0000	.0000	.0000	.0000	.0001	.0004	.0016	.0052	.0139
	13	.0000	.0000	.0000	.0000	.0000	.0000	.0001	.0003	.0010	.0032
	14	.0000	.0000	.0000	.0000	.0000	.0000	.0000	.0000	.0001	.0005
	15	.0000	.0000	.0000	.0000	.0000	.0000	.0000	.0000	.0000	.0000
16	0	.4401	.1853	.0743	.0281	.0100	.0033	.0010	.0003	.0001	.0000
	1	.3706	.3294	.2097	.1126	.0535	.0228	.0087	.0030	.0009	.0002
	2	.1463	.2745	.2775	.2111	.1336	.0732	.0353	.0150	.0056	.0018
	3	.0359	.1423	.2285	.2463	.2079	.1465	.0888	.0468	.0215	.0085
	4	.0061	.0514	.1311	.2001	.2252	.2040	.1553	.1014	.0572	.0278
	5	.0008	.0137	.0555	.1201	.1802	.2099	.2008	.1623	.1123	.0667
	6	.0001	.0028	.0180	.0550	.1101	.1649	.1982	.1983	.1684	.1222
	7	.0000	.0004	.0045	.0197	.0524	.1010	.1524	.1889	.1969	.1746
	8	.0000	.0001	.0009	.0055	.0197	.0487	.0923	.1417	.1812	.1964
	9	.0000	.0000	.0001	.0012	.0058	.0185	.0442	.0840	.1318	.1746
	10	.0000	.0000	.0000	.0002	.0014	.0056	.0167	.0392	.0755	.1222
	11	.0000	.0000	.0000	.0000	.0002	.0013	.0049	.0142	.0337	.0667
	12	.0000	.0000	.0000	.0000	.0000	.0002	.0011	.0040	.0115	.0278
	13	.0000	.0000	.0000	.0000	.0000	.0000	.0002	.0008	.0029	.0085
	14	.0000	.0000	.0000	.0000	.0000	.0000	.0000	.0001	.0005	.0018
	15	.0000	.0000	.0000	.0000	.0000	.0000	.0000	.0000	.0001	.0002
	16	.0000	.0000	.0000	.0000	.0000	.0000	.0000	.0000	.0000	.0000
17	0	.4181	.1668	.0631	.0225	.0075	.0023	.0007	.0002	.0000	.0000
	1	.3741	.3150	.1893	.0957	.0426	.0169	.0060	.0019	.0005	.0001
	2	.1575	.2800	.2673	.1914	.1136	.0581	.0260	.0102	.0035	.0010
	3	.0415	.1556	.2359	.2393	.1893	.1245	.0701	.0341	.0144	.0052
	4	.0076	.0605	.1457	.2093	.2209	.1868	.1320	.0796	.0411	.0182
	5	.0010	.0175	.0668	.1361	.1914	.2081	.1849	.1379	.0875	.0472
	6	.0001	.0039	.0236	.0680	.1276	.1784	.1991	.1839	.1432	.0944
	7	.0000	.0007	.0065	.0267	.0668	.1201	.1685	.1927	.1841	.1484
	8	.0000	.0001	.0014	.0084	.0279	.0644	.1134	.1606	.1883	.1855
	9	.0000	.0000	.0003	.0021	.0093	.0276	.0611	.1070	.1540	.1855
	10	.0000	.0000	.0000	.0004	.0025	.0095	.0263	.0571	.1008	.1484
	11	.0000	.0000	.0000	.0001	.0005	.0026	.0090	.0242	.0525	.0944
	12	.0000	.0000	.0000	.0000	.0001	.0006	.0024	.0081	.0215	.0472
	13	.0000	.0000	.0000	.0000	.0000	.0001	.0005	.0021	.0068	.0182
	14	.0000	.0000	.0000	.0000	.0000	.0000	.0001	.0004	.0016	.0052
	15	.0000	.0000	.0000	.0000	.0000	.0000	.0000	.0001	.0003	.0010
	16	.0000	.0000	.0000	.0000	.0000	.0000	.0000	.0000	.0000	.0001
	17	.0000	.0000	.0000	.0000	.0000	.0000	.0000	.0000	.0000	.0000
18	0	.3972	.1501	.0536	.0180	.0056	.0016	.0004	.0001	.0000	.0000
	1	.3763	.3002	.1704	.0811	.0338	.0126	.0042	.0012	.0003	.0001
	2	.1683	.2835	.2556	.1723	.0958	.0458	.0190	.0069	.0022	.0006

TABLE 1 *(Continued)*

n	x	.05	.10	.15	.20	.25	.30	.35	.40	.45	.50
	3	.0473	.1680	.2406	.2297	.1704	.1046	.0547	.0246	.0095	.0031
	4	.0093	.0700	.1592	.2153	.2130	.1681	.1104	.0614	.0291	.0117
	5	.0014	.0218	.0787	.1507	.1988	.2017	.1664	.1146	.0666	.0327
	6	.0002	.0052	.0301	.0816	.1436	.1873	.1941	.1655	.1181	.0708
	7	.0000	.0010	.0091	.0350	.0820	.1376	.1792	.1892	.1657	.1214
	8	.0000	.0002	.0022	.0120	.0376	.0811	.1327	.1734	.1864	.1669
	9	.0000	.0000	.0004	.0033	.0139	.0386	.0794	.1284	.1694	.1855
	10	.0000	.0000	.0001	.0008	.0042	.0149	.0385	.0771	.1248	.1669
	11	.0000	.0000	.0000	.0001	.0010	.0046	.0151	.0374	.0742	.1214
	12	.0000	.0000	.0000	.0000	.0002	.0012	.0047	.0145	.0354	.0708
	13	.0000	.0000	.0000	.0000	.0000	.0002	.0012	.0044	.0134	.0327
	14	.0000	.0000	.0000	.0000	.0000	.0000	.0002	.0011	.0039	.0117
	15	.0000	.0000	.0000	.0000	.0000	.0000	.0000	.0002	.0009	.0031
	16	.0000	.0000	.0000	.0000	.0000	.0000	.0000	.0000	.0001	.0006
	17	.0000	.0000	.0000	.0000	.0000	.0000	.0000	,0000	.0000	.0001
	18	.0000	.0000	.0000	.0000	.0000	.0000	.0000	.0000	.0000	.0000
19	0	.3774	.1351	.0456	.0144	.0042	.0011	.0003	.0001	.0000	.0000
	1	.3774	.2852	.1529	.0685	.0268	.0093	.0029	.0008	.0002	.0000
	2	.1787	.2852	.2428	.1540	.0803	.0358	.0138	.0046	.0013	.0003
	3	.0533	.1796	.2428	.2182	.1517	.0869	.0422	.0175	.0062	.0018
	4	.0112	.0798	.1714	.2182	.2023	.1491	.0909	.0467	.0203	.0074
	5	.0018	.0266	.0907	.1636	.2023	.1916	.1468	.0933	.0497	.0222
	6	.0002	.0069	.0374	.0955	.1574	.1916	.1844	.1451	.0949	.0518
	7	.0000	.0014	.0122	.0443	.0974	.1525	.1844	.1797	.1443	.0961
	8	.0000	.0002	.0032	.0166	.0487	.0981	.1489	.1797	.1771	.1442
	9	.0000	.0000	.0007	.0051	.0198	.0514	.0980	.1464	.1771	.1762
	10	.0000	.0000	.0001	.0013	.0066	.0220	.0528	.0976	.1449	.1762
	11	.0000	.0000	.0000	.0003	.0018	.0077	.0233	.0532	.0970	.1442
	12	.0000	.0000	.0000	.0000	.0004	.0022	.0083	.0237	.0529	.0961
	13	.0000	.0000	.0000	.0000	.0001	.0005	.0024	.0085	.0233	.0518
	14	.0000	.0000	.0000	.0000	.0000	.0001	.0006	.0024	.0082	.0222
	15	.0000	.0000	.0000	.0000	.0000	.0000	.0001	.0005	.0022	.0074
	16	.0000	.0000	.0000	.0000	.0000	.0000	.0000	.0001	.0005	.0018
	17	.0000	.0000	.0000	.0000	.0000	.0000	.0000	.0000	.0001	.0003
	18	.0000	.0000	.0000	.0000	.0000	.0000	.0000	.0000	.0000	.0000
	19	.0000	.0000	.0000	.0000	.0000	.0000	.0000	.0000	.0000	.0000
20	0	.3585	.1216	.0388	.0115	.0032	.0008	.0002	.0000	.0000	.0000
	1	.3774	.2702	.1368	.0576	.0211	.0068	.0020	.0005	.0001	.0000
	2	.1887	.2852	.2293	.1369	.0669	.0278	.0100	.0031	.0008	.0002
	3	.0596	.1901	.2428	.2054	.1339	.0716	.0323	.0123	.0040	.0011
	4	.0133	.0898	.1821	.2182	.1897	.1304	.0738	.0350	.0139	.0046
	5	.0022	.0319	.1028	.1746	.2023	.1789	.1272	.0746	.0365	.0148
	6	.0003	.0089	.0454	.1091	.1686	.1916	.1643	.1244	.0746	.0370
	7	.0000	.0020	.0160	.0545	.1124	.1712	.1844	.1659	.1221	.0739
	8	.0000	.0004	.0046	.0222	.0609	.1144	.1614	.1797	.1623	.1201
	9	.0000	.0001	.0011	.0074	.0271	.0654	.1158	.1597	.1771	.1602
	10	.0000	.0000	.0002	.0020	.0099	.0308	.0686	.1171	.1593	.1762
	11	.0000	.0000	.0000	.0005	.0030	.0120	.0336	.0710	.1185	.1602
	12	.0000	.0000	.0000	.0001	.0008	.0039	.0136	.0355	.0727	.1201
	13	.0000	.0000	.0000	.0000	.0002	.0010	.0045	.0146	.0366	.0739
	14	.0000	.0000	.0000	.0000	.0000	.0002	.0012	.0049	.0150	.0370

TABLE 1 *(Continued)*

n	x					p					
		.05	.10	.15	.20	.25	.30	.35	.40	.45	.50
	15	.0000	.0000	.0000	.0000	.0000	.0000	.0003	.0013	.0049	.0148
	16	.0000	.0000	.0000	.0000	.0000	.0000	.0000	.0003	.0013	.0046
	17	.0000	.0000	.0000	.0000	.0000	.0000	.0000	.0000	.0002	.0011
	18	.0000	.0000	.0000	.0000	.0000	.0000	.0000	.0000	.0000	.0002
	19	.0000	.0000	.0000	.0000	.0000	.0000	.0000	.0000	.0000	.0000
	20	.0000	.0000	.0000	.0000	.0000	.0000	.0000	.0000	.0000	.0000

Reproduced with permission from National Bureau of Standards, *Tables of the Binomial Probability Distribution*, United States Department of Commerce (1950).

TABLE 2 Values of $e^{-\lambda}$.

λ	$e^{-\lambda}$	λ	$e^{-\lambda}$	λ	$e^{-\lambda}$	λ	$e^{-\lambda}$
0.00	1.000000	2.60	.074274	5.10	.006097	7.60	.000501
0.10	.904837	2.70	.067206	5.20	.005517	7.70	.000453
0.20	.818731	2.80	.060810	5.30	.004992	7.80	.000410
0.30	.740818	2.90	.055023	5.40	.004517	7.90	.000371
0.40	.670320	3.00	.049787	5.50	.004087	8.00	.000336
0.50	.606531	3.10	.045049	5.60	.003698	8.10	.000304
0.60	.548812	3.20	.040762	5.70	.003346	8.20	.000275
0.70	.496585	3.30	.036883	5.80	.003028	8.30	.000249
0.80	.449329	3.40	.033373	5.90	.002739	8.40	.000225
0.90	.406570	3.50	.030197	6.00	.002479	8.50	.000204
1.00	.367879	3.60	.027324	6.10	.002243	8.60	.000184
1.10	.332871	3.70	.024724	6.20	.002029	8.70	.000167
1.20	.301194	3.80	.022371	6.30	.001836	8.80	.000151
1.30	.272532	3.90	.020242	6.40	.001661	8.90	.000136
1.40	.246597	4.00	.018316	6.50	.001503	9.00	.000123
1.50	.223130	4.10	.016573	6.60	.001360	9.10	.000112
1.60	.201897	4.20	.014996	6.70	.001231	9.20	.000101
1.70	.182684	4.30	.013569	6.80	.001114	9.30	.000091
1.80	.165299	4.40	.012277	6.90	.001008	9.40	.000083
1.90	.149569	4.50	.011109	7.00	.000912	9.50	.000075
2.00	.135335	4.60	.010052	7.10	.000825	9.60	.000068
2.10	.122456	4.70	.009095	7.20	.000747	9.70	.000061
2.20	.110803	4.80	.008230	7.30	.000676	9.80	.000056
2.30	.100259	4.90	.007447	7.40	.000611	9.90	.000050
2.40	.090718	5.00	.006738	7.50	.000553	10.00	.000045
2.50	.082085						

TABLE 3 Cumulative distribution function of the standard normal distribution.

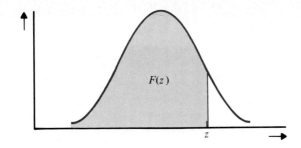

The table shows the probability, $F(z)$, that a standard normal random variable is less than the number z. For example, the probability is 0.9750 that a standard normal random variable is less than 1.96.

z	$F(z)$	z	$F(z)$	z	$F(z)$	z	$F(z)$
.00	.5000						
.01	.5040	.31	.6217	.61	.7291	.91	.8186
.02	.5080	.32	.6255	.62	.7324	.92	.8212
.03	.5120	.33	.6293	.63	.7357	.93	.8238
.04	.5160	.34	.6331	.64	.7389	.94	.8264
.05	.5199	.35	.6368	.65	.7422	.95	.8289
.06	.5239	.36	.6406	.66	.7454	.96	.8315
.07	.5279	.37	.6443	.67	.7486	.97	.8340
.08	.5319	.38	.6480	.68	.7517	.98	.8365
.09	.5359	.39	.6517	.69	.7549	.99	.8389
.10	.5398	.40	.6554	.70	.7580	1.00	.8413
.11	.5438	.41	.6591	.71	.7611	1.01	.8438
.12	.5478	.42	.6628	.72	.7642	1.02	.8461
.13	.5517	.43	.6664	.73	.7673	1.03	.8485
.14	.5557	.44	.6700	.74	.7704	1.04	.8508
.15	.5596	.45	.6736	.75	.7734	1.05	.8531
.16	.5636	.46	.6772	.76	.7764	1.06	.8554
.17	.5675	.47	.6803	.77	.7794	1.07	.8577
.18	.5714	.48	.6844	.78	.7823	1.08	.8599
.19	.5753	.49	.6879	.79	.7852	1.09	.8621
.20	.5793	.50	.6915	.80	.7881	1.10	.8643
.21	.5832	.51	.6950	.81	.7910	1.11	.8665
.22	.5871	.52	.6985	.82	.7939	1.12	.8686
.23	.5910	.53	.7019	.83	.7967	1.13	.8708
.24	.5948	.54	.7054	.84	.7995	1.14	.8729
.25	.5987	.55	.7088	.85	.8023	1.15	.8749
.26	.6026	.56	.7123	.86	.8051	1.16	.8770
.27	.6064	.57	.7157	.87	.8078	1.17	.8790
.28	.6103	.58	.7190	.88	.8106	1.18	.8810
.29	.6141	.59	.7224	.89	.8133	1.19	.8830
.30	.6179	.60	.7257	.90	.8159	1.20	.8849

TABLE 3 *(Continued)*

z	F(z)	z	F(z)	z	F(z)	z	F(z)
1.21	.8869	1.71	.9564	2.21	.9864	2.71	.9966
1.22	.8888	1.72	.9573	2.22	.9868	2.72	.9967
1.23	.8907	1.73	.9582	2.23	.9871	2.73	.9968
1.24	.8925	1.74	.9591	2.24	.9875	2.74	.9969
1.25	.8944	1.75	.9599	2.25	.9878	2.75	.9970
1.26	.8962	1.76	.9608	2.26	.9881	2.76	.9971
1.27	.8980	1.77	.9616	2.27	.9884	2.77	.9972
1.28	.8997	1.78	.9625	2.28	.9887	2.78	.9973
1.29	.9015	1.79	.9633	2.29	.9890	2.79	.9974
1.30	.9032	1.80	.9641	2.30	.9893	2.80	.9974
1.31	.9049	1.81	.9649	2.31	.9896	2.81	.9975
1.32	.9066	1.82	.9656	2.32	.9898	2.82	.9976
1.33	.9082	1.83	.9664	2.33	.9901	2.83	.9977
1.34	.9099	1.84	.9671	2.34	.9904	2.84	.9977
1.35	.9115	1.85	.9678	2.35	.9906	2.85	.9978
1.36	.9131	1.86	.9686	2.36	.9909	2.86	.9979
1.37	.9147	1.87	.9693	2.37	.9911	2.87	.9979
1.38	.9162	1.88	.9699	2.38	.9913	2.88	.9980
1.39	.9177	1.89	.9706	2.39	.9916	2.89	.9981
1.40	.9192	1.90	.9713	2.40	.9918	2.90	.9981
1.41	.9207	1.91	.9719	2.41	.9920	2.91	.9982
1.42	.9222	1.92	.9726	2.42	.9922	2.92	.9982
1.43	.9236	1.93	.9732	2.43	.9925	2.93	.9983
1.44	.9251	1.94	.9738	2.44	.9927	2.94	.9984
1.45	.9265	1.95	.9744	2.45	.9929	2.95	.9984
1.46	.9279	1.96	.9750	2.46	.9931	2.96	.9985
1.47	.9292	1.97	.9756	2.47	.9932	2.97	.9985
1.48	.9306	1.98	.9761	2.48	.9934	2.98	.9986
1.49	.9319	1.99	.9767	2.49	.9936	2.99	.9986
1.50	.9332	2.00	.9772	2.50	.9938	3.00	.9986
1.51	.9345	2.01	.9778	2.51	.9940	3.01	.9987
1.52	.9357	2.02	.9783	2.52	.9941	3.02	.9987
1.53	.9370	2.03	.9788	2.53	.9943	3.03	.9988
1.54	.9382	2.04	.9793	2.54	.9945	3.04	.9988
1.55	.9394	2.05	.9798	2.55	.9946	3.05	.9989
1.56	.9406	2.06	.9803	2.56	.9948	3.06	.9989
1.57	.9418	2.07	.9808	2.57	.9949	3.07	.9989
1.58	.9429	2.08	.9812	2.58	.9951	3.08	.9990
1.59	.9441	2.09	.9817	2.59	.9952	3.09	.9990
1.60	.9452	2.10	.9821	2.60	.9953	3.10	.9990
1.61	.9463	2.11	.9826	2.61	.9955	3.11	.9991
1.62	.9474	2.12	.9830	2.62	.9956	3.12	.9991
1.63	.9484	2.13	.9834	2.63	.9957	3.13	.9991
1.64	.9495	2.14	.9838	2.64	.9959	3.14	.9992
1.65	.9505	2.15	.9842	2.65	.9960	3.15	.9992
1.66	.9515	2.16	.9846	2.66	.9961	3.16	.9992
1.67	.9525	2.17	.9850	2.67	.9962	3.17	.9992
1.68	.9535	2.18	.9854	2.68	.9963	3.18	.9993
1.69	.9545	2.19	.9857	2.69	.9964	3.19	.9993
1.70	.9554	2.20	.9861	2.70	.9965	3.20	.9993

TABLE 3 *(Continued)*

z	F(z)	z	F(z)	z	F(z)	z	F(z)
3.21	.9993	3.41	.9997	3.61	.9998	3.81	.9999
3.22	.9994	3.42	.9997	3.62	.9999	3.82	.9999
3.23	.9994	3.43	.9997	3.63	.9999	3.83	.9999
3.24	.9994	3.44	.9997	3.64	.9999	3.84	.9999
3.25	.9994	3.45	.9997	3.65	.9999	3.85	.9999
3.26	.9994	3.46	.9997	3.66	.9999	3.86	.9999
3.27	.9995	3.47	.9997	3.67	.9999	3.87	.9999
3.28	.9995	3.48	.9997	3.68	.9999	3.88	.9999
3.29	.9995	3.49	.9998	3.69	.9999	3.89	1.0000
3.30	.9995	3.50	.9998	3.70	.9999	3.90	1.0000
3.31	.9995	3.51	.9998	3.71	.9999	3.91	1.0000
3.32	.9996	3.52	.9998	3.72	.9999	3.92	1.0000
3.33	.9996	3.53	.9998	3.73	.9999	3.93	1.0000
3.34	.9996	3.54	.9998	3.74	.9999	3.94	1.0000
3.35	.9996	3.55	.9998	3.75	.9999	3.95	1.0000
3.36	.9996	3.56	.9998	3.76	.9999	3.96	1.0000
3.37	.9996	3.57	.9998	3.77	.9999	3.97	1.0000
3.38	.9996	3.58	.9998	3.78	.9999	3.98	1.0000
3.39	.9997	3.59	.9998	3.79	.9999	3.99	1.0000
3.40	.9997	3.60	.9998	3.80	.9999		

TABLE 4 Probability that a multiserver queueing system will be idle.

For a system with s servers, Poisson arrivals at rate λ, and exponential service times at average rate μ, table shows probability P_0 that there are no customers in the system, for given s and system utilization ratio $\lambda/s\mu$.

$\dfrac{\lambda}{s\mu}$	NUMBER OF SERVERS(s)						
	2	3	4	5	6	8	10
.02	.9608	.9418	.9231	.9048	.8869	.8521	.8187
.04	.9231	.8869	.8521	.8187	.7866	.7262	.6703
.06	.8868	.8353	.7866	.7408	.6977	.6188	.5488
.08	.8519	.7866	.7261	.6703	.6188	.5273	.4493
.10	.8182	.7407	.6703	.6065	.5488	.4493	.3679
.12	.7857	.6975	.6188	.5488	.4868	.3829	.3012
.14	.7544	.6568	.5712	.4966	.4317	.3263	.2466
.16	.7241	.6184	.5272	.4493	.3829	.2780	.2019
.18	.6949	.5821	.4866	.4065	.3396	.2369	.1653
.20	.6667	.5480	.4491	.3678	.3012	.2019	.1353

TABLE 4 *(Continued)*

$\dfrac{\lambda}{s\mu}$	NUMBER OF SERVERS(s)						
	2	3	4	5	6	8	10
.22	.6393	.5157	.4145	.3328	.2671	.1720	.1108
.24	.6129	.4852	.3824	.3011	.2369	.1466	.0907
.26	.5873	.4564	.3528	.2723	.2101	.1249	.0743
.28	.5625	.4292	.3255	.2463	.1863	.1065	.0608
.30	.5385	.4035	.3002	.2228	.1652	.0907	.0498
.32	.5152	.3791	.2768	.2014	.1464	.0773	.0408
.34	.4925	.3561	.2551	.1821	.1298	.0658	.0334
.36	.4706	.3343	.2351	.1646	.1151	.0561	.0273
.38	.4493	.3137	.2165	.1487	.1020	.0478	.0224
.40	.4286	.2941	.1993	.1343	.0903	.0407	.0183
.42	.4085	.2756	.1834	.1213	.0799	.0347	.0150
.44	.3889	.2580	.1686	.1094	.0708	.0295	.0123
.46	.3699	.2414	.1549	.0987	.0627	.0251	.0100
.48	.3514	.2255	.1422	.0890	.0554	.0214	.0082
.50	.3333	.2105	.1304	.0801	.0490	.0182	.0067
.52	.3158	.1963	.1195	.0721	.0432	.0154	.0055
.54	.2987	.1827	.1094	.0648	.0381	.0131	.0045
.56	.2821	.1699	.0999	.0581	.0336	.0111	.0037
.58	.2658	.1576	.0912	.0521	.0296	.0094	.0030
.60	.2500	.1460	.0831	.0467	.0260	.0080	.0024
.62	.2346	.1349	.0775	.0417	.0228	.0068	.0020
.64	.2195	.1244	.0685	.0372	.0200	.0057	.0016
.66	.2048	.1144	.0619	.0330	.0175	.0048	.0013
.68	.1905	.1048	.0559	.0293	.0152	.0040	.0011
.70	.1765	.0957	.0502	.0259	.0132	.0034	.0009
.72	.1628	.0870	.0450	.0228	.0114	.0028	.0007
.74	.1494	.0788	.0401	.0200	.0099	.0024	.0006
.76	.1364	.0709	.0355	.0174	.0085	.0020	.0004
.78	.1236	.0634	.0313	.0151	.0072	.0016	.0004
.80	.1111	.0562	.0273	.0130	.0061	.0013	.0003
.82	.0989	.0493	.0236	.0111	.0051	.0011	.0002
.84	.0870	.0428	.0202	.0093	.0042	.0009	.0002
.86	.0753	.0366	.0170	.0077	.0035	.0007	.0001
.88	.0638	.0306	.0140	.0063	.0028	.0005	.0001
.90	.0526	.0249	.0113	.0050	.0022	.0004	.00007
.92	.0417	.0195	.0087	.0038	.0016	.0003	.00005
.94	.0309	.0143	.0063	.0027	.0011	.0002	.00003
.96	.0204	.0093	.0040	.0017	.0007	.0001	.00002
.98	.0101	.0045	.0019	.0008	.0003	.0005	.00001

TABLE 5 Some uniformly distributed random numbers.

85387	51571	57714	00512	61319	69143	08881	01400	55061	82977
84176	03311	16955	59504	54499	32096	79485	98031	99485	16788
27258	51746	67223	98182	43166	54297	26830	29842	78016	73127
99398	46950	19399	65167	35082	30482	86323	41061	21717	48126
72752	89364	02150	85418	05420	84341	02395	27655	59457	54438
69090	93551	11649	54688	57061	77711	24201	16895	64936	62347
39620	54988	67846	71845	54000	26134	84526	16619	82573	01737
81725	49831	35595	29891	46812	57770	03326	31316	75412	80732
87968	85157	84752	93777	62772	78961	30750	76089	23340	64637
07730	01861	40610	73445	70321	26467	53533	20787	46971	29134
32825	82100	67406	44156	21531	67186	39945	04189	79798	41087
34453	05330	40224	04116	24597	93823	28171	47701	76201	68257
00830	34235	40671	66042	06341	54437	81649	70494	01883	18350
24580	05258	37329	59173	62660	72513	82232	49794	36913	05877
59578	08535	77107	19838	40651	01749	58893	99115	05212	92309
75387	24990	12748	71766	17471	15794	68622	59161	14476	75074
02465	34977	48319	53026	53691	80594	58805	76961	62665	82855
49689	08342	81912	92735	30042	47623	60061	69427	21163	68543
60958	20236	79424	04055	54955	73342	14040	72431	99469	41044
79956	98409	79548	39569	83974	43707	77080	08645	20949	56932
04316	01206	08715	77713	20572	13912	94324	14656	11979	53258
78684	28546	06881	66097	53530	42509	54130	30878	77166	98075
69235	18535	61904	99246	84050	15270	07751	90410	96675	62870
81201	04314	92708	44984	83121	33767	56607	46371	20389	08809
80336	59638	44368	33433	97794	10343	19235	82633	17186	63902
65076	87960	92013	60169	49176	50140	39081	04638	96114	63463
90879	70970	50789	59973	47771	94567	35590	23462	33993	99899
50555	84355	97066	82748	98298	14385	82493	40182	20523	69182
48658	41921	86514	46786	74097	62825	46457	24428	09245	86069
26373	19166	88223	32371	11570	62078	92317	13378	05734	71778
20878	80883	26027	29101	58382	17109	53511	95536	21759	10630
20069	60582	55749	88068	48589	01874	42930	40310	34613	97359
46819	38577	20520	94145	99405	47064	25248	27289	41289	54972
83644	04459	73253	58414	94180	09321	59747	07379	56255	45615
08636	31363	56033	49076	88908	51318	39104	56556	23112	63317
92058	38678	12507	90343	17213	24545	66053	76412	29545	89932
05038	18443	87138	05076	25660	23414	84837	87132	84405	15346
41838	68590	93646	82113	25498	33110	15356	81070	84900	42660
15564	81618	99186	73113	99344	13213	07235	90064	89150	86359
74600	40206	15237	37378	96862	78638	14376	46607	55909	46398
78275	77017	60310	13499	35268	47790	77475	44345	14615	25231
30145	71205	10355	18404	85354	22199	90822	35204	47891	69860
46944	00097	39161	50139	60458	44649	85537	90017	18157	13856
85883	21272	89266	94887	00291	70963	28169	95130	27223	35387
83606	98192	82194	26719	24499	28102	97769	98769	30757	81593
66888	81818	52490	54272	70549	69235	74684	96412	65186	87974
63673	73966	34036	44298	60652	05947	05833	27914	57021	58566
37944	16094	39797	63253	64103	32222	65925	64693	34048	75394
93240	66855	29336	28354	71398	45118	01454	72128	09715	29454
40189	76776	70842	32675	81647	75868	21288	12849	94990	21513

Reprinted from page 259 of *A Million Random Digits With 100,000 Normal Deviates*, by the Rand Corporation. New York: The Free Press, 1955. Copyright 1955 by The Rand Corporation. Used by Permission.

TABLE 6 Cutoff points of the chi-square distribution

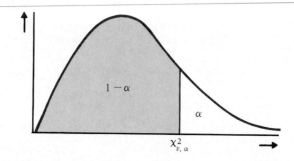

For selected probabilities α, the table shows the values $\chi^2_{\nu,\alpha}$ such that $\alpha = P(\chi^2_\nu > \chi^2_{\nu,\alpha})$, where χ^2_ν is a chi-square random variable with ν degrees of freedom. For example, the probability is 0.100 that a chi-square random variable with 10 degrees of freedom is greater than 15.99.

ν	α									
	.995	.990	.975	.950	.900	.100	.050	.025	.010	.005
1	0.0^4393	0.0^3157	0.0^3982	0.0^2393	0.0158	2.71	3.84	5.02	6.63	7.88
2	0.0100	0.0201	0.0506	0.103	0.211	4.61	5.99	7.38	9.21	10.60
3	0.072	0.115	0.216	0.352	0.584	6.25	7.81	9.35	11.34	12.84
4	0.207	0.297	0.484	0.711	1.064	7.78	9.49	11.14	13.28	14.86
5	0.412	0.554	0.831	1.145	1.61	9.24	11.07	12.83	15.09	16.75
6	0.676	0.872	1.24	1.64	2.20	10.64	12.59	14.45	16.81	18.55
7	0.989	1.24	1.69	2.17	2.83	12.02	14.07	16.01	18.48	20.28
8	1.34	1.65	2.18	2.73	3.49	13.36	15.51	17.53	20.09	21.96
9	1.73	2.09	2.70	3.33	4.17	14.68	16.92	19.02	21.67	23.59
10	2.16	2.56	3.25	3.94	4.87	15.99	18.31	20.48	23.21	25.19
11	2.60	3.05	3.82	4.57	5.58	17.28	19.68	21.92	24.73	26.76
12	3.07	3.57	4.40	5.23	6.30	18.55	21.03	23.34	26.22	28.30
13	3.57	4.11	5.01	5.89	7.04	19.81	22.36	24.74	27.69	29.82
14	4.07	4.66	5.63	6.57	7.79	21.06	23.68	26.12	29.14	31.32
15	4.60	5.23	6.26	7.26	8.55	22.31	25.00	27.49	30.58	32.80
16	5.14	5.81	6.91	7.96	9.31	23.54	26.30	28.85	32.00	34.27
17	5.70	6.41	7.56	8.67	10.09	24.77	27.59	30.19	33.41	35.72
18	6.26	7.01	8.23	9.39	10.86	25.99	28.87	31.53	34.81	37.16
19	6.84	7.63	8.91	10.12	11.65	27.20	30.14	32.85	36.19	38.58
20	7.43	8.26	9.59	10.85	12.44	28.41	31.41	34.17	37.57	40.00
21	8.03	8.90	10.28	11.59	13.24	29.62	32.67	35.48	38.93	41.40
22	8.64	9.54	10.98	12.34	14.04	30.81	33.92	36.78	40.29	42.80
23	9.26	10.20	11.69	13.09	14.85	32.01	35.17	38.08	41.64	44.18
24	9.89	10.86	12.40	13.85	15.66	33.20	36.42	39.36	42.98	45.56
25	10.52	11.52	13.12	14.61	16.47	34.38	37.65	40.65	44.31	46.93
26	11.16	12.20	13.84	15.38	17.29	35.56	38.89	41.92	45.64	48.29
27	11.81	12.88	14.57	16.15	18.11	36.74	40.11	43.19	46.96	49.64
28	12.46	13.56	15.31	16.93	18.94	37.92	41.34	44.46	48.28	50.99
29	13.12	14.26	16.05	17.71	19.77	39.09	42.56	45.72	49.59	52.34
30	13.79	14.95	16.79	18.49	20.60	40.26	43.77	46.98	50.89	53.67
40	20.71	22.16	24.43	26.51	29.05	51.81	55.76	59.34	63.69	66.77

TABLE 6 *(Continued)*

ν	α									
	.995	.990	.975	.950	.900	.100	.050	.025	.010	.005
50	27.99	29.71	32.36	34.76	37.69	63.17	67.50	71.42	76.15	79.49
60	35.53	37.48	40.48	43.19	46.46	74.40	79.08	83.30	88.38	91.95
70	43.28	45.44	48.76	51.74	55.33	85.53	90.53	95.02	100.4	104.2
80	51.17	53.54	57.15	60.39	64.28	96.58	101.9	106.6	112.3	116.3
90	59.20	61.75	65.65	69.13	73.29	107.6	113.1	118.1	124.1	128.3
100	67.33	70.06	74.22	77.93	82.36	118.5	124.3	129.6	135.8	140.2

Reproduced with permission from C. M. Thompson, "Tables of percentage points of the chi-square distribution," *Biometrika, 32* (1941).

answers to selected even-numbered exercises

CHAPTER 2

2. **(b)** $(0, 0), (0, 320), (84, 264), (150, 0)$; **(c)** $x_1 = 84, x_2 = 264$; **(d)** 348

4. **(b)** $(0, 0), (0, 750), (300, 450), (600, 0)$; **(c)** $x_1 = 0, x_2 = 750$; **(d)** 2250

6. **(b)** $(0, 0), (0, 600), (400, 300), (600, 0)$; **(c)** $x_1 = 400, x_2 = 300$; **(d)** 2500

8. **(b)** $(0, 0), (0, 450), (3300/7; 1500/7), (600,0)$; **(c)** $x_1 = 3300/7, x_2 = 1500/7$; **(d)** 20,700/7; **(f)** Let s_1, s_2, s_3 be slack variables $x_1 = 3300/7, x_2 = 1500/7, s_1 = 0, s_2 = 0, s_3 = 300$

14. The second and third constraints are redundant.

16. $x_1 = 80, x_2 = 20, s_1 = 0, s_2 = 100, s_3 = 0$, Profit $= \$2800$

18. **(a)** 400 large color, 450 portable black and white; **(b)** No slack in storage capacity, No slack in available budget, 50 sets slack in color T.V. limit

20. **(c)** 15 square feet national, 5 square feet generic; $950 profit

22. $14,000 high risk fund, $56,000 low risk fund, $30,000 fixed interest securities

24. $30, $120

26. $0.75, $3, $6

28. **(c)** 375 bottles of A, 250 bottles of B, profit $825; slacks are 0 for essence 1, 50 ounces of essence 2, 100 ounces of essence 3, 0 for essence 4

30. $45

32. **(b)** $(20, 60), (30, 50), (50, 40)$; **(c)** $x_1 = 30, x_2 = 50$; **(d)** 210

34. **(b)** $(10, 60), (30, 40), (60, 30)$; **(c)** $x_1 = 30, x_2 = 40$; **(d)** 110; **(e)** Let s_1, s_2, s_3, s_4 be surplus variables: $x_1 = 30, x_2 = 40, s_1 = 0, s_2 = 0, s_3 = 20, s_4 = 10$

38. Problem now has multiple optimal solutions satisfying $x_1 + 2x_2 = 16$, for $2\frac{2}{3} \le x_1 \le 8$. Minimum cost is 32 cents. Surplus variables depend on choice of solution for s_1, s_3, s_4, but $s_2 = 0$.

40. Lowest cost $505 with 7 operators on first shift and 5 on second. Time period surpluses are 4, 3, 0, 0, 3.

42. $5\frac{2}{3}$ cents

44. **(b)** 3000 to 1, 2500 to 2, 4500 to 3

CHAPTER 3

2. $x_1 = 450, x_2 = 0$

4. $x_1 = 400, x_2 = 0, x_3 = 300$

6. **(a)** $x_1 = 0, x_2 = 500, x_3 = 300$; **(b)** 1300

8. **(a)** $x_1 = 800, x_2 = 0, x_3 = 0$; **(b)** 2400

10. **(a)** 80 desks, 0 bookcases, 80 chairs; **(b)** 30 man-hours in finishing, none in assembly and inspection; **(c)** $3680

12. **(a)** 5000 small, 0 medium, 1500 large; **(b)** $725; **(c)** None in beans limit, none in small limit, 500 in large limit, 3500 in medium plus large limit

16. **(a)** $x_1 = 5, x_2 = 5$

18. $350, or 0.35 percentage points

20. 1300 units product 1, 0 units product 2, 600 units product 3

22. $x_1 = 150, x_2 = 200$

24. $x_1 = 600, x_2 = 150$

26. **(a)** $x_1 = 400, x_2 = 0, x_3 = 400$; **(b)** 800

28. 0 large color, 800 small color, 1,000 portable black and white

39. 900 units product 1, 0 units product 2, 800 units product 3

32. $x_1 = 150, x_2 = 100$

34. $x_1 = 50, x_2 = 100$

36. $x_1 = 200, x_2 = 200, x_3 = 300$

40. $37 17/24

42. 275 sets from plant 1 to center A, 0 from plant 1 to center B, 25 from plant 2 to center A, 250 from plant 2 to center B

CHAPTER 4

4. **(c)** zero

10. **(c)** zero

12. **(a)** 1.4545 grams additive I, 2.9091 grams additive II, 4.3636 grams additive III; **(c)** 0.0136 (26.67 to 320); 0.2909 (61 to 160); 0 (to 94.5155); 0.0045 (37.33 to 132.41)

14. **(a)** 0 units product I, 2,000 units product II, 0 units product III; **(c)** $0.50, $0, $0, $1.50; **(d)** 4000–6000, above 2000, above 2000, 2000–2400

16. Minimize $\quad\quad\quad\quad\quad 400\,y_1 + 600\,y_2$
subject to $\quad\quad\quad\quad 2y_1 + 3\,y_2 \geq 1$
$$y_1 \geq 2$$
$$y_2 \geq 3$$

18. **(a)** $x_1 = 84, x_2 = 264$
(b) Minimize $\quad\quad\quad 960\,y_1 + 600\,y_2$
subject to $\quad\quad\quad 2\,y_1 + 4\,y_2 \geq 1$
$$3\,y_1 + y_2 \geq 1$$

(c) $y_1 = 0.3, y_2 = 0.1$

20. **(a)** $x_1 = 30$, $x_2 = 50$

(b) Maximize

$80\,y_1 + 130\,y_2 + 20\,y_3 + 40\,y_4$

subject to

$y_1 + y_2 + y_3 \leq 2$

$y_1 + 2y_2 + y_4 \leq 3$

(c) $y_1 = 1$, $y_2 = 1$, $y_3 = 0$, $y_4 = 0$

22. **(a)** Minimize

$6000\,y_1 + 4000\,y_2 + 3000\,y_3 + 2000\,y_4$

subject to

$y_1 + 2y_2 + 2y_3 + y_4 \geq 2$

$3y_1 + y_2 + y_3 + y_4 \geq 3$

$2y_1 + 2y_2 + y_3 + y_4 \geq 2$

(b) $y_1 = 0.5$, $y_2 = 0$, $y_3 = 0$, $y_4 = 1.5$

24. **(b)** Minimize

$8000\,y_1 + 320{,}000\,y_2 + 500\,y_3$

subject to

$8y_1 + 360\,y_2 + y_3 \geq 50$

$5y_1 + 300\,y_2 \geq 40$

$4y_1 + 80\,y_2 \geq 20$

$y_1 = 3.5$, $y_2 = 0.075$, $y_3 = 0$

26. **(d)** Minimize

$640\,y_1 + 540\,y_2 + 100\,y_3 - 50\,y_4$

subject to

$8y_1 + 4y_2 + y_3 \geq 30$

$4y_1 + 6y_2 + y_3 - y_4 \geq 20$

$3y_1 + 2y_2 + y_3 \geq 12$

$y_1 = 0$, $y_2 = 0$, $y_3 = 30$, $y_4 = 10$

CHAPTER 5

2. **(b)** **(i)** 500 units product 1, 200 units product 2, 300 units product 4, 200 units product 5; **(ii)** $500

4. **(b)** **(i)** 1000 units product 1, 600 units product 2, 600 units product 4, 200 units product 5

6. **(b)** **(i)** 50; **(ii)** 659.72 of 1, 263.89 of 2, 37.04 of 3, 388.89 of 4

8. **(b)** 10 cents

10. **(b)** October: 200 small normal time, 50 small overtime, 100 large normal time; November: 120 small normal time, 180 small overtime, 180 large normal time; December: 125 small normal time, 195 small overtime, 175 large normal time

12. **(b)** January: 1800 man-hours normal, 500 man-hours overtime; February: 2000 man-hours normal; March: 2000 man-hours normal, 600 man-hours overtime; April: 2400 man-hours normal, 600 man-hours overtime

16. **(b)** Numbers assigned to the six shifts, in order, should be: 20, 10, 25, 0, 30, 20

18. **(b)** 2000 man-hours overtime department I, 750 man-hours overtime department IV; Product mix should be 1000 pounds drug A, 2250 pounds drug B, and 500 pounds drug C

22. **(b)** 250 from plant 1 to center A, 150 from plant 1 to center B, 300 from plant 2 to center C, 50 from plant 3 to center B, 150 from plant 3 to center C

24. **(b)** 882 portable color TVs, 1411 microwave ovens

26. **(b)** $100,000 newspapers, $100,000 magazines, $50,000 radio, $250,000 television

28. **(b)** 2000 to libraries, 1000 to professors in North America, 2000 overseas

30. **(b)** October: 245 desks, 150 bookcases; November: 240 desks, 160 bookcases; December: 240 desks, 160 bookcases. All output sold in month of production, except 30 October bookcases sold in November, 40 November bookcases sold in December

CHAPTER 6

2. **(a)** Atlanta–San Francisco 5, Atlanta–Washington, D.C. 35, Atlanta–Cleveland 25, New Haven–Boston 35, New Haven–Cleveland 40, Dallas–San Francisco 45
 (b) Atlanta–Washington, D.C. 35, Atlanta–Cleveland 30, New Haven–San Francisco 5, New Haven–Boston 35, New Haven–Cleveland 35, Dallas–San Francisco 45
 (c) $1080

4. **(a)** I-A 260, II-B 40, II-C 200, III-A 50, III-D 200, IV-A 10, IV-B 290; **(b)** No; **(c)** $10,550

6. **(b)** I-B 250, II-A 70, II-B 10, II-D 180, III-A 240, IV-B 80, IV-C 220; **(c)** $11,620

8. Atlanta–San Francisco 50, Atlanta–Washington, D.C. 15, New Haven–Washington, D.C. 20, New Haven–Cleveland 55, Dallas–Boston 35, Dallas–Cleveland 10

12. **(a)** I-A 260, II-B 280, III-A 50, III-D 200, IV-A 10, IV-B 50, IV-C 200; **(b)** Plant IV

14. **(a)** I-A 100, II-C 180, III-A 30, III-B 100, III-C 10; **(b)** Plant II

16. Purchase 380 in January, 400 in February, 430 in March, 450 in April

18. Unaltered from Exercise 17

20. **(a)** New Orleans–Baltimore 20, New Orleans–Milwaukee 75, Boston–Philadelphia 70, Boston–Baltimore 40, Seattle–Los Angeles 75, Seattle–Baltimore 5
 (b) New Orleans–Baltimore 65, New Orleans–Milwaukee 30, Boston–Philadelphia 65, Boston–Milwaukee 45, Seattle–Los Angeles 75, Seattle–Philadelphia 5; **(c)** $7110

22. **(a)** Newark–Boston 250, Newark–Minneapolis 70, Seattle–San Francisco 260, Detroit–Minneapolis 180, Charlotte–San Francisco 80, Charlotte–Dallas 200, Charlotte–Minneapolis 20; **(b)** Solution in **(a)** is optimal; **(c)** $41,860

24. **(a)** I-A 270, II-B 250, III-A 50, III-D 200, IV-B 80, IV-C 190; **(b)** No; **(c)** $50,590

26. There are multiple optimal solutions. One is General Motors Common Stock $40,000, Mobil Common Stock $10,000, IBM Preferred Stock $5000, Mobil Preferred Stock $20,000, IBM Bonds $25,000

28. 1-D, 2-A, 3-B, 4-C or 1-D, 2-B, 3-C, 4-A

30. 1-B, 2-E, 3-C, 4-D, 5-A

32. **(a)** 1-Dilley, 2-Randall, 3-Willis, 4-Edmonds; **(b)** $109 thousand

34. **(a)** 1-E, 2-B, 3-D, 4-A, 5-C; **(b)** $203 thousand

36. 1-Moore, 2-Charlton, 3-Banks, 4-Wilson

CHAPTER 7

2. 6 grams additive I, 5 grams additive II

4. 500 units product I, 600 units product II

6. 6 operators on each shift

8. 40 desks, 60 bookcases

10. 52.5 desks, 55 bookcases

12. 5 grams additive I, 5.5 grams additive II

14. 125 units product I, 175 units product II

16. 700 units product I, 500 units product II

18. 400 bottles of A, 200 bottles of B

20. 6 operators on each shift

CHAPTER 8

2. **(c)** $x_1 = 5$, $x_2 = 6$
4. **(c)** $x_1 = 3$, $x_2 = 3$
6. **(c)** $x_1 = 2$, $x_2 = 6\frac{4}{5}$ or $x_1 = 3$, $x_2 = 6$
8. **(c)** $x_1 = 8$, $x_2 = 2$ or $x_1 = 9$, $x_2 = 0$
10. **(b)** $x_1 = 1$, $x_2 = 0$, $x_3 = 0$, $x_4 = 1$
12. **(c)** $x_1 = 4$, $x_2 = 4$
14. $x_1 = 4$, $x_2 = 4$
16. 4 units product I, 4 units product II, or 5 units product I, 3 units product II; $48,000
18. Projects 1,4
20. Television, newspapers and magazines

CHAPTER 9

2. **(a)** 1–3–6–9–10; **(b)** 355 miles
4. **(a)** 1–2–5–8–11 or 1–2–6–8–11; **(b)** 485 miles
6. **(a)** 4 of type A, 2 of type B (There are multiple optimal solutions)
8. 2 of type D and 2 of type C (There are multiple optimal solutions)
10. 2 life, 2 business (There are multiple optimal solutions)
12. $1000
14. 1 to territory A, 2 to territory B, 3 to territory C, 4 to territory D (There are multiple optimal solutions)
16. Invest all $10 million in project 4

CHAPTER 10

2. **(a)** ¼; **(b)** 1/13; **(c)** 1/52; **(d)** ¼; **(e)** Yes
4. **(a)** 0.95; **(b)** ⅔
8. 0.80
10. **(a)** 0.30; **(b)** 0.75; **(c)** 0.50
12. **(a)** 0.95; **(b)** 0.9175; **(c)** 0.875
14. **(a)** 0.64; **(b)** 0.0229
16. **(a)** 0.5; **(b)** 0.36
18. 0.2784
20. 0.5526
22. **(a)** $P_X(0) = 0.31$, $P_X(1) = 0.33$, $P_X(2) = 0.28$, $P_X(3) = 0.06$, $P_X(4) = 0.02$; **(b)** 1.15; **(c)** 0.9937
24. **(a)** 0.3456; **(b)** 0.66304; **(c)** 2
26. **(a)** 0.3685; **(b)** 0.4780; **(c)** 0.6
28. **(a)** 0.8291; **(b)** 0.5491; **(c)** 0.1671
30. 0.9337

32. 0.6577

34. (a) 0.8413; **(b)** 0.0228; **(c)** 0.3085; **(d)** 0.9332; **(e)** 0.1464; **(f)** 0.7698

36. (a) 0.0228; **(b)** 0.0808; **(c)** 0.1018

38. 734.4

40. (a) 0.632121; **(b)** 0.606531; **(c)** 0.085548

CHAPTER 11

2. (a) $P(\text{Low}|\text{Poor}) = 0.24$, $P(\text{Moderate}|\text{Poor}) = 0.60$, $P(\text{High}|\text{Poor}) = 0.16$ **(b)** Process C, with EMV \$124,600; **(c)** $P(\text{Low}|\text{Fair}) = \frac{1}{15}$, $P(\text{Moderate}|\text{Fair}) = \frac{2}{3}$, $P(\text{High}|\text{Fair}) = \frac{4}{15}$; **(d)** Process A, with EMV \$138,000; **(e)** $P(\text{Low}|\text{Good}) = \frac{2}{45}$, $P(\text{Moderate}|\text{Good}) = \frac{1}{3}$, $P(\text{High}|\text{Good}) = \frac{28}{45}$; **(f)** Process A, with EMV \$167,556; **(g)** \$950; **(h)** Yes; **(i)** \$5500

4. (a) a_3 is inadmissible; **(b)** a_4; **(c)** a_1; **(d)** a_1 or a_2; **(e)** a_1 with EMV \$5.6 million; **(g)** At least \$12.5 million

8. (a) $P(\text{Very Successful}|\text{Good}) = \frac{24}{39}$, $P(\text{Moderately Successful}|\text{Good}) = \frac{9}{39}$, $P(\text{Unsuccessful}|\text{Good}) = \frac{6}{39}$; **(b)** New center, with EMV \$86,153.85; **(c)** $P(\text{Very Successful}|\text{Fair}) = \frac{4}{11}$, $P(\text{Moderately Successful}|\text{Fair}) = \frac{4}{11}$, $P(\text{Unsuccessful}|\text{Fair}) = \frac{3}{11}$; **(d)** New center, with EMV \$59,545.45; **(e)** $P(\text{Very Successful}|\text{Poor}) = \frac{1}{7}$, $P(\text{Moderately Successful}|\text{Poor}) = \frac{9}{28}$, $P(\text{Unsuccessful}|\text{Poor}) = \frac{15}{28}$; **(f)** Established Center, with EMV \$71,785.71; **(g)** \$12,850 per year in profit; **(h)** \$34,500 per year in profit

12. (b) Mount campaign, with EMV \$30,000

14. (c) Bid \$475,000 and attempt to solve problem internally, with EMV \$13,500

18. (a) $P(\text{Very Successful}) = 0.5$, $P(\text{Moderately Successful}) = 0.3$, $P(\text{Unsuccessful}) = 0.2$; **(b)** Mount campaign with EMV \$160,000; **(c)** $P(\text{Very Successful}|\text{Favorable}) = 20/27$, $P(\text{Moderately Successful}|\text{Favorable}) = 2/9$, $P(\text{Unsuccessful}|\text{Favorable}) = 1/27$; **(d)** Mount campaign with EMV \$264,815; **(e)** $P(\text{Very Successful}|\text{Not Favorable}) = 5/23$, $P(\text{Moderately Successful}|\text{Not Favorable}) = 9/23$, $P(\text{Unsuccessful}|\text{Not Favorable}) = 9/23$; **(f)** Mount campaign with EMV \$36,957; **(g)** zero; **(h)** \$30,000

20. (b) Yes, with EMV \$18,600; **(d) (i)** Yes, with EMV \$18,142,86; **(ii)** No, with EMV \$18,697.67; **(iii)** No

22. (a) Retain patent, with EMV \$182,500; **(b)** Retain patent, with EMV \$104,605; **(c)** zero

24. (a) $\frac{100}{37}$, $\frac{400}{37}$, $\frac{900}{37}$, $\frac{1900}{37}$; **(b)** $\frac{1}{37}$, $\frac{4}{37}$, $\frac{9}{37}$, $\frac{19}{37}$

CHAPTER 12

2. \$3.76 for each future year

6. 531, 543, 556, 568

12. $Y = 13.89 - 1.408\,X$; 3.33

CHAPTER 13

2. **(a)** Means: 1, 1.25, 2.5, 2.25, 3, 2.25, 4.5, 3, 5.5, 4, 2.25

Variances: 0, 0.1736, 0.6944, 0.1736, 0.25, 0.1736, 1.3611, 0.1111, 0.6944, 0, 0.3404

(b) (*ES, EF*): (0, 1), (1, 2.25), (1, 3.5), (3.5, 5.75), (5.75, 8.75), (5.75, 8), (5.75, 10.25), (8.75, 11.75), (10.25, 15.75), (10.25, 14.25), (15.75, 18)

(*LS, LF*): (0, 1), (2.25, 3.5), (1, 3.5), (3.5, 5.75), (7.25, 10.25), (9.5, 11.75), (5.75, 10.25), (12.75, 15.75), (10.25, 15.75), (11.75, 15.75), (15.75, 18)

(c) A–C–D–G–I–K

(d) 0.5

4. **(a)** Means: 2.25, 2, 3, 2.5, 4.5, 4.25, 3.5, 5.5, 2, 5, 3, 5.42, 4.25, 5

Variances: 0.3403, 0.1111, 0.1111, 0.6944, 1.3611, 0.8403, 0.6944, 0.6944, 0.1111, 0.4444, 0.1111, 0.3403, 0.3404, 0.1111

(b)

ACTIVITY	ES	EF	LS	LF	SLACK
A	0	2.25	1.50	3.75	1.50
B	0	2.00	0	2.00	0
C	2.25	5.25	3.75	6.75	1.50
D	2.00	4.50	2.00	4.50	0
E	2.25	6.75	6.17	10.67	3.92
F	5.25	9.50	6.75	11.00	1.50
G	4.50	8.00	4.50	8.00	0
H	6.75	12.25	10.67	16.17	3.92
I	9.50	11.50	11.00	13.00	1.50
J	8.00	13.00	8.00	13.00	0
K	12.25	15.25	16.17	19.17	3.92
L	13.00	18.42	13.00	18.42	0
M	15.25	19.50	19.17	23.42	3.92
N	18.42	23.42	18.42	23.42	0

(c) B–D–G–J–L–N

(d) Practically one

6. **(a)** Means: 1, 2, 1, 4.5, 3.5, 2, 3, 2, 2

Variances: 0.0278, 0.0278, 0.0278, 1.3611, 0.6944, 0.1111, 0.1111, 0.0278, 0.0278, 0.1111

(b)

ACTIVITY	ES	EF	LS	LF	SLACK
A	0	1	0	1	0
B	1	3	1	3	0
C	3	4	3	4	0
D	4	8.5	4	8.5	0
E	4	7.5	5	8.5	1
F	4	6	6.5	8.5	2.5
G	8.5	11.5	8.5	11.5	0
H	8.5	11.5	10.5	13.5	2
I	11.5	13.5	11.5	13.5	0
J	13.5	15.5	13.5	15.5	0

(c) A–B–C–D–G–I–J

(d) 0.3520

8. (a) $200, $600, $500, $200, $600, $300, $100

(b) Minimize $\quad 200\,y_A + 600\,y_B + 500\,y_C + 200\,y_D + 600\,y_E + 300\,y_F + 100\,y_G$

subject to
$$x_7 \leq 10$$
$$y_A \leq 1$$
$$y_B \leq 1$$
$$y_C \leq 2$$
$$y_D \leq 1$$
$$y_E \leq 3$$
$$y_F \leq 2$$
$$y_G \leq 1$$
$$x_2 + y_A \geq 2$$
$$-x_2 + x_4 + y_C \geq 4$$
$$-x_2 + x_3 + y_B \geq 3$$
$$-x_4 + x_3 \geq 0$$
$$-x_2 + x_5 + y_D \geq 3$$
$$-x_4 + x_5 \geq 0$$
$$-x_3 + x_6 + y_E \geq 5$$
$$-x_5 + x_6 + y_F \geq 4$$
$$-x_6 + x_7 + y_G \geq 2$$

(c) Optimal solution calls for one week of crashing for each of activities A, C, and G

10. (a) $200, $100, $300, $400, $200, $500, $300, $400

(b) Minimize $\quad 200\,y_A + 100\,y_B + 300\,y_C + 400\,y_D + 200\,y_E + 500\,y_F$
$$+\, 300\,y_G + 400\,y_H$$

subject to
$$x_8 \leq 18$$
$$x_9 \leq 18$$
$$y_A \leq 2$$
$$y_B \leq 4$$
$$y_C \leq 1$$
$$y_D \leq 4$$
$$y_E \leq 1$$
$$y_F \leq 2$$
$$y_G \leq 4$$
$$y_H \leq 2$$
$$x_2 + y_A \geq 6$$
$$-x_2 + x_3 + y_B \geq 7$$
$$-x_2 + x_4 + y_C \geq 5$$
$$-x_3 + x_4 \geq 0$$
$$-x_3 + x_5 + y_D \geq 6$$
$$-x_4 + x_6 + y_E \geq 3$$
$$-x_5 + x_7 + y_F \geq 4$$
$$-x_6 + x_8 + y_G \geq 8$$
$$-x_7 + x_9 + y_H \geq 6$$

(c) Optimal solution calls for 2 days crashing activity A, 4 days B, 4 days D, 1 day E, 1 day G, and 1 day H: total crash cost is $3300

12. (a) $2000, $-$500, $10,000, $1500, $-$500, $2000, $750, $500, $0, $0, $0, $0; **(b)** 11.19%

14. **(a)** $-$500, $1500, $3000, $-$1000, $4000, $2500, $1000, H–N zero; **(b)** 4.88%
16. **(a)** 18 months
    (b) (*ES, EF*): (0, 3), (0, 2), (3, 7), (2, 4), (3, 5), (7, 11), (7, 10), (7, 9), (11, 16) (10, 14), (11, 13), (16, 18), 13, 17)
    (*LS: LF*): (0, 3), (5, 7), (3, 7), (7, 9), (16, 18), (7, 11), (9, 12), (10, 12), (11, 16), (12, 16), (12, 14), (16, 18), (14, 18)
    (c) $15,000, $30,000, $44,000, $67,000, $83,000, $91,500, $100,000, $129,000, $158,000, $178,000, $195,500, $220,000, $244,500, $268,000, $283,000, $298,000, $318,000, $329,000
    (d) $7000, $14,000, $21,000, $29,500, $38,000, $54,500, $71,000, $87,000, $103,000, $123,000, $152,000, $178,000, $202,500, $227,000, $250,500, $274,000, $301,500, $329,000
18. **(a)** 210 miles; **(b)** 1–2–4
20. **(a)** 170 miles; **(b)** 1–4–6–9–10
22. 20 miles
24. **(a)** $47,000; **(b)** Either lease for four years at beginning of year 1, or lease for three years at beginning of year 1, and for 1 year at beginning of year 4.
26. 1–2, 2–3, 3–4, 4–5, 5–6, 6–7, 7–8
28. 1–2, 2–3, 3–4, 3–5, 5–6, 5–8, 6–7, 8–9 is an optimal solution
30. **(a)** 8000 vehicles per hour; **(b)** 1–2, 3 thousand; 1–3, 2 thousand; 1–4, 3 thousand; 2–5, 3 thousand; 3–5, 2 thousand; 4–6, 3 thousand; 5–8, 3 thousand; 5–7, 2 thousand; 6–7, 3 thousand; 7–8, 5 thousand
32. **(a)** 10,000 vehicles per hour; **(b)** 1–2, 3 thousand; 1–3, 3 thousand; 1–4, 4 thousand; 2–5, 2 thousand; 2–6, 1 thousand; 3–6, 3 thousand; 4–7, 4 thousand; 5–8, 2 thousand; 6–8, 3 thousand; 6–9, 1 thousand; 7–9, 4 thousand; 8–10, 5 thousand; 9–10, 5 thousand
34. **(a)** 12,000 gallons per hour; **(b)** 1–2, 5 thousand; 1–3, 7 thousand; 2–4, 1 thousand; 2–5, 4 thousand; 3–4, 5 thousand; 3–6, 2 thousand; 4–5, 1 thousand; 4–7, 5 thousand; 5–7, 1 thousand; 5–8, 4 thousand; 6–8, 2 thousand; 7–8, 6 thousand

CHAPTER 14

2. **(a)** 316 cases; **(b)** 16; **(c)** 158 cases; **(d)** 80 cases
4. By 25%
8. A reduction of 13.4%
10. **(a)** 3381 lamps; **(b)** 986 lamps; **(c)** 35, **(d)** 49; **(e)** $5916
12. **(a)** 4536 tires; **(b)** 1361 tires; **(c)** 45; **(d)** 68; **(e)** $2,204.54; **(f)** Yes
18. Receiving at a steady rate over time, provided this rate exceeds the demand rate
20. **(a)** 642; **(b)** 135; **(c)** 10; **(d)** 507; **(e)** $2026; **(f)** $254
26. Optimal order quantities: 765, 675, 624, 614
    Maximum backorder levels: 340, 193, 104, 85
    Minimum total costs: $1700, $1927, $2082, $2117
    Total costs with $Q = 642$, $S = 135$: $1884, $1955, $2097, $2168
28. $5.985 per case
30. Week 1: Order 530 units of E
    Week 2: Order 320 units of D, 230 units of E
    Week 3: Order 440 units of D, Begin production of 210 units of B
    Week 4: Begin production of 210 units of C
    Week 5: Begin production of 80 units of A

32. Week 1: Order 900 units of G
Week 3: Order 400 units of G, 300 units of F
Week 4: Order 900 units of F
Week 5: Order 400 units of F, 300 units of E, Begin production of 300 units of D
Week 6: Order 400 units of E, Begin production of 300 units of C
Week 7: Begin production 200 units of B
Week 8: Begin production 100 units of A

34. **(a)** 5.7; **(b)** 0.002

36. **(a)** 7.9; **(b)** Practically zero

38. **(a)** 69.5 cases; **(b)** 4,343.75 cases; **(c)** 466 cases; **(d)** 14.50, 10.00, 6.00, 2.75, 1.00, 0.25, 0 cases; **(e)** $101, $70, $42, $19, $7, $2, $0; **(f)** $0, $12, $24, $36, $48, $60, $72; **(g)** 70 or 75 cases

40. **(a)** 25.5 cases; **(b)** 6375 cases; **(c)** 545 cases; **(d)** Possible demand levels over lead-time period are 40, 45, 50, 55, and 60 cases, with probabilities 0.04, 0.20, 0.37, 0.30, 0.09; **(e)** 11.00, 6.20, 2.40, 0.45, 0 cases; **(f)** $96.50, $54.39, $21.06, $3.95, $0 **(g)** $0, $15, $30, $45, $60; **(h)** 55 cases; **(i)** $0.66 to $2.85 per case

44. 522

CHAPTER 15

2. **(a)** 0.017353; **(b)** 0.848781; **(c)** 10 seconds; **(d)** 0.135335

4. **(a)** 0.776870; **(b)** 0.135335

6. **(a)** 0.5; **(b)** 0.125; **(c)** 0.5; **(d)** 1; **(e)** 10 minutes; **(f)** 0.5; **(g)** 5 minutes

10. **(a)** 0.2; **(b)** 0.4096; **(c)** 0.8; **(d)** 4, **(e)** 1 hour; **(f)** 3.2; **(g)** 48 minutes

12. **(a)** True; **(b)** True; **(c)** False; **(d)** True; **(e)** False

14. **(a)** 0.5; **(b)** 0.875; **(c)** 0.5; **(d)** 1; **(e)** 6 minutes; **(f)** 0.5; **(g)** 3 minutes

16. **(i)** **(a)** $\frac{1}{7}$; **(b)** $\frac{9}{14}$; **(c)** $3\frac{3}{7}$; **(d)** $5\frac{5}{7}$ minutes; **(e)** $1\frac{13}{14}$; **(f)** $3\frac{3}{14}$ minutes; **(ii)** **(a)** 0.07477; **(b)** 0.5678; **(c)** 3.9534; **(d)** 6.59 minutes; **(e)** 1.7034; **(f)** 2.84 minutes

20. One

22. Four

24. **(a)** 0.05618; **(b)** 0.809; **(c)** 0.647; **(d)** 0.518; **(e)** 0.956; **(f)** 4.989; **(g)** 0.416 hour; **(h)** 2.589; **(i)** 0.216 hour

30. **(a)** 0.27865; **(b)** 0.13438; **(c)** 0.919; **(d)** 12.7 minutes

34. **(a)** 1.53; **(b)** 2.6833; **(c)** 12.75 weeks; **(d)** 26.833 weeks; **(e)** 0.93; **(f)** 2.5833

38. 4

CHAPTER 16

2. **(c)** **(i)** 1.875 parts; **(ii)** 3.75; **(iii)** 0.25

8. **(b)** 0.2

10. Evidence against claim is not strong: test statistic is 4.29

12. **(a)** 0.8, 0.2, 0.8, 0.2, 0.8, 0.2

16. **(b)** 0.4

CHAPTER 17

2. **(a)** 0.61; **(b)** 0.556; **(c)** 0.64; **(d)** 0.49; **(e)** ³⁄₇

6. 0.7

8. ¹⁄₁₈

10. **(a)** 0.7425; **(b)** 0.18; **(c)** 0.2725; **(d)** 0.457, 0.257, 0.286

12. 42.6%, 28.225%, 29.175%

16. 0.7927

18. **(a)** 0.0975; **(b)** 0.71; **(c)** 0.8625; **(d)** 0.2143, 0.2857, 0.3571, 0.1429

20. **(a)** 0.48; **(b)** 0.16

index

699